Fairleigh Dickinson University Library
Teaneck, New Jersey

EDINBURGH UNIVERSITY PUBLICATIONS
HISTORY PHILOSOPHY AND ECONOMICS

INDEPENDENT AFRICAN

John Chilembwe and the Origins, Setting and Significance of the Nyasaland Native Rising of 1915

BY GEORGE SHEPPERSON
AND THOMAS PRICE
at the University Press EDINBURGH

©

EDINBURGH UNIVERSITY PRESS 1958
22 George Square, Edinburgh
85224 002 3
North America
Aldine Publishing Company
529 South Wabash Avenue, Chicago
Printed in Great Britain by
R. & R. Clark Ltd, Edinburgh
reprinted 1963, 1967, 1969

John Chilembwe : drawing from photograph taken c. 1897

PREFACE

No book is entirely the work of one or even two pairs of hands. This book, in particular, owes more to the help of others than its authors can adequately express. To the Edinburgh University Press for its encouragement, advice, and generous assistance we are especially indebted. The Carnegie Trust for the Universities of Scotland, with that generosity which is sometimes taken too much for granted, provided a guarantee towards the cost of publication of this book. We must also acknowledge gratefully the contributions of the Carnegie Trust and the University of Glasgow which promoted field trips to Nyasaland and the Yao country of Tanganyika, some of the material from which has been used in this work. To the Earl of Moray Fund for the Promotion of Original Research, University of Edinburgh, for grants which have made possible the photographing of a number of documents, we must express our gratitude.

Our thanks are due to the following: Thomas Nelson and Sons, Ltd., for permission to quote from the Revised Standard Version of the Bible, copyrighted 1946 and 1952; the Universities' Mission to Central Africa for permission to quote from *Central Africa*, 1916 and 1917; the Hogarth Press, Ltd., for permission to quote from Norman Leys, *Kenya* (London, 1924); Routledge and Kegan Paul, Ltd., for permission to quote from Jessie Monteath Currie, *The Hill of Goodbye* (London, 1920), and from Lucy Mair, *Native Policies in Africa* (London, 1936); Chatto and Windus, Ltd., for permission to quote from Sir Harry Johnston, *The Man Who Did the Right Thing* (London, 1921); the Stirling Tract Enterprise for permission to quote from Emily Booth Langworthy, *This Africa Was Mine* (Stirling, 1952); Oxford University Press for permission to quote from *The Empire at War*, volume iv (London, 1924); William Blackwood and Sons, Ltd., for permission to quote from L. S. Norman, 'Rebellion', *Blackwood's Magazine*, 1931; the *New Statesman* for permission to quote from Sir Harry Johnston, 'The Bitter Cry of the Educated African', *New Statesman*, 1916; Hodder and Stoughton, Ltd., for permission to quote from Sir Hector Duff, *African Small Chop* (London, 1932); Faber and Faber Ltd. for permission to quote from W. M. Macmillan, *Africa Emergent*

v

(London, 1932); *The Journal of Negro History* for permission to quote from Robert Hughes Brisbane, Jnr., 'Some New Light on the Garvey Movement', *The Journal of Negro History*, 1951; *African Affairs* for permission to quote from J. E. T. Phillips, 'The Rising Tide of Colour, I', *The Journal of the African Society*, 1921–2.

We must express our indebtedness to Miss Isabel Geddie, Miss Elizabeth Whitelaw, and Miss Elizabeth Blyth for untiring help with the many awkward jobs of typing which the work has necessitated; and to Mrs. G. Shepperson for assistance with the proofs.

We are most grateful to those persons who have provided us with the photographs which form the illustrations to this book and to whom acknowledgement is given under the photographs as they appear in the text.

A detailed list of acknowledgements to persons and institutions who have helped us to find materials appears at the end of this book in the statement on sources.

Finally, we would point out that we have been helped in the difficult task of tracking down and assembling the scattered materials out of which this study has been made by so many persons and institutions that, in all cases, it has not been possible, for reasons of space, to give detailed acknowledgements. To all those, therefore, whose names are not mentioned in our statement on sources, we offer our apologies, but we hope that they will understand that we are none the less grateful to them for their assistance.

G. S.
T. P.

CONTENTS

CONTENTS

ILLUSTRATIONS

Maps at end of book

NOTE ON SPELLING AND PRONUNCIATION

In the pioneering period, Central African words were spelt in a confusing variety of ways, according to the highly individual tastes in phonetics of the writers. Our practice, on the whole, has been to follow the more generally accepted modern usages, except in those cases where there is a possibility of their confusing the reader. But, in quotations from contemporary sources and in the employment of proper names, we have kept to the original spellings. This may mean that a word is sometimes spelt in one way in the main text and in another in a quotation : e.g. 'Chiradzulu', 'Chiradzulo'; 'Zambezi', 'Zambesi'; 'Mathaka', 'Mataka', etc. The variations of such spellings are usually so slight that the reader should have no difficulty in following them.

All African names and terms here used are to be pronounced on the general Bantu pattern, stressing the syllable before the last. There are no silent letters, and every syllable is open, ending in a vowel : e.g. 'Chi-le-mbwe'. The vowels have the Italian values as in '*Il Trovatore* by *Giuseppe Verdi*'. 'l' and 'r' are used interchangeably, though 'l' tends to displace 'r' in modern spelling. Initial 'm' or 'n' before another consonant is lightly pronounced as a rule.

I

INTRODUCTION

Why do the nations conspire, and the peoples plot in vain?
Psalm ii (Revised Standard Version)

INTRODUCTION

SOME years ago [wrote a contributor to a missionary magazine of the First World War] the well-known writer Mr. John Buchan published a romance called *Prester John*, the theme of which was a great native rising in South Africa. The leader of this rising was a native clergyman who had been educated abroad and had returned full of the determination to found a great native empire and to drive the hated white intruders into the sea. The tale of its preliminary success and ultimate failure, those who have read it are not likely to forget. It is not often that fact plagiarizes fiction. Those who have enjoyed Mr. Buchan's excellent yarn probably never dreamed that there was the slightest chance of anything approaching to it really happening. The idea seemed bizarre and utterly impossible, excellent for the plot of a story, but out of the question as a plot in real life.

They will have been much surprised, then [went on this war-time writer] if they came across any account in the newspapers of the rebellion of John Chilembwe in Nyasaland.[1]

It is unlikely, however, that citizens who opened their *Times* on Monday morning, 1 February 1915, and read that the Secretary of State for the Colonies had been informed by the Governor of Nyasaland that an outbreak of natives had taken place in the Shire Highlands between Zomba and Blantyre, were much inclined to question this fact or to indulge in literary exercises about it. A new week's work was beginning and spirits were not unduly high a month after that Christmas which was to have seen the end of the war against Germany. Casualties were beginning to pile up on the Western Front; life was becoming more restricted at home; and there was little incentive to think about the difficulties of the forgotten army that was fighting far away in East and Central Africa against the Germans, or to worry much about the embarrassments of the Scottish outposts of Christianity and commerce in Nyasaland.

Anyway, the whole thing was over so quickly : most of the rebels' successes had taken place in little more than twenty-four hours. By the time that the few carefully censored, official press releases were making their unobtrusive way into the British newspapers at the beginning of February, the body of the fugitive native parson who had led the rising, still adorned with his gold-rimmed spectacles, was found near the border of Portuguese East Africa. The perturbed settlers of southern Nyasaland could rest quietly again.

But a week before, most of them had drawn in their breath very quickly when they heard what had happened to the manager of one of the largest estates in the country, a member of the clan of the great David Livingstone, symbol to the world of patience and good-will in relations with Africans. Some time about nine o'clock on Saturday evening, 23 January 1915, as he was lying in bed watching the baby while his wife was having a bath, armed Africans had broken into his house, cut off his head, and dragged his wife and children away into the bush. There were a few other European casualties during the early Sunday morning, but what took place later in the day indicated that, for the rebels at least, his was the most important casualty, and a symbol of their whole rising against the Europeans. For their leader, the Reverend John Chilembwe, held at that time what would have been his normal Sunday service—except for the manager's head stuck up on a pole in church, and the sermon which he preached to his congregation of conspirators on its significance.

It is this event which gives the short Nyasaland native rising of 1915 an intimate drama that Buchan's *Prester John*, for all its great pageantry of African revolt, lacks ; and which makes its leader, the Reverend John Chilembwe, so much more of a puzzle than Buchan's 'Reverend John Laputa'. For Chilembwe had been for most of his life a man of peace, and on one occasion had even journeyed as far as the United States in the cause of friendly relations with the Europeans.

But the Nyasaland rising of 1915 was more than a dramatic clash of personalities. It was a piece of a pattern of human relations stretching across the African continent south of the Sahara, along the axis of the great Rift Valley of Kenya, down to the very tip of the ill-named Cape of Good Hope itself.

This was certainly how the rising appeared to a Medical Officer who had served in Nyasaland, and had interviewed in jail some of the African rebels who had got off with a prison sentence instead of the death penalty. He was Dr. Norman Leys, author of one of the first books to bring to public notice many of the dangers of European rule in Kenya, which was published shortly after the first important African political movement there, the Kikuyu Central Association of

1922, had suffered defeat with the imprisonment of its leader, Harry Thuku, for subversive activities. Leys compared the two movements, Thuku's in Kenya and Chilembwe's in Nyasaland, and came to a conclusion which must have seemed fantastic to many when it was written over a quarter of a century ago but which, for the second half of that century, has lost all its attributes of fantasy. Writing in 1924, Leys said :

> Little likely, then, as any native rising may be for some years, either in Kenya or Nyasaland, it is far from impossible that it may happen some day. If, some morning . . . readers . . . open their morning paper over their breakfast coffee and read of some other Chilembwe or Thuku, they must not expect that some particular act of policy or the unwisdom of some Governor is the cause. They should look upon the rising as a by-product of the system under which the very coffee they are drinking is produced.[2]

It is the purpose of this book to provide material and analysis of the Nyasaland movement of 1915, that small but significant link in the great chain of faith, hope, and tragedy which Leys and others like him saw was being forged in the Africa of the early years of this century. But to bring out the full qualities of the story, and to demonstrate that the Native Rising in the Nyasaland Protectorate of 1915 was the end-product, not of a short sequence of events, but of a long train of causes going back many years, it is necessary to begin the narrative in the early years of British rule in Central Africa. This has meant a long and involved investigation in order to bring to light the mass of detail which makes up the raw material of this story. It has meant researches in three continents, Africa, America, and Europe, of a prolonged and persistent type which, because of the relatively recent character of many of the events in this book, has often had to probe into the private lives of many people, and perhaps, by dragging to the surface old and often unpleasant memories, has caused them pain. If so, we apologize to them very sincerely, and thank them for their co-operation much more than the list of acknowledgements at the end of this work would suggest. But there may be some who read this book who would say that, because of the unhappy memories which we may be resurrecting, we should have let sleeping dogs lie. We shall let our answer be that, even if we left the dogs alone, someone else would soon turn his attention to them. Already a legend-making process around the events that led to the Nyasaland disaster of 1915 is at work amongst both Europeans and Africans.   Surely it is better that some serious and diligent attempt should be made to unearth the scattered records and, by analysing them to the best of one's ability, provide at least an approximation to truth, rather than that it should lie hidden in clouds of conflicting testimony, or that it should receive the over-persuasive stamp of partisan print ?   And, in Africa, irrespective of what academic Europeans may do, sleeping dogs have a way of waking up suddenly and snarling.   It is our belief that there is little to be lost and much to be gained by our giving them an airing now.

Finally, we feel that we must defend the large number of quotations and references which are scattered throughout this book.   It has been our purpose, wherever possible, to let the figures of this story speak for themselves—hence the variety of quotations.   Furthermore, we hope that the range of references and quotations may act as a stimulus and something of a guide to others who may wish to unravel the tangled skeins of this and similar African protest movements.   We are sure that what we have written cannot be taken as the last word on the subject of native discontents in British Central Africa in its formative period, and we must expect that, with the best will in the world, errors and misjudgements must have slipped into our story.   Our references, then, may supply both the curious and the carping with guides for further investigations into the tortuous territories of these movements.   And for the long-suffering general reader, who takes so much on trust, it is our hope that, as some compensation for stopping so often the smooth-running of the text with quotation and reference, we may perhaps communicate something of the excitement, some of the thrills of the chase which we ourselves have experienced in tracking down the strange collection of facts that makes up this tale.

II

ORIGINS: JOSEPH BOOTH AND JOHN CHILEMBWE
1892–1897

Ethiopia shall soon stretch out her hands unto God.
Psalm lxviii. 31 (*Authorized Version*)

. . . they could not quite agree with the discipline or ideals of the different churches or sects and preferred evangelizing East Africa on a plan of their own. They had private means at first until they ran through them in founding mission stations . . .
Sir Harry Johnston, *The Man Who Did the Right Thing* (London, 1921)

ORIGINS: JOSEPH BOOTH AND JOHN CHILEMBWE

1892–1897

1. CANNIBALISM AND CULTURE-CONTACT

ONE of the commonest European symbols of racial misunderstanding and suspicion is the cannibal stewpot. From the times when Victorian mammas used it to scare their children, down to its present-day vogue of music-hall joke and advertisement cliché, it has had much to do with conditioning the white man's attitude towards Africa by making it appear, more often than not, a dark and savage continent of human sacrifice and cannibalism.

It is, then, sardonically interesting that, in East Africa at least, many Africans, from their early days of contact with the white man, have had a very similar picture of Europe.[1] To them it has often been presented as the homeland of sophisticated cannibals, as hungry for Africans' flesh as for their lands.

In small tribal societies, where the dead who are properly buried are still part of the community, and where soul depends upon body for life even beyond the grave, such a fear would be a very real one. David Livingstone himself summed it up in 1872 when writing of some of the peoples in the Nyasa regions :

> great agony is felt in prospect of bodily mutilation or burning of the body after death, as that is believed to render return to one's native land impossible. They feel as if it would shut them off from all intercourse with relatives after death.[2]

The great explorer witnessed this fear being turned to account by the Arab slave-masters, whose terrible trade he had used in his writings and speeches to make the world conscious of the problem of Africa. The Arabs were spreading the rumour that the Europeans who were entering East and Central Africa in the nineteenth century had no intention of freeing the African slaves : the European wanted only a change of masters—to grab the slaves for himself, ship them abroad, and then eat them.[3]   It was magnificent propaganda—effective because it rooted itself in a deep-seated fear.

In one form or another it is recorded from all over East and Central Africa.   It seems to have been widespread around Lake Nyasa where it was linked to the idea of white men as sea-bleached, less-than-human creatures who hid in pools to ambush and kidnap passing Africans, according to the 'spirit-ridden' folk in the north, or who simply took the victims they wanted by straightforward assault, as the people along the Zambezi highway believed.[4]

This rumour was made even more terrible for many of these southern tribes because it added to the feelings of insecurity which were then only too plentiful among them.   Throughout the nineteenth century the great parent people of modern Nyasaland, the Maravi, and many other tribes, had been witnessing a slow disintegration of their traditional cultures.   Ravaged on all sides by Arab slave-raiders and their native middlemen, the Yao ; by the marauding Ngoni, faithful imitators of the great Zulu warrior, Shaka ; by the avaricious frontiersmen of mixed blood, and the adventurer or deportee officials on whom Portugal mainly depended for holding and administering the East African colony she had claimed for the past three and a half centuries and by a new generation of British, German, and Belgian missionaries and traders, the old way of life (as David Livingstone witnessed so forcibly) with its sufficient if primitive agriculture and iron-working was being savagely torn apart.   *Chifwamba*, the sudden swooping of armed bands on villages, often stealthily and secretly by night, to spirit men away as captives, for purposes the very mention of which brought terror, was a word echoed all too frequently.

A few threads in this complicated web of suspicion and fear are revealed by the chance remark in an account by a missionary's wife of life during the last decade of the nineteenth century on a small Scottish mission station in the area of southern Nyasaland where the 1915 rising took place :

> It was commonly asserted [she said] that our chief . . . had eaten his child by a slave wife.   Some of our boys believed us capable of this abominable practice ourselves.   When a very stout white man, a land surveyor, called by the natives 'Che Chimimba' [*Mr. Big Stomach*] visited our Station and stayed in the Doctor's house, [the] table-boy there fled in terror lest he should be eaten by the fat man.   And another time when the Msungu [European in charge] was smoking a piece of

wild boar in a barrel, a boy believed firmly that the 'nyama' [meat] was one of his comrades.[5]

It was 1892 when these events took place : the year in which John Chilembwe, leader of the 1915 rising, met another missionary, Joseph Booth ; and it was to be this meeting and this strange cannibal rumour that was to change his whole life and bring him eventually to a fugitive's death.[6]

2. BRITISH CENTRAL AFRICA IN THE EARLY 1890's

In 1892 some semblance of formal administration and order was beginning to appear in British Central Africa. On 1 February 1891 its first Commissioner and Consul-General had been announced ; and between 14 May 1891 and 22 February 1893 a Protectorate was defined and declared over the country that was to be called officially, from 1907 onwards, Nyasaland.

Harry Johnston, the first Commissioner, was a little man who made up for his lack of size by his tremendous vitality. His interests were enormous—he was scholar, soldier, and statesman, and, later in his life, Shaw was to give him permission to write a novelistic sequel to *Mrs. Warren's Profession*—and there was little doubt of his abilities or enthusiasm. But the Nyasaland of the 1890's was enough to try a man of superhuman capability.

The sullen Arab slave-raiders at the northern end of Lake Nyasa were still making difficulties which, in 1895, were to cause another war with them. There was still trouble with their African henchmen and allies, such as the Yao, in other parts of the country, angry that the white man's rule was seeping away the profits which they derived from the slave trade. The wild Ngoni were bursting out from time to time with a resentment not unlike that which their Zulu ancestors had felt in South Africa when the European came to destroy their pride and power, and to reduce them to humbled dwellers in tribal reserves. Immigrants from neighbouring Portuguese territories, the Nguru, in search of land and loot, added to the general disturbance, and over all these old-fashioned tribal and slave wars hung the shadow of the new industrial conflicts of the future : the shadow of the gold and copper mines of South Africa and the Rhodesias, which were eventually to take away under contract for a season so many

Nyasaland African labourers and to send them back with new and disturbing habits and ideas . . . the shadow of Cecil Rhodes.

It was Rhodes who added to Johnston's troubles at this time. He was bitterly disappointed with Johnston, the British Administration, and the whole of the Lake Nyasa region. He had seen this part of the world as an essential segment of the highway of British advance northwards from the Cape to Cairo. He had no doubt that it would be very useful as a possible entry-point into the rich mineral lands of Katanga in the Congo area, which he envisaged as a valuable addition to his personal mining empire in South Africa, and as an area which would round out the new frontier that his private army of the British South Africa Company (chartered by the Queen in 1889) was at that very moment pushing into the country that was later to bear his name. Rhodes had already paid heavy subsidies to a bankrupt Scottish pioneer trading organization, the African Lakes Company, to keep the colour of the Nyasa piece of his pattern red, and it was his money that had helped Johnston's new administration. And here, in the 1890's, was the British Government letting the rich copper and rubber country of the Congo slip into the hands of Leopold of the Belgians ; giving way to the Germans in East Africa ; and being far too soft towards the Portuguese, much of whose South African possessions, after centuries of feeble administration, would be far better off, he believed, under an efficient business régime like his own. It was obvious that Rhodes, with his *idée fixe* of a new British empire on the longitudinal axis of Africa, could not appreciate that Africa was only one part of a wider, world policy, inside which the British Foreign Office had to be prepared to make concessions if it was to safeguard its interests in other parts of the world in face of new imperial and industrial rivals in 1892. But he never saw it that way. He felt that he had been let down very badly, that Britain should have had the lion's, not the jackal's, share of the European scramble for Africa ; and he let some of his animus against authority fall on the new Commissioner for British Central Africa, on whom he had looked for so long as his unofficial agent.[7]

While Johnston was being embarrassed and embittered by the characteristically laconic and indirect way which Rhodes had of communicating his disfavour to his satellites, others on the spot in Central Africa were adding to his difficulties with fresh criticisms. From Johnston's point of view, some of the most annoying of these came from missionaries of the older-established stations in the country. There were three main groups of them : the Anglican and largely English missionaries of the Universities Mission to Central Africa at the centre of Lake Nyasa ; the predominantly Scottish missionaries of the Livingstonia Mission of the Free Church of Scotland, up in the Ngoni lands that bordered on the west of the Lake ; and the Church of Scotland Mission in the country along the Shire River to the south of Nyasa. They all had their roots in the great period of David Livingstone's explorations of Central Africa between 1853 and 1873, and their effective beginnings in the second half of the 1870's. Not all of their missionaries were critical of Johnston. For all his personal push and self-assurance, many of them welcomed him as representative of an official administration which would relieve them of the unhappy necessity of taking the law into their own hands, in the arbitration that was forced on them by the clash of cultures of their own Christian-European way of life and the pagan habits of the surrounding African peoples. But others of the missionaries, notably those of the Church of Scotland, who were nearest to the seat of government, and held themselves most directly responsible for having turned the scale when the British Government was hesitating whether to undertake the responsibility of a Protectorate, were critical of the new Administration. They had done Johnston's job for two decades before he appeared—and over three if one considered the first seeds of Christianity which David Livingstone had sown personally in Central Africa, in the short-lived station which the Universities Mission, in response to his famous 1857 appeal, had tried to set up at Magomero in the highlands to the south of Lake Nyasa. (Ill-fated Magomero which had seen the end of missionary pioneering hopes through slave-raiding, tribal warfare, and fever in 1862, and from which, in 1915, the head of another Livingstone was to be carried away into the night !) The missionaries had represented British ideas and ideals to the African tribesmen. They considered that they had pledged themselves for the behaviour of the administrators ; and they were not prepared to admit arguments of expediency and of ends justifying means. In their schools, from which Johnston and his successors took their native agents and officials, they had trained what they hoped were Christian leaders of new, peaceful, and industrious African communities. They saw no reason to forgo what they considered to be necessary authority to protect and direct those inexperienced Christians, now that Britain had resumed political responsibility. And as much as anything else, they were intensely suspicious of the subsidies which Rhodes was paying to the new Commissioner.

But Johnston, like all consciously talented men, and like most who are faced with a new situation in which there are no helpful precedents, expected to be allowed to do things in his own way, and to be given co-operation only when he asked for it. He read the situation as one of resentful disappointment on the part of proud priests. It did not occur to him to think of it as a change of government without an election, or to suppose that the missionary opposition was an Opposition almost in the parliamentary sense. When the missionaries criticized his tax policy, his punitive measures, and his relations with European commercial interests, he took it as clerical officiousness of a kind that had long been tamed out of Anglicanism. The clash of personalities may have been unfortunate. It was probably unavoidable in days when only strong personalities, ecclesiastical or lay, could make any mark in raw Africa.

At the heart of all of the new Commissioner's problems lay the one question still in the centre of that triangle of troubles among native Africans, European settlers and administrators in modern Africa: the ownership of land. In the years between the mid-1870's and the arrival of Johnston, land in many parts of the Nyasa regions had been changing hands very rapidly. Some had been taken away in tribal forays from one set of Africans by another, and the Arabs had stolen it from all. Tribesmen were filtering in from Portuguese East Africa to squat on any land they could find, and half-caste owners of estates or *prazos* from there were encroaching on the borders of the Shire Highlands itself, playing off African against Arab against white man for their own aims. At the same time, a few Indians, petty traders, and soldiers, had come to stay. And right into the middle of these Nyasa highlands, which David Livingstone had seen as such admirable centres from which selected European settlers could spread the civilizing influences of commerce and Christianity, numerous European concerns (mission stations, traders, planters, white hunters, mineral concession-seekers) mainly of Scottish origin had established themselves. They had secured land from native peoples and chiefs by a variety of means: purchase from native authorities who had no right to alienate the land from the tribal commonalty; purchase from native authorities who had; gifts from native chiefs and peoples; outright filching from native chiefs and peoples. The process had speeded up after the Conference at Berlin in 1885, when the scramble for Africa may be said to have begun formally. The Powers of Europe had given a definite signal to their roving, unofficial representatives in Africa to start, and the great treaty race was on. British, French, Germans, Portuguese, Belgians, Italians rushed into the fray, armed with treaty-making forms, intent on securing the marks of at least a few native rulers and thus of acquiring some form of 'title-deeds' to land which would enlarge the boundary in Africa of their national spheres of influence. Private interest became a matter also of patriotic concern, and the pattern of land-holding assumed the aspect of a kaleidoscope, the pieces of which had a tendency to fly violently out of their container under the centrifugal force of international and internal manœuvre and war, in order to make way for other and even more complicated designs which were to provide profitable employment for future generations of special commissions, anthropologists, historians, journalists, and politicians in the attempt to find the original pieces. Nowhere, perhaps, in East and Central Africa was the pattern more complicated than in the little Protectorate that was left to the British in the Nyasa regions after the international share-out.

This was the *mêlée* Johnston faced in 1892 when, in order to lay the foundations of a stable official administration, it was his duty to try to sort out the whole matter by holding an inquiry into the European ownership of land and by making arrangements, under the aegis of the Crown, for the remaining land to be held in trust for the future inhabitants of the country. It was a task before which any ordinary man might quail—or at least want to carry out leisurely. But Johnston, who had not flinched before Rhodes's criticisms, was no ordinary official. And, anyway, he wanted to get the job finished quickly so that he could pour his enormous energy out of the confines of the office and the consular bag into the great new frontier of opportunity which he believed British Central Africa held out for African, Asiatic, and European alike. He called on all Europeans who held land in the Protectorate to show reason for their tenure, and threw himself into the task of assessing the tatterdemalion collection of claims they produced. Between 1892 and 1893 he gave to most Europeans in the country 'certificates of claim' which assured the freehold tenure of their lands. A few claims, the result of apparent sharp practice and chicanery, he refused outright. Others, which he believed were based on insufficient purchase price, he granted upon payment of an additional sum to the natives concerned. In the areas of the 1915 rising, Blantyre and Mlanje, threepence an acre was the maximum increase he enforced; in less settled parts of the Protectorate it was as low as a halfpenny an acre. To some Europeans, who had no proper claims at all but who wanted land, he granted it at much the same low rates out of the Crown land which he had demarcated when all the original European claims had been considered and assessed. He had made, according to his lights, a fair and honest—though perhaps rather rapid—attempt to clear up the mess of land-holding in British Central Africa, in spite of all the criticisms he received while he was engaged in the task from missionary and secular elements alike.[8]

Johnston did two things in this year of land assessment which were to work out their strange logic twenty years later in the rising of 1915: he inserted a 'non-disturbance clause' in many of the certificates of claim, the interpretation and infringement of which was to provide John Chilembwe in 1915 with much of his African following; and he granted land to the new missionary from Australia, Joseph Booth, and thus provided Chilembwe with a contact which was to lead him to America and to set his feet, unknowingly and unwillingly, on the path leading to intrigue and revolt.

The 'non-disturbance clause', at this stage, may simply be stated and its implications left for detailed examination later. On most of the certificates of claim issued in 1892–3 to European land-holders, it ran:

> That no native village or plantation existing at the date of this Certificate on the said Estate shall be disturbed or removed without the consent in writing of Her Majesty's Commissioner and Consul-General, but when such consent shall have been given the sites of such villages or plantations shall revert to the Proprietor of the said Estate. No natives can make other and new villages or plantations on the said Estate without the prior consent of the Proprietor.[9]

Before the arrival of Joseph Booth and his taking-up of land in the Protectorate is examined, it is perhaps pertinent to end this section that has introduced the British Central African missionaries with some account of and some words that were written at this time by one of the greatest of them all. He was David Clement Scott, of the Church of Scotland at Blantyre in British Central Africa, the unofficial missionary capital of the Protectorate, which had been named after the little industrial township in Scotland where David Livingstone was born. Over a year before Joseph Booth began his journey up the Zambezi into the Shire Highlands where Blantyre was set, Scott had seen the opening of the new church of his mission : 'an edifice which', according to the *Illustrated London News* of that day, 'would be creditable to any town or city in Great Britain, and which is said . . . to be the handsomest church in Africa'.[10] Scott had designed and erected the great ornate building, more like a cathedral than a church, by himself, with only two European assistants and the rest of his labour from the native Africans. When Johnston was checking the land-claims and Booth was moving into Blantyre, it stood as a symbol of two decades of missionary enterprise and achievement. It was also a mark of European power and status, and it may be this which decided Chilembwe, perhaps even when he made his first acquaintance with Booth in 1892, to build his own church—that was to be blown up after the 1915 rising.[11]

The Blantyre church was not the only memorial to Scott's labours that appeared in 1892. In this year his *Cyclopaedic Dictionary of the Mang'anja Language* saw publication. It was a sensitive study of the language which Chilembwe's mother spoke, and which he himself used to his congregation in the years when he was an independent preacher. It summed up over twenty years of pioneer missionary work on the African languages, without which the activities of Johnston's new Administration and of Booth's mission would have been infinitely more difficult. And it was a study which foreshadowed a new conception of the dignity of the original people of the Protectorate (a fact which might have disposed Chilembwe, if Scott had been alive in 1915, to cross him off his list of doomed Europeans). For Scott wrote of Chilembwe's mother-tongue :

> It bids fair for a high place in the kingdom of heaven ; and anyone who would surpass it must be as broad and as courteous as this language and this people declare the genius of Africa to be.[12]

It was this concern with the spirit of the African peoples, exemplified in his church and his Dictionary, which must have led Scott to write an article on 'The Situation in the Shire Highlands' for a British missionary magazine in 1892. Looking back over the work of the missions, Scott expressed fears of the new interests that were coming into British Central Africa :

> She has had fifteen years of *vested interests* of the highest kind. . . .
> Dare we [now] 'divide and crush' the native tribes according to the

formula of *divide et impera* which we have seen advocated as an effective African policy . . . are we to set aside native and mission rights and conquer a country with no provocation, and take what is not our own and yet be just ? . . . The African is the key to Africa . . . let the Church know that the natives are threatened with the worst evils of the vast records of spoliation and slavery and moral degradation. . . Protection has too often meant the protection of the aborigines against ourselves.[13]

By using similar words, Joseph Booth, a stranger to the Protectorate at this time, was, not long after, to be accused of adding fuel to the native fire of African resentment against the European occupation of their country. Yet, in order to get both Booth and the Africans he influenced before 1915 into perspective, it is important to remember that words like these of Scott show that other Europeans had anticipated him in some of his criticisms of white rule in British Central Africa.

3. JOSEPH BOOTH—EARLY LIFE

When Joseph Booth arrived, on 11 August 1892, in the Shire Highlands of British Central Africa to look for land for the mission station which he had sketched so ambitiously in imagination the year before in Australia,[14] it would have seemed fantastic to him if he had been told that, twenty-three years later, his name would be raised in the House of Commons in connection with a rising of Africans against Europeans in the new land that he had chosen for his missionary experiment. For Booth went into Africa with a mind firmly set against war and with a predisposition towards religious pacifism which events of the next twelve months in Nyasaland were to strengthen. Yet there was a link between him and the rising of 1915, although the chain of circumstances leading up to these events had been forged before he entered British Central Africa, and was to continue long after he had left it. Therefore, in order to gain some understanding of its bizarre causes, some inquiry into the life and work of Joseph Booth is essential.

He was born in Derby, England, in 1851,[15] the year of the Great Exhibition, watershed of an age of faith and an era of fighting between science and religion, whose bitter contradictions found little resolution in that literature of troubled spirits which the next half-century thrust upon the reading public. There is not a little of the feeling of this literature in the account which Booth left of his early religious experiences and, indeed, in the whole of his later life. It has much of the painful personal searching of Mark Rutherford's *Autobiography* and *Deliverance*, and even elements of *The Way of All Flesh* and of Edmund Gosse's *Father and Son*.

John Booth, his father—so far as can be gathered—was some form of real estate agent and a man of strong religious convictions. It was his custom, Booth related,

> on Sunday afternoons, from the time when I was ten years of age, to require my three sisters and myself to repeat from memory the Ten Commandments ; and, at my mother's request the Catechism. Mother was a devout follower of the Church of England and Father a thoughtful and fearless Unitarian. Both lived an equally good and busy life but agreed to differ religiously and uphold their respective convictions. On one thing they both agreed and taught their children to believe, as beyond doubt : that the Ten Commandments were the sure rule of life and God's own words.[16]

In this early environment, perhaps, was formed Joseph Booth's lifelong habit of religious questioning, which made him move from denomination to denomination like a 'religious hitchhiker',[17] with an unsettling uncertainty of belief which communicated itself to many hundreds of Africans in Central Africa, at a time when the old tribal foundations of life were cracking, and were forcing upon them the harsh necessity of chaos or choice of the faiths, morals, and occupations of the new white man's culture.

Booth's first important religious question struck right into the roots of this culture : its practice of a warfare which made the old tribal fighting look like child's play. His account is characteristic :

> My Grandfather Booth, a fine old man who had fought for thirteen years in the Wars of Napoleon's time and my two uncles who had fought in the Crimean wars, were never tired of telling how many and in what way they had killed scores and scores of French and Russians. Indeed, it was frequently Grandfather's boast that he slept the soundest whenever he had a dead Frenchman for his pillow on the battlefield. . . . I remember that long before I spoke to Father about it, the repeating of the short definite Command, 'Thou shalt not kill' gave a strange jar to my nerves, but it was a long time before I felt I must tell my father what I was thinking. Early in my fifteenth year (mother

having died four years before) I said to my father, when would the time come that I should be free to choose for myself what to believe and what to refuse. My father asked if his religion was not good enough for me. I asked for permission to put a few questions. Father agreed. I asked if he and his father had been born in China, or India, or Turkey, would he have chosen his father's religion : he said, Yes, he thought so. I asked was it not best to take time and search out what was the Truth. He said perhaps so. I replied that was what I wanted to do, for I saw much I could not believe in Mother's faith and some things I could not receive in his faith. He asked what. I asked did he firmly believe the ten Laws of God. He said most certainly, every word. I asked, what about the Law 'Thou shalt not kill', did he believe that ? Yes, he said. I then asked were grandfather and my uncles very wicked men for killing so many and if so why did we not tell them ? Father said it was quite right to kill the enemies of your King and our country. I said that proved nobody believed that Command, neither did I, for I saw no proof that God spoke such words, since neither preachers nor anyone known to me really believed them. So I asked again when could I be free to choose for myself and father said, just as soon as I could keep myself and never ask him for one penny for food or clothes. On the Wednesday after, I got a situation as booking clerk at Buxton, Derbyshire. I have been free in such matters ever since.[18]

This extract reveals much of that volatile spirit of religious independence, fundamentalism, pacifism, and the tendency to criticize established authorities and institutions which, in the little world of British Central and South Africa twenty-five years later, was to bring Joseph Booth into conflict with the ruling Powers and on the side of those Africans already in dispute with them. And for long after the time of this account, he passed under influences which increased his questioning and critical turn of mind, and must have sharpened the edge of his spirit for conflict with the authorities of Africa. Leaving his father's faith, he became an agnostic and for many years nourished his appetite for 'Truth' with the lectures and writings of men like George Jacob Holyoake, old Chartist, atheist, and author of *Sixty Years of an Agitator's Life* ; R. Ingersoll, the American propagandist for agnosticism ; John Watts, the English reformer ; and Charles Bradlaugh, who refused so dramatically in the House of Commons on his appointment as Member of Parliament to take the oath on the Bible. It was an informal university for a religious radical.

For that is what Booth eventually turned out to be. He could not accept the over-statements of the atheists and agnostics and returned to Christianity through the works of the last person who might be expected to fulfil such a role—and yet was himself, surely, the greatest of all religious radicals whose work had stirred up the whirlpool of revolution in two continents—Tom Paine. 'He said that it was useless or dishonest to deny that Jesus Christ lived', noted Booth. 'This was my first step back.'[19]   And from this time (somewhere before his thirty-fifth year) Booth went slowly back to a highly personal form of Christianity, through an exhaustive search of all the evidence which would be available to a man who was mainly self-educated.   The search must have bred in him that habit of intense, comparative examination of Scriptural texts which he found well established among the natives of British Central Africa when he first arrived there, and to which he was to add later, with such unsettling consequences for the Administration.

In 1880, at the age of twenty-nine, Booth seemed to have found clerical work in England a fetter on both his pocket and spirit, and had removed himself to New Zealand.   Like Samuel Butler, he then took to sheep farming.   By 1886 he had achieved a reasonable competence as a sheep and dairy farmer and was living in Auckland, where he had become a member of the Tabernacle and a close friend of its pastor, the Reverend Thomas Spurgeon, son of the famous Charles Spurgeon, whose efforts in his Metropolitan Tabernacle, London, amongst the working and lower-middle classes, had made him one of the greatest popular preachers of his time—and, no doubt, an annoyance to many of the established clergy, who saw in his harvest the result of their own work, and resented his intrusion into fields which they considered their own, as Booth was himself resented later by many members of the older-established missions in Central Africa.

It was in Auckland that Booth's reconversion to Christianity was completed.   It was a deep and genuine conversion, the result of many years of scriptural study and of attendance at popular services and public baptisms at Spurgeon's New Zealand Tabernacle.   Out of this slow process of conversion came a sudden spirit of dedication to whatever form of Christian work should be brought before him. It was, to employ his own language, a 'call', and afterwards, when recounting the decisive stages in his African career, he was to typify each one with the term 'call'.   This first 'call' came on his thirty-fifth birthday, 26 February 1886.   His young son, John Edward (who was to die of fever in Africa in 1894), came suddenly into his room, and in Booth's own words :

> placed his arms round my neck and kissed me, saying . . . 'Here I am the first to remember your birthday, even before mother (Booth's wife was a Yorkshire girl, whom he had married in 1872). Get up and see my birthday card with your favourite text.' He half pulled me out of bed to go to the window and read it. The text was : 'Acknowledge Him in all thy ways and He will direct thy path'. The words pierced me as though I had been swiftly stabbed. I looked into the boy's dear brown eyes and asked, 'Eddie, why did you call this my favourite text?' He answered, 'Because, father, you have given it to me so often to write for a punishment'. True, I had done so and thought nothing of it. . . . But now . . . was it the power of God confronting and convicting me, and repaying me for what I had said twenty years back to my father ? . . . I could no longer speak or look my son in the face. Neither could I take breakfast or go out after my normal business. I was seized with such trembling and weeping that I was compelled to go back to my room overwhelmed and speechless, unable to pray, but only to sob in a paroxysm of shame at the appalling self-centred, superficial life I had led up to that day.[20]

It is no object of this book to comment on the psychology of religious conversion. Whatever its origins, there is little doubt that Booth's conversion was sure enough. In his agony it was completed in a manner which has, under similar circumstances, brought comfort and a feeling of assurance to many. He took up his Bible, put his finger at random on one of its pages and found the words of Isaiah xli, 10, 'Fear thou not, for I am with thee : be not dismayed, I am thy God : I will help thee : Yea, I will uphold thee'. It was enough : 'I went forth to a new life, to find what God would "show" he had for me to do'.[21]

That work, it seems, was to rest ultimately in Africa. But, before that, much else was to happen in Booth's life. He was to leave New Zealand for Melbourne, Australia, the year after his conversion, and to go into partnership in running a number of restaurants. By all accounts, he seems to have been a successful small business man. And all the time he was carrying his faith out into the streets and meeting-places of the North Brighton suburb in which he had settled with his wife and son and small daughter.

It was in this *milieu* that the next 'call' came to take him away far off into the African mission field. The influence of Spurgeon's son in New Zealand had brought Booth to a more or less orthodox Baptist position, and between 1887 and 1891 he was a deacon in the North Brighton Baptist Church of Melbourne. His thoughts had already been turned towards overseas missions as a vocation, by a missionary who stayed at his house on one occasion. He even made two journeys to England in 1891-2, leaving his business for the time in his partner's hands, to offer himself to the China Inland Mission and other missionary societies. But they refused him because he was then forty. So he returned, disappointed, to Australia to await a new direction. Little is known of these trips ; but they illustrate Booth's habit, if his conscience seemed to call him, of going to the ends of the earth, almost, in search of satisfaction—a habit which was eventually to annoy and perplex so many in Africa.

If China was to be denied him—as it was earlier denied to David Livingstone—happenings in Australia in 1891 indicated that Africa was the field for him. The Australia of the 1890's was still a rowdy, turbulent country, with a restless frontier, and an urban population of miners and industrial workers, organized into radical unions and groups who had little respect for the 'nicer' things of life. Amongst the Australian labour movement at that time there were strong currents of free-thought which Booth, in his street-corner preachings, could not avoid. As one who had already run a personal gamut of atheists' debates, Booth was not afraid to take up their challenge to cross swords with them in their 'Hall of Science' in Melbourne, where so many of the militant workers met each Sunday night, on payment of a shilling, to listen to lectures and to take part in debates. Their hero was one Joseph Symes, a former Wesleyan minister, who had deserted the chapel for the platform of the atheist lecturer and who seemed, to Booth, 'to be but little inferior to Charles Bradlaugh' [22] himself. It is said that Symes had thrown down the gauntlet to Christian ministers in Melbourne to debate and that only Booth had accepted. These debates took place every alternate Sunday and provided him with big audiences of hostile Australian miners and others over a period of years which must have increased his self-confidence and brought out the latent strength and persistence in following his convictions, whatever the odds, which he was to display later in many parts of Africa.

Some time before May 1891 the debates took a sudden dramatic turning. One night his atheistic adversary, Symes, before a critical audience of over a thousand, turned round to him and asked if he had never heard the Biblical injunction not to lay up treasures for oneself on this earth but in heaven alone where moth and rust do not corrupt or thieves break through and steal. Apparently not, according to Symes, for

> 'you are exploiting the labour of many and laying up your "little pile" like the rest of us and therefore a good secularist, with whom we are quite ready to shake hands'. Symes' attack mounted: 'Of course, you never heard or read Christ's final orders, "Go ye out to the uttermost parts of the earth—Lo I am with you"?'

And then came his decisive stroke at Booth:

> 'Are there no savages in Central Africa, and if so, why do you not go to them instead of casting these doubtful pearls where no one wants them? Why don't you go, without purse, without weapons, without societies? Is not "Lo I am with you" good enough? Have you forgotten this Christ's message to men of possessions, "Sell all thou hast and give to the poor"? When is the sale coming off? When shall you start to be a Christian?' [23]

It was savage, but it stung Booth to consider again the fundamentals of his religion; it confirmed his mind in the missionary direction in which it had been running for long; and in May 1891 the 'sale' did 'come off', and six months later Booth, with colleagues in Australia, had matured plans for an African mission. His inspiration was confirmed by a meeting with Dr. John Paton, the great missionary from the New Hebrides, who turned his attention to the Livingstone country. For his organizational model he went back to the springs of Baptist missionary effort: the industrial mission ideal of William Carey.

A century before, the independent missions of self-help and self-support which Carey and his Baptist followers of humble origins had built up in India had been accused by the Government of preaching the disturbing doctrine of levelling caste and thus of fomenting mutiny and civil disobedience.[24] Booth, throughout his African career, was to be charged similarly, time and again. There was something about his missionary ideal, even, which went back beyond Carey to the independent 'Diggers' and 'Levellers' of the English 1648 Revolution. It was a tradition, perhaps, which had been handed down from that time onward, through a multitude of sturdy, independent little sects, through the era of Evangelical and Wesleyan storm, into the mid-nineteenth century with its working men's 'tabernacles', such as Booth had supported in New Zealand. It did not scorn the established churches' missionary efforts; but it had an urgency and a spontaneity about it which did not find co-operation with them easy.

A statement that Booth published in 1892 (but which was probably written earlier) gives some of this feeling, as well as outlines his missionary ideal.[25] It has importance because it shows his attitude of mind when he went into Africa and when he first made contact with John Chilembwe. The statement declared that it was rooted in William Carey's ideal of 'self-supporting and self-propagating' missions. And it struck what was to become a characteristic Booth note with a special warning against relying too much on patronage:

> Beware of expecting too much from the wise, the mighty, the noble, or the rich, knowing that they have special hindrances and temptations.

Part of it almost has the ring of 'missionary sovietism', using the word 'soviet' in its original meaning of 'a council of workers':

> Has not the special time come for Christian working men of this generation to come forward and give their working power to God and His great redemptive work? Farmers, artisans, engineers, miners, mechanics, and tradesmen who, while supporting themselves, proclaim the Gospel in word and work?

One can almost see Booth in these words replying to the taunts of his working-class audiences in the Melbourne 'Hall of Science', and, at the same time, catching much of their militant spirit, when he went on to say in his first missionary manifesto:

> Is not the working man of the world the great wealth power?

In the working man might, perhaps, be found the salvation of Africa, which Booth proceeded to draw in typical Victorian terms of darkness and enlightenment:

> Take earth's darkest picture, cruel, bleeding, chaotic Africa, with its average of eight to ten thousand victims every day to slave-raiding, tyranny, and cannibalism. What is needed to transform that picture and to develop Africa's vast resources, and to rightly apply the earth's fulness God has stored there?
>
> Is it to be the 'children of this world' who, without society aids or a 'Go Ye', will presently take possession, fill their pockets, button them up, degrade the native, and make the missionary's work harder?
>
> Or shall it be what the British and American Christians are able to

give and be the better for it—viz. some thousands of consecrated missionary working men?

Then followed a plan to put these ideas into effect. If initial funds could be raised, a small band of missionary workers should be able in two years to become self-supporting by the growth and sale of some suitable crop. (In his early years, Booth placed great reliance on coffee.) The first base should be in the territory of Cecil Rhodes's British South Africa Company: the Zambezi regions. (From this was derived the name of Booth's first missionary experiment, the Zambesi Industrial Mission.) But this was only to be a first base. Supported by an international prayer-union, it would eventually spread in self-supporting communities all over the world. Young men dedicated to the task should sell all they had and go throughout Britain and America to bring in others for the cause. Units of two or three families or about six young men should go out to live amongst the Africans and to share with them their industrial and agricultural experience. They were not to be allowed to trade privately or to invest in the territories in which they settled; all capital was to be held by the mission trustees. There was to be no colour bar: black and white should work side by side, and every effort was to be made to convert the missionary units into models of 'simple Christian civilization transparent by contrast with paganism'. And then Booth inserted a principle which never left him for the rest of his African life:

> Train and cultivate native converts' spiritual gifts and lead to self-reliant action in preaching and planting industrial missions in the 'regions beyond'.

It was all part of his plan for taking the African into active co-operation with the European as soon as possible.

The plan contained many more provisions, couched often in the evangelical language of the 'tabernacles', but its essence lay in the creation, as soon as possible, of mission stations as nuclei from which others would spread, on an absolutely co-operative and non-discriminatory basis. And, perhaps, because the emphasis was so much on speed, Joseph Booth included a final provision that

> in the early stages of the mission special care be taken to secure good climatic and fair commercial, agricultural, or manufacturing conditions, as far as may be consistent with nearness of native population for mission work.

It was this conception of getting off to a good start which certainly led Booth to set up his first stations near missions which had had two decades of existence in British Central Africa, and which drew from them the cries that he was trying to reap where he had not sown on their own hard-won fields of work, when there were fresh and uncultivated fields farther out.

But, when the plan was originally written, Booth was not certain which part of the Livingstone country should be chosen for it, north or south of the Zambezi. It is also doubtful if all of it was his work—though undoubtedly the drive and enthusiasm behind it came from him. He had the assistance of some Australian comrades, one of whom was to die in his service of fever, and others who were eventually to break with him and to set up fresh 'industrial missions' of their own. And, when Booth was forming his ideas, winding up his business, and trying to secure additional funds for his enterprise from philanthropic and religious bodies in Australia, Great Britain, and the United States, his practice, if not his vision, must have been disturbed when he lost his wife from pneumonia on 19 October 1891. She had shared all his ideals—had even, at one time, had a strange dream of a woman from a far-off land standing at the foot of her bed and asking, 'Won't you come and help us?'—and had created for him a feeling of family atmosphere and security which had helped him in many battles. Now she was gone, leaving Booth with a little daughter of nine and a son in his teens. Many would have hesitated under such circumstances to set sail for the new continent to which he had dedicated his life. But that dedication had been so profound, the culmination of such a troubled and searching emotional life, that Booth was not to be daunted.

On 31 October, three weeks after his wife's death, he took his two children with him aboard the s.s. *Oroya* and set off for Great Britain, the first lap of his journey.

4. BOOTH GOES TO AFRICA

Booth had been well provided by his Baptist friends in Australia with contacts in Great Britain. One of them was the Congo missionary, Dr. Grattan Guinness, with whom he left his son to begin training as a medical missionary while he himself went in search of funds and support. He was able to secure a good deal of influential help for his plans, but was advised by Robert Caldwell, who eventually became the first Secretary of the Zambesi Industrial Mission, not to spend too much time initially with such canvassing but to get out to Africa, to survey the land and to come back with a more concrete scheme. Booth was not slow to take this advice.[26]

However, before he set out for this initial survey, there occurred two of those many incidents in his life which added to his conviction that he had been 'called' to the work and which were to have considerable consequences for those Africans with whom he came into contact. The first of these took place while he was staying a week with the Grattan Guinnesses. A missionary arrived at their house from West Africa and, in Booth's own words:

> he said I must take certain guns and weapons which he named, assuring me I should not live six months in Central Africa without them. I said I was not going as a soldier and that my trust was not in guns but in God. He said God expected us to defend ourselves. I replied I would go back to business in Australia, if I had to put my trust in such weapons: but I would pray that night and decide. My decision was never to use a weapon and if God could not or would not protect me from any and every danger I had nothing more to live for and preferred to die. Thus, unwittingly, I became what is now called a pacifist.[27]

This decision had sprung logically from Booth's conversation with his father over twenty-five years ago and out of it was to spring his first brush with the British authorities in Central Africa.

The second incident showed that he was still perplexed, even after his conversations about the Livingstone country with missionaries in Australia, as to which part of Africa to choose for his work. It was such a vast continent and its needs so great, that could he be certain that he had chosen the right place from which to start? Booth overcame this difficulty in a typical manner:

> I resolved whilst at the Leeds Midland Railway Station that if God did not within one hour make it plain what part of Africa he wished me to go to, I would hold myself excused from going at all. I would indeed go to get lunch and try to speak to no one until the hour was out. I walked into a quiet-looking restaurant and pointed out on the menu the food I wanted and opened my pocket Bible to read. The man who served me watched me eat, and read my Bible. He had a newspaper in his hand and commenced to ridicule me for reading that 'foolish old book', adding that he should think what he had just

been reading would interest a man like myself. I asked what did he mean. He said here was an account of two 'Nigger' chiefs from East Africa calling for missionaries from England and they were being taken about by Mayor Beckwith and they were now staying quite near at the Queen's Hotel with an interpreter sent by the Chartered Company. Would I like to see them, if so he would take me there. I was in their presence within the hour and talked to them through Mr. Boyle the interpreter : the conversation would take too long to record but it satisfied me. These natives came from Portuguese East Africa. By the month of April 1892 I had reached the delta of the Zambesi.[28]

If this incident had shown Booth that his field lay along some axis of advance through the Portuguese East African territories, he did not limit his survey to them during his first reconnaissance of Africa. He left London on 2 January 1892 and arrived at Cape Town on 7 February. Before the autumn, by his restless energy, he had carried out an examination of the missionary prospects of 'Cape Colony, Natal, Zululand, Gazaland, the Zambesi Valley, Mashonaland, Manicaland, Matabeleland, and the Shire Highlands', of the whole 'Eastern Coast of Africa, as far north as Mozambique and Lake Nyassa' ; [29] and by November he had sent home a carefully prepared report which, issued in the form of two business-like 'schedules . . . designed to show what £1000 (and £3000) would probably accomplish on Reproductive Lines applied to industrial missions—Industry—Coffee Planting—District—Shire Highlands—Nyassaland',[30] had brought in the funds needed to start his work. The influential Hely-Hutchinson family had supplied the money to buy the first plantation. And, as a measure of Booth's enthusiasm, of his supporting staff in England, and of the business-like character of his 'schedules', one may look forward two years and instance the five and a half thousand pounds which the Zambesi Industrial Mission trustees could set out by January 1894 in their list of contributions. This did not include the initial capital from the Hely-Hutchinsons or the loans on easy terms to the Mission, or the gifts in kind from leading British firms such as Cadbury's, Burroughs & Wellcome, Huntley & Palmers, and many others.

Booth's choice of the Shire Highlands in 1892 may have been motivated by two considerations. The first was that it was already a missionary and commercial base and could be used to reach into the north along the Lake's line, and out to the west down the Congo ;

it might also provide opportunities for evangelists in the Portuguese territories, along the line of the Zambezi entry into British Central Africa. The second was that Booth had already been discouraged from direct attempts to work in the lands of the two chiefs whom he had met so appropriately in Leeds, by the Portuguese authorities themselves, who were at this time still not too well-disposed towards subjects of the country with whom they had nearly gone to war over the disposal of the Nyasa hinterland in 1890.

'I had reached', Booth says, 'the delta of the Zambesi river and stayed in that region about a month, trying to learn something of the language. At Quellimane the Portuguese authorities imprisoned me and refused to allow any kind of Protestant out-door mission effort.'[31] This is the first record of his unfriendly reception by colonial authorities, and although his handling on this occasion by the Portuguese may have been nothing more than a reflection of the international situation as well as of the traditional Portuguese Catholic domination of Mozambique, it is also possible that, at this early moment of his direct African career, Booth showed some of that independence and unorthodoxy of missionary approach which were to lead later to his expulsion from British Central Africa.

Between Booth's arrival at the Cape in February and his ascent of the Zambezi in August 1892, to take him into the Shire Highlands, he had listened to many points of view on East Central Africa and had read as widely as he could in its growing literature. He had heard from the Scottish Free Church missionary, W. A. Elmslie, of the difficulties of colonization in the new country and had been warned by him not to take into British Central Africa his little, motherless, nine-year-old daughter, Emily, whom he had left in Durban while he was spying out the land.[32] The dangers of fever were pointed out to him; but he was not to be put off from his purpose. While in South Africa, Booth had listened to the Scottish missionary, Dr. Robert Laws, even then a veteran, who was at that time on furlough and fresh from a meeting with Rhodes in Natal. Laws was addressing a gathering at which he pointed out the opportunities for settlement in British Central Africa.[33] This seems to have counterbalanced the advice Booth had received from Laws's co-worker, Elmslie.

Backwards and forwards Booth went, across the whole coastal range of South-East Africa, picking up ideas for his mission. His industrial mission ideal was strengthened by accounts of and visits to missions of this type organized by Moravians in South Africa and, at the other end of the scale, by the

> Benedictine Order of Romanists. From one parent station planted ten years ago at Pinetown, about twenty miles from Port Natal, they have now twelve stations, ranging from ten thousand to forty thousand acres each. They produce all the food required for about one thousand, two hundred persons—priests, pupils, etc.—and realise a large income from the sale of surplus products. What has been done well may be done again.[34]

Booth's determination was strengthened. And, in a recently published book on the regions he had in mind for his experiment, he found passages to whet his egalitarian spirit, which may, as has been seen, have caused him some trouble already at Quilimane :

> I had with me Professor [Henry] Drummond's book on Nyassaland [*Tropical Africa*, London, 1889] describing his visit there in 1889. He said, 'What can be done with such a people ? Give them one stick and they will make a spear ; two sticks and they will rub them together and make a fire ; fifty sticks and they will build a hut and there is no more you can do. What can be done with such a people ?' I resolved to go and see.[35]

It was in this determined, assertive, and highly independent frame of mind that Booth went up the Zambezi in August 1892. He took with him a load of personal problems. There was first of all his little daughter, who had been entrusted to him by his wife as she lay dying in Australia. 'Don't ever force Dot away from you, Joseph', she had said to him, referring to their daughter, Emily, by her pet-name.[36] He knew very well that he was taking her into a difficult and dangerous country, but the bond between them was too strong to be broken : the bond between a lonely and troubled man who needed human affection to supplement his new mission vision, intense and untried, and a sensitive, highly strung little girl who had always enjoyed a close personal relationship with her father and who could not bear to be left alone in England with her aunt. Then there was his son, John Edward, who was very young to remain behind in England in training for the mission. Finance was still a matter of concern, in spite of all the money which was coming into the headquarters of the Zambesi Industrial Mission in London. Already the panic conditions that were to develop into a bank slump in Australia in 1893 were visible : and Booth had all his personal capital tied up in the new venture, and was drawing on it freely. And there was the supreme fact that, in spite of the small business successes he had had in Australia, he was entering a country with no previous experience of its pioneer commercial conditions—conditions which had to be manipulated in favour of his mission if his great evangelistic plans were to be a success.

So that when Booth arrived at the commercial capital of the Shire Highlands, the 'Mandala' stores and headquarters of the African Lakes Company in Blantyre, on 11 August 1892, it did not seem likely that he was going to find things easy. He was a man who needed a great deal of help and advice, but who, like so many other visionaries, often find unforeseen difficulties in their way which prevent its being given—or taken.

The first of these difficulties was the attitude towards him and his enterprise of some of the Scottish missionaries in Blantyre. They resented his intrusion into their spheres of work, those 'vested interests of the highest kind' which David Clement Scott had contrasted with the new secular interests in the Central Africa of 1892. They had seen the country and its people change in twenty years. They knew how promising plans had 'gone agley', and saw no reason why the Africans whom they had come to direct, when there were no others who were prepared to do so, should now be distracted by the exhortations and promises of an enthusiast who recognized the discipline of no church. Why should he not go beyond the head of the easy transport line which they had developed, and test his ideas among the pagans who had no other European direction? The Scottish missionaries could not appreciate Booth's hasty insistence on acquiring land, so that a self-supporting mission nucleus could be built up as soon as possible. The Scottish missions in the Blantyre area and farther north at Livingstonia had built up their settlements over almost two decades: why should he not move on into fresh fields? But for Booth, with his vision of self-supporting mission units, staffed by humble men who took no thought for the morrow, it was essential that the first unit should be in operation as soon as possible. And furthermore, as he pointed out later, he had originally intended to go 'at least fifty miles from any existing Mission station, but man proposes and God disposes'. Sickness and an initial 'failure of resources' walled him up in

the vicinity of the Blantyre Mission, and that neighbourhood (about five miles away) became the theatre of an infant effort, not as a recognised

Mission, but as an individual matter. Naturally enough this nondescript effort, taking to itself such a locality for its experimental home,
excited indignation near and far.[37]

Booth measured this indignation by his uninhibited expression of
the contrasts which he noted between the snug mission life at the
centre of the Shire Highlands and the poverty of the African peoples
around them :

> Candidly now [he wrote to the secretary of the Zambesi Industrial
> Mission in London], is it not a marvellous picture to see elegantly
> robed men, at some hundreds of pounds yearly cost, preaching a gospel
> of self-denial to men and women slaves, with only a very scrap of goat
> skin round their loins, compelled to work hard from daylight to dark
> six, but more often seven days in a week, for calico [then the currency
> of British Central Africa] costing fivepence per week the men, and
> twopence-halfpenny the women, and this calico not theirs but their
> owners ? [A reference, presumably, to Ngoni and other native chiefs,
> who sent out their slaves as labourers.—AUTHORS.] I have never felt
> so utterly ashamed of myself and my fellow countrymen as I have
> since coming here. Either we ought to stop spreading the Gospel or
> conform to its teaching amidst such a needy cloud of witnesses as
> Central Africa presents.

For Booth, a European missionary ought to have been able to get
along with £50 a year—or less :

> As I gaze into the yawning gulf of Africa's needs, its hundred
> million helpless . . . I despise myself that I cannot do with less and
> accomplish more.[38]

To all of which, some of the Blantyre missionaries could have
replied that they had been out twenty years before Booth and that
they knew the situation and he did not. Furthermore, most of them
were of good Scottish artisan stock, and had had ample experience
of plain living at home and abroad. But Booth had the enthusiasm
of a convert, fresh to the missionary outlook. He had all the zeal of
a crusading friar anxious for quick results, while many of the older
missionaries looked for slow growth, based on the quiet accumulation
of solid achievement. And before both sides was the frightening
prospect of the development of the new secular interests. While
Booth protested that the missions were using their influence with
their fellow Scots to make his purchase of land difficult, they could
reply that the whole land situation, at the time of Harry Johnston's

survey, was in a flux and that, anyway, they were as uncertain as he was in face of the new concerns.

Little is known of the intimate, on-the-spot aspects of Booth's rubs against the thin skin of civilization over British Central Africa. From the beginning he seems to have clashed with Alfred Sharpe, the Vice-Consul, who was slow to respond to his claims for land, and whom Booth criticized for his habits of rapid punishment of native offenders and his readiness to put them into chains. It was a quarrel which was to last the whole of Booth's time in Nyasaland, and it was Sharpe who first deported him from the Protectorate in 1899. There is little doubt that more than an element of bitterness developed on both sides; Sharpe was a 'practical' man of 'no nonsense' who wanted to see a firm civil administration built up as soon as possible, and Booth was a visionary to whom the hierarchical society which he saw developing in the Shire Highlands was utterly abhorrent. With Johnston, Booth maintained good relations—for there was something of the visionary, too, in Johnston, though of a very different kind from Booth—and it was from him that he secured the ratification of his first land grant at Mitsidi, near Blantyre.

With the secular employers of labour in the Highlands, Booth fell into immediate disfavour because he paid much higher wages to his workers, particularly to the all-important few who had had a little schooling from the missions and were needed desperately for minor clerical posts. And for those who had come to make a fortune and to live as masters of men, Booth's egalitarian emphasis was anathema.

Many of these criticisms of Booth were summed up in a letter which Alexander Hetherwick, a pioneer Scottish missionary, wrote home a year after Booth's arrival. The two men were on very prickly relations and Booth accused Hetherwick, from the beginning, of resenting him and of refusing to give him native guides into the interior. Hetherwick wrote on 2 October 1893, 'He has purchased close to Blantyre—a mile and a half from it—a piece of land'. Here Booth had begun to plant coffee. Hetherwick went on:

> He pays his men enormous wages, as much as eighteen shillings a month (where the ordinary pay is three shillings). He is enticing our Mission boys to join his mission by the offer of enormously increased wages. One boy who got seven and sixpence at the Mission, now gets forty-five shillings at Mr. Booth's. He sent our printing boys a circular showing his increased rates of pay. . . . Two have gone to him who were

our church members and were asked by him to be re-baptized. You may imagine what all this means in a small Christian community such as ours. He intends bringing out more people and to build a Baptist chapel, and this when there are millions on millions of people in Africa who have seen neither missionary or church. . . . There is a great and immense indignation among the European community at Booth's attitude. He is ruining the labour question by his preposterous wages, and all classes—planters, traders and Administration—see the injury he is causing the natives by his way of working.[39]

Nothing less than a minor economic revolution was threatened by Booth's introduction amongst the Africans of the old European habit of seeking higher wages, '*ku tsata mtengo*, to follow price, as the natives call it'.[40] To many of the Scottish missionaries it must have seemed that Booth was spending his backers' money rashly, not on settling himself down but on offering Africans who had been trained by the older missions rates of pay which their own carefully husbanded funds could not meet.

The controversy was taken further later when Booth's mission activity had sought fresh fields, on the western side of Lake Nyasa, where the Livingstonia Mission was at work amongst the Ngoni and Tonga tribes. In May 1894 one of their missionaries, William Elmslie, published an article in a mission paper with the provocative title of 'Strikes Among Natives'.[41] In this he accused Booth of drawing away workers from the mission by his offer of higher wages, and even of touching off a strike among Africans at that time in training as teachers at Livingstonia. Booth was giving the African all the social status of belonging to a mission by the easy entry of quick baptism—not through the long preparatory period which the Scottish missions enforced—and the added incentive of higher wages. Furthermore, went on Elmslie, he was attracting those natives who were loath to labour and who looked for an easy life as a teacher—for Booth's evangelical plans envisaged large numbers of teachers. Booth resented the accusations and claimed that his mission had turned away more native Christians than it had taken from other missions. His reply was characteristic : 'Some day the native view of the case may have to be considered'.[42] And, from the whole controversy, arise two points of considerable significance for Booth's link with the 1915 native rising : first, that the existence of his missions in the early days of the Nyasaland Administration precipitated some native labour discontent, which the economic structure and habits of the country could not satisfy; second, that much of his appeal was to Africans who had aspirations beyond the labouring classes, Africans who had received a little schooling and sought increased status as a consequence.

And, in addition to the dramatic egalitarianism which his example and eloquence helped to spread in the country after 1892, Booth's early years in Nyasaland provided the Africans with another disturbing thought: the fact that the missionaries who had spoken to them so often about loving each other were capable of losing little love amongst themselves. Africans had noted conflicts of ideals within the Scottish missions from the beginning,[43] and now the quarrels of some of the older-established missionaries with Booth provided them with another example of inter-mission conflict. It was not a happy situation and, in the same year as Booth and Elmslie were crossing swords, the Church of Scotland, in Great Britain, in response to representations from their missionaries in British Central Africa, had lodged complaints against Booth and the Zambesi Industrial Mission with the Eastern Section of the Foreign Missionary Council of the Alliance of Reformed Churches holding the Presbyterian System. But the appeal to this informal supreme court had little effect and the squabbles still went on in the territory. Well might some Africans, according to Booth, inquire, 'Why are mission headmen against one another and speak many hard words?'[44]

It was, perhaps, another symptom of the fact that the progressive paternalism of a closed society of predominantly Scottish missions was breaking up in Nyasaland rapidly after 1892, under the impetus of the new secular Administration and interests and under the blows of men like Joseph Booth, who were bringing in radical currents which the world outside, still in the grip of the Great Depression, was, in the days ahead, to thrust even more violently into its once relatively calm waters. For the Africans, a second phase of 'culture-contact' had begun, a phase which was not to end until the Rising of 1915.

5. THE MEETING OF BOOTH AND CHILEMBWE

If pacifist Joseph Booth had been warned that the gentle African, with his few quiet words of English, who came to seek work from him in the autumn of 1892 was to become the leader of that Rising he might well have put it down as just another manifestation of European unfriendliness. Those first days were hard ones for a man, alone with a small daughter in the new British Central Africa. They were living in an old native hut not far from Mandala, and the few provisions Booth had brought up the Zambezi were hopelessly inadequate. While he was out looking for land or arguing himself into some sort of acceptance by the local society, his meagre stores were plundered by a succession of native 'boys' whom he had hired to help him and the little girl, Emily. It was obvious that if he was to go forward in his work at all, Booth would have to have some reliable native servant whom he could trust to tend the small base that he was building up for himself and on whom he could rely to look after his young daughter, for he could not always be carrying her around with him. To fill this need John Chilembwe came along.

Years later, the daughter, Emily, was to write an account of this which deserves extensive quotation, as it is important testimony for the character of Chilembwe, which, when judged only by the context of the immediate events of 1915, has seemed very different from what she has to say. She writes :

> Father was despairing of ever being able to find a dependable boy, when out of heaven's blue the right boy came to find us. His name was John. He was a very black boy with white teeth and a gleaming smile. John's English was limited. But at a mission school somewhere, he had learned to speak and write a few English words. On a scrap of paper he brought to Father a pencilled note. There could be no misunderstanding of either his hopes or his motives. 'Dear Mr. Booth', the note read, 'you please carry me for God. I like to be your cook boy.' Thus did our dear black boy John come into our lives.

> The coming of John was to mean to us much more than merely having found, at last, a dependable cook-boy. In that capacity he did all that could be expected of a native boy who had acquired only a little something of the ways of the white people. He had a great desire to learn and write, and to gain the Truths of Christianity. Being a cook-boy was only a means to an end.

> While neither his cooking nor his English were astonishing in their perfection, they served both our need and his. It was in greater qualities than these that our John excelled.

> Our black boy was a Yao. He was the product of a strong and aggressive race who knew what they wanted and went after it. He knew his own mind and was not easily to be turned from his purpose. But

somewhere there must have been a strain of the gentle Manganja in John. He was so kind and true—so thoughtful and unselfish. Without his faithfulness and dependability I doubt very much if I could have survived, or if Father could have completed the seeking-out, and the buying of land for a mission station. A sick little girl could have been a great hindrance—but John was there. Years later, my brother Eddie might well have died in the Elephant Marsh near Chiromo, instead of reaching Mitsidi before he died, had it not been for his beloved friend, John, who never forsook him—as he had never forsaken us. John had come to us of his own choice. He had heard of Father as a kind white man, and he had heard of our need for a house-boy. He came to give help as well as to receive it.

It wasn't long before we found how trustworthy this black boy was. No longer did our provisions disappear, nor did the knives, spoons and clothing take unto themselves wings. When my malaria recurred, and it seemed impossible for Father to go about his business of finding suitable land for the Mission, John proved himself invaluable. Father was able to leave me in his care. He was kind and infinitely patient, making beef-tea and broths for me, trying to tempt my appetite and give me strength. He could not more gently have tried to comfort me, and help me to be unafraid, if he had been my big brother.

The days were very long with Father away. I was weak and some-times half delirious. Late one afternoon—it has, somehow, stayed clearly in my memory—I woke up and found that Father had not returned. Unreasoning panic possessed me. I got out of bed and went out-of-doors in my nightgown. I started to run down the path, calling for Father. My strength gave out and I fell in a heap. John, who had tried to restrain me, came and gently picked me up. He carried me in his arms and laid me down on my cot. 'You no cry, Miss Dot,' he said, 'your father come back soon.' I must have slipped off to sleep for a brief time, and when I woke up again in restless longing for Father, John was sitting on a packing-box beside my camp cot. His soothing voice said, 'I no leave you, Miss Dot. I stay till your father come.' I was comforted and at peace. Gradually, I came out of my malaria. Gradually, with John's help, Father and I were able to feel the Mandala hut was something of a home.[45]

Well might Booth, then, at this time have echoed the Gospel and cried out, 'There was a man sent from God whose name was John'! And many, years later, would have commented that it was an appropriate name for the Negro Baptist, Chilembwe, of whom hearsay accounts have reported that he looked upon himself as 'the voice of one crying in the wilderness', the preacher in secret of a gospel of hate against the European that 'every tree which bringeth not forth good fruit is hewn down and cast into the fire' and the levelling doctrine that 'every valley shall be filled and every mountain and hill shall be made low'. But the truth of the matter seems to be that Chilembwe had chosen his own Christian name as an adjunct to his tribal names—a practice of many Africans in the new world of European nomenclature—not from John the Baptist but from John, the disciple whom Jesus loved.[46]

Of John Chilembwe's origins, before he came to Booth, there is the greatest uncertainty. Vital statistics and records were rare in Africa at that time, except amongst the Europeans, and even theirs were scant. It is not clear whether or not John Chilembwe had seen much of formal mission schooling before he came to Booth. Admittedly, there is a record from the Blantyre Mission of the baptism of a Chilembwe on 19 June 1888. But this appears to have been the adult baptism of another Chilembwe—though one who may probably have been related to John—who worked for John Buchanan, the artisan missionary-made-good, to whom had fallen the task of proclaiming the first Protectorate of the British in Central Africa in 1889, and who had built up prosperous estates and was in 1892 employing in a clerical capacity Edward Mangin, Booth's Australian assistant, who had gone with Booth into the Shire Highlands and was to die there of fever so pathetically, and to add yet another worry to the burdened Booth. But the fact that Chilembwes are thus recorded does suggest that some family influences may have brought John to the Scottish missions before he met Booth, as well as his own ranging curiosity to learn the white man's creed and ways. It is also possible that he had come into contact with teachers from the Church of Scotland mission school at Chiradzulu, near to which some say he was born, twelve miles or so along the road from Blantyre to Zomba.[47]

Chiradzulu was a particularly troubled area that was raided over by all and sundry. At Magomero, in the Chiradzulu district, the scene a quarter of a century later of Chilembwe's own Rising, David Livingstone had been forced, for the first time in his life, to use a gun against hostile Africans.[48] In 1884 Ngoni had swept over it, and many of the local population had sought refuge on the slopes of the great Mlanje Mountain. The Portuguese were continually interested in the region at this time of international competition, because of its useful strategic position. And, always, the people of

the area, the native Nyanja (or Mang'anja or Wanyasa, as many
Europeans called them), knew well the threat of being sold into
slavery by the infiltrating Yao, dour middlemen of the coastal Arabs.
Robert Cleland, the Scottish missionary who opened up the little
school at Chiradzulu in 1888, has fittingly described the difficulties
of the missions and the local people :

> After conversing with groups here and there and asking them to
> come to 'talk about God', we get all gathered under one village tree.
> Just as the service is beginning we hear far away up on the hillside a
> woman calling with that peculiar strained voice—strained to suit the
> distance. All is silence. Then we hear again, and this time we distin-
> guish plainly the word *ngondo* [war], and soon several of the men rush
> up. It is news of the war. Some of the boys from the other side of the
> hill have been captured at Lake Shirwa [to the east of Chiradzulu] when
> fishing with their fathers. All is excitement, and we hear them say,
> 'They will be taken to Matapwiri', a great Arab centre on Mlanje,
> whence they will be driven to the coast, sold, and perhaps shipped off
> who knows where ? In a little someone suggests, 'Let us be quiet
> until the white man speaks about God and then we will hear about the
> war'.[49]

Whether John Chilembwe was born in this area or not, and
whether or not he actually attended its Church of Scotland mission
school, there is no doubt that he spent the greater part of his boyhood
and youth in this Chiradzulu district, with all its rumours of war
and slavery and its prevailing atmosphere of insecurity. He must
have realized that this was one reason for the chiefs (Mangoche Yao)
of the district signing a treaty with the British the year after the
little struggling mission school was opened there. By agreeing to
this treaty they brought themselves under British protection. But
it was not an altogether unmixed blessing. It meant the payment of
taxes and the decline of much of the old local autonomy, insecure
though this may have been, and often unjust, with its widespread
practice of highway robbery.

Two months or so before Chilembwe joined Booth, incidents had
taken place in his district which must have stamped themselves on
his mind. Some of their implications were recorded in the primitive
little Blantyre Mission paper which had been outspoken for long
on the matter of taxation, claiming that many of the chiefs who
signed treaties of Protection had no idea that they were committing
themselves to the payment of taxes. Writing in June 1892, in an

'Extra Supplement' which it had issued for the purpose,[50] the Mission paper recorded :

> On the 1st inst. H.B.M. Vice-Consul for this district [Blantyre] accompanied by another officer of the Administration left with a large armed party of Zanzibaris professedly for Zomba [the settlement at the foot of Mount Zomba about forty miles to the north which became the capital of the Administration]. Their real destination, however, turned out to be Chiradzulu. On one end of that mountain there dwells a chief who refused to pay the gun-taxes and to hoe the Zomba road when ordered to do so by the Administration officer of the district. The expedition consequently proceeded to deal with him. Of course the people fled to the hills on the rumour of 'war', and only two were found and captured in the village. One of them was the chief's brother. Mitochi himself refused to come down from the hill above where he sought refuge. So the expedition proceeded to loot the village and burn several houses in it. . . . After dealing with Mitochi, the Expedition proceeded to the village where Chipasala lived. [Chipasala was the brother of a headman who lived on the other side of Chiradzulu hill. He was accused of selling two people to a slave caravan bound for the coast but had refused to come when called to account for his action.] The people fled at the first shout of 'war' [ngondo], and the expedition occupied the village. This they did by burning to the ground every hut in it, together with all the food stores. Newly reaped maize was burned inside, or else was emptied out to the ground and then set fire to.

The paper then went on to give its comments :

> We cannot conceive under what form of justice an act such as this should have been perpetrated. Because one man living in his brother's village did not come when called, that the village, houses, food and all, should be destroyed so wantonly is not English law. Neither is it native unless it be that of the Angoni or Arab raider. . . .
>
> A Native chief said to us the other day : 'You English have come and you have seized our country. Well, we give it to you, only we wish to live at peace with you. If you burn our houses, we will build again ; if you seize our property we will work and get more ; but if you destroy our food we must die. You will only drive us away from the Europeans altogether.'

Thus it may be inferred that John Chilembwe spent his early years in an atmosphere of great insecurity and change. It was an atmosphere full of the keenness of the contrasts between the new gospel of peace and brotherhood which the missions were preaching and the evident injustices and disturbances of both European and African society at a time of rapid social change. The new education which the missions had brought with them provided much of the stimulus and the means for observant Africans like Chilembwe to apprehend these contrasts. It is such facts, rather than the exact place or time at which he was born, which need emphasis in trying to build up a picture of the evolution of John Chilembwe's mind before 1915.

Nevertheless the search for Chilembwe's origins has some value, in addition to the normal requirements of biography : it throws light on the tribal traditions within which he may have set himself and from which he may have drawn support in his later years ; and it helps in the appreciation of the myth of John Chilembwe which grew up after his death. It is complicated by the fact that few records survive. Official records of births and deaths did not become effective until many years after the establishment of the Administra-tion—and are still not reliable—and the native peoples themselves were illiterate. There was, perhaps, some use of Arabic by the slave-raiders, and Swahili—the *lingua franca* of the East African coast—in the Arabic script was employed by a few rulers who did well out of the trade. But, before the 1890's, the only workable sources are native traditions and the scattered statements and observations of white men.

A beginning may be made with two of these. The first comes from America, from a small pamphlet put out by the American Negro missionary body which, after the train of events that Chilembwe's meeting with Booth set in motion, was to finance for fifteen years his career as a native preacher. It says that he was born at Sangano, Chiradzulu, June 1871.[51] The second is by Booth himself and refers to Chilembwe's father as a Yao and to his mother as a 'Mang'anja slave, caught in war by his father'.[52] Native accounts may now be used to supplement these statements.

According to some, John Chilembwe's father, the Yao, was named Kaundama and his mother, the Mang'anja, Nyangu.[53] It was by no means an unlikely union. Since the 1850's, groups of the Yao had been moving into the Shire Highlands area, often as the result of a wave of pressure that had been built up by the wars of the turbulent Makua peoples of the Portuguese territories with the central Yao on the Lujenda River. It was a typical process of 'infiltration'. At first, the Yao who had been thrown into the area sought to make themselves acceptable to the local headman of the Mang'anja people and, as the central and coastal Yao were already engaged in the Arab slave trade, tried to get rid of undesirables, such as delinquents and orphans, to the profit of their Mang'anja patrons. But it was the thin end of the wedge for these patrons. Yao and Arabs outside the community, their appetites whetted by these sporadic sales, stimulated the trade now for its own sake, especially as the Zanzibar slave market, to which all their purchases and captives eventually went, was at that time suffering from shortage of supplies. The pattern was complicated by the southern sweep of the Ngoni from the eastern shores of Lake Nyasa. The Mang'anja political structure began to break up, and its great chief in the Shire Highlands, Kankhomba, a rain-maker, is said to have died of starvation. Headmen began to intrigue against each other and to enter into a maze of alliances with the infiltrating Yao. And at the time when David Livingstone was reporting so dismally the sad state of a once flourishing Mang'anja population, the drought and famine of 1862 set the seal on a process of disintegration. It seemed that the only real chiefs left were the Yao captains of slaving bands.[54]

It was, then, quite likely that Chilembwe's Mang'anja mother had been captured by his Yao father in a slave foray.[55] It is also very probable that Kaundama, the father (if such was his name), belonged to that section of the Yao who had settled at Mangoche Hill just south of Lake Nyasa, one of the four groups of this people who migrated into the Nyasa regions. The Mangoche Yao had inter-married readily with the Mang'anja, to the extent that their native Yao speech took into itself so much of the indigenous Mang'anja vocabulary that it was barely intelligible to later and less mixed groups of the Yao who came into the Chiradzulu area. Such a group were the Yao from Mandimba Hill to the south-east of Lake Nyasa, who were ready to treat the mixed Mangoche Yao chiefs as they themselves had treated the indigenous Mang'anja. Thus, to the general *mêlée* in the area, was added competition between competing groups of the Yao. But even with pressure from a rival section of their tribe, the Mangoche Yao chiefs could not hold together. To the south of Blantyre, around Soche Hill, Kapeni had built up his little 'empire' of tributary headmen and villages. At Zomba mountain to the north-east, Mlumbe had carved out his own territory. And, in between, at Chiradzulu Hill, Mphama held sway over his group of client headmen. Belts of no-man's-land, overgrown with bush and infested with wild beasts, separated their petty 'empires'. Other Yao chieftains of different groups complicated the pattern outside the Shire Highlands.

As for the Mang'anja people themselves, there is some slight evidence that they were indirectly descended from the ancient Monomotapa Kingdom which the Portuguese heirs of Vasco da Gama had found in south Central Africa in the seventeenth century. A 'princess, daughter of Monomotapa', is said to have married a 'Maravi chieftain'. The name 'Maravi' is a mysterious one, but whatever its significance, geographical or ethnic or both, it was one which had great relevance for Chilembwe's mother's people. Though Livingstone had found them calling themselves Mang'anja, and others used the expression Nyanja, they were undoubtedly 'Maravi' peoples.[56]

The name which some Africans attribute to Chilembwe's mother, Nyangu, was not without associations for these peoples. It is the title of the ancestress of the northern branch of the Maravi people, and Livingstone himself noticed a Nyangu as the 'lady paramount' of the 'Upper Shire Valley'. In her dominions, he noted, 'women rank higher and receive more respectful treatment than their sisters in the hills'.[57] She was a woman of great power and influence in the area, and it is not altogether impossible that she may have been in the line of descent from the princess of Monomotapa. So that, for some Africans at least, it is not difficult to see why she has acquired some of the attributes of a symbol of the Maravi past.

Whatever the real truth of the matter—and it is deep in the mists of legend—it is probably this aura attaching to the name Nyangu which has created the tradition amongst some Africans that Chilembwe was the son of the traditional Nyangu of the Maravi. Certainly, David Clement Scott in his pioneer dictionary defined 'Chilembwe' as 'a chief, a headman ; a name of honour'.[58] Whether John Chilembwe was or was not the descendant of a mythical chieftainess of the Maravi, he would have known, if Scott's definition is to be believed, that his name was one to which some prestige was attached. It is possible that he had turned over in his mind from his early days the 'name of honour', Chilembwe, and, if his mother really did bear the name of Nyangu—and she could have had it without actually being the 'lady paramount' herself—he might have relished also its significance for her people, the parent people of the Shire Highlands, a people older than the more recent intruders to the area, the Yao, the Ngoni, the Nguru, the Arabs. Did this fact help to build up in Chilembwe's mind the concept of an 'oppressed people' who had suffered enough without having to bear the further 'indignities' of the Europeans?

Whether, from such facts, one may draw the conclusion that Chilembwe, when he first met Booth in 1892, had already in his mind an inkling of the idea that he would eventually become the 'deliverer' of his peoples is very doubtful—though it would be unwise to discount altogether the fact that the associations of his names may have had some meaning for him.[59] Certainly, if he had originally chosen his European name from the disciple beloved of the white man's God, some of his followers in times nearer to 1915 —and perhaps even John Chilembwe himself—may have invested it with a 'John the Baptist' mantle: 'to give light to them that sit in darkness'. There is more than a little suggestion of this in a story that has been attributed to his mother of his manner of birth.[60]

She knew that he was a child marked out for wondrous things, for he came out of her womb feet first: an unnatural and portentous manner of birth. More than any other of her children, he enjoyed great strength and was continually twisting and turning inside her; it was a sign that he would 'turn' events as he had turned inside the womb itself. It is all so similar to the miraculous circumstances attending the birth of John the Baptist. Perhaps Chilembwe had been told that he was a troublesome child in the pre-natal stage, and these facts, communicated to his followers, had in the days after 1915—perhaps even in the days immediately leading up to the events of 1915—been responsible for the growth of legends. 'And all they that heard them laid them up in their hearts, saying, What manner of child shall this be! And the hand of the Lord was with him.' But Chilembwe's mother was no Christian, with echoes of mission-school teaching of St. Luke in her mind, and when she— according to this particular legend—felt him leaping in the womb, her reaction was to dub him 'antelope', *chilembwe* in the Chewa-Tumbuka language of Nyasaland. 'Chilembwe' may also be construed as 'what is written'. If, then, Chilembwe was prone to meditate on the meaning and significance of his name, he would have had material enough in this fact, and the 'antelope' story, as well as in the 'name of honour' meaning and the association of 'Nyangu', to provide the etymological elements of a 'man of destiny'

45

for himself. All this, however, in the absence of more definite evidence, remains very much in the realms of speculation.

Whether Chilembwe thought like this or not, if African testimony is to be believed there does not seem much doubt that as a young child he moved around very much before his parents came to settle in the Shire Highlands. He himself may have told the American Negroes who financed him that he was born in Sangano, Chiradzulu, June 1871—otherwise where did they get the information from? But this could very possibly have been merely his first memory of time and place. How he or anyone else in the 'seventies could have calculated 'June 1871' so exactly is difficult to say. There is no evidence to suggest that his Yao father had adopted Islam, like so many of his tribe, in emulation of their Arab slave-masters, and that he might therefore know the Muslim calendar. Without this guide, it seems difficult to see how the figure could have been worked out. The only statement of secure evidence which seems to have been left by Chilembwe was that he was a native of Nyasaland, born at 'Chiradzulo in the days of David Livingstone, the great African's friend'.[61] By this standard, his date of birth could have been at any time after the 1850's (and before 1873, the date of Livingstone's death), which is, indeed, the time that one of his African followers has calculated.[62] And the statement that he was born at Sangano,[63] Chiradzulu, is worth bearing in mind again, for the same African who has calculated that Chilembwe was born in the 1850's claims that he did not arrive at Sangano, Chiradzulu, until the mid-1860's, by which time he was in his early teens. Prior to this, so the African story has it, he had been following the random flight of the Maravi of the Upper Shire, under his mother Nyangu, from the west of Lake Nyasa down into the Shire Highlands. Harried by the Yao, these peoples had split into several groups, one of which crossed the Shire River with Nyangu and, after a number of years of wandering, stopped finally in the Highlands area. Nyangu herself, with the young Chilembwe, settled finally not at Sangano but at Chilimoni's village in the hills around Blantyre, at a time when the Scottish-named missionary capital was just being built up by the pioneers' labours of the 1870's. It is a picture of a 'chilembwe', an 'antelope', leaping and bounding in no uncertain sense!

But some of Chilembwe's kinsfolk have painted a much more migratory youth for him. According to one account he was born at Zanzibar itself, heart of the slave trade.[64] The picture is not altogether a fantastic one, for another Chilembwe family story says that his parents came from outside Nyasaland.[65] It has been said that they came from Mombasa. Certainly, groups of slaves from the Nyasa regions existed along the coast, as Rebmann, compiler of a 'Kiniassa' dictionary from one of them in the 1850's, knew ;[66] and the Yao had for generations been trading as far afield as the Arab settlements at East Coast anchorages. Nevertheless it is a story, like, perhaps, the whole 'Nyangu myth', which is very likely to have been the wish-fulfilment of Chilembwe supporters, after the death of their hero had set in motion a legend-making process. It is highly likely that Chilembwe's youthful movements were restricted to the Fort Johnston-Michiru-Chiradzulu area of Nyasaland.[67] But to see Chilembwe as a wanderer far afield would set him with the notable Yao—and give him something of a similar prestige—who had accompanied Livingstone's body to England, or with those whom the great explorer had taken as far away as the Nassick Mission at Bombay.[68]

Whatever truth lies behind this tissue of rumours and stories, there is plenty of evidence to support the view that the young Chilembwe, in his own person, felt the force of the wanderings of the Yao, the sufferings of the Mang'anja, and the generally disturbed state of the people of the southern Nyasa regions in the period from the 1850's until the *pax Britannica* brought order—and a new kind of unsettlement. Perhaps it was this, as much as natural curiosity and friendliness, which may have made him seek some slight mission education, formally or informally, from the little school in Chiradzulu before 1892 or, perhaps, from the main Blantyre Mission station itself ; and which, after Booth's arrival, drew him to the new missionary with his great schemes and promises.

When Chilembwe met Booth first, in the autumn of 1892, there is little evidence that he was in any formal sense a Christian. He may have taken his name from the Gospels but, as we have seen, he does not appear to have undergone any form of baptism. It is true that the Church of Scotland Mission at Blantyre early accused Joseph Booth of attracting to him five of their converts, but it is not certain that John Chilembwe was one of these.[69] There is no record whatsoever of him in their publications ; and it may be surmised that whatever influence the Scottish missionaries exercised over John Chilembwe before he went to Booth was not of the most direct kind. Indeed, Chilembwe himself stated that his conversion was not until 1893.[70] And Booth has given the first firm date in his story : 17 July 1893,[71] when he records John Chilembwe as his first convert and notes his baptism. Knowing Booth's practice at this time, it would seem that this was a form of baptism by total immersion, possibly in a river. This is certainly the way Chilembwe himself later baptized his own converts and it may have been a strand in the creation in his mind of the 'John the Baptist' picture— if, of course, he ever held such a view—of himself. Some further evidence of this is provided by a story from a publication of the American Negro Baptist organization into whose hands Chilembwe fell later. It states that he had remained outside the Blantyre Mission for two years because he had read in St. Matthew's Gospel that Jesus was baptized in a river, the Jordan ; and from this Chilembwe had conceived the belief that baptism meant something more than the sprinkling of water on the head. The arrival of the total-immersing Booth was, then, very propitious for him.[72]

Before this date, other stages in Chilembwe's development may be inferred. Between the autumn of 1892 and the early months of 1893, he had been Booth's greatest help. The death of Booth's Australian assistant, Edward Mangin, from malaria, on 25 August, was to deprive him of any further European assistance for his mission until well into 1893. Chilembwe, moreover, was constantly improving his English, and with the two native languages of his mother and father, Yao and Nyanja, became increasingly useful to Booth as an interpreter. During this time, he was to nurse Booth and his daughter during spells of fever. One can only speculate what effects this growing intimacy with Europeans had on him. Tending Booth and his daughter, with their impoverished life in an African mud-hut, perhaps helped to impress on Chilembwe's mind the different social levels of the Europeans. It certainly does not seem to have made him more critical of Europeans—that was a much later development.

As time went on, Chilembwe was not Booth's only African helper. He was joined by a small but growing group of Africans, many of them from the neighbouring Blantyre Mission, much to the chagrin of the missionaries there. One of these helpers, who was to prove especially useful, had joined Booth shortly after Chilembwe, and probably went to him when, thanks to a member of the African Lakes Company, he and his little daughter had been allowed to use one of its European houses for a while—simple accommodation certainly, but a welcome change from a mud hut. It may have been Chilembwe's first introduction to the interiors of European dwellings.

This new-comer was one 'David Livingstone', a Mang'anja who lived under the control of the Makololo people whom Livingstone had brought with him as porters and servants into the Lower Shire regions, and who had eventually settled there, and, by taking advantage of the fluctuating state of African politics, had made themselves masters of bodies of the local people. He had chosen his European names from the great explorer's, and he and Chilembwe together became the Booths' boys in the new house. Emily Booth left an interesting comparison of the two of them which merits quotation for the light it throws on Chilembwe at this time. As she saw them,

> John was typically Yao, intelligent and quick in his thought processes ; his face and eyes were alert. He moved with assurance and decision. David was just as typically Mang'anja as John was Yao. He was a big, kindly chap, gentle in manner and with a slow-moving mind . . . but once he knew a thing, he knew it. He made me think of a good-natured Newfoundland dog, he was so big and clumsy, but altogether lovable and trustworthy. That was the major quality in which John and David were so much alike.[73]

The comparison along tribal lines may be forced—though many at this time made such contrasts between Yao and Mang'anja [74]—but it does give a valuable sidelight on Chilembwe's character and suggests an independence of bearing in him remarkable even at this early time.

Perhaps it was this trait which made him tell Booth that he was reluctant to go with him when Booth wanted to visit the village of Maseya (David's Makololo chief) which was situated a little below Katunga's, the river station for Blantyre on the Shire. The villagers were almost all Mang'anja, for whom the Yao, in spite of all their intermarriage with them, felt some of the scorn of a dominant people. The incident indicated that, despite his Mang'anja mother, Chilembwe looked upon himself as a Yao [75] and had originally many of their prejudices. (It also suggests one reason why he failed to gather behind him a fully representative selection of the Nyasaland tribes to fight the Europeans in 1915.)

Booth had been introduced to Maseya by Johnston in the August of 1892 when he was entering British Central Africa. But the Makololo chief had, at that time, been cautious of opening his heart to Booth in the presence of the representative of the new and untried Administration. He had his chance, however, in December, when Booth went back to his village to see if he could borrow a canoe and some men for his mission reconnaissance. Even if Chilembwe was not present at this meeting, he must have heard about it from his fellow house-boy, David, who went along with Booth as interpreter. It was a meeting which showed that, even in the few months he had been in the Shire Highlands, Booth's independence had made him unwelcome to some of the Authorities ; and it illustrated the uneasiness which even the Makololo, the first people of this area to have contact with the white man, felt at the coming of the Administration.

The story is best told in Booth's own words :

> The Chief Maseya called Chief Katunga and a large concourse of people, placed mats on the ground and for three days, one after another, rose, questioned and cross-questioned self and child [Booth had taken with him his little daughter] in a way that caused me great surprise and admiration of their natural insight and ability. Some of the questions I did not like and could only answer with difficulty, such as : 'Why did the "Zinganga" [Doctor] Livingstone first come ? Did the White Queen send him ? Who paid him and helped him with goods and money ? Did he come with a soft tongue to spy out the land and open the way for these men of guns and taxation, to steal the land and make slaves of them ? Who sent this smooth-tongued man "Johnsoni" [Harry Johnston] ? Why did the White Queen send him ? Why did he bring more men with guns ? Why were they to make his roads or carry his loads and work one month for him for nothing ? [A reference to the hut-tax of three shillings, which was equivalent to a month's labour.] Were white men preparing to steal all Africa ? Did I not think my nation was a nation of robbers ? Had we stolen any other countries ? Were we going to make them a nation of slaves ? What would the end of it all be if they did not fight and stop us ? Who and what was I ? Who sent me ? Who found the payment for the journey and paid for my goods ? Did the Queen send me ? What was the difference between "Johnsoni" and myself ? Must I obey him ? Who was "Sharpi" [Alfred Sharpe, the Vice-Consul, who so disliked Booth], his chief servant ? If "Johnsoni" told me to take a gun and fight a black man, should I do so ? Why should I refuse to fight ? Would white men kill me if I would not stand and fight with them ? Would I fight for and help the black men ? Why would I die myself rather than fight at all ?

Was I a coward ? Why would I not have or use a gun ? Was there a nation or tribe of white men of that kind ? If I went back home anytime would I seek out and tell that tribe of no guns to come and share their land as friends, bringing no guns ?' And endless more questions, till I felt almost ill with heat and worry.[76]

It was a dramatic meeting : the tall black man, with his garment of dark blue calico, worn like a toga ; holding in his outstretched hand a long black staff of ebony, with a heavy gold band at the top, which he claimed Queen Victoria had sent to him when she had heard the story of Livingstone's Makololo ; and before him, the isolated white man and his ten-year-old, motherless daughter.[77] Booth's answer to all the questions was to produce his Bible and to read the first two verses of the sixty-first chapter of Isaiah. Maseya recognized them instantly and remembered that David Livingstone, the explorer, had read them years before. But in these changed circumstances, did the old chief find a fresh significance in the words Booth was reading to him : 'he hath sent me to bind up the broken-hearted, to proclaim liberty to the captives and the opening of the prison to them that are bound ; to proclaim the acceptable year of the Lord and the day of vengeance of our God' ? Out of their context, there was something ambiguous about the words : they might evoke memories of Livingstone ; they might support Booth's claim that he was a man without guns, a man of peace ; but they could also be taken to suggest that Booth, this new, independent man, free from associations with the established missions and the new Administration, was a potential ally in a conflict with the new order, with its unwelcome demands and its threat to the Makololo position as overlords of groups of Mang'anja. Certainly for some in that new Administration, the news of this three-day palaver between a difficult newcomer to the Protectorate and two chiefs who were asking awkward questions was something that could not be tolerated. Booth goes on :

On the third day, a Zanzibari native soldier arrived with a letter to the chiefs from one Bohill, a white officer of Mr. Johnston's. This letter the chiefs could not read so my interpreter, David, translated it into both Makololo and English. It ordered this meeting to be dispersed by the soldiers if the chiefs did not stop it and told the chief to send me away. 'There were good and bad mission men. I was a bad and dangerous one and must be sent away. I had no authority to speak or teach : no Church sent me ; I had no authority but an old Book.' [78]

And so the meeting was dispersed as ordered. But, before Booth left on the following day, Maseya gave him a piece of land

> for the men of my kind, whom I must call the men without guns, a good piece of land with river frontage for boats to use, which he did deliberately soon after daylight, cutting with his own axe a deep mark in each boundary-tree and for which he firmly refused any form of payment or present.[79]

Then Booth left with his daughter and they were back at their house near Blantyre late in the morning.

The daughter records that 'John came over in the afternoon and was glad to find us back from our journeyings'.[80] Perhaps the most interesting time of that day for Chilembwe was the moment that is cherished by all African house-boys, in the evening when the sun is down, and the Europeans have been fed, and the servants can gather around the fire outside and just talk . . . and usually the talk is of the *bwanas*, the Europeans themselves. It may have been in such a setting that David, bursting with the news of his part as interpreter between Booth, Maseya, and Katunga, told him what had passed between them, and how the soldiers came to break up the meeting. How much of this talk of peace and war, of taxation and land, of white and black, remained with Chilembwe in his later days when he began his own fight with the 'men with guns', cannot be determined. But it is evident that his career with Joseph Booth in the 1890's influenced him in countless ways in his later years.

Apart from the general religious-radical attitude which it imparted, it may well have been an object lesson to Chilembwe of the dangers of mission rivalries and of the necessity of taking a strongly independent and assertive line if missionary independence was to be obtained. For, shortly after Booth's return from the meeting with Maseya, the land which had been given to him was taken away, after, according to Booth, missionary criticisms at Blantyre that he had cajoled the old chief into giving him the plot had brought the matter to Johnston's notice and had caused Maseya a journey into the court at Blantyre.

Yet, from this inter-missionary fracas had sprung one good result: Johnston, with whom Booth seems always to have been on good terms, gave him a piece of land to make up for what he had had to surrender. Booth could now go on to build up his Zambesi Industrial Mission at the place he called Mitsidi, after the stream by which it stood, near Blantyre. John Chilembwe, of course, went with him.

Operating from this centre, Booth had by about March 1893 built up at least eight other missionary bases. Five lay to the west of the Shire River, in the Ngoni country dominated by the paramount chief, Gomani. Booth seems to have established these by himself, in another episode which must have come to Chilembwe's ears, though he was not with Booth at this time.

According to Booth, the 'mouthpiece' of Gomani, Zidama, had told him that it was death to enter into his wild country without his consent. Booth's reply in pacifist terms seems to have caught his fancy :

> This man came every day for seven days to 'kucheza', chat, about the way of peace and friendship : then went back to his great chief, brought a cow as present and said the land was now open to choose . . . payment of any kind was refused.[81]

Johnston ratified the transaction. And Booth recorded the moral and sequel thus :

> This grand native Zidama . . . said simply their fathers only knew the way of war, now they were utterly sick at heart of war and longed for white men without guns to teach them the way of peace and friendship— sad to say the head chief, Gomani, two or three years later, whilst the writer was away in the Zulu country, was invited and came to the Domboli station. One of those same 'men of guns' was there, the result being that the chief was killed and buried there, which soon after nearly cost the writer his life as being the first man to open the way for 'men of guns'.

It is a puzzling account. Gomani was certainly captured and shot in 1896 when a British expedition invaded his country after he himself had raided British territory in search of refugees from his own government. Yet in what way this fact led up to Ngoni resentment against Booth is not clear.[82] But the whole episode has two consequences : first, it shows what was to become a familiar feature of Booth's career with Africans, the way in which they often broke with him and moved on to another alliance to serve their purposes, while he transferred himself to another group to support his ; and second, the constancy of his pacifist attitude which must have been contrasted by the Africans who met him with the punitive methods of the new Administration, which was still struggling to maintain itself in the face of tribal, Arab, and Portuguese resentment and rivalry.

Booth's entry into the Ngoni country on the borders of Lake Nyasa and on the other side of the Shire had the result of taking John Chilembwe there as an interpreter. Throughout 1893 Booth's movements are difficult to trace in detail. He had moved rapidly up and down the Shire: to Natal for supplies; to London on a flying visit to discuss finances with his colleagues at home; and backwards and forwards over the whole range of his nine or ten bases in British Central Africa, advising, supervising, bringing new Africans to him from heathen territory—and from the older missions. Some of his colleagues from Australia, undeterred by the death of Edward Mangin, had joined him in the Likabula Valley in the neighbourhood of Mitsidi to build up the nucleus of what was later to be known as the Nyassa Industrial Mission; and reinforcements of Europeans had come out from Great Britain in response to the campaign which the Zambesi Industrial Mission was then conducting at home. During this time Chilembwe must have been left very much to his own resources.

In the intervals during which his master, Booth, was at Mitsidi, Chilembwe had at least four experiences which deserve mention, not only because they eke out the meagre record which is left of his life but because they may have helped to build up his imagination for the events of 1915. One was a wedding. Two Africans at the Mitsidi station were married in Christian fashion, with full European-style honours; veil, frock-coated clergyman, wedding march, cake, reception, and all. Much of it was the work of a European female missionary who had just joined the station, and it created a great impression amongst the Africans.[83] Even if Chilembwe was not present at it—and he probably was—he would have heard about this nine-days' wonder from his fellow house-boy, David, who interpreted at the ceremony. It may have increased his fascination with the surface phenomena of European society— proper dress and respectability—which, when he had his own congregation after 1900, he tried to enforce with so much vigour upon his flock.

And after a wedding, death. Two Europeans who came out in 1893 went down with fever and were 'properly' buried near Mitsidi, in coffins that were made by a native carpenter under instruction, and with the Christian form of ceremony.[84] It was a new jolt into the strange European world, the world of exits as well as entrances, as formal in its last rites as those of Chilembwe's Yao fathers, but a new experience and a new form of intimacy with the European.

Chilembwe was next to witness how the pacifist Booth would be found to break his word and put a gun into his hands and into the hands of another Yao, Gordon Mathaka, who had joined Mitsidi perhaps in July, and with whom for three years Booth was to be closely linked. Booth had on one occasion befriended a girl from a near-by village whose father, having accepted a bride-price, had agreed that she should marry a man older than herself to whom she felt no degree of attraction whatsoever. To the independent Booth it was an intolerable situation and he refused to surrender her to the irate father. When this parent's response was the threat to burn down the mission station, Booth gave Chilembwe and Mathaka guns and the job of sentry-duty day and night, and saved the situation.[85]

But for Chilembwe's fourth recorded experience at this time at Mitsidi there was no gun, though the situation might well have demanded it. As the mission station grew, Booth began to encounter exactly the same problems of native relations which the Blantyre missionaries had met over a decade ago. A woman and her child were stolen from land belonging to the mission, and it was Booth's duty to go to the village of the envious chief who had stolen her and get her back.[86] This time he took Chilembwe as well as David with him, and it may have been the first time that he used Chilembwe as interpreter. Perhaps this was because, under the new conditions of the mission, some of Chilembwe's Yao prejudice was breaking down. It is more likely, however, that it was an indication of his increasing command of English.

It seems that Booth may have been preparing Chilembwe for the role of independent interpreter to the mission ; for, about this time, Chilembwe was going out with parties of recently arrived missionaries from Great Britain to help them with their language difficulties and to witness the effects of their new enthusiasms in the African bush. One of these was a raid on an African 'beer-drink' at Mbinda's village on Michiru Hill around Mitsidi : the zealous newcomers held up the proceedings in order to evangelize while Chilembwe interpreted. But what Chilembwe may have been learning most at this time was not the effects of the new missionary enthusiasm but the power of the interpreter, the voice of the alien.[87]

The next occasion when Chilembwe witnessed the strange effects of the newcomers' enthusiasms was during a trip lasting two or three months, some time shortly after the middle of July 1893, when a young and zealous missionary, Alexander Hamilton, arrived at Mitsidi. Hamilton had been stirred by Booth's description in the British literature of the Zambesi Industrial Mission of how the Ngoni west of the Shire tyrannized over the older inhabitants. Booth had prepared the way, with his establishment of five bases in the territory of Gomani's Ngoni, and he had dependable Africans ready to take the young newcomer into the area. They were Chilembwe and his fellow Yao, Gordon Mathaka. One wonders if this was the first time that Chilembwe had been in predominantly Ngoni country, though, of course, it was by no means his first contact with this warrior people, for his own Chiradzulu had suffered enough from their raids. Perhaps, if the story of his wanderings with his mother Nyangu is true, he had already been in that country. But it seems more likely that this was his first trip there, and therefore it is regrettable that the records of it are so scant.

What does emerge from the brief testimony of Chilembwe's visit to the Ngoni country, however, is further evidence of his familiarity with guns. He and Mathaka, on this trip, went along not only as the interpreters of Alexander Hamilton but also as his gun-bearers, for he seems to have been a man with ideas on big game. His first encounter with them, however, was not a fortunate one. One of the Ngoni villages the party visited was terrorized by a lion. Hamilton saw this as his first chance for blood. It was arranged that he, with Chilembwe and Mathaka, should stand behind a clump of trees in a comparatively open space outside the village. The villagers would then beat the surrounding bush and drive the lion into this field of fire. However, the lion moved too quickly from the bush to the clearing and the swiftness of its sudden bound into the open had Hamilton up the tree in no time! Mathaka and Chilembwe stood their ground. Mathaka wounded the lion with one shot and Chilembwe with another, while the Africans who had been beating the bush rushed in to finish it off with their spears.[88]

This incident, together with the story of Chilembwe on armed sentry-go, raises the question of what knowledge he had of firearms before he met Booth and the Europeans of the Zambesi Industrial Mission. Guns were no rarity in the disturbed Chiradzulu of his boyhood and youth, and many of the Yao, with their slave-trading

Arab contacts, were no strangers to firearms.[89] In the incident recorded, Chilembwe sounds like a practised hand. But, whatever stage it marks in his evolution as a big-game hunter, there is not much doubt that he later became one, as will be seen. Furthermore, the point deserves raising at this stage as it adds to the evidence that Chilembwe was no mean hand with a gun—a fact to be borne in mind in judging his tactics in his pathetic campaign of 1915.

If his independent ventures as interpreter illustrate a growing self-reliance on Chilembwe's part, in reality he was drawing yet closer to the Booths. While Joseph Booth was away on his many errands, Chilembwe was, it seems, the most useful African member of his household. Although the arrival of female missionaries at Mitsidi meant that Booth's little daughter did not lack for supervision, by the second half of 1893, it is reasonable to suppose that her bond with Chilembwe was closer than it had been the year before when he had saved her from fever. He had shared her pathetic attempts to celebrate her father's birthday earlier in the year on 26 February,[90] and had been close to her all the time when he was not away interpreting. When Booth wrote home to the secretary of his mission in June 1893, refusing an offer to look after the little girl, one of the reasons he gave was that she wanted to stay in British Central Africa 'partly for the natives, whom she looks upon as her friends now'.[91] There is not much doubt that Chilembwe was the main person he had in mind when he wrote that.

Chilembwe's bond with the Booths was strengthened in the October of 1893 when Booth's son, John Edward, a youth of eighteen, who had left England with a party of twelve Zambesi Industrial Missionaries and their children, arrived in the Shire Highlands. The daughter has left an account of his arrival that October which underlines the closeness of Chilembwe's connection with the Booth family :

> I best remember his meeting with our black boy John who was also growing to be a young man. Father introduced them saying, 'Ned, I've often written to you about our friend, John. Now I want you to know him.' I stood beside them, wondering if they would like each other. As they clasped hands, looking into each other's smiling faces, they seemed always to have been friends with no need for words.[92]

It seems that it was a genuine friendship. Booth went back to England at the end of the year to raise funds for the mission ; he took his little daughter with him, in spite of all her protests, because, no doubt, of the necessity of giving her some sort of education and of protecting her health, already sorely tried. During Joseph Booth's absence Chilembwe was one of the few personal connections in British Central Africa with his father and family that Edward Booth had left, for the European missionaries there had no very personal relationships with the elder Booth, apart from the small Australian group who were not in Mitsidi. The two young men, white and black, drew closer together and John Chilembwe was to be with Booth's son at his death, when Joseph Booth himself, tramping over England, Scotland, and Wales on speaking tours about the mission, had no idea of what was happening to his son.

Some time at the beginning of 1894, John Edward Booth had set out on the long journey from Blantyre to Chiromo, the trading post at the confluence of the Shire and Ruo rivers, and from there down the Zambezi to the Portuguese town of Quilimane. Chilembwe went along with the young Booth as his guide, protector, and companion. The son's object was to clear a shipment of food and supplies through the customs at Quilimane, and he was away two months. On his return, fever overtook him at Chiromo. There was only the flimsiest of accommodation at the African Lakes Corporation's post there and John Edward Booth was advised to get back to Mitsidi, away from the rainy season at Chiromo, as soon as possible. With Chilembwe's help, he managed to make the journey back to Mitsidi in a week, and he died there on 22 February 1894. Without Chilembwe he might well have died in the humid Elephant Marsh north of Chiromo through which part of his journey lay. And Chilembwe was with him at the end.[93] His bond with the Booths was sealed by this death, news of which came unexpectedly to Joseph Booth when he returned to the Shire Highlands some time before May 1894.

Booth's isolation was now acute, with his wife dead in Australia, his only son buried in Africa, and his little daughter far away in England, and increasing trouble with the established missions. (This was the time of his controversy with Elmslie of Livingstonia.) He had plenty of incentive to draw closer to friendly native helpers like Chilembwe.

The extension of the Zambesi Industrial Mission activities kept him busy. On 30 August 1894 the Mission steamer *Glad Tidings* (*Mtenga Wabwino*) was launched at its headquarters at the Chinde mouth of the Zambezi. Between this time and the May of the following year, when it was sold to the African Lakes Corporation,[94] Booth was using it constantly on his various trips up and down the Shire and Zambezi. A native story that Chilembwe served as captain of this river steamer may be discounted,[95] but he may well have seen some service on it.[96]

If this was the case, one result may have been to bring Chilembwe into touch with the African who, in 1915, was to play something of the role of his second-in-command. This was John Gray Kufa. On 20 July 1890 this African, whose home was at the Kongoni mouth of the Zambezi, had been baptized by the Church of Scotland Mission at Blantyre, after having been with the mission for five years.[97] He proved one of their ablest converts. By December 1892 John Gray Kufa was on twelve months' probation as one of the Scottish Church's first native deacons in British Central Africa, and a year later he had been entrusted by the Blantyre Mission with the responsible task of evangelizing amongst his own people.[98] At the time when the *Glad Tidings* was running its brief eight months' career for the Zambesi Industrial Mission he was living at the junction of the Zambezi and Chinde rivers in a little hut beside his small school, which served twelve native pupils.[99] Although one tradition claims that Chilembwe and John Gray Kufa first encountered each other while Chilembwe was out hunting, it is just as likely that they may have met originally at the coast. Another tradition of this period, which is open much more to question, is a European account that Chilembwe lived disreputably for a while at the coast. Chilembwe was far too busy in Booth's service to have time for sensual orgies in the Portuguese territories.

Indeed, some time after Booth's return to British Central Africa from England in 1894, Chilembwe was selected to go with him on a mission into what Booth called the 'Mang'anja' country to the west of the Shire. Booth had read of the people here, in a book written by Lieutenant Edward Young, who had gone out in 1867 with an expedition to the south end of Lake Nyasa to examine reports that Livingstone had been murdered there by the Ngoni.[100] Young had visited this branch of the Maravi and had said that they claimed a special revelation from God. This whetted Booth's curiosity to visit them but he had to wait his opportunity, which seems to have come to him in 1894. He found them immediately to the south of Lake Nyasa, 'on the plains around and in the valleys . . . lying between the Shire and the Zambesi rivers with Tete to the West and Blantyre to the East'.[101] They were not fighting folk. It was this which impressed Booth about them : they were 'a particularly peace-loving people'.[102] His encounter with them strengthened his pacifist convictions and reinforced his belief that Europeans could do nothing effective with the Africans unless they negotiated with them on equal terms without guns. Booth felt that yet another 'call' had come to him from the natives to impress this point of view on him, and he found it, looking back later, one of the most remarkable of all such 'calls' which he received. Therefore, as Chilembwe was with him at the time, the episode deserves more than a passing mention. It shall be treated, as much as possible, in Booth's own words.

When he arrived in this country he inquired carefully into the sources of their own religious beliefs before he gave his own testimony :

> 'Mlauli' [probably a mishearing of 'Malawi', Port Herald mountain] is the name of their sacred mountain, where they have built their 'Nyumba ya Kalubvi' or House of Worship. The two chiefs, each of a group of villages, with whom the writer had to do, were named Chatyika and 'Kucha-wa-dzua', 'the break of day'. Neither of them would have anything to do with the writer at first, but treated his requests for a hearing with quiet and dignified contempt. Chilembwe, whose mother was of this tribe, was with the writer as interpreter, where needed. Nothing that we could say secured a hearing. In despair [for the writer had gone a five days' journey purposely to inquire about this people and their worship] before leaving, beaten out for the very first time, the writer chose out a tall dense tree, stood under it, took off his helmet, placed it on the ground, closed his eyes and sang hymns in the Chinyanja, their language, from memory, as solemnly and heartily as possible.[103]

Chilembwe seems to have joined him in this hymn-singing, for in his next sentence Booth changes into the plural and relates :

> At first the people were ordered into their huts, taking children, dogs, and fowls with them and so the singers had the place to themselves for a short space.[104]

Chilembwe's eyes must have been open, however, for Booth changes back sharply to the singular :

> But as the closed-eyed singer did not stop, or go, a sudden change took place and all burst forth with tom-toms, clapping of hands, circling

round, stamping of feet, singing of River and other songs, so that the writer's voice was drowned out and he resolved to beat a retreat as soon as the hymns of memory were run out : and thus the noise of the people was forgotten till the end of the memory hymns was reached, perchance thirty or forty minutes all told. By this time all was perfect silence, so that the writer concluded they had gone away in disgust, his eyes having been scrupulously kept closed, so as to keep close to God and take any consequences.[105]

What Chilembwe must have thought of what was going on as he stood, open-eyed, helping Booth with his hymns is not recorded. For Booth, however, it all came as a complete surprise, for

on opening his eyes he found hundreds of people standing in silence. Taking prompt advantage of this he commenced the usual Gospel about God's love in sending his Son, etc. etc., Chilembwe translating carefully. After twenty minutes of this the writer stopped, said he had finished and was now ready to go unless they had something to say. To this the swift response came from Chatyika : Yes, they had a deal to say—What I had told them was 'Mwambi wa Chabi', a tale of nonsense. They knew that God had spoken to them by the skeleton head of Mbona, which they kept in their house of worship. His messages were spoken in the darkness. But perhaps God the creator had spoken to white men also. Had the writer heard him speak ? If not, how could he know that God *had* spoken ? Did I myself know God's message to white men and how and what ? [106]

Booth then took out the small Bible he habitually carried in his pocket and showed it to the two chiefs : 'this holds the Message God himself spoke to white men'.[107] They asked him to open it and to read out this message and they would know if God had spoken or not. Chilembwe was interpreting all the time.

Then slowly and carefully we read and translated the Ten Commandments. These caused great excitement and very much talking amongst the chief men. After some considerable time, a chosen spokesman stood up to speak for all. He said, The chiefs and people of the Mang'anja have examined the Message of God to white men and it was very good. Their hearts told them that no white man or black man could or would make such a message. It was hard for white men, very hard—and also for black men—the black man or chief would say men must not covet cattle, or land, or woman and that if they had power, they should not take or steal them. But hardest of all that they should not fight, or kill those who did these things. Yes, to-day they had heard a message that could not be from either white men or black men but only from the Great God and Father who made them both.

Even Mbona centuries ago, the Father of their tribe, had spoken much the same and forbid them to spill the blood of men upon the ground and this they tried to do till the 'Zinganga' Livingstone brought guns and left them with the Makololo who fought them and stole their women : also the Yao got guns from the Arabs and stole both lands and women. Why did white men come with guns if they knew God said they should not kill ? Was the writer a man of guns or not ? Did he not have a small gun hidden in his pocket ? [108]

To all this Booth replied with his usual pacifist arguments, and continues :

> This was very carefully and repeatedly gone over by Chilembwe, my friend and interpreter. The effect on this people was remarkable. They said this message was like the break of day to them. Maybe God who spoke these words would choose out a people who would refuse the way or power of guns and send them to show black men the same good way. Indeed they would by and by go with others to the chief white men of Government and ask them to give up the use of guns and the way of killing those who did not understand their ways of taxing, etc.[109]

Booth counselled them against this, probably fearing that such a deputation would be looked upon as a deputation in force and received with arms by the Administration. He advised sending a letter or a petition. In later years he was to be associated in particular with this manner of criticizing the Authorities, and one of his petitions was to be linked by them with the circumstances leading up to the 1915 Rising. (Perhaps it was from such suggestions of Booth's that Chilembwe took his tactic of writing letters to the government for redress of grievances—a habit that was to bring him into trouble with the Nyasaland Government when the First World War broke out.)

The people who heard Booth that day did eventually take up his suggestion of petitioning the Government. It must have been some time after Booth, having refused to take up the land which they offered him and to stay with them, had left. They appear to have sent some sort of a delegation to visit his station near Blantyre. Booth was away at the time but they stayed to discuss these matters with Yao and others there, and eventually drew up a mild petition and sent it to the authorities. It was from this that Booth believed the initial warrant for his arrest in British Central Africa, which drove him into his first exile from the country, was issued at some time towards the autumn of 1899. He saw in it the origin of all his subsequent troubles with the governments of Africa. And when, in later years, he was to review all these troubles, still very far away when this melodramatic meeting on the other side of the Shire took place, he commented that the oddity of it all had been that the governments consistently accused him of stirring up the natives, whereas he had merely been following the lead given by the natives themselves in their criticisms of the authorities.[110]

Whatever is the truth of this particular matter, one thing is certain : that, in the two years he had known Joseph Booth, John Chilembwe had gone through a range of experiences beside which even the wildest accounts of his boyhood wanderings with his parents seem flat. He had seen a European build up a mission from which he must have drawn many lessons for the years when he was to try similar experiments himself. He had been in close contact with that European, as, through personal disposition and force of circumstances, Booth was forced into a highly pro-African viewpoint on the key subjects of land, taxation, and the use of punitive expeditions and force. There can be little doubt that Chilembwe was influenced by this attitude. But Booth's greatest effect upon him was yet to come : his trip to America.

6. Booth's First Essay with American Negroes ; Chilembwe writes a Letter

Booth visited the United States for three months in the middle of 1895. Though at this time, because of the poor crops of coffee which his main industrial missions shared with the rest of British Central Africa between 1892 and 1895, the depressed conditions in Australian finance between 1892 and 1896 and the over-ambitious planning in which he had indulged, it might at first sight appear that Booth had gone to America mainly to elicit further funds for his missions, it seems just as likely that he made the journey in search of new allies for his missionary vision.[111] Already in 1894, he had been concentrating more of his energies on the area around the Likabula station which he had founded for the Australian Nyassa Industrial Mission group that had arrived in Africa in 1894 than on the main Zambesi Industrial Mission stations. It seems, indeed, that some rift was then emerging between Booth and the trustees of his parent body, the Zambesi Industrial Mission, in Great Britain. New missionaries from England to the bases which he had established often had new and different ideas from Booth on how they should be developed and felt critical of his over-liberal native policy. And rumours were going back that Booth had over-reached himself and that his mission finances were in a bad state. Perhaps, too, some of the estrangement may have been due to changes in Booth's religious opinions. He had gained widespread support for his initial mission idea in Britain on the basis of a scheme for an inter-denominational mission. But in the mid-1890's his beliefs, which had changed so often from his boyhood to the time when he deserted the agnostic position to challenge the atheist's citadels and bring himself eventually to Africa, seem to have been asserting themselves to the detriment of the inter-denominational ideal. Some change was simmering under the surface. The same fundamentalism which had brought him to an uncompromising Christian pacifist position was bringing him, slowly, to a 'seventh-day' attitude on the Sabbath—a belief which, when it finally began to spread amongst his African followers after 1900, was to add to planters' grievances against him, for it meant that their workers who took up the 'Sabbath position' would want to stop work on Saturday, which to them was the true 'seventh-day' or Sabbath.

Whether or not these changes of belief were elements, with the other factors, in cooling relations at this time between Booth and the Zambesi Industrial Mission in London,[112] it is certain that those relations were no longer of the warmest. Furthermore, an appeal which Booth, at the beginning of 1895, had launched amongst Baptists in Great Britain resulted at the end of 1895 in another mission station being set up at Gowa, to be known as the Baptist Industrial Mission of Scotland.[113] A difference of opinion between the first European sent out to the new mission and Booth matured, and the newcomer broke with him. All this complicated matters and must have made Booth long for new support.

His reason for going to the United States in the middle of 1895, therefore, may well have been to seek new allies. It was an American periodical which had issued his first radically religious missionary plan [114] and which had defended him against the criticisms in Dr. James Johnston's *Romance and Reality in South Central Africa*, in which the doctor, after a short tour of British

Central Africa in the autumn of 1892, had accused Booth of a fanaticism which disregarded the welfare of others. Whether Booth made contact with the editor of this periodical, or what other connections he had at this time in America, is not clear. But certainly in 1895 he did make new acquaintances in the United States which were to be invaluable when, later, he was to take Chilembwe there. One of them, probably, was the head of an American Negro school in Washington—for Booth visited that city in 1895—who certainly gave hospitality to Chilembwe in America and who may have been the very man who paid for the education which Chilembwe eventually received in a Negro theological college, and which changed the whole course of his life. Though little is known of Booth's movements there at this time, he undoubtedly came into contact with numbers of American Negroes who had been turning their eyes towards Africa. For many of them it was with a genuine desire to see some of the benefits, however imperfect, which they themselves had achieved, extended to what they considered their less fortunate African brethren ; for others it was part of a trend to increase their own status which discriminatory laws and practices in the United States restricted ; for most it was with a combination of both of these motives. It was also part of an old desire amongst the American Negroes, only three decades out of slavery at this time, to get back to the 'African Fatherland'. Many schemes sprang up to give substance to these desires : old projects to ship all the American Negroes back to Africa, once the pet ideas of white reaction, were being revived by the Negroes themselves ; Negro American churches were taking an increasing interest in African missionary effort ; disgruntled intellectuals plotted schemes of mutual advancement for Negroes in both hemispheres. There was, then, a fruitful soil prepared amongst American Negroes for Booth's ideas when he first went to the United States in 1895.

But this is mainly speculation—as are the stages of Chilembwe's life during 1895. It seems that he may have carried on with odd jobs on board the *Glad Tidings* until it was sold in May 1895—the sale itself was a measure of the loss of confidence of the Zambesi Industrial Mission headquarters in their representatives in Africa— and with his work as interpreter for the mission. It is highly probable that he felt the loss of close contact with the Booth family at this period, for Booth was not only in America in 1895, but he also spent some time in Great Britain. And for the first five months of the year, Booth, in administrative and financial difficulties, had probably kept his nose close to the books and documents of the mission, and would have little time to spare for Chilembwe.

Between November 1894, when he arrived at Chinde, and May 1895, the secretary of the Zambesi Industrial Mission was in British Central Africa investigating Booth's mission stations. He was Robert Caldwell, a Fellow of the Royal Geographical Society, and a man of some attainments. (Two years later he was to publish a practical grammar of Chinyanja which ran into two editions.) The journal of the Scottish mission at Blantyre noted his arrival in January 1895 and observed laconically that he had 'already made several changes in the Mission and its working'.[115] The break between Booth and the Zambesi Industrial Mission was obviously in the offing, though it would take some time to mature.

It is likely that Caldwell was helped on some of his trips of investigation in 1895 by John Chilembwe—though whether Chilembwe knew of the impending rift between him and Booth, or what he thought of it if he did, cannot be gauged. Chilembwe certainly met Caldwell when he was in Africa, and the secretary of the Zambesi Industrial Mission must have thought enough of him to write to Chilembwe when he got back to London. The letter which he wrote to Chilembwe would be of little interest if it had produced no response. But it did bring out some response from Chilembwe in the form of a reply to Caldwell, that was then published by the Zambesi Industrial Mission in the little paper which it occasionally issued to its supporters as proud manifestoes of the improvement of its native converts. It is an important letter. Not only does it seem to be the first direct evidence available from Chilembwe's hand, but it demonstrates the state of his mind in the months before Booth's decision to take him to America had matured. In it, Chilembwe's English is shown as fluent and colourful, though very broken. But, more important, it reveals a proud and independent feeling for equality between white and black. Yet the letter gives no sign that this might take a militant turn against the Europeans, for the note is obviously a friendly one, the product, it seems, of an African mind which was still prepared to believe the best of Europeans, and which had not yet reached the *impasse* that the conflict of cultures and interests in the years shortly before 1915 was to produce in it.

Some time after his return to England, Caldwell had sent

Chilembwe a small broadsheet on which he had printed some verses which he had written about Africa. That they were shockingly bad verses, written in trite octosyllabics redolent of Longfellow's *Hiawatha*, is immaterial. What is important is that they were headed 'The Land of Ham' and began with a versified rendering of the curse placed on Ham, the dark brother, that he should serve others eternally. Though the poem had gone on to suggest that the Gospel had now come to bring about the redemption of Africa, this was not enough for Chilembwe. He seized upon the point of the servitude of Ham. His letter runs :

DEAR SIR,—MR. CALDWELL, I hope you are well, but we are well and in good health, with our white brethren and sisters all right at MITSIDI here. But am very pleased for the booklet which you sent to me. Therefore I am glad when I read it out and to understand all ; and I hear some words is this—that about HAM and his sons, said—

'Cursed let HAM be, and HAM'S son,
CANAAN to ages unending ;
Servants of servants they shall be ;
Servants to SHEM and to JAPHETH !'

Yes, that is true to be so, if it was long times ago, but by this time, is not so to be, says one of HAM's sons. Now HAM's son they shall be servants not to them now, dear white brothers and sisters. Yes, our Father was indebted long time ago, therefore now we are not servants any more to them who are SHEM and JAPHETH's sons, for many knoweth that Our LORD had paid all about us, through His exceeding bad death. We are in peace ; we are saved by HIM ; all is done ; we are no more servants to SHEM's son and to JAPHETH's son ! No more. But one thing is this to be all the same, and be servants to Jesus.

Blessed are the white people who keeping pray for our darkness, and send some more out to tell the good news about JESUS, that my people may be saved. GOD be with them who willing to send their sons and their daughters to die for us that we must be saved ; and for of that I thank to the LORD very much, and you big men who love us and pray for us and send some to help us. May LORD JESUS be to all Friend.

I am not write much in English, but you will judge for yourself.

I am yours boy in faithful to Jesus,

JOHN CHILEMBWE.

P.S.—Give my love to all who are with you, and remember darkness of here ; and pray for us that we may be true servants to JESUS for ever, and willing to do His work with one eye.[116]

The letter, though it was probably written much before, was published in the Zambesi Industrial Mission paper in England for July and August 1896.

How much of the incipient egalitarianism and radicalism which may be seen in this letter was the result of Booth's influence can only be guessed. There is some evidence to suggest that at least an element of it came out of Chilembwe's family. In a book which he published in America perhaps eighteen months later, Booth recorded a story that probably had its origins at this time. He writes:

> An earnest Native convert, by name John Chilembwe, recently narrated the following:
> 'I often preach in my native village but the chief and many people will not hear now. One day after preaching my elder brother (James Chimpele [117]) came to me and said, "You preach just now that God's message is to go to all people and tell a good message to them. How do you know?" I answered: "Because I can read it for myself both in the English tongue and in my own language. I have God's book." He said, "But perhaps white men have altered God's book to suit themselves and so they preach peace to us. Perhaps God's book does not say this to white men; perhaps it says to them, 'Go to all people, take their land, kill the people, I give you power'. If God's word said to them what they preach to us, not to steal, not to kill, would they not do it? I cannot receive the words which the white men have brought."' [118]

Whether this episode happened when Booth was away in America for the first time or not is immaterial. Its value is that it indicates that Chilembwe was probably being subjected to radical influences other than Booth's. New lessons in Chilembwe's political education were to take place, however, when Booth came back from America.

Booth returned to British Central Africa at the end of 1895. He fell into difficulties straight away, not only with the new Baptist Industrial Mission which had been set up at about the time when he was leaving for America but also with the Zambesi Industrial Mission. His relations with this had reached breaking-point. One of the mission's trustees, Sir Brampton Gurdon, followed Caldwell on a tour of inspection in February 1896, and seems to have reported against Booth's leadership in British Central Africa. Booth went back to England early in the year to sort matters out, and appears to have made the break fairly amicably, though he must have felt bitterly the isolation from the Europeans in Central Africa which it enforced upon him.   It may have been this growing spirit of loneliness which contributed much to bring about his second marriage. He had met Caldwell in the Isle of Wight to discuss the severance of relations, and there, on 4 March 1896, he married a nurse, Annie Susan Watkins, whom he had probably got to know during his visits to the home base in 1894 and 1895.   No doubt this second marriage brought some ease to Booth's spirit, after the break with the Zambesi Industrial Mission had dealt such a blow to the great schemes that he had made four years before in Australia for self-propagating expanding industrial missions.   It was true that he still had the new Baptist Industrial Mission of Scotland to rely on, despite the inauspicious beginning of his relations with it ; but something was to go wrong even with that during the course of the year, and Booth was to sever also his connections with the Baptist Industrial Mission.   Some new scheme was an urgent necessity to keep his spirit alive with the hope of the eventual fulfilment of his great mission ideal.

Booth was not a man who was easily cast down.   In May 1896 the Scottish mission paper at Blantyre noted that 'the latest Commercio-Missionary venture we hear of is that of a [African] Missions Transport Company Limited which we see has been registered in London, to conduct traffic on the Shire and Zambesi rivers', and added, 'Our old friend, Mr. Joseph Booth . . . is at the head of it '.[119]   What this announcement signifies it is difficult to say, for the Company seems to have been little more than a paper one.   It is likely, however, that it was intended as a step forward in a scheme which Booth may have hatched while on his short visit to the United States in 1895.

The Missions Transport Company may well have had its origin in one of the American Negro schemes for bringing new African blood and ideas back from the slave communities of the New World, to Africa itself.   That American ideals of Negro improvement did influence his projects in 1896, however, is obvious from Booth's movements later in the year.   They indicated a widening of his vision : a shift from European support to actual attempts to get Africans to set up their own self-propagating mission stations.   Some time in August 1896 he went down into Natal, taking with him Chilembwe's fellow Yao convert, Gordon Mathaka.   The circumstances and the outcome of this visit parallel so closely what happened when Booth took Chilembwe to America that it merits detailed treatment.

7. BOOTH, CHILEMBWE, AND THE AFRICAN CHRISTIAN UNION

Back in Africa in the middle of 1896 after his second marriage, Booth was no doubt at a loose end after his break with his parent mission and the failure of his leadership in the scheme for a new Scottish one. His new African Missions Transport Company was little more than a paper project. Perhaps he spent the time in strengthening his contacts with the little band of Africans that was left to him and in searching out fresh fields among the tribes of British Central Africa. But whatever he may have done in detail, one thing in general is certain : he found the Protectorate still in a state of unrest. If by this year Commissioner Johnston had broken down the last stand of the slave-trading Arabs, their informal influence was not lost. It survived amongst those tribes they had influenced, such as the Yao, and through these made itself felt amongst other peoples of the Protectorate.

One form in which it manifested itself was through the old cannibal rumour that the Europeans had secret plans for eating the Africans—traditionally a powerful one, as the Arabs realized when they tried to stir it up against the British in their last stand against the forces of the Protectorate. Booth came across this rumour amongst groups of the Yao whom he visited. In some way, as he puts it, they had expressed to him a 'desire, when the whites were charged with cannibalism by the Arabs, to send a messenger to the other tribes in the south who had known the white man a long time, to find out what they thought'.[120] Booth was not a man to stand in the way of such a desire and he offered to take anyone whom they chose. They picked Gordon Mathaka, 'a fine Yao young man, six feet tall and of pleasing demeanour. He was clothed and booted and generally fitted with suitable trappings to commend him to the more advanced Zulu people' [121]—whether the Yao or Booth had picked out the Zulu for questioning about the white man's 'cannibalism' is not clear—and he and Booth set off down south. It was August when Booth left, and he was away in Natal at least three months.

If it was distrust of the Europeans' intentions in Central Africa that had sent Gordon Mathaka south with him, when Booth and he arrived in Natal they found amongst the Zulu a suspicion of the

Plate 1. Joseph Booth and family. Taken in Australia, probably between 1890 and 1892. (*Left to right :* Emily Booth ; Joseph Booth's first wife, who died shortly before he left for Africa ; John Edward Booth, who died in Nyasaland not long after Booth's arrival in Africa ; Joseph Booth)

Plate 2. A typical mission settlement, with grass church in centre, Nyasaland, 1912

white man which had reached the point of bitterness and hatred. Slowly, throughout the nineteenth century, the frontier of white settlement and influence had advanced north. The great days when the Zulu chief Shaka had laid claim to the whole of Natal were over. In 1879 the Zulu at Isandhlwana under their chief Cetewayo had slaughtered eight hundred of the British. But it was to be the last great victory of this military people. Six months later they had been defeated at Ulundi and the dynasty of Shaka abolished. An administrative settlement was made in Zululand and Cetewayo was banished. His son, Dinizulu, had taken up the struggle against the British, but by 1887 the remains of Zululand had been annexed and he, too, had been driven into exile. It was a tale of contrasting hopes and ambitions, of broken promises and pledges, and it confined the Zulu, no longer a military people, to the eroding soil of crowding native reserves or to the fate of a landless, libertyless, urban pro-letariat. It was, then, a bitter tale that they poured into the ears of Gordon Mathaka when they had him to themselves.

Booth took him to gatherings of Zulu native ministers at Pietermaritzburg. From them and from other Zulu, Mathaka heard that no white man could be trusted : 'there was no white man living who was a safe guide for native African people'. Bishop Colenso of Natal ('Sobantu'), adviser of Cetewayo,

> was the last of the race of true white man friends, and . . . no matter what the Yao thought, no living white man, whether carrying guns or not, would in the end, when war came, be friends of black men. Indeed he himself was only a puppet in the hands of the white man who brought him : and . . . if he asked to go back home he would find no way back, but . . . he was even then in a prison whilst thinking he was free.[122]

It was no wonder that Mathaka, catching some of their distrust and afraid of not being able to go back to his own people, should tell Booth that he wanted to go home. Booth let him go and records that he was never able to regain Mathaka's confidence.

What Mathaka told his people when he got back to the Shire Highlands is not known ; that it was bitter and distrustful of the Europeans is certain. It could have done nothing to quell their fear of the cannibal rumour. Chilembwe would have heard all this, either directly from Mathaka or from the neighbouring Yao. It seems that he was not to be persuaded against Booth and continued to uphold, through his attachment to him, belief in the integrity of

Europeans in Africa. Perhaps also Chilembwe caught other exciting news from Mathaka, for Mathaka must have been one of the first Africans from British Central Africa to make the journey down south [123]—a journey with which hundreds of other Africans from the Nyasa regions were to become familiar when, after 1900, the great mines began to call for their labour power. Perhaps he was an early link in that human chain which has bound Nyasaland to the Rhodesias and South Africa and which, before 1915, was to bring in new and dangerous ideas to swell the currents of native discontent. Mathaka's tales of life in Durban and Pietermaritzburg could well have provided strong and attractive food for the young Chilembwe's thought in the three months that his master was away.

Booth would have even more startling news to disclose when he returned. For when Gordon Mathaka left him, Booth had stayed on determinedly in Natal to confront the embittered and humbled Zulu with a plan by which they might recapture their lost dignity and advance to new power and prestige. Later in his life when he was to write of this time he spoke of these activities in terms of racial co-operation :

> to stem this tide of prejudice against the white race, pointing out the hopelessness of the African race ever being united and capable of making the best of their noble heritage by their own unaided efforts.[124]

But others were to see his 1896 schemes in Natal from a very different angle. To them, his ideas were to set off currents of native discontent and black nationalism which would eventually lead to a resurgence of revolt. This growing black nationalism was to be called 'Ethiopianism', a loose and unsatisfactory term which was also to be applied by many in 1915 to Chilembwe's movement. It is therefore necessary, before looking into the exact nature of Booth's activities in Natal when Mathaka left him, to bring out some of the implications of this term.

Etymologically, it took its origins from Biblical texts such as the thirty-first verse of the sixty-eighth Psalm, 'Ethiopia shall soon stretch out her hands to God', and later, at the time of the Abyssinian defeat of the Italians at Adowa in 1896, it may have taken on direct tones of political nationalism from the existence of the black state to the north. But for most of the last three decades of the nineteenth century and for the first two of the twentieth, it was to stand for a form of religious African nationalism which always threatened to oil over into revolt against European rule. Ethiopianism had its origins in South Africa in the 1870's when colour prejudice had tung many Africans to set up their own churches rather than face egregation and humiliation in the white man's places of worship. This humiliation was felt particularly by the black ministers and eading members, such as deacons, of the Christian churches that ad been set up by the European missionaries. So thorough had een their work that, by the 'seventies, a class of black ministers had rown up in South Africa, men who had taken every advantage of he little education that was afforded them and who had all the ttributes of the rebellious intelligentsia of European countries, hough their arguments and criticisms of the white man's rule were ouched in Biblical phrases. Like the Anabaptists and other re-ellious sects of the early Reformation church in Europe, they found o difficulty in finding Biblical passages to drive home their meaning. The Ethiopian movement began properly among the African Wesleyans in 1884 when a Tembu minister, Nehemiah Tile, founded separate tribal church; and it reached its first peak in 1892 when nother African Wesleyan preacher founded a general 'Ethiopian' hurch. It was almost inevitable that such a body should seek ffiliation with the denomination which had had such a similar areer amongst the Negroes of America: the African Methodist piscopal Church. This was in process at the very moment that ooth was putting other schemes to leading Africans in Natal; for ames M. Dwane, another former black Wesleyan minister, was arrying out negotiations in the United States in 1896 which made ossible, two years later, the triumphal tour of Henry M. Turner, merican Negro bishop of this body, amongst South African Negro eparatist churches, which was to create the affiliation. Turner was man full of the concept of the 'manifest destiny' of coloured mericans to redeem their unhappy brethren in Africa. After the nid-1890's, American Negroes of like persuasion were to have a rowing influence in South Africa and the regions to which it was llied. They added a new nuance to the concept of Ethiopianism, nd for many whites in South and Central Africa their schools and olleges in the United States became nests of agitators, American r African Negro, who brought growing elements of political con-ciousness of a rebellious nature to the African separatist churches, rom which, through the influence of the Negro minister, they pread out amongst the masses of the native peoples who only

73

wanted inspiration and organization to raise them anew against their white masters. That the African separatist movement often acted as a safety-valve for the discontents of leading African elements often escaped the notice of white critics of Ethiopianism; and they could not see at this time that sectarianism, the growth of numerous little black churches, often made combinations amongst their members for common aims of revolt more difficult.[125]

It is into this movement of growing African religious nationalism that Booth's 1896 schemes in Natal must be fitted. He proposed what he called an 'African Christian Union' and soon found Africans south of the Zambezi to support him. One of them was John Navuma Tembula, the first South African Native to qualify—overseas, of course—as a medical doctor. (This was characteristic of Booth's appeal to Africans at all stages of his career; though his call was to the masses, he usually appealed most to what may be called—at the risk of introducing foreign categories into the African social structure—the 'petty-bourgeois' elements.) With Tembula as his treasurer and one Solomon Kumalo as his district agent in Durban, Booth issued, on 10 September 1896, the prospectus of the 'African Christian Union'. It began, typically, with a passage from Isaiah:

> Cry aloud, spare not . . .
> Warn my people of their transgressions, . . .
> A little one shall become a thousand
> And a small one a strong nation.
> I the Lord will hasten it.

Its plans were in true line of descent from the self-propagating industrial mission schemes that he had outlined in Australia in 1892. The organization would work and pray for the unity of the denominations amongst African Christians and for the day when the African would become a Christian nation. Capital was to be raised for industrial mission stations. Some of this was to be acquired by asking the United States Government to pay one hundred pounds for each adult 'Afric-American' who would volunteer or be asked to return to the African Fatherland. This was only fair, considering the wrongs which the Negroes had suffered in America. Other capital would be raised from Native Christians, and

A total of 12,000,000 African Christians is to give at least 1d. a day—£3,000,000 a year. The African Christian Union will issue 100,000 £ shares paying 5 p.c., all surplus to become its own property. Zambesi

Blantyre transport will give £16,820 on a capital expenditure of £12,000 (a reference, presumably, to the mission transport company which Booth had on paper). Buchanan's plantations (the estates of the late Shire Highlands planter which the Union was to buy) will, only half worked, yield a profit of £45,500 on a cost of £54,360. The coasting trade (a reference to a proposal to use a steamer to ply between Natal and the African ports) will cost £15,000 and yield an annual profit of £14,473.[126]

Such capital, continually expanding, should be used to build up African industry and commerce ; and to 'mould and guide the labour of Africa's millions into channels that shall develop the God-given wealth of Africa for the uplifting and commonwealth of the people, rather than for the aggrandisement of a few already rich Europeans'. European co-workers were to make this possible by training the African in the various forms of industry and commerce : reaping the fruits and building up a huge native opulency and a 'skilled native trades union'. All Africans, chiefs and commoners, were to be drawn in, and Africans were to be encouraged to 'demand by Christian and lawful methods' equal privileges with Europeans. The scheme envisaged European help to restore Africans in America to their Fatherland and to place on record the great wrongs which Africans in both continents had suffered at the hands of Europeans and asked for restitution. Finally the scheme's aim was

to pursue steadily and unswervingly the policy AFRICA FOR THE AFRICAN and look for and hasten by prayer and united effort the forming of the AFRICAN CHRISTIAN NATION by God's power and in his own time and way.[127]

The plan had all the attributes of Booth's original 1892 project but with this difference—that the emphasis was now on the African as his own evangelist and uplifter. The European was to help ; but a significant shift of emphasis had taken place. Some of this, of course, must have been due to Booth's break with European missions. It is conjectural how much of it Booth brought back from his first trip to America in 1895 and the Negro contacts which he made there : the references to American Negro co-operation suggest that they had had some influence. But it was the emphasis on the African which mattered. Even the Blantyre mission paper, when criticizing Booth's plan, drew attention to this : 'He has got the right sow by the ear in the Native Question of which few in this country know the significance, and upon which as upon a stone of stumbling they will come to grief'.[128] It was the leading principle from this time on in Booth's life, and however impractical his future schemes might be—as the African Christian Union of 1896 surely was—and however much disunity the difficulties of his own personality might create among his African followers, at the base of his projects was the appeal to the African to unite and work for his own redemption, political, economic, and spiritual.

Yet at this time amongst the embittered Native intellectuals of Natal, it was just this emphasis on the African that broke up the scheme. Booth had brought a hundred and twenty educated Africans together, and after a twenty-six-and-a-half-hour session they rejected his scheme, not because of its visionary character, but on the simple grounds that no white man was fit to be trusted, not even Booth himself. Bishop Colenso, the last honest white man, was dead. No trust or reliance at all could be placed in any representative of 'the blood-stained white men, who had slain scores of thousands of Zulus and their Matabele relations'.[129] (It should be remembered that the Matabele Rebellion against the British South Africa Company took place in 1896. About three thousand African rebels were killed.[130]) The final disintegrating thrust of criticism had been made by Solomon Kumalo, Booth's own district agent. It was a bitter and painful moment for him. Sadly, he went back to the Shire Highlands.

Booth's experience of the Zulu was confirmed a few weeks later when he set out for England. The main reason for his visit, it seems, was to seek out fresh sources of support for new missionary ventures that he had in mind; but he also took with him on his journey a young Yao who was interested in sounding the mysteries of the white man's country. *En route*, Booth stopped to pay a tourist visit to St. Helena. He was surprised to find that his attention was taken not only by the memorials of Napoleon but by a board with the heading 'Zulu Notice' which stated that a penalty of £20 would be inflicted on any visitor who spoke to the Zulu prisoners on the island without the Governor's permission. They were two brothers, a son, and two sub-chiefs of Cetewayo, paramount chief of the Zulu who, between 1879 and his death in 1884, through a complicated triangle of British, Boer, and Zulu politics, had kept Sir Garnet Wolseley and his men busy. In 1889 the son, Dinizulu, with the two brothers and the sub-chiefs, received sentences of imprisonment from the Imperial Government for their part in the Zulu disturbances of 1887–88, and were deported to St. Helena. Booth's interest

in the Zulu having been stimulated by his recent experiences with
the African Christian Union, it was certain that he would try to
speak with them.

He had no difficulty in securing the Governor's permission, and,
as the prisoners were in exile rather than captivity, was easily able to
get into touch with them. Through their interpreter, he and his
Yao companion spoke to Dinizulu and his followers. 'The few
minutes' talk', wrote Booth later, 'revealed the same deep-seated
conviction (as he had found in Durban in September) that there
was no hope of generous treatment from the white race of men.
"Their words were sweet, but their deeds were bitter."' [131]

It would be tempting to imagine that Booth's Yao companion at
this time was Chilembwe, and to suppose that he met and heard
the bitter words of Dinizulu, whose name was to be linked so con-
troversially with the last great Zulu rebellion of 1906 in Natal.
There is, indeed, just the faintest possibility that Chilembwe may
have been with Booth. Yet it seems more likely that his Yao companion was one George Kulimbika who had been living at Kimberley,
and whom Booth may have met for the first time in South Africa.[132]
Nevertheless, whether Chilembwe was with Booth or not, his closeness to the radical missionary, and the fact that the young Yao who
was present with Booth at the St. Helena meeting and on his subsequent trip to Great Britain reported on his experiences to groups
of Nyasaland Africans,[133] makes it most probable that the story of
Dinizulu's bitterness reached Chilembwe's ears. If so, it might
have passed into his memory and have influenced that growing sense
of Ethiopianism, the foundations of which were being laid by his
early association with Booth, and which was to increase during his
stay in America, and to mature when he was the leader of his own
mission.

There are further indications of the growth of Chilembwe's pro-
African spirit under Booth's influence in an independent native
missionary venture to which he joined his name at this period. At
the beginning of 1896, eight months before he had entered Natal
with Mathaka on his African Christian Union scheme, Booth had
given back the lands which he had acquired at Likabula near
Blantyre for the Nyassa Industrial Mission, to the group of
Australians who made up its staff. This had been incorporated,
in September 1896, into a separate mission. At the same time the
backers of Booth's Baptist Industrial Mission of Scotland took the

opportunity to regularize their own land position, after it was obvious that their association with him was ending. Out of this complicated series of transactions which was probably started when Booth was in England in the early part of 1896, a hundred acres, somewhere in the Likabula area, were given to him at his own request. On this land Booth planned to build up a completely African mission on self-propagating lines, with a ban on private trading and a typical scheme for mutual improvement and welfare. The trustees were to be Booth himself and seven of the Africans whom he had drawn to him since his arrival in British Central Africa. Amongst them, three names stand out: Morrison Malinki, who was eventually to become the first Seventh-day Adventist African pastor in Nyasaland and who, until the middle of 1897, was in many ways the most promising and active native member of the Zambesi Industrial Mission; [134] Gordon Mathaka, who obviously dropped out of the scheme after his Zulu-inspired disillusionment with the white man, Booth; and Chilembwe himself, whose name begins the list of African trustees of the proposed mission.[135] Little is known of its fate, but the mutilated and incomplete deeds which exist [136] are valuable not merely as indications of the ideas of its founders but also as documentary evidence for the Chilembwe story. The kind of mission which they envisaged may have been something of a model for Chilembwe when he came back from America, and they contain a theological statement which appears to represent his own and Booth's views at that time.[137] They are normal Baptist beliefs, and if either Chilembwe or Booth showed later any signs of Adventism, they are not manifest in this document. It has another value, too, for it seems to point to what must have been the first independent African church in British Central Africa. That Chilembwe had a hand in this is, then, a mark of his increasing independence of mind towards the end of his Nyasaland apprenticeship to Booth.

The seal, however, was to be set on this, not by the independent African church experiment, important though this surely is for Chilembwe's development, but by his participation in a Nyasaland version of the African Christian Union scheme which Booth had failed so miserably to put to the Zulu intelligentsia of Natal. At Blantyre on 14 January 1897—by which time Booth, always a rapid traveller, had apparently returned from his trip to Great Britain with his Yao companion—Chilembwe put his hand, together with Booth,

Morrison Malinki, and the English Zambesi Industrial missionary, Alexander Dickie, whom he may have known on the river steamer the *Glad Tidings*, to a document which follows almost word for word Booth's African Christian Union project of the previous September.[138] Having failed with the South African Zulu, Booth was obviously determined to make a beginning somewhere, and what could be better than amongst his own first converts ? It is probable that he had explained some elements of the scheme to Chilembwe before he went on his fruitless errand amongst the Zulu with Mathaka. But when Booth returned to Blantyre, it is clear that he must have gone much more carefully into it with him, for Chilembwe's name appears immediately below his own in this version of the project. The importance of the document is, therefore, that it gives a summary of the ideas which Chilembwe had picked up in the course of his five years' apprenticeship with Booth. Some of the newer ideas which had been discovered by Booth during his first 1895 trip to America, such as the role which the American Negro could play in Africa, were perhaps at that time strange to Chilembwe. They would have to wait until he himself went to the United States and had brought back from there Negro helpers for his own mission, before he would realize their full implications. But others would be familiar to him : equal rights, political, social, and economic, for Africans as well as Europeans ; the development of African education along the technical lines of the European world ; independent African activity in all economic fields ; a just land settlement ; the encouragement of a pro-African press and literature ; and the growth of independent African Christianity. It was a policy that was summed up at the end of this new African Christian Union manifesto in the same way as in the first : by the simple but appealing slogan, 'Africa for the African'. That some Africans were critical of the scheme was apparent from a letter which Joseph Bismarck, an African smallholder of the Blantyre Mission, published in the local press at the beginning of March 1897. He had a feeling that the exploited might well become the exploiters : 'Will these Africa-American Christians do anything good in our country . . .? Won't they sit down in their houses and read their books when they come out here, and make us poor Bantu to do their work instead of themselves ?' [139] But Chilembwe had, it seems, no such scruples. And even if he had possessed any such qualms, by March, Booth was preparing to take him to America ; and April 1897 was to find

Chilembwe in the capital of the United States, ready to test the metal of the Negro American people for himself. Thus the African Christian Union manifesto, to which he had affixed his name at the beginning of the year, is like a seal set on the first phase of Chilembwe's career—a seal that impressed a pattern which now seems to point clearly to the crisis and catastrophe of 1915 but which, at that time, if other factors had been absent, might have indicated different, more peaceful developments for Chilembwe.

A crucial factor, however, had already been brought into the situation. Between 1893 and 1897, a large, new European estate had been opened up at Magomero, in Chilembwe's home country, from which the ill-fated party of the Universities Mission to Central Africa, the first attempt to establish a Christian mission station in Nyasaland, had withdrawn in 1864. Here, as has been noted, David Livingstone himself, while visiting the chief of this area for the party, was attacked for the first time in his missionary career by Africans, an advance section of the invading Yao, and was forced to use a revolver in his own defence. It is not surprising, then, to learn that the manager of the new estate, who also bore the name of Livingstone, should have had numerous attempts made on his life during the first years of his settlement in Nyasaland.[140] But this did not deter him from his business of developing the estate that had been entrusted to his charge. He was a practical planter, and experimented with cotton as well as coffee. The local paper noted that he had put in seventy thousand plants in the 1896 season.[141] Obviously he had earned his leave, and the same journal observed in February 1897, the time at which Chilembwe was getting ready to go to America, that the enterprising manager was taking it.[142]

He was going back to Scotland where his family had had roots for centuries in the lovely island of Lismore, off the west coast and within sight of Mull, from which David Livingstone's ancestors had come. The ancestors of this Livingstone from Lismore, William Jervis, as far back as there is a record, had been the custodians of the Bachull Mor, the pastoral staff of Saint Moluag, to whom tradition gives the honour of introducing Christianity to the island.[143] William Jervis Livingstone himself was later to become the Baron of Bachull, the hereditary custodian of Moluag's crozier. He was a proud Gael, in a proud tradition : [144] throughout Lismore's recorded history his family had borne many offices of honour and responsibility on the island, and in the nineteenth century, of course, David

Livingstone's explorations had brought a new glory to the clan. It was fitting, then, that this Livingstone, as a distant relation of the great explorer, should have gone out to manage the extensive estates of Alexander Low Bruce, who had married Agnes, David Livingstone's daughter. His employer was a keen Scottish business man, a partner of the brewers, William Younger & Company, and a director of other concerns, among which was the African Lakes Company of Nyasaland.[145] Bruce had strong Imperialist sentiments : he was one of the founders with Sir William MacKinnon of the Imperial British East Africa Company,[146] and he had written appreciatively of Rhodes's Cape-to-Cairo ideas.[147] (Alexander Low Bruce, who died in 1893, should not be confused with his younger son who had similar initials. It was this son, Alexander Livingstone Bruce, who was owner of the Bruce Estates in Nyasaland in 1915.)

There are clearly apparent elements of irony in W. J. Livingstone's story : it is surely ironical that he, a relation of the great missionary, should lose his life in Nyasaland at the very place where David Livingstone had fought to save its first Christian mission. But there is yet a further touch of irony to his tale. His father, Alexander, himself the Baron of Bachull at the time the manager of the Bruce estates was going home on leave, was for long a Baptist missionary in Skye and later pastor of the small Baptist church on Lismore.[148] There is not a little irony in the fact that his son should have met his death through the activities of another Baptist minister and missionary—for this is what John Chilembwe became through his association with American Negroes.

But the story of William Jervis Livingstone is only another of the factors that were emerging in 1897 that seem now to point to this end. Yet before it could fall into the pattern to make these terrible events possible, another would have to be added : Joseph Booth would have to take John Chilembwe to the United States of America.

III
CHILEMBWE AND BOOTH IN AMERICA
1897–1900

> . . . John, John, de holy Baptist,
> Sittin' on de golden order,
> To view de promised land.
>> *American Negro Slave Song*

III

CHILEMBWE AND BOOTH IN AMERICA
1897–1900

1. CHILEMBWE AND BOOTH TOGETHER

BOOTH's departure with Chilembwe to the United States in 1897 does not seem to have been noticed at the time by members of the British Central African Administration or by the missionaries. No doubt they had too many problems on their hands to worry about yet another of the moves of a rather troublesome and erratic individual, as Booth appeared to so many of them. Besides, although he had had his brushes with authority, Booth had not yet been put on the official 'black list' and was perfectly free to come and go as he wished, without having any special notice paid to his movements. Chilembwe was a relatively unknown character. Both the Blantyre and Livingstonia missions, with their two decades of educational activity, were concerned with their own bright boys rather than with Joseph Booth's particular discovery. They were much more interested in Africans like John Gray Kufa who, in the following year, was to become the first African to get 90 per cent marks in the special Blantyre surgical examination,[1] and was looked on as the prototype of the African doctor, the fruit of the care and skill of Scottish kirk and medical school overseas. The Blantyre Mission's attention was naturally centred on two of its own boys whom, by the end of 1897, it had sent overseas to England on a carefully arranged journey.[2] They had indeed too much work of their own in hand to question the journeyings of one insignificant African whose actions, eighteen years later, were to call into question the whole character and value of missionary achievement in British Central Africa.

Indeed on all sides, in 1897, in the little Protectorate, there was a certain air of smugness. Johnston had finished his job of pacification. Back in England he had published his *British Central Africa*, a virtuoso volume which told everything there was to be known about the new addition to the British Empire, and gave helpful advice to intending settlers. As far as he was concerned, all opponents of

British rule—Portuguese, Arab, Yao, Ngoni—had been put in their places, and the foundations of a stable community had been laid. His second-in-command, Alfred Sharpe, could now take over the Commissionership. Johnston was off to put things straight in Uganda. Blantyre itself caught the mood of confidence, declared itself a township, and elected a Town Council. Its missionaries, in their journal, marked the transition from the old days of war to the new era of peaceful Christianity and commerce with musical metaphor :

> We hope soon to be listening to sweet music in Central Africa—not the harsh grating of the maxim gun, nor the crackle of burning huts, nor the groan of dying men, all hideous noises to our ears—but the gold waltz, and the rubber gavotte, and the ivory fugue.[3]

Indeed they had some grounds for complacency, when they turned their eyes south, and saw Rhodesia still in the throes of its struggle with the Matabele ; and South Africa not yet recovered from the effects of the Jameson Raid, and its Zulu still restless. The achievement of Crown Colony status in 1897 set the seal on this process of pacification for British Central Africa. For it, at least, there was nothing to mar the splendour and optimism of Victoria's Diamond Jubilee Year. And so, Booth and Chilembwe slipped unnoticed out of the Protectorate.

Why did Booth take his first native convert to America ? An African story says that it was because Booth was pleased with Chilembwe's work for him and thought that he would become more effective as an evangelizer and teacher if he studied for a while in America. But he took him in the face of his reluctance to leave his mother, Nyangu ; only when she had given her consent was Chilembwe willing to go.[4] It would be a plausible story if Booth had not left his own record of the adventure. His account goes, in essence, right back to the early days of white settlement in Central Africa, when the 'cannibal rumour' had been a symbol of the tension between the races. He shows that it was still very much alive in 1897 and provides evidence which suggests that, if the Europeans then in British Central Africa were so sure of their new state, the native peoples were not entirely of the same mind. In Booth's words :

> When the Arabs told Kawinga, Liwondi, Makanjira, and Kapeni [four Yao chiefs] that the whites were cannibals, that their pretended

Plate 3. Rev. John Chilembwe and family

Plate 4. The first American Negro missionaries in Nyasaland. Thomas Branch and family (Seventh-day Adventists) who arrived in Nyasaland in 1901

friendship towards the slaves was only so as to get them for food, this bold youth [Chilembwe] withstood them, his own parents, and his chief. When a slave woman and a child helped to freedom and protected by the writer, was kidnapped and the writer charged with having killed and *eaten* her and her child, this brave youth exposed the falsity of the charge.[5]

The episode to which Booth refers is obviously the one of 1893 (see page 55) when he had taken John Chilembwe and 'David Livingstone' to recover a woman and child stolen by a jealous chief from the land of the Mitsidi mission. Booth's young daughter, Emily, was enamoured of the little baby Booth had brought back with its mother from the chief; and, when she was later to write of her Central African experiences, she added this gloss to his story :

> It was the only little black baby that I ever remember kissing in Africa, but it certainly was sweet enough to kiss. . . . But it occurs to me that . . . some native who saw me kiss the baby might have misinterpreted it. . . . Natives did not kiss each other : they didn't even rub noses as a sign of affection, as the Maoris of New Zealand do. [It should be remembered that Booth's daughter had been born in New Zealand.] The story went around that the white man and little girl took the black baby and ate it ![6]

Chilembwe must have had the opportunity many times after 1893 to defend the Europeans against such charges, for, as Booth goes on :

> . . . when the Arabs filled the Yao mind with the story that for hundreds of years whites had taken shiploads of slaves to U.S.A. and other places and eaten them there, for they never came back—perhaps trying to bring about a massacre of all whites then north of the Zambesi [7] . . . John Chilembwe was one of the few to believe the writer that the descendants of these slaves still lived in U.S.A. and as freemen, and *he volunteered* to go with the writer, after learning English, and so prove the Arabs of Tanganyika [who from the north end of Lake Nyasa threatened British rule in Central Africa until 1896] to be false and the 'Chinglese' [English-speaking whites] to be true friends and no cannibals.[8]

This passage merits two comments. First, it seems to show that Booth's decision to take Chilembwe to America was not a one-sided affair ; that Chilembwe may well have put the idea into his head, and that the two of them only waited the opportunity to go to the United States. It appears that the idea did not suddenly arise in

1897, but went back almost to the earliest times of their friendship. But until Booth's hands were less tied with Zambesi Industrial Mission work, it was not possible. The great opportunity came when Booth broke with his mission and its satellites in Central Africa. It should be noticed, too, that he undertook the journey after his bitter disappointment in Zululand in 1896 where he had seen a complete lack of confidence in the white man widespread amongst Africans, and where his first 'Yao messenger' to other peoples, Gordon Mathaka, had been turned against him by the embittered Zulu. Thus, after his return to Blantyre in the early part of 1897, a good opportunity presented itself for doing something to stem the tide of this prejudice which the whites were helping to create for themselves in Africa.[9] Booth was freed from his mission ties and Chilembwe, untouched by the returned, embittered Mathaka, had already volunteered to go and disprove rumours antagonistic to the white man.

It is this fact that supplies a second comment of terrible irony that this same African, whose bitterness against European rule was to manifest itself in the 1915 Rising, should have been brought to the position which made it possible for him to head this revolt through his initial friendship towards the Europeans. For if Chilembwe had not gone to the United States, he could not have become minister of an American Negro Church : and, if he had not been such a minister, he would not have been able to build up, in his own country, with American Negro backing, the mission from which, in 1915, the Rising against the whites in the Shire Highland would be launched. There is, too, a second irony in the situation that Booth, who three years after he had taken Chilembwe to America, would be deported from British Central Africa as a disturber of the peace between African and European, had made the very great personal sacrifice of paying his own passage and some, it seems, of Chilembwe's, to America in 1897 in order to make a contribution, however small, towards re-establishing confidence between white and black.

That it was a sacrifice hardly appears in this bald understatement of Booth's :

> He (Chilembwe) and the writer had great difficulty to raise enough for deck and steerage passages from the Shire and Zambesi rivers to London, thence to Liverpool, thence to New York and forward to Richmond and Baltimore, U.S.A.[10]

But sacrifice it was. Chilembwe could have had little personal money of his own, however much greater than the normal Nyasaland rate may have been the wages that Booth paid to his Africans. And, although Chilembwe may possibly have worked some of his passage —using to advantage, perhaps, some of the experience he may have gained on the *Glad Tidings*—Booth must have financed him most of the way out of his own money.

Let the double irony of the situation be underlined by another quotation from Booth's account of Chilembwe :

> He was charged in my presence by his parents and many Yao friends to become 'eyes, mouth and ears' for them and quickly write to those who could read Yao what he found and how he was received by these lost and forgotten black people. Chilembwe wrote in the Yao language to his father's people and in the Chinyanja language to his mother's people (a former Mang'anja slave caught in war by his father) and to educated Yao natives so that all evidence in the Arabs' effort to create hatred of the English was utterly destroyed.[11]

Booth, however, had intentions other than the taking of Chilembwe to America. Though he had received rather discouraging treatment from Negroes there during his 1895 visit,[12] he still had hopes that they would help to forward his ambitious schemes, and by now he had some expectation of support from white groups in the States. Furthermore, the voyage to America would take him by way of Great Britain, and there was always the possibility that additional sources could be tapped in that country.

Mention of Great Britain raises the difficult question : how far did Chilembwe travel in Europe and the British Isles ? From the passage of Booth's quoted above, it is clear that he touched, at least, at London and Liverpool. The real issue is whether or not he got much further than the restricted port areas. There is some reason for supposing that he did. Chilembwe himself claimed that he travelled 'considerably' [13] in England—though his employment of this adverb might not have had then the same extensive significance which it would have had for a European—and his American Negro backers stated later that he accompanied Booth in his campaigns 'both in Europe and America'.[14] But of the full extent of Chilembwe's European travels in 1897—or on his return voyage from America—no record seems to exist. Perhaps some clue to their character may be glimpsed if the mysterious 'Yao messenger' is recalled whom Booth had with him at St. Helena, *en route* for England after his African Christian Union fiasco in South Africa in 1896. This African had succeeded in visiting Bradford, York, Glasgow, and Edinburgh, as well, presumably, as the normal ports of call.[15] It is not unlikely that Chilembwe did the same on his way over to the States, for all of these places had become well known to Booth on previous finance-gathering visits for his missionary experiments. If so, one would like very much to know what Chilembwe's reactions had been to them, for they would have represented his introduction to the white man's countries outside of Africa, and some of the impressions which he took away from them would undoubtedly have influenced his attitude to Europeans when he went back to British Central Africa.

Would he have been impressed in the same way as the two Nyasaland Africans whom the Church of Scotland Mission had sent to Great Britain in 1897? They wrote:

> some of the things which we wondered at [were] the houses, crowds of people and buses, cabs . . . the underground train, the 'Flying Scotchman' . . . the machine for making electric light . . . the iron works. . . . It would take us years to tell it all.[16]

Yet the introduction of these Blantyre Mission boys to the white man's wider world had not been wonders all the way: at Durban before they went ashore, they said:

> We saw a detective coming on board and [he] asked the Captain to lock us up. The Captain allowed him, and we being strangers to Durban did not quite understand their laws to the Natives. We were taken up to the water police office and our bags examined. Then they gave us *pass tickets* for a month's time.[17]

If Chilembwe had made his voyage by way of South Africa,[18] similar experiences would undoubtedly have awaited him. Did he altogether avoid the white man's discriminatory practices on his way over to America? Certainly, as will be noted, experience of them awaited him in the United States. But all these are largely matters for speculation, and it seems that little will ever be discovered of the effects in detail of the first impact of the European way of life beyond Nyasaland on John Chilembwe.

Though the character of American influences upon him may be estimated with some assurance, there is still tantalizingly scanty evidence of his movements in the United States. It is, however, clear that Booth and Chilembwe must have left the Shire Highlands for America in the early months of 1897, for by the first week of April of that year they appear to have been firmly based in its capital.[19]

Booth's 1895 trip had obviously given him the opportunity to provide for something of a firm base in Washington. When he arrived there in 1897, he found fifty dollars waiting for him from a supporter whose interest he had captured on his previous visit. The money was handed to him by the Principal of the Lincoln School, a Negro institution, in Washington, whose address Booth was using at this time for correspondence.[20] The character of this support may be surmised because Booth had travelled in the Southern states during his first visit to America : in Virginia, Maryland, North Carolina, and the colour-conscious American capital. Knowing Booth, it was unlikely that he would have thrown himself zealously upon the Southern whites for companionship. Instead, he had made some contact with that growing movement of coloured Americans which, after the First World War, was to give new hope to many disillusioned American Negroes under the leadership of Marcus Garvey by suggesting that their salvation lay in an increased interest in and an eventual return to Africa.[21] For Booth wrote to his daughter on 9 April 1897 : 'There are many signs that a great work will spring from this side of the ocean also. I am lecturing on "Africa for the Africans"'. And, from the same letter, it is apparent that Chilembwe was speaking with him at meetings on this theme.

If Booth's 1895 trip had given him a base in the capital, his association with African intellectuals in Natal in 1896 had provided him with another important contact in America. This was John L. Dube. Dube became, much later in his life, one of the most respected Africans in the Union of South Africa—or one of the most reprobated, according to political standpoint. To many South African whites he was an admirable type of African, an obvious choice as one of the first members of the Native Representative Council ; leader of a 'reasonable' native political organization ; one whose attempt to put into practice, in his training institute for Africans at Ohlange, Natal, the educational ideals of the American Negro, Booker T. Washington, warranted him the honorary doctorate which he received at the end of his life from the University of South Africa. To many Africans, however, Dube was a man who had 'sold out' to the whites his early promise to lead a genuine South African reform movement. But when Booth and Chilembwe met him in 1897 he was still a radical : the man who, later, would found the militant native paper *Ilanga lase Natal* (*The Sun of Natal*) which was to bring him into trouble with the authorities for its criticisms of Government measures of repression against the Africans who took part in the great Natal poll-tax rebellion in 1906, when nearly four thousand lost their lives.[22] Some time in 1897, Booth, Chilembwe, and Dube, in Booth's own words, 'were together in Brooklyn, U.S.A., on the same errand—all pleading for the commencement of Native Independent Missions. Dube then had seven or nine years U.S.A. education and he quickly found . . . his supporters'.[23] These supporters came from the African Methodist Episcopal Church, whose native adherents in South Africa were creating so much fear among the European population with their 'Ethiopianism'. But Chilembwe's fate was not to lie with this denomination—though his association with Dube gives some ground for comment.

Though little is known about it, it is unlikely that Chilembwe would not increase his radical ideas from this association. Whatever he may have heard or believed of unrest in Natal, his suspicion of Europeans may well have been confirmed by Dube. Some of Dube's earlier radicalism is indicated in such phrases as these, the spirit of which is well in accord with that of Chilembwe's when he returned to his own country : 'The reason that the Christian native has a bad name, among the lower classes of Europeans especially, is that he does not submit to being treated like a dog' : [24] 'If the Europeans wish to know the true cause of native unrest they may find it in their own administration of native affairs'.[25]

Thus, in both Brooklyn and Washington, Chilembwe had been plunged into a *milieu* that was highly critical of the white man. Yet all the time his constant companion was a white man. The incongruity of Booth's position is revealed by him :

> In Richmond, Virginia, he [Chilembwe] found hosts of educated black ministers and others : but mobs of white young men followed us and frequently stoned us for walking together, sitting on the same public seats in the park and for living in the same Negro house.[26]

The web in which Booth had been caught in Natal was stretching itself over into the United States. In Natal, Booth, for all his attempts to identify himself with the coloured man, had been discarded by him and had lost his Yao comrade. In America, faced with similarly embittered groups of Negroes in the big cities, the pattern was to repeat itself.

The first stages of his separation from Booth were certainly unintentional on Chilembwe's part. 'The Negro preachers wished him to leave the writer', says Booth, 'as we became very poor.' But Chilembwe was loath to leave him. All of his closeness with Booth, his little daughter, and his dead son, must have asserted themselves at this moment. 'He would not leave me in poverty', Booth goes on, 'to be made comfortable himself.' But Booth begged him to take the advice of the Negro preachers; they could do so much more for him than the impoverished Booth. And so Chilembwe 'was then for two years put into a Negro college in west Virginia; after which he returned as a full-blown, round-collared, long-coated "Reverend" of the regulation type'.[27] The climax of the separation had been reached.

Its setting was Philadelphia. 'At a large gathering of Negro ministers', Booth reports, Chilembwe said openly to him :

'Mr. Booth we must now part. God has brought me to good friends. I am now a man and can walk alone. For ten years you have been kind to me and carried me like a baby, for which I shall be thankful till I die.' Henceforth he should walk in another path. His new friends would care for him and send him back when ready. They knew well the ways of the whites towards blacks better than [Booth] did.[28]

The 'ten years' of the passage is an obviously convenient, round figure of conversation. So far as can be gathered accurately, Chilembwe parted ways with Booth in the United States some time in 1899. But to introduce this date at this stage is to skip over two years of Chilembwe's stay in America. A somewhat more detailed estimate, therefore, must now be made of the effects of American Negroes on making the separation of Booth and Chilembwe certain, and on setting Chilembwe's feet in the way that led to the 1915 Rising.

2. AMERICAN NEGRO BACKGROUND

The official Commission of Inquiry into the Rising linked the American Negro to it in two ways : first, by indicating that one of its causes was 'the political notions imbibed by Chilembwe . . . during his education in the United States in a Negro Baptist seminary'; and secondly, by claiming that the movement had been affected by 'a class of American Negro publications imported by Chilembwe, the tendency of which was to inflame racial feeling'.[29] Much of the evidence on which this Commission based such assertions was burnt by an accidental fire at the Secretariat, Nyasaland, in 1919, and little is now available on either side of the Atlantic to check in detail such statements. But what is known of the American Negro environment at the time of Chilembwe's stay in the United States, and later, supplies very good circumstantial evidence to show that it had an extremely important influence upon him.

Race relations in the United States at the end of the nineteenth century were not good. The period from 1877, when the Northern troops who had occupied the defeated Confederate States after the Civil War were withdrawn from the South, to the beginning of the twentieth century has been called by one responsible American Negro historian 'the nadir'.[30] As a result, the Negro in the United States felt an acute bitterness about his lot, and often responded in kind to his white brother's discrimination. As Booth put it, after his 1895 visit:

> the pendulum of distrust [had], in its reaction, swung overfar, and left the Negro in need of the gentle reminder, 'If ye have respect to persons, ye commit sin'.[31]

Amongst American Negroes there was a widespread sense of disappointment because the hopes of the Civil War and emancipation from slavery had not been realized. Politically, the promises of the Fourteenth and Fifteenth Amendments to the Constitution, that the Negroes would be granted full rights of citizenship, had not matured. The withdrawal of Northern armies from the former Confederate States was a guarantee to reactionary elements in the South that the Federal Government would not back Negro rights by force if necessary. White Supremacy rode back in the saddle of the Ku Klux Klan, and kept itself there by violence, intimidation, bribery, and the manipulation of the States' political structures. In this way, the more liberal constitutions of the days of Reconstruction (the term usually applied in American history to the period 1865–77, when the North, backed by its armies of occupation, attempted to change the political and social framework of the conquered South) were overthrown, and new, pro-white ones put in their places. By 1898, when Booth and Chilembwe were in America, the pattern for the disenfranchisement of the Negro had been outlined. Poll taxes, literacy tests, property laws, 'grandfather clauses', and other spurious devices were called into action to keep the Negro from the polls, and to rivet control by white elements over local and state assemblies in the South. By 1910 the Negro had been excluded from the vote in all of the major Southern states. Virginia, where Chilembwe spent much of his time, was no exception. In the 1890's white manœuvres were eclipsing the influence of the Negro in Virginian politics. Intimidation and graft were rife at elections, and violence was not unusual. A Negro candidate for the State senate in 1892 was shot dead by a white man in Charlotte county.[32] At the turn of the century, when Chilembwe was getting ready to return to Africa, the Negro had been virtually eliminated from Virginian politics. Delegates to the State constitutional convention of 1901, which overthrew the Reconstruction constitution, adopted a poll tax and 'understanding' requirement for prospective voters, and wildly cheered a white member, Carter Glass, when he declared, 'This plan will eliminate the darkie as a political factor in this State in less than five years. . . . The article of suffrage . . . does not necessarily deprive a single white man of the ballot, but will inevitably cut from the existing electorate four-fifths of the Negro voters.'[33] The *Lynchburg News*, local paper of the home town of Carter Glass and the place in which Chilembwe received his formal American education, found in 1905 that, of the 147,000 Negro voters qualified under the former Virginian constitution, only 21,000 were registered, and less than half of these had paid their poll taxes and qualified under the new, discriminatory dispensation.[34] It was impossible that this process of keeping the Negro away from the polls could have escaped Chilembwe's attention.

Socially, of course, white discrimination against Negroes increased; segregation became the counterpart of disenfranchisement. Beginning in Tennessee in 1870, laws against intermarriage were enacted in every Southern state. Segregation in trams, depots, wharves, white hotels, barbers' shops, restaurants, theatres, schools, and all places where the twain might meet followed. The whole process was helped forward when the American Supreme Court outlawed the Civil Rights Act of 1875, a Reconstruction measure which had tried to enforce the Fourteenth and Fifteenth Amendments to the United States Constitution. And though for some Negro business men the situation was, relatively speaking, less disheartening because they could concentrate on the internal Negro market from which White Supremacy, by the contradictions of its own conventions, excluded itself to a great extent, nevertheless, economically, for the mass of Negroes, discrimination continued both in rates of pay and in the kind of jobs open to the coloured man.

The fear and hatred that arose from this spate of discrimination was expressed in violence. A minor expression of this has already been noted in the mobs of young white men at Richmond, Virginia, who stoned Chilembwe and Booth for consorting together. For Chilembwe it must have been a personal proof of what he was hearing continually from his American Negro acquaintances : that violence was the *leit-motiv* of White Supremacy. In 1898, when Chilembwe and Booth were on the brink of separation, there was a striking manifestation of this. Tension arising from campaigns for white suffrage flamed up into a miniature race war at Wilmington, North Carolina, neighbouring state of Virginia. Three white men were injured, eleven Negroes killed and twenty-five wounded. It is highly unlikely that this display of intolerance would have escaped Chilembwe's attention. Even if he had not read of it in the newspapers, it must have come to his ears through a witness of the Wilmington outbreak, the Rev. Charles S. Morris, a Negro Baptist and an 'Ethiopian'-minded minister who seems to have travelled back to Africa with Chilembwe. 'We have waited two hundred and fifty years for liberty', said Morris, in January 1898, to the Interdenominational Association of Colored Clergymen, 'and this is what it is when it comes.'[35]

Indeed, Chilembwe was in the States at the time when the incidence of lynching was mounting. In the last sixteen years of the nineteenth century more than 2500 Negroes had been lynched, and in the first year of the new century, when Chilembwe was going home, there were more than a hundred lynchings. (And, indeed, during the decade and a half before his Rising, the lynching rate in America amounted to over 1100—a fact which presumably would not have escaped Chilembwe either from the 'class of American Negro publications he imported' or from the racially conscious Negroes from the United States who visited him in Nyasaland.) The terror was not limited to Southern towns, and there were not a few moments when white passion could hurl itself at Negroes in the larger Northern cities, such as Philadelphia, where Booth and

Chilembwe separated, or New York, where Chilembwe was a member of a Negro church for a while.[36]

From all this it is not difficult to see why Chilembwe, however amicably he may have broken with the radical Booth, chose to entrust himself to the protection and training of American Negroes. If Chilembwe could write home to his Yao and Nyanja kinsmen and friends that the Arabs were wrong and the descendants of the slaves in America were most certainly alive ; and if he could report that their political, social, and economic status offered hopes for much more rapid advancement than the Africans in Nyasaland could then envisage, nevertheless, he was not able to present an altogether rosy picture of the American Negroes' situation. Thus, as Booth witnessed, Chilembwe's Negro acquaintances in the United States had plenty of reasons for persuading him that 'they knew well the ways of the whites towards the blacks'. Their centuries-old traditional knowledge of race relations contrasted tellingly with Booth's mere eight years' study of these problems. This, and the fact that many of them were much better off than Booth at that time, made a break almost certain.

From them, too, Chilembwe would learn that the American Negroes' response to White Supremacy was not merely passive. The manner in which they were adjusting themselves to the post-Reconstruction discrimination offered him a pattern of strategy and tactics from which he could draw lessons for his own reactions to the less drastic but none the less effective discriminations against Africans in his own native land.

A favourite form of American Negro reaction to white rule had its roots in the slave days, when the Negro had shown the spirit, if not the fact, of independence through the organization of his own forms of worship.[37] Before Emancipation, as far back as the days of colonial slavery, independent groups of Negro Baptists and Methodists had been formed amongst the slaves. Although the Baptists were the first in the field, their very distrust of centralized control kept them for long from acquiring a wider organization; not so the Negro Methodists, who created in 1816 the African Methodist Episcopal Church which, although it drew heavily on the support of free Negroes, gained widespread allegiance from the slaves themselves. The Negro Baptists did not begin such a separate organization until 1880 ; indeed, the National Baptist Convention of the United States of America, the particular Negro body which sponsored

Chilembwe, was not created until 1895.[38]   Yet the local congregations of Negro Baptists made up in spirit for their lack of a more centralised organization.   In Chilembwe's Virginia they were particularly strong : the first African Baptist Church in Richmond, for example, had five thousand members at the beginning of the century.   And to these Negro Methodists and Baptists must be added a host of infinitely less orthodox sects with their 'prophets' and 'messiahs', which flourished in the atmosphere of open-air, river baptisms, with their associations of John and the Jordan.   Chilembwe's 'total-immersion' convictions could only have been strengthened by his period in Virginia.

For all of them, Negro Baptists, Methodists, and independent 'messianic' groups, the reasons for setting up separate religious organizations were the same : resentment at discrimination in white churches ; a direction into a 'neutral' field of energies that lacked appropriate political channels ; a desire for corporate ownership ; and, through independence, however limited, an advancement of status.   If these tendencies could be expressed in the period after Emancipation in other than religious fields—and many 'advanced' Negroes were sceptical of the churches—nevertheless religious separatism continued to be an important part of American Negro reaction to white discrimination.[39]

Through the churches which the American Negro had made peculiarly his own, his wish for independence could function in other directions than simple domestic evangelization.   The Negro church, before and after the Civil War, took a leading part in bringing education in primary and higher fields to the Negro.   The Baptists led with over a hundred educational institutions of very varied levels of efficiency ; [40] and Chilembwe, with a mind set on education before he ever saw the States, would receive in them further lessons for the aspiring Negro in the importance of schooling. In addition, many of these Negro schools and colleges taught doctrines and inculcated attitudes which some call politely 'racial radicalism', and others, more bluntly, 'sedition'.   In this they anticipated the later trend of independent native schools in Africa ; and while it would be wrong to believe that Chilembwe derived his idea of African schools, independent of Government and European mission, from these American Negro bodies, it is not unreasonable to suppose that his conception of them was influenced by his experiences in the United States.

The American Negro churches after the Civil War extended their activities by entering the foreign mission field on an increasing scale. Even before 1861 they had been active in this sphere, and here again the Negro Baptists had taken the lead. In 1783 George Lisle, going from Georgia to Jamaica, was the first American Negro missionary overseas; and another former slave, David George, became the first American Negro minister in Africa, when he went in 1792 to the new British settlement of Sierra Leone and organized its first Baptist church. Lott Carey, an ex-slave of Richmond, Virginia, followed him to Sierra Leone in 1821 and extended Negro missionary activity into Liberia. The year before, African Methodism had reached the new British colony in the persons of another former slave, the Rev. Daniel Coker of Maryland, and a body of American Negro colonists. It was, however, in the post-Emancipation period that Negro foreign mission work from the United States, naturally, increased. A tremendous stimulus had been given to this by the 1898 tour in South Africa of the African Methodist Episcopal Church Bishop, Henry McNeal Turner.[41] (It was to this church, it will be remembered, that the first important separatist 'Ethiopian' church amongst the natives of South Africa had sought affiliation in 1892.) But the Negro Baptists of America did not lag far behind. At the beginning of the new century they sent out the Rev. Charles S. Morris, eye-witness of the Wilmington riot, to organize and encourage the native Baptists of South Africa.[42] Like Bishop Turner, Morris was strongly convinced that it was the destiny of the American Negro to redeem his less fortunate African brethren; as he said at the 1900 Ecumenical Missionary Conference in New York:

> I believe that God is going to put it into the hearts of these black boys and girls in the schools of the South to go with the message to South Africa and West Africa, and vindicate American slavery as far as it can be vindicated by taking across the ocean the stream of life.[43]

These were, indeed, the hopes of David Livingstone himself, who had written at the time of the American Civil War and the emancipation of the American slaves: 'The day for Africa is yet to come. Possibly the freedmen may be an agency in elevating their fatherland.'[44] Certainly, by the late 1890's, the American Negro churches had realized this hope to the extent that they had created mission nuclei in the Pacific, the West Indies, and in West and South Africa. It was no mean achievement.[45] Thus, Chilembwe could take from the Negro churches of the United States not only lessons in strategy and tactics for his own separate African church but also the feeling of operating within a great tradition of independent and expanding Negro evangelism—a feeling which must have been of no small value to one from a land that was noticeably lacking in traditions of independent Negro activity under the conditions of the new, white man's world. It became, no doubt, a powerful element in Chilembwe's morale when he returned home. He was not, he knew, entirely alone.

The American Negro's reaction to the conditions in the United States after Emancipation did not limit itself to the church and its allied activities. The overthrow of slavery opened up to the Negro a new world beyond the narrower bounds of traditional religion, and he meant to take advantage of it. There were, however, very distinct divisions amongst Negroes as to how this might be done. One powerful school of thought was represented by Booker T. Washington, a former Virginian slave who had been freed, when a young boy, by the Civil War, and had acquired sufficient education and training to found in 1881 in Alabama the Tuskegee Normal and Industrial Institute, which soon achieved fame both in the United States and overseas as a school for accommodating Negroes to the changed circumstances of a post-Civil War America. Booker T. Washington's ideas were simple, practical, and persuasive : let the Negro work his way to the top from the bottom upwards ; let him first learn properly the humblest jobs (farmer, mechanic, domestic servant) before aspiring to the higher positions in business and politics. It was a doctrine of industrial education that had not a few points in common with the practice of the Scottish Blantyre and Livingstonia missionaries in Nyasaland. It sought to avoid the complications and dangers of politics, and to change the average Southern white's conception of the educated Negro as a dangerous agitator decked out 'with a high hat, imitation gold eye-glasses, a shiny walking stick, kid gloves, fancy boots and what not' [46] to a person who was prepared humbly and cheerfully to take his place in the economy and to work for better conditions from there. As Booker T. Washington put it in his famous Atlanta Exposition address of 1895 : 'The wisest of my race understand that the agitation of questions of social equality is the extremest folly. . . .' [47] His theories gained strong support for him from the white community, and his own personal status assured him a deep respect from his own people, so that his figure dominated the American Negro scene from the 1880's to the First World War.

His doctrines, however, did not go unchallenged, and from the controversies which sprang from them may be seen another response by the American Negro to his position in the United States, a response which is certain to have been known to Chilembwe. Opposition to Booker T. Washington crystallized around the figure of William Edward Burghardt DuBois, a Massachusetts-born Negro of free and Huguenot origins who had received a thorough University education at Fisk, Harvard, and Berlin, and whose 1896 publication, *The Suppression of the African Slave Trade to the United States, 1638–1870*, the first work in the new Harvard Historical Series and the first monograph in the spirit of the new history by an American Negro, placed him in the front rank of Negro intellectuals. Although the DuBois-Washington controversy had not reached its crisis when Chilembwe was in America, there were indications that it was imminent during his stay. In 1895 DuBois dubbed Booker T. Washington's Atlanta Exposition address the 'Atlanta Compromise' with white society. And his and other Negro criticisms of Washington's ideals touched off a series of movements which asserted that the Negro must fight for full integration in the American community through all available channels, political, social, cultural, and economic. The Negro should not wait until his economic position had been consolidated before demanding the full privileges of American citizenship. To this end there had been formed: in 1896, the short-lived National Association of Colored Men; in 1897, the American Negro Academy; and in 1899, the Afro-American Council, which demanded an end to lynching, and the enforcement of the Fourteenth and Fifteenth Amendments. This was the year of the Spanish-American War which gave the United States the Philippines; and DuBois and other Negro intellectuals, together with a large section of the Negro press, actively supported the recently formed Anti-Imperialist League, castigated the war as unjust, and linked it to their own struggles with the demand that America should put itself in order at home before expanding overseas. This Negro campaign against American imperialism did not stop with the acquisition of the Philippines; and, in 1900, many voices—including that of the African Methodist Episcopal Church Bishop, Henry M. Turner— were raised against the use of Negro troops in the United States' effort against the Boxer Rebellion in China.[48] They were all indications that leading groups of American Negroes did not intend to sit down quietly and follow the advice of Booker T. Washington, but were determined to make themselves heard on all matters which affected their interests. When Chilembwe was leaving for home, the anti-Washington trend had set in motion forces that were to culminate in the Niagara Movement of 1905 and the National Association for the Advancement of Colored People, through which the American Negro moved right out into the open in politics.[49]

All this criticism of American home and foreign policy by Negroes could not have left Chilembwe untouched, particularly as the college he attended was poles apart from the simple, 'industrial' methods of Booker T. Washington.

All types of American Negro response to the new conditions, however, could join together in at least one task: the search for elements in the Negro's past in which he could take pride, and by which he could give himself a feeling of confidence, distinct from the centuries-old stigma of inferiority. It was an attempt to face the future with a hope rooted in an historical tradition: a form of 'cultural nationalism'[50] which expressed itself in many fields, and which for African witnesses of the movement such as Chilembwe or John L. Dube must have provided background for the growing Ethiopianism of their own countries—a tendency that was, to some extent, the equivalent of this American Negro movement. Indeed, the slogan of South African Ethiopianism was echoed in some of the cultural nationalist writings of Negro Americans. In the words of one American Negro Baptist minister:

> If it be here shown beyond reasonable doubt . . . that the ancient Egyptians, Ethiopians and Libyans . . . were the ancestors of the present race of Ham, then the Negro of the nineteenth century may point to them with pride; and with all who would find in him a man and a brother, cherish the hope of a return to racial celebrity, when in the light of a Christian civilization, Ethiopia shall stretch out her hands unto God.[51]

And on the more scholarly level, DuBois and other gifted Negro writers were publishing books with the aim of boosting the racial consciousness and pride of the Negro.[52] No evidence exists of Chilembwe's reading in the United States,[53] but it is not unreasonable to suppose that some of the literature of this movement later formed part of that 'class of American Negro publications' which was sent to him when he returned to British Central Africa.

Out of this cultural nationalism and the many other schemes to improve the American Negro's position there arose, at the time when Booth and Chilembwe were arriving in the United States, a wider movement of cultural nationalism : Pan-Africanism, an attempt to find the general elements in the problems of Negroes of all countries, and to remedy them through multi-national Negro action. In 1897 DuBois had asserted that if 'the Negro were to be a factor in the world's history, it would be through a Pan-Negro movement'.[54] From this time, through the first Pan-African Congress in Paris in 1919 to the inclusion of Pan-Africanism in the Gold Coast Convention People's Party platform of 1951,[55] the movement has had the character of an informal, irregular Negro International.[5]

Such a movement did not exhaust the range of Negro reaction to American conditions after Emancipation. When things were difficult, there was always one solution : getting away from them ; migration, internal and external. Before the Civil War this had mainly taken the form of escaping from slavery to the free states or the North or to Canada, and sometimes as far afield as the West Indies or Europe itself. After 1865 the general northward movement continued, and was supplemented by a drift from impoverished agricultural areas to the more hopeful and exciting environments of the growing American cities, whether of the North or the South. Thus foreign visitors, like Chilembwe and Booth, would find amongst their heterogeneous Negro populations every degree of despair and hope, bitterness and faith, ignorance and knowledge, scheme and counter-scheme for improving the conditions which had driven them to uproot themselves and seek new homes. Many still had memories, at the time of Chilembwe's visit, of the days of the 'Exodusters' of 1879–80 when numbers of Negroes, of varying estimates from 6000 to 25,000, under the leadership of Benjamin 'Pap' Singleton, emigrated to the western lands of Kansas.[57] Yet, if formal and informal internal migration had been the major way by which the American Negro, both before and after the Civil War, had attempted to ameliorate his lot, it is his migration overseas, theoretical and practical, that has the most relevance for the study of Chilembwe, Booth, and Central Africa.

For the American Negro, emigration overseas usually meant one thing : back to Africa, back 'home'.[58] As early as 1788, groups of free Negroes had been discussing a general Negro exodus to Africa. The movement was first dramatized in 1815 when the black sea captain, Paul Cuffee, took thirty-eight American Negroes to Sierra Leone. Within a year the American Colonization Society had been founded, under white leadership, to relieve pressure on the slave problem by shipping Negroes back to Africa. Though such movements received bitter criticism from Negro leaders as a device for ridding the United States of possible agitators against slavery, nevertheless the concept of the return to Africa had something of the appeal for many American Negroes of Zionism for the Jews : it meant 'home'. And so, before Emancipation, free coloured men in the States hatched schemes for Negro colonization in Africa or other coloured communities, such as the West Indies, Cuba, and Haiti. After the Civil War, though the vision of a return to Africa was checked by the increased possibilities of internal migration, it did not die out until the 1920's and the failure of the Marcus Garvey movement, for conditions in the new places inside the United States to which Negroes moved were still dominated by White Supremacy. Thus, in 1877 hundreds of Negro families in South Carolina signed up to go to Liberia, and the Liberian Exodus Joint Stock Company was formed ; a ship was purchased for six thousand dollars ; and a trip was made to Africa in 1878 with two hundred and six emigrants.[59] It was the prototype of many similar schemes down to the 1920's.

Such schemes were not limited to United States Negroes : they existed, too, amongst the coloured people of the West Indies. One of them is relevant for the story which will be told later of Booth's and Chilembwe's interests in the repatriation of Negroes to the African fatherland. This was the so-called African Colonial Enterprise of Dr. Albert Thorne, a West Indian graduate of Edinburgh University : a scheme for the settlement of West Indian Negroes in British Central Africa.[60] Thorne, like Booth and Chilembwe, was touring the United States in 1897 for support, and, though there is no evidence that they encountered each other, it is by no means impossible ; and, anyway, the African Colonial Enterprise forms part of the contemporary climate of opinion on African colonization in which the ideas of Booth and Chilembwe were nourished.

It was the American Negro at this time, rather than the West Indian, who had the most to do with the creation and extension of this climate of opinion ; and it must be pointed out that the coloured American looked upon Negro colonization of Africa not only as a means of relieving the pressure on Negro populations in America but also as a part of a Negro-American 'manifest destiny' to uplift his less fortunate brother in Africa. Here, of course, the American Negro missionary societies played an important role. Bishop Henry M. Turner, whose part in the stimulation of South African Ethiopianism has been noted, was an enthusiastic protagonist of Negro colonization. His address on 'The American Negro and the Fatherland' at a Conference on Africa at Atlanta, Georgia, in 1895 bears witness to his enthusiasm.[61] Indeed, he believed that the Negro had no future in America at all. Similar thoughts were expressed by National Baptist Convention officials and missionaries, especially Chilembwe's acquaintance, the Rev. Charles S. Morris, in whose orations the note of Negro 'manifest destiny' has already been indicated.[62] In spite of all its failures, its often self-seeking and corrupt leadership and its unrealistic appraisal of African conditions, colonization seems to have had a much deeper basis amongst American Negroes than is often supposed.[63] Whether for reasons of pure self-help or of 'manifest destiny', the 'Back to Africa' movement was well launched during Chilembwe's three years in America, and, as a member of the 'fatherland', he could look forward to a welcome from its many adherents.

Yet all of these Negro responses to the post-1865 conditions that have been examined—church, educational, economic, political, cultural, Pan-African, migratory — worked within the existing American frame of reference, however fiery they may have become at times. And so there remains one last response to be considered, the ultimate reaction of Chilembwe himself after he had tried out in his own country many of the other American Negro ideas : revolt against the existing order. After the Civil War the coloured man in the United States was very conscious of his own weaknesses when it came to the point of conspiracy against the Government, state or federal. Furthermore, the counter-revolution of the Ku Klux Klan and terrorism in individual states of the Union made him more than hesitate should he ever consider so drastic a step ; and he was, after all, not merely nominally free, for obviously greater opportunities existed after Emancipation than before, especially for former free Negroes and the Negro intelligentsia, the natural leaders of rebellion. Nevertheless the coloured American had a great heritage of revolt against slavery, and it was not forgotten in the years after the Civil War, especially by those exponents of cultural nationalism who were set on proving that the Negro was not, and never had been, a docile, inactive creature in the face of white oppression. Because a revolt was Chilembwe's final political act, and he had lived for three formative years of his life amongst Negroes with a tradition of insurrection and rebellion, some examination of its history is necessary for his story.

From the earliest times of slavery in the sixteenth century to the closing years of the Civil War, a conservative estimate of the number of slave risings in the United States would set the figure at over two hundred and forty.[64] For the state of Virginia in which Chilembwe spent much of his time, the total of over forty is equally conservative.[65] It must also be noted that the 'Old Dominion', the Negro's first home in the British North American colonies, was the scene of two of the three greatest slave revolts of the nineteenth century in the United States : the Gabriel Prosser revolt at Richmond, Virginia, in 1800 ; Denmark Vesey's South Carolina movement of 1822 ; and Nat Turner's rising of 1831 in Southampton Country, Virginia, which touched off slave insurrections all over the United States. And it was, of course, at Harper's Ferry in Virginia, on the evening of 16 October 1859, that John Brown, with Negro associates, raided the Federal Arsenal and hoped to precipitate a general rising of American Negroes against the institution of slavery.[66] Chilembwe was thus, for three years, not only in a country with a strong tradition of Negro insurrection but, more particularly, in a section of that country which had played a very important part in the creation and development of that tradition.[67] It was a tradition, furthermore, which was by no means isolated, and which set itself solidly in the long history of Negro revolt against white domination in the Caribbean and farther afield. An example of this may be seen in the aid which the Vesey conspirators of 1822 expected from San Domingo,[68] scene, at the end of the eighteenth century, of the greatest of all slave risings, Toussaint L'Ouverture's revolt, and of the establishment by King Christophe,[69] at the beginning of the nineteenth century, of Haiti, the first independent Negro state of the modern world. Indeed, the Vesey conspiracy looked as far afield as Africa for help. In this primitive Pan-Africanism the connection between American and West Indian Negro slave risings must not be passed by, especially in the 1830's, when Nat Turner was plotting his rebellion, and when the dream of emancipation in the British West Indies was to become a reality in 1833, and hope passed backwards and forwards across the sea in some strange way between dissatisfied Negroes in the United States and the islands of the Caribbean.[70]

Indeed, fresh spirit and new centres for Negro revolt in the British West Indies had been provided by the development of independent native churches amongst free and slave Baptists, themselves the offspring, as has been noticed, of the first Negro Baptist missionaries from the United States to the West Indies. More than once the levelling character of their teaching had brought them into trouble with the authorities.[71] They had, indeed, touched off an 'Ethiopian' movement in much the same way as their fellow Negroes in South and Central Africa nearly a century later. The tradition is all the more significant for Chilembwe's American period when it is recalled that George Lisle, the first of these Baptist missionaries to arrive in Jamaica and to build its original dissenting chapel, was himself an emancipated slave of the 'Old Dominion', and that Virginia's Negro Baptists supplied more than one ex-slave missionary for the little but spirited independent African churches of the islands.

From the tradition of the Caribbean and mainland Negro risings against their white masters, some elements which have much in common with Chilembwe's own movement in 1915 may be singled out, and the question asked—though not, unfortunately, answered— how far his actions at this time were influenced, consciously or unconsciously, by these Negro insurrections in the New World, and how far they were, in the main, a part of a general pattern of Negro reaction to European domination. (The latter seems the more likely answer to this question, though, in Nyasaland in 1915, echoes of the New World tradition of Negro revolt should not be dismissed as improbable.) First, the role of the independent Negro churches must be noted. In Jamaica their connection with the frequent revolts and disturbances there in the first seventy years of the nineteenth century is clear. In the Denmark Vesey conspiracy of 1822 in South Carolina, the African Methodist Episcopal Church played no small part. Its most able leaders were from the local church of this denomination; and the pioneer African Methodist Bishop, Morris Brown, a secret counsellor and active sympathizer of the plot, was forced to leave the state when his part was made known.[72] Furthermore, in each of the three great slave risings of nineteenth-century America, in 1800, 1822, and 1831, scriptural support, especially from the Old Testament, was used by the leaders to justify their revolts. They called on the examples of the Jews to escape from bondage, and on eschatological texts to give a kind of divine aura or sanction to their movements. Above all, it should be noted that the leader of the greatest of them, Nat Turner, was a Baptist local preacher who had been won over to Christianity, like Chilembwe, by a kind master. To them all, Baptist and Methodist alike, Christianity had brought the Bible, and the Bible had proved a mine of religio-political texts which seemed to justify their actions.[73]

There must also be noted in these risings the element of white support and influence : the four white men who were imprisoned for aiding Denmark Vesey ; [74] the master who had brought Nat Turner to the Baptist denomination ; the white man who was hanged near Lynchburg, Virginia, Chilembwe's American 'home town', for allegedly attempting to interest slaves in an uprising in 1835 ; [75] the criticisms that the white missionaries had sown the seeds of revolt in America and Jamaica ; [76] and numerous other examples may be quoted, amongst which John Brown must obviously be given first place. There were, indeed, many men in America and the West Indies with the same radical-religious spirit as Joseph Booth, and their effect on their Negro associates was, it seems, not unlike his on John Chilembwe.

There was, too, the ingrained Negro habit of the secret meeting, from the illegal gatherings of the slave plantation days to the more peaceful but still conspiratorial proliferation of fraternal orders, lodges, and secret societies at the time of Chilembwe's visit to America.[77] It was a tradition as old almost as Africa itself.

In sum, if John Chilembwe was in his early twenties when he went to America,[78] he was obviously at an impressionable age. He had gone, it will be recalled, with explicit instructions from his family and friends to observe closely the ways of the descendants of the slaves. His three years with them coincided with a period of intense reaction to white discrimination against Negroes. It is fairly clear, therefore, that he went home with more than a few new ideas. And yet, in one sense, their seed-bed had been laid before he ever entered America : for, between 1895 and 1897, his master, Booth, was writing a book in which he himself surveyed some of the American Negro scene, and commented on its relation to Africa and the lessons which might be drawn from it for African development It is very probable that Chilembwe read the book, as he was in close contact with Booth throughout this period. If he did not, its matter would be familiar to him through his five years of association with Booth before they left for the United States. It forms a link, therefore, between his early work for Booth in Africa and his visit to America with him; it indicates how their initial friendship had prepared Chilembwe's mind for the reception of new ideas from American Negroes; and it includes a range of schemes for Africa, and a religious and political perspective which Chilembwe retained after his formal break with Booth at Philadelphia, down to his last days in 1915. And the book itself was published while Chilembwe and Booth were together in the United States : it stands as something of a symbol between Chilembwe's formative years with the Zambesi Industrial Mission in his own country, and the new world which residence with American Negroes had opened up before him. For all these reasons, Joseph Booth's book must now be examined.

3. BOOTH'S BOOK

The title of Booth's book is revealing : *Africa for the African*.[79] At first sight it seems to hark back to the end of 1896 and the use of the slogan in Booth's African Christian Union prospectus to the disillusioned Zulu of Durban. In reality, however, it is more likely that it had its origin at the time of the three months' visit that Booth made to groups of American Negro Baptists in 1895. The slogan, 'Africa for the African', would probably then have had the meaning for the American Negro simply of his return to his 'fatherland'; it is with such connotations that the phrase appears to have originated in the middle of the nineteenth century. But Booth had adopted the slogan when the European partition of Africa was well advanced, and his use of 'Africa for the African' in his book is coloured more by this than by its traditional associations with American Negro colonization. He thus enlarges its scope to cover not merely plans for resettling New World Negroes in Africa but also to include a vigorous protest against the whole European Scramble for Africa.[80] To this end, although the greater part of his study is biased in favour of his British Central African experiences, he widens its horizon to take in South, East and West Africa as well. *Africa for the African* becomes, then, Booth's own highly personal critique of the African situation in the 1890's.

Supplementing his African experiences with reading drawn from missionary, Negro, and Governmental sources, Booth arranged his book in three parts. The first is a general criticism of the European partition of Africa : the acquisition of African lands by private companies and speculators ; the use of taxation to force the African to work for the European ; the employment of natives in European wars ; and a determined assertion of the African's potentialities if given the training and the chance—both of which Booth considered the African's right as a recompense for the horrors of the slave trade and slavery. He advocated three schemes to right these wrongs : an extended version of his 1896 African Christian Union proposal ; specific American Negro colonization of Africa ; and the development of self-propagating, industrial missions. Throughout all of these ran the triple themes of the necessity of a change of heart, and a new and more generous attitude towards the African by the European ; the special role which the American Negro could play in Africa if he so desired (and Booth had no illusions that he would be over-willing to take on this task) ; and the setting of the African on the path to full political independence as soon as possible, by returning his lands to him, and by encouraging him to develop his own economic enterprises.

The second section of the book is 'The Author's Apology' in which Booth gives a brief biographical sketch of himself, and stresses his African experiences as a justification for the views that he has outlined in the first part of *Africa for the African*. And the last section is a series of 'schedules' in which Booth develops his individual schemes for Africa in greater detail.

The whole work has much of the Christian radicalism of the criticisms of Rhodes and the British South Africa Company that were made by the great South African writer, Olive Schreiner, in her polemical story, *Trooper Peter Halket of Mashonaland*, which was published in the same year as Booth's own book. The primary problem is 'bridging the gulf between the European and the native'.[81] Booth described this gulf in much the same way as he had done in his numerous manifestoes and occasional writings over the past five years :

> . . . the ingenious heartlessness to which the modern spirit of greed can descend in the exploitation of African ignorance and helplessness. Whether we look at the government, mining capitalists or the planter class the spirit is the same. . . . Even missionaries, many of them need teaching that the African is inferior in opportunity only.[82]

Yet Booth, unlike Olive Schreiner, was not content to try to bridge the gap by a mere protest, however forceful. He had his three schemes, the latest of which was the 'effort to get the educated black man to his needy black brother. He at any rate cannot hold the deadly belief in the black man's born inferiority.' [83] It was this newer element, then, that Booth stressed most in his book. Someone must help the African to help himself : the European was failing in this task ; let the New World Negro now have his chance.

Despite his initial slow start with the coloured man of the United States in 1895, by 1897 Booth, as has been seen, had obviously interested a number of influential American Negroes in his work. One, indeed, had apparently sponsored the publication of *Africa for the African*. He was Dr. John F. Wagner, President of Morgan College, Baltimore, Maryland, whom Booth claimed as 'the first man in America to stand for the African Christian Union programme',[84] and who permitted the book to be printed on his College press.[85] To his growing number of bases amongst American Negroes Booth had added another of which Chilembwe could, and did, take advantage.

Chilembwe was obviously in Booth's mind as he wrote the book. He gives as evidence of the treacherous character of the Scramble for Africa the story that has already been quoted in the first chapter, of Chilembwe's brother's suspicions of Europeans ; [86] and he prints in full the African Christian Union schedule of 14 January 1897, which Chilembwe signed immediately after Booth. A close examination of this document [87] shows that almost all the ideas which Chilembwe may have developed whilst amongst Negro Americans must have been in his mind, through his association with Booth, before he left Nyasaland. His stay in America strengthened but certainly did not create them. (Perhaps, indeed, Chilembwe made his own contribution to the growth of these ideas amongst American Negroes.[88]) Booth's programme, then, at this time, was also Chilembwe's. It was a programme which each was to adapt to his own way in the years before 1915 : Chilembwe, with the constant backing of a Negro American organization ; Booth, through a maze of conflicting religious alliances, along a line of increasing isolation, yet still with the ultimate aim in view which *Africa for the African* summarized thus :

> Let the African, sympathetically led by his more experienced Afro-American brother, develop his own country, establish his own manufactures, work his own plantations, run his own ships, work his own mines,

educate his own people, possess his own mission stations, conserve the wealth accruing from all sources, if possible, for the commonwealth and enlightenment of the people and the glory of God.[89]

For Booth the difficulties of realizing all these aims were many : personal temperament and the prematureness of his ideas being but two of the greatest. But Chilembwe in 1897 was infinitely less well equipped. For him there was, above all, the terrible handicap of lack of education. How he obtained this, therefore, and what its character was, must now be determined.

4. CHILEMBWE AT LYNCHBURG

Some reasons for Chilembwe's separation from Booth have already been noted : Booth's poverty, and the increasing effect on Chilembwe of criticisms of white men by Negro American ministers. But, together, Booth and Chilembwe had toured many parts of the United States in an attempt to raise money for a new industrial mission. Booth perhaps hoped for too much—thirty thousand dollars, according to one source of information [90]—and his hopes were increasingly deflated. Between September and November 1897 he tried to interest white American Baptists in his work. But, though they showed interest, they were slow to move in a more positive and practical direction.[91] Finally, Booth appealed to the American Baptist Home Mission Society and the American Baptist Missionary Union in New York.[92] To this white gathering he invited the secretary of the Negro National Baptist Convention, Dr. Lewis Garnett Jordan. It was an auspicious invitation, for the white Baptists could offer Booth only good advice. In these circumstances the impoverished Booth handed John Chilembwe over to the care of Dr. Jordan. In this way Chilembwe's formal association with the National Baptist Convention, and the first stage of his separation from Booth, began. Yet it was much more than a circumstantial transfer ; it sprang logically from the whole trend of Booth's thinking —as his *Africa for the African* demonstrates—that the American Negro was marked out to be the best custodian of his African brother.

In Jordan, Chilembwe found a friend and a mentor on whom he relied heavily almost until his last days in 1915. Jordan obviously had a good deal of sympathy with him. Chilembwe's mother, according to Booth, had been a slave at first, and Jordan knew well what slavery was. His own grandmother, of the Choctaw Indian tribe, had been a slave in Alabama. His grandfather had been brought to America from Africa at the age of eighteen, and Jordan himself had been born into slavery in 1858.[93] Emancipation had given him the opportunity to educate himself, and he soon became a Baptist minister and secretary of the Foreign Mission Board of the National Baptist Convention, a position which he held for a quarter of a century. Jordan was thus well situated to advise Chilembwe about educating himself.

A preliminary step was to secure financial backing for him. And so, early in 1898, Jordan took Chilembwe to Roanoke, Virginia, where William W. Brown was the pastor of the High Street Baptist Church. Brown, who later became an influential 'preacher of the social gospel'[94] and minister of the important Negro Metropolitan Baptist Church, New York, seems to have taken to Chilembwe immediately. 'The coming of that African into my home', he said, 'brought me face to face, as never before, with my responsibility for the redemption of all the world and especially Africa.'[95] Brown, therefore, paid the expenses for Chilembwe's schooling.[96]

The next step was the school itself. An obvious choice was a Negro Baptist institution in Virginia; and conveniently at hand, fifty-odd miles from Roanoke, was the Virginia Theological Seminary and College at Lynchburg, an important market town in Campbell County.[97] Its head was Gregory W. Hayes whom Jordan was later to describe as a 'great scholar, a good teacher, a maker and leader of men';[98] and he handed Chilembwe over to Hayes's personal charge. The College itself had been founded in 1888, though it was not opened until 1890, by the Virginia State Baptist Convention 'to prepare Christian preachers, teachers and workers for work among Negroes'.[99] Disappointingly little can be discovered about Chilembwe's two years there.

It is possible that he was given special tuition by the head of the College, as he would not fit easily into any part of a curriculum that was designed primarily for American Negroes. This comprised a three years' course of elementary education; two secondary courses, a 'normal' course of three years, and an 'academic' course of four years; with some teacher-training and instruction in theology. Chilembwe's main centre seems to have been the theological department. Some idea of the teaching at Lynchburg at this time may be seen in an American Government report of 1917 on Negro education. The Virginia Theological Seminary and College is described in this as 'a school of elementary and secondary grade. Excessive time is devoted to foreign languages and exaggerated claims are made for the courses offered.' [100] It is clear from this report, which recommended the reorganization of the College, that it tried to do more than it could with the teachers and equipment at its disposal, and that it stressed the academic rather than the 'industrial' side of education. It certainly seems to have been the reverse of the careful step-by-step, practical approach of the Livingstonia and Blantyre missionaries. Furthermore, though its numbers probably did not exceed two hundred when Chilembwe was there, the students and staff seem to have been zealous proponents of the causes of Negro American and African 'improvement' and 'freedom'. Highly independent in spirit, they believed that the Negro peoples were perfectly capable of carrying on with their work without the white man always at their elbows. Whatever radical-religious ideas Chilembwe may have taken to Lynchburg, he would certainly not have lost them at the College.

Chilembwe obviously cut quite a figure amongst the student body at Virginia Theological Seminary. One of the students of the school, Anne Spencer, who later became an interesting American minor poet,[101] has noted

> his general unlikeness to the other students. In all, his air. I saw him long enough for a mind as questing and impressionable as mine was in those days to trace unforgettably his fine-boned face, his grey suit, grey-black complexion, his thin erect body; the tightness with which he clamped a large flat book under his arm when marching into chapel for devotions—and suspect the book of being a 5th grade geography! [102]

The last remark suggests a certain amount of pretentiousness in Chilembwe at this time—a by no means unlikely characteristic, because, although Chilembwe was amongst coloured people, they were folk who had tasted for long the white man's culture, and were worlds removed from the tribal societies of Chilembwe's Africa, and he would no doubt feel as uneasy among many of them as he would in white society itself. It is, then, understandable that he should guard himself with a protective pose. He invariably signed himself 'Che John Chilembwe', using the Yao prefix of politeness. But he interpreted this very differently from the normal translation of 'Mister' or 'Esquire'. Anne Spencer testifies of this :

> In one of those intervals between something—a group was on the front steps—I asked Mr. Chilembwe, 'What does *Che* mean ?' . . . He stiffly replied, 'It means *Prince*. My father is a King.'

Certainly, as was pointed out in the previous chapter, one of the meanings of 'Chilembwe' is 'a chief, a headman, a name of honour', and too little is known about Chilembwe's parents and their ancestry to accuse him of deliberate falsification.[103] Yet there seems little doubt that in such episodes he was guilty of some exaggeration.[104] The story suggests one who felt keenly on questions of status, and who might be stung to indignant action if he felt that his status had been attacked or insulted. It was a tendency, again, which could only be strengthened by a stay amongst American Negroes at this time.

Chilembwe's period at Lynchburg, therefore, was obviously quickening his imagination and stirring his pride ; and, as so many Europeans complained later when he was back in Nyasaland, was giving him 'ideas above his station'. Furthermore, it is very likely that he read fairly widely while he was at Lynchburg, not merely because he was in a *milieu* which would put into his hands 'advanced' Negro literature but also because the National Baptist Convention to which he was affiliated had in its Publishing House one of the largest Negro ventures of the period.[105] Yet how much technical equipment Lynchburg gave him for the realization of his ideas is doubtful. To the end of his life, for example, his command of English, although fluent and colourful, was by no means complete— though, by comparison, it was certainly very much better than the proficiency in his own tongue of many Central African Europeans. An example of his English at this time is provided by Chilembwe's own brief account of his American experiences which he sent in a letter to the local paper on his return to Nyasaland :

> In 1893 Chilembwe was converted to Christianity, and after his confession he was inspired to visit civilized countrys, then he took notion of crossing the deep deep mighty ocean. He had traveled through England and America considerably, and to the conclusion of his travelling he was burned with great desire for Education though it was little deflecluty on his part having no money to pay for his instruction. Yet he trusted to God that He will help to get his erudition.

Doubtless the merciful Creator had provided friends who sent him into Seminary, and after attended the College few years he was ordained to ministry of the Gospel.

Last year he was emit under the auspices of the National Baptist Convention of America to labour amongst his benighted race.[106]

The way in which Chilembwe's Lynchburg period came to an end with his ordination is puzzling. The Seminary records that he took A.B. and B.D. degrees in 1901.[107] If so, they must have been awarded *in absentia*, as he was back at Chiradzulu by this time.[108] Furthermore, the nature of the Seminary's authority to grant degrees of this kind is not clear. Nevertheless, at the end of two years at Lynchburg, in Booth's evocative phrase, 'he returned as a full-blown, round-collared, long-coated "Reverend" of the regulation type'.[109] Chilembwe's formal education had come to its end.

On leaving the Seminary he went, apparently, to Philadelphia, where he joined the Mount Zion Baptist Church of Germantown, a suburb of Philadelphia.[110] Booth was waiting for him in Philadephia, and the climax of their separation, which has been described in the first section of this chapter, took place. While Chilembwe had been in Lynchburg, Booth, by 1898, seems to have succeeded in interesting groups of Negro Baptists in his mission proposals, and he had become field secretary of an African Baptist Society or African Baptist Industrial Mission with its headquarters in Philadelphia. But the direction of their proposed mission by a white man did not suit the Negro Baptists, or else Booth left them of his own accord : for he soon surrendered his position as field secretary to the Rev. Charles S. Morris,[111] eye-witness of the Wilmington race riot, whose Negro 'manifest destiny' feelings for Africa have been quoted. It was with Morris that Chilembwe returned to Africa : the American was to take over the general supervision of the National Baptist Convention's missionary activities in Africa, and Chilembwe, under their auspices, was to set up his own mission in British Central Africa.[112] However, in the origins of Chilembwe's own mission, a factor of great importance is Booth's winning over of Negro members of the National Baptist Convention by 1898 to his African Baptist Industrial Mission scheme. In this scheme the beginnings of Chilembwe's Providence Industrial Mission at Chiradzulu may be observed. It was the first fully independent African Baptist industrial mission which Booth had struggled so hard to realize.

But there remains to be considered one other scheme with which

Chilembwe was associated during his stay at Lynchburg, a project of which Booth may have been aware but of which Chilembwe seems to have been one of the prime movers, for his name appears on its prospectus as its chief officer. This was the so-called African Development Society.[113] It was headed by G. W. Hayes, Principal of the Virginia Theological Seminary and College, and a number of other Negroes from Virginia and Washington, D.C. (Though L. G. Jordan's name is not included in the prospectus, the scheme may well have had his backing, for he was interested in Negro business ventures and is known to have been associated with a number of steamship projects.[114]) Chilembwe's name appeared in large type at the head of the prospectus as 'CHE JOHN CHILEMBWE, of EAST CENTRAL AFRICA, Gen. Solicitor'. In outline, this African Development Society followed closely Booth's ideas on African industrial missions and the settlement of American Negroes in Africa ; it was most likely modelled on the 'schedules' at the end of his *Africa for the African* ; and was interfused with a similar note of religious radicalism. The one new note was an obvious reference to Chilembwe himself in the opening paragraph of the prospectus which stated that 'certain Christian natives of East Central Africa have sent messengers to the Afro-American people, bearing a petition, asking their co-operation and direction in the development of the rich resources of their own country'. The only 'messenger' in question could have been John Chilembwe.

Though the scheme does not seem to have progressed much further than a paper prospectus, its existence none the less provides yet another indication of the ambitious and radical cast of Chilembwe's mind after his apprenticeship with Booth and his stay in America. It is not unlikely, too, that it owed something to the interest in African colonization which there had been for long amongst white and Negro alike at Lynchburg.[115] If this is so, it would appear to indicate that the influence of the Virginian city on Chilembwe was not restricted to the purely academic and institutional.

His schooling there may have been inadequate ; but his education in America had been a wider one than could have been found within the walls of the Seminary and College. He had travelled through England to many parts of the United States. One may note a few of the places which it is certain that he visited, and where he may have given public addresses, either for Booth's projects or for his own and those of the National Baptist Convention : the capital city of the United States, Washington ; New York ; Durham, North Carolina ; Richmond, Virginia ; Philadelphia ; Louisville, Kentucky, where the Foreign Mission Board of the National Baptist Convention had its headquarters ; Roanoke and Newport News in Virginia ; Baltimore, Maryland ; and, of course, Lynchburg itself. This skeleton list means that Chilembwe travelled in at least six American states, and it is very likely that he visited more. It was no mean itinerary for the first Nyasaland African to go to the United States. In itself, irrespective of what the Virginia Theological Seminary and College may have given him, it was an education. And, as he went along, Chilembwe learned that what Booth had originally taught him was proved true by his own experiences amongst American Negroes at a particularly difficult stage in their emergence from slavery. He did not fail to draw from it all the lessons which seemed most appropriate to him for his own people. Chilembwe was equipped, at least in spirit, to go home.

5. Booth's 1899 Petition

During Chilembwe's last year at Lynchburg, Booth was making his way back to British Central Africa where he was to produce another document that carried further his ideas for a radical change in the Protectorate. Chilembwe must have had some knowledge of this, and it is likely that it influenced the subsequent development of his ideology. The document was a petition for African self-government and it led to Booth's arrest and the threat of his deportation from Nyasaland. For Chilembwe the episode appears to have a twofold significance. First, it was taking place as he was about to return home, thereby ensuring that, as a known convert and former assistant of Booth, he would not exactly be welcomed with open arms by the Protectorate Government or by the greater part of the white settler community. Secondly, it represented a more exact formulation of the demand for African self-government in British Central Africa than the general statements of Booth's *Africa for the African*, and it looked forward to the kind of programme which, so far as can be gathered, Chilembwe was putting forward on the eve of 1915.

When Booth went back to Nyasaland in 1899 he was the agent of a body that called itself 'The Sabbath Evangelizing and Industrial Association'. It was sponsored by an American sect with whom Booth had come into contact in July 1898, when he was still nominally connected with the proposed African Baptist Industrial Mission of the Negro National Baptist Convention. This sect was the Seventh Day Baptists, a very old American religious grouping which is too often confused with the more widely known Seventh-day Adventists. But it was through the Seventh-day Adventists of the Rhodesias that Booth had been introduced to the idea that the true Sabbath is the seventh and not the first day of the week.[116] Meetings with fundamentalist Africans of Nyasaland had kept this idea before his attention. (At one such meeting, Chilembwe was with Booth, though he does not seem to have been attracted to the sabbatarian doctrine.[117]) But Booth was not yet ready for the Adventists' eschatology, and he found in the ideas of the Seventh Day Baptists a more amenable combination of his old Baptist principles and the new idea that the true Sabbath was the seventh day. And so, on 24 September 1898, Booth became a member of their Plainfield, New Jersey, Church. It was a convenient change of faith for him because it brought him into touch with a small but relatively prosperous American sect, at a time when he had broken with most of the missions he had established in Nyasaland between 1892 and 1897, and when the National Baptist Convention, looking, not for a white, but for a Negro field secretary for its proposed South and Central African missions, was placing its emphasis on Chilembwe, not Booth, as its pioneer in Nyasaland. Long interviews with leading Seventh Day Baptists resulted in the incorporation, on 30 January 1899, of the Sabbath Evangelizing and Industrial Association, with a capital stock of twenty thousand dollars, of which three thousand were quickly reached. It was an industrial mission similar to Booth's previous ventures, from which it differed only in that it proposed to teach the seventh-day Sabbath doctrine.[118] With this backing, Booth, his wife, and second small daughter left New York on 19 April 1899. Back in the Protectorate by 16 July, Booth proceeded to establish a base thirty miles south of Blantyre from which, when his brush with the authorities was over, he would set up a mission station for his new Association with the name of 'Plainfield', after the Seventh Day Baptist Church in New Jersey which he had joined.

His tour of the surrounding country, however, soon taught him that there was a more directly political task on hand. Therefore he set himself to draw up and circulate for the signature and assent of Africans a petition to Queen Victoria 'to influence the Powers That Be in favour of a suggested Native Policy more in keeping with the Commandments of God than the present'.[119] It had attractions for both the illiterate tribal African and the new and aspiring literates like Chilembwe. Briefly the petition asked : first, that the entire amount of the hut tax in the Protectorate should be spent on African education 'to the point of equality with the average British education'; secondly, 'That a pledge be given from your Government that this Protectorate shall never pass from the direct control of your Home Government unless it be to restore the Territory to an approved Government' ; thirdly, that free higher education should be provided for not less than 5 per cent of the African population to qualify it for 'Government, professional, mechanical, or mercantile operations' ; fourthly, that the whole Protectorate should revert to native ownership after twenty-one years ; and fifthly, that Africans from British Central Africa should not be forced to bear arms against neighbouring tribes or elsewhere in Africa.

Booth approached the local paper, the *Central African Times*, with his petition, and it printed it in its issue of 22 July 1899, with the comment that 'in the interests of the native, and of law and order, we would therefore ask H.M. Commissioner to take such steps as seem necessary to him to put a stop to this propaganda which can only end in mischief'. The Government was obviously of a like mind, for, in the words of a subsequent Deputy-Governor of the Protectorate to one of Booth's backers :

> It may be necessary to explain to you that Nyasaland was at this time beginning to settle down to peaceful conditions after centuries of intertribal wars and after the wars against slave raiding chiefs which followed the institution of British rule. You will therefore readily understand that such propaganda was considered dangerous to the peace of the country. Mr. Booth was asked for a promise to desist from the objectionable propaganda ; after some evasions he refused, and on issue of a warrant [August 1899] for his arrest and deportation he fled to Portuguese Territory and remained there in hiding until the beginning of November 1899 when he again approached the Government and having signed an undertaking to abstain from political teaching and given substantial security for his good behaviour he was permitted to re-enter the Protectorate.[120]

These few unemotional, official words cover for Booth nearly four months of wandering. They comprise, like so many episodes in his career, a confused period, when he was forced to flee into the neighbouring Portuguese territories with his wife and second little daughter. It was for him and his a period of great personal hardship, and the outcome was that at some date before the end of 1899 he lost his baby son, John Gordon, one month old.[121]

Despite all of Booth's sacrifices for his beliefs during this un-happy period, his petition, through the prompt efforts of the British Central African authorities, seems to have secured little open and immediate support amongst Africans—though its clear formulation of native grievances may well have acted as a focus for the subsequent political thinking of many more Africans than at first sight seems probable. Of these, Chilembwe would be an important but by no means isolated example, for there were many Africans at the end of the nineteenth century who could read in English the terms of the petition and the discussion about it in the Nyasaland press, and who might be expected to agree silently with many of the things Booth had stated in it, and to turn them over in their minds as future political material.

To some of Booth's American backers the issue was simple : 'in partial explanation of the harsh action of the British [against Booth], it should be said that at that time all British Africa was in a fever of uncertainty in fear of a native uprising to take advantage of the English troubles with the Boers'.[122] This was something of an over-statement, but it did have the virtue of seeing the issue in its wider context of native grievances.

The fiasco of Booth's 1899 petition was, indeed, a strange episode, as a result of which a nice constitutional argument developed between Zomba and London about the validity of existing deportation orders should it become necessary to use them against him.[123] But he solved the authorities' dilemma when he gave surety for his future behaviour, and by the beginning of the new century was back again in the Protectorate. Yet it had been a sharp warning to Booth to watch his step in the future. And for Chilembwe, in spite of all the new and liberating ideas which he was at this time bringing back from America, the episode may have had the same lesson.

6. Chilembwe leaves America

While Booth was making his peace with the authorities and was being allowed to re-enter British Central Africa, Chilembwe was also preparing to return to the Shire Highlands. Like Booth's, there is a certain dramatic quality about his story at this time, if the account left of it in colourful American Negro idiom by Jordan, the Secretary of the National Baptist Convention Foreign Mission Board, is to be believed. In his words :

> Two years having gone by, and this bright-eyed, opened-hearted young African had made rapid strides in his studies, but had become a victim of asthma. By order of his physician, he must return to Africa. We can never forget, at a farewell meeting at Newport News, Virginia, about 2 o'clock in the morning, with the rain coming down in torrents, the thunder fairly shaking the house wherein we dwelled, and the lightning playing about on the electric wires on the front of the building, we supposed this young African dying. We had propped up his head with a chair to see him die. As we stood, after looking into his face with pity, we remember having said to him, 'Bro. Chilembwe, if anything should happen, to you, what must I write to your people ?' He was then to us breathing his last. Rolling his eyes towards us, unable to speak scarcely, he said 'Bruddur Jordan, I no going to die. God bring me to this land to get light to take back to me people. He is not going to kill me here.' Deep in our hearts we admired his faith but would not have given a ten cents for his life. But the next morning he was yet living. . . .[124]

Thus John Chilembwe went back home, with the financial support and blessings of leading sections of American Negro Baptists. To them he was not only an attractive figure in his own right, but also a John the Baptist making in the wilderness of Central Africa a path for American Negro missionaries. Such a missionary venture, they felt, would afford further evidence to the whites of the United States and the world in general that the Negro could succeed as well as they in any sphere of his choice. It would be part of the great protest that was then sweeping through Negro America against its loss of civil rights since the failure of Northern Reconstruction of the Southern States after the Civil War, and a proud assertion of the independent Negro spirit. Indeed, by the end of 1904, when the National Baptist Convention had given to its members an account of its stewardship during the first phase of its relationship with Chilembwe's missionary enterprise, this point was made very clear :

> We serve notice on the world to-day that there will be no more begging for our own, there will be no more selling out below cost, there will be no more courting of favours, there will be no more divorcing ourselves from this soil, but there will be a standing until either Shiloh or our rights as American citizens come. Nothing but the gospel of Jesus Christ ruling every heart, in black and white alike, will bring these rights. . . . Jesus will not come to this earth until at His appearance the world will sing this chorus and the world will not sing this chorus until black men and white men who preach the doctrine of the brotherhood of man and the fatherhood of God believe so supremely in that gospel that one shall not deny the other inalienable and sacred rights.[125]

It was in this spirit that John Chilembwe went back to Africa.

IV

THE FIRST WAVE OF ETHIOPIANISM
IN BRITISH CENTRAL AFRICA
1900-1912

Oh John, Oh John, what do you say—That'll be there at
    the coming day—
John said the City was just four square—And he declared
    he'd meet me there—
Oh, I want to be ready to walk in Jerusalem like John.
American Negro Spiritual

Affrick never more abounded with New Monsters than
Pennsylvania does with New Sects, who are continually
sending their Emissaries around.
CHARLES WOODMASON, 1765

THE FIRST WAVE OF ETHIOPIANISM
IN BRITISH CENTRAL AFRICA
1900–1912

1. CHILEMBWE GOES HOME

CHILEMBWE arrived at Mbombwe, Chiradzulu, some time in 1900,[1] and began work on his little church and schoolhouse. How much of the specifically American side of the ideology of the Negro in the United States he had taken to heart it would be difficult to say, though there is little doubt that he was deeply moved by its application to Africa. There is evidence of this in the independent spirit of a letter about his proposed school-work which he wrote to the local paper of the Shire Highlands at the end of the year. In his fluent but still erratic English, he claimed that

> by giving the children of Africa good training they will be able to possess an indomitable spirits and firm dependence upon God's helping and sustaining hand. And make observations which will be of greatest use to different tribes of African Sons, who only need the quickening and enlightening influence of the Gospel of Christ to lift them from this state of degradation, and make them suitable members of the Great human family.[2]

Some clue, perhaps, as to the native and foreign elements which went initially to the making of his mission may be suggested by an examination of its original title.

Originally it was known as the Ajawa Providence Industrial Mission.[3] Chilembwe had undoubtedly taken his general concept of an industrial mission from Booth's Nyasaland experiments between 1892 and 1897, and this had been sanctioned by the National Baptist Convention Foreign Mission Board which, even if it had had no contact with Booth, would most certainly have been aware of the discussion on industrial missions in the American religious press. But where the adjective 'Providence' came from it is difficult to say. Was it the reflection, simply, of a pious hope? It is more likely that the term has American Negro connotations, and it may well have been suggested by the Providence Missionary Baptist District Association, the first grouping of United States Negro Baptists in Ohio, 1836 ; [4] or by the facts that there were Negro Baptists at Providence, Rhode Island, as early as 1774, and that in a different Providence (New Providence, the Bahamas) American Negroes had been active as far back as the last decade of the eighteenth century.[5] If this is so, the originators of its use for the title of Chilembwe's mission may have hoped that his centre would take its place in the Afro-American tradition of Negro Baptists—a tradition of highly independent activity that was set on increasing Negro status—which Chilembwe, in a land where there were few Negro traditions other than tribal ones, may have welcomed as a support to him in his self-ordained work of advancing the position of his people in the culture of the new, technical West.

There remains the particularized tribal adjective, 'Ajawa' (Yao) in the original mission title. This choice could have been none other than Chilembwe's own : but it is a puzzling one in view of the general sentiments of African improvement in his 1900 letter to the local press. Was his reason for choosing this epithet that he wanted to administer especially to his own people because of their bitterness and jealousy of the white man, which had been reflected in the circumstances of his own trip to America with Booth ? Or was it selected out of motives of tribal chauvinism,[6] because Chilembwe believed that it would give a particular mark of distinction to his work ? Whatever the reason, it was his own specific African contribution to the ambitious little mission.

Little mission it must certainly have been in those early months of his establishment in Chiradzulu, for Chilembwe had many other problems to distract his attention from the difficult enough task of building huts for churches and schools, and of finding a congregation and scholars. An overriding initial problem was his relationship with the local community. He was the first African from his part of the world who had been to America, and returned. He had come back from overseas not as slave or soldier or servant but as an independent minister, with the backing of one of the greatest forces of organized Negroes in the world.[7] If the teaching and training of the Virginia Theological Seminary left much to be desired, it had put on Chilembwe the mark of increased social status. He had come back clothed in full clerical respectability more than a decade before the neighbouring Blantyre Mission would ordain its first African ministers. Indeed, at a period when, as the Blantyre mission paper put it, 'the direction of native wages [was] upward, especially skilled labour [, and] in native life the horizon of ideas [was] widening every year',[8] he was for many Africans an example of a successful man : one who had taken advantage of the opportunities which white society offered to reach out and claim a position of equality with the European himself. He was an object of respect and envy : both of which attitudes would add to Chilembwe's difficulties in starting mission work. Respect would make some of his first followers expect more from him than he could give, and envy would turn against him many who might secretly hope to emulate his achievements. Furthermore, difficulties might be expected with some of the local chiefs who could be expected to resent the intrusion into their midst of an African representative of the new white-collar class which threatened to supplant their traditional power.

Above all, there was the problem of his relations with the local Europeans. It would be wrong to suppose that they would all apply to him the scornful categorization of the contemporary *Central African Times*, 'a pitiable travesty of Christianity', though a mixture of scorn and suspicion for the African clergyman was not uncommon amongst them.[9] Missionaries of the Zambesi and Nyassa Industrial Missions, despite past contretemps with Booth, gave the struggling little mission some help. Perhaps they remembered Chilembwe as one of their earliest converts and saw in his experiment some small fulfilment of their original, pioneering hopes for self-propagating industrial missions. The Blantyre and Livingstonia missionaries seem to have preserved a neutral attitude. If their papers do not mention the Providence Industrial Mission (P.I.M.) until 1903, at least they contain no criticisms that Chilembwe was drawing away converts from their stations, as they had done in the original days of Booth's ventures.[10] Some of their silence may, perhaps, have been the result of a discreet 'wait and see' attitude ; and much of it may have been because they did not see Chilembwe as relevant to any concerns of theirs at the time. And there may also have been in it a certain tremulousness when they remembered the results of the 'Mzimba schism' at Lovedale which had been taking place while Chilembwe was in America.

Lovedale was a missionary venture on the eastern boundary of the Cape Colony with which the Scottish churches had been connected for over half a century. In 1870 James Stewart, a founder of the original Livingstonia Mission in British Central Africa, had become Principal of its educational institution and had begun to make of the Lovedale experiment one of the outstanding achievements of mission work and industrial education in the whole of Africa. In 1875 an African named Pambani J. Mzimba had been ordained minister in charge of its native congregation. Mzimba was a model minister until Lovedale sent him abroad in 1893 to attend the jubilee of the Free Church of Scotland. While in Scotland he had been given considerable sums of money by sympathizers for Lovedale, which, on his return to the Cape Colony, he insisted on using for mission objects which seemed desirable to him, against the wishes of the local Presbytery. The Presbytery denounced him, and Mzimba left the Lovedale Mission in 1898 and founded his own 'Presbyterian Church of Africa', taking with him two-thirds of the native congregation, the title-deeds of his church, and mission property to the value of £1361. The action was a considerable embarrassment to the Free Church of Scotland—especially at a time when it was undergoing a schism in its own ranks in Scotland—and, although it took the case to the South African Supreme Court, it never succeeded in regaining the whole of the property that he had taken. Mzimba, an African who 'felt keenly what he considered a slight either on himself or his people', was an outstanding example of the dangers of native church separatism to the established missions,[11] and, with this in mind, it is just possible that the Scottish missions in British Central Africa concluded to tread warily in their relations with Chilembwe on his return to the Protectorate. He had not been ordained by them, and his Providence Industrial Mission, unless it were handled carefully, might easily become a centre to which discontented elements from their own could drift, to the detriment of the three decades of work and their own ideal of an African native church.

Since Chilembwe had some support from independent European missionaries in the area and the backing of the National Baptist Convention in America, it is unlikely that he worried unduly about the lack of response from the established Scottish missions. His much more serious problem *vis-à-vis* Europeans at the time was his taking up land in one of the parts of the Protectorate most convenient for European planters. It is true that he was not the first African to buy land in British Central Africa, and that his demand in 1900 was modest, a mere ninety-three acres. Nevertheless it was some time before the deed to the land which he had selected and purchased for £25 : 18s. (about $130 in American currency) was properly completed. Emissaries of the National Baptist Convention complained that this had been the result of deliberate delay by the Commissioner, Alfred Sharpe, who first forced Chilembwe to have a Power of Attorney from the Foreign Mission Board of the Negro Baptists and then conveniently 'lost' it until another was made available.[12] It is impossible to get at the truth of this allegation : but the Administration may well have taken its time over the matter of Chilembwe's land transaction. Chilembwe, after all, was known to be one of Booth's first converts and the Commissioner had just finished dealing with Booth after his 1899 petition. There was little love lost between the two of them : to Sharpe, Booth was a 'shifty, undesirable, dangerous man' ; [13] to Booth, the Commissioner was a petty tyrant, ready to put an African into chains for the slightest offence. Sharpe could hardly be expected, therefore, to go to undue pains to see that Chilembwe's land transaction went through quickly. Indeed, it is probable he was annoyed with Chilembwe personally not only because he came back to the Protectorate at a difficult time and was, anyway, the type of African not likely to take without question the directives of the Administration but also because, as it appears, he had offered him some form of office work and Chilembwe had refused it.[14]

Furthermore, Chilembwe's land lay near to the growing A. L. Bruce Estates at Magomero where W. J. Livingstone was manager. During his seven years in the Protectorate, Livingstone had proved himself an extremely practical planter.[15] In August 1900 he had written to Sharpe asking that, as a relative of David Livingstone and 'the first of his name to make the country which he practically discovered my home', he should be given a grant of land. The letter had been forwarded to the home government with the recommendation that Livingstone should be given five thousand acres. The request was refused on the grounds that, if it were granted, 'a large number of persons will claim relationship with the worthy deceased Doctor'.[16] How W. J. Livingstone may have received this refusal it is impossible to know. He may, however, have noticed that land near the area that he was managing was being sold, if only in very small lots, to ambitious Africans like Chilembwe at a time when a grant of land was refused to himself. Whether he drew from this any animus against such Africans it would be impossible to say. Nevertheless, despite the fact that, when Livingstone's application for land was sent home, he was described as having 'very friendly relations with the natives', he seems to have been involved in a case of assault against a native of the area in August 1900. The native concerned had been a prisoner of the Administration and had threatened Livingstone repeatedly. Because of this and his 'good private character', Livingstone was dismissed with a fine of £5 and costs, though the judge pointed out to him that 'in England the punishment would be imprisonment without the option of a fine'. The circumstances of the case are veiled in a brief official report.[17] The fact, however, that the name of the prisoner assaulted by Livingstone was 'Souza'—a Portuguese-sounding name—suggests that he was one of the scores of unruly, landless labourers then streaming into the Protectorate from Mozambique, squatting on private and Crown land and creating a host of labour problems for estate managers like Livingstone.[18] When, after all this, Chilembwe's missionary activity threatened to spill over into the Bruce Estates, it can be imagined that the manager did not view the prospect with complete equanimity. It may be possible that the tense relations which are known to have existed for long between Livingstone and John Chilembwe had their beginnings in the very year in which the latter returned to the Protectorate.

Closer personal problems than this now faced Chilembwe : the problem of resuming relations with his family. The suspicions which some of them felt towards Christianity and the Europeans have already been indicated. What could they be expected to feel now, when John had returned clothed in unmistakably European garb, and as an ordained minister of the white man's religion ? There was, for example, the question of his wife. Some have claimed that Chilembwe married before going to America, and had one child. On returning, he found that this 'wife' was already married and so he took another. Others make out more probably that he did not marry until after he came back, while another story has it that he married in America and that his wife was a Negro American.[19] Whatever the truth may be, there was some problem of personal readjustment for him in 1900, not the least of which was making his wife—or future wife—into 'a lady of the manse'. Existing photographs of her, her family and her mission activities at a later period suggest that, in this respect, Chilembwe succeeded very well.

To all these personal problems which beset him on his return home must be added the poor state of health which had forced him to leave America. Yet his mission work was not neglected, in spite of all these difficulties. Notwithstanding the land troubles, by the end of the year he had built sufficient hutments at Chiradzulu for a school of about a hundred, and a little mud church where he had baptized fifteen, and had begun to employ labour for more ambitious buildings.[20] And he had not let these domestic considerations turn his attention away from wider issues.

In the middle of 1900, three hundred Nyasaland native troops of the Central Africa Regiment had gone to the Gold Coast for the campaign against the Ashanti. Earlier, Nyasa soldiers had been used as garrison troops in Mauritius and in many campaigns against rebellious tribal elements in the Protectorate ; while another contingent had been sent into Rhodesia to deal with the recalcitrant Lunda chief, Kazembe. Booth, in his 1899 petition, had protested against the recruitment of troops in the Protectorate for such purposes. Whether Chilembwe knew of this protest of his old master or not, in 1900, after the dispatch of troops to the Gold Coast, he followed suit. Chilembwe's protest may, at this stage, have been a purely vocal one, but it was intense. He complained that Africans who lost parents or husbands in the Ashanti war were not being compensated ; and objected that the Government was making widows of native soldiers pay taxes.[21] His protest may have reached but a tiny circle in 1900 ; none the less, it demonstrates that, from the beginning of his return to the Protectorate, he had begun to criticize the employment of Africans in European wars. It looked forward to his protest against the use of Central Africans in the Mad Mullah campaigns in Somaliland and, above all, to his criticism of recruitment of Africans for the World War of 1914—an event that was closely linked with his Rising in the following year. Thus, by the end of 1900, yet another strand had been run into the pattern of 1915.

2. AMERICAN NEGROES ARRIVE

Another element in this pattern was the actual arrival in the Protectorate of Negroes from America. Though Booth's scheme of large-scale West Indian and American Negro settlement in British

Central Africa had collapsed with the failure of his 1899 petition, he had not altogether given up the hopes of his *Africa for the African*. At the same time as Chilembwe was beginning mission work, Booth, having made his peace with the Government, had entered again the Nyasa mission field. This time, with the assistance of the Seventh Day Baptists of Plainfield, New Jersey, whose Sabbath Evangelizing and Industrial Association had backed him during the fiasco of the petition, he had selected at Cholo, about thirty miles south of Blantyre, a plantation of 2001 partly cultivated acres, and between May and September 1900 the American Seventh Day Baptists had purchased it for about $15,000.[22]   It was to be the centre for another of Booth's industrial mission experiments, and, as has been noted, he called it the Plainfield Mission, after the New Jersey sabbatarian church where he and his wife had been converted to the doctrine that the Sabbath is the seventh day.   How far he intended to make this new mission a distributing centre for American and West Indian Negroes is not clear, though there is some evidence to show that he tried to interest American Seventh Day Baptists in this project.[23] Under their auspices, however, Booth had little chance to put such schemes into effect.   Despite the fact that he soon had a labour force at work planting coffee, a local blight on the crop speedily put an end to many of his ambitions.   Furthermore, the events of the Zambesi Industrial Mission's early pioneering period were to repeat themselves.   Booth quarrelled with the Seventh Day Baptist Missionary, Jacob Bakker, who had been sent out to help him ; and, enthusiastic and over-ambitious with a new base from which to try out his original ideas, he 'did not always follow principles of business prudence in his administration of finances', and involved his American backers in debt.   On 13 December 1901 the Seventh Day Baptists in the United States terminated their contract with Booth.[24]

Booth was not finished with the scheme.   Having gone to the United States to explain the initial difficulties of his projects to his sponsors, he found the Seventh-day Adventists ready to listen to him when he had broken with the Seventh Day Baptists.   By the end of 1901 the Adventists had bought the Plainfield Mission from its original owners, and Booth had shifted his allegiance to them. Like so many of his volatile movements, the details of this switch in religious allegiances are obscure, though it is clear that he had made some contact with the Seventh-day Adventists in the United States before he had broken his contract with the Seventh Day Baptists.

Plate 5. Rev. L. N. Cheek, the second American Negro missionary to land in Nyasaland, and Rev. John Chilembwe ; probably taken in 1901. (Chilembwe is standing)

Plate 6. Chilembwe's American Negro helpers : Rev. L. N. Cheek and
Miss Emma B. DeLany

The result was that the Adventists sent out an American Negro, Thomas Branch, together with his wife and family, to open the first effective Seventh-day Adventist mission in the Protectorate.[25]

Thomas Branch was apparently the first American Negro in British Central Africa. Arriving at the beginning of April 1901, he and his family seemed to be the start of the realization of Booth's dream of Negro colonization. It is, however, not altogether certain that Booth had persuaded the Seventh-day Adventists to send him. It is true that, shortly after Branch's arrival, Booth had written a letter in defence of 'Afro-American' Negroes in the Protectorate to the *Central African Times*.[26] But later in the year a rift began to emerge between him and Branch, which appears to have been due to Booth's resentment that he, with all his previous experience, had not been made director of the new mission in place of Branch.

Branch, by all accounts, was a quiet sort of man, unlikely to cause trouble to the whites of the Protectorate. Yet the local press, fearful of the political implications of the Ethiopian scare in Natal at the beginning of the new century, did not hesitate to link his name with the entry of the Ethiopian spirit into British Central Africa. Since he and Booth entered the Protectorate, it claimed, local Africans had grown impertinent and spoke of the rape of their land by the white man.[27] Later, Booth himself was to be accused of secretly propagating Ethiopian doctrines amongst Africans under the cover of the Plainfield Mission, and, because of this, at some time between 1902 and 1904, official pressure was to be brought upon him to leave the Protectorate, to which he never returned.[28]

All the blame for the entry of the Ethiopian spirit and what seemed to be its Negro American agents into British Central Africa at the start of the century should not be placed on Booth. The *Central African Times* of the period reflected a certain minor hysteria amongst some Nyasaland Europeans on the subject of Ethiopianism. It spoke, in the middle of 1901, of the feeling of Natal newspapers that Ethiopian American Negroes might soon cause a 'general native rising' in Natal, and went on to stress that the Protectorate had been free of such subversive elements until 'the mistaken kindness of our old friend Joseph Booth' introduced two such into their midst.[29] However, Booth's rift with Branch and the fact that the Negro missionary had originally been chosen by a white American missionary organization, the Seventh-day Adventists, make it fairly clear that, from this quarter at least, Booth must be absolved from any direct role in the introduction of subversive elements in the form of American Negroes into Nyasaland—though, of course, indirectly, his interest in Afro-American emigration to Central Africa may have played no small part in this.[30]

With the second American Negro to which the *Central African Times* referred, Booth had nothing to do whatsoever. Indeed, the paper itself, on 20 April 1901, noticed his arrival in East Central Africa :

> by the s.s. *Induna* there arrived in Chinde an American Negro who comes to BCA as a sort of emancipator of his people and we learn that he has settled in that hornets' nest, Chiradzulu. The cloud [commented the paper gloomily, with its eye on Ethiopian developments in Natal] is small now, as a man's hand, but it is there.

Between Chilembwe's mission at Mbombwe, Chiradzulu, to which the new arrival had gone, and the work of Branch and Booth at Cholo there was a distance of over thirty miles ; and there appears to have been little contact, if any, between these two suspected centres. Any collusion between Africans of the two areas lay well in the future. In the middle of 1900 the missions were too concerned with internal questions to worry much about anything else.

Chilembwe, no doubt, was hoping that the American Negro newcomer to the P.I.M. would take some of the burdens of work from his shoulders. The new arrival was the Reverend Landon N. Cheek,[31] who had ranged the full gamut of training as an American Negro Baptist minister. Cheek was born at Canton, Madison County, Mississippi on 8 December 1871—he was, thus, of much the same age as Chilembwe—when the bungling Reconstruction of the Southern states of the American Union still had six years to run ; and he must have drawn from the circumstances of his boyhood some feelings of resentment against the white man. After a successful schooling, he had passed into the little Negro college at Jackson, Mississippi, for some higher education, and then to Western College, Macon, Mississippi, for theology. His early interests had been in Y.M.C.A. work for Africa, and the transition to a desire for African mission work on his part was, therefore, natural. The plan of the National Baptist Convention for a Nyasa mission was to be his chance. In 1899 Cheek applied to the Convention for a missionary post, was accepted, and after a peripatetic year of appealing for funds from American Negro churches, set out from New York in January 1901 for British Central Africa.

There was no doubt of his enthusiasm, and though, perhaps, some of his education and theological training, by stricter standards, may have left much to be desired, Cheek had had more formal education than some Europeans in the Protectorate. When he reached Blantyre in May 1901, these facts, together with the mood of misgiving amongst many Europeans because of the Ethiopianist developments in Natal, ensured suspicion of him. Cheek had known neither Booth nor Chilembwe in America; but he was a Negro minister, and that was enough! As Cheek was later to write:

> My English friends (?) were eyeing me as a veritable hornet who within thirty years would incite the natives against English rule. To the last day of our long and weary years they tried to trump my every move, even to build up our station, hoping that any day I would be discouraged and return to U.S.A.[32]

If there was little genuine justification for such an attitude amongst Europeans towards him, some of Cheek's actions, in an atmosphere heavy with suspicion, could easily be misinterpreted. For example, as he himself noted:

> The paramount chiefs of our time at the Providence Industrial Mission were Kumtaja and Malika. They have a minor power amongst their subjects, jealously guarded by the English since they established the Protectorate. . . . They were friendly with me and often exchanged visits with us, even with the hope of having me to become one of their chiefs and lead them into autonomy.[33]

Such visits would not pass unnoticed by loyal Europeans, especially as the Yao chiefs of the area were not distinguished for their pro-British sentiments. Again, when Cheek published in an American newspaper an article critical of the British in Central Africa, it was natural that the Protectorate press should show some suspicion of his activities. A passage from the article indicates the kind of criticism that many Europeans resented:

> The negroes are looked upon with suspicion. These brethren here need a start in civilization, and that at most is a few ploughs and farming implements. The plough and mule are unknown. While the native bends down with a hoe-handle about one and one-half feet in length and digs in the earth, making his hills for corn and beans, we cannot expect him to dream of heaven and a higher ideal. When the village hut-life is broken up and the Government will run schools with some of the tax-money used for standing armies and Imperialism, we can hope for a

great change. Will we really hope for this change from any other race
[but the Negro]? Can we expect the foreigners in Africa to plead for
higher wages and more education while they still sell barter goods to
natives and get the majority of them for seventy-five cents per month?
Is there no power to save? Who will make a move for justice and
mercy? [34]

Such words, when drawn to the attention of the local European
press, were not likely to leave it without comment.

The next American Negro to arrive at the P.I.M., however,
evoked no comment from the local paper. This was probably
because she was a woman: Miss Emma B. DeLany.[35] The same
age as Cheek, and much the same age as Chilembwe, she had been
born at Fernandina in Florida. After an education at its Convent
School, Emma DeLany had entered the Spelman Seminary (now
the undergraduate college for women at Atlanta, Georgia) in 1889,
where she spent six years for further education, nursing-training—
for which she was awarded a gold medal—and preliminary instruction for the mission field. For some time after this she had worked
as a matron at Florida Institute, Live Oak. Miss DeLany, then,
was a young Negro American woman of some accomplishments, all
of which could be put to good use when she arrived at the P.I.M.
in 1902, a year after Cheek. There was nothing Ethiopian, in the
British Central African sense, about the practical Miss DeLany,
though she had the new pride of her people. But she was the third
American Negro missionary to set foot in the Protectorate within
two years: and for Cassandras amongst white settlers, with their
suspicions of Ethiopianism, that was enough!

3. FOUNDATIONS OF THE PROVIDENCE
INDUSTRIAL MISSION

Yet, for Chilembwe, Miss DeLany had not arrived too soon. In
spite of the presence of Cheek at Mbombwe for a year, the foundations of the P.I.M. were still weak.[36] There was still trouble about
the land on which its permanent buildings were to be erected—this,
indeed, was not settled until, at least, 1904. Furthermore, famine
and disease in Portuguese East Africa had increased the number of
native emigrants from Mozambique into British Central Africa in
search of food and work. This increase in the potential labour force

of the area presented a challenge to Chilembwe, his hands already
full with the problems of proselytizing his own people. He seems
to have met it. An African story [37] has it that Chilembwe soon
built up a following amongst these migrant workers by actual penetration into their own homelands. He had gone into the Portuguese
territories, so the story goes, during 1901, on a hunting trip.
(Chilembwe, as will be seen later, relied on his skill as a hunter to
eke out the mission rations and to contribute to its finances.) While
there, he found that many Africans were being thrown into prisons
with execrable conditions, where native women, indeed, had often
to give birth in the presence of men. By approaching the keeper of
one of these prisons, and by pointing out to him that such things
were not good in the sight of God, Chilembwe succeeded in getting
the release of some of these Portuguese African captives. Whatever
apocryphal elements of *naïveté* this African story may contain, a
moral has been drawn from it : that for many Africans, from this
time on, it was obvious that Chilembwe had come to deliver his
people from their bonds. And if he was gaining, in episodes of this
sort,[38] the confidence of the emigrant workers from the neighbouring
Portuguese territories, as they poured as labourers and squatters on
to the European estates near his mission, then the fact has some
significance, as it was from such elements that a considerable part of
Chilembwe's following in the 1915 Rising was to be drawn.

That Chilembwe was frequently out shooting [39] in the bush at
this time underlines what is only too clear from other sources : that
in the period before he had both Cheek and Miss DeLany with him,
his little mission was in financial difficulties. The P.I.M. had only a
modest beginning, yet even a mud school requires skeleton supplies,
and a wattle-and-daub church needs some accessories. And
Chilembwe, it should be noted, had begun work on a more permanent brick building. But the difficulty about hunting to increase
his finances — the sale of elephant tusks was then a profitable
business—was that gun and game licences were expensive too. The
arrival of the two American Negroes, therefore, meant to him that
the National Baptist Convention was ready to give him more
tangible support.

Their work was apparent in two years. Regular cheques began
to come from the United States. Chilembwe and Cheek divided
up between themselves the tasks of teaching and proselytizing, and
extended their congregations and influence not only in the immediate

Chiradzulu area but through the neighbouring district of Mlanje into the Catholic Portuguese territories, and in some cases, it seems, as far afield as the Rhodesias.[40] New teachers were added to the mission, amongst which were Chilembwe's nephew, Morris, who went down in the 1915 Rising, and his elder brother's daughter, Mary Chimpele. A start was made on a women's movement, in which, though Miss DeLany was the major influence, Mrs. Chilembwe played some part; and weekly sewing classes—possibly with sewing machines, a great native luxury at that time—were established in several quarters. Regular forms of social life were springing up at the P.I.M., and the celebration of Christmas was on its way to becoming a recognized feature of the mission's life, with *nyama* (meat—another great luxury in an area that was often touched by scarcity of food) and games, to which the Africans in Chilembwe's following could look forward. At his mission, indeed, small though it still was, a corporate feeling and pride was emerging. It was, by the time the American Negro missionaries had been there for two years, simply the Providence Industrial Mission, or P.I.M. as it was coming to be known popularly. The more restrictive prefix, 'Ajawa' (Yao), had been dropped from its title. Chilembwe was now preaching in the *lingua franca* of the Shire Highlands, Nyanja, and his appeal was clearly being made to the widest circle of Africans that he could find.[41] The corporate feeling that was growing up at the P.I.M. at this time must have helped by providing Chilembwe with a firm base from which he could extend his activities.

By 1904 this corporate spirit and pride had become recognizable. Miss DeLany expressed it very well in a letter to the women of the National Baptist Convention in America who had financed the first major brick building to be erected at the mission. She wrote:

> If I may compare the place to-day with the place two years ago, I would say that . . . we have already reached a degree of civilization. In front of the house where one year ago only stumps, thorns and crooked trees were growing you will find to-day scarlet geraniums, a few bloom-ing roses and other flowers, while the red leaf hedge forms the walks and divides the yard into squares. On either side of the walks in the back yard the thick soft grass that was planted in December has covered the place and the red hedge around it gives the appearance of a green velvet arch square with a red border. This with a few flowers gives the back yard a pretty appearance. Beyond the kitchen where the tall grass flourished and was burned each year simply to come up again, I had

about an acre and a half of cotton planted. Certainly it is not growing nor bearing yet, but it makes the place look neat. . . . To the right of the house a few hundred yards were delapidated huts and another field of grass, trees, etc. ; to-day you will find a brick church, certainly not a very handsome building, for architects here are self-taught, and native labour very crude, but nevertheless God's Temple reared to his glory.[42]

With its cotton, the P.I.M. had no greater success than many of the other planters of the area. But the fact that it was planted at all was a measure of the mission's aspirations. Indeed, by 1905, Cheek and Chilembwe had experimented with coffee, tea, pepper, and rubber, as well as cotton.[43] Chilembwe was preaching to his congregations that they must be prepared to work with their hands in the new society, and was obviously exerting all his energies to emulate the white industrial missions. A detailed economic history of the mission does not seem possible, but there is some evidence to indicate that, although the P.I.M. had fewer resources to fall back on than the European missions or estates in times of climatic or economic fluctuation, it managed to struggle along in face of economic difficulties. Furthermore, it had the advantages over the European missions that it had means of subsistence culture, a staff which, on the whole, was brought up in that tradition, and less alien supporters to persuade that their subscriptions were producing quick results. What figures exist for the mission's growth suggest that, for all the initial enthusiasm of its founders, its development in terms of actual members was small in the early years—105 in 1905—though this, of course, is no guide to the ramifications of its influence.[44] Chilembwe and his American Negro helpers seem to have concentrated at this time on building up the permanent stock of the mission rather than on going for quick, initial enrolments which would fade away hastily afterwards. If this is true, it suggests that Chilembwe, unlike his old master, Booth, was not over-ambitious at first, and contented himself with building on small but secure foundations.

Thus, by 1906, the two American Negro missionaries, in their five years in British Central Africa, had helped Chilembwe to create a promising little mission.[45] Cheek, indeed, had become closely attached to the Chilembwe family. He had married Chilembwe's niece, Rachael, and had become the father of three children, one of whom, Ada, died in Africa. Both he and Miss DeLany had learned the local vernacular, and had built up their own little personal following amongst P.I.M. Africans. When, therefore, the mission foundations were secure, and the time came for them to leave, in June 1906, it is not surprising that some of this following, through Cheek and Miss DeLany, managed to find their way over to America. The opportunities there would have been contrasted with those in the Protectorate, or even in South Africa, not only by the American missionaries but also by Chilembwe, whose pioneering example these new emigrants hoped to follow. Cheek himself took two of the mission boys home with him, Matthew and Fred Njilima, and gave them an education; and Miss DeLany was persuaded to send back from the United States for one of her own special followers. He was Daniel Malekebu who, after Miss DeLany left, had made his own unaided way down to the Cape, and from there had appealed successfully to her to send for him. (After many years in America, where he eventually took a medical degree, Malekebu was to return to Nyasaland in 1926 as the head of a new Providence Industrial Mission.) Thus the early years of Chilembwe's mission, like the early years of Booth's, had introduced aspiring Africans from British Central Africa to the New World, and had added to the intricacies of the already ramified native emigration from the Protectorate.

4. Chilembwe builds his Mission alone, 1906–10

By the end of 1906, then, John Chilembwe was in sole charge of the Providence Industrial Mission, whose history now enters into a new phase. The Protectorate, too, was moving into a new period. In 1907 its title was changed to 'Nyasaland', its Commissioner and Consul-General became 'Governor', and provision was made for the creation of Executive and Legislative Councils, the latter of which was to include nominated, unofficial members. And, as if in anticipation of the change, in 1903 the Commissioner, Alfred Sharpe, had been knighted.

How much these changes were noticed by Chilembwe is not known. Neither he nor any of the politically conscious Africans seems to have commented on the fact that no provision was made for direct African representation amongst the nominated members of the proposed Legislative Council. His attention, perhaps, was diverted by more human manifestations of the price which had to be paid for the Protectorate's rise in the scale of the British Empire.

Chilembwe, for example, does not appear to have remained silent in face of the loss of over a hundred and fifty African soldiers from Nyasaland in the Somaliland campaigns against the 'Mad Mullah'. Indeed, an incident at the reception given to these troops on their return to Zomba in 1904 could hardly have escaped his attention. As the Blantyre Mission paper put it :

> An old woman had come eighty miles to welcome back her six sons. Standing amid the cheering crowds she saw the troops march past and enquired after her boys. She then learned for the first time that all of them had been killed.

The journal commented :

> War has its price of sorrow even for the untutored African who takes his share unwittingly in the burden of Empire. And there still remains the question to be answered, 'Is it right ?' [46]

Chilembwe, it seems, had no hesitation about the matter, for he complained in some way—the manner of which is not clear—against the use of African troops in this campaign.

This, indeed, raises a point about the character of his teaching in the early years of the P.I.M. Before Cheek arrived, as has been noted, he had protested about the employment of African troops outside the Protectorate, and Cheek himself had not been uncritical of local conditions. Did this tendency increase when Chilembwe was in sole charge of the mission ?

Certainly, between the time of his return home and the departure of the American Negro missionaries, marked changes were taking place in Nyasaland which Chilembwe, as an intelligent African with some European-style education, could not have failed to notice and on which he may well have commented to the Africans in his classes and congregations. Population, European and African, was concentrating, if not increasing rapidly, in the Shire Highlands,[47] and was adding to problems of land-labour relations. If Nguru emigrants from Portuguese East Africa were complicating these, difficulties were not lessened by the emigration of indigenous Protectorate workers to the South African mines. Between 1903–4 attempts had been made to solve at least part of these problems by giving some fixity of tenure to Africans on the land, and by encouraging a settled agricultural population in the Protectorate. Most important of all these attempts had been the Nunan Judgement of 1903, which commented on 'the growing tendency to treat the native, whether he is an old or new settler, and whether any rights were secured to him under the Certificates of Claim [of Harry Johnston's land settlement] [48] or not, as a tenant at will or even as an unfree *villein* or *scriptus glebae*'; [49] and which tried to bring some equitable perspective into this confusion of land problems. (The constant shifting of African population in response to the conditions of the European-dominated society that created much of this confusion, is illustrated by a young Ngoni chief, Makwangwala, who shifted his whole village about 1900 in order to be near the Baptist Industrial Mission of Scotland, that Booth had founded, in order to take advantage of its school.[50] In 1915 he was found to be implicated in Chilembwe's conspiracy.)

Such attempts may have created as many problems as they solved. There was, for example, the Native Locations Ordinance of 1904 which tried to introduce some fixity of tenure on the land for unsettled Africans by providing for the European principle of rent, which the African could pay either to the Government or to a private European landowner. But, as the Blantyre Mission paper commented :

> On the face of it, it is an anomaly that the native should in this way have to buy back land which was once his own. Where he once had fixity of tenure he now has to pay for it at the rate of four shillings per annum. It is an anomaly but one of those anomalies which must be allowed for. The introduction of the white man with his new notions of private property in land was the predetermining cause, and this must be accepted as something which has come to stay.[51]

All Africans, however, could not be expected to adopt this comparative point of view, though a few were to take advantage of the situation to become small landowners themselves.

On one point, though, all could agree : the inconvenience of the new taxes. Between 1902 and 1903 the original hut tax of three shillings had been increased to six, with a labour rebate of three shillings, equivalent to about a month's work for wages with a European. It was all a very disturbing situation for Africans.

Furthermore, in the year when Chilembwe was consolidating the initial achievements of his mission, serious native revolts occurred in neighbouring territories : revolts which gave cause for thought not only to those Nyasaland Africans who heard about them but also to many Europeans in the Protectorate. The first had broken out in 1905–6 in German East Africa. In this 'Maji-Maji' Rebellion, as it is often called from the belief of African participants that those who possessed a certain medicine had the power to turn bullets into water ('maji' in the Swahili language), 120,000 are said to have died. The second revolt took place in British Natal in 1906, under the leadership of Bambata, and was the last militant stand of the Zulu against the inroads of the European way of life. Its casualties have been estimated at four thousand.[52] For Nyasaland Europeans the outbreak verified all the prophecies about the effects of Ethiopianism in Natal which the local papers had been making since Booth's 1896 African Christian Union scheme. Furthermore, the converts of American Negro missionaries were linked at the time—and later by the official Commission of Inquiry into the Bambata Rebellion—to the disturbances. To many Europeans it was all evidence that the African was getting out of hand.

If statements in the *Central African Times* on these changing conditions inside and outside the Protectorate are any guide to white settler opinion in the Shire Highlands, Chilembwe, from his own mission, might have been expected to produce some reactions. In 1906 the paper commented on the refusal amongst some Africans to perform 'such manual work as was assuredly designed for the ordinary tribesman. They regard themselves as of a better class.' It then noted that 'education makes the native aspire to something better and hence must be discouraged, because cheap labour is the main desideratum at the present time'.[53] The upshot of it all was, according to one correspondent, that 'No one should be kind to natives. They do not understand it, they do not wish it, and it is not good for them. . . .'[54]

In face of such statements, Chilembwe was unlikely to be silent before the Africans of his churches and schools.

To this kind of criticism the African intellectual from Natal, John L. Dube, whom Chilembwe appears to have known in America, could react in the native newspaper which he had founded in 1906, *Ilanga lase Natal* (*The Sun of Natal*). Indeed, he was arrested for a short period for making radical statements in his paper at this time. But no such channel existed for Chilembwe. Yet there is not much doubt that he used both the churches and schools of the P.I.M. to complain about the many changes in the air. An African who entered the Providence Industrial Mission in 1904 and passed into Chilembwe's class (Standard III) in 1907, has expressed this succinctly :

> Chilembwe taught us a good deal about planters and white settlers. He complained about the planters [European] who were cruel to their African tenants, stopped them from collecting firewood and cutting trees from their estates, etc. Many of the tenants were Christians in his church. Indeed, the Europeans did not seem to like him because they used to send detectives to his Mission to find out what he was doing.[55]

But negative criticism of local Europeans, particularly of the adjacent Bruce Estates, was not Chilembwe's only response to the changing conditions of Nyasaland society at this period. He seems to have set himself a more positive ideal as an answer to European attacks on native education. And, despite the academic cast of Chilembwe's Lynchburg education, there is not a little of the Booker T. Washington technique about his mission training in these years. He would show the Europeans how wrong they were about educated Africans by building up a clean, neatly dressed community at the P.I.M., with industrious and sober habits. His teaching stressed respectability and deportment on the European model, and his simple curriculum included basic agricultural teaching along the lines of the famous Tuskegee Institute and other American Negro industrial schools. In this way, by about 1910, Chilembwe succeeded in producing such a well-dressed and drilled community that he invited local Europeans to come out and photograph them ; and many of them were surprised at the standard he had attained. A glance at one such photograph that was taken then (see p. 166) indicates that, although his flock was obviously in its 'Sunday best', it was something of a personal achievement for Chilembwe. Indeed, if, as this picture suggests, Chilembwe's ideal at this moment was the Booker T. Washington industrial-educational prescription for the advancement of Negro status, it may explain why he made no criticism of the lack of African representatives among the nominated members of the new Legislative Council. It would suggest, too, why, in spite of all his criticisms of the European-wrought changes in the Protectorate, he indulged in no propaganda to subvert the white man's rule : because, despite all the imperfections, from a native point of view, of white rule, Chilembwe felt, like Booker T. Washington before the society of the contemporary United States of America, that if the opportunities afforded the African were fully utilized by him, they offered prospects for individual and collective advancement that would otherwise have been utterly impossible. Certainly there was no 'black republicanism' about John Chilembwe and the P.I.M. at this time.

He may, it is true, have been incensed with one of the local officials at Chiradzulu around 1908, who confiscated his gun when he was about to set out with his nephew on a hunting expedition. The details of the episode are obscure, but Chilembwe seems to have written a letter to the Governor or some member of Government above the local Chiradzulu officials. He received back a reply which stated that the gun would be returned to Chilembwe but that he must then sell it. African accounts of the trouble are confused; but, although there is a record that gun licences were issued to Chilembwe from 1902 onwards,[56] he appears to have taken a sense of grievance from this official interference with his freedom of hunting on which, as has been seen, he depended for some of his mission's finances. Yet his grievances were controlled, and, at this stage, there was no indication that they would spill over into rebellion.

In this period, indeed, despite an occasional outburst from him, any potential threat to European law and order in Nyasaland came not so much from the well-dressed Chilembwe and his respectable congregation but from other quarters.

5. Joseph Booth, Elliott Kamwana, and the Watch Tower Movement

This threat to European rule in Nyasaland at the end of the first decade of the twentieth century came from other African religious bodies which, in spite of Booth's departure from the Protectorate about 1902, had experienced a fresh influence from him. Chilembwe, it should be remembered, had switched his direct allegiance from Booth in 1897-8, when he had entrusted himself to the National Baptist Convention of America. It would be wrong to suppose that he ever lost his affection for his old master; yet, after 1897-8, there is little evidence of any very direct connection between them,[57] though Booth, to the end of his life, took a deep interest in Chilembwe, his first convert. From this time onward, Booth's major influence was to be exercised on other Africans; and it was to be the product of further changes in his religious convictions.

After his semi-official deportation from the Protectorate at some time between 1902 and 1904 on charges of the secret preaching of Ethiopianism, Booth had no centre from which to carry out his schemes for African religious and social change. He was adrift in the world again, as he had been so often since he first took up missionary work. It is true that he still had his relationship with the Seventh-day Adventists, although he had broken with their Negro missionary, Branch, at Cholo, and the Nyasaland Mission which he had started for them had passed into other hands than his. Yet this relationship was not to last long and could provide little of a steadying centre.

In this new period of his life, Booth, as an independently minded missionary, was to exceed even the degree of independence he had assumed when the Zambesi Industrial Mission had withdrawn whatever slender control it had over him. Somewhere between 1904 and 1906 he had gone up into the Kikuyu country of British East Africa and Uganda, perhaps in an attempt to begin his radical industrial missionary experiment on a new soil. He seems to have had a sharp and unwelcome reception from the authorities there.[58] Undeterred, he had wandered into South Africa, and again overseas into England, Scotland, and Wales, renewing old contacts and seeking new sources of support for his schemes. On one of these trips, 1903–4, he had taken with him a young Ngoni, Peter Nyambo,[59] whom he had first met at the Seventh-day Adventists' mission in Cholo. It was Nyambo's introduction to the great European world overseas, and some might have thought that he would have returned to Nyasaland as a second John Chilembwe. But Nyambo, despite his close relationship with Booth, was to remain for many years a paid worker of the Seventh-day Adventists, though his story, as will be seen, comes close to John Chilembwe's on the eve of the First World War.

Booth, unlike his Ngoni protégé, was not to maintain his connection with the Adventists. In 1906 he was 'dis-fellowshipped' by them,[60] probably because of his previous association with South African Ethiopianism : for at the time of the Bambata Rebellion of 1906 in Natal,[61] the Seventh-day Adventists in South Africa, like every other small religious group with American connections, were under suspicion. Yet part of the break, too, may have come from Booth's side ; from a feeling that they no longer offered facilities for the realization of his dreams of religious and social change in Africa.

Certainly, in 1906, all accounts of his movements suggest that he was looking around for new sources of support. In this year he had got into touch with the British Churches of Christ, off-spring of the mid-nineteenth century 'primitive Christianity' thinking of the American, Alexander Campbell, and a grouping which, by the twentieth century, was well established amongst British nonconformists. (Lloyd George was a member of one of the Welsh Churches of Christ at this time.[62]) Booth had put to the British Churches of Christ a proposal for Central African missionary activity which received at first some friendly support but was eventually rejected by them. One of the reasons for their rejection throws light on the character of Booth's thought at this time. According to the British Churches of Christ, his proposal involved 'matters of grave political importance'—nothing less, in fact, than a development of the suggestion in his 1899 petition to the Queen that Nyasaland should revert to native ownership after twenty-one years. The British Churches of Christ, with a typical analogy from primitive Christianity, commented gravely :

> We do not find that the Apostles organized the churches to secure that the Roman Government should restore its territory to former inhabitants.[63]

Undeterred, Booth turned to the Cape Town branch of the South African Churches of Christ and succeeded in interesting some of their members in a Nyasa mission.[64] One of them, George Hollis, who had come to Africa from Australia like Booth, was to be the prime mover in setting up a Churches of Christ mission in Nyasaland between 1906–9 at Booth's old Chikunda station. (Although, at this moment his name may seem of little consequence, it should be noted that he was to be deported from the Protectorate in 1915 on charges of foreknowledge of the Chilembwe Rising.) Lack of adequate finances as well as its own principles of local control meant that the Churches of Christ Nyasaland Mission relied heavily on native preachers and teachers, a fact which was not displeasing to Booth, and he eventually made contact with many of them for the fulfilment of his schemes.

If, through the South African Churches of Christ, Booth had indirectly introduced another denomination into the already patch-work quilt pattern of Nyasaland missions, 'all of which [was] dis-concerting and puzzling to the native catechumen' [65] and was to be a factor in the breakdown of that pattern in 1915, it is clear that he felt that it was only a very small contribution to the realization of his hopes. By the end of 1906, removed from the fellowship of the Seventh-day Adventists, discouraged by the Churches of Christ, and cut off from his old bases in Nyasaland, Booth was now turning to a new source of support: the Watch Tower Bible and Tract Society, forerunner of the modern Jehovah's Witnesses, with its headquarters in the United States. Because this religious movement was so closely connected by contemporary observers with the origins of the Nyasaland Native Rising in 1915, it is necessary at this stage to give some indication not only of Booth's associations with it and the effect which these had on the first wave of Ethiopianism in Nyasaland, but also of its tenets.

Booth was introduced to the movement in Scotland, to which he had gone towards the end of 1906,[66] probably with the object of seeking fresh help from the kind of people who had supported him in 1895 at the inception of the Baptist Industrial Mission of Scotland. But he must have had other things on his mind during this Scottish visit than questions of mission finance. In Africa at this period, it appears, he

> had felt so depressed by the conditions surrounding him there and by the thought that all who were not brought to a knowledge and love of the Saviour were going to eternal torment, that his mind was greatly distressed and he felt sure that something was radically wrong with his message.[66]

Groups of followers in Scotland of the Watch Tower Bible and Tract Society helped him to overcome this problem by putting into his hands copies of the 'Millennial Dawn' writings of Charles Taze Russell of Pennsylvania.[67] These works contained a hopeful philosophy of history that was rooted in the Scriptures, and had already received considerable publicity in Scotland through the preachings and writings of Dr. John Edgar,[68] Professor of Midwifery at Anderson's College, Glasgow, whose pamphlet, *Where are the Dead?*, had helped to smooth the way for much of Russell's teaching into Great Britain.

Charles Taze Russell (1852–1916)[69] was born in Pittsburg, Pennsylvania, of Scotch-Irish descent, and had revolted against the concepts of everlasting punishment that had been preached in the Congregational churches to which he had been taken as a boy. To him death brought total annihilation; but he believed that in the

Plate 7. Inside an African independent mission church, Nyasaland, 1912

Plate 8. Livingstonia revival meeting—taken at about the time of the
Kamwana movement

Millennium—and Russell's teaching was firmly set in the American millenarian tradition [70]—the dead would be re-created and an evangelistic campaign carried out amongst them. Those who proved worthy would stay to inherit the Kingdom; the remainder would relapse into annihilation. From his own reading of the Scriptures, Russell claimed that Christ had returned invisibly to earth in 1874 and that this process had already begun:

> The buds will thrive but will bear no perfect fruit before October 1914—the full end of 'Gentile Times'. . . . The time of trouble or 'day of wrath' which began October 1874 . . . will cease about 1915.[71]

(The coincidence of this date with that of the Chilembwe Rising may be noted here in anticipation of further examination.) Out of these troubled times—to attempt to summarize a very complex body of Scriptural interpretations—would come the Battle of Armageddon, the Millennium, the Final Judgement, and the ultimate and everlasting reign of God's Kingdom, when the forces of Evil would be defeated for ever, mankind purified and fitted for the Kingdom, and those unrepentant souls who had not taken advantage of the second chance would be consigned to final, irrevocable death.

Russell and his followers denounced existing churches as rejected by God, and envisaged contemporary governments as agencies of the Devil. 'They hold to the present arrangement of society with a death-clutch, and seem instinctively to dread the promised Kingdom of Messiah. . . .'[72] To Russell, all the signs of change were at hand: wars, depressions, class violence, Imperial expansion, and conflict. It should be noted, too, that the movement had its origins at the time of the Great Depression, 1877–1896, which affected particularly the agricultural areas of the United States, then adjusting itself to the new post-Civil War industrialism and finance. It was a moment when more than one American looked on socialism as a solution of these troubles. Russell shared some of this sympathy for socialism.[73] His conception of the Kingdom had distinctly Utopian socialist elements:

> the mechanical devices . . . will encourage labour and provide the world in general with time and conveniences, which under Christ's reign of righteousness, will be a blessing to us all.[74]

But the change would not come through peaceful evolution:

> for by the increase of knowledge among the masses, giving to all a taste of liberty and luxury, before Christ's rule is established to rightly

regulate the world, these blessings will gradually become agencies of class-power and will result in the uprising of the masses and the overthrow of Corporation Trusts, etc. . . . ; [75] a still more general and widespread dissatisfaction will finally express itself in a world-wide revolution and the overthrow of all law and order ; in the midst of all this confusion the God of Heaven will set up his Kingdom.[76]

Blessed are the poor, for theirs is the Kingdom of Heaven !

By the mid-1890's Russell had been instrumental in welding together all the Bible classes in America and elsewhere (which had sprung from his original Bible class at Alleghany, Pennsylvania, in the 1870's) into the Watch Tower Bible and Tract Society, and had completed the original volumes of the Millennial Dawn message before Booth set out for Africa from Australia. By the time that Booth's mind was being turned towards the new teaching in Scotland in 1906, Russell had further elaborated this message in *Studies in the Scriptures*, and had created for the Watch Tower Society a powerful publishing organization which was distributing through an enthusiastic body of converts in many countries copies of Russell's own works, a journal, *The Watchtower*, Bibles with Millennial Dawn commentaries, and a host of pamphlets and leaflets. Though there is evidence that the Russellites had interests in Africa from the beginnings of their Society, these seem to have been into traditional areas of American penetration, such as Liberia, or amongst scattered groups of whites. To Booth was to fall the task of introducing their ideas amongst broader masses of African peoples in South and Central Africa.

The message of the Watch Tower Society which Booth had received from the Millennial Dawn volumes presented to him in Scotland had fired him with a new enthusiasm, and had revealed a fresh American channel which might help him in his schemes for the redemption of Africa. So, once again, towards the end of 1906, Booth was *en voyage* for the United States : this time to confer with Russell himself at his Alleghany, Pennsylvania, headquarters. Booth left no very detailed record of his meeting with Russell ; but the founder and editor of *The Watchtower* noted it in his periodical in an account which leaves no doubt that Booth had made a deep impression on him.[77] Though Russell explained to him his less active conception of mission work than Booth's—a fact which may explain Booth's eventual break with Watch Tower—Russell recorded that 'Brother Booth's zeal for the black brethren has had the effect of stimulating our own interest in them',[78] not only in Africa but also amongst the coloured people of the United States. And so Booth went back to Africa with Charles Taze Russell's blessing.

Despite some very slight evidence that Booth returned to Nyasaland [79] to establish at Chikunda a Watch Tower mission station under the leadership of a native convert, Alexander Makwinja—one of the many Booth converts who later fell under suspicion at the time of the 1915 Rising—it seems much more likely that, warned by his previous contretemps with the authorities, he went straight back to South Africa by the beginning of 1907 ; and, through the chain of contacts that he had established in South and Central Africa by his years of wandering since 1892, directed from afar the introduction of Watch Tower ideas and literature into Central Africa. One medium of distribution was, of course, the post ; and Booth was a perfervid writer. Another and, perhaps, more successful channel was the stream of Nyasaland native labourers and servants in South Africa, who either met Booth at his firm base in Cape Town or during his peregrinations to the mining centres farther north. Such men would take the new message home with them when they had served out their terms of contract. By the middle of 1909, Russell reported in his journal that seventy-six Nyasaland natives had subscribed to *The Watchtower* [80]—no very large number by absolute standards but an impressive one in a country which was new to a money-economy, and to whose natives the ideas of a subscription to an overseas periodical was a considerable novelty. But more important than forms of subscription or even the excited perusal of literature which Booth was sending from the Cape, was the propagation of the new ideas by word of mouth. 'The method', noted Russell,

> is singularly applicable to the conditions of native towns. Every village has a Bwalo for the hearing of matters of public interest. The itinerant brother reading English translates the paragraphs in simple style into the vernacular of the people. Questions are entertained, etc.[81]

If Booth from afar supplied the literature and the initial inspiration for this oral method, the director on the spot was an African : Elliott (sometimes called Kenan) Kamwana. Kamwana was a Tonga who had been educated by the Livingstonia Mission at Bandawe on the western shores of Lake Nyasa. For a while he had attended the Mission's Overtoun Institute at Kondowe farther to the north. At the time that the first Watch Tower proselytizing was beginning in Central Africa, the Overtoun Institute had been supplying further education of a semi-secondary, semi-technical form to the brighter pupils of the area for thirteen years. Some had even seen in it the nucleus of a future Central African University. Certainly it had drawn to it a number of Africans who, with their fellows like John Gray Kufa of the Blantyre Mission, were becoming increasingly conscious of the economic and social possibilities of the white man's culture, and who manifested this by an increasing preoccupation with status, at the same time as they felt keenly the burdens, often irksome, which the new culture was bringing to the old tribal life.

Kamwana was such a man, and the Watch Tower movement he touched off amongst the tribes of his area, though it had obviously old-style tribal elements in it, marked the beginning of the newer type of African reaction to the Europeans in Nyasaland, and brought to a head its first wave of Ethiopianism.[82] He had broken with the Overtoun Institute when it introduced fees—an important point to notice because it demonstrates the appeal which free education, unhampered by taxation mechanism, had for the proto-intellectuals of Nyasaland at this time—and had gone down to Blantyre where he met Booth in 1900 at the Plainfield Mission. Two years later Kamwana was baptized either at the Seventh Day Baptist or the Seventh-day Adventist Mission. From the Shire Highlands he moved down into South Africa, worked in the mines for a time, visited Durban and Pretoria, and then, later in 1907, made contact with Booth at the Cape. For about six months Kamwana remained with him, and was instructed in the Watch Tower teachings. Then, in 1908, he set off back for Nyasaland. Arriving there in September, he found in his own country to the west of Lake Nyasa a disturbed social situation of which he could take advantage.

Kamwana's tribe, the Tonga, had once been dominated by the Ngoni. But, after the coming of the Livingstonia Mission, many Tonga put themselves under the mission's safe-keeping. The arrival of the new Administration, through the control of Ngoni military power which it achieved, added to this protection. The Tonga, then, like many a formerly oppressed group when opportunity presents itself, had gone ahead faster than their former masters, and had made full use of the new opportunities and education. As a result, they had become the most important element amongst the Nyasaland migratory labourers to South Africa, and a channel whereby new ideas could be introduced into the Protectorate from the world outside. It is no accident, therefore, that the first Ethiopian movement in Nyasaland which came near to the pitch of militancy should have come from them. (It may be noted, too, in passing, that it was a Tonga, Clements Kadalie, who was just starting his education at Livingstonia when the Kamwana agitation was in the offing, who became the organizer of the first powerful South African native trade union, the Industrial and Commercial Workers Union, which caused the nearest approach yet to a general strike of African workers in South Africa, and a Cabinet crisis in 1927.)

Kamwana's apocalyptic and revolutionary preaching was given in the Livingstonia area, though it is reasonable to assume that Chilembwe and the independent native sects to the south of the Lake in the Shire Highlands would know what was going on there. Tonga bound for the mines under the contract system passed through Blantyre *en route* for South Africa, where they were, in fact, known generically as 'Blantyres'; there were Tonga boys in domestic service, on the plantations, and in the army in the Shire Highlands; and Booth was posting Watch Tower literature to all of his African acquaintances in the Protectorate. Through all of these sources Chilembwe and the independent African sects south of the Lake would learn of Kamwana's activities.

His movement, though the greater part of its members came from the up-to-date Tonga, seems to have influenced most of the tribes of the Livingstonia sphere. A marked feature was its dramatic, open-air baptisms; a Livingstonia witness claims that in his key year, 1909, Kamwana baptized as many as ten thousand Africans in a few months.[83] To them, baptism was a simple Open Sesame to the new Kingdom he preached. The emotional wave that he touched off was often accompanied by attempts to return to the old, pre-European tribal ways. This was noted with horror by the local missionaries who spoke in their publications and letters of a return to polygamy, of the revival of 'obscene dances', and the immoral old customs.[84] They claimed, moreover, that the absence of any punitive concept of Hell in Kamwana's teaching added a distinct element of sexual licence to the movement.

If these factors appealed to the less detribalized elements in his following, his claim that the new order which he preached would bring free schools for all had a very strong attraction for the more up-to-date converts. His quick and freely offered baptism, too, opened the way to the rapid acquisition of the status of church membership for those who had not the patience or inclination to accept the longer and more arduous route that the Scottish missionaries offered. It became a short and easy road, an *nthowa ifupi* into at least one prized aspect of the new, European-style world.[85] And that Kamwana could back his claims by reference to Booth at the Cape and Russell in Pennsylvania added enormously to his appeal : for Booth's reputation as the possessor of many profitable American connections, and his habits of paying high wages and dispensing money liberally not only from these but from his own personal funds, were well known to large numbers of Africans.

Kamwana seized one element which could unify behind him both old and new groups from the Africans who flocked to hear him : the question of the hut tax. The 1901 increase with its hated labour rebate had already produced throughout the Protectorate much criticism of the Europeans and their Government. In 1907 a Chikunda prophetess, Chanjiri, had arisen, who preached that by the end of the year the Europeans would have to leave the country and that no more tax need be paid.[86] At the same time as she was saving the Government the trouble of apprehending her by fleeing into Portuguese East Africa, Kamwana was returning to carry on the agitation, backed this time by a new and attractive apocalyptic teaching.

He preached the coming in October 1914 of the new age, in true Russellite fashion. Christ would come, all the whites would have to leave the country, and there would be no more oppression from tax-gatherers. Pointing to the Residency, he would say,

> These people you soon will see no more. . . . We shall build our own ships, make our own powder, and make or import our own guns.[87]

It was fiery talk. The authorities, with mission backing, stepped in to silence Kamwana. He was imprisoned, and, in June 1909,[88] deported from the Protectorate until 1914, when he would be allowed to return after the danger period of his prophecy had passed. It was a hasty reaction on the Government's part and did not pass unnoticed at home, for on 1 and 8 September the pioneer Labour Member, Keir Hardie, raised the matter at Question Time in the House of Commons. But the Government, hasty or not, had controlled the agitation. Though the impetus of the original Watch Tower movement in Nyasaland was not spent until 1912,[89] the removal of its leaders broke its façade, and it split into a number of petty congregations, some wishing to follow the American Society and others preferring an independent African movement. Moreover, at this time, Booth was again modifying his religious opinions; he was moving back to his initial Baptist position, with strong leanings towards the seventh-day Sabbath concept. His change of opinions helped to disintegrate still more the original Watch Tower congregations in Nyasaland.

In 1910, therefore, Pastor Charles Taze Russell decided to send an investigator to Nyasaland: William W. Johnston of Glasgow,[90] a joiner by trade who had been to America. Johnston reported soberly on the extent of the work and the way in which it had increased the number of independent African congregations, each with its own mud church, some big enough to hold five or six hundred people. Having made peace with the Government, Johnston believed that Watch Tower work had considerable prospects in Nyasaland. But he added a number of afterthoughts which throw light on the social forces that ran through the first Watch Tower movement— and perhaps on some of its later adherents who were accused of complicity in the 1915 Rising. Amongst all the native Watch Tower pastors, said Johnston:

> there is manifest a spirit of cupidity and self-seeking. . . . I pointed out that our work was the gathering-in of the Lord's saints together out of Babylon and their instruction in the words of the Lord only.

But many thought that he had come only to offer them 'lucrative employment' with the Society. Johnston went on:

> I regret to say that in almost every case . . . their interviews ended with an appeal for financial assistance in some shape or form.

And then Johnston added significantly:

> Many of them . . . proposed that I should sign their labour certificate, a document indicating that they had worked for me for one month and were therefore entitled to three shillings in their hut tax.[91]

(That Booth had some inkling of the economics of this matter is suggested in a remark of Johnston's that, having again switched his allegiance, Booth was now trying to win back some of the Kamwana-ite Watch Tower leaders by sending them, from the Cape, Seventh Day Baptist Year Books with a £5 note inside each volume!) But Johnston refused all these demands—and he was jeered as he left the Livingstonia Watch Tower congregations, whereas cheers had greeted him on his arrival.

All of these points were noted by the Scottish missionaries at Livingstonia in their paper. But they added others which may be taken as additional commentary on the Kamwana movement and the end of the first militant wave of Ethiopianism in Nyasaland. The first was a defence against the view-point of the Governor, Sir Alfred Sharpe, when he visited Livingstonia in 1910. The Livingstonia missionaries reported that he thought the movement had been a revolt against their own strict discipline, and that, but for this, it would not have taken place.[92] Certainly, went on the Livingstonia witnesses of Kamwana's agitation,

> intense bitterness has been shown to the missionaries and their old associates[93] [with the aim] more at undermining the position of the white man's teaching than from any definite desire for or indeed, knowledge, of, the propaganda whether of the 'Watch Tower' or 'Seventh Day Adventistism'.[94]

It was, indeed, claimed the pioneer Livingstonia missionary, Elmslie, the direct result of emigration to the labour centres of South Africa, and of contact with the Ethiopianism of that country. Another Livingstonia witness was very emphatic :

> No one who looks into the matter carefully will fail to see that in the minds of the leaders and no doubt in the minds of many others there is a revolt against the new order of things in the country. It is a symptom of a common African disease 'mafumu onse' (chiefs all). . . . The native can jump into a white man's clothes and fancy that he is every whit as good as he is, so the next step is to think that he no longer needs his presence and aid . . . it is an accomplishment of partial education which hostile critics are so ready to notice but which competent judges of the work see as bringing into sharper contrast the many instances of successfully educated natives.[95]

As another Livingstonia observer put it, it was 'the flush of mistaken nationalism'.[96] Some of the missionaries wondered, especially after the Governor's visit to Livingstonia, whether the final result would be not only the deportation of Kamwana but also an attempt by the Government to regulate the European missionaries themselves.

This Livingstonia missionary opinion supplies not only a useful analysis of the Kamwana movement but it is also significant in that

ate 9.   An early Providence Industrial Mission group.   (*Seated, left to right :* John
Chilembwe; the African in the cap has been identified by some as David Kaduya,
who followed Chilembwe in the 1915 Rising; Rev. L. N. Cheek;   Chilembwe's
niece, Rachael, whom Cheek married)

Plate 10. Chilembwe baptizing (from Chilembwe's own photograph album)

March 17 - 1912   Chipata.
                                   Ngoniland
                                   Mzimba P.O.

Dear Pastor, and Brother in our Master.

I have taken myself into the danger of writing or asking for a Bell and Clock. True we are in need of a Bell: the drum which we use in calling the people for Services, Sabbath School as well as Day School is partly torn and hardly can sound at all. We have no Time i.e. Clock to see what we are doing, and when we start our business we don't know when to end our work. Therefore we are asking you to appeal in America to Seventh Day Bros., and Sisters that we are in need of these two things very badly. There are many things we can cry for however time will show its duty. It took 430 years, and the Israelites were rescued; it takes long time to possess jewels of gold or so. It may take sometimes to possess jewels of Independance among we the Nyasas

                        Yours, lovely
                        for Africa C. r. Domingo

Plate 11. Letter from Charles Domingo to Booth

Plate 12(*a*).   Charles Domingo in his study

Plate 12(*b*).   Charles Domingo and his congregation

it raises most of the questions that were to come to the surface again after the Chilembwe-led outbreak of 1915.

Yet Chilembwe at this time was still, apparently, no threat to authority; and the Blantyre missionary, Alexander Hetherwick, in 1912 commented on him as one of the ablest Africans in the country.[97] The banner of Kamwana-ite militancy may be said to have passed, at this moment, to another Livingstonia convert : Charles Domingo.

6. CHARLES DOMINGO

Charles Domingo,[98] as his name suggests, seems to have been originally a native of Portuguese East Africa. He was brought to British Central Africa in 1881 by William Koyi, a Lovedale-trained evangelist who had been seconded as a pioneer native missionary to Livingstonia. Returning from a furlough in South Africa, Koyi found Charles Domingo a helpless waif at Quilimane, where his father, an habitual drunkard, was a cook for the African Lakes Company, with its traditional Livingstonia associations. Domingo was introduced into the household of Laws of Livingstonia as a house-boy, and, as he grew older, became something of a protégé of the veteran Laws, who noticed his natural ability. Soon Domingo grew to be one of the most promising pupils of Livingstonia, and was promoted to first native assistant at the Overtoun Institute and an elder in the congregation. A visitor to Livingstonia in 1907 observed that he took the Sunday service and commented on his standing at the mission.[99] Domingo had become one of the great hopes of the Livingstonia missionaries : a pillar, on orthodox Scottish foundations, of the native church.

However, Domingo had other ideas. The exact source of these it is difficult to trace, although his growing independence of mind may be illustrated as early as 1901 by a paper he read in October, as a Livingstonia native representative, to a conference of African elders at the semi-jubilee celebrations of the Blantyre Mission. At the session devoted to native life, he spoke on African dancing, a subject on whose morality many of the missionaries had very strong views. Although Domingo expressed some support for the usual missionary opinion, he was not slow to point out that all native dancing was not necessarily the work of the Devil, and that much of it had a definite function to play in the lives of the tribes.[100] Yet the independence of mind which he demonstrated in such episodes did not implicate him in the Kamwana movement : though, as this had taken place in the Livingstonia area and Domingo was acquainted with all its principals, he could not have been untouched, at least, by its social teaching. Furthermore, by 1909 Domingo was to be found in Blantyre, where his second child was born, and there is some evidence that by this time he had had dealings with Chilembwe himself.[101] But Domingo did not enter the camp of the Providence Industrial Mission. He became, rather, the premier agent in Nyasaland of Joseph Booth, at the time when Booth was returning to the Seventh Day Baptist allegiance after his stormy period as introducer of the Watch Tower doctrines into the Protectorate.

Domingo was well equipped to act as intermediary for Booth. At some time between 1907 and 1910 he had broken with Livingstonia and had set up his own native following in an independent African church.[102] Laws felt the defection in much the same way as Stewart had received Mzimba's secession at Lovedale years before. But Domingo was launched on an independent course, and nothing could stop him. Whether his introduction to Booth was personal or by proxy is immaterial ; the important point is that Booth now placed his hopes for an independent African sabbatarian church in Nyasaland on Charles Domingo.

The *Livingstonia News* for December 1910 noticed the transition and commented on the emergence of a new 'society of Sabbath keepers'.[103] It was the result of yet another trip by Booth to America and the headquarters of the Seventh Day Baptists in this year. Despite the failure of the hopes they had placed on his mission during the 1899–1902 period, Booth's amazing persistence again persuaded them that there were considerable numbers of Africans in Nyasaland who still adhered to the practice of Seventh Day Baptism : all they needed was organization and encouragement, and their ranks would swell rapidly. His scheme was daringly simple : 'visitation not residence' was its keynote ; the work of evangelization and organization should be carried out on the spot by Africans like Domingo ; Booth himself would direct from afar at the Cape, and the parent body in America should send out an occasional visitor to check on the progress of the work. It was all part of Booth's plans for thrusting as much responsibility as possible on to the African. Between 1910 and 1912 he, Domingo, and a native staff on the spot claimed to have increased the numbers of African Seventh-day

Baptists in the Protectorate to over two thousand—some native witnesses, indeed, put the total as high as five thousand.[104] Though a pair of investigators from the parent body in America claimed that these figures were exaggerated—as undoubtedly they were—their report itself [105] bears witness to the multitude of tiny native congregations in 'pretentious mud churches' under native pastors all over the southern part of Nyasaland, and in not a few areas to the west in the Livingstonia sphere. (Out of many of them, on the eve of the 1915 Rising, were to come important cadres of Chilembwe's movement.)

To this bizarre tangle of independent native churches that came into existence in the 1910–12 period under Booth's and Domingo's coaching, no clear doctrinal or organizational bounds can be set. Though some of the money Booth received from the Seventh Day Baptists at this time was going into them, part of it came from his own personal labours and the efforts of his wife in South Africa. Furthermore, he was sending to these little Nyasaland churches not only orthodox Seventh Day Baptist literature—the translation of which into the vernacular may have been helped by Chilembwe,[106] not because Chilembwe was a sabbatarian but out of his general sympathy with African independent church activity—but also Bibles with Watch Tower commentaries. Though Booth had broken with Watch Tower, his line of reasoning appears to have been that the Russellites produced Bibles as cheaply as anyone else ; the Nyasaland African was hungry for any sort of reading material which, in the absence of effective Government encouragement to education, was in short supply ; and, anyway, he had a stock on hand, so why should he not use them ? Yet the introduction of such material must have complicated the doctrines of these little churches. And their teaching and allegiance were complicated further by the fact that they often called themselves 'Churches of Christ',[107] though with little genuine connection with the European-led mission of that name. Booth's connection, however, with Watch Tower, the Seventh Day Baptists, and the Churches of Christ within a short period added elements from the teachings and methods of organization of all three to the superficially sabbatarian churches under his and Domingo's supervision. Booth was producing a native church—and that rapidly !—but it was not the kind of African church that the Scottish missionaries had dreamed of. To them the African church members of the Booth-Domingo following had seized only on the outward and visible signs, Baptism and the Seventh-day Sabbath, and had left aside the inward and spiritual graces of Christianity. A witness at Livingstonia put it another way :

> No doubt in the transition stage the sudden inrush of new ideas upsets the balance of certain minds, and produces the phenomenon of the half-educated, self-concerned native, impatient of foreign control.[108]

Stripped of its superciliousness, and bearing in mind the fact that such comments have had no small validity for European society too, in times of rapid social change, there is not a little truth in this statement.

In this desire for freedom of action a cardinal element was the movement for independent African schools.[109] Each little church tried to build one, and Booth at the Cape was continually pestered for money for school materials in curious letters, a cross-breed of pidgin English and Biblical quotation. To such schools may be applied the common modern assertion that education is not merely a means of instruction but also a form of social conditioning. For these little independent schools along the Booth-Domingo axis taught other things beside the 'three R's'—as indeed (as has already been seen, and as will be examined again later) did Chilembwe's own schools.

The independent African schools under Domingo and Booth's leadership became centres where the policies of the Europeans, missions, and Government—even Booth himself [110]—were called in question. Most of the teachers could struggle through the local press. And the ramifications of the Nyasaland labour system ; the fact that Domingo and others, both through Booth and independently, were in touch with South African native intellectuals, such as John L. Dube or John Tengo Jabavu ; [111] the dissemination of Russellite literature with its criticism of established orders, religious and secular ; and news from the new Nyasa expatriates in the United States—all of these provided ample material for political discussion. Above all, in the hands of the independent native pastors, the Bible became, as it has so often become in moments of social tension, a great source-book for the criticism of established institutions, and a mine of authoritative texts which soon acquired the character of political slogans.

Charles Domingo summed up all these tendencies at this time better than Chilembwe ; though the contacts which are known to have existed between the two of them suggest interesting patterns of cross-fertilization of ideas. By 1911 Domingo had become the Nyasaland editor, with Booth as editor-in-chief at the Cape, of the *African Sabbath Recorder*, a slender magazine, often little bigger than a small leaflet, which was circulated amongst their South and Central African following, and in which doctrinal, organizational, and social problems were discussed.[112] Furthermore, Booth sent from the Cape, for distribution, additional supplementary leaflets in which he printed *in extenso*, with comments, letters from Domingo and other native leaders of the independent churches. From these Domingo's feelings may be gauged.

One incident that was reported in this ephemeral literature was the result of the so-called Lebelezi Sabbath Conference of 26 August 1911, which was apparently held under Domingo's leadership. The holding of such an African conference to propagate the Sabbatarian doctrines was itself a measure of African development at this time. The result of it was a decision to send out a number of African sabbatarian evangelists. One of them who went out to preach at Lundazi, just over the Northern Rhodesian border, had been inhospitably received by the local Resident, partly because he wanted to begin African schools, and partly because he was the agent of an African, Charles Domingo. Domingo's reaction was typical :

> Poor Resident, he thinks too much of his skin and not of his heart. What is the difference between a white man and a black man ? Are we not of the same blood and all from Adam ? This startles me much—is Europe still Christian or Heathen ? [113]

Other criticisms by Domingo of European society went further, and struck at the basis of the Administration. Perhaps the little leaflets in which they were expressed never fell into the hands of the authorities, otherwise Domingo might have been dealt with as drastically as Kamwana. The tenor of his criticism was the contrast between Christian theory and practice. Despite the picturesqueness of his English, he makes his meaning clear :

> There is too much failure among all Europeans in Nyasaland. The three combined bodies, Missionaries, Government and Companies, or gainers of money—do form the same rule to look upon the native with mockery eyes. It sometimes startles us to see that the three combined bodies are from Europe, and along with them there is a title 'CHRISTENDOM'. And to compare or make a comparison between the MASTER of

the title and his servants it pushes any African away from believing the Master of the title. If we had power enough to communicate ourselves to Europe we would advise them not to call themselves 'Christendom' but 'Europeandom'. Therefore the life of the three combined bodies is altogether too cheaty, too thefty, too mockery. Instead of 'Give' they say 'Take away from'. From 6 A.M. to 5 or 6 P.M. there is too much breakage of God's pure law as seen in James Epistle, v. 4.[114]

Domingo's use of James v. 4 is important in this context, for it appears to be nothing less than a criticism of the condition of African employment on European lands in the Protectorate. The verse runs : 'Behold the hire of the labourers who have reaped down your fields, which is of you kept back by fraud, crieth, and the cries of them which have reaped are entered into the ears of the Lord of Sabaoth'. The text, it seems, became something of a popular political slogan amongst disgruntled natives, and four years later Africans who had been accused of complicity in Chilembwe's revolt quoted it in court.[115]

Perhaps one reason why Domingo's criticism of established authority did not draw down the full wrath of the Administration on him was that he had good references from Livingstonia. To the Resident Magistrate at Mzimba he was 'an exceptionally good and competent native'.[116] Indeed, he had offered Domingo the job of postmaster at Mzimba ; but Domingo had refused it in order to carry on with his mission work. Moreover, the local European officials may have been tolerant of Domingo because he seemed to be nothing more than a dupe of Booth, an innocent mouthpiece for his radical views. Yet, with all these excuses, Domingo was no one's dupe. As one Livingstonia missionary said, 'He had a spirit of extreme independence and spiritual pride'.[117] This certainly explains Domingo's attitude to the local society.

But, by 1912, his star had begun to set. In this year the American Seventh Day Baptists sent out two investigators, N. O. Moore and Wayland D. Wilcox, to look into the state of their Nyasa missions. As a result of this inquiry the American body decided to withdraw its support from Booth's work, partly for personal and partly for administrative reasons.[118] After this, though Booth and Domingo continued to correspond, Domingo was just another leader, albeit an influential one,[119] of an African independent church, without the support and status of a foreign missionary organization. Chilembwe, on the other hand, despite all his financial difficulties, still had the backing of the National Baptist Convention in America. And, furthermore, there was evidence that, by 1912, Chilembwe's work was taking on a new proportion and direction.

7. FURTHER DEVELOPMENTS OF THE P.I.M., 1910–12

It would be wrong to suppose that Chilembwe had felt none of the influence that emanated from Kamwana or Domingo. Indeed, with the passing of mining boys and other workers through the Shire Highlands, his own reading of the European and primitive native press, and his indirect connections with Booth to the south, he could hardly escape it. But between 1908 and 1910, when Kamwana's influence began its brief rise and fall and Domingo started to launch his criticisms of the European, Chilembwe, for all the dislike he drew upon himself from local white settlers, seemed to be growing respectable and was acquiring a definite status and prestige, not only in his immediate Nyasaland environment but out in the wider world.

The high-water mark of his respectability was undoubtedly the brief mention of him and his mission in the report of the Commissions of the first World Missionary Conference at Edinburgh in 1910. Chilembwe appeared in the list of correspondents who had filled in questionnaires on the 'church in the mission field' as 'The Rev. John Chilembwe (National Baptist Convention), Blantyre'.[120] At this time, too, although the literature of white Nyasaland missionaries does not abound with references to Chilembwe, the P.I.M. was beginning to be noted as a normal part of the Shire Highlands mission scene.[121] It must be pointed out, however, that the Government Census for 1911 did not mention the P.I.M. amongst its statistics, although it included the other, smaller white sectarian missions.[122] Was this apparent lack of recognition by the Government, when other European groups were beginning to take notice of him, noted down as another grievance against it by Chilembwe? Whether accidental or not, it was an unfortunate oversight on the Government's part: for Chilembwe was now, quite obviously, a man with a position, and his mission had a native following and overseas support not far behind that of many of the non-Scottish missions of the Protectorate.

This was reflected in the contemporary literature of the National Baptist Convention where the stock of the P.I.M. at this time appears as :

1 Missionary, 5 Churches, 800 members, 7 native helpers, 625 pupils. Superintendent, Rev. John Chilembwe.[123]

It was a claim which was by no means exaggerated ; for, although the European-run missions continued to attract greater numbers of Africans because of the superior facilities, status, and stability which they offered after the failure of the Kamwana movement, and while doctrinal, disciplinary, and financial difficulties were encumbering Domingo's Seventh Day Baptist churches, the P.I.M. continued to grow in strength. By 1912 Chilembwe could report to his American headquarters over nine hundred Africans at the schools which he and his wife had set up.[124] His main Chiradzulu brick chapel that had been built in Cheek's and Miss DeLany's days had become too small for his congregation, and some time towards the end of 1911,[125] Chilembwe and his followers began work on the large brick church of ornate design which they finished by 1913. It could not stand comparison with the Blantyre church which the Scottish missionary, David Clement Scott, had built ; but, for an African, untutored architecturally, it was a remarkable achievement, as all the photographs of it show (see pp. 214, 311). The Negro National Baptist Convention made it the proud boast of their missionary propaganda.

This growth in the status and strength of Chilembwe's mission was reflected in the widening of its activities. The centre of the P.I.M. at Mbombwe, Chiradzulu, was obviously becoming a meeting-place for Africans with an independent turn of mind. An outstanding example of this was the discussion which took place there about the formation of an 'African Industrial Society', a sort of producers' and consumers' co-operative.[126] All of the Africans who met to talk over this venture were later implicated in the 1915 Rising. The project does not seem to have got much further than discussion, but it has considerable importance as evidence not only of the growth of Chilembwe's mission but also of the role it was beginning to play, in the second decade of the new century, as a focus and forum for the new, aspiring Africans of southern Nyasaland, the 'marginal men' between the two worlds of traditional tribal society and the promising new forms of economic, political, and social activity which thirty years of European rule had brought to the Shire Highlands.

Courtesy Mr. W. Sanderson

Plate 13(*a*).   P.I.M. group (from Chilembwe's own photograph album) :
probably taken about 1912

Courtesy Pastor Leon R. Lawton

Plate 13(*b*).   House of an educated native, Nyasaland, 1912

Plate 14. Mrs. Chilembwe and two sisters of the P.I.M.
(from Chilembwe's own photograph album)

The meeting was held on 30 July 1911, and opened and closed, characteristically, with 'praise and prayer'. The chairman, D. C. Njilima—a relation, apparently, of the two Africans whom the Rev. L. N. Cheek had taken to America with him—'expressed his dis-appointment that so few had come to the meeting' but 'nevertheless, considered that the object for which they had gathered would in time show that they were on the right lines'. He made a plea for the creation of independent native capital. It was wrong, he said,

> for people to go to South Africa in search of employment when work could be got in this country, and he pointed out that many natives in the country were in receipt of wages varying from 3s. to £3 per month, every penny of which they spent and no thought given to thrift.

Chilembwe himself elaborated this point :

> He appealed to the better educated natives to do something more with their money than to put it into the hands of their Bombay brethren, who do nothing for the country but ship every penny to India.

It was an open attack on the Indian storekeepers, the main petty traders of the Protectorate, in competition with whom some enter-prising Africans had been setting up small retail stores as early as 1904.[127] Chilembwe's appeal seems to have had independent African production in mind : but production which could succeed only if it were backed by sufficient capital. Perhaps, in this context, he was speaking with his own experiments in cultivation at the P.I.M. with Cheek in mind.

It appears that the real fear of the meeting for this 'African Industrial Society' was not so much the economic difficulties that would have to be met as the attitude of the Government towards their project. (Was it for this reason, perhaps, that the report of the meeting was put out by members of the Society in the form of a leaflet in English, rather than in Nyanja or Yao ? Did they hope in this way to reach more easily the ears of the authorities, and thus to impress them with their respectable intentions ? Or was their use of English a sign of a problem of communication amongst the Africans themselves, with their differing languages ? Or was it, as is not un-likely, another mark of their intention to emulate the white man in as many ways as possible ?) One member, Robert Msosa of Songani, said

> that one of the reasons why they had not got a bigger attendance was that people were afraid of gathering lest the Government might not approve of their object.

A question was put about the legality of the experiment, and 'it was explained that the Society would be registered'. But, at the end, nothing seems to have come of it, although a leaflet for circulation was printed on a near-by mission press.

The Administration, with its by now habitual dislike of Booth, may well have looked askance at the project. Indeed, copies of the leaflet reached Booth at the Cape, and he sent one to his Seventh Day Baptist backers in America to demonstrate the extent of his connections with leading Africans of Nyasaland. Annotations made by Booth on this leaflet afford valuable evidence of the extent of the connections between him and Chilembwe at this time. Booth claimed that he was adviser to the proposed 'African Industrial Society', and then added that 'its members and leaders for 19 years past' had been 'in sympathy with his efforts'. Indeed, many of them were members of the 'Shiloh Sabbath Station'. This station seems to have been part of the land that was left over for Booth from the first mission which he had established in the Cholo area for the Seventh Day Baptists at the time of his Sabbath Evangelizing and Industrial experiment of 1899–1901. It had become, by 1911, a centre for a group of Seventh Day Baptist Africans whom Booth was then supervising with so much difficulty from the Cape. Between them and Chilembwe's Chiradzulu following there was obviously a good deal of contact. Furthermore, in his correspondence with his American backers, Booth dealt with pride on the way in which his religio-economic co-operative experiments of the 1899–1900 period were now bearing fruit in the attempts of Chilembwe and Njilima to set up the 'African Industrial Society'. He referred to them as 'my old First Day Baptist converts', and added that the Shiloh Sabbath Station from which so many of them came

> was originally bought with money earned by the Seventh Day Baptist Plainfield Natives Industrial Association on Co-operative lines after the style that these my old First Day Baptist converts are again attempting.

From such a statement it is obvious that Chilembwe and Njilima's project had its roots in Booth's type of religio-co-operative experiment that he had adumbrated as early as 1892, had elaborated in his Natal 'African Christian Union' scheme with scant success in 1896, and had tried again on his return from America, 1899–1900, when Chilembwe was founding his own mission.

Yet, from all this, it would be wrong to suppose that Chilembwe was a regular and close correspondent of Booth at this period. Indeed, because of Chilembwe's preoccupation with the internal affairs of the Providence Industrial Mission, their correspondence was the result more probably of Booth's than Chilembwe's soliciting, as the letter printed in Appendix 4, pp. 537-8 suggests. But there was no need for much correspondence between Booth and Chilembwe; through correspondence with Domingo and other Seventh Day Baptist followers, Booth would be kept informed of Chilembwe's doings and ambitions and vice versa. That such an indirect channel existed between Booth and Chilembwe is suggested by the fact that Chilembwe's backers, the National Baptist Convention, wrote at this time to the Seventh Day Baptist headquarters about Chilembwe and his good work.[128] Occasional letters may have passed between him and Booth,[129] although Chilembwe's informal and intimate connection with the many Africans of different denominations who used the P.I.M. as a general meeting-place meant that, for all practical purposes, this was unnecessary. He would learn from many of them who were members of Boothian Seventh Day Baptist churches or who had come into contact with his activities outside Nyasaland the general outlines of his old master's work.

In 1911, in spite of Chilembwe's break with him in America nearly fourteen years ago, Booth clearly looked upon the African leader of the P.I.M. as one of his 'young men'. There is little doubt that at this time Booth still had hopes that many of Chilembwe's flock, if not their leader himself, would come over to his Seventh Day Baptist position. But Chilembwe had relatively little interest in doctrinal matters : [130] to the end of his life he was a 'First Day' Baptist. His main interest in the second decade of the new century, when his mission was well-established and growing, was to promote schemes like the 'African Industrial Society', and to make the African, through economic and social responsibility, conscious of his power.

It is important to notice here that the 1911 leaflet about the 'African Industrial Society' meeting refers to it as having taken place in the 'first African Baptist Church, Chiradzulu'. That Chilembwe should have described the P.I.M. in this way suggests that he saw it as the nucleus of something not unlike the National Baptist Convention itself amongst the Negroes in America : the organizing centre of a group of independent African Baptist churches. His emphasis, it seems, was on unity rather than division amongst the African churches.[131]   In this, as in his opposition to the Indian traders of Nyasaland, there is some element of growing national consciousness.

Even so, such increasingly political consciousness had no militant signs at this time. Chilembwe, indeed, at the meeting to establish the 'African Industrial Society', expressed

> the thanks of all the natives to the Missionaries for the gospel of peace and to the Government for their encouragement in cotton-growing.

The whole cast of his appeal and activity was then completely legal. Perhaps he remembered the treatment which the Government had meted out to his old master, Booth, and recalled the firm deportation of Elliott Kamwana. No doubt Chilembwe's criticisms of the Europeans to his schools and congregations continued, and there is some native testimony between 1907–9 to suggest that his relations with the near-by Bruce Estates were worsening. Yet these criticisms and his relations with the Bruce Estates were kept, there seems no reason to doubt, within legal bounds. His attitude at this time is the Booker T. Washington, 'petty-bourgeois' ideal, not that of the militant revolutionary.

In this respect it is significant that the leaflet on the 'African Industrial Society' gives Chilembwe his status-title of 'Rev.', and refers to the other members as 'Che', the African equivalent of 'Esq.' And Chilembwe's respectability is indicated, again, by the considerable amounts of personal property—for an African of the Shire Highlands in this period—that he was acquiring. He continued to place great emphasis upon dress and the formalities of a man who was intent on rising in the social scale. His colleague, Duncan Njilima, too, had a small store, and his relations in the United States would give him additional prestige.[132] A. M. Chisusi, another follower, was the African photographer of Blantyre. His set of pictures of Chilembwe, his family and flock, would have graced any contemporary European album. (Chisusi, it seems, like Njilima, went down in the 1915 Rising.) Indeed, an examination of the 1911 attempt at the P.I.M. to form an 'African Industrial Society' provides a valuable gauge for judging the character and ideals of the leadership of the 1915 movement. If the Industrial Society experiment failed through the immaturity of its movers, they may still have taken away from this increased anti-European grievances, by projecting their resentment at their lack of success on the white man and his Government.

The 'African Industrial Society', for all its significance, was not Chilembwe's only scheme, and its failure does not seem to have disheartened him very much—though it is possible that he did take away from the episode some feelings of frustration, for, as will be seen later, at the end of 1912 and the beginning of 1913, a certain despair was taking possession of him—a despair that was to pass over into desperation in 1915. Yet, on the whole, between 1910 and 1911, the steady growth of the P.I.M. seems to have stimulated hope rather than despair in Chilembwe, and to have nourished his imagination with schemes for African betterment.

Foremost amongst these was, of course, the development of independent native schools to give the African the knowledge and skill by which he could integrate himself successfully into the new community. That these schools could and did become centres of anti-European agitation does not mean that, initially, their aim was not purely educational—in so far, that is, as there is ever such an entity as 'pure' education, devoid of any political content at all. In the year after the two American Negro missionaries had left him, and before 1913, Chilembwe had been strengthening the schools of his mission. He could report to his American headquarters in 1912 a total of 906 Africans under his teachers, an increase of nearly 300 on the figures he had given them two years before. He could report of his teachers with their schools radiating out from his main Chiradzulu base :

> This is about the number of scholars they teach as follows : Namkundi school, W. Kustia, 168, 8 miles from the main station; Matili school, D. Loweza, 190, 15 miles ; Ndunde school, T. Nowazi, 82, (6) miles ; Tumbwe school, T. Ngokwe, 120, 10 miles ; Malika school, A. Jamali [who became Chilembwe's 'secretary' during the period of the 1915 Rising], 60, 2 miles ; Sangano school, H. Chese, 86, 3 miles. The main school, 200, teachers, S. L. Mkulichi and I. Z. Chilembwe.[133]

The last-named was Mrs. John Chilembwe, and she gave a practical touch to the women's side of the schools, with her classes in sewing and deportment. For this purpose the mission possessed a number of sewing machines—no mean capital for Nyasaland Africans at that time. The character of all this teaching was, of course, at a very elementary level by European standards. Yet it would be a mistake to pass it off as merely pretentious. Many of Chilembwe's teachers had received some training in the European-run

Blantyre Mission; and Chilembwe's travels and the limited but by no means negligible schooling he had acquired in America gave some degree of 'background' to the curricula. Moreover, the four to five years of organizational help that the Rev. L. N. Cheek and Miss DeLany had given to the P.I.M. helped to strengthen its system of instruction.

The plan of Chilembwe's schools, however, does not seem to have been based completely on an American Negro model. Much of it followed the normal, British seven-standard elementary course. Chilembwe's nephew, Morris, taught for some years the First Standard, and Chilembwe himself the Third and some elements in other Standards. 'He taught me', says one African, 'English, Arithmetic, Bible, Geography, History and Agriculture.' It was an ambitious programme, but the inclusion of agriculture—following the traditional pattern of European missions in South and Central Africa—shows that it did not neglect the practical element. This was emphasized, too, by the fact that Chilembwe sent one of his scholars in 1911 to the Henry Henderson Institute of the Blantyre Mission for hospital training.[134] At the end of his course he was to return to the P.I.M. to work for Chilembwe's mission. In all, it may be said that the group of independent schools under John Chilembwe's leadership provided one of his main hopes for the advancement of Africans. By 1912 he does not seem to have looked upon them as in competition with other mission schools but as complementary, for at that time there were no Government-supported schools.

Chilembwe himself must have realized how immature his staff was. This is indicated in a 1912 report which he sent to his American Negro headquarters, and which casts light not only on the level of his teachers at this time but also on his own desire to improve standards amongst them:

> Please note, these teachers are still under instruction three months during each vacation. I am trying to give them the art of teaching the Bible by various helps while engaged in their teaching. My desire is that each teacher should be properly fitted and an expert in Bible teaching, as in our other branches. I hope to see in this country and in the confines of our work, some young men to be qualified in the preliminary steps to the ministry of the church in this land; possessing [a] certificate as a teacher or schoolmaster to be a qualified native pastor.[135]

It was an aim for a native pastorate not unlike that of the Scottish missions themselves ; though no doubt this pastorate, as time went on, would have taken upon itself an increasingly political role.

Chilembwe himself, perhaps, might not have envisaged this clearly then. But it is not difficult to see that a group of independent African Baptist pastors *vis-à-vis* the ministers and clergy of the established European missions would have played a part not so very different from their European forebears at the time of the Reformation. That the authorities noted a political element in his schools at this time is clearly evident from a change of tone in the few references to Chilembwe and his mission which appear in the Chiradzulu District Book. In 1910 the District Commissioner had commented sardonically on the harmlessness of the P.I.M. : it exists, he claimed, 'more I think for the benefit of the person after whom it is named than for the natives in general'. But by 1912 a marked change had come into the official note. After giving a list of Chilembwe's schools, the District Commissioner went on to notice the P.I.M.'s ambition to start more of them. But, he added, 'they have been severely repressed'. And then he commented in warning fashion :

> This mission requires careful supervision and should not be allowed to spread.[136]

To what exact elements in Chilembwe's plans these over-succinct official notes refer, is not, unfortunately, clear.

There was one certain element in Chilembwe's teaching at this time, which if it was by no means absent from the other missions, did not seem to have the same note of urgency for them as it did for Chilembwe : the training and development of African women. This does not mean that Chilembwe had in mind a women's movement for political emancipation like Mrs. Pankhurst's in the Britain of that day. His ideas were simpler and far more difficult to realize : to pull the African women of Nyasaland out of the tribal state, and to model them on the contemporary European woman, as a progressive ideal. His concept had all the shades of the European female respectability of the time : 'correct' deportment ; 'proper' style of dressing ; a 'decent' manner of arranging the hair ; faithful church membership—a veritable Bantu 'Angel in the House', in fact ! [137] Existing photographs of the female members of his flock, and of the standards of dress of his own wife, stress the character of his feminist ideal far better than any verbal description (see p. 167). Such a concept, however, if limited by the standards of a Mrs. Pankhurst, was revolutionary for the African society of Chilembwe's country—though it must be noted that in this, as in many other of his activities, Chilembwe was following the lead of the Blantyre missionaries who had encouraged the education of African women, from the mid-1890's. A quotation from a letter Chilembwe wrote to the Foreign Mission Board Secretary of the National Baptist Convention in 1912 illustrates further the character and problems of his ideal for African women. Though it is coloured by his picturesque English, it does nevertheless allow some of the urgency of his feeling on this matter to make itself felt :

> Brother Jordan, what about the mothers of the race—shall I forget them ? God forbid ! There is a special work to do. I lay the needs of our benighted wives and mothers before you and upon the great Baptist family and Christian ladies who love Christ and believe that an African woman has a soul to be saved . . . please allow me to plead that more may be done for the women. . . . I feel safe in saying that I am doing good to my countrymen, as it is true everywhere the men are developing faster than the women. But there can be no healthy progress if such is the case. We believe there is an urgent need for special work to be done among the wives of the people, whom you are privileged by God's grace to bring out of darkness into light, because an African woman, [un-? AUTHORS] like her American sister, does not exert an influence for good or evil on her husband. The ordinary African woman in her heathen state is ignorant, uninteresting and unloveable. I almost despair when I think of her ignorance, her utter lack of ambition. I believe and pray that God may rule someone to lay the foundation for the future of the race. It is sad to see a young mother, little more than a girl, with an infant on her back and know that she is thrust into responsibility for which she is quite unfit, and that at a time when she should be taken care of, and she ought to have been left to the joys of young womanhood . . . as my little wife, one night after my prayer she said when she heard my cry that the women and girls are very difficult to work amongst. She said, 'Change your cry and say that the women of Africa for Christ's cause and king-dom, there is nothing too hard for the Lord ; the gospel that transforms and uplifts is sufficient for her needs'—amen, that ours is the privilege of bringing this gospel to her. Please help us. Mrs. Chilembwe needs good friends to help her in her undertaking. She needs to teach our young women that God has a purpose in creating man, male and female, and that women have work to do that man cannot do. She is teaching

day school and taking the sewing department and also visiting her sisters in her surroundings with her Bible in hand. She is seeking to prevent early marriage among our girls, telling them that marriage has meant too little among our parents for generations, and telling them that it is not thus that happy homes are made and a strong race reared. . . . The world will not go forward as it should till women have been taught and have learned to take the place God has ordained for them as man's helpmeet— his equal, not his slave.[138]

Women's movements, independent schools, native co-operatives, and church-building did not exhaust Chilembwe's activities at this time. There was still the problem of financing all these schemes. Between 1910 and 1912 Chilembwe's letters to his American headquarters were full of urgent appeals for more money, because his own people could raise comparatively little for his ambitions. A typical appeal asked for more funds for church-building :

At this writing we are digging the foundations for a new chapel [the brick church, apparently]. Our church now consists of 492 membership [the congregation of the main, Mbombwe centre of the P.I.M., it appears]. . . . Our chapel will cost not less than $500 to complete. It will cost that much on account of tin roofing. Our church in her rags has managed to collect $157.27 to make bricks and burn them. We are looking to you for the $350 by October or November next ; to fail to get that amount by that time is certain to be in trouble with Government. For the men are working on credit and you said we must not make any debts until we notified you.[139]

Trouble with the Government was, clearly, the last thing that Chilembwe wanted at this moment. It was issues of this kind which obviously forced him out into the bush to hunt game for sale. (On many such trips he seems to have been accompanied by John Gray Kufa, the medical assistant of the Blantyre Mission,[140] whose interest in Chilembwe and his work was to cost him his life in 1915.) The extension of such activities, however, may have brought Chilembwe into further difficulties with the Government : he may have got into trouble again over the question of a gun licence.[141] There is some evidence, too, that at least one of these trips was in Portuguese territory, where Chilembwe combined duty with business, preached to the natives, got himself into trouble with the Portuguese authorities, and was imprisoned for a while.[142]

Yet whatever discomfort and annoyance such episodes caused

Chilembwe, they demonstrated the rapid growth of the P.I.M. in many fields. But the extension of its activities brought corresponding problems of organization. One of them (what to do with the increasing numbers of the P.I.M. when staff was small and ill-trained, buildings few in number, and money to meet the growing necessities in short supply) was suggested by a remark of the Blantyre missionaries in 1912 that Chilembwe, like his old master Booth, was 'constantly receiving and baptizing suspended and expelled members from the [other] missions'.[143]   That Chilembwe had not done this in the early years of the P.I.M. has been suggested. When, however, the physical assets of the Providence Industrial Mission increased, and Chilembwe's own reputation was spread more widely abroad, it is very likely that more and more lapsed and disgruntled members of older-established missions made their way to him. But, for all this, Chilembwe seems to have remained on good terms with the Scottish missionaries, as the fact of their receiving members of his mission for training at their Henry Henderson Institute witnesses. Indeed, the leader of the Blantyre Mission in 1912 was quoted on Chilembwe in terms which, if critical, are not antagonistic or unsympathetic, and afford some testimony of the status that Chilembwe then had gained for himself :

> Dr. Hetherwick regards John Chilembwe . . . as above the ordinary type of mission native, but says that his work is sadly suffering from want of European control and superintendence.[144]

How far Chilembwe's work really was 'sadly suffering' is a debatable point. If it did not seem to Hetherwick to be progressing as rapidly as it might have done, this was due less to lack of European superintendence, perhaps, than to other causes. Another comment of Hetherwick's at the same time suggests what these were. He claimed that Chilembwe 'was continually neglecting his mission work to go on long elephant hunts for the revenue he may derive'.[145] Such a statement illustrates one of Chilembwe's major problems by 1912 : the financial difficulties which the rapid expansion of P.I.M. activities had brought in its train. Although the P.I.M. had received new additions to its funds between 1910 and 1911,[146] Chilembwe's American Negro backers, even though they were one of the most powerful coloured denominations in the United States, represented also a subordinate social group and did not have the financial resources of the large white missionary societies.

However important these administrative problems may have been, some of Chilembwe's keenest difficulties at the end of the first dozen years of his independent mission work sprang from more intimate, personal causes. At the beginning of these personal problems may be placed his own health. The chest trouble which had forced him to leave America was still, apparently, with him, and with the passing of time his eyesight got steadily worse. Some have claimed that at his death in 1915 he was suffering from cataract. Others believe that, about 1908, he was cured of this by one of the Scottish medical missionaries, Dr. Macfarlane.[147] Yet whatever may have been really wrong with his eyes, it is obvious that they were getting worse. All pictures that were taken of him after the early days of his return from America show him to be wearing spectacles, and his eyes in them seem to be puckered and peering. Is it unreasonable to suppose that these physical difficulties increased Chilembwe's feelings of frustration which, even if they derived basically from other causes, combined to produce in him that desperate state of mind that made him lead the 1915 Rising?

Other personal troubles of this kind concerned Chilembwe's own family. At some time during the second decade of the new century he lost his little daughter, Emma. There is every reason to suppose that Chilembwe had considerable affection for the members of his family, and that he felt this loss keenly. And then there were the difficulties that faced his wife. Whatever her origins, she was obviously a woman of some accomplishments, and no mean helpmate for Chilembwe. Yet, as his eloquent testimony on the position of African women shows, she must have been even more isolated in the local African society than Chilembwe himself. There is little evidence that she received any sympathetic consideration from the neighbouring European women,[148] and her position must have been extremely difficult, and one which Chilembwe took very much to heart.

There is some indication of Chilembwe's domestic difficulties at this time in a rather pathetic, begging letter which he wrote, on 31 June 1911, to the Secretary of the National Baptist Convention Foreign Mission Board:

DEAR BROTHER: I regret to write to you of an accident which has just occurred. Yesterday, my little wife, industriously, did her washing and at close of day, put the clothes in a room, forgetting to put out a lamp. About midnight it exploded [it must have been a pressure-lamp] and we were unable to extinguish the flames. The people were afraid to come to our rescue because of the leopards who are engaged in destroying our live stock around the station, and my eyes being so weak and bad, I cannot hunt and kill them.

Alas, all our clothing burnt to ashes. Wife had nothing but night garment and me in pyjamas. My children are all naked.

Please Brethren, some good friends send us a box of clothing—second-hand, torn garments such as shirts, trousers and jackets will cover our bodies.

We thank God that the building did not take fire. Only our clothing was destroyed. Oh, how it will rejoice my heart if some brother will send me a baptizing suit as I have a larger number awaiting baptism before the year closes.

Yours sincerely,

JNO. CHILEMBWE.[149]

This unhappy little letter reduces to more human proportions the devilish agitator whose origins some have traced to this period. Yet, for all this, the grievances that were to make Chilembwe a militant rebel against the Government in 1915 were now coming into existence. With his own personal problems and the administrative difficulties that arose at this time of his mission's rapid expansion, they served to confirm and focus all the criticisms of the Europeans in the Protectorate which he had been acquiring since the beginning of his association with Booth, his trip to America, and the early troubles of getting land for the P.I.M.

These grievances that were now coming to the surface for Chilembwe centred around the neighbouring Bruce Estates. An African member of his 1915 following has claimed that Chilembwe's trouble with the Estates began in 1909, and some have set the date as early as the first days of the P.I.M. But whenever it may have been—and 1909 seems as reasonable a guess as any other—there is no doubt that trouble between Chilembwe's people and this European-owned plantation was increasing as the first decade of the new century drew to a close. The character of this trouble has been conveniently summarized by the same African who suggested 1909 as its starting date. It takes the form of a series of charges against the Europeans of the Bruce Estates.[150]

First, it is claimed that they burned the small grass-hut churches that members of Chilembwe's flock erected on the Estates. These members were all workers on the Bruce plantations, and they had built their little meeting-houses on this European land because of their distance from Chilembwe's main Chiradzulu church. That such burnings did take place is undisputed. The reasons for this on the Europeans' part were not simply an animus against the congregations of 'that upstart' Chilembwe, and, also, perhaps, a general feeling against 'mission boys'. They were, in essence, part of the complicated squatter problem which had grown up since Harry Johnston's land settlement in the 1890's. The African squatters on these European-owned estates, whatever traditional claims they could produce to the land that they had taken up—and many who were Nguru immigrants from Portuguese East Africa could obviously produce none—were lumped together as a block and treated to a rigorous labour discipline. An essential part of this, as has already been noted, was the 'thangata' or labour-rent, whereby an African squatter on European-owned land paid for his holding through a period of labour-service for the white owner rather than by money rent. Because of all the labour problems of the Shire Highlands, and the attractions of the higher wages and adventure in South Africa, most European planters wanted their African squatters to pay for their little patches of land by labour rather than a simple money payment. It was at the time of checking on the amounts of labour due to them from their squatters by the officials of the Bruce Estates that the little Chilembwe-ite churches were noted and burned down. It seems to have been part of a policy of making the African understand that he was a squatter on alien-owned land, and that he would not be permitted to build up settled communities which might contest with the European the use and ownership of that land. As a result of instruction at the P.I.M. in their 'rights' many of Chilembwe's following would be aware of the legal position. They would know of the 'non-disturbance clause' in the Certificates of Claim which had been granted to European landowners at the time of Harry Johnston's land settlement. This knowledge would increase their natural indignation over the destruction of their little church buildings which were, in part, their way of asserting that they were more than mere 'labour'. The fact, then, that the 'non-disturbance clause' stipulated that no 'native village or plantation' that existed on a European estate at the time at which its owner had received his Certificate of Claim should be 'disturbed or removed' without the consent in writing of the Government [151] might have been construed by some of Chilembwe's Africans on the Bruce

Estates, who watched their churches burn to the ground, as an indication that the management was proceeding illegally against them, for they were not all Nguru from the Portuguese territories, and some of them may well have had valid grounds for protesting that they and theirs had been part of the original land at the time it fell into European hands. But, for their part, the European officials of the Bruce Estates could have quoted back at the indignant Chilembwe-ite 'barrack-room lawyers' that another part of the 'non-disturbance clauses' usually stated that 'no natives can make other and new villages and plantations on the said Estate without the prior consent of the Proprietor'. Both sides, indeed, if they felt inclined, could quote the law. But, for the ordinary rank-and-file Chilembwe-ites, legalistic squabbles would mean little. They construed the burning of their churches as an act of simple and unmitigated injustice.

Secondly, it has been claimed that the Europeans of the Bruce Estates objected to Africans in European dress. If so, they would have ample material on which to exercise their objections, for, as existing photographs of the P.I.M. show, Chilembwe's people had been taught by their leader to adopt European styles. Women he had told to wear dresses, and to bind up their hair, after the Pauline injunction ; and the men of his congregations had been persuaded to don trousers, shirts, jackets, and hats. It was the hats which caused so much of the trouble. If they wore them—presumptuous though this may have seemed to many of the Europeans—they were expected to raise them to a white person. Failure to do this could mean a number of minor indignities, from the European's knocking-off of the offending object to his implanting his boot on the seat of those other equally offensive articles in his sight, European-style trousers. To many Europeans an African in white man's clothing was 'getting above himself' ; and, as some Africans have claimed, they were whipped when found in European dress and told to get into their own native garb again. How much truth there is in such 'horror' stories it is difficult to determine, though they were wide-spread. What does seem certain, however, is that Chilembwe and the members of his mission felt that the Europeans of the Bruce Estates were strongly against their attempts to 'improve' themselves, and they resented it bitterly.

Thirdly, African testimony has it that the wages of the labourers on the Estates were small : two coils of tobacco a month, according to one informant. Wage payments to Africans at this time in a transitional stage from their indigenous tribal economies to the new, European way of economic life, form a complicated subject, and it is difficult to assess the truth of such charges. But the important fact for the development of Chilembwe's grievances against the Europeans was that many members of his flock on the Bruce Estates believed that they were underpaid, not only in the actual amounts that were given to them, in cash or kind, for work done when they were labouring directly as hired hands but also as a result of various manipulations by the management of the 'thangata' (labour-rent) squatter system so that the African labourer often gave to his employer more work than he was legally bound to do. In fact, in the opinion of African witnesses, at this time the Africans on the Estates were becoming no more than cattle.

Finally, African testimony reports a growing animus in this period by the Europeans of the Estates—particularly their manager —against Chilembwe himself. A slight against their leader would be taken by many of the P.I.M. following who worked for the Bruce Estates as an insult to themselves, and a further indication of the way in which Europeans resented the African's 'bettering' of himself. It was noticed that they disliked especially Chilembwe's hunting—though this European feeling was not, perhaps, a resentment at Chilembwe's desire to 'ape his betters' but was rather part of an habitual European objection to native hunting on the grounds that it was indiscriminate and tended to spoil the game for everybody.

By 1912 it is clear that these grievances were beginning to focus themselves in the figures of John Chilembwe and William Jervis Livingstone, manager of the Bruce lands. Livingstone was eager to develop the Estates on the best 'industrial' lines as rapidly as possible. Faced with an unstable and reluctant group of African workers who were distrustful of the new European economic system, and many of whom sought alternative leadership in the person of a critical and independently minded African preacher, the theories and practices of whose associates and following tended to upset the pattern of efficient, smooth-running management, Livingstone, it may be appreciated, was often guilty of impatience which sometimes turned into harshness in the treatment of his labour force. Chilembwe, perhaps, became a personification to him of all these difficulties.

There is a widespread anecdote which still exists in many forms amongst Africans in southern Nyasaland that illustrates the character of Chilembwe's and Livingstone's relationship. A popular version of it tells the story of how Chilembwe had received from America a bell for his mission, the task of which was to call his flock to church. But, in some way, it did not ring as loudly as was desired. And so, one day when Chilembwe met Livingstone, his advice was either requested, or proffered without asking, on the best manner of treating the faulty bell. Livingstone advised hardening it in a fire to make it ring more loudly. The experiment was tried, and the bell cracked and would not sound again. It was all, said the Africans of Chilembwe's following, a malevolent and typical plot on Livingstone's part to rid them of something which they prized as an example of their standing and progress. Other versions of the tale point the moral more directly : they claim that Livingstone destroyed Chilembwe's bell himself. Of course, the story has obviously apocryphal elements : but they point to the symbolism of the two men as representatives of a European-African conflict of interests.

This hostility between Chilembwe and his following and the Bruce Estates did not, it seems, give any indication in 1912 that it would provide the occasion for the first African attempt to set up an independent state in Nyasaland. An examination of the growing pains of Chilembwe's mission, his own personal problems, and his relations with the Estates up to 1912, suggests that his ambitions were still legitimate, and that those who have seen in his 1915 Rising the final result of a deeply laid plot that went back many years have simply allowed their suspicions to run beyond the evidence.

8. ETHIOPIANISM IN NYASALAND BY 1912

The 'safeness' of Chilembwe's activities up to 1912 was stressed by a Blantyre missionary in an important article on 'Ethiopianism'. He wrote with assurance that

> up to the present Ethiopianism has gained no footing in this country. . . . I do not think that we have much to fear from the emissaries of Negro Churches in America. The native here does not take much to his black brethren if we may judge from the success of their mission.[152]

The statement was certainly an underestimation of the growth of the P.I.M. but it was sound in its assessment of the Ethiopianist threat in Nyasaland at that time. There had been Kamwana ; there was

Courtesy Mr. W. Sanderson

late 15(*a*). Mrs. Chilembwe's sewing class (from Chilembwe's own photograph album). Standing at the left of the table is Morris Chilembwe, a nephew of John Chilembwe, who was killed following him in the 1915 Rising

Courtesy Pastor Leon R. Lawton

Plate 15(*b*). Ringing the church 'bell' of an independent mission church

Plate 16. Mrs. John Chilembwe and family (from Chilembwe's own photograph album). The Chilembwes had three children : Emma (who died as a child before 1914), Charlie and Donald. The young African standing at the right is either a relation or—probably—a Providence Industrial Mission follower who acted as a servant to the Chilembwes

always Booth ; Domingo was still in action ; and anti-hut tax seers, like the Chikunda prophetess of 1907, might arise again ; but the Europeans appeared to have the situation well in hand. Chilembwe's mission, then, was quickly dismissed as a possible source of trouble.

In 1912, and, indeed, very much earlier, the threat seemed to come from another source : Islam, which in a diluted and barely orthodox form had been widespread in Chilembwe's part of the world from the first days of Yao contact with the Arab and half-Arab slavers. In the Protectorate, memories were still alive of the strength of militant Mohammedanism in the Mahdi's outbreak in the Sudan of the 1880's ; and there were continual reports of the troubles with the Muslims and their 'Mad Mullah' in Somaliland. As early as 1900 the Livingstonia paper, *The Aurora*, had analysed the Islamic situation in Nyasaland and had drawn the conclusion that

> the spirit that has led to the formation of the Ethiopian Church in South Africa would operate here for the establishment of Islam.[153]

Indeed, the paper even went so far as to suggest a general native rising under the banner of Islam. The Blantyre missionaries were no less alive to the implications of its spread, and noted that, by 1907, this tendency had resulted in

> 'Chinasala' . . . a spurious kind of Mohammedanism . . . [that pandered to the African's] pride by giving him a status or distinction which separated him from the common run of natives.[154]

Thus Mohammedanism was becoming in Nyasaland another *nthowa ifupi*, another short road to the social status of belonging to a religious group outside the rut of traditional tribal faith : a rival to the quick baptism and advancement of status which Booth, Kamwana, Domingo, and Chilembwe all held out at one time or another to the kind of aspiring and discontented African who might become the centre of political agitation.

But what the missionary [155] and secular critics [156] who commented on this process failed to observe was that, before the Turkish and Egyptian Revolutions, Islam had not fused itself with the economic spirit and technology of the West. It could not, therefore, hold out the same promises as Christianity which had been linked with the commerce and the new economic spirit of the West as a liberating force in Africa by David Livingstone himself. Western culture had obviously much more to offer in the way of technical improvements and creature comforts than the traditional ways of life of the Mohammedan countries, however attractive in other respects their religion might seem to Africans. This should have been obvious from an examination of Madhism in the Sudan, which, as General Gordon and the young Winston Churchill [157] had both seen, offered a form of primitive communism that looked back nostalgically to the days before the rise of European power : an ideal as anachronistic and unrealistic as the attempt to re-create in the early twentieth century the teachings of the medieval Catholic Church on usury. The aspiring Nyasaland African who wanted some faith to integrate him into the new, European-style society, had to seek it in Christianity, either through the white man's missions or in some independent African church.

An examination of Islam or of any of the other rival movements to Chilembwe's for the allegiance of Africans of this type shows some of the reasons for the failure of his Rising against the Government in 1915 : reasons which will be examined in more detail later in this book, but whose indication at this stage serves the purpose, too, of casting some further light on the course of Ethiopianism in Nyasaland between 1900 and 1912. First, such movements drew away potential support from Chilembwe's, and, where they might be willing to unite with him in a general, anti-European rising, were so independent that they split the unity of his effort. Secondly, the prompt manner in which the Government had already dealt with some of them—especially Kamwana's agitation and Booth's 1899 petition—provided a salutary lesson for others who might have thought of joining Chilembwe. And, thirdly, more secular alternatives were, even at this time, beginning to engage the attention of Africans. It has been suggested that it is to 1912 that the Nyasaland African Congress may trace its origins.[158] Certainly, Africans who were interested in this form of political organization would have no difficulty in finding out about the South African Native National Congress which was founded in this same year. And perhaps some of Booth's followers may have learned that, on one of his trips to America about 1912, he had discussed theoretically the possibility of a native revolt in the South and Central African regions with the American Negro political leader, Dr. William B. DuBois.[159] If so, it might have been connected in their minds with one of the more secular revolutionary political creeds : there was enough discussion of socialism and allied issues in the South and Central African press [160] for some Nyasaland Africans, at least, to be aware of its existence; and, indeed, one volume of Charles Taze Russell's *Studies in the Scriptures, The Battle of Armageddon,* which would have circulated in Nyasaland with other Watch Tower literature, contained some detailed discussion of the various secular reform movements of the period, with many quotations from the liberal American press of his day. At this time, too, the implications of more secular forms of political struggle can be seen in the fact that Clements Kadalie was getting ready to leave the Protectorate for South Africa, where he was to become a pioneer trade-union militant. All of these new ideas and practices, in varying degrees of realization, were alive amongst Nyasaland Africans. But, in spite of these other channels of development, Chilembwe's following increased until he had, as the 1915 Rising demonstrated, a potential force at his command should he take the way of violent protest.

By 1912, then, it will be seen that there had been created the conditions inside and outside Nyasaland which would precipitate Chilembwe's final political action, the Native Rising of 1915. If the first wave of Ethiopianism in the Protectorate had split on the rock of Kamwana-ism, there were many places left into which it could flow, and in which it could keep itself alive. Though Nyasaland was relatively isolated, this isolation was by no means complete, and it felt, and in the future was to feel still more, the influences of the wider world outside its borders. As one Nyasaland missionary pointed out correctly in the Blantyre paper and its Scottish equivalent in 1911–12:

> Ethiopianism is caused by forces that are operating all over the world. At home we have the Irish Nationalists, and the Wee Frees who are largely the Celtic remnant of the old Free Church. Abroad we have grave unrest in India and Egypt caused by the desire of nations to have separate existence untrammelled by foreign supervision, so we need not blame the African if into the brain which we have educated, the feeling of Patriotism comes, and [if] the first step is the formation of a Church that is peculiarly their own.[161]

The four years before 1915 were to prove that, in Nyasaland, one such church had been created in John Chilembwe's Providence Industrial Mission.

V

PRELUDE TO REVOLT

1912–1915

Many plans were formed and rejected by us, and it affected my mind to such a degree that I fell sick, and the time passed without our coming to any determination how to commence—still forming new schemes and rejecting them, when the sign appeared again which determined me not to wait any longer.

Confessions of Nat Turner
(Southampton, Virginia, 1831)

V

PRELUDE TO REVOLT

1912–1915

1. CHANGE AND STRESS IN THE PROTECTORATE

THE arrival of a new Governor, Sir George Smith, in 1913, was a time for general self-congratulation among the Europeans of Nyasaland. For the first time in its history, exports exceeded imports in value, and work had begun on that portion of the railway which, by linking the existing limited system with the coast, was expected to cause a further extension of trade. The Mayor of Blantyre could speak with assurance at the reception to the new Governor when he declared that 'In Nyasaland we are all optimistic'.[1]

There was, however, a certain air of unreality about his address of welcome. In particular there was the phrase, 'We rejoice to bear testimony to the harmonious relations that have always existed between the European settlers and the natives of the Protectorate'.[2] Not only was this less than accurate historically but its general optimism about native relations was not to prove true, as Chilembwe and the future would show.

In the two years before the outbreak of the War, continuing changes in the Protectorate were creating the conditions within which Chilembwe's plans for an anti-European revolt matured.

First, beginning at the end of 1911, continuing during 1912 and coming to a head in the early months of 1913, famine had attacked many parts of Nyasaland.[3] Its original cause was the intermittent drought that was particularly severe at the start of 1912. Though the crop-failure was especially acute in the Lower Shire district, few parts of the Protectorate had much food to spare. Export of maize was forbidden in 1912 in order to husband resources, and the Government made plans for relief. The seriousness of the conditions was noticed by a young district officer who entered Nyasaland in the first week of January 1913 to take up service with the Administration : 'It was an unusually bad famine and had even led to some cannibalism'.[4] Traditional African carelessness had done little to prevent the famine. And yet there seems no doubt that the new economic relations which the Europeans had brought into the Protectorate made it more difficult for the Africans to resist the failure of the food supply. As a missionary at Zomba noticed : 'It is extraordinary nowadays to what extent the native trades with his own foodstuffs. He takes the produce of his garden and sells it in the townships or the market-places now to be found on the highways where native carriers and travellers abound. The word *gain* has been naturalized in the phrase *ku chita gain* (to make profit by trading).'[5] Furthermore—though the point must not be over-emphasized—dislocation of the African labour force by the attractions and demands of the European wage system, inside and outside Nyasaland, had not helped African capacity to forestall the onset of famine.[6] And, since prices of foodstuffs rose, as a natural concomitant of the shortage of crops, the African had less money to spend on other commodities, large stocks of trade goods accumulated, and something like a slump developed in the native trade.[7] The situation, indeed, had the makings of a vicious circle. To make matters worse, after long drought, the sudden coming of torrential rain made famine relief very difficult.[8] And, although there was an improvement throughout 1913, nature was still unreliable. For example, the terrific rainstorm at the beginning of March 1914 did serious damage to crops in the Blantyre and surrounding districts, washed away parts of the railway line, and wrecked bridges.[9]

Chilembwe's own part of the Protectorate did not escape. It seems that these disturbed conditions set back somewhat the development of the Providence Industrial Mission which, as noted in the previous chapter, had been making steady progress up to 1912. During 1913 Chilembwe wrote two letters to his American Negro sponsors which reflect the seriousness of the situation for his flock. The first, of 24 March, is the most graphic :

> We are still doing all we can for our Master and brethren and sisters out here. The spiritual work is still prosperous, but work in general is poorly managed on account of lack of sufficient means, above all the famine is raging near all around B.C.A. [British Central Africa]. The people are starving, great numbers of the people are dying with hunger. All missionaries have closed schools, for having nothing to feed their pupils. . . . Oh, famine is raging !
>
> It is a serious thing to report that we are persuaded to make a debt for $100 in order to save our lives and also of those around our reach.

We call your attention to the fact that we are earnestly looking to you to come to our rescue, as you know the system of famine when it is around the country.

This trouble will continue until next year. Nearly all people had planted, but they are not able to clean the weeds. And those who are able both planters [sic], they fail to keep up their plantations, for people are wandering to and fro seeking for employment when they can get food instead of money. . . .[10]

Chilembwe's last point was echoed by the Blantyre missionaries, who stated in their journal for April-June 1913 that they had never seen such a scarcity of native labour at that time of year, and commented that 'unless a large number of workers come down to the Shire Highlands in the next three months the prospects of next year's crops will be far from bright'.[11] Chilembwe, however, sounded a slightly brighter note in his second letter of 1913. He wrote in June to ask for further financial assistance from the National Baptist Convention to meet the demands of the famine, but added :

Last Sunday we had a very, very delightful day, so that we all had forgotten about Njala [famine] for one hundred souls were added to the church by baptism, out of those there was an old lady almost about sixty or seventy years old. The wonderful thing about her is that she walked every Sunday before [for] the distance of twenty miles accompanied by her own two grandchildren to her baptism class. And four of them we are glad to say . . . had been converted from Mohammedanism to Christianity.[12]

One feature of this statement which deserves special attention is the figure of a hundred at baptism. No doubt this would have been at one of the open-air baptisms in a near-by stream which Chilembwe, in the 'Jordan' tradition of Negro Americans, favoured.[13] It was probably an occasion for a gathering of many other Africans from his neighbourhood, not only actual members of his congregations but also the merely curious. Chilembwe, despite increasing lack of funds, was still preaching far and wide from his main base at Chiradzulu and was attracting many Africans to his meetings. As has already been noticed, he had made several preaching trips into nearby Portuguese East Africa and his following among peoples from there was increasing. It is this fact which necessitates further mention of the emigrant Nguru from the Portuguese territories into Nyasaland, and, in particular, into the areas near Chilembwe's sphere of work, where the prospect of employment on European estates was good.

Though there is some doubt about the rate of growth of the African population in Nyasaland at this time and later,[14] it is beyond dispute that in those parts of the Protectorate which bordered on the Portuguese territories there was a very apparent and rapid increase of population. Some have estimated that in the first twenty years of the twentieth century at least 100,000 Nguru entered Nyasaland.[15] It is very probable, too, that this emigration increased in intensity as the War approached, owing to the abuses of the semi-feudal system still in existence in the Portuguese territories, the demands of the chartered companies, the increased maladministration which attended the overthrow of the Portuguese monarchy and the disruption of their colonial policy,[16] and the comparative attractions of the more pro-gressive economic and political life in Nyasaland. The significance of this fact for Chilembwe and his mission in the three years before the Rising appears to be that, at a moment when intermittent famine was already making things difficult for him and his flock, increase of Nguru emigration meant further mouths to feed and less food for the indigenous inhabitants of this area : and the numbers of Nguru who actually joined the P.I.M. or used its facilities as primitive social centres, created for Chilembwe a serious problem of organiza-tion at a time of depletion of resources—as well, of course, as a restless *lumpenproletariat* who might make useful material for any contemplated revolt.

Consideration of the difficult conditions created by shortage of food in the Protectorate in the 1912–14 period is not complete without some mention of how well equipped physically, as well as economically, the African was to meet this. It has been claimed that 'in the first two decades of this century, owing mainly to the greater mobility of the natives caused by the advent of the Europeans, the state of health deteriorated. Unfortunately the medical and sanitary staff was insufficient to cope with the situation.'[17] Chilembwe's awareness of the problems of health was clear from the fact that he sent an African to the Blantyre Mission for medical training in 1911. In 1913 local shortage of food had put a temporary stop to his training, though he returned later to take up his course.[18] How seriously, then, did Chilembwe consider an extension of the primitive first-aid and medical facilities which his mission provided? His friendship with John Gray Kufa, the chief medical assistant of the

Blantyre Mission, may well have riveted in his mind the necessity of some sort of a hospital at the P.I.M. But the point at issue is rather how much notice Chilembwe and Kufa took of the Africans' lack of resistance in face of intermittent famine, not merely because of their own traditional neglect of reserves against shortage of food, or the influence on their native economy of the new European system, but as a result of the deterioration of the state of native health in a period of transition from one way of life to another. It is possible that some considerations of this sort passed through Chilembwe's mind, when the famine came and he might have been stimulated to speculate on his own physical deterioration, which a comparison of the photographs of Chilembwe as a young man in America and as an elderly looking preacher in the second decade of the new century illustrates. Though he had, it seems, been cured of cataract, his eyesight was very bad, and he may still have had vestiges of the asthma which beset him when he was leaving America. The death of his daughter Emma, too, at some time before 1914, may have reinforced his thoughts in this direction. Though these points are, of course, speculation, nevertheless, as has been noticed in the previous chapter, they should not be overlooked in any estimate of the personal frustrations which Chilembwe may have felt, and which, together with factors of a wider implication, may have driven him to open revolt. Certainly the periods of intermittent famine before he took that step must have prompted his thought along many avenues, which, if they were not altogether unexplored, in the 1912–14 period, were investigated increasingly by Chilembwe.

Some of the Government's measures in this period may have increased the feelings of uneasiness about the new order of things amongst many of the natives, and may have turned some of them to Chilembwe, at a time when his thoughts were moving in the direction of leading them in rebellion. Apart from the recruitment of troops and porters which will be considered later, three official actions at this time deserve consideration.

The first was the District Administration (Native) Ordinance, 1912, an attempt to supply 'a salutary measure of discipline and control in village life to replace the old system of tribal rule by chiefs which [had] fallen into decay with the evolution of native life and the passage of time'.[19] The 'archaic system of tribal rule' was to be supplanted 'by the gradual formation of subsidiary local government by means of Sectional Councils of Headmen chosen as far as possible by the natives themselves and presided over by the District Resident'.[20]   From these quotations alone, it may be suggested that at least one element of the native society of Nyasaland was likely to take umbrage against the new measures : the leading elements of 'the archaic system of tribal rule' which were to be progressively eliminated.   Though the new Councils of Headmen, when created, did in fact contain many of the old chiefs and tribal worthies, it was an underlining of the writing on the wall against the old ways of life, which had become increasingly clearer as the Administration entrenched itself in British Central Africa.   Chilembwe himself was not likely to have been influenced by a desire to return to the old ways of life, though he may have felt some sympathy for any Yao chiefs who were affected by the new legislation, for, as has been observed when considering the original 'Ajawa' title to the P.I.M., Chilembwe had a good deal of Yao patriotism.   Furthermore, the Ordinance was not introduced into the districts of the Shire Highlands, Chilembwe's *milieu*, 'where most of the land was in private ownership'.[21]   But it was introduced on 31 May 1914 into the Ncheu district to the north.   And it was from this area that plans were made for some dissident Ngoni forces to join up with Chilembwe in his attack on the main centres of European rule in 1915.   For a long time the Ngoni had been sulky over the decline of their power in Nyasaland as a result of successive punitive expeditions against them, and it is possible that the threat to the old tribal way of life which the 1912 Ordinance and its gradual application brought to a head had something of the effect of a 'last straw' for some of them.

This attempt to bring more system into the intricate complications of Nyasaland tribal life and eventually to supplant it altogether probably had one effect on Chilembwe.   The point was suggested by a writer in the first analysis of Chilembwe's rising printed by the Livingstonia Mission paper :

> One great bar to the progress of Africans in the past had been their lack of self-discipline and their desire for power, however limited. The result has been the multiplication of weak tribes and the breaking-up of those under petty chiefs and headmen. The advent of British rule has changed this for Nyasaland, but the tendency still remains among natives and, since a pushing man cannot now set up as an independent chief, he is apt, unless controlled by higher principles, to seek to gain his object by trying to become a chief inside a Church. This seems to have been the mental process with John Chilembwe. . . .[22]

Following this line of analysis, it could be argued that Chilembwe saw in the kind of attempt to shape native society, which the 1912 Ordinance represented, an increasing control of such portions of local independent authority as he might hope to attain.[23] An analysis of this sort would suggest that Chilembwe saw himself as a thwarted 'man of destiny'. There is some reason to suppose that this was not so to any great extent, as will be seen later. Yet the point deserves consideration for there may be some small element of truth in it—and it is the accumulation of such small elements which, together with greater precipitating factors, may well push a man along the path of revolution.

It is more likely, however, that what annoyed Chilembwe in such measures as the 1912 Ordinance—and what probably annoyed members of his following much more—was their aim of building 'up an organization to control the rising generation of natives who, finding themselves without the restraining influences to which their parents were accustomed, have of recent years evinced an inclination to emancipate themselves from the disciplinary responsibilities of village life and obedience to authority. . . .'[24] To Africans already suspicious of European intentions towards them, such an ideal might well be construed as an attempt, through a hierarchy of 'puppet' headmen, to direct their activities into political, social, and economic channels which the Administration considered 'safe'. The Administration in its Report for 1912–13 hoped that 'the people [will] recognize that they are being given some measure of responsibility for their own affairs and that they will be afforded full opportunity of following a path of progress'.[25] But for the kind of politically conscious African who came under Chilembwe's influence, as 1915 approached, there was a sting in the tail, for the Report concluded by referring to 'a path of progress on lines which Government will control and regulate'. This was not the only contradiction which might have been observed in the Government's native policy of which this 1912 Ordinance was a fair sample. It claimed to be an attempt to maintain 'the responsibilities of village life' and the traditions of 'native family life', yet at the same time its object was to clear away the 'archaic system of tribal rule' of which, of course, both traditional village and family life were an integral part. The Government could not have it both ways; and it is important to notice that the Ordinance broke down and had to be redrafted after the War.[26] For all its emphasis on local native government, the onus of selection of the Sectional Councils of Headmen fell on the District Resident, and Principal and Village Headmen had to be approved first by the Governor himself. The Ordinance thus represented an attempt to introduce more direct rule into the Protectorate and the Government seems to have been somewhat hasty in judging when the time was ripe for this. Whatever the rights and wrongs of the measure, it provided a focus for African political discontents, and offended some elements of the traditional tribal way of life and some of the new, politically conscious Africans who were already beginning to appraise legislation and administrative action by political concepts which they had learned from contact with the Europeans.

A second official action at this time which has some relevance for the background of the Rising was the increase of the hut tax. In 1912 the rate of the hut tax was raised to 8s., with a 4s. labour rebate, an increase of 2s. on the figure of 1911.[27] To anyone studying them to-day, the regulations, with their provisions for labour and produce rebate and their varying scales of taxation, are difficult enough to understand. To the Nyasaland African of 1912–14, the raising of the hut tax rate in 1912, the culmination of a series of complicated taxation changes, cannot have been any easier to comprehend. Though pre-War reports stated that the hut taxes were being paid quietly,[28] there is not much doubt that they were a source of considerable grievance for many Africans, though few contemplated going to the lengths to which Kamwana had gone. The labour rebate made it seem that the hut taxes had been instituted with the express purpose of getting the African to work for the European. Abuses grew up in the issuing by Europeans to Africans of the labour certificates which, on the statement that a native had worked for a month for a European employer, entitled him to a rebate of half the hut tax.[29] Often more than the statutory minimum of labour was taken from the African by unscrupulous employers. The perplexity of the continuing series of regulations did not make it easier for the African to defend himself against this, and as most of the regulations were in English, not in the native vernaculars, confusion and resentment were natural. (This point applied to most regulations and ordinances and its general significance for the background of the 1915 Rising may be seen in the recommendations on native grievances of the Commission of Inquiry into this : 'publication in the native languages of those Ordinances and Regulations which more directly affect the native, and . . . [the taking of] means to explain to him the reasons for such legislation'.[30]) The increase of hut tax created for the more affluent natives such as Chilembwe and those who became his staff in 1915 a more particular cause of grievance, because, as they were engaged in their own enterprises, they were not able or willing to work for a European in order to gain a certificate for labour rebate. They would thus have to pay the full rate of tax and the regulations had for them something of the character of an indirect income-tax.[31] And, for all classes of native society, there was the grievance that the taxes were often collected indirectly by chiefs and local headmen—a system which could easily be abused—instead of directly by Government officials.[32]

If taxation regulation has importance in the background to the Rising, even more significance must be attached to the third official action in the 1912–14 period in Nyasaland. 'Action is perhaps the wrong word, for in dealing with the Government's attempts to bring some order into the chaos of the land system of the Protectorate contemporary critics would have had no hesitation in changing the term to 'inaction' or something stronger! In 1911 the Crown Lands Ordinance had brought some system into the land question as it affected primarily the European settlers; but 1912 and 1913 still found the Government fumbling its way forward to overcome the failure of its previous legislation and attempts to bring some security of tenure to the Africans of the Protectorate. Johnston's 'non-disturbance clauses' of the 1890's, as had been seen, had proved impractical when confronted with the development of European land-holding and the immigration of natives from other parts of Nyasaland and from Portuguese East Africa into the estates where paid employment was available. The Land Ordinance (Native Locations) of 1904, which followed on the Nunan Judgement of 1903, had tried to secure some protection for the African tenant on European land but became a dead letter almost as soon as it was passed.[33] The crux of the matter was twofold. First, for those African dwellers on European estates who might claim protection against eviction on the ground of Johnston's original 'non-disturbance clauses', it was well-nigh impossible to prove who was or was not an original African settler on the land before the Certificates of Claim were issued. To complicate matters here, the mobility amongst Africans who were never static as a result of their traditional methods of shifting cultivation had been influenced by the demand of the new European economic system—and, of course, there were the migrations into the affected areas from Portuguese East Africa, which added to this mobility. And secondly, when the Government attempted to regularize the rent paid by African tenants to European estate owners, the attempt was by-passed by the Europeans concerned, for 'what the landlords wanted was not rent but work'.[34] Thus, if an African resident on a European estate did not provide his quota of labour as rent-in-kind (the 'tangata' system), many Europeans felt that they ought to resort to their only means of disciplining their labour force : eviction from his land-holding. The point became even clearer when, in the period under review, the Government spent many anxious hours considering what could be done to ameliorate the abuses of the existing land system, and formulated a Native Tenants (Agreement) Ordinance that was debated in 1914 in the Legislative Council, but was allowed to lapse because of the outbreak of the War and was not reconsidered until 1917. At the 1914 debate, A. L. Bruce, managing director of the Bruce Estates, was particularly outspoken, and stated clearly that the extension of economic cultivation on his land depended on the number of African tenants who settled on it, for only in this way, through the labour-rent they would have to pay, was it possible to secure an adequate labour force ; and if the Africans concerned would not co-operate, then he was frank enough to recommend eviction.[35] From even this very brief review and previous mention of the problem in other chapters, it is obvious that, in areas such as Chiradzulu where Chilembwe had his mission and where Bruce's estates were one of the biggest land units, trouble between employer and native tenant was almost an everyday occurrence.

The new Administration under Sir George Smith as Governor could perhaps have done little to remedy the situation in 1912–14 without alienating either the Europeans or the Africans. Like most colonial governments, it tried to compromise, and the result was ineffectiveness and a continual chagrin to Africans who were affected. The Blantyre Mission paper was, then, by no means unfair when it drew attention to the anomalies of the situation as a sober point for reflection at a time when the Mayor of Blantyre was welcoming so optimistically the new Governor to the Protectorate :

> The place and permanency of the native on the land has not yet been settled. Time is passing and we look to the opening of the line to Beira and the south to bring us an influx of Europeans and demands for land to settle on and cultivate. It is time that this subject was dealt with and

the position of the native as regards the land defined with some degree of finality.

At present, with the exception of a few—very few—natives who have got grants of land from the Government or have secured them by purchase or lease, no native has any security of tenure for himself or his crops. If he has a house or garden on an estate owned by a European, he may be moved any day after certain notice, or he may have to make such arrangements as regards rent or services to make it suitable for him to move elsewhere. If he is on Government land he may have the land he is settled on transferred to some private purchaser ; and though the deed of transfer secures his rights, yet the new conditions are such as he will no doubt prefer to move elsewhere. In neither case is there permanency of occupation guaranteed him which alone can induce him to put his surroundings on a permanent basis. He will not build a permanent house nor will he care to plant and cultivate slow maturing plants, crops or trees.[36]

That Chilembwe was very well aware of these conditions was clear, not only from his observation of local African society but also from his own difficulties when he and the Negro minister from America, Cheek, had had trouble in getting a legal title for the land on which their mission stood—a title which, from some of his letters to the National Baptist Convention in America, it seems he was always afraid might be taken away at any time by the Administration that had so reluctantly granted it in the first place. And not only would Chilembwe have his mind drawn consistently to these problems by their exposition in the Blantyre Mission journal but also by their airing in the *Nyasaland Times* itself.[37]

Yet in spite of all these changes and stresses, there was a general feeling of complacency amongst almost all members of the Nyasaland European community, Government, settlers, and missionaries, at this time. Despite famine and an increase in the hut tax the Administration could observe in 1912 that 'the natives as a whole have met their obligations in a favourable manner' ;[38] and in 1913, when the intermittent shortage of food was still dangerous, the tax still onerous, and the District Administration (Native) Ordinance was being put into practice, the Government could state complacently in its annual report that 'nothing has occurred to vary the good opinion formed in the past of the general law-abiding character of the Nyasaland native in his ready compliance with constituted authority'.[39] Even the Blantyre missionaries, in spite of their worry over the land question, were able to note that the African reception to the new Governor in 1913 'gave the newcomers an excellent object lesson in the happy relations that exist between the Government of the Protectorate and the protected'.[40] And when the greatest change and stress of all for Nyasaland occurred, the outbreak of the Great War in 1914—to be examined in more detail later—assurance about native relations was widespread, and the *Nyasaland Times* was speaking not only for itself when it declared, scarcely a month after hostilities had begun, that 'There is not the slightest fear of disaffection among the natives'.[41]

Perhaps there was a certain centenary feeling in the air—a hundred years (no matter of what) for a young country often has the effect of a confident coming-of-age—that may have been touched off by the celebrations at Blantyre, on 19 March 1913, of the hundredth anniversary of the birth of David Livingstone. At the celebration service for Europeans, Government, settlers, and missionaries were represented, and A. Livingstone Bruce of the Magomero Estates presented to the Blantyre church on behalf of Livingstone's grandchildren a bronze memorial plaque. In the commemoration of this occasion there seems to have been something of that sounding of emotions, that consciousness of community and assurance of tradition which, for example, the Lincoln Memorial Day often represents in America. Yet some may have had unconscious fears that, beneath the façade of optimism, all was not well; and when the Blantyre missionary journal as part of the celebrations carried an article on the pioneering journeys of David Livingstone, its comment on the site he chose for the first party of white missionaries to enter the Protectorate seemed to have ominous overtones. (This site, it should be remembered, became, after the failure of the preliminary missionary attempt of David Livingstone and the Universities Mission to Central Africa in the 1860's, the centre of the estates of the great explorer's son-in-law, A. L. Bruce.) The Blantyre paper asked:

> Why Livingstone ever led the Mission party to stay in such an unhealthy site as Magomero plainly showed itself to be, we have never been able to understand. One cannot help thinking that had they established themselves [elsewhere] . . . the whole history of the Shire Highlands . . . would have been changed.[42]

Yet this was not the only note of unconscious irony that the optimistic commemoration of David Livingstone's centenary produced, for present on the occasion [43] was William Jervis Livingstone, the Baron of Bachull, from Lismore, the heir of a long tradition of respect amongst the Livingstones of the Western Isles of Scotland, and manager of the great explorer's grandson's estates. And though W. J. Livingstone was more than suspicious of Chilembwe, he could hardly have thought, at that moment of celebration, that Magomero would prove for him something more than an 'unhealthy site'.

But before that could be, other links had to be forged in the fatal chain of events, and for one of those links, again, Joseph Booth was indirectly responsible.

2. BOOTH'S SECOND PETITION

In 1912 Booth was adrift again. The American Seventh Day Baptists, suspecting that missionary activity in Central Africa by an agent at the Cape might not be up to their standards, had, it has been seen, sent a two-man commission of inquiry to investigate Booth's work. Booth had rushed over to America to defend his efforts but his explanations were rejected by the Seventh Day Baptists, and they broke with him. So, when he arrived back in Cape Town at the end of 1912, he was completely without sponsors. But although dejected for a while, Booth was not a man to remain inactive in those causes of African advancement to which he had dedicated his life.

That his egalitarian principles were still clearly before his eyes was noticeable in the way in which he upheld them even at the risk of his principal source of livelihood after he was deprived of American finances. This was the income from his house at Sea Point, Cape Town, where he and his wife took in boarders. Naturally most of these were white ; but Booth, when it seemed necessary, was always willing to give shelter to an African, though this might antagonize his other boarders who, according to the structure of prejudice in South Africa, objected to living under the same roof with a black man. One of Booth's lodgers was D. D. T. Jabavu, later Professor of Bantu Studies at Fort Hare Native College, and he has borne witness to the fact that Booth was always prepared in such cases to support the African against the white's objections.[44] Naturally, this did not help Booth's income.

It seems that Booth did not remain long without a pro-African cause to which to attach himself. In February 1913 he had issued leaflets for a 'British Christian Union': a variant of his African Christian Union scheme of the late nineteenth century. Though the project tried to make an appeal to Africans beyond the borders of the Union of South Africa, Booth, after his experiment of trying to convert Nyasaland Africans from afar, seems to have decided that the preliminary emphasis should be on activities nearer home; and so his new scheme was based on South Africa. Its immediate object was to establish 'British Christian Union Native Training Institutes' in order that Africans might be trained speedily in a variety of professions to secure a rapid, peaceful development of British Africa. As usual, there were many utopian elements in the project and it appears that these Institutes got no further than a small group of Africans meeting at Booth's own house. But the appeal was not altogether in the clouds and had an element of practical vision:

> As a matter of sheer expediency Britain cannot afford to ignore or undervalue the enormous latent possibilities of mutual advantage, blessing and power, available in the awakening of the fifty millions constituting her African family. . . . It should be remembered that the British African family occupies an estate thirtyfold the area of Britain, with an equal or greater productive capacity, and that a just and co-operative development will draw many millions from the backward regions of non-British Africa, so that twenty years hence the British Family may well be a hundred millions.[45]

The project had many of the features of Booth's earlier ventures· There was the attempt to secure the interest of Americans, in particular Negro Americans; and it was probably the aim of re-patriating 'spiritually and industrially qualified Negroes, on Peace Principles, to their African Fatherland' that was the reason for Bishop H. M. Turner's name appearing in the American 'Repatriation Auxiliary' which the prospectus outlined.[46] But the most general appeal of Booth's British Christian Union lay in its declared aim 'to discover and unite such persons as are wishful to uplift and give equality of opportunity and freedom to the whole of our Indian, African and other coloured races'. It must have been this which secured for him the support of at least one West African native intellectual and a number of South African. Thus, one of his supporters at this time was Solomon T. Plaatje, Tswana treasurer of the South African Native National Congress (formed in 1912), and author of *Mhudi*, a historical novel in English, and a translation of some of

Shakespeare's plays into Tswana ; [47] and another was John L. Dube, then first president of the South African Native Congress, and comrade of Booth and Chilembwe in America for a brief period. Support from leading African politicians indicates how Booth in this period was attempting to work through the newly formed South African Native National Congress.

Running throughout the whole British Christian Union scheme was a strongly pacifist note :

> to positively refuse to shed each other's blood, or countenance the same, in order to retain, or regain, territory acquired or held by forceful methods . . . [and] to declare the Gospel of peace and Goodwill to every tribe and people within the British Empire, and to solemnly seek to substitute the rule of love and co-operation for that of brute force.

This note has importance not merely for Booth's own story in showing pacifism as a constant element in his thinking but also for the Rising, because it demonstrates, with other evidence, that Booth was prepared under no circumstances to countenance the use of force.

How much Chilembwe may have heard of the scheme is uncertain, for it has been noticed that he and Booth were in no very close contact at this time. It is possible that he may have heard something about it from Nyasaland emigrant labourers in the Union of South Africa on their return to the Protectorate. But he can have had no very direct connection with it. The scheme, however, was linked directly to Nyasaland by one figure : and it was his connection with Booth which was to link Booth, if only indirectly, with the immediate circumstances of Chilembwe's Rising, though the conception of armed revolt was anathema to him.

On the February 1913 prospectus of the British Christian Union, as the 'Secretary of the Central African Committee' appeared the name of 'Peter Nyambo of Nyassaland'. Nyambo's own story is a fascinating one and deserves a separate biography : but only those elements of it may be mentioned here which affect the background— and the foreground—of the Nyasaland Rising of 1915. Peter Nyambo was a Ngoni, born in the Ncheu district of Nyasaland about 1884.[48] After five years at the Blantyre Mission, he joined Booth in 1901 at his Plainfield Mission at Cholo. Two years later Booth introduced him, as he had introduced Chilembwe and other Africans, to the great world outside Nyasaland : and from that time onwards Nyambo was to see as much of it as many of Booth's other converts—though an American trip was denied him. In 1903 Booth took him to England, where he improved his education and in 1904 came into contact with the Seventh-day Adventists. From this time until 1911 he worked as a paid African missionary for this American denomination and travelled in Britain, Holland, Germany, Belgium, Switzerland, the Mediterranean countries, and East Africa. Nyambo spent over a year in British East Africa, as Kenya was then called, as assistant to its first Seventh-day Adventist missionary. Home, however, called him back, and in 1908 he returned to Nyasaland, where he served in his role of missionary assistant at Malamulo, as the Plainfield Mission, now under Seventh-day Adventist control, had been called from 1907 onwards. But he had his disagreements with the director of the mission there, and decided in 1910 to return to his native Ncheu district.

In view of the fact that a supplementary native rising was planned at Ncheu to link up with Chilembwe's in 1915, it is interesting to see how Nyambo's career at this time throws some light on this. He was, it should be remembered, a Ngoni, and Ngoni discontents with the Government of Nyasaland have already been noted. Though Nyambo knew only at second hand of Filipo Chinyama, Ngoni leader of the supplementary rising, his readiness in the first place to link himself with Booth, his travels, and his criticisms—to be noticed later—of European rule, indicates that not all Ngoni at this time were still stagnating in the old tribal mould. In the Ncheu district some of them, at least, were looking to new ways and methods of protest against the hardships—real or imagined—of European rule. Furthermore, Nyambo's own account of conditions in the Ncheu district gives some evidence for the short-lived movement of revolt which misfired there in the first year of the Great War. He states that he witnessed 'the miscarriage of justice and the whippings of the people'.[49] But not wishing to stay and agitate against the Government in order to stop this—no doubt remembering the punishment which the Nyasaland Government had meted out in the past to recalcitrant Ngoni—he took himself off to South Africa.

It was here that he met Booth again, after a separation of about nine years. The two soon picked up their old friendship, and Nyambo's position on the prospectus of Booth's British Christian Union of 1912 demonstrates that Booth lost no time in putting this to use in his schemes. Though Nyambo had left Ncheu in Nyasaland

to avoid embarrassments with authority, he was quite clear and outspoken about the conditions of Africans as he saw them. His
command of English was as good as Chilembwe's and he put his
talents to work in South Africa in order to vent native grievances
against European rule on a wider basis than the narrower agitations
of Nyasaland would have afforded him. Typical of his sentiments
at this time is this extract from a letter he wrote to the press in
1913 :

> In Central Africa there are fully 2,000 Natives to every White Man,
> but we do not try to trouble them. We reason that if the British Govern-
> ment were so generous with the Dutch (who refused them reasonable
> freedom and voting power and so caused a bitter and horrid war)—a
> reference to the Boer War and the Treaty of Vereeniging—will they not
> also see to it that we of British Africa, in the sections of Cape Colony,
> Transvaal, Orange River State, Matebeleland, Barotseland, Nyasaland,
> Ugandaland [sic] and all British East Africa, have just peace . . . and
> educational treatment, such as the good Missionary pioneers assured us
> of and which we still confidently look for.[50]

Letters to the press, however, were not enough for Nyambo. In
1913 he conceived the idea of petitioning the King,[51] as Booth had
tried to address the Queen in 1899, for a general redress of African
grievances. Though the idea of a petition was his own and Nyambo
had not heard of Booth's 1899 attempt, nevertheless the finished
document that he produced in 1914 was strongly influenced by
Booth in both form and content, and many identified it with him,
not with Nyambo. Booth's name indeed appeared on the printed
petition forms with Nyambo's as one of the main signatories.[52] It is
this petition which, according to the Commission of Inquiry into
Chilembwe's Rising, had some effect on the outbreak in 1915 :
'Joseph Booth's petition of May 1914, sent for circulation and to
some extent circulated, among Nyasaland natives'.[53] The extent
of circulation is not clear and Nyambo himself claimed that he sent
only three copies into Nyasaland and that few signed it. Nevertheless, even three copies passing carefully from hand to hand in the
vital months before the War, when other events in Nyasaland were
helping to turn some to Chilembwe's leadership against the Government, could have had an effect in persuading vacillating Africans to
join his standard by formulating more clearly their grievances. One
can imagine its being discussed in small, clandestine groups, many
of them probably meeting in the independent African churches,

with a leading African who could speak some English translating slowly into the native tongue.

The petition was entitled 'The Rhodesia-Nyasaland Appeal of May 1914'. It began with a criticism of the British acquisition of the Rhodesias and Nyasaland 'without giving any public or definite pledge as to the manifest rights and future status of the numerous native owners found in possession thereof',[54] and went on to complain that 'the right of native [land] ownership throughout these vast and valuable regions' had been 'extinguished or [made] of negligible importance'. Such statements could not fail to find some support amongst Africans of the Shire Highlands, with its thorny problems of land-holding. The petition then described how, until recently, Africans of the Rhodesias and Nyasaland had acquiesced in and trusted the rule of 'educated white men' over their areas. But, when many of them had gone down into South Africa and had found a country where British rule over the natives was completely established, they discovered a situation which did not merit much future trust in the good intention of local whites : complete discrimination against the African, the hampering of all his movements, and assignment of him to a distinctly subordinate status in society. Faced with such conditions, the petition went on, Colonial officials and the British Government itself disclaim responsibility. A criticism of this kind is an important indication of how the peripatetic Central African was using conditions in South Africa as a yardstick with which to measure the potential development of his own country. Booth's case was then quoted as an example of what happens to a European who attempts to stop the worsening of race relations. And, finally, after this series of complaints about the dangers of European rule, the petition came to its main demands. It asked first that, in order to bring about a 'state of peace and mutual goodwill' between white and black, the British Government, in those territories of Central Africa over which it still had control, should 'from the close of the current year, 1914 . . . see to it that' all revenue from these countries should 'be administered in equal amounts and just proportions' for both Natives and Europeans alike. Then came a demand which could have had great attraction for men of the calibre of Chilembwe and the leaders of his movement : 'that educated, civilised natives, as they become available in any part of British African Dominions, shall have equality of representation upon the Legislative Councils, and in the Assemblies in the respective

territories, and be fully eligible for official posts of trust, administrative, financial, military and otherwise, subject to the same tests of
fitness as those applied to British officials and other servants'. (As
has been seen, Chilembwe himself had never at any time protested
against the European domination of the Governmental organs of the
Protectorate. Perhaps he thought that the time was not ripe for
Africans to assume such responsibilities until they were fitter
economically and politically for them. This may well have been so
for the first decade of the P.I.M. Afterwards Chilembwe's attitude
towards Europeans may have hardened so much that he distrusted
anything savouring of them at all. So what attraction this part
of the Rhodesia-Nyasaland Appeal of May 1914 would have had
for him in particular it is very difficult to say.) The final demand
was for the establishment of 'Native Advisory Councils' to promote
co-operation between natives and Administration in the affairs of
the countries concerned. Though this part of the petition was
anticipated at least in part by the councils which the Government of
Nyasaland proposed in its 1912 Ordinance, nevertheless the Appeal
went further in its scope for African government, and if it did not
propose complete ultimate autonomy, as Booth's 1899 petition had
done, it obviously looked in that direction.

Though the knowledge of such a petition and its circulation in
the period shortly before war broke out in Europe could not have
been welcome to any colonial government—particularly to the
Nyasaland Government with its brash optimism at that time—
nevertheless it may have done as much to keep down discontent,
amongst Africans who discussed such matters, as to promote it. For
it should be observed that the petition was addressed to the Sovereign
of Great Britain, a figure whom many Africans, from the first times
of British occupation in the days of the 'good Queen', had felt was
somehow above all the hurly-burly of local African-European
politics, and who could be relied upon, when asked, to intervene and
see that justice was done. It was certainly in this spirit that Nyambo
sailed to England in May 1914, intent on getting as close as possible
to the King to present his grievances. He was given, indeed, a
tactful and friendly reception by some official. In this way, Africans
with knowledge of the petition in Nyasaland may have felt that in
the approach to the King, rather than by the path of conspiracy and
armed revolt, lay the solution to their problems ; and so, perhaps,
some were kept away from Chilembwe's overtures to rebel against

the Government. But this point must not be pressed too far, for there is another way of looking at the petition which suggests that, apart from making some Africans more articulate about their grievances and thereby drawing them indirectly to a militant course of action, the Rhodesia-Nyasaland Appeal of May 1914 may have driven some directly into Chilembwe's arms.

From this point of view it is important to notice that the petition asks that its terms shall come into operation 'from the close of the current year, 1914'. Therefore, when 1 January 1915 arrived, it would be apparent to any Africans who may have placed their hopes on the petition that its terms had not been granted, and some, in disillusionment, may have gone over to Chilembwe. It is also just barely possible that Chilembwe held his fire until he saw what was the outcome of the petition. For, although there was no connection between Chilembwe and Nyambo—he did not at any time meet Chilembwe and by his constitutional approach was obviously unsympathetic to the use of force—Nyambo was from the Ncheu district, where the fortunes of himself and his petition may have been followed more carefully by local Africans. Chilembwe could very well have heard of all this from his contacts in the Ncheu district. Whatever is the validity of this hypothesis, is it no more than a coincidence that the Rising followed within a fortnight of the time when the sponsors of the petition had asked that its terms should come into operation, if at all ?

After the joint ventures of the British Christian Union and the Rhodesia-Nyasaland Appeal, Booth and Nyambo did not meet again until 1917. Nyambo stayed in England for two years before returning to South Africa in 1917. Booth at the end of 1914 went into Basutoland, where he carried out independent missionary work and apparently financed himself by acting as a Native Agency for the International Correspondence Schools, an educational organization in which he saw hopes for the advancement of Africans in a country where the opportunities of higher education open to them were very limited. It was lonely work, and often Booth's thoughts would turn nostalgically to those early days when he had first entered British Central Africa ; to his little daughter, Emily, and his faithful servant, John Chilembwe. In his wildest dreams he could not have imagined that Chilembwe was then plotting revolt against the Nyasaland Government. The only rebellion which caught Booth's attention at that moment was the Boer Rebellion of 1914 in the Union of South

Africa,[55] for he saw in it a danger of attempted Dutch annexation of Basutoland. He was old and tired and dispirited at the failure of so many of his hopes. His work for Nyasaland was nearly over ; the petition of 1914 with Nyambo was his last direct attempt to influence the Protectorate. Yet some Europeans there, in the months before and after Chilembwe's Rising, still believed he had a direct hand in it.

To the Nyasaland authorities, however, it was not Booth who seemed likely to stir up the Africans. They knew that he was safely outside Nyasaland and not likely to return. It was a newcomer from America about whom they were worried.

3. AN INNOCENT ABROAD

This newcomer was as American as the Stars and Stripes itself. He was, in his own words, a 'backwoods boy' and had been born in 1886 near the small country town of Berlin, Wisconsin, when the West was still officially a 'frontier' area, and the Mid-West, of which Wisconsin was a key state, was in the opinion of many the most American of all American regions : a centre of democracy, equality, old-time religion, progress, and plain-speaking. His name was Walter B. Cockerill [56] and he had been brought up in the faith that was represented by the little Seventh Day Baptist country church at Berlin, Wisconsin, of which he became a member on 7 June 1898, at the age of twelve. In 1913 he was 27 years old and, as he puts it 'left college after one year in search of adventure, and I found just that—and then some !' It was Nyasaland which was to supply him with this adventure and he was to take there in 1914 some of the restless, honest-to-goodness, fundamentalist, democratic spirit of the Mid-West which was to be, in part, the cause of his troubles.

On the last Saturday of December 1913, Walter Cockerill was admitted to membership of the Seventh Day Baptist Church at Plainfield, New Jersey : the same church which Booth had joined sixteen years before this and which had financed him in two of his missionary ventures. Cockerill's object in becoming a member of this church—the centre of the Seventh Day Baptist faith in the United States—was, presumably, to gain from it a preacher's licence so that he might go overseas as a Seventh Day Baptist missionary. This was granted on 3 January 1914, and within three weeks of this date he had set sail for Nyasaland and adventure. He went entirely of his own volition and means, and received no financial assistance from the American Seventh Day Baptists, who had, no doubt, unpleasant memories of their past ventures into Central African missions and wished to see, first of all, how Cockerill fared in Nyasaland before committing themselves to his monetary support. Booth, after all, had had a warrant issued for his arrest within eight months of his return to Africa the first time he was in their service. Within a similar period, history was to repeat itself in Cockerill's case.

On his way out to Africa and especially after his arrival at Chinde, in the mouth of the Zambezi, in March 1914, Cockerill took pains to inform himself further of the mission history of Nyasaland, of which he had learned the elements before he left America. He soon became aware of the confused situation which existed in the Ngoni and Tonga regions to the west of Lake Nyasa, where between 1907 and 1910 the Watch Tower maelstrom of Joseph Booth and Elliott Kamwana had thrown so many into a panic, and where Charles Domingo, with his little church at Mzimba, was still a centre of the Seventh Day Baptist faith. Kamwana himself was at Chinde when Cockerill was there, and he was still preaching the Watch Tower doctrine from the books of Pastor Charles Taze Russell. No doubt he was waiting for Russell's prophecy that the Millennial Age would begin in October 1914. If so, he had just over six months left to wait. Kamwana seemed in no hurry to communicate any of these matters to Cockerill, who tried to arrange an interview with him but failed. Nevertheless the very fact that Cockerill had tried to see Kamwana, although only as a matter of general interest, may have reached the ears of the Administration in Nyasaland. If so, it would not have been a good mark in Cockerill's favour, for even after his deportation in 1909 Kamwana was still remembered as a fierce critic of the British régime and as a defier of the hut tax ; and, as the zero-hour of the Watch Tower prophecy drew nigh, it seems to have been feared that he might take pains to hasten the arrival of the Millennial Age in Nyasaland by less passive measures than merely those of waiting and preaching at Chinde.

This was not the only possible black mark against Cockerill as he went up the Zambezi in the latter days of March 1914. He was, after all, following in Booth's footsteps, and he was entering the Protectorate to put some new life into the tangle of sabbatarian, independent native churches which Booth had brought into being. The last thing that the Administration of Nyasaland wanted at this time was new life in the independent African churches, which seemed to them, in the expression often applied to frontier churches by the British Government on the eve of the American Revolution, veritable 'sedition shops'.[57] It would have preferred nothing more than for these little meeting-houses to have passed into quiet oblivion. Despite the complacency which beset so many in Nyasaland in these days, international war was in the air—and no colonial government looks for trouble. It did not want a repetition of Booth's activities. So, when Cockerill arrived at Blantyre on 31 March 1914, it was clear that his movements would be watched. He based himself on Booth's old Shiloh station at Blantyre and spent four months in the Shire Highlands area. Here he went through the usual gamut of a missionary novice : learning enough of the language to get his bearings ; employing 'boys' and building himself some sort of a base ; going down with fever ; finding out the temper of his immediate European neighbours ; making his first essays in preaching and teaching amongst the Africans. What the Government thought of him at this time is uncertain, though it may well have heard that Cockerill, as an outspoken Mid-Westerner, was not afraid to air his opinions of the social conditions which he found in the Protectorate, or to vent his criticisms of any actions that seemed, to his code, unjust. He spoke out to his Africans against the obvious disfavour in which officialdom held the independent native churches, and gave a sympathetic ear to their many grievances—such as the story he was told by an African woman from a village ten miles from the Shiloh station that her people had voluntarily taken down their own independent sabbatarian church lest they should get into trouble with the Administration. Yet none of these things was likely, by itself, to bring Cockerill into open disfavour with the Government. It was only when, on 6 August 1914, he left Blantyre *en route* for the north of Nyasaland to make contact with the further remnants of the chain of Seventh Day Baptist African churches which were left after Booth's break with their parent American body in 1912, that Government suspicion passed over into open disfavour and hostility towards him. For Cockerill was going up into the Kamwana country, into the regions of the Tonga and, more especially, the Ngoni.

On his way north Cockerill would pass through two important groups of Ngoni. The first of these, which lay to the south-west of Lake Nyasa, was known generically as Gomani's Ngoni ; [58] the second and larger group to the north of the lake comprised the main body of Ngoni in the Protectorate, and was called after the great chief of the old days, Mombera.[59] Of these proud offshoots of the Zulu, the Administration could never be certain. It was true that there had been no great trouble with the Ngoni in recent years but one could not be sure in the times of change and stress inside Nyasaland before the War : and with the coming of the War itself, there was no telling what might happen. With both groups of Ngoni there had been friction and fighting before and after the establishment of the Protectorate. Mombera's Ngoni had been 'granted certain privileges at a time when the authorities were busily engaged in suppressing slave raiding and their antagonism was not desired' and 'had ever been disposed to regard themselves as of a superior race to their neighbours'.[60] Of these neighbours, the go-ahead Tonga particularly irked them. And it was a Tonga, Elliott Kamwana, who was sitting at the Chinde mouth at this time, waiting for the coming of the Millennial Age. Ngoni and Tonga views on such a golden age differed considerably : the one looked back to their past as tribal overlords ; the other forward to the new conditions which had freed them from Ngoni suzerainty. In all, the country into which Cockerill was going presented a very complex picture to the Administration, whose last wish was to see old tribal feuds and ambitions touched off again.

Within a week Cockerill was in the area of Gomani's Ngoni and here he met Filipo Chinyama at Ncheu on 9 and 10 August 1914.[61] The European War, it should be remembered, was by this time just over a week old and had already opened on the borders of German East Africa with Nyasaland and British East Africa. Whether at this time, when he met Cockerill, or earlier, when friendly letters had passed between them, Filipo Chinyama was plotting a rising against the Government, in conjunction with John Chilembwe to the south, and with the knowledge of at least one Ngoni headman of the area (Makwangwala of Dedza), is not certain. The American missionary, however, was not concerned with latent African conspiracies when he encountered Filipo Chinyama and discussed mutual interests with him. From Cockerill's point of view there was nothing disgraceful in the association. He had heard of Chinyama as a preacher of the Seventh Day Baptist faith and naturally went to see him. (While he was at Ncheu he officiated at the funeral of a native woman.[62]) Cockerill was not to know the suspicion in which Chinyama had for long been held by the authorities—or if he did know, it was a fact which would disturb him little, for, as a very American American, he had his own suspicions of the motives of British Imperialism. Chinyama had come under the influence of at least four European missions which Booth had founded : the Seventh Day Baptists, of course ; the Seventh-day Adventists ; [63] the Churches of Christ ; [64] and the Baptist Industrial Mission of Scotland.[65] It was from this last mission that he had seceded some time before Cockerill arrived, and he appeared to be planning a 'settlement' on the lines of Chilembwe's P.I.M., though Saturday would be observed as the Sabbath. The District Resident had had his eye on Chinyama's potential Ethiopianism for some time, and although he could not prevent his carrying out informal teaching and preaching, despite repeated requests, he had refused to allow Chinyama to build a church, as this might give his African 'Church of Christ', as he referred to his mission, a definite standing in the area : a status which might draw more followers to him, as Chilembwe's did in the Shire Highlands. No doubt all this was bitterly resented by Chinyama, just as the refusal by the Bruce Estates to allow him to have churches on their land was resented by Chilembwe. If so, Chinyama communicated none of this to Cockerill : and their association was simply that of fellow members of a denomination. Thus, in the area of Gomani's Ngoni, Cockerill might have appeared to the Administration as a nuisance ; but his activities seemed harmless and he was not there long enough to run into any trouble. (But, after the Rising, when Chinyama's part in it was revealed, Cockerill's association with him would be remembered by the Government against the American.) By 18 August at the latest he was out of the area and heading farther north.

All this time the local struggle between British and German forces was taking shape. The British, having gained command of Lake Nyasa by the disablement and capture on 13 August of the German vessel, the *Hermann von Wissmann*, at the moment when Cockerill was on his way to the potential trouble area of Mombera's Ngoni, were sending further forces to the north end of the Lake. By August 22 they had concentrated these at Karonga, some fifteen miles south of the boundary between Nyasaland and German East Africa. Between then and the second week of September, British and German forces manœuvred into positions which resulted on 9 September in the defeat by the British of a German attack on Karonga and the retreat of the German forces.[66] Yet, though the

Germans had been defeated, and this engagement was to prove decisive in maintaining the security of the Nyasaland northern border with German East Africa, it was for long expected that they would return with larger forces to avenge their defeat at Karonga and would possibly sweep down into the Protectorate along the west side of Lake Nyasa. It was towards this troubled region that Cockerill was now moving.

The area, then, in which he arrived about 24 August 1914, was something of a strategic approach to key territory at the extreme north of the Lake. If the Government wished to maintain its military successes there and to stave off possible German counter-attack, it was essential that there should be no trouble in their rear. Mombera's Ngoni were already restless and the paramount chief, Mbalekelwa, or Chimtunga as he was more familiarly known, was ready to direct the other Ngoni chiefs to refuse to supply the military with carriers and other services, and was prepared, when the British Resident of the area sent for him, to send back the defiant answer of 'fetch-him-if-he-could'.[67] Apart from this fear of Ngoni re-calcitrance, trouble between them and the Tonga was also possible in the veiled form of rivalry between the Watch Tower factions who were dominated by the Tonga and looked to the fulfilment of Kamwana's prophetic message, and the Seventh Day Baptist group of Africans, amongst whom was a sizable number of Ngoni. Cockerill's arrival amongst them could have had the effect of touching off conflict between the two rival groups, by creating jealousy amongst that section which was deprived of the status and prestige of association with a white man—and one from America, too, with which, as Booth had often said, the Africans were more likely to find a better future than with Britain. It was a situation pregnant with trouble.

Cockerill spent over six weeks in the area, and then, on 5 October, was called to the office of the Resident at Mzimba. Here he was cautioned about his activities. Four days later this caution had become an informal process of deportation from the region, and within a week he was packed on to a ship on Lake Nyasa and bundled down south to have an interview with the Governor : an interview that was clearly aimed at curtailing all his activities in potential danger spots of the Protectorate. The full details of this strange process are not clear, and the literature of the time, official and un-official, has hardly anything to say about it. Nevertheless the episode is significant for the Chilembwe Rising, not only because, at the

Plate 17(*a*).   Chilembwe's church in construction

late 17(*b*).   Side-view of Chilembwe's church in construction.   Both of these photographs are from Chilembwe's own album and were, presumably, taken between 1911 and 1913

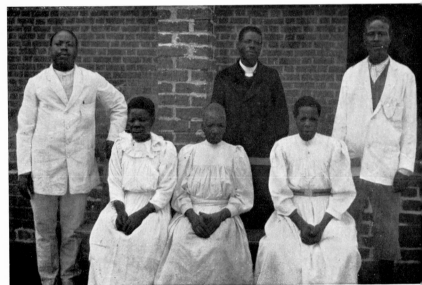

Plate 18. Some members of the P.I.M. (from Chilembwe's own photograph album) *The three men standing are :* Morris Chilembwe; John Chilembwe; Stephen Mkulichi. The women have not been identified

time of it, Cockerill was associated, however innocently, with one of Chilembwe's leading supporters, in the person of Filipo Chinyama, but also because it seems to demonstrate that for the first six months of the War the Government feared that trouble was coming from other quarters : from the Ngoni ; from the regions in which Elliott Kamwana had had the greatest effect and in which his prophecy that the world as it was known then would come to an end in October 1914 would be likely to have the most unsettling effect on the natives. It is this fact which may explain why it was that, despite previous warnings that Chilembwe was planning an insurrection, the Government did not take pains to apprehend him before it was too late : because its attention was diverted to the possibility of more serious native trouble elsewhere in the Protectorate.

In considering Walter Cockerill's deportation from the Ngoni country—there was a second deportation from the Protectorate itself which will be considered later—it is noticeable that not only had he tried to meet Kamwana and had actually met another suspect of sedition, Chinyama, but that, on 4 September 1914, he visited Charles Domingo, supposedly then Booth's chief African follower in the Protectorate, whose piquant criticisms of the Administration have already been noted. Cockerill preached at Domingo's church, which was not far from Mzimba, and the Resident there could not have failed to notice this. That Cockerill did not meet nor, until after the Rising, was apparently interested in Chilembwe, but concentrated on other former African followers of Booth, may also have had something to do with diverting Government suspicions from Chilembwe.

Cockerill himself gave his own account of the circumstances of his first deportation in two letters to his people at home—letters which the censor would have seen and from which he may have passed on passages critical of the Europeans in Nyasaland to the Administration and thus have predisposed them further towards Cockerill's second deportation. In the first, of 10 October 1914, Cockerill wrote :

> I am compelled to stop work for a time, however, as the Government has become suspicious of me and thinks that I am connected with Booth, so the Governor has sent for me. . . . It seems that there is a law that one cannot squat on Government land or stay in native villages and when I asked for land the Government practically refused to sell land for a mission. Then they say they do not wish another mission in Angoniland. We have people here all right and churches but the Government refuses to recognize them and are trying to keep me out of

the country. . . . The Government taxes the natives more than they can stand, for there is practically no work in this country and no good way to earn money. If the natives cannot pay their two dollars per year they are taken by the magistrate and compelled to work about six months in irons.[68] Many natives want me to stay very much but of course they are powerless. . . . The natives of the Watch Tower Mission about Bandawe are very strong and are inclined to make trouble with our people there and the Government is afraid there will be uprisings. . . .

On 20 October, the day after he had seen the Governor, Cockerill wrote home :

. . . a state of war exists between England and Germany and battles have been fought at no great distance from where I was staying, and I have been seized by the British Government as a cause of disturbance. . . . My part of it comes in this way. There is a big tribe of negroes called the Atonga along the shores of Lake Nyasa who have some ideas of freedom from white rule mixed up with some ideas of the Christian religion to such an extent that the Government is much afraid of an uprising among them. The Russellites or Watch Tower people have been sending them native teachers, and literature saying that the world or at least the present order of things would come to an end in October 1914. They are expecting that the Europeans will all leave the country at this time and a black government will be set up. The War and many other things tend to make them think so, as some Europeans have left the country. Now wasn't it romantic for me to drop in among them just at this time in my work of looking up our own people a few of which are scattered among this tribe ? So the Resident Magistrate in this troublesome district wrote to the Governor of Nyasaland to have me removed from his district for fear that my teaching would inflame the natives to revolt against the Government. They thought that I was connected with Booth, and the Watch Tower natives had told everybody that I was coming to see them. There are very few Whites in this district so the Magistrate became alarmed and sent for me. Then Mr. MacDonald, Resident at Mzimba, sent me a letter which I received while at Lusari in Atongaland near So[a ?]nga saying that he had received important information concerning me and wished me to report to him. That was all. I went to him and he put me in charge of an armed native soldier, and sent me to the Resident in the Lake district where the trouble began. This man [Murray of Chintechi] explained to me that it would be better for me to leave the district until after the War. . . . Well, I was placed on board a Lake steamer called the *Chauncy Maples* at Nkata Bay with some soldiers who had come down from the fight at Karonga—two were wounded and sent to Fort Johnston. . . . I had four Ngoni boys with me. Two of the boys are teachers of our Mission who wished to come with me to see the Governor. . . . Monday, October 19, I went to see the Governor. He is an old fellow and a typical George III. He gave me to understand that I was not to return to the North country until after the War. He gave me no satisfactory reason but said I was under grave suspicion. Then he said he thought he had made himself clear which was a signal for me to go. I then intimated to him that he had insulted me and my country whereupon he said he was sorry that I took it that way but said he was obliged to warn me not to go North. That was all. I was summoned without a summons and tried without a trial.

Though the last statement was very correct, the Governor's action was presumably within his powers, under the emergency regulations of war-time. Nevertheless the whole episode was very hastily and high-handedly conducted, and it revealed a state of semi-panic in the official mind which did not augur well for Europeans who fell under disfavour in the aftermath of the Chilembwe Rising, amongst whom Cockerill was to be numbered.

Cockerill and the Governor were obviously at cross-purposes and neither was in a mood to appreciate the other's point of view. In addition to all the causes of confusion which have been reviewed, there was possibly a further factor which would not exactly have reconciled them. It may have grown up around the word 'Ethiopian'. To the Europeans of the Protectorate this word had at that time much of the significance of 'Bolshy' after the War : a general vague term which existed in an atmosphere of combined fear, suspicion, hatred, and indignation at a set of forces that were supposed to be creating subtle and fiendish plots to overthrow the established order. Enough has been said so far about 'Ethiopianism' and its history to make unnecessary a more accurate estimate of exactly what these forces were. For the Administration, then, the term had political connotations. For Cockerill, though he was not unaware of its use in this sense, the word had rather an ethnic and religious significance. He tended to identify it with the actual Ethiopia where the ancient Abyssinian church had sabbatarian beliefs similar to those of his own denomination.[69] Many Africans at the time, though they often used the word in its political form, also employed it in a racial sense with the object, no doubt, of conferring an increase of status upon themselves. Thus, when Cockerill visited certain peoples and chiefs in the area of the Ngoni and Tonga, he was often told that they were

Ethiopians by his African interpreters and others, who employed the term, it seems, in a combined racial and political sense.[70] Cockerill, on the other hand, gave it his religious and ethnic slant, and felt that the Africans he met were either descendants of the Ethiopians or else long ago had been very strongly influenced by them. And so a chain of cross-purposes began. Many of the peoples whom Cockerill met in this way were glad to see him, and expressed the hope that he would stay with them. Naturally, Cockerill was equally friendly. But to the Administration in the far-off Shire Highlands, when the news of this fraternization of Cockerill and 'Ethiopian' Africans was received, it may well have appeared that an extension of an 'Ethiopian' subversive plot was in the making. For observers with semantic interests it all forms an instructive example of the distortion of communication.

For Cockerill it meant that he was debarred from visiting again the more active centres of Seventh Day Baptist activity in Nyasaland. Though he was given permission to live in the Shire Highlands at Chikunda, his field of activity was considerably restricted. But if the Government thought it was finished with him it was mistaken; for his name was to come up again in conjunction with Chilembwe's Rising in 1915, and once more his work was to be misunderstood and he was to be set wandering again. Yet for a little while, perhaps, the Government was to forget about him altogether, as its mind became more and more occupied with the task of raising troops and supplies for the fight against von Lettow-Vorbeck and his soldiers in German East Africa; and its attention, when October 1914 passed and the world remained much as before, was drawn away from the possibility of revolt in the country west of the Lake down into the south where that revolt was actually to take place.

It is, then, more particularly, to this region, to John Chilembwe and the Providence Industrial Mission, that it is necessary to return.

4. THE CHARACTER AND PLANNING OF THE RISING

Between the foreground of any insurrection, where its actual physical results are achieved, and the background in which lines of force that lead to the ultimate outburst may usually be traced with some certainty, there lies a perplexing and frustrating middle distance inside which men with grievances become in turn potential rebels, conspirators, and active insurgents. It is a region which, for even the best-documented rebellions, is full of concealed places and shady corners, that must leave serious gaps in the understanding of the processes whereby a group of people move from the passive to the active mood of revolt, and in the appreciation of the manner in which they organize themselves to this end. In particular, there is always the cardinal problem of trying to explain what goes on inside the heads of the leaders of a conspiracy when they decide at last to stake their all on the desperate outcome of insurrection. Even the worst-organized revolts do not commit too much to paper and the testimony of those who have actually taken part in one, or of officials and others who may have helped to suppress it, if it was a failure, is rightly suspect of partisanship. It is the perennial problem of an insufficiency of documentary materials and of the difficulties of trying to interpret oral evidence. For the Chilembwe Rising the description and analysis of this middle distance is of particular difficulty.

From the documentary point of view there is the irksome fact that what papers were seized in the rebels' houses in 1915 appear to have been lost in the fire of February 1919 in the Nyasaland Secretariat at Zomba. Of these papers, the *Nyasaland Times* wrote that apart 'from the information thus obtained it would have been very difficult to piece together and assign to their true place the various items' that came to hand in the interrogation of the rebels.[71] If this was so but a month after the Rising, how much more difficult must it be forty years later—though, happily, time brings one compensating factor : that African witnesses of the events of 1914–15 are no longer so afraid to hand on their knowledge to the investigator for fear of official displeasure. Yet even this knowledge must come through the blurred focus of memory.

With the realization, then, of all the difficulties of finding one's way through the middle distance, a hesitant step must be taken into this territory, and some attempt must be made to cross it, though it will be obvious that many of its important features will be veiled, and some missed because they have become, by now, almost completely invisible.

A beginning may be made by taking a statement by the 1915 Governor of Nyasaland as a bearing. He wrote of Chilembwe's plans that:

> The movement was designed for the massacre of the whites in the
> Shire Highlands, where they are principally congregated, and for the

suppression of white rule, and there can be no doubt that it had been in the course of preparation for some years by John Chelembwe [*sic*] and the members of the religious fraternity which he had established under the name of the African Baptist Church and Provident [*sic*] Industrial Mission.[72]

With the Governor's description of the object of the rebellion we are not greatly concerned, though it presents too violent a picture of destruction to do justice to Chilembwe's intelligence. Norman Leys, whose impressions of the Rising have already been mentioned in the introduction to this book, gave a more detailed picture of Chilembwe's schemes, which he derived from African participants in prison nearer to the time of the Rising, that seems more accurate:

> His plan was to get the people on the estate [A. L. Bruce lands at Magomero] to murder their masters, and then to bring about a general rebellion. He had a list of all the Europeans in the country, of whom some were to be killed out of hand; others, including the women and children, were to be expelled from the country; while a few, men and women, were to be allowed to remain as teachers, but without political authority.[73]

Such a statement suggests that Chilembwe had some rudimentary picture of an African state which could be set up in Nyasaland, should his plot prove successful. But what is of concern here in the discussion of the Governor's statement is less the character of the object than the time factor involved in it: the Governor's assertion that 'there can be no doubt that it had been in the course of preparation for some years'. If this statement is correct, then the middle distance of the Rising obviously goes back some years.

However, it seems that the Governor, as in his conception of a total massacre of the Europeans, was guilty of exaggeration. (A further indication of the accuracy of his statement may be taken from the fact that he could not get the name of Chilembwe's mission correct, but referred to it as 'Provident' instead of 'Providence Industrial Mission'.[74]) The expression 'some years' suggests over two years and indicates a more carefully laid plot than can have been the case. Though the Rising did have an organization, much of its failure may be attributed to the fact that it was hastily arranged: a fact which does not suggest years of planning. It may, perhaps, be interjected here that a long time would have been needed for the planning of the revolt if Leys' statement that Chilembwe had a list of all the Europeans in the country is correct, for the composition of this list would take some time in the conditions of Nyasaland before the First World War. In 1914–15 it has been estimated that there were 831 Europeans in Nyasaland. But of these, 741 were in the Shire Highlands in the areas of Zomba and Blantyre.[75] As both of these areas were close to Chilembwe's sphere of work, and as a perennial topic of African conversation was the movements and habits of Europeans, such a list would not take long to compile. If evidence is needed for the longevity of Chilembwe's planning of revolt, it must be sought elsewhere.

A more convincing piece of circumstantial evidence for this is the character of the large brick church which Chilembwe built on his mission land and which was the pride of the P.I.M. and its American Negro backers.[76] Though the building could not compare with the great Blantyre church designed by David Clement Scott for intricacy of structure and design, it was none the less a remarkable achievement, for it seems that Chilembwe himself conceived the idea of it and supervised the construction in every detail (see photographs, p. 214). The building was opened formally by some of the near-by missionaries from the Zambesi Industrial Mission, it appears, in 1913.[77] Its construction was very sturdy and the walls were built three bricks thick. It was this fact which was commented on by many Europeans after the Rising. They claimed that Chilembwe had done this deliberately so that his church could be used as an arsenal and fort for his projected rebellion.[78] The sturdiness of the building was illustrated further by the trouble which had to be taken to blow it up after the Rising. Yet these circumstantial facts seem to prove nothing else than that Chilembwe had to build the walls of his church substantially because it had two towers and a large roof to carry, and that he felt that he should build as solidly as he could in order to follow in the tradition of European respectability which so often demonstrated itself in the size and solidity of its places of worship. It is true that Chilembwe often called his church 'Jerusalem' or 'New Jerusalem', and that this might be taken as an echo of the Jerusalem, Virginia, to which Nat Turner, the Negro Baptist insurrectionist, had turned his attention in 1831.[79] But such a construction would be as fanciful as to suppose that, in building his big church, Chilembwe was using other memories of his American stay and was harking back to the construction of the great citadel in Haiti by the Negro revolutionary, King Christophe![80]

It is more in accordance with what has been indicated of Chilembwe's 'respectable' character so far, to suppose that his brick church was an expression of his own status and of what he felt should be the standing of his mission and its congregations. It certainly reveals an ambitious cast of mind—but it must also be remembered that other Africans in the Protectorate, though on a less ambitious scale and with backing from the Scottish and other missionaries, were building their own brick churches.[81]   The fact, too, that some of the Zambesi Industrial Missionaries were interested in his work and were present at the church's opening in 1913, may be taken as additional evidence that Chilembwe's intention in building the church was completely legitimate and in no way connected with a long-term plan of insurrection.

One other fact must be considered in deciding how far back to date the planning of the revolt.   This is a Biblical text which Chilembwe is said to have used when, in the months before the Rising, his teaching to his P.I.M. flock became clearly militant.   It was from Acts ('Macitidwe', to the Africans of Nyasaland), xx, 29-32.   Verse 31 of this text reads : '. . . remember, that by the space of three years I ceased not to warn every one day and night with tears'.[82]   If this verse in the context of nearness to the Rising was used as Biblical backing for militant teaching some time towards the end of 1914, or the beginning of 1915, it suggests that Chilembwe's warning to his Africans—presumably of the encroachment of the neighbouring Europeans on their lands and liberties—went back to 1911 or 1912.   This, however, cannot be taken to mean that Chilembwe had started an anti-European conspiracy three years before the Rising took place.   What it seems to mean is that, by this time, he was becoming increasingly critical of Europeans in the Protectorate, and was pointing out to his Africans what their rule might ultimately mean.   It could also be taken to suggest that, after the apparent failure of his African Industrial Society in 1911, when, as has been seen, Chilembwe thanked the Government for what it had done to promote cotton-growing amongst Africans and had been more critical of the Indians than the Europeans in the Pro-tectorate, he began to feel increasingly that all schemes for African betterment in Nyasaland were doomed to failure unless great changes took place.   But this is mere supposition, though the increase of Chilembwe's 'warnings' over a three-year period may well have been connected with the failure of this scheme for African co-operation.

What is really at issue is when Chilembwe's feelings towards the Europeans passed from those of cool co-operation, through criticism, to bitter anger, hostility, and finally conspiracy. By 1912 his attitude towards many Europeans had much in common with Charles Domingo's : [83] but nothing more militant. In 1913 changes and stresses in the Protectorate may have acerbated his feelings and made him more critical, but the evidence of actual conspiracy at this stage is still negligible. It is possible that at this point Chilembwe said privately to his friends many rash things, such as that he wished all the Europeans were dead and out of the Protectorate ; [84] but rash statements do not constitute a conspiracy. In his case, however, they do perhaps mark a turning-point which led easily into plotting and insurrection, for in 1914 Chilembwe appears to have been advocating secretly to his African congregations the non-payment of taxes,[85] and in July 1914 clear warning was given to the authorities that he was plotting a rebellion. This warning will be examined later : [86] but it may be said at this stage that it is still not clear proof that an actual organization of insurrection was emerging. It could have meant merely that Chilembwe was suggesting rebellion to his African followers as one amongst several alternatives for improving their status and conditions. Organization in the strictest sense does not appear to have come into being until after the European War had broken out in August 1914 and, by the battle of Karonga, had made itself felt to Africans in Nyasaland.

Thus the middle distance between the foreground and background of the 1915 Rising, sketchy though the analysis may be, can be divided into two parts. First, there is the period opening somewhere in 1913 when Chilembwe's feelings towards selected Europeans in the Protectorate became increasingly bitter and hostile and when the concept but not the carrying-out of a conspiracy may have occurred to him ; and secondly, there is the generalization of these feelings towards the greater part of the Europeans in Nyasaland during 1914—a process in which the outbreak of the War played a major role—and their passing over into actual concrete plotting against the British. In the first part, the 1913 period, the worsening of relations between the Bruce Estates at Magomero and the Providence Industrial Mission was responsible for the dynamic of Chilembwe's feelings at this time.

That relations between Chilembwe and his following and the manager and European members of the A. L. Bruce Estates were not good has already been indicated, and the suggestion has been made that they began to worsen about 1909. In 1913 these relations appear to have deteriorated further. It does not seem unreasonable to suppose that in this year the owners of the Estates decided to tighten up their administration: 1913 was, after all, despite all the optimism at official and unofficial celebrations, a year of intermittent famine, when labour was scarce, and labour relations, testy at the best of times, became even more difficult. And on 2 May the A. L. Bruce Estates at Magomero and Lukulezi were formally incorporated and a share capital of £54,000 issued. In the Memorandum of Association of the new company wide terms of business were outlined and it seems clear that it was the intention of the owners to advance considerably the cost price of the Estates which was at that time quoted as £41,220 : 12 : 6. The manager, W. J. Livingstone, had a clear interest in this, for he had 500 £1 shares in the new company.[87] But to achieve these aims at a time of change and stress in the Protectorate would mean a tightening of the Estates' administration. When A. L. Bruce, their head, spoke in the Legislative Council in April 1914 in favour of a labour rent for tenants on European Estates, he had more than the general land situation in Nyasaland in mind. As he put it: '. . . at Magomero the extension of the area under cultivation very largely depends on the number of new tenants who settled the land', and if these did not pay their rent, then the labour force should be disciplined by the evacuation of unreliable tenants.[88]

This was the major problem of the Estates at a time of declared economic expansion: how most effectively to organize and discipline their labour force. The labour force also had its own ideas about the process, which was conducted with a rigorous rationalization not unlike that in the Scottish Highlands after the '45, and rival concepts of land tenure of the newer, more sophisticated owners and the more primitive, less settled peoples of the areas concerned, clashed with each other as they had done a century and a half before in the Highlands of Scotland.[89] That W. J. Livingstone, on whom as manager fell the task of settling these problems, was himself a Highlander of a traditional group which was more used to giving than to taking orders, added to the parallel and also indicated the difficulties which lay in the way of a solution. For many Africans who were to follow Chilembwe 'Bwana Liston' or 'Listonia', as Livingstone came to be called by the local people, grew to be a focus for their discontents. But undue concentration upon him has drawn attention away from the fact that he was not the only European on Chilembwe's list for liquidation. If W. J. Livingstone had not attracted the animus of many Africans before and especially after 1913,[90] he and the Estates he managed might still have been the centre of attack, for he was the most tangible representative of the administration of what the rebels conceived the most typical and threatening of the new European economic units which had come to challenge their traditional way of life on one hand, and their hopes of surmounting this by emulation of the Europeans themselves on the other. And when the owner of the Estates, A. L. Bruce, son of the founder, at the beginning of the War went away to the north of Lake Nyasa to serve with the Army, W. J. Livingstone became even more isolated as a representative of the Estates. Thus not only his own often domineering attitude towards his employees and local Africans, but actual economic forces within the Protectorate and on the Estates themselves were making it more than likely that if a rising was decided on, the blow would, in all probability, fall first of all on him.

His task as manager of one of the largest European land units in the Protectorate was no easy one. The overrunning of the Estates by Nguru from Portuguese East Africa was an outstanding disciplinary problem for the labour force, though it seems that nothing was done to discourage them from settling on the Estates as tenants who would pay their rent in kind with labour. The popularity of sabbatarian doctrines amongst some Africans was a further problem, for it meant that many of them would not work on Saturdays, or, if they were forced to work, did so reluctantly and half-heartedly. That Chilembwe's P.I.M. was non-sabbatarian in its teaching would make little difference, for Chilembwe was known as one of Booth's 'boys', and that would be enough to brand his followers as potentially sabbatarian and seditious. Furthermore, a general habit amongst the Africans of cutting down timber or hunting game indiscriminately had to be stopped if the resources and amenities of the Estates were to be preserved, and erosion prevented.[91] And to add to all of W. J. Livingstone's difficulties, the months between November and March, the rainy season, appear to have been a general time of labour shortage for the Shire Highlands.[92] It is not unlikely, therefore, that the Estates' management found it necessary to 'tighten the screws' on its depleted labour force during these months. This, with other factors that will be examined, clearly had much to do with the timing of the Rising. And then there were disputes with other European land-holders : for example, the case between the Bruce Estates and the neighbouring Blantyre and East Africa Company in March 1914, about their mutual boundaries.[93] All added to the manager's difficulties.

He was determined to keep churches off the Estates : because, as in so many of the plantations in the Old South, by disturbing their native labour force, through providing potential centres of agitation against the management, and by establishing claims to land which might be needed in the course of development, they interfered with what the management considered to be the most efficient way of handling the Estates. Chilembwe's conflicts with W. J. Livingstone over the building of churches have already been noticed. In 1912 two P.I.M. churches on the Estates had been burnt down. Then, to quote African testimony :

> In 1913, Chilembwe built another church at Cikomwe on Government land next door to Magomero Estate. Livingstone also burned this down. This time Chilembwe went to the Government in Zomba to complain, but the complaint was not received with any sympathy. This made him angry, but to pacify him he was told to leave it to the Government to deal with the matter. Nothing was ever done. . . .[94]

An official European version of such a process notes that complaint was made 'to Mr. Cruise, Assistant Magistrate at Chiradzulu, who supported Mr. Livingstone's action'.[95] Thus it would appear that, from a local dissatisfaction, Chilembwe's bitterness widened to include the Government itself, which seemed to be doing nothing to rectify what he considered to be just grievances. When it is remembered, too, to what extent the building of churches symbolized for many Africans the advancement of their status, to curtail their erection seemed tantamount to a bar on African progress.

Such infringement of status, trifling as it might have seemed to many Europeans, showed itself in other ways that caught the imagination of numerous potential Chilembwe followers as much as their purely economic grievances. Some of these manifestations have already been noted in Chapter IV, but their accumulation on the eve of the Rising and the manner in which they were bitterly resented by the Chilembwe-ites justify some recapitulation and expansion now. One manifestation was resentment at a widespread

European insistence that the African, if he had the temerity to wear a hat and 'ape the European' should raise it whenever he came into contact with a white man, or that he should give some equally respectful form of salutation. There was the prejudice, too, that many Europeans felt about Africans who wore European clothing—and the Chilembwe flock, with their pastor's insistence on high standards of European dress, would be particularly bad offenders in this respect. Chilembwe, too, annoyed many in the neighbourhood by his habit of entering European stores and buying articles of clothing for his wife, such as silk stockings, which many considered to be the prerogative of Europeans only.[96] And there were other ways than pure, overt rudeness to make Chilembwe and Africans like him who had 'ideas above their stations' feel resentful. These forms of social prejudice were not proscribed in the Protectorate and there is no doubt that they were widespread. African accounts suggest that they were particularly notable on the A. L. Bruce Estates where the acute problems of maintaining, extending, and disciplining a comparatively large labour force seemed to the management and owners to require a type of African who 'knew his place', and numbers of African 'horror stories' grew up about the steps to which the manager would go to ensure this.

If such social manifestations of worsening relations between African and European in the neighbourhood of the Magomero Estates were often evidenced in the symbolic way in which they revealed themselves to Africans, these relations had a clear economic base. Whatever the rights and wrongs of ownership, or the almost unbelievable difficulties in the way of resolving them that had been created by the so-called land 'settlement' of the first Commissioner-General, Africans could not help noticing that the Bruce Estates, with the labour force of a thousand Africans, covered some three hundred square miles,[97] a great block of land over which many of them—though certainly not the immigrant Nguru—had at one time been accustomed to move as they wished but on which their movements were now subject to all manner of restrictions. That some restrictions were necessary if efficient and progressive production was to take the place of the traditionally anarchic and wasteful native methods of cultivation was disregarded by most Africans. Those who considered them, such as Chilembwe and his lieutenants, were prone to ask bitterly in whose favour ultimately such regulations worked : the African's or the European's. Had these regulations, however, been administered with a little more sympathy towards the African view-point, irritating though it often seemed to be, much friction could have been avoided and, perhaps, the eventual flame which grew out of it might have been prevented. The summary of African economic grievances about the Magomero Estates by the official Commission of Inquiry into Chilembwe's Rising supports this point, and indicates not only their character but also the basis for the worsening of relations between African and European in this area shortly before the outbreak of the War :

> We think although the grievances of natives on these estates was no doubt exaggerated by Chilembwe for his own purposes that in certain respects their treatment was not satisfactory. We are of the opinion that Mr. Livingstone's treatment of natives was often unduly harsh, and apart from this the general system of estates management was unsatisfactory. The tenant system was that natives living on the land were compelled to work for the estates. No money rent was accepted. Natives were compelled to work one month in the wet season for rent and anothe month also in the wet season for Hut Tax, that is two months' work. A month was reckoned at twenty-eight days' actual work, and it was stated before the Commission that by various devices natives were compelled to work considerably longer periods, e.g. if a native did not complete his day's task, no credit was given to him for the time he had worked, and occasionally he had to work several days extra to make up for the day lost. The labour roll books of the estates were exhibited to the Commission and it clearly appeared from them that the safeguards laid down in the 'Employment of Natives Ordinance' for ensuring the proper payment of natives were not complied with. It was impossible to discover from them either the rate of pay of an individual native or the days on which he had worked, or in some cases whether he had been paid or not. While the native evidence must be received with caution, the Commissioners are of the opinion that the treatment of labour and the system of tenancy on the Bruce Estates (labourers and tenants being practically interchangeable terms) were in several respects illegal and oppressive and that the conditions on the estates more especially in the Magomero estate directly conduced to the rising.[98]

The official statement provides a conclusion for the first part of a tentative analysis of the 'middle distance' of Chilembwe's rebellion. The second part, the effect of the outbreak of the War on his potential conspiracy, may now be examined.

The effect of the Great War on the Rising was, in general, two-fold. First, as a new and terrible phenomenon which brought to the African fresh rigours and responsibilities that he had no inclination to experience, it helped to generalize Chilembwe's feelings from an animus against a relatively closed society of Europeans to a bitterness against the whole principle and practice of white rule in the Protectorate. And, secondly, the embarrassment which the outbreak of War brought to the Nyasaland Government provided Chilembwe with an opportunity to bring out into the open a conspiracy which may only have been latent before 4 August 1914, when the War was declared.

Despite the hopes raised by certain clauses of the Berlin Act of 1885 (the first important international agreement to try to formalize the European scramble for Africa) that in time of war the African territories would be neutralized,[99] the Great War, with all its unsettlement and uncertainty, did not spare Nyasaland. It 'struck the black man like a thunderbolt. It was beyond his comprehension altogether. Yet though he was soon to learn that he had nothing to do with it, it had everything to do with him.'[100] At the outbreak of the War, the King's African Rifles was considerably below strength in Nyasaland,[101] and rapid recruitment was the order of the day. Not only soldiers were needed but also carriers for the munitions and supplies for the kind of war that was developing in German East Africa. Porters, or *tenga-tenga* as they were generally known, were indispensable, because the communications and transport of East and Central Africa were primitive and totally inadequate for the military tasks at hand. Economic inducements often rallied recruits, but sometimes they were appointed by chiefs or headmen as part of a quota assigned to them by the Government. As a result, in Nyasaland, at the beginning of the war prices rose, and although these were stabilized after a few months, they were always fluctuating and often the cause of discontent. Many of the carriers suffered considerable hardships as a result of the arduous conditions of service, and the folk at home tended to suffer with them and their soldier companions, for the relatively large number recruited drew away from the villages vitally important labour that was needed for the growing of general subsistence crops.[102] The coming of the War, indeed, had something of the same drastic effect on native society in Nyasaland which the first sudden thrust of Europeans into the country had produced.

And, as on that occasion, when some Central Africans had had premonitions that something was about to happen, before it actually did,[103] so on the eve of the Great War, rumours were circulating among them that a conflict between the European Powers was imminent, and speculations, mostly unsettling, were the consequence. The Livingstonia missionaries noted this and observed that 'The official confirmation of the news, however, caused great commotion among the people'.[104] In the Dzunje-Ncheu areas, where a supporting rising to Chilembwe's under Filipo Chinyama's leadership was being plotted, the character of this commotion amongst Africans was analysed by an independent European missionary :

> They can't understand the war, and ask such questions as 'Are the Germans Christians ? Why have the Christian countries gone to war ? Have the evil spirits got into the hearts of the Kings ? ' They know more about this war than they did about the war in South Africa [the Boer War]. . . . Now thousands of natives are in Rhodesia and further south in the mines and many of them can read their own and the English language to know all that is taking place in the world.[105]

Africans themselves left their own record of the unsettlement which the War had brought to them. It seemed, indeed, to many that the Watch Tower prophecy that the world would end in October 1914 was about to come true. As one African in his faltering English wrote to *The Watchtower* magazine of September 1914 in America :

> Surely we are living in the Time of the End, according to the Scriptures. We are seeing the clergy people turning the word of God into tables. They think they can stop the Christian people from sinning— as they call it—by whipping and putting them in prison and by making them pay so much money. Can this stop the people sinning ? No : not at all ! . . . But we learn in the Bible that the deliverer shall come. . . People may remember that our Lord found the people of Israel doing wrong against the word of God, and they were proud. But we never see a single line in the Bible saying that he took everyone of the Jews to the Roman Governor, to be put in prison. . . . In Nyassaland we see many things which have been preached in our churches, and what we are learning [from] the Volumes (Pastor Russell's *Studies in the Scriptures*) and WATCH TOWER—all these things are now being fulfilled.

This letter from a Nyasaland African adherent of the Watch Tower affords evidence not only of the way in which the coming of the War seemed to many Africans an event of apocalyptic magnitude, and of the manner in which they coupled to this impression many of their grievances against the European and his Administration in

Courtesy Mr. W. Sanderson

Plate 19.   A group at the P.I.M. (from Chilembwe's own photograph album) : probably
taken about 1911 or 1912.   Chilembwe is seated at the extreme left

PROVIDENCE INDUSTRIAL MISSION,
CHIRADZULO,
BLANTYRE.

The bearer Nelson is one of our scholars, during the school vacation he wishes to work any where. We shall be much obliged if he can get some employment.

John. Chilembwe

Plate 20(*a*). Specimen of Chilembwe's best handwriting

Plate 20(*b*). Churches of Christ meeting-house built by Africans the Protectorate, but it may also be taken as a convenient moment to pause and ask what was the connection between the American Watch Tower belief and the Chilembwe Rising.

Chilembwe himself has often been accused with varying degrees of odium of being an adherent of Watch Tower. The designation of him in the official *History of the Great War* as a 'religious fanatic . . . of the so-called "Watch Tower" sect' [106] is one of the less derogatory variations on this theme.[107] But it should be noticed first of all that nowhere in the Report of the official Commission of Inquiry into the Rising was Watch Tower specifically connected with Chilembwe. Certainly, the circulation of its literature in Nyasaland was mentioned as affecting the Rising and its prohibition from the Protectorate on the grounds of its being 'inflammatory' was recommended : [108] but the Report does not link Chilembwe directly with the movement. In fact, though some of Chilembwe's following may have been swayed by Watch Tower publications [109] and preaching, there is no direct available evidence to suggest that he himself was in any way influenced by them. His theology appears to have been constantly of the more orthodox Baptist kind, and does not seem to have developed much beyond that of the 1896–7 separatist church which he and Joseph Booth had planned.[110] It is true that the quotations from the Epistle of James, Chapter V, which have already been noticed,[111] and which were used, no doubt, as a description, accusation and threat for the conditions on the Magomero Estates— '. . . the hire of the labourers who have reaped down your fields, which is of you kept back by fraud, crieth . . .'—were also construed in a similar sense in the *Studies* of Pastor Russell.[112] But this may be no more than a coincidence ; and if it is not, this does not presuppose any causal link between the leader of the Rising and the American body. Though the subject will be discussed again, the real fact of the matter seems to be that the Watch Tower interpretation of history affected some of Chilembwe's followers [113] and no more. The Watch Tower magazine circulated to some postal subscribers in Nyasaland and may have been brought in by mining boys returning from South Africa. 'Berean Bibles', or copies of the King James version of the Scriptures to which was attached a Watch Tower commentary, were in the possession of some Africans ; and Russell's volumes were used as teaching material for the learning of English in some of the little schools of the African independent churches not so much, perhaps, because of their doctrine but because they were cheap or often obtainable free. That any African who read them would have brought before his eyes a wide range of political thinking and sampling,[114] or that this thought was often strongly critical of established institutions, secular and religious, is undeniable. But it must also be noted that nowhere in the Russell volumes was it suggested that the believers in his teachings should take active steps to hasten the overthrow of these institutions in preparation for the Millennial Age : rather they were recommended to wait patiently for divine intervention.[115] In sum, Chilembwe's function was to act as a rallying-point for a number of groups of Africans from independent churches and some from the established European missions. Amongst these groups, African adherents of Watch Tower, some of the rump of Kamwana's following, comprised one section but by no means the most important. Its distinctive feature was its prophecy for October 1914. But Chilembwe, while he was doubtless aware of this, seems to have been in no way influenced by Watch Tower eschatology, which had always had its main influence in Nyasaland to the west of the Lake and not so much in the Shire Highlands.

Had Chilembwe indeed been a genuine follower of Russell's teachings he would have had much clearer convictions about the character of the War than he appears to have had. He would have seen it as the inevitable fulfilment of the Scriptures, the disintegrator of the established orders and the herald of the New Millennial Age. As it was, the advent of the War at first appears only to have brought the greatest confusion and fear to Chilembwe : complex feelings which suggest not that he saw it as a portent of hope but rather as a harbinger of dreadful forces which could bring nothing but unhappiness and further 'bondage' for his people. It had caused a rise in the price of all essential commodities and Chilembwe was already financially embarrassed. Though he had collected large sums of money from local Africans for the building of his brick church—over £300 according to one informant, and very much more according to others [116]—its final erection had been completed at a time when labour was expensive in the Protectorate owing to the scarcity of food, and it is very likely that Chilembwe was heavily in debt over it. Certainly, in 1913 his own testimony has recorded that he was forced to run into debt for ' $100 ' because of the famine conditions.[117] He may well have been deprived of the means for supplementing his income either by the refusal of the authorities to issue him with a gun licence or by the fact that his over-spending on his mission—and probably on himself and his family, for he identified them all closely with the P.I.M.—meant that he did not have enough money to buy a licence so that he could go out shooting game for sale and elephants for their ivory as he had done in the past.[118]   It should also be noted that in 1913 Chilembwe lost what was probably a substantial section of his income, when a three-year period of donations from an American sympathizer came to an end.[119]   There is certainly a note of mingled fear and desperation in the last letter which he seems to have written to his American Negro sponsors :

> I am afraid of the war, which exists between Great Britain and Germany, war the results of which are world wide, and which has already paralyzed all business in Africa.   I don't know how you can help us, but by all means try to send us something to sustain our lives and bodies, for we, as well as those who are taking part are greatly in need.   Please in some way send us help, or leave us to die if you choose. At this writing I am penniless.   Pray that God in his Chariot may bring messengers of peace and that the Nations may be brought back to the Temple of Peace.[120]

This letter was printed in the National Baptist Convention missionary journal for October 1914, and, as there was usually a gap of a month or so before they published Chilembwe's letters, it is likely that it was written in the early days of the War.   The War had not been in existence for six weeks, when the Nyasaland contingent of the King's African Rifles at the northern end of Lake Nyasa was in action on 8 and 9 September against the Germans at Karonga. 'The casualties on both sides were heavy for the forces engaged, each about 400 rifles' : [121] the British lost sixty men, of whom forty-nine were Africans ; and the Germans a hundred and twenty-two, of whom a hundred and more were Africans.   Some of the action was fought in dense forest and the whole Karonga affair had something of the uncertainty and horror of jungle warfare.[122]   Though both casualties and horror seem slight beside the losses of more recent wars, it was the first battle of modern, international war in which Nyasaland forces were participants and it made a deep impression on Africans in the Protectorate.   Politically conscious Africans like Chilembwe read of it in the local paper and may have heard first-hand accounts of it from any wounded who were brought south. They did not fail to notice that the majority of casualties were African. Once again Chilembwe was stung to protest against the employment of native troops in European wars, as he had done on his return from America about the use of Nyasaland *askari* in the Ashanti and Somaliland campaigns. This time his protest carried his additional force of increased bitterness against the Europeans, and a feeling of despairing confusion about the new World War. It also provided the last public document to which Chilembwe set his hand.

This took the form of a letter which Chilembwe wrote to the *Nyasaland Times*. The paper so handled the publication of this as to bring down upon it the wrath of the censor and the Government, and it seems that copies of the offending issue were seized. But at least one copy of the letter has survived. Because the document has considerable importance for the determination of the dating and the character of Chilembwe's conspiracy, it must be published in full :

THE VOICE OF AFRICAN NATIVES IN THE PRESENT WAR

We understand that we have been invited to shed our innocent blood in this world's war which is now in progress throughout the wide world.

On the commencement of the war we understood that it was said indirectly that Africa had nothing to do with the civilised war.[123] But now we find that the poor African has already been plunged into the great war.

A number of our people have already shed their blood, while some are crippled for life. And an open declaration has been issued. A number of Police are marching in various villages persuading well built natives to join in the war. The masses of our people are ready to put on uniforms ignorant of what they have to face or why they have to face it.

We ask the Honourable government of our country which is known as Nyasaland, Will there be any good prospects for the natives after the end of the war ? Shall we be recognised as anybody in the best interests of civilisation and Christianity after the great struggle is ended ?

Because we are imposed upon more than any other nationality under the sun. Any true gentleman who will read this without the eye of prejudice will agree and recognise the fact that the natives have been loyal since the commencement of this Government, and that in all departments of Nyasaland their welfare has been incomplete without us. And no time have we been ever known to betray any trust, national or otherwise, confided to us. Everybody knows that the natives have been loyal to all Nyasaland interests and Nyasaland institutions. For our part we have never allowed the Nyasaland flag to touch the ground, while honour and credit have often gone to others. We have unreservedly stepped to the firing line in every conflict and played a patriot's part with the Spirit of true gallantry. But in time of peace the Government failed to help the underdog. In time of peace everything for Europeans only. And instead of honour we suffer humiliation with names contemptible. But in time of war it has been found that we are needed to share hardships and shed our blood in equality. It is true that we have no voice in this Government. It is even true that there is a spot of our blood in the cross of the Nyasaland Government.

But regarding this world-wide war, we understand that this was not a royal war, nor a government war, nor a war of gain for any description ; it is a war of free nations against a devilish system of imperial domination and national spoliation.

If this were a war as above mentioned such as war for honour, Government gain of riches, etc., we would have been boldly told : Let the rich men, bankers, titled men, storekeepers, farmers and landlords go to war and get shot. Instead the poor Africans who have nothing to own in this present world, who in death, leave only a long line of widows and orphans in utter want and dire distress are invited to die for a cause which is not theirs. It is too late now to talk of what might or might not have been. Whatsoever be the reasons why we are invited to join in the war, the fact remains, we are invited to die for Nyasaland. We leave all for the consideration of the Government, we hope in the Mercy of Almighty God, that some day things will turn out well and that Government will recognise our indispensibility, and that justice will prevail.

JOHN CHILEMBWE,

In behalf of his countrymen.[124]

So far as can be gathered, this strange but moving document was written at some time between the Karonga affair on 8-9 September and 4 December 1914. The latter date is chosen as a limit because it was the day on which Walter Cockerill, still cooling his heels in a limited mission sphere around Blantyre, wrote home to his family in America, and included a few lively comments that seem to refer to the circumstances of the publication of Chilembwe's letter or to some very similar issue, and which conclude with an implicit prophecy that was soon to be realized. He said :

The Editor in Blantyre published something that was not sent to the censor first, and the paper was seized . . . and proclamations were tacked up the same as if the town was under martial law. You may be glad you do not live in the Old World. This government is the pettiest one on earth and most officious and despotic. It doesn't give a hand for individual rights. They are so deadly afraid of a native insurrection.[125]

Using these dates as a guide, a check of the files of the *Nyasaland Times* makes it appear highly likely that the issue of the paper which caused all the trouble was No. 48 of 26 November 1914.[126] In the following issue, the editor referred in veiled terms to what appears to be this episode. After regretting the inconvenience caused 'by the holding up in the post of the last issue of the *Nyasaland Times* by the Resident', he added that at 'about the hour of publication a police guard was placed round the "Print" and the papers not already distributed, seized'. Rhymed commentary by a local wag was added :

> Remember, Remember,
> This month is November
>   The Gunpowder Treason and Plot.
> I see no reason,
> Any trumped up Treason
>   Should ever be forgot.

Four verses in the same vein followed, each of them harping ironically on the 'plot'. Had the author possessed at this time even the slightest suspicion that a plot really was in the offing at the P.I.M. he would have been much less inclined to levity !

Indeed, if this hypothesis about the date of composition and printing of Chilembwe's letter is correct, it suggests a number of considerations about his conspiracy. The first clear warning to reach the authorities that he was preparing for a rebellion came at the end of July 1914. A native teacher of the Roman Catholic Montfort Marist Fathers Mission at Nguludi, Eugenio of Matuta Village, told his Superior that Chilembwe was planning a rising, and that he intended to kill all the Europeans of the country, as well as those Africans who would not join him, and then make himself spiritual and temporal head of Nyasaland. He was, said the teacher, holding secret meetings at night, and was gathering arms for a first objective : a march on Zomba and Blantyre where he would obtain further arms and ammunition. The story had come to him from another teacher, one Paulos of Masanjala Village who, in his turn, had heard it from a certain Morson, a member of Chilembwe's mission. Both men were instructed to inquire discreetly in neighbouring villages about such rumours. Meanwhile the Superior had received a letter from his mission station at Zomba in which these rumours were again mentioned. He reported what he knew to Mr. Mitchell, who was then in charge of Chiradzulu sub-district, who in turn referred it to the District Resident, Mr. Moggridge. Morson was called to the Residency to be cross-examined, but he denied all accusations against the P.I.M.; and more direct inquiries were made at Chilembwe's mission itself but nothing was revealed and the Government was unable to take any very direct action.[127] Though the whole chain of rumours was most indirect and the Government could find no substance in them, this does not necessarily mean that they had no validity, for it is perhaps significant that one of the first actions of Chilembwe's men, after the murder of W. J. Livingstone, was to sack and burn the Nguludi Mission and half-kill one of its priests. This action may have been a simple one of revenge against the mission for its part in giving warning to the authorities. But it may just as well have been motivated by a knowledge of the Roman Church as an inveterate enemy of all forms of separatist churches.[128]

Thus, it seems that the July 1914 warning cannot be taken as clear evidence that Chilembwe had a definite conspiracy in progress. But if it was correct, and Chilembwe in July 1914 really was plotting rebellion, then what is one to make of his two letters on the War that have just been quoted: the one to his American Negro backers and the one to the *Nyasaland Times*? While it is just possible that the confused and despairing letter which he sent to the National Baptist Convention could have been written while a plot was in progress, for that missionary body was far away, is it likely that he would have written the letter to the local paper which drew down the wrath of the censor and the government: a letter which, despite its patriotic references and its resigned note at the end, would be looked at askance by the Government and would lead them to investigate further the possibility of his leading an insurrection, as the July rumour had suggested? Is it probable that Chilembwe would have invited a second investigation of his mission station, and thus have jeopardized any plot that he had brewing? Certainly, as it will appear, Chilembwe's Rising was not a model of revolutionary organization, but is it likely that he would be so inefficient a conspirator as to go out of his way to invite exposure? Of course, it is possible that the letter was written with the intention of suggesting just such considerations to the Authorities so that they would leave him alone. If this is true, it suggests that Chilembwe was capable of a greater degree of sophisticated intrigue than is apparent from the general tenor of his insurrection. It is much more likely that he wrote this letter with the full knowledge that it could lead to his arrest under the summary emergency powers which the Governor had taken on himself. Perhaps, some may say, he sought such arrest so that he could pose as a martyr and provide an occasion for an outburst of popular feeling to support a secret movement for insurrection, under the actual leadership of others, which he had planned long ago. This, again, makes him out to be a much more clever conspirator than he apparently was.

Unless other evidence is produced to the contrary, the circumstances of his two war-time letters—particularly the second—make it seem very probable that Chilembwe's actual conspiracy was hatched only a few months before the Rising in January 1915, and that it had been precipitated by the War itself. Indeed, after reading Chilembwe's anti-War letter to the *Nyasaland Times*, who can doubt that the assertion in the official *History of the Great War* that the Rising was 'unconnected with the war' is very far from the truth? [129] The War provided Chilembwe not merely with an opportunity to strike when the Government was embarrassed by military considerations; [130] but, because of the confusing and depressing circumstances of the international struggle, especially after the Nyasaland casualties at Karonga, it also brought to a head all his feelings against the European State, and made him convinced that some gesture was necessary, however liable it was to fail, in order to demonstrate to the Europeans that there was a limit to which they could drive the Africans. This does not mean that Chilembwe did not envisage the possibility of success and that he had no plans for some form of native state with himself as head, and cadres of selected Europeans to help him, in the case of victory. Nor does it mean that, after 1912–13, when his feelings towards Europeans in the Protectorate seem to have become progressively embittered, he did not discuss an insurrection as a possible reaction to British rule in the Protectorate with the tried and trusted of the P.I.M.[131] It is very probable that it was such a discussion, much coloured and melodramatic in dress, which was reported in July 1914 to the Marist Fathers at Nguludi. Yet it is more likely that Chilembwe's animus against the Europeans did not come to the head of concrete conspiracy and preparation for revolt, did not pass from the theory to the practice of insurrection, until after his letter to the *Nyasaland Times* had failed to produce any other response from the Government than the suppression of the issue in which it appeared. If this letter was produced immediately after the Karonga fighting and Chilembwe's disillusionment in reaction to its reception manifested itself in quick succession, this would leave a bare four months [132] for the actual organization of the revolt—a fact which may explain the slender successes which it achieved. Though, as will be seen, the planning of the Rising was as thorough as it could be in the circumstances, and in consideration of the relative inexperience of the main actors in the intricacies of conspiracy under modern conditions, it had all of the character of a quick, desperate gesture—of something which was likely to achieve symbolic rather than material results.

This is certainly the impression left by one of the members of Chilembwe's 'army' who saw in his letter to the local press an indirect question to the Government on what it proposed to do about its complaints. As he put it :

> To this question the answer was thus, 'The top men refuse to answer the question but they are arranging to visit him'. . . . He [Chilembwe] knew by these signs that the coming of the top men to him would not be a peaceful visit. But they would come with a small army.[133]

That is to say, Chilembwe feared arrest after the affair of his anti-war letter—a fear which was not, apparently, unjustified, for the Governor, Sir George Smith, seems to have made plans at this time to deport him.[134] So, 'He then began strong teaching' [135]—an African litotes for the organization of revolt. He exhorted his followers to be strong and of good courage, and they all read together from the twentieth chapter of the Acts of the Apostles some warning passages from Paul of the dangers of dissension and the difficulties of unity (verses 29-32), especially when deprived of a leader—in this case Chilembwe himself. This story suggests that Chilembwe looked upon himself more as a martyr in the cause of the Nyasaland Africans rather than as a sort of 'Emperor Jones' over the Protectorate. (There is, indeed, apparent here not a little of the psychology of John Brown at Harper's Ferry.) And so, concluded this African witness, 'He strengthened them [his followers] with these words, "We ought to suffer persecution . . ."' [136]

Wherever in the 'middle distance' of the Chilembwe rebellion future research may allocate the emergence of the actual conspiracy, a place for it has now been found in this narrative, and, as the foreground of the Rising becomes distinctly visible, some space must be provided for a consideration of its actual organization. A good place to begin is with an examination of the Africans who rallied to Chilembwe's standard in the days when the Rising was being plotted.

The official Commission of Inquiry into the Rising had three things to say about Chilembwe's African following which help to open up the subject of its character : first, 'the fact that there were in his immediate neighbourhood a number of discontented educated natives who imbibed his ideas and acted as his assistants' ; second, that the Rising was 'chiefly confined to natives connected with independent native Christian sects or associations' ; and, third, that 'the rebels were drawn from various different native tribes' and that the Rising was not 'connected in any way with any tribal movement'.[137] Nowhere does the Report refer to the Nguru and other African emigrants from the Portuguese territories into the Shire Highlands. This is a point of some importance, for numerous accounts of the Rising have polarized it into the twin forces of Chilembwe, the isolated, vengeful leader, and an undifferentiated mass of ignorant Nguru and emigrant African *lumpenproletarians* from Portuguese East Africa. But the forces of the Rising were much more complicated ; and though the Commission of Inquiry's three points help in the appreciation of this fact, Chilembwe's following was more variegated than this body acknowledged.

Six groups at least may be distinguished amongst those Africans who supported Chilembwe's plans : the 'educated natives' or 'proto-intellectuals' who provided the leadership and the general staff of the Rising ; a similar but less qualified group from the independent African churches who assumed the lesser positions of command ; the Nguru and other African emigrant labourers from Portuguese East Africa who supplied a large share of the rank and file ; the Ngoni from whom came special supporting forces, and whose members were also distributed amongst the first two groups ; chiefs, headmen, and other persons and groups from other tribes to whom Chilembwe made appeals for support, which were sometimes successful ; and finally, perhaps, a few simple adventurers whose motives may have been loot and excitement.

Of all these sections, it is undoubtedly the first two which give to the Rising much of its interest and most of its importance as a 'new kind of unrest' [138] for Nyasaland and East Africa as a whole. Both had some connection with the independent African churches of the Protectorate, of whose doctrines most Europeans in the Protectorate were so ignorant that they were usually lumped under the abusive generics of 'Watch Tower' or 'Adventist' to the detriment of a clear analysis of their character. Enough has been said in this study so far to indicate what the independent churches were on the eve of the Rising : Chilembwe's own Providence Industrial Mission ; a chain of independent African Seventh Day Baptist churches, of which Charles Domingo's was the most important, that had been nurtured by Booth from the Cape ; potentially fissiparous groupings from the European-led Seventh-day Adventist and Churches of Christ missions which were always liable to form separate congregations, and which in the case of Filipo Chinyama and his tiny mission at Ncheu actually did so ; and the rump of Elliott Kamwana's Watch Tower following which, if it influenced mostly the west of Lake Nyasa, had some sway in the Shire Highlands through itinerant preachers and the fact that it afforded channels for the entry into Nyasaland of Watch Tower literature from the United States. These independent African religious groupings provided intricate avenues whereby Africans who were discontented with the more orthodox and longer established European missions could find means for self-expression and leadership and for the advancement of their individual status in accordance with the religious and 'respectable' norms which over three decades of missionary, particularly Scottish missionary, activity had established in the Protectorate. Like the separatist churches of the European Reformation, such as the Anabaptists, or of the times of the Industrial Revolution, such as the first Wesleyans, they easily and logically became channels through which political, economic, and social grievances could be vented usually, but not always, under a religious guise ; and they continually threatened to turn themselves into centres of more militant agitation that might disturb the fabric of British 'law and order'. For all the vagaries of their doctrine and their often pathetic pretentiousness, they represented the first effective stirrings in Nyasaland and Central Africa of a spirit of African independence, not of the old tribal kind of reaction to the white man's way of life but of a new kind of response to European culture along what they considered to be the lines of that culture's main elements as they saw them in their own little localities. Chilembwe had not created them ; Booth had not created them—though he had given to them much of their characteristic form and focus—and they might well have come into existence if neither Booth nor Chilembwe had existed, for they sprang from internal conditions in Nyasaland which, even if they had needed a precipitant, could have found this in the 'Ethiopianism' of South Africa and kindred movements amongst Negroes in other parts of the world, particularly America.

By themselves, these independent African churches were mere channels for all manner of currents. It is these currents which must be examined amongst Chilembwe's following if the effect is not to be mistaken for the cause. Their sources should already be clear from what has been written so far. Of their agents, the 'educated natives' are of primary importance. Yet it must be noticed that all the members of these independent African religious groups did not necessarily follow Chilembwe. Charles Domingo was a conspicuous example of this. Though, as has been seen, he had close relations with Chilembwe, and although he 'went down' [139] in the general Government assault on the separatist churches after the Rising, yet in spite of his previously expressed radicalism, he had no part in Chilembwe's insurrection. Nor, indeed, was Chilembwe able to recruit his old friend of the Zambesi Industrial Mission days and of Booth's 1895–7 separatist church, Morrison Malinki, then a Seventh-day Adventist pastor under European tutelage.[140] Nevertheless, a considerable number of Africans, who had received some education and training in the independent churches and schools, did converge on Chilembwe's movement as a centre.

The level of the 'educated natives' who followed Chilembwe, even of those who had gone through the whole gamut of the Scottish missionary schools or, as in Chilembwe's particular case, had sampled what Negro America had to offer, was not high by conventional British standards. But it is not good enough to dub these men 'half-educated' and to expect that phrase to explain their dilemma : for it raises the vexed question of what is education anyway ? They had all the general problems of 'marginal man' [141] in any society, and the very special ones of their own time and place—not the least of which was that they wanted more education on the European model when they saw what personal and social advantages it could bring, but the economy and policy of Nyasaland failed to provide it. Let it be remembered, too, as a standard of comparison, that elementary and secondary education were then of comparatively recent growth in most European countries. It was Nyasaland's privilege and its perplexity that its taste for education had been formed by men from a country which had pioneered the spread of common schools : Scotland.

Typical of Chilembwe's educated lieutenants, and one who was said to be his second-in-command, was John Gray Kufa. Unlike Chilembwe, whose contact with the Scottish missions is something of a puzzle, John Gray Kufa was a pure product of the Blantyre Mission. His career has already been noted in passing [142] and it may be recalled that he had had an uninterrupted association with the Blantyre Mission at least from 20 July 1890, the date of his baptism by the Scottish missionaries from whom he had received his European first names. Within three years his rate of progress at the mission school had been so fast that he was sent back to his home at the Kongoni mouth of the Zambezi as an evangelist among his own people.[143] It was here that Chilembwe may have met him if he was working on the Zambesi Industrial Mission steamer. In 1898 John Gray Kufa passed the surgical examination set by the Blantyre medical missionaries with 90 per cent marks, and was clearly marked out as the nearest thing to an African doctor in the Protectorate. Work in school and church, and proficiency in medicine approved by the Scottish doctors with their high standards, gave him a position of special trust in the Blantyre Mission. He was soon the foremost native assistant in its hospital and was entrusted with work in the dispensary. On the eve of the Rising he was an elder in the Blantyre Church. Yet by this time his connections with the Providence Industrial Mission were obvious. He had been friendly with Chilembwe for a long time : as far back, apparently, as the relatively untroubled days when Chilembwe could go hunting for business and pleasure with an easy mind, John Gray Kufa accompanied him on many of these trips. That Chilembwe thought a good deal of him is shown by the fact that his own personal photograph album—another mark of his status and respectability—sported a fine photograph of John Gray Kufa (see p. 374). It is a striking photograph : not only does it show that he wore his elegant European clothes with much greater ease than Chilembwe but it seems to reveal a personality at once sensitive and intelligent, in the fine lines of his face and the set of his lips. It is not the face of one who would be rushed easily into any madcap scheme ; nor does it suggest a person who would submit passively to the kind of social distinctions which the management at Magomero practised. John Gray Kufa seems to have been a man who was conscious of his own achievements and who felt he was worth more than the contemporary society afforded : a man, indeed, very much like Chilembwe himself. He had been friendly long enough with Chilembwe for both of them to have discussed their respective conditions and ambitions and to have come to the conclusion that they were incapable of realization under the political and economic system of Nyasaland before the Great War. It will perhaps never be known what were their exact relationships in the conspiracy,[144] though John Gray Kufa seems to have been put in charge of a party that was to attack Blantyre.[145] He was apparently drawing closer to the leader of the P.I.M. in 1913 when Chilembwe's feelings against the Magomero Estates were growing very bitter, and the first phase of the Rising's 'middle distance' was developing. At this time John Gray Kufa was actually working for the Bruce Estates at Magomero, to which he had been recommended as Estate hospital dispenser by Dr. Robert Macfarlane of the Blantyre Mission ; and he was going so far as to ask his employer, A. L. Bruce, for permission to visit Chilembwe at his Chiradzulu church. Bruce noted : 'This was the first time that I had heard of Chilembwe'.[146] (From this statement it is obvious that he was the owner and not the manager of the Estates—though the fact illustrates again that, although W. J. Livingstone and Chilembwe had fallen foul of each other before 1913, relations between the P.I.M. and Magomero did not begin to deteriorate rapidly until this year.) And so Bruce asked John Gray Kufa many questions about Chilembwe and received in return the impression 'that he was uncomfortable about answering'. As a result of this impression, Bruce made private inquiries about Chilembwe and reported his scant findings to the Governor. He found no evidence for a conspiracy against Magomero at this time. John Gray Kufa was still an efficient dispenser who caused little trouble. It may well be, however, that it was his period of employment on the Magomero Estates that brought him closer to Chilembwe's point of view during 1913 and 1914 than he would otherwise have come under the mild day-to-day tutelage of the Scottish missionaries' hospital at Blantyre.

A. L. Bruce was to meet John Gray Kufa again when he had hurried down from Karonga, where he had been serving with the Nyasaland Field Force, after the Rising had taken place and his Estate manager had lost his head, and when, for all Bruce knew, the general security of his property was threatened. This time the setting was very different. John Gray Kufa had been tried, found guilty, and was awaiting execution in the prison at Blantyre. Here A. L. Bruce saw him, and John Gray Kufa told him about the conspiracy. If Bruce's account of this meeting is correct—and there is no reason to suppose that it is not—it throws a valuable light on the aims and procedures of Chilembwe and his henchmen. In Bruce's words :

> He said that Chilembwe preached 'Africa for the Africans' in his Church, but was always careful before starting on that theme to make sure that he knew every member of his congregation. When issuing orders for the Rising he said he wished W. J. Livingstone's head to be brought to his church as he was so well known to the natives, he being one of the first Planters in Nyasaland, having been sent out by my father in 1893. Gray swore to me that there was no personal vendetta against W. J. Livingstone or Magomero.

A cynic might interpret this account as a desire on Bruce's part to exonerate his Estates and their management from the blame which fell upon them after the Rising. Yet his statement is in accordance with evidence drawn from African and other sources which supports the interpretation that has already been offered : that Chilembwe's attack on the Magomero Estates, with its decapitation of their manager, was as much a symbolical action as a bid for political and economic power ; a desire to make a gesture against what the conspirators considered to be the abuses of European rule and to gain such recognition for an independent African view-point as would bring these abuses into the open.

John Gray Kufa's participation in the rebellion was a blow to the Blantyre missionaries. It seemed even more difficult to understand because he had taken up land in the Protectorate at Nsoni and had set up as a small estate owner. He even had his own *capitao* (African foreman), one Lemeck of Mwandama's Village, who had formerly been employed at Magomero and was himself implicated in the Rising.[147] Gray had his own brick house, with a veranda [148]—a mark of social standing to an African at the time—and seemed destined for the quiet and relatively distinguished career of one of the new African 'petty-bourgeois'. And yet he gave it all up to follow Chilembwe, as Chilembwe himself threw away his own hard-won status in a desperate gamble. Mention of John Gray Kufa's small estate raises a further point about the 'educated natives', the lieutenants of the Rising : their role as small property-owners.

It would be wrong to over-estimate the amounts of property which some of them owned. By the standards of the white property-owners of the Protectorate it was small, though it was probably much greater than that which most of the European missionaries possessed at that time. Nevertheless, although independent African land-ownership and production for the market along the lines of the European economy was not as far advanced by 1915 in Nyasaland as the enthusiastic Harry Johnston had hoped originally [149]—itself a reflection of the fact that the relatively isolated Protectorate, with its lack of easily exploitable minerals, had not fulfilled the economic dreams of the early pioneers—some advances had been made. The small native capitalist was a feature of the Nyasaland scene by 1915 : the product of a process which had much earlier origins.[150] His lot was not an easy one, for he faced the competition of the Indian storekeeper and trader on his own level ; and, should he aspire to higher forms of production and trade, he found that not only did his own lack of training and tradition hamper him but, in an economy like Nyasaland's, though labour was cheap, amounts of capital beyond his command were needed to maintain and increase production because of the natural and artificial hazards to which the economy was subjected. That Chilembwe and many of his supporters were aware of these facts is clear not only from Chilembwe's own independent attempts at production at the P.I.M., in the days when the American Negro, Cheek, was with him, but also from the attempt in 1911 to found an 'African Industrial Society' when the difficulties which confronted Nyasaland's aspiring native capitalists were discussed. It will be recalled that the chairman of the meeting about this Society was one Duncan Njilima, who had been very much aware that, if the African was to progress economically along European lines, the formation of a native capital would have to be encouraged. He was one of Chilembwe's fellow conspirators, and a man of no small substance ; had taught for some time at the Blantyre Mission, and had been to Rhodesia and South Africa.[151] This was witnessed by a European, who as part of the Nyasaland Volunteer Reserve helped to round up some of the rebels in 1915, and had the task of sacking Njilima's house :

> a fine brick building with veranda, etc. . . . . We went through the house and everything was taken out—tables, chairs, chest of drawers, fine tin boxes, a bath, a sewing machine, in fact everything under the sun, silk dresses, boxes of books, pictures, etc. . . . my assistant bagged a fine new ladies cycle, a Swift, which had never been ridden, valued at £12 : 10 . . . we have some swell natives in Central Africa.[152]

Njilima's estate had its own sheep and cattle, fowls, ducks, and pigeons in the European manner. Similarly, another one of Chilembwe's plotters was Hugh Mataka,[153] owner of a small store. The same witness to Njilima's relative prosperity sacked one of such stores that belonged to a member of Chilembwe's following, and estimated the value of its goods at about £150, no small sum for an African of the period. Chilembwe himself, John Gray Kufa, Duncan Njilima, and Hugh Mataka, were probably the most substantial of the African property-owners amongst the conspirators but there were many lesser men of property amongst the rebels, such as Thomas Lulanga, owner of a small estate on Mbombwe stream, close to Chilembwe's.[154] All of the small African capitalists of the Shire Highlands, of course, were not implicated in the Rising,[155] and those who conspired with Chilembwe were probably but a slight percentage of this group. Nevertheless he seems to have attracted to himself a number of them,[156] and this fact gives to the Rising a partial economic motivation which has not been commonly recognized. It was true, as Hector Duff, Deputy-Governor of Nyasaland for part of the Great War, pointed out, that Chilembwe had amongst his collaborators none of the more 'prominent' Africans of the Protectorate.[157] But, as 'prominent' was applied at that time to Africans, it usually meant chiefs and well-known headmen : and most Europeans of Nyasaland would have hesitated to apply it to any of the small native capitalists, who seemed so insignificant in comparison with European enterprises that they were often regarded as silly upstarts who were unworthy of any serious recognition. It was no doubt, in part, this attitude which forced some of these native capitalists into Chilembwe's forces. For their motives in this, there is little direct evidence. But it is not unreasonable to suppose that many of them felt a strong sense of frustration, part of which may have been the result of a sense of their own failure to adopt European methods and manners as effectively as they wished, and part from the economic, political and social circumstances of the Protectorate which did not operate in favour of the rapid advancement of aspiring Africans.

Allied to them here would be those Africans who, while they possessed little other than personal property, had some degree of education and wanted more, or for whom a little learning was to prove a dangerous thing. That the educational facilities of the Protectorate were inadequate was clear from the whole history of the Booth-inspired separatist churches, which had drawn many Africans to them because they seemed to offer a free education. The demand on the established churches' missions for schools was greater than the supply, because of over-strained finances and difficulties of creating quickly cadres of native teachers—for it was impossible to attract or support enough teachers from Great Britain. The small annual grant of £1000 which, from 1908 to 1918, the Government gave to the missions on whom the burden of education fell was not enough and did little to improve the situation.[158] Furthermore, some Africans resented the discipline and the standards of the Scottish mission schools, which did not offer a quick and easy road to the status they desired.[159] The over-all result was a multiplication of independent African schools, side by side with the separatist churches. The P.I.M. schools were the most important and probably the most effective of these. Out of them came men like Andrack Jamali, who acted as Chilembwe's church clerk and secretary for the conspiracy,[160] and Filipo Chinyama of Ncheu who tried to organize the supplementary revolt, and who was running his own independent school up to the time of the Rising. On such men undoubtedly fell the burden of 'non-commissioned officers'' tasks, and they can be imagined working to maintain the security of Chilembwe's conspiracy in the months before the Rising. They proved themselves no mean exponents of this art, for, in spite of the warnings given to the authorities and others in Nyasaland, it came as a complete surprise to most of the inhabitants of the Protectorate, especially to the established missionaries who claimed to know the Africans better than anyone else.[161]

Below Chilembwe's lieutenants and his N.C.O.s came, obviously, his rank and file. How he organized these is conjectural. Though his church was large, it certainly would not have taken all the rank-and-file members of his conspiracy. They must either have been divided into groups which were brought separately to his brick church for instruction in their tasks, or else others were contacted either individually or in sections by him or his leaders. It is likely that both methods were employed. How many he contacted in these ways is, again, uncertain. Estimates have varied from several thousand to a few hundred. The number who actually went out on the night of 23 January when the Rising began is no guide to this —if it could be accurately ascertained—for many lost heart at the last moment. It is quite likely that Chilembwe had contacted enough to have the makings of a fair-sized battalion if all went well: perhaps eight or nine hundred.[162] Many of them were Nguru and the sources of Chilembwe's following amongst them are not difficult to find. It has been seen how he had made, throughout the history of the P.I.M., frequent trips into their territories of origin in Portuguese East Africa, and had, on one occasion, suffered some slight imprisonment, so the African story goes, for speaking out against their conditions. He had carried out, too, many evangelizing tours amongst them when they emigrated into the Protectorate. As something of a pariah people amongst the local Nyasaland tribes, many of them were undoubtedly moved by the fact that they received a welcome from Chilembwe's churches. It was natural that any grievances which those of them who were employed at Magomero felt against the Bruce Estates should be aired at the P.I.M. to Chilembwe. Yet, as it has been stated, though they gave him major support it is wrong to place the emphasis entirely on them.[163]

A much more remarkable feature of the Rising was the support for it which came from the Ngoni. It is true that much of this misfired, but that it existed at all, that Ngoni men actually took part in Chilembwe's conspiracy side by side with members of other tribes which they, with their heritage of conquest and suzerainty, were accustomed to despise, was a demonstration of the difference between the 1915 Rising and the older, tribal movements of reaction to British rule.[164] Some of this Ngoni support may have been looked upon by them as a tactical alliance against the British, for they had known tactical alliances in the past. Yet this does not explain the number of individual Ngoni in Chilembwe's following, and their motives are not explained by sheltering under the adjective 'detribalized', a term which creates as many difficulties as it solves. From the first day of the P.I.M. it is likely that Chilembwe numbered Ngoni amongst his followers, for a base had been prepared for him whilst he was still in America, it appears, amongst Gomani's Ngoni who were adjacent to Portuguese East Africa. This seems to have been the work of his elder and only brother, James (Chimpele to some), who had been teaching at one of the outlying schools of the Zambesi Industrial Mission in Ngoniland in 1899.[165] This elder brother is something of a mystery man in Chilembwe's life, and his influence on him may have been greater than is apparent at first sight. He put into his head seeds of suspicion about European motives before Chilembwe left for America; [166] and he was obviously in the conspiracy, for he was arrested and shot instantly after the Rising at Blantyre.[167] Another and possibly stronger pillar of Chilembwe's influence amongst the Ngoni was Stephen Mkulichi, a Yao teacher at the P.I.M., who had also taught for the Zambesi Industrial Mission in Ngoniland and had married there.[168] But, of all Chilembwe's contacts with the Ngoni, the most immediately important for the Rising was Filipo Chinyama, himself a member of this tribe.[169]

Some details of Chinyama's career have already been noted, while discussing Walter Cockerill's visit to him in 1914.[170] It is obvious that he was a kindred spirit with Chilembwe, John Gray Kufa, and Hugh Mataka. He had had his small share of travel and had been down to Bulawayo in Rhodesia to work.[171] Chinyama seems to have been passionately keen on education, and he worked hard to set up his own school at home in Ncheu. Here he came into contact with another Ngoni enthusiast for education : the minor chief Makwangwala of Dzunje, who had removed himself and all his people to this section in 1900 from their home in the Portuguese territories for the reason that the Portuguese would not allow him to have a school.[172] Because of Chinyama's previous contacts with four European missions who had influence in the area (the Seventh Day Baptists, Seventh-day Adventists, Churches of Christ, and Baptist Industrial Mission of Scotland) he was able to influence some of their African members, as well as to disturb the work of the Church of Scotland missionaries in Makwangwala's country.[173] Out of the discontented from these missionary centres, and with the knowledge and co-operation of Makwangwala himself, Filipo Chinyama built up a force that consisted largely of Ngoni. While it was by no means as large as Chilembwe's own force, it was not small—this is suggested by the fact that about a hundred of Chinyama's men were captured at the time of the Rising,[174] and that an uncounted number of them escaped into the neighbouring Portuguese territory. It does not seem, from the fate of Chinyama's rebels, that he and Chilembwe had good communications, otherwise the synchronization of their advances would have been better. That they had made some attempt to work together was clear ; but the details and staff-work of their joint-conspiracy apparently left much to be desired. It is also possible that Chinyama's effective planning was developed much later than Chilembwe's : [175] perhaps because he was waiting to see how much progress was being made in the Shire Highlands before he committed himself too deeply.

Other tribal elements in Chilembwe's following were represented largely by individual or small group attachments to himself and his lieutenants. It may appear at first odd that he secured no widespread support among his own people, the Yao. There seem to be three main reasons for this. To begin with, there were the traditional divisions amongst the Yao themselves. Chilembwe's people, it appears, were of the Mangoche branch of the Yao : a section which traditionally was at loggerheads with the Machinga Yao. Secondly, there was undoubtedly some jealousy of Chilembwe by Yao chiefs and headmen who, at a time when their own indigenous political system was being put into a straight-jacket by the new European Administration,[176] watched enviously Chilembwe's progress up the social ladder. This was largely the attitude of the Machinga Yao chief, Malemia, who sent a guard of spearmen to look after the Reverend James F. Alexander, Church of Scotland missionary at Domasi, when the Rising broke out. 'I am not going to let Europeans get killed', Malemia is reported to have said, 'just to make John Chilembwe the Governor.' [177] And then there was the strong influence which the Church of Scotland missionaries possessed amongst leading Yao of the Shire Highlands, from the earliest times of the British in Central Africa, which helped to counteract Chilembwe's attempts to win them to his side.

Indeed, apart from the Ngoni, Makwangwala, Chilembwe had scant success with chiefs or headmen, though he made an attempt to get some of the neighbouring Mlanje chiefs on his side. A plot was hatched with them and they were assigned the task of attacking the Boma (administrative centre) at Mlanje, and of seizing its rifles and ammunition.[178] With one Zomba headman, Kimu (Makwangwala [179]), Chilembwe had more success, and he made him an integral part of his conspiracy. These figures largely represent the limit of Chilembwe's influence on direct tribal representatives. Yet, through his effects on individuals who did not have leading positions in the traditional tribal administrations, Chilembwe numbered Africans from most of the leading tribes of the Protectorate amongst his followers, with the exception, it appears, of the Tonga—though, even of the Tonga, at least one representative has been traced in Chilembwe's following.[180]

The reason for Tonga lack of support to Chilembwe may have been that their main habitat was to the west of Lake Nyasa, and far away from the Shire Highlands. But it could not have been the only reason, for the peripatetic Tonga passed regularly backwards and forwards through Blantyre on their way to the mines of the south, and many came to the Shire Highlands for work in the main plantations and only industrial areas of the Protectorate. As they formed something of the backbone of the small industrial working-class of Nyasaland which was coming into being at that time, this raises the question of Chilembwe's influence amongst the Nyasaland industrial working-class and of the role it performed in his Rising. Indirectly, some of the ideas which migrant African industrial labourers brought in from South Africa and the Rhodesias played, as has been seen, a considerable part in creating the 'Ethiopian' tradition in Nyasaland, of which the 1915 Rising was to be the most important manifestation. In this respect the Commission of Inquiry into the Rising no doubt underestimated their role, though it was correct about their immediate influence on the Rising.[181] But Chilembwe tapped some elements of support from amongst wage-labourers on the plantations inside the Protectorate, particularly amongst the field hands and skilled workers on the Magomero Estates,[182] and some of his adherents, like Chinyama or Njilima, if they had not themselves worked on the mines down south, were acquainted with their conditions. Perhaps the main reason why Chilembwe did not cast his net more effectively into the emigrant Nyasaland mining population, the distinctive element of its industrial working-class at this time, is simply that it was emigrant, its members constantly moving backwards and forwards under contract and the rival pulls of the urban centres to the south and the homeland to the north. A migrant labour force is always difficult to organize, and even the radical American union, the Industrial Workers of the World, which had some success with a similar migrant labour cycle in the United States around this time, might well have quailed before trying to organize the tatterdemalion rovers who made up this Nyasaland social grouping.

As for the Tonga, if they made their discontents felt at all at this time they probably did it in their own home territory to the west of the Lake and in concealed mutterings which never reached, in 1915, the pitch of militancy because of the effective way in which the Kamwana movement, with which they had been allied, had been stamped out amongst them. Radical and ambitious ones amongst them, like Clements Kadalie, were casting their lot with the working-classes outside the Protectorate, in South Africa in particular, where hopes of advancement and change, because of the more enterprising character of the economy, were more apparent, and where the more militant and less religiously veiled forces of the contemporary white man's labour movement offered themselves as a direct model. Furthermore, from a pan-African point of view, South Africa was at that time the obvious place for action, and it is significant that Booth at the time of the 'middle distance' of the Rising was exerting himself to influence the African Congress movement there, not so much perhaps because he had given up all hopes of getting back into Nyasaland or of influencing it effectively from a distance but because it was in South Africa that 'things were happening'. A similar criterion may have occurred to Chilembwe, and he may well have not troubled to contact the Tonga, not merely because of the physical difficulties of reaching them to the west of the Lake, or because of ignorance of Livingstonia, its Overtoun Institute at Kondowe, and the lively Africans emerging from it, but because he himself was concentrating on the place where 'things were happening' in Nyasaland—the Shire Highlands, where the majority of the European population resided and where the major centres of economic life were concentrated. If so, this was sound strategy.

Because most of the documents of the conspiracy have been lost or destroyed, and what few official records are in existence are not readily available,[183] it is not easy to appreciate Chilembwe's strategy. Much of it, too, was obviously not committed to paper. Thus, it can only be inferred from some slender threads of evidence and from what took place during the Rising itself: an unhappy procedure, because the Rising, apparently, did not go according to plan—a fact which makes the strategy of the original plan doubly difficult to determine. Some critics of Chilembwe who have looked upon him as a simple, bloodthirsty fanatic, might interject that it is pretentious to give a high-sounding appellation like 'strategy' to the actions of his mobs. But this would be a rash assertion, for there is no doubt that, within his limits, Chilembwe had given quite definite thought to matters of strategy and tactics.

Any consideration of his strategy must start with an inquiry into the ultimate aim of the conspirators. It has already been noticed that the 1916 Commission of Inquiry's assertion that the object of the Rising was 'the extermination or expulsion of the European population' is probably an exaggeration; and that Norman Leys's claim that Chilembwe would have allowed carefully selected cadres of

Europeans to remain in the Protectorate to assist him in the building up of his new state is more likely to be correct, for Chilembwe had seen enough of the Euro-American world to know that European help was indispensable. Which Europeans he would have spared to this end, it is difficult to say.[184] Even more difficult to determine, however, is the character of the state which he proposed to set up. The 1916 Commission referred to the setting up of a 'native state or theocracy of which John Chilembwe was to be the head'.[185] The use of the word 'theocracy' is important here, especially as the Commission also noted that it was part of his scheme to form a union between the P.I.M. and the independent native churches.[186] In the movement against foreign control, Chilembwe seems to have had some conception of the role which an independent African church throughout the Protectorate could play, and his struggle for African church unity, under the leadership of himself and the P.I.M., has not a few points in common with similar processes at the heart of the Reformation in Europe. The ascription, therefore, of 'theocracy' to the character of the state which he may have hoped would supplant European rule in the Protectorate seems very apt. Yet it would probably be wrong to imagine that his ideas or the ideas of his followers on this score were at all clear. That the concept of 'Africa for the Africans', tinged with not a little pan-Africanism, had been growing in Chilembwe's mind from the time of his first association with Booth is obvious : but as a simple slogan its emotional appeal discouraged rather than encouraged clear thinking on the character of the state which was to achieve this. In the absence of other documentary evidence, it seems very likely that any aims which Chilembwe may have had for a native state to supplant British rule would have followed closely the Christian-commercial schemes for independent African political activity which Booth had set out as appendices to his book, *Africa for the African* [187]; and that these ideas would have been supplemented by Chilembwe's own knowledge of independent Negro American political, economic, and cultural practices.

But to leave—as did the 1916 Commission of Inquiry—the aims of the Rising as simply anti-European and pro-independent-African government in Nyasaland would seem to be a harmful simplification. No doubt these were the objects which Chilembwe and his lieutenants, as well as the majority of his convinced following, set themselves, if the Rising should prove successful. Yet it is by no means clear that

Chilembwe believed it would be successful, and one aspect of the Rising, as a symbolical gesture to show that Africans in the Protectorate would not always accept passively the spate of changes and discriminations which the rush of European rule was heaping on them, has already been suggested. It was one way—perhaps the only way—of forcing upon the Government and settlers of the Protectorate an independent African view-point. Thus the aims of the Rising appear to have been twofold : first, if successful, the creation of an African state in Nyasaland, with strongly theocratic elements and selected European guidance ; second, if unsuccessful, a gesture of protest, in the early months of the new and frightening war, against what were conceived as the intolerable aspects of European rule. With the Government embarrassed by war, there was just a chance that the first aim would succeed.

It was with this possibility in mind, no doubt, that Chilembwe looked around for allies to support his strategy. Inside the Protectorate he probably took no Europeans into his confidence, for he knew very well that, however sympathetic some of them may have been to some of his ideas, they would come together in a firm front of white solidarity at the first suggestion of a native rising. His main European allies would have to be sought outside Nyasaland, amongst those who were engaged in fighting against the British. It was this matter of military necessity which forced him to get into touch with the Germans. Nothing short of military necessity would have driven him to seek their councils, for Chilembwe was not ignorant politically and he must have known of the harsh treatment that they had meted out to their own rebels after the Maji-Maji rising of 1905, and of the generally rigorous conditions of German colonial rule.

Africans who knew him have claimed that he never got into touch with the Germans. But this assertion does not do justice to his strategical sense ; for Chilembwe, like any other revolutionary, was prepared to take his allies where he could find them. The whole matter has been shrouded by defensive attitudes on all sides. Some African supporters of Chilembwe, conscious of British feelings about the Germans, have tried to make out that Chilembwe was not guilty of such 'treachery'. Other Africans, such as the migrant Nyasas working in the Congo who had no wish to be labelled by their employers as subversives, shortly after the Rising took an opposite view-point and claimed that the whole thing was due to German intrigue.[188] And some officials in the Protectorate, it seems, used the German 'scare' to blacken Chilembwe's reputation and to alienate African support from his memory.

Chilembwe's degree of collusion with the Germans, though slight, was definite. If many of his followers were not aware of it, this, it seems, was because Chilembwe and his leading lieutenants naturally took great pains to keep their contacts with the Germans on the 'top secret' list. Shortly before the Rising broke out, Chilembwe sent a letter to German East Africa by a messenger who could travel in Yao tribal territory all the way from Chiradzulu, through Portuguese East Africa, to Tunduru, where he apparently had an interview with a German official.[189] The official sent back an answer with the same messenger, which was written in Kiswahili and couched in the terminology of the German administration. It ran :

> To the Sultan John Chelembwe,
> P.I. Mission at Chiradzulu near Blantyre.
>
> I let you know that your man . . . arrived here with your letter, thank you.
>
> I have sent your letter to the Chief Judge at Lindi and to the Governor at Dar es Salaam. We are all very pleased to receive your news. Also I have received an order from the Chief Judge at Lindi to write you thanking you for your letter. The news you tell me about the war is true. In Europe the Germans have conquered the English, many were killed, many wounded, many taken into German territory. In Europe on the sea the German Navy is the best. Every time English ships have been sunk. As to what concerns about German territory here in Africa this man of yours . . . will inform you, having heard all the news.
>
> My compliments to all your people. WASALAAM,
> —Chief Judge at Tunduru.[190]

If this letter and the verbatim message had reached Chilembwe safely, they would have indicated that the Germans were sympathetic to his venture but could give no direct support.[191] Nevertheless, there are grounds for supposing that the letter and information did not reach Chilembwe,

> for the man had scarcely left German territory on his return journey when, learning of Chilembwe's death and the collapse of the rebellion, he turned about and fled back to his friend, the enemy, in such a des-

perate hurry that he dropped the 'Chief Judge's' letter on the road, where it was soon afterwards picked up and sent to Zomba.[192]

Yet, that the Germans would be sympathetic to his plans must have been clear to Chilembwe before he sent this letter, and at the very least he could hope that, indirectly, by their pressure on the British troops at the north end of Lake Nyasa, they would keep the main forces of the Protectorate locked up around Karonga and out of the Shire Highlands area where he would make his main thrusts against the Europeans.[193]

Had he known that for some time the Germans had had plans for Portuguese Nyasaland as a 'shadow colony' through financial control of the Companhia de Moçambique,[194] he might have been more suspicious of their ultimate intentions ; though the fact could only at that time have reinforced his convictions that the Germans would do anything in their power to embarrass the British in Central Africa. This was becoming apparent from the intrigues amongst Muslims in Allied territories which the Germans were known to be conducting ; [195] and Chilembwe, with his connections amongst the Yao, the main Nyasaland tribe to be influenced by Islam, may well have been aware of these subversive activities, and may have drawn from them the conclusion that at least some measure of support could be expected from the Germans. The German answer to his overtures, however, must perforce have been non-committal. Not only were they unsure of the disposition of their forces near Nyasaland, especially after their defeat at Karonga, but they did not know much about Chilembwe's plans, other than what he had told them, and they were obviously waiting to see what the outcome of these would be before they committed themselves further to his support. Furthermore, though they wished to embarrass the British as much as they could, they must have known that native revolts could be two-edged weapons, and they had their own very strong concepts of white solidarity, which revealed themselves when German prisoners of war in Nyasaland during the course of Chilembwe's insurrection rallied to the side of the British Government in the Protectorate.[196] Thus, from Chilembwe's point of view, the Germans were not very trustworthy allies. Yet they were at least adequate for his purpose ; and, if the Germans had made the counter-thrust into Nyasaland that was expected of them after their defeat at Karonga, the Shire Highlands might have been deprived of further Europeans who would have been needed as hasty reinforcements to check German activity to the north. Under such circumstances Chilembwe's plans might have had much greater success.

With the prospect of German indirect support to the north—a support which could, under favourable circumstances, become direct —Chilembwe could concentrate the weight of his proposed attacks on the Shire Highlands : a course which he would obviously wish to pursue, as it was in this area that the main centres of European power, political, economic, and social, were concentrated. His plan seems to have fallen into three parts. First, there was to be a series of attacks on European centres in the Blantyre-Zomba-Magomero area. As these were the main centres of the Protectorate, as well as being near to Chilembwe's own P.I.M. base, they were to be the main thrusts against European power. Second, Filipo Chinyama and his Ngoni and other associates were to embarrass the Dzunje-Ncheu area and move down south to link up with Chilembwe and his main forces. Third, there was some hope of an attack coming from a group of chiefs on the Governmental centre in the Mlanje area to the east. In all of these ventures, surprise was to play a main role, and there is no doubt that, despite the few warnings that were given of seditious activity at Mbombwe, once Chilembwe's conspiracy was launched, he and his colleagues were remarkably successful in maintaining secrecy to the last moment. Should the attacks fail, an escape route into Portuguese East Africa—and possibly from there into German East Africa—was indicated. With these main outlines of Chilembwe's strategy in mind, a little more detail may now be added to the various sections of his plan.

The main thrusts in the Blantyre-Zomba-Magomero area were organized carefully. Though some help was expected from Kimu, the Zomba headman, and an attack on the Zomba ammunition store seems to have been considered,[197] the attacks which mattered in this area were in three groups. The first two were to fall on Magomero, the centre of the Bruce Estates, and on Mwanje, an out-station of the Estates, about six miles to the south-east of Magomero and nearer to Chiradzulu. It is likely that these two attacks were planned to take place simultaneously,[198] not only because the Bruce Estates—in particular, their Magomero centre—were a focal point for African grievances in the area, but also because they were in a situation that had some strategical significance for the control of the whole region, and also because the shooting range of the Namadzi section of the Volunteer Reserve was on the Bruce Estates and there was, therefore, some hope of obtaining arms from there. Thus, though the main reason for attacking Magomero and its environs was that it had become something of a symbol of African grievances in the Shire Highlands, the supporting reasons of its strategical position and its arms supply should not be underestimated. But it was the third of the main planned attacks in the Blantyre-Zomba-Magomero area which afforded most hope for an arms supply. This was to be a raid on the ammunition and European store of the African Lakes Corporation at Blantyre. It had something of the character of a fighting patrol, and was clearly worked out carefully in advance. Some say that John Gray Kufa was assigned the leadership of this venture, a fact which shows the importance that was assigned to it tactically and logistically, for there is little doubt that, from this raid, the rebels hoped for a considerable increase in their arms supply. Others, however, claim that the leader of this attack was David Kaduya, one of Chilembwe's main followers.[199] After these two main raids on Magomero and Blantyre, the participants had instructions to go back to Chilembwe's brick church at Chiradzulu, no doubt for reorganization and for the dumping and allocating of arms and ammunition which may have been secured. To assist all the ventures in the Blantyre-Zomba-Magomero area, the telephone wires were to be cut.[200]

A controversial point of the main planning of the Rising in the Shire Highlands area is the question whether an attack on the Roman Catholic Marist Fathers' Mission at Nguludi was actually planned in advance. Such an attack did take place on the third day of the Rising. Reasons for it have already been suggested : revenge and an attack on the main enemy of independent churches.[201] In view of the theocratic elements in the conspiracy, the second factor may have had considerable importance, and, from this it is not unlikely that some measure of prior planning, if not in full detail, went into the attack on the Nguludi Mission station.

In all of these actions, and in the ventures of Filipo Chinyama and Makwangwala amongst the Ncheu Ngoni, the element of careful timing was essential to success. Timing must certainly have been considered, and if, ultimately, synchronization of the various thrusts did not have the almost complete measure of success which the element of surprise achieved, it is nevertheless a guide to the amounts of preliminary planning which went into the Rising.

Mention of time introduces a fundamental point of Chilembwe's tactics : why did the Rising break out on the night of Saturday, 23 January 1915 ? No clearly documented answer can be given to this question. It is highly unlikely, however, that the date was arbitrarily chosen. Two possible reasons may be suggested. First as has been noticed, the Government, who were suspicious of Chilembwe, appear to have been ready—no doubt after the affair of his anti-War letter—to deport him to the Seychelles.[202] Chilembwe seems to have got wind of these intentions and, according to African testimony,[203] anticipated the Governor's action by setting his Rising in motion. If this theory is correct, the choice of that particular Saturday evening, has no more special significance than that it came near to the time when Chilembwe felt he was due for deportation. While it is doubtful whether a simple cause-and-effect relationship may be seen in these two facts, it is very probable that the threat of deportation, in the long run, made Chilembwe more anxious to start the insurrection than he would otherwise have been. A second reason may be found in the fact that the night of 23 January 1915, was the date of the annual general meeting of the Blantyre Sports Club. This was a customary time for general festivities amongst most Europeans in the Shire Highlands at the Blantyre Club. Though it has been suggested more than once [204] that events connected with this annual festivity at the Blantyre Sports Club had something to do with frustrating the rebels' attacks in this region, this point of view has had the effect of disguising the fact that it was very much to Chilembwe's advantage to begin his attacks when a large part of the Europeans in the Shire Highlands were away from home, and in a condition of festive conviviality which was not the best physical and moral state for the defence of their lives and property. It is not unreasonable to suppose that such considerations passed through Chilembwe's mind when he issued the final orders for the Rising. It is most likely that a combination of both reasons was responsible for his choice of this date : that, knowing that he would have to bring forward the time of his proposed action because of the imminence of deportation, he showed his tactical sense by making the best of a bad job and choosing the week-end of 23 January, when many of the Europeans of the Shire Highlands would be celebrating at the Blantyre Club and then recuperating after their festivities ! [205]

From a consideration of Chilembwe's strategy and tactics some of the organization of the Rising may be inferred. And there are a few facts which have slipped through the net of accident and secrecy so that a slightly more substantial picture of this may be attempted. The organizing centre was the brick church at Mbombwe, Chiradzulu. Here all the carefully checked secret meetings were held in which the leaders and cadres of the Rising made their plans and were assigned their tasks.[206] It was from this church that, through Chilembwe's personal influence and the work of his P.I.M. colleagues, large numbers of the local Africans were prepared for the Rising. If few of them came to Chilembwe's side at the actual time of the insurrection, informers against him were negligible ; and there is little doubt that if his initial successes had been greater, he could have expected a considerable increase amongst his following. But the P.I.M. brick church was more than a centre of conspiracy and propaganda. It was to be the General Headquarters of John Chilembwe and his staff during the Rising. Chilembwe himself does not seem to have been present in person at any of the attacks which actually took place. He was, it seems, directing and co-ordinating activities from the Mbombwe church. The 1916 Commission of Inquiry noted that he had 'undoubtedly, for a native, exceptional administrative gifts',[207] and this was no over-statement. In the short time at his disposal and with the untrained material which he had to hand, Chilembwe's organizational work was no mean achievement. Had he been better supported by his leaders he might have achieved greater success. There was no doubt that he had given considerable thought to military matters : a much-thumbed military manual was found in the P.I.M. church after the Rising which showed evidence of this.[208] He had made some plans for the storing of guns beforehand ; and if the raid on the African Lakes Store and at Magomero had been more successful his armament would have been much greater. The failure of some Mlanje chiefs to support him was another disappointment in this respect, for Chilembwe had hoped that they would bring in arms from that district. His planning was further illustrated by the stretcher-bearers he is said to have trained for the care of the wounded ; [209] and by the use for some of his conspiratorial correspondence of Government stationery which one of his supporters, an Administration clerk at Zomba, appears to have purloined.[210]

At first sight there does not appear to have been much discipline amongst Chilembwe's following during the Rising. This is probably because most of the accounts of actual fighting come from the victorious European side. If one looks through and beyond these, however, a greater degree of discipline is apparent amongst the rebels both before and during the Rising. For one thing, Chilembwe's clear orders that European women and children were not to be harmed were scrupulously followed.[211] Furthermore, some of the fire discipline of the rebels was good, as their repulse of the first European attack on the P.I.M. church indicated. This may have been due to a few ex-soldiers amongst Chilembwe's African following,[212] though his influence amongst the King's African Rifles was on the whole negligible.[213] In the few actions which the rebels fought, there were further indications of discipline. The secret manner in which the group who attacked the ammunition store in Blantyre arrived on their objective was evidence of effective march discipline.[214] In the absence of looting,[215] and in the careful withdrawals from Magomero, their most successful action, Chilembwe's men showed a rare restraint and an uncommon degree of discipline and conviction. How much of all this was due to Chilembwe's personal efforts and how much to the conviction of his lieutenants and men it is difficult to say. But of the existence of a degree of discipline amongst a very variegated following there is no doubt. Despite its few successes, Chilembwe's 'army' was no rabble.

The one fact above all which has often given rise to accusations of this sort was the decapitation of W. J. Livingstone in his own house and before his own family at Magomero. This singular action seems to have been on Chilembwe's order,[216] and it is doubtful whether it was quite the result of personal vendetta which is often assumed.[217] There was something of a symbolical quality about it and Chilembwe seems to have received the news of the decapitation in a mood of sad resignation.[218] Though the cutting off of heads of one's enemies was part of many tribal traditions in Nyasaland,[219] and had led as far back as 1884 to the decapitation of at least one other European, the infamous George Fenwick,[220] it is by no means certain that such traditions influenced Chilembwe. It is not unlikely that, like Oliver Cromwell, who also issued an order for a man's head, he did it very reluctantly, at the instigation of his followers and from a conviction that, terrible though it was, it was the logical result of their actions, the inevitable outcome of their grievances, and a symbol of their whole protest.

The comparison with Cromwell is apt in another sense: there was a mixture of religion and politics in the whole movement of the Nyasaland independent African churches which culminated in the 1915 Rising that is not unlike the fusion of religious and political ideologies which characterized the English Revolution of the 1640's. The atmosphere of the Chilembwe-ite rebels' meeting was a combination of religion and politics : for the African, like the revolutionaries of the seventeenth century, had not yet learned the convenient divorce between the two which, as the twentieth century approached, became characteristic of so many Europeans. Chilembwe, too, often taught his politics straight from the Bible [221] like many a good Covenanter ancestor of the Scots who had tutored Nyasaland ; and, as has been noted, the slogans which inspired his men came from such radical scriptures as James's Epistle.[222]

It seems that Chilembwe possessed little, if any, of the 'prophetic' element which distinguished some of the 'Saints' of seventeenth-century Britain. Nor, indeed, had he much in common with the type of Central African 'prophet' such as the so-called 'Son of Man' who appeared at Kasungu in the Livingstonia sphere in 1913 and gave out the tidings of a new religion, so that, as one of the missionaries put it, 'the whole church was shaken'.[223] Chilembwe certainly created no new religion, and his theology appears to have been simple Baptist to the end of his life. Furthermore, there was nothing of the 'messiah' about him.

For all this, Chilembwe did not lack the feeling that he had to give the lead in the 'deliverance' of his people : the same kind of sentiment which had inspired many a Negro agitator on the slave plantations of the New World. The special circumstances of Chilembwe's life, his travels, all reinforced this conviction that he had a special destiny. These elements have to be understood if the strength—and the weaknesses—of Chilembwe's leadership are to be appreciated. For, though the 1915 Rising was much more than a one-man or one-group affair, nevertheless it was John Chilembwe who provided much of its immediate force. He was its general, its high priest, its martyr, all in one.

VI
THE RISING
23 JANUARY–4 FEBRUARY 1915

A Bleeding Head, where they begun . . .
> ANDREW MARVELL, *Horation Ode upon*
> *Cromwell's Return from Ireland*

·

THE RISING

23 JANUARY–4 FEBRUARY 1915

JOHN CHILEMBWE'S conspiracy flared into revolt on Saturday evening, 23 January 1915 ; it was extinguished less than a fortnight later, on 3 February, when his body was found by Government troops. In this short period Chilembwe's forces had killed three Europeans and seriously wounded two others. His following had broken up quickly, and no other Africans inside the Protectorate came to his support. For a rebellion against foreign rule, it had been, on the face of it, singularly ineffective. But, as has already been suggested, it was the quality rather than the quantity of Chilembwe's movement which gave it significance. Before a final estimate can be made of that quality, some attention must be given to the quantity of the Rising and its immediate aftermath.

To Europeans who were living in the Shire Highlands in the last week of January 1915, the Chilembwe outbreak was at first a cause for serious alarm. Despite all the optimism of the years immediately before the War, they were conscious that they were but a small island of whites amid a great sea of blacks ; and at no time, since the beginning of the European scramble for Africa, had any of the occupying groups been altogether sure of their safety.[1] The boast of many Nyasaland settlers that relations between them and the natives were better than anywhere else in Africa had much truth in it. But even this feeling of relative confidence was seriously disturbed by the coming of the Great War and its extension to the African colonies : for such a conflict was unprecedented, and ignorance was accompanied, naturally, by apprehension. By January 1915 it was still an open issue whether the Germans would launch a large-scale counter-attack after their repulse at Karonga ; and Nyasaland, at least psychologically, was still very much in the front line of the War. For all these reasons, it is understandable why many Europeans in the Protectorate felt more than perturbed when the news of the Rising reached them.

Their perturbation was enhanced by the suddenness of the movement. It came as a complete surprise :[2] though some would later shield behind a 'not surprised, told you so' attitude, when the few previous warnings about Chilembwe and his plot were called to mind. Yet if most of the Europeans of Nyasaland were to be honest about it, they could not but admit that it came as a shock to them. Though the imminence of the outbreak was known to many Africans of the neighbourhood, there was, with one exception, no observable change in their attitude towards the Europeans from which the nearness of the Rising could be judged. The one exception is indicated by the testimony of L. S. Norman, a planter in the Mika-longwe hills on the southern margin of the district that was involved in the conspiracy : and his evidence supplies only a partial exception to the rule of silence and secrecy which preceded the Rising, for it was noted by him on the day after the main attacks. On this day he felt something was wrong with the labourers on his tobacco plantation :

> Instead of the usual long row of bending men in each furrow all moving forward, some stood conversing and gesticulating, while others were openly and defiantly doing the work anyhow, though a few carried on as usual. In most eyes was a gleam of suppressed excitement as they furtively, or boldly, watched my movements.[3]

To get a measure of the situation, he called his overseer and asked him if he had heard anything of the rebels' fighting. The overseer told him that the Africans knew all about it ; and then added a story which suggests that certain officials of the district had received information, or had had some experience which confirmed a state of uneasiness amongst them. He informed Norman that 'a few days ago' a native policeman passed by his plantation on his way to Chiradzulu with a letter to warn the magistrate there that the 'trouble' was coming, and that the policeman had told him about it. The policeman, it seems, was 'murdered only a few miles away by some natives to whom he had communicated the nature of his errand' ; and so the secrecy of the Rising was maintained. At its best, the story is slender evidence that the secrecy around the conspiracy had been infringed but very slightly.

This is apparent from the fact that the magistrate at Chiradzulu was away in Blantyre on the day of the outbreak, and that he had taken no pains at all to warn his European neighbours. He, seemingly, had no apprehensions, or nothing he had seen or been told had brought them to a head at this stage.[4]   And yet the scene of the trouble, when it came, was literally under the eye of this magistrate.

Chiradzulu mountain dominates the road from Blantyre to Zomba. In the early days of the Administration, as was noted in Chapter II, it had been a lair of highway robbers, and the centre of a traditionally troubled district. The Administration's post, therefore, had been built on the mountainside : partly in the interests of the magistrate's health ; and partly to have a centre which would be uninviting to attack and, at the same time, at the head of a fan of approaches to potential seats of disaffection and recalcitrance.   It was on the side of Mount Chiradzulu away from the line of the Blantyre-Zomba road, facing eastward over a thirty-mile-wide plain to the mass of Mlanje mountain on the Portuguese frontier. Like all other Administrative posts, it was called *Boma* by white and black alike, after the Swahili term that was used by the first Zanzibari and Makua soldiers of the Queen's Commissioner for the stockaded 'forts' from which they dominated the district.

Some five miles or so from the Boma, just beyond the fringing foothills of Chiradzulu mountain, lay Chilembwe's church and head-quarters. His rising, then, had been planned right under the eyes of the district magistrate. And with that official absent from his post, on the night of Saturday, 23 January 1915, to the surprise and alarm of the unprepared European community, John Chilembwe and his people broke into armed insurrection.

From their centre at Mbombwe the two main attacking parties set off in opposite directions. The first went north on a short march of some eight miles to Magomero and the heart of the A. L. Bruce Estates. Its primary objectives were the dwellings of the general manager and the field staff of the Magomero section of the Estates. And foremost amongst these primary objectives was William J. Livingstone, the manager, himself.

On this Saturday night, guests were being entertained at Mago-mero. Mrs. Ranald MacDonald, wife of the Director of Customs at Chiromo, was on a visit to the Livingstones ; and Mrs. Emily Stanton of Zomba, with her young child, was visiting her brother's wife, Alice Roach.   J. T. Roach was Engineer on the Bruce Estates, and had been with them some four years after a brief spell with the Zambesi Industrial Mission. He had left his wife and his two young children with his sister while he went to attend a jumble sale for the Belgian Relief Fund in Blantyre on the Saturday afternoon. Roach stayed overnight in Blantyre, and so probably escaped the fate of William Jervis Livingstone and another European, Duncan MacCormick, who was employed as a planter by the Bruce Estates.[5]

Thus there were eleven Europeans at Magomero that night : the Livingstones and their two children (a daughter of five years and an infant son of five months) ; Mrs. Roach and her sister-in-law, with three young children ; the visiting Mrs. MacDonald, and the estate employee, MacCormick. All of them had retired early for the night, keeping the early hours of those who have no resources but paraffin lamps when darkness falls at six, and who must be up at the crack of dawn. It was a perfectly normal night for all of them ; and the house servants, who seem to have been innocent of what was to take place—though suspicion fell later on some—gave no signs that anything out of the ordinary was imminent.

The staff quarters at Magomero were built on the shoulders of a fairly steep, wooded knoll and were seventy or eighty feet above the offices, stores, and working yards that were the main concern of the watchmen. They could be approached from the other side of the knoll and each house was sufficiently secluded from the other for what happened at the one not to attract attention at the other. Thus the attackers were able to approach Livingstone's house without too much danger of notice.

At the time, he was lying on the bed playing with his baby son, while his wife was having her bath. The attackers got quickly and silently into the house, although it was apparently locked up for the night. How they managed to do this is not clear but they may have had accomplices within, and it is obvious that they knew the lay-out of the building and were not making their assault without previous reconnaissance. Yet even if the assailants had no accomplices among the house-boys, mosquito-gauzed windows could be readily forced, and door fittings were, as a rule, flimsy adjuncts to light and warped timbers. It was about nine o'clock in the evening when the blow fell.[6]

The details of the assault are not clear, for the whole incident was over in a matter of minutes and by its very rapidity left little impression on European memories. Livingstone tried to defend himself and obviously put up a good fight, using a clubbed rifle—he had no ammunition handy [7]—and fighting his way through three rooms before one of the assailants drove an axe into his head. In the presence of his distraught wife, his head was cut off.[8] She and her children were then bundled out into the dark, with their personal servant, Hinges, while the party of Africans who had conducted the assault, with Livingstone's head stuck on a pole, got ready to go back to Chilembwe [9] and their headquarters at Mbombwe.

Meanwhile the personal servant of Mrs. MacDonald was coming to her rescue. She had been getting ready to go to bed, when she noticed from the window of her room large numbers of natives gathering outside. But she had no time to speculate on the significance of this unusual sight, for the attack was delivered almost immediately.[10] She called for her native servant, and he came speedily to her aid. He held her down while the attackers were in the house ; and then, taking advantage of the distraction caused by Livingstone's fight, pushed her—in her nightdress—through a window and out into the surrounding bush, which was close to the house and afforded cover for her, as it had, no doubt, some hours previously helped the advancing rebels. The native servant then guided Mrs. MacDonald across the country away from the line of march of the attackers until they reached the village of headman Jumbe, who was a *capitao* (foreman) in the employ of the Bruces and lived outside the boundary of their Estates, about two miles away from the centre of the attack. He gave her a *machilla* (carried hammock) and some carriers, who took her to the nearest European planter, at whose house she arrived in the early morning. The planter, a Mr. Charles Carmichael of Nachambo, went with her into Zomba. It was in this way that the news of the attack on Magomero was made known to Government headquarters in Zomba, early on the Sunday morning, 24 January. Had Mrs. MacDonald not escaped in this almost miraculous manner to Zomba, it is possible that the rebels' effort might have been more protracted.

While she was thus making her escape, further fatal events were taking place at Magomero. The house-boys of Duncan MacCormick had come and informed him that there was trouble at Livingstone's. MacCormick was a fellow islander of Livingstone's, from Baligarve in Lismore, and had been brought out by him in 1908 to help on the Estates.[11] There was thus a bond of sympathy, as well as of interest to make MacCormick rush to Livingstone's assistance. Yet, for all his readiness to help, he did not bother to take firearms with him. MacCormick is said to have told his anxious house-boys that he could settle any trouble with his bare fists [12]—a remark which was symptomatic of the general planter's attitude that a gun was the last resort in dealing with people, and that truculence could be outfaced by truculence. But on this occasion the people were something more than truculent. They were carrying out an operation—and MacCormick was speared on his way to the main disturbance. His body, unmutilated, was found with Livingstone's by the first reconnaissance parties from Zomba.

The two white men having been killed, the remaining ladies, Mrs. Roach and Mrs. Stanton and their three children, were brought out barefoot and in their night attire, to join the distracted Mrs. Livingstone, with her little son on her back, and her small daughter by her side.[13] Their personal servants were allowed to go along with them : an arrangement which may have prevented them from becoming utterly demented, for it was a dark night, and the whole affair of the decapitation and capture was so sudden and mysterious that they could have little idea of what was going on. Chilembwe's men apparently intended to march them all off to Mbombwe, the rebel headquarters. What Chilembwe intended to do with them then is not clear : they believed that they were to be held as hostages. Yet Chilembwe never showed any signs that he wanted to use them to extract favourable truce terms or any other advantages for his following. It is possible that they were simply being taken out of the way so that they should not interfere with the rebels' activities, or become hurt in the course of their operations. It is likely that they were to be held at his headquarters until he saw which way the Rising was going : their ultimate fate would then be decided. Certainly, they were not to receive harsh treatment. Indeed, they suffered no further aggression nor any injuries apart from the hardships of a march on foot in the dark over broken ground and the shock which the frightening and uncertain circumstances through which they were passing thrust on them. Had pure blood-lust and atavism played the role in the rebels' plans which subsequent critics have claimed, there was nothing to stop Chilembwe's men at the Magomero attack from perpetrating any manner of outrages on the women and children. As it was, once the worst part of the attack was over, the decapitation of Livingstone and the spearing of MacCormick— which was probably no part of their original plans—the rebels withdrew in order. They made no further attempt to attack other isolated European houses, in spite of the success of their first essay and the long period of darkness which still remained. This seems to have been more than restraint, for not only did the insurgents do no further harm to the women and children whom they were escorting to Mbombwe but, indeed, they seem to have practised positive kindness towards them. Weary children were carried; in some cases wet nurses were provided; and, in the later stages of captivity, banana leaves were held over the heads of the Europeans to shield them from the sun.[14] Whatever the original intention for abducting them may have been, they had, in fact, been removed from possible irresponsible attack and pillage by anyone who might decide that, with the men killed, the women and children left at Magomero were fair game. In all this there seems no reason to attribute the rebels' attitude to prudence and the wrath to come, and the fact deserves some notice when judgement is made of the character of John Chilembwe and his men. For it has too often been charged against them that, for a people professing Christianity—a Christianity which such critics in other contexts have not hesitated to point out could hardly be anything but superficial—they had not only treacherously killed a man but had then cut off his head. The symbolical quality of this action has already been suggested in the previous chapter; and, without in any way wishing to excuse it, one cannot help noting the restraint which enabled the insurgents to control the emotional eruption due to the culmination in bloodshed of a dangerous con-spiracy—conditions which not uncommonly drive those who are subjected to such influences to unrestrained assault on the helpless and weak.

Concentration on the human aspects of the assault on Mago-mero should not be allowed to conceal the material advantage which the rebels had derived from their attack. Not merely had they killed the manager of the Estates—a concrete and symbolic action which might have been expected to bring them some support from local Africans—but also they had taken all the rifles and ammunition they could.[15] Most, if not all of the small but not insignificant arms supply which they captured came from Roach's house. Roach was secretary of the local Volunteer section, and had stores of cartridges at his home—a fact that was surely known to the rebels before they attacked it. They made away with his two rifles and nearly a thousand rounds of ammunition, although his Mauser pistol and another thousand rounds escaped their notice.[16] If the Rising were to be extended, it was not a contemptible haul, though perhaps Chilembwe had hoped for more.

While Livingstone and MacCormick were losing their lives and the women and children at Magomero were being ushered into the dark, a further attack was in progress on another part of the Estates. This was at Mwanje, the section of the Estates nearest to Chilembwe's centre. It was here that the section manager, John Robertson, a Lowlander from the family farm of Ochiltree Castle, near Linlithgow,[17] was attacked at an hour which he estimates as 8 P.M.[18] If this is correct, the attack in this section came about an hour before the raid on Magomero. It is unlikely that this was in accordance with a prearranged plan, for there seems nothing to be gained by having the one attack earlier than the other. It is likely, therefore, that both attacks were planned for the same time but failed to synchronize properly, perhaps because Mwanje was nearer to Chilembwe's headquarters and, therefore, was more easily reached. Perhaps, however, both attacks did take place at much the same time, and this time has been confused by European witnesses because of the suddenness and the surprise by night of the rebels.[19]

Robertson's assailants at Mwanje were apparently a separate party, though under the same central control as the Magomero attackers. At Mwanje there were two European houses. In one of them the stock manager, Robert Ferguson, was lying on the bed reading his mail which he had only received that afternoon. (Ferguson was another Lowlander, a native of Dumfriesshire, who had been eighteen months in Nyasaland.[20]) He had not yet troubled to lock up his house for the night, when a group of insurgents rushed upon him and speared him in the chest. The attack failed to kill him and he was able—and permitted, it appears—to make his way to the Robertson house, where the first attempt to force an entry had failed, and the attackers had withdrawn temporarily. A curious feature of the attack on Ferguson is that, unlike Livingstone and MacCormick at Magomero, or his neighbour, Robertson, at Mwanje, it is reported that he had been warned—presumably by an African— that an attack was likely to be made ; but he did not appreciate the seriousness of the situation and left his house completely unlocked.[21] If this is correct, why Ferguson alone of the Magomero-Mwanje group of Europeans should have been singled out for such a warning is another mystery of the Rising—especially as he is known to have been ordered by W. J. Livingstone one Sunday to destroy a P.I.M. church on the Bruce Estates,[22] a fact that was not likely to endear him to Africans.

Conditions in the Robertson household were similar to those in

Magomero : they were getting ready to go to bed. Mrs. Robertson was having a bath, and her husband was completely unaware of what was impending. Suddenly there was a knock on the bedroom door. Robertson asked who it was, and received the reply, 'Come to the door. I have something to tell you.' The night before he had had some difficulties with the cattle in his section, and, on this occasion, he thought it was the watchmen who had come to tell him of more trouble with them. He went to the door. But, before it was half open, the assailant outside thrust a spear at him which went through his right arm into his chest. Fortunately for Robertson, he had been standing sideways to his assailant ; otherwise, he would have got the full force of the spear in his chest. Checked in its course, the spear broke. But the force of the blow was enough to send Robertson reeling across the room with the iron spearhead sticking in his arm. Luckily for him, however, the attack could not be followed up : for, as he fell backwards, the reaction of the door as it slipped out of his left hand—in which he appears to have held it— was enough to shut it with a bang. The bolt then dropped and fastened the door. The very precipitancy of his assailant had created the means whereby he was prevented from following up his attack.

The delay was sufficient to save Robertson's life. Alarmed and out of her bath, his wife rushed to his aid, helped him to pull out the spearhead, bandaged his arm and stopped the bleeding. Robertson could now take stock of the situation. It was clear that there were no other attackers in his house, for he, unlike the assistant manager Ferguson, had locked up before going to bed. (This fact raises the problem of how the assailant had got so secretly into the house in the first place, for, afterwards, Robertson had no reason to suspect either of his two house-boys of collusion with the Chilembwe-ites. The whole affair had taken place too quickly for Robertson to know who his assailant was.) From noise outside the house, it was obvious that there was a crowd of natives around it. This body was obviously less disciplined than the attackers of Magomero,[23] for they were dancing around the house and breaking all the windows. Robertson by this time had recovered enough to seize his rifle, get out on to the veranda of his house and fire a few shots at the attacking Africans. Unfortunately this was too late to prevent the roof from being set alight. At this point Ferguson came staggering over to the Robertson's with the spear that had been thrust at him still sticking out of his chest. The resourceful Mrs. Robertson managed to get him on to a sofa in their sitting-room and pulled it out. But, for Ferguson, it was too late, and he died almost immediately.

The fire in the Robertson's house was now threatening. So they rushed into their kitchen, a grass shack away from the main building. No thought could be given to Ferguson's body in the danger of the moment, with a blazing house all around them and a mob of assailants outside. The dead Ferguson, therefore, was left on the sofa in the sitting-room and was burned so completely that all that was found of him later was a thigh-bone, which was buried at Mwanje.

In the grass kitchen outside, the Robertsons were joined by their house-boy, who proved completely loyal. Robertson had his two rifles with him ; his wife loaded them, because of his wounded right arm, and he pressed the trigger. One of these rifles was given to the house-boy and he was told to go outside and discover what was happening. No sooner had he done this than he was speared. Recovering the rifle, Robertson fired at the attackers through the grass walls of the kitchen. It seems that they were now concentrating on the kitchen, having been driven back for a short time by the fierceness of the flames from the main house. So Robertson and his wife decided to try to escape through a near-by garden of cotton, whose plants, then about two feet high, offered some cover. They did what they could for the wounded house-boy, and then bolted for the shelter of the cotton. When they were about a hundred and fifty yards away they saw the kitchen go up in flames. Mrs. Robertson's innate military sense, which had been admirable up to this time, then deserted her and she was all for shooting at the Africans who could be seen silhouetted against the flames of the burning kitchen. But Robertson had had some actual military experience—he had been at the Karonga battle—and he realized that to shoot at the Africans from the cover of the cotton plants would only reveal that he and his wife had escaped. It was far better to let the Africans think that they had been burned in the kitchen. This ruse succeeded, for after the kitchen burned to the ground, the attacking party seemed to go back in the direction of Chilembwe's church. Robertson and his wife had escaped the fate of the Europeans at Magomero.

For Robertson it had been a much more frightening experience than the battle of Karonga. On his return from the northern war front he had found the neighbouring natives friendly and had had no suspicion that any conspiracy was being launched. Thus he was taken completely by surprise. On his escape from his burning house, however, he would have little time for such thoughts. He and his wife were now intent on making for Magomero where they believed they would find succour from the Livingstones, for they had no idea that, at much the same time as they themselves were fleeing from assaulting Africans, Livingstone's head and his trembling wife and children were being paraded into the night. Like Mrs. Livingstone and her children, the Robertsons were clad only in their night-clothes.

By the time the Robertsons felt that it was safe to move, after shivering for an hour in the dark amongst the covering cotton plants, it was two o'clock on Sunday morning. A small action still awaited them. When they were four miles on their unsuspecting way to Magomero, at a place called Chimwaliro, they came across three natives standing at the side of the road. Robertson asked them what they were waiting for. On receiving no answer, he ordered them to move away from the road. They made no response, so he fired at one of them and apparently killed or wounded him. The other two ran away. It is not unlikely that Robertson had met a party of Chilembwe's scouts, a kind of primitive standing patrol. Two miles farther along the road, Robertson met a herd-boy whom he knew. He refused to help the wounded and exhausted Europeans ; but, on the other hand, did nothing to impede them. Yet the meeting with him was fortunate for he told the Robertsons that it would be useless for them to go to Magomero, and gave them all the news of what had happened there. The ambivalent attitude of this herd-boy suggests that he was like other Africans of the area at the time of the outbreak of the Rising : desirous of giving neither offence nor help to either side until they were sure of the final outcome of the insurrection.

Warned of the fate of Magomero, the Robertsons made for the estate of a private planter named Kemper over by the Zomba road at Namiwawa, about six miles away. (Namiwawa, 'mahogany tree stream', is a common Nyasaland place-name. The Namiwawa to which the Robertsons were making their way should be distinguished from the Church of Christ mission station over the opposite (northern) border of the Bruce Estates.) They journeyed through the small hours of Sunday, 24 January 1915, and in the early morning, just when they were but a mile away from the Namiwawa estate, met Kemper himself who had come out to look for them. Though his property was fairly close to Magomero no attempt had been made on Kemper's life—a further piece of evidence which indicates that general massacre was no part of the rebels' plans at that time. He had got up in the normal manner, early on Sunday morning, when his boy had brought in the morning tea and the garbled news that Livingstone had killed himself. So Kemper had gone over immediately to Magomero and found not the suicide of Livingstone but the evidence of a native rising. Other Africans had told him that the Robertsons had been killed at Mwanje, so he had set out for there to see what had happened.

It was typical of the reactions of Europeans very close to the situation that Kemper, as soon as he heard that there was trouble, did not turn to barricade himself in his quarters but promptly set off alone to investigate and to bring what help he could. Like MacCormick at Magomero before he was speared, Kemper did not think in terms of a hornet's nest but of a situation that probably needed cooling down. It was a different attitude from that of the Government at the capital of the Protectorate, which could only view the situation in terms of the War and of the future of the British in the Protectorate, and showed many signs of panic and hasty action. The episode revealed, too, the attitude of the Africans of the district, for Kemper encountered no hindrance or threat on his journeys of investigation. But the immediate needs of the Robertsons, by this time utterly exhausted and in need of medical treatment, turned him back, and thereafter investigation became a matter for official action alone. Robertson was taken on the Sunday afternoon into hospital in Zomba and his part in the Rising was over.

It was the end, too, of the major thrusts of John Chilembwe and his men against the Bruce Estates. They made no further attacks on any of the other Europeans of the Estates or on the neighbouring private planters,[24] who were not even in pairs like the Magomero and Mwanje men. Yet, though it was obviously limited in its aim, the night's work of the rebels in the area of the Bruce Estates had been disturbingly successful. Of the four potentially well-armed and competent Europeans in key economic positions whom they had attacked, three (Livingstone, MacCormick, and Ferguson) were dead, and the other, Robertson, might at first be presumed dead in the fire that had been set to the point from which his last shots had come—though that presumption would not last long in view of the number of natives who had met the Robertsons on their way to Kemper's. Furthermore, as has been noted, it appears that the Magomero raiders had taken the opportunity—presumably after the murder of

Livingstone and MacCormick—to get as many arms as they could from the armoury of the Namadzi section of the Nyasaland Volunteer Reserve. Thus, on the night of 23 January 1915 and the early morning of the following Sunday, despite the escapes of the Robertsons and of Mrs. MacDonald, Chilembwe's men seem to have achieved their immediate objectives, at least as far as Magomero was concerned. The increase in their armament would mean strength for any subsequent attacks which they cared to launch, and the capture of the European women and children apparently provided, should they care to use them, excellent hostages. In that period of the Rising, then, there was some justification for the panic which was prevalent in official quarters and amongst some private persons, too, in Nyasaland.

In their other objective for that first night of the Rising, however, the rebels had not been so successful. This was the walled enclosure which held the principal warehouse and trading store and the armoury of the African Lakes Corporation at Blantyre. There were firearms in the store for sale, and in the armoury a stock of arms and ammunition for the use of the Corporation's agents. The approach to Mandala (the traditional name for the Corporation's headquarters) was along a much longer route of some fifteen miles from Chilembwe's main base and in a different, and, for some members of the party at least, a less familiar direction from his centre. There seems to be no means of ascertaining the exact size of the force which was used on this occasion ; but, from available evidence, it appears to have been a bigger one than the groups that were employed for the attacks on Magomero and Mwanje. Though still relatively large, with, according to some suggestions, numbers over the hundred or hundreds mark, the force which actually reached the Blantyre objective seems to have been thinned out by preliminary desertions and wastage *en route*. Nevertheless, in spite of the relatively long approach to the objective and the desertions, a remarkable degree of secrecy was maintained and it was not until the raid was launched on the African Lakes Corporation's armoury that the element of surprise was lost. Though the fact that many of the Europeans were congregated together in mutual entertainment at the annual general meeting of the Blantyre Sports Club helped to divert the attention of many of them from the massing on Blantrye of a large number of Chilembwe's supporters, there were others who were not at the Club and they were deceived equally.[25]

The raid on the Corporation's ammunition and general stores did not take place until about half-past two on the Sunday morning [26] of 24 January, when the Magomero and Mwanje Europeans were already dead, captive, or fugitive. Whether this delay between the raids on the two centres was intentional or a matter of the more difficult circumstances of the Blantyre attack is not clear. Chilembwe certainly seems to have taken precautions to keep the news of the various attacks from reaching the Government prematurely. Telephone lines were cut between Blantyre and Mikalongwe, Zomba and Tete ; [27] and, according to one account, armed Africans were stationed at the fronts of all the houses near the African Lakes Corporation's stores to ensure that any man who ventured out 'to inquire into the unusual occurrence' [28] could be silenced effectively.

The ammunition store of the Corporation, its retail store in which rifles for sale to Europeans were kept, and the houses of the headquarters staff occupied the Mandala estate that was practically a suburb of the Blantyre township, from which it was divided by the steep banks of the Mudi stream that was bridged at two points. Despite its successful arrival on the objective, the actions of the raiding party, once the scheme had begun, were clumsy and confused. Some of this confusion may have been due to the numbers in the party for whom the area was not well-known territory ; and some to the fact that the leaders of the individual sections that carried out the various tasks on the objective were not of the calibre of the general leadership which had so successfully brought them there. Who composed this leadership, as has been seen, is not clear. If, as some maintain, the Blantyre raid was in charge of John Gray Kufa, then the story from the same source, that his heart failed him at the last moment,[29] may be a further explanation—perhaps the main explanation—of the clumsiness and confusion of the attacks that were made on the property of the African Lakes Corporation. Nevertheless this emphasis on clumsiness must not be carried too far, for the first attack went off without a hitch.

This was the raid on the buildings of the European store, where the rebels were successful in finding a few rifles. A native watchman of the Bank of the African Lakes Corporation was roused but he did not interfere immediately nor give any general alarm : no doubt because he feared for his own safety. The main point and hope of the attack, however, appears to have been the ammunition store about four hundred yards away, in the midst of the European bungalows. The raiders set off for this, and on their way noticed the night watchman, who was following them, presumably with the object of helping the other night watchman at the ammunition store to raise an alarm. It was here that the raiders made their first serious mistake. In a moment of panic or apprehension, they shot the watchman.[30] The shot gathered together all the staff of the Corporation,[31] with the exception of a few who were out of hearing. Amongst those alarmed was the custodian of the armoury key, who immediately left his house and sought the company of others. The rebels now had no choice but to break directly into the ammunition store,[32] however much previously they may have intended to take it by stealth. (There is no clear evidence of the exact technique they proposed to use in getting into it, though, in view of the silence of the first raid on the European stores, it is likely that stealth was their intended method.) By the time the entry into the ammunition store was achieved, the alarm had spread amongst the Mandala men, and the raiding band broke up in disorder, discarding in their flight some of the stolen arms. When, eventually, the African Lakes Corporation employees had had time to recover the arms and ammunition that were left around Mandala by the raiders in their hurried flight, and to make a check on the situation, it was found that, from the attack on the European retail stores, they got away with three 0·303 Martini-Enfield and two Snider rifles, and that from the hurried raid on the ammunition store they had taken six hundred and five rounds of 0·303 soft-nosed cartridges. It was a poor haul for what seems to have been originally a carefully planned night's work. And, in the departure from the objective, there was none of the careful, orderly withdrawal that had marked the attack on Magomero.

It was clear that, at this stage, the Blantyre raiders were badly scared. Too often the cause of this has been attributed to a European legend, not supported by African recollection. The legend is that the panic of the raiding party, after its hasty foray on the ammunition stores, was caused by the break-up of the last revellers of the annual general meeting of the Blantyre Sports Club in the small hours of the Sunday morning. The staccato explosions of early model motor-cycle engines rattled in the clear night air across the Mudi stream like gun-fire, and the uninhibited good-night yells of the combiners of business and pleasure at the Sports Club, so the story goes, sounded to the Africans of Chilembwe's band like the war-cries of the white men in counter-attack.[33] The story has all the elements of a legend, and while it is possible that the break-up of the Club meeting may have added to the fears of some of the rebels, it seems most unlikely that it caused them. No more cogent explanation of their origin is needed than that of the appearance on the scene of a concentrated group of Europeans from the Corporation's staff who had been alerted by the shot that killed the night watchman. It is too much to claim that the Blantyre clubmen, as such, nipped the Rising in the bud !

An urgent message from an alert Mandala man soon brought the Assistant District Resident on the scene, and, with the help of a squad of native police, a sweep was made of the villages around the African Lakes Corporation's centre. In the event of resistance being offered, more drastic measures were to be taken. But none were found necessary, for the raiders were in full flight along the line of the main road as far as Mpingwe hill on the Zomba road about six miles from Blantyre, and then on to Chilembwe's head-quarters at Mbombwe, Chiradzulu. It was in this rout that Chilembwe lost his first men as prisoners. They were four in all, and one of them was said to be an uncle of his.[34] One had been found badly cut with glass as a result of the mad scramble of the raiders to get into the ammunition store, once the alarm had been given, only a couple of hundred yards from the manager's house. The four prisoners admitted their guilt straight away. From Chilembwe's point of view the Blantyre raid raised the questions as to whether the loss of four of his men and the general premature alarm which had been given was worth the five rifles and six hundred rounds of ammunition. Clearly it was not, and his losses at Mandala on the early morning of Sunday, 24 January 1915, must be set against his successes at the Bruce Estates the night before.

And, if the report given in one account is correct, the Mandala raid brought in its train another, possibly more serious loss for Chilembwe : the alienation of some Ngoni who, other things being equal, might have formed an alliance with him. The story goes that the native watchman who was shot at Mandala was 'the son and heir of Kampelusa, an Angoni chief of considerable importance'. He is said to have been an attractive young man, 'immensely popular with his tribe', whose 'murder immediately roused up bitter hostility towards Chilembwe throughout the Angoni tribe in Western Nyasa-land'.[35] It is a story based on hearsay evidence and how much credence should be attached to it is uncertain.[36] Yet it deserves

mention, if only as a further slender shred of evidence for the unfortunately thinly documented episode of Chilembwe's relations with
the Ngoni.

But, if the murder of this watchman may conceivably have given
offence to one particular tribal group, the general African populace
of the Blantyre area seems to have done nothing to help or hinder
either side. It would, perhaps, be wrong to call the Blantyre Africans
apathetic, since they no doubt, like their fellows at Magomero and
other areas of the Rising, were waiting to see how things turned out
before committing themselves definitely to the one group or the
other. Personal ties in this difficult period, such as those which had
kept Robertson's boy with him to the death, or the support of the
faithful Hinges to Mrs. Livingstone, decided most Africans' attitudes.
Where these were lacking, a 'canny' frame of mind was maintained.
Typical of this personal element was the warning given to a Roman
Catholic missionary. He was going unknowingly into the line of
movement of the party which had attacked Mandala—it can hardly
be called a march on its return journey—when he was warned by
friendly villagers of the danger in his way.[37] There was, indeed, no
general action amongst Africans to take advantage of European un-
preparedness to deal the hardest possible first blow, nor any tendency
to be swept into headlong fanaticism.

Thus, by daylight on the Sunday morning, the Europeans of
Blantyre found no difficulty in calling together a detachment of the
Volunteer Reserve to follow up the retreat of the raiding party from
Blantyre. Though some were mounted on motor-cycles, they had
something of the zeal of a 'posse' in the days of the Wild West,
and had soon swept the area to a point eight miles from Blantyre,
where a path forked off that led to Chiradzulu and the rebel headquarters. By this time the Europeans would have some knowledge,
because of the four prisoners they had taken, of who was behind the
attack. It was, then, natural that they should make this point where
the Blantyre-Zomba road branched off in the direction of Chiradzulu
into a base, a kind of standing patrol, from which they could hold
any further attacks that the rebels might launch towards Blantyre
and from which they could scout for further information. Shortly
after their arrival at this base, the Blantyre force encountered dispatch
riders on their way from the seat of government at Zomba, where, as
has been seen, warning had been conveyed of the attack on Magomero in the early hours of Sunday morning—though, because of the

cutting of the telephone lines, news of the Mandala attacks did not reach Zomba 'until later in the day'.[38] When the two parties had exchanged news, it was becoming apparent to them that they were faced with a conspiracy which, even if it had—in one of the initial phases, at least—gone off at half-cock, was yet sufficiently dangerous to be taken seriously. And until news could be gathered from the outlying estates, there could be no certainty that there were, or would be, no more casualties.

Rumour, naturally enough, was spreading amongst these estates. Beyond Zomba, a private planter, G. V. Thorneycroft,[39] was told that the Germans had reached Mlanje and that John Chilembwe had risen in their interest. Rumours that the Germans 'were behind it all' were perfectly understandable and reasonable at a time when the war in East Africa was still very uncertain from the British point of view. Yet, as was to be seen, the Germans in Nyasaland had regard to the call of 'white solidarity' rather than embarrassment of their opponents in war. Indeed, in Mlanje itself, where the rumour of their invasion of the Protectorate was in the air, a German officer, Lieutenant von Veltheim, who had been wounded and captured at Karonga the previous September and then brought to Mlanje as a prisoner of war, 'placed his services at the disposal of the British magistrate there, organized the defence and virtually assumed military command of the station'.[40] Veltheim and a fellow prisoner, although they were not allowed to carry rifles, went about the whole defence with typical German thoroughness—even to constructing wire foot-traps along all native paths which led to the Boma![41]

Nevertheless, in this early period of the Rising, rumours were still rife. At the other end of the planting country, for example, L. S. Norman had received a very panic-stricken report from an Indian storekeeper—who doubtless realized that, if there was an anti-foreign rising amongst the Africans, he and his countrymen, just as much as the Europeans, would be an object of attack—that on the Sunday afternoon three Europeans had been murdered, and that fighting was going on in Blantyre.[42] Yet all was not panic and rumour. At the Nguludi station of the Montfort Marist Fathers' Mission, a bare five miles away from Chilembwe's main church, news had been received of the events of Saturday. But the priests did not feel that it was necessary to evacuate their station, in spite of the warning they had been given before the Rising that Chilembwe proposed to clear out foreign missions with the rest of European agencies from the Protectorate. Nor did the District Magistrate, when he communicated with them, consider it necessary to do more than warn the Marist Fathers to keep a good look-out through the Sunday night.[43]

In fact, despite evidence of panic and rumour on both sides, cooler counsels seem to have prevailed with both Chilembwe and the Europeans. Sunday, 24 January, was spent by both groups in assessing the situation with very little action.[44] If Chilembwe had been keen on a sweeping military victory, it is likely that he would have made advances into the surrounding countryside, while the European forces were still relatively unorganized and the Government had had little opportunity to bring in further reserves from outside the areas affected. In fact, Chilembwe did nothing of the kind. At Mbombwe he held his usual Sunday morning church service, during which the head of William Jervis Livingstone, which had been delivered to him by a member of the party that attacked Magomero, was exhibited on a pole to the African congregation. Local European tradition says that Chilembwe preached a fanatical anti-European sermon, rich in the imagery of the Old Testament, full of vengeful triumph and incitation to further slaughter. Other European accounts claim that Livingstone's head 'was exhibited on the altar, and was a subject of certain hideous rites performed by the officiating high priest and his mission-boy congregation'.[45] According to a native who was present, however, the sermon advocated resignation and courage in face of the retribution which would surely fall on them for this act, necessary though it had been in a situation which, from their point of view, could not be allowed to develop unchecked and without protest.[46] All this while, the European women and children from Magomero were being looked after at Mbombwe, and Chilembwe, it seems, was taking a decision on their fate. If the African informant mentioned above is correct, this was to send them back to the District Commissioner at Chiradzulu with a letter to say that

> we have accomplished what we set out to do, and we are waiting for our deaths. In proof whereof, we have sent his wife alive to explain to you what she saw this night about her husband's death.[47]

It was a note of resignation. Whatever hopes Chilembwe may have had originally, it does seem that on this Sunday, after the three attacks on Magomero, Mwanje, and Mandala, he had come to realize—as, indeed, he may well have foreseen from the very start of his enterprise—that further successes were unlikely, and that the most he could do would be to make the best of a very bad situation. (It must be remembered here that the three attacks had only provided the rebels with seven rifles and 1605 rounds of ammunition.) It has been suggested that his decision to send the European women and children back to their own people was taken out of fear and in the hope that this might persuade the Government to give him better surrender terms.[48]   But there is no evidence that Chilembwe at this time or later contemplated surrender.   From subsequent actions it appears that he and his closest associates had decided that, if the Government wanted them, they had got to take them.   Otherwise, there was just the hope of escape into Portuguese East Africa.   And was there, perhaps, for Chilembwe the feeling that he might get down to the coast and away, surreptitiously, to his Negro friends in America ?   It is most likely, however, that he realized, with his followers, that they were doomed.

This would have been apparent from intelligence that came into Chilembwe's headquarters of the lack of any great African support for his venture, and of the preparations which the Europeans were making for the emergency.   Although, as has been noted, news of the Mandala affair did not reach the Government until late in the day, in Zomba action was immediately taken when the news of the Magomero attack reached it.   A force of about 150 [49] men was made up from local Europeans and recruits at the depot of the King's African Rifles in Zomba and placed under the command of Captain L. E. L. Triscott of the 1/K.A.R.   This was sent out to the Magomero area, and later on the Sunday morning, when it had been joined by a reinforcement of Volunteer Reservists, to the Boma at Chiradzulu.   As Zomba became more aware of the extent of the movement, when news came in of the Blantyre episode, a message was sent to the Officer Commanding the troops at Karonga for a force of seasoned troops as insurance against the development of the Rising.   How long this message took to reach Karonga is not certain : but if it went by wire it would have reached there on the Sunday evening.   The Officer Commanding lost no time in sending from Karonga a double company, 'F' and 'H', of the 1/K.A.R., with a machine gun and a 7-pdr. M.L. gun, under Captain H. G. Collins.[50] It is by no means impossible that Chilembwe heard that this message had been sent off to Karonga : for though he received no active support from Africans who were not directly attached to his force he had a number of passive African supporters who would be in a position to pass such news on to him. If so, with the failure of any hopes that he may have had of getting a good supply of arms and ammunition from Mandala, it would demonstrate fully to him the precariousness of his position.

The situation, however, was still very uncertain, with rumour correspondingly rife. The force which had been sent on the Sunday morning from Zomba to investigate the Chiradzulu Boma had no news whether it had been occupied by insurgents or not, for the magistrate was still absent. Thus it advanced very cautiously towards the Boma. Caution was increased when scouts observed a number of natives moving about in the neighbourhood of the magistrate's house. For all the investigating force knew, the moving natives might have been Chilembwe's men who had taken and were guarding the Boma. It is not without significance as well as humour that the movements proved to be those of convicts from the Boma prison, who were detailed to keep the house and grounds in order. They were carrying on with their routine tasks in the absence of the magistrate, in spite of the outbreak of a 'war of liberation' at the foot of the hill. They could hardly have been ignorant of the outbreak; yet they had neither broken jail nor called on the insurgents to rescue them.[51]

This minor scare is typical of many others in the early days of the Rising. A good example is the tale from Mponda's, the site of a Universities Mission to Central Africa station, some three miles from Fort Johnston at the southern end of Lake Nyasa. A padre from Malindi, about nine miles from Mponda's, rushed into the mission station, out of breath and exhausted, having run almost all the way, to tell the Anglican missionaries that an armed party of raiders might at any moment descend upon them. The missionaries prepared themselves as well as they could to receive an attack, and sat up all night in expectation of it. But nothing happened; and, the following morning, another messenger arrived with an explanation. It seems that a group of friendly Africans had given warning of an attack after they had seen a party of men who were carrying what they took to be some kind of weapon, and who were coming over the hills towards the Lake. The supposed raiders, however, were nothing more than a party of touring photographers equipped with the old-fashioned folding tripod cameras![52] The farther north the rumours went, the more weird and wonderful they became. Presumably because it was known that Chilembwe was associated with American missions, the story was spread around amongst some Africans that the Americans had invaded the Protectorate![53] One would like to know more of the actual scope and distribution of this rumour, for it may well have been not merely the result of Chilembwe's known links with the United States but also an echo of the sentiments which Booth had often aired amongst Africans : that they would be better off under American than British rule.

But to the Zomba detachment that was charged with ascertaining the facts and with checking the trouble at its known source at Chiradzulu, it was Chilembwe himself that mattered, not any remote support which he might have had. Still unsure of the situation, the detachment planned a reconnaissance in force to Chilembwe's headquarters at Mbombwe. It was not to take place immediately but on the following day. There seem to be no grounds for the assumption that Government forces attacked and were repulsed from Mbombwe on the Sunday, 23 January.[54] The Government was taking stock of the situation before committing itself. Precautions, however, were taken. In Blantyre on the Sunday night, the town was patrolled by Volunteers, and people in the more isolated houses came in to stay with friends at the centre. But no official concentration in laagers was yet ordered. Perhaps until Government forces had fought at least one engagement with Chilembwe's men and been repulsed, the Administration did not feel that any very great action was necessary. Or it may be that, taken by surprise, the Government was still recovering from the shock of the Rising, and was wondering what exactly would be the most appropriate action to take.

Certainly, in Blantyre and Zomba and their environs, there seems to have been none of that atmosphere of sullen expectation which L. S. Norman, the planter, professed to find among the domestic servants and labourers on the Mikalongwe estates.[55] The only evidence of disaffection among domestics appears to be provided by the plot against C. E. Ingall of the British Central Africa Company who, on information supplied by his pantry boy, ascribed a violent illness on the Friday night, the night before the first organized attack by the Chilembwe-ites on Europeans, to poison in his food.[56] It seems that the greater part of Ingall's house staff were in a conspiracy against him, and had set an ambush for him by placing a tree across the road : so that when he returned, as they expected, from the Blantyre Sports Club meeting to which he had gone on the Saturday in spite of his sickness of the night before, he would be easy meat for the armed party that lay in wait. Fortunately, like Roach of Magomero, he stayed in Blantyre over-night, and thus frustrated the plans of the conspirators. But when he went home after an absence of a few days, during which he served with the Volunteers in the second attack on Chilembwe's stronghold, the loyal pantry-boy and others revealed the whole story to him; and he took his cook, house-boy, and kitchen-boy to be tried at Blantyre. They were all found guilty, along with two other natives from Chisombezi, and were shot by a firing party of the Mikalongwe section of the Nyasaland Volunteer Reserve. It is a mysterious episode—rather like 'the Chiradzulu police [who] saved the lives of two Europeans by a timely warning' [57]—and there are many details about the episode of which one would like to have more information. Why was Ingall, alone of the Europeans in the area, singled out for this attack? How far were the conspirators linked to Chilembwe in the relation of sub-plot; and how far did they act independently of him? Is this episode—as it certainly appears to be—the same as that which was noticed by another planter of the area, L. S. Norman? In this, the details of the ambush have a ferociously efficient character:

> A native armed with the gentleman's rifle and ammunition, waited in an outhouse to shoot him should he escape the first trap; and to make doubly sure, another, armed with a bayonet, lay hidden on the verandah of the dwelling.[58]

But, with this exception, unless Norman's account is of some other plot, all other references to servants at the time of the Chilembwe insurrection suggest that they not only discharged faithfully their responsibilities in looking after property that was left to their care by employers who were away in the hunt for the rebels, but also that, in the comparatively few dangerous situations in which the Europeans found themselves, some of their servants ran—not always with impunity—serious risks to themselves.

This consideration of the measure of support which Chilembwe received from some of the local Africans provides a convenient place to pause and examine what effective help he was given from other Africans. As has already been noted when considering his con-spiracy, Chilembwe had hopes of support from three quarters: from some Mlanje chiefs; from some Zomba headmen; and from Filipo

Chinyama and Ngoni and allied groups around Ncheu. What hopes Chilembwe had from the first of these parties for an attack on the Mlanje Boma and a seizure of its arms were soon dashed to the ground, for one of the Mlanje chiefs to whom he had apparently made overtures turned King's evidence.[59] In the Zomba area, though most of the overtures which Chilembwe had made to chiefs and headmen were refused, he appears to have gained some support amongst a few of the headmen. The *Nyasaland Times* for 4 February 1915 notes the execution of Makwangwala, a Zomba headman who had been implicated in the Rising. It is not clear who this man was, and, as has been seen,[60] it is just possible that the paper was confusing him with an Ncheu African. But, of one of Chilembwe's Zomba supporters, there can be no doubt.

An elder of Chilembwe's church had succeeded to the headmanship of Kimu village, a dozen miles out of Zomba itself, on the way to Lake Chilwa and near the road going east between Machemba and Mlanje mountains. It was in the area which had been swept originally by the slave wars, and at this time it was being re-populated by African immigrants from Portuguese territory. To secure their effective adherence to Chilembwe's cause, some bravado was perhaps thought necessary. And so, when the local estate-owners were called into laager in Zomba, Kimu indulged in some wild talk of leading his people to the sack of Zomba. This was reported to the Administration; and two planters, G. V. Thorney-croft[61] and A. J. Williams, who asked for and were given the Governor's permission to deal with this threat to the peace of the area with the help of their estate employees, returned home and armed a force of Ngoni and Tonga labourers. They operated for about a week between Pirimiti hill and the north end of Mlanje; but, after an opening running fight with Kimu's people, who were in retreat but who shot arrows at the pursuing force as they withdrew, no resistance was encountered. Written evidence was found at Kimu's village to show that he was in league with Chilembwe: yet his activity had contributed nothing to the success of the Rising. Unlike the other Zomba headman who, according to the *Nyasaland Times*, was shot, Kimu escaped with a prison sentence, and, when the whole affair had died down and he had served his term, was re-instated in his office and grew into an old man, reluctant to speak of his past misadventures.

If the support which Chilembwe received from the Mlanje and

Zomba headmen and chiefs was small, there are indications that his following among the Ncheu Ngoni was much larger, and that, if the Rising there had been organized better and had then gone according to plan, the threat from the Ncheu area to the security of the Shire Highlands might have been greater. Some of the background of Filipo Chinyama and the Dzunje chief, Makwangwala, the moving insurrectionary spirits in the Ncheu area, has been noticed in the previous chapter. The actual effect of their conspiracy remains to be considered.[62] Their influence seems to have been limited to the Dzunje section of Chief Makwangwala, and the Africans of the other seven sections of the district appear to have had no part or interest in the Rising. This may have been due to local rivalries or to a persistence in the Ncheu area of the same 'canny' attitude towards the outcome of the Rising which has been observed elsewhere. Ncheu itself lies west of the Shire, some seventy miles from Zomba, and a little more from Blantyre, by a different road. This distance factor, together with some inefficient communications work on the part of Chilembwe's staff, may have been the reason for the failure of Chinyama's and Makwangwala's men to strike south-west and give the main Rising in the Shire Highlands more effective support. One African informant states that the revolt was badly timed,[63] and suggests that if the Ngoni from Ncheu had been given more time they would have been more able to help Chilembwe. As it was, some failure of co-ordination and control between Chilembwe and Chinyama, and between Chinyama and his own men, is apparent. The day before the Ncheu outbreak occurred,[64] the District Resident, C. A. Cardew, had received word that Africans at Dzunje were holding meetings and that trouble might be expected. From his previous experience of Chinyama's independent church and school activities, he reacted immediately and sent three of his police to inquire into the situation. Later in the evening he received a message to say that a large body of armed natives was advancing on the Boma. Reports from the Shire Highlands that this was 'several hundreds'[65] in size were probably correct, for a hundred were captured eventually, and the numbers of desertions from this force, once the news of its bad timing with the main scheme and its slender subsequent hopes were realized, suggest that the original body was substantial. The intentions of this group are still not clear, because of the paucity of evidence about the whole Ncheu-Ngoni side of the Rising. Was it their intention to capture the Boma and then strike south to join

Chilembwe; or did they merely intend to create trouble in their own area so that this would act as a diversion in favour of Chilembwe's main force? Whatever their objectives, they seem to have realized none of them, though they no doubt added to local European apprehensions. The American Seventh Day Baptist missionary, Walter Cockerill, who had known Chinyama, was still confined to the neighbourhood of Blantyre after his brush with authority. It was here that he picked up, from some source or other, an account of the Ncheu side of the Rising which may be quoted at this stage because, while some of his details may be incorrect, he does seem to have a grasp of the numbers involved, and, anyway, his account seems representative of the story of the insurrectionary movement which was circulating amongst Europeans in parts of the Protectorate that were more directly influenced by Chilembwe's plots. Cockerill stated:

> At the same time a curious event took place at Ncheu in Angoniland. Three hundred natives armed with spears, made a demonstration for two nights before the office of the resident magistrate, breaking the windows but doing no further harm. They were finally dispersed by half a company of native soldiers, and a hundred captured.[66]

The Resident had taken pains to meet any threat. On the night of the warning he had taken all the police, himself, his Assistant and wife into his office building, as a precautionary defensive measure. The following day he received news that the rebels had reached Chimwala village three miles from Ncheu, and that, on hearing of his defensive measures, they had decided to join forces with Chilembwe. As Chinyama's band was equipped largely with spears and seems to have had very few guns, this was no unwise alternative manœuvre, when it is remembered that the Residency was something of a concentrated defensive point, moderately well fortified, and in possession of rifles and ammunition. Some of the rebels, according to one official source, appear to have been moving in the direction of Matandani, where there was a Seventh-day Adventist Mission station—though what this fact is intended to convey is not clear.[67] (Matandani station was in the hill country near the Portuguese border, some seventy miles west of Blantyre; and it is possible that some of Chinyama's men were seeking it as a friendly place from which to escape from the wrath of the Nyasaland authorities.) At some period, then, near the time of Chilembwe's main attacks

Chinyama and Makwangwala's forces were moving on the Ncheu Boma ; and later in the direction of the Shire River. Precise dating of their march does not seem possible.

But Cardew's actions from the Boma were enough to frustrate them. In the absence of telegraphic communication between Ncheu and Zomba, he had got word through by motor-cycle to the seat of government about the intended march. This seems to have had the effect of bringing up native soldiers from Zomba to guard the Shire at points where Chinyama and his men might have been able to cross it in their move southwards. And within twenty-four hours Cardew had succeeded in enrolling about two hundred spear-men from the three most powerful chiefs of the district, so that his own slender force of twenty native policemen could be supplemented effectively. No doubt some of the spearmen, since they were Ngoni [68] who had been unemployed in their traditional military fashion after the pacification of the district, found it all a salutary exercise. Perhaps, indeed, some of the other Ngoni who had joined Chinyama were in the fray for the same reasons ! Whatever the motives of them all, Cardew's own Ngoni auxiliaries, together with his regular force, were responsible for following up Chinyama's body of men, taking about a hundred of them prisoner, and dispersing the rest into the neighbouring Portuguese territories. Chinyama himself was captured by 4 February 1915,[69] and the whole affair of the Ncheu rising was over at the same time as the main Rising. However badly timed at the start Chilembwe's and Chinyama's affairs may have been, at least they both finished together !

When the Rising had begun, Chilembwe's and Chinyama's men do not seem to have made effective contact, though, perhaps, a scout or runner managed to get messages through to both parties. It is this lack of contact which gives to the abortive Ncheu insurrection an even more isolated appearance than the main attacks at Magomero and Blantyre. Some of this isolation colours European accounts of the events at Ncheu, for it was farther away from the main centres of Government than the other areas affected. This feeling is shown very clearly in the contemporary record of Alexander Smith. Smith had gone out for the Baptist Industrial Mission of Scotland in 1900,[70] and had become its main representative at Gowa, some three miles from Ncheu Boma. Like W. J. Livingstone, he was from the crofting country. But unlike the Magomero manager, his father was a crofter. Some of this difference of social position may have been responsible for their different attitudes towards the Africans. Certainly no such fate awaited Alexander Smith as had been meted out at Magomero : for it was rumoured that he was one of the few Europeans of the Protectorate who had been placed on the rebels' list of those who were to be saved. From this long and friendly period of relations with local Africans he had gained the title of 'Bambo' or 'Father'. For all his friendship with Africans, however, Smith was by no means happy when the news reached him of the call to arms which Chinyama sent out to his people :

> Yesterday [he wrote home from Gowa on 26th January, 1915] he [Chinyama] . . . threatened to kill all the Europeans in this district, and all Christians who go to the White Man's schools. I don't look at it as very serious, but it is so easy to carry away some of the discontented natives that one never knows what length they might go. We are only seven white men in this district just now, and two at Mlanda makes nine men, but we are scattered, and from Mlanda to Ntanda is between fifty and sixty miles, so we can't give each other much help. The natives could clear us out if we had no friends among them, but we hope we have not lived so many years among them for nothing.[71]

Smith then quotes from a copy of a letter which he had received from the superintendent of the Zambesi Industrial Mission at Chiole, half-way between Gowa and the Ncheu Boma, which indicates that the Resident, Cardew, had warned them that it would be safer for them to concentrate at the Boma in Ncheu, but had pointed out that no word of these moves should be allowed to reach the Africans. It was the careful action of a small group of men who were still living in frontier conditions, amongst a people, Gomani's Ngoni, whose memories could still go back with some bitterness to the days of 1896 when the British had shot their chief.

Happily for Smith, his confidence in his own Africans was merited. A few old boys of the Baptist Industrial Mission of Scotland were found to have had connections with Chinyama ; but all of them had left the mission for breaches of discipline some years ago. In his account of these old boys, Smith provides an important piece of evidence which suggests that conditions on, and grievances from the Bruce Estates at Magomero were felt even in Ncheu, and may have had something to do with helping to bring about the 'rising' there. He notes that one of the Ncheu rebels who was executed for his part in Chinyama's effort was 'an old sawyer' who had gone to

Courtesy Mr. W. Sanderson

Plate 21. A later P.I.M. group (from Chilembwe's own photograph album): probably taken after 1912. *Standing, left to right*: Damson Bolowoza; Lee German Chimumbi; John Nkhawazi; Andrack Jamali (said to be Chilembwe's secretary during the Rising); Wallace Kampingo; John Chilembwe. *Seated, left to right*: Stephen Mkulichi (killed in 1915); Douglas Mankhokwe; Wilson Kasitu (killed in 1915 with the Ncheu section of the Rising); Harrison Chehe; Mrs. John Chilembwe

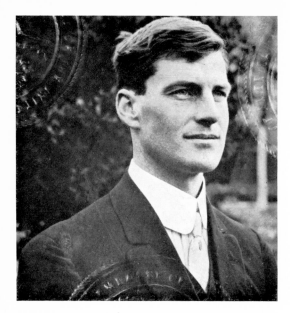

Plate 22(a). Walter B. Cock
Seventh Day Baptist missior
Chikunda, Nyasaland, 1915

Plate 22(b). Mr. and
Mrs. George H.
Hollis, Churches of
Christ missionaries,
Namiwawa, Nyasa-
land, 1915

Courtesy Mr. Walter B. Cockerill and Mrs. G. H.

work with the Bruce Estates at Magomero. 'He had been promoted to be a native foreman there, but was dismissed some time before the trouble occurred.' [72]   Perhaps one will never know the exact degree of relationship which existed, as this episode suggests, between the aggrieved Ncheu Africans and the Bruce Estates. It forms another of the many problems of the Rising.

But nothing is more problematic for the Ncheu revolt than the role and fate of Chief Makwangwala of the Dzunje section of Ncheu. It has already been noted that the *Nyasaland Times*, which reported the execution of a Zomba headman, Makwangwala, on 4 February, may have been confusing this man with the Dzunje chief.[73] If so, it seems that he was executed after a trial by Judge Lyall Grant of the Protectorate service. Yet Smith reported that Makwangwala of Dzunje, from whose area (especially from Ntanda village, two or three miles from Dzunje) much of the force of the Ncheu revolt had come, committed suicide. 'The Chief shot himself at the time of the Rising . . . two or three days after the Rising of Philip and his people . . . he sought the quickest way to get out of trouble to his way of thinking.' [74]   The mystery was why Makwangwala shot himself, for although there is record of at least one important Nyasaland chief who took his own life—Mwasi of Kasungu in 1895 [75]— suicide was not the normal way out of problems in that part of the world, and Portuguese East Africa was adjacent to Makwangwala's territories and could have provided him with an escape route. Yet Smith was sure that there had been a suicide :

> . . . we saw the grave of the chief. It was covered with calico of every kind, and a number of flags flying on the little roof where the grave was. Chiefs are always buried in the village which they govern. The idea of putting a lot of calico is to honour the dead.[76]

It is now time to take up again the thread of narrative of the events of the main Rising in the Shire Highlands. This has been allowed to slacken while some examination has been made of the character and value of the support which it received from other areas, particularly from Ncheu.

Sunday, 24 January 1915, was, as has been seen, a day for stock-taking on both sides. By the morning of Monday, 25 January, it was apparent that the rebels had made no further move. Therefore the troops and volunteers at Chiradzulu went out towards Chilembwe's village. When they were close to Mbombwe, they met the ladies and children who had been taken away from Magomero on the Saturday night. What then followed forms another mysterious and confused episode of the Rising.

From all accounts, quite understandably, the ladies themselves were in a dazed and shocked condition. They came into contact with the troops from Chiradzulu, when the soldiers apparently had just reached one side of the Mbombwe stream, which was about fifteen feet wide and lay in the path of their advance on Chilembwe's village. The ladies themselves seem to have been about to cross the stream. It must have appeared to them that they were about to be liberated by Government soldiers. Yet from both European and African accounts [77] it seems that they had already been given their liberty by Chilembwe who had made up his mind the day before to send them back to the District Commissioner at Chiradzulu. He had given them into the hands of the same Nguru who had first brought Livingstone's head to him, with instructions that they should be taken back to Chiradzulu and that a note should be handed to the District Commissioner there which said that the rebels had accomplished what they had set out to do and were waiting for their deaths, in proof of which they were sending their captives back to him.[78] It was this party, it seems, which met the troops out from Chiradzulu on the other side of the Mbombwe stream. Yet the story is complicated further by an account which states that, on their way from Chilembwe's village, the party was joined by another force from Mbombwe which handed to them another note. This time the letter was given to Mrs. Livingstone. It was very clearly and correctly written and said : 'Go back to the Boma. Tell the white men there we are going to kill them all, because they have taken our native land.' [79] Who was the author of this letter ? Was it Chilembwe ? The evidence of the careful handwriting cannot be taken as proof that he wrote it, for although Chilembwe could write a clear copperplate, other Africans from the local missions did not lack this skill. Was, then, the letter written by some other member of his following ? If this story and the account of the letter written in a spirit of resignation are correct, they suggest a similar ambivalence of attitude towards the Rising which has been noted in the analysis of the conspiracy in the previous chapter.

Something like a skirmish seems to have taken place between the Africans who were in charge of the Magomero ladies, and the troops on the other side of the Mbombwe stream. In this, Hinges, the servant of Mrs. Livingstone, who had been with her since her capture, was killed, presumably by the troops who at that time were exerting themselves to liberate those who had already been liberated. When the ladies were in the hands of the Government forces, the troops made a slight attack on Chilembwe's village with the aim of finding how strong were the defending forces. The village seems to have been a relatively strong position, with a stream in front and an encirclement of dense maize gardens. It was from the cover of these maize gardens that the insurgents were able to keep up a rate of fire which brought the Government forces to a standstill. The troops replied with some volleys but found it impossible to advance farther or to gauge effectively the strength of the rebels. When their ammunition was running low, the Government forces withdrew. Two native soldiers of the King's African Rifles were killed and three wounded, and it was rumoured that twenty of Chilembwe's men had been killed and some thirty taken prisoner,[80] though there is no means of checking these latter figures and it is possible that they were exaggerated.

If the Government forces were compelled to withdraw from this encounter, it was a lesson to Chilembwe and his men that they could not hope for any mutiny amongst the native soldiers of the Protectorate to assist them. Indeed, the only recorded support which they enjoyed amongst these was the instance of a sergeant of the King's African Rifles at Karonga who was later charged with complicity in the Rising and was brought down to Zomba to stand trial. But even he was only temporarily employed by the Nyasaland Field Force.[81] Thus, apparently, no Chilembwe supporters were discovered amongst the regular soldiers of the Protectorate. And, whether this thought occurred at the time or not, it was clear that, since the native troops of the Protectorate had not turned their rifles against the white men when they found the rebels capable of checking them, only two prospects remained to the insurgents : to make a destructive last stand at Mbombwe ; or to disperse, either to carry on guerrilla warfare, or else with the eventual hope of escape. One group, indeed, decided to break away—whether by direct order or on its own initiative is not clear—and on the Monday evening went off to the south-east, diametrically away from the Government base at Chiradzulu, in the direction of the Nguludi Roman Catholic Mission, the seat of the Bishop of the Shire.

It was clear that the Europeans now took the position seriously.

Before noon on Monday the trial of the four prisoners, who had been taken after the Blantyre attack, began before the District Resident. It was then remitted to the High Court at Blantyre, where judgement of death was given at half-past four in the afternoon. Almost immediately, the sentence was carried out. The culprits were lined up with their backs to the wall of the European prison and shot by a firing party of eight from the European section of the Nyasaland Volunteer Reserve.[82] As one contemporary reporter noticed :

> The shooting was done in the presence of a huge crowd of natives as a warning. The prisoners were chained, marched out to a wall, blindfolded and shot. It must have been a ghastly business. The bodies were left lying out until next day.[83]

It was the first of a number of similar quick trials and it was meant to teach other potential supporters of Chilembwe a lesson in advance. The lesson was indeed learnt by the locals. In after years little African children would come up and stick their fingers into the bullet-holes in the walls, and, in this way, children's play would help to keep African memory of the shootings alive.

At much the same time, the European residents of Blantyre and the surrounding district were moving into laager at the head offices of the African Lakes Corporation at Mandala. Behind Mandala House there was a large enclosed compound, a kind of defensive store around a square which made an excellent shelter for the Europeans at this time of alarm. It was not the first time that this defensive store had served the European community. In 1884, after the murder of the Makololo chief Chipatula by George Fenwick—who paid later with his head for it—his warriors threatened the country right up to Blantyre, and the store provided shelter then for the alarmed Europeans. Similarly, when in 1884 the Ngoni chief Chikusi raided the country from the north-west, Mandala compound was again transformed into a European refuge. 1915 was to be the third and last time that it would fulfil this role.[84]

On Monday, 24 January, Mandala became the centre of a motley assembly. The upper floor of the offices, the clearing house and the motor accessories portion of the European store, and part of a large goods shed were given over to women and children for sleeping accommodation. The French Sisters, Roman Catholic nuns, with their wards, from Nguludi, had the rice store placed at their disposal. The Italians of the Blantyre community had the packing room and a small store at the east end of the square ; the Indians had the transit shed ; while the bulk store at the north end of the square and the *tenga-tenga* (transport) office were devoted to the nursing staff as hospitals. European men had the use of a long shed on the northern side of the African Lakes Corporation compound, and proceeded to make up long rows of makeshift beds from full bales of calico and other piece goods. The German residents and two prisoners of war had their quarters in a large marquee tent in the square itself. Temporary corrugated iron shelters within the compound housed the cooking arrangements and the native police, and some frantic work added to the defensive strength of the compound.[85] As a contemporary noted :

> About 300 people slept here each night—in all kinds of places, on
> bags of cement, trusses of calico, bales of goods on floors, etc. It must
> have been a sight.[86]

It was, indeed, a demonstration that the Europeans meant business.

Further evidence of this was ably provided by the European Volunteers from Mikalongwe. The telephone line which had been cut by the rebels between Mikalongwe and Blantyre was soon repaired, messages put through to Blantyre, and a train with an armed guard sent down the single-track line to pick up the women and children gathered at Mikalongwe section, who included the Nguludi Sisters, to take them to the safety of Blantyre laager. Then it was decided by the Mikalongwe Volunteers to reconnoitre the homes of three of the suspected ringleaders of the Rising, John Gray Kufa, Duncan Njilima, and Hugh Mataka, which were only some five or six miles from Mikalongwe. Using native scouts, an approach was made in the direction of Hugh Mataka's place. A hundred friendly natives were recruited and a first raid was made on a mud-and-wood store that belonged to one of the rebels. After the capture of documents and some permitted looting by the friendly natives, the store was fired and the force moved on. The next visit was to Duncan Njilima's house, a substantial brick building whose relative prosperity has been noted in the previous chapter as a gauge of the amounts of property of some of the leaders of the Rising.[87] The house was looted by Europeans and natives alike in a very short time ; its poultry, sheep, and cattle were carefully taken into possession ; and the whole property was then fired. The next call was to another native store that belonged to one of the rebels. It was treated in the same way as the first two buildings that were visited. The last venture was to the house of John Gray Kufa himself, and a great quantity of correspondence was captured, and the pride of John Gray's property, brick building and all, was consigned to flames. By this time the moon was coming up, and the determined Mikalongwe detachment could look back on a successful day. So they retired to the firm base which they had set up for themselves in the morning, about five miles from Mikalongwe, in the iron-roofed store belonging to a European planter, Fiddes.

Their work for the day, however, was not finished. The Volunteers took up a defensive position in an iron-roofed building a few miles away from the Marist Fathers Mission station at Nguludi, and guarded some of the mission personnel, including Sisters and children, who had been evacuated to Midima [88] during the day by another group from the Mikalongwe Volunteers. By half-past ten in the evening the refugees had reached their destination.[89] The night was passed by the Volunteers in various bouts of restive sentry duty. At daybreak came another scare of the Rising. It seemed, by the movement of groups of Africans some eight hundred yards away on the brow of a tobacco field, that a dawn attack was imminent. A nervous stand-to was ordered, until scouts discovered that the approaching natives were 'friendlies'.[90] The episode had almost distracted attention from the reflection of a fire that the Mikalongwe Volunteer sentries had seen in the sky over in the direction of the Nguludi mission. In a little while, their worst suspicions were confirmed. A native from the Marist Fathers Mission brought in the news that the rebels had attacked the Nguludi mission, killed one of the Fathers and burnt the buildings.[91] It was the last Chilembwe-ite attack of the Rising : so its course and causes must now be examined.

In the previous chapter it has been noticed that there is a certain mystery about the attack on the Nguludi mission.[92] Had it been premeditated ; and, if so, what were the reasons for this ? Was it due to a feeling of revenge against the Marist Fathers for the warning they had given the authorities of the impending Rising? Or was it because the Roman Catholics were the main enemies of religious separatism in the Protectorate, and known opponents of over-rapid education for the African ? Was it, as one European Volunteer suggested later, 'the rebels' method of retaliation for the capture, that day, of their own church and headquarters by the Government forces' ? [93]   This seems unlikely, as the attack on Nguludi was made some hours before the Europeans captured Chilembwe's Mbombwe centre, and those members of his forces who attacked the Catholic mission had clearly been waiting around it for some time before they launched their assault, and would be unaware that a Government seizure of their own headquarters was impending.   If the attack on the Nguludi mission must be linked with the immediate circumstances of the Rising, rather than with the conspiracy which preceded it, it is not improbable that it was made because the Marist Fathers Mission lay in the path of that group of Africans who had broken away from Chilembwe's headquarters on the Monday, and who were, apparently, in retreat.   If this theory is correct, the problem yet remains : was the attack made on Chilembwe's instructions as a tactical manœuvre of retreat, or was it simply the impetuous decision of the commander—he seems to have been David Kaduya [94] —of the group of retreating Africans ?   But whatever were its causes, the assault on the Nguludi mission brought no advantages to the rebels whatsoever.

The attack fell at about half-past three on the morning of Tuesday, 26 January 1915.   The only people in the buildings then were Father Swelsen, four armed Africans, and a little native orphan named Alicia.   Father Swelsen had stayed behind because he had misunderstood the order of his Superior.   The little girl had been left in the flurry of evacuating the mission the day before.   When this had been discovered, the Superior, Bishop Auneau, had sent four armed Africans to fetch her.   They found the little girl asleep, and, as they themselves were tired and afraid—it was dark, and not only was there the possibility of meeting with Chilembwe's men on their return trip through the bush, but also there were wild beasts to be taken into consideration—they stayed at Nguludi for the night.   The rebels had been hiding in the bushes around the mission.   The moon was down at half-past three in the morning [95]—a fact which suggests that the attack followed some sort of a plan.   Suddenly the rebels emerged from their cover and attacked the Fathers' house.   Father Swelsen, who had been lying fully dressed on his bed, was aroused from sleep by the uproar and went to the door of his quarters.   As soon as the rebels saw him, they set upon him, and clubbed and speared him into unconsciousness.   He may well have appeared to be dead, and it seems that the insurgents put him in the graveyard [96] of the mission, where he was found later by some of the African adherents of Nguludi who lived around the mission and who had hidden themselves while the attack was in progress. One of the Africans who had been sent for Alicia tried to offer some opposition but was shot and wounded—mortally, as it proved later.

When the rebels had satisfied themselves that there were no other Europeans on the station, they prepared to destroy the property. They went into the mission church and sang hymns [97]—a detail which suggests a religio-political interpretation of the attack. Then they fired the thatched roof and burnt other buildings in the area. The little orphan, Alicia, was a victim of the conflagration. She had apparently taken refuge under a bed in the corner of one of the rooms, for it was there that the returned missionaries later found her bones. The amount of destruction was considerable : the Fathers' house with its library and store ; the Sisters' house with its chapel and linen store ; the children's house with its store ; the school and main store ; and the kitchen, together with all the poultry.[98] The blaze must have been extensive, and it was not surprising that the Mika-longwe detachment, who were guarding the mission evacuees a few miles away at Fiddes's place, could see its glare in the early morning sky. One of the Mikalongwe Volunteers, William Sanderson, em-ployed at Gotha Estate, visited the ruins later in the day and left an account of the devastation :

> The Mission station presented a very sad sight. All the houses were burnt to the ground except the small church and cattle kraal ; in the hen and duck houses the animals had been roasted alive.[99]

All that was left was a 'large new church which had been in the course of construction, which was so new that there seemed nothing to burn'.[100] When it was all over, the insurgents were not heard of again as a group, but broke up to seek asylum amongst their African acquaintances and fellow clansmen in the villages. Their leader David Kaduya, was subsequently mortally wounded by a shot from Ben Yomani,[101] one of the Ngoni members of the band of Africans who had rallied to the Mikalongwe Volunteers' call.

It was dawn when the raiders left. The mission's African adherents came out of their hiding-places, found Father Swelsen in the grave-yard in a serious condition but still breathing, put him in a *machilla* and carried him over to the main body of the Nguludi evacuees under the guard of the Mikalongwe Volunteers. By this time the evacuees had been taken to Mikalongwe itself, some five miles away from their shelter for the night, with the object of catching the train for Blantyre and safety, as soon as a wire could be sent for one. The sight of the blaze in the sky from the burning buildings at Nguludi had convinced them and their Volunteer guards that this was the safest course to follow, for at that moment none could tell what the attack on Nguludi might signify. There was still no clear news of Chilembwe's movements, and for all they knew this new attack might be the beginning of a push by the rebels into other regions. So, it was better to be off to Blantyre and the safety of the laager there. Ten minutes after the party of evacuees had arrived at Mikalongwe station, an African came up with the news that Father Swelsen had not been killed after all, and that he was being brought to them. Within a few minutes, a party of about twenty Africans from Nguludi arrived with him in the *machilla*.

> It was a terrible sight. His head which had been battered with knobkerries was about twice its usual size, and just below his eye was a long flesh wound made by a spear. He lay groaning . . .[102]

Fortunately for him, Father Swelsen was a man with a strong constitution and he recovered eventually. But at that moment, still early in the day of Tuesday, 26 January, to the crowd of mission evacuees waiting for the train to Blantyre, the sight of the bloody and wounded Father Swelsen must have seemed a portent of many dangers ahead, and they must have welcomed the train that soon came up to take them to the refuge of Blantyre. They could not have known that the withdrawal of the rebels from Nguludi after the attack on Swelsen and the mission property was the last effective foray of Chilembwe's men ; an armed guard of Europeans and local Indians, therefore, went with them for protection.

Reports of the attack on Nguludi decided the Government to insist that all the Europeans in the Shire Highlands must go into laager.

The concentration at Mandala compound, Blantyre, has already been noticed ; and the attempts which were made to bring the local Europeans into the Boma at Ncheu have been described. At Zomba, accommodation was found in the depot buildings of the King's African Rifles. Mlanje, the social and administrative centre of a planting district, provided a laager which was simply a sleeping-place for men who went about their estate business by day, while their boys, who cooked in the kitchens of neighbouring estates, brought dinner along to them in the laager in the evening. No one suspected treachery among the cooks ; and nobody suffered for his confidence. The planting district of Cholo also had its laager, but the area was not closely involved in any stage of the Rising, and the concentration there seems to have passed without incident. This was not true of some of the other laagers, however, and not all Europeans were treated alike in them. This was especially true of those Europeans from the smaller missions—some of which were at this time suspected of complicity in the Rising—whose experiences will be noted later. For all, the greatest trouble was discomfort ; [103] and for some, such as the Zambesi Industrial missionaries who lost their little girl from malaria contracted while in laager at Mandala,[104] this discomfort could pass over into a danger greater than anything which the rebels at any time offered them.

While these arrangements were being made for the safe-keeping of the European population in the Shire Highlands, other developments were taking place which spelt the doom of Chilembwe's conspiracy. The Mikalongwe Volunteers, having armed a group of about sixteen local Africans with whatever guns they could find, and having called to their aid a much larger force of natives who were equipped only with spears, patrolled the area of the Nguludi mission. They could report 'all clear' : a situation that may have been due to the heavy rain that had set in during the day and which may have discouraged Chilembwe's men from any further attempts in the area ; but that is more likely to have been the result of the force which attacked Nguludi having achieved its limited object. Like the attack on Magomero on the Saturday evening, once the object had been achieved, a withdrawal by the rebel attackers was in order. When they saw that no further trouble was to be expected at that moment from Nguludi, the Volunteer patrol bedded down there for the night. One flank, at least, of the supposedly threatened area was secured to the Europeans. While all this was in progress, the troops which had been dispatched from Karonga in answer to the Governor's request were steaming down Lake Nyasa *en route* for Fort Johnston at the southern end, and a rapid march to the main centres that the Rising threatened. Their nearness would give new heart to any Europeans in the Shire Highlands who felt disturbed.

Yet, on the Tuesday, 26 January, the event which really gave heart to the Europeans was the news that Chilembwe's village was clear of rebels. The re-munitioned military detachment at Chiradzulu under Captain Triscott, supported by Volunteer reinforcement, had profited by its experience of the previous day, when it had experienced its unsuccessful brush with Chilembwe's men outside Mbombwe, to launch an attack on the village. The attack went in, apparently, at dawn.[105] Beaumont, a planter, justified his African nickname of 'the Black Ant' by the infiltrating skill he showed on this occasion. He had told the party that he knew the district well and could take it into Chilembwe's place without the rebels' knowing. By moving well out on to the right flank, and then coming in from the rear through the high maize that surrounded this part of Mbombwe (see plate 236 on p. 310), he took the regular troops and the Volunteers right on to the objective, so that the rebels would know nothing of the attack until their look-out was fired on.[106] No resistance was met. It was not, however, until Chilembwe's brick church, the rebel headquarters, was rushed that it was known that the village had been entirely vacated.[107] The troops went on to sweep across the whole area of Mbombwe and found it utterly empty of people. It is not clear how the evacuation had taken place. But one thing is apparent : that there had been little system or plan about it. Huts and homes were found in various stages of hurried abandonment, and there were plenty of evidences of demoralization. From the attack on Nguludi it is clear that one group had left Chilembwe on the Monday night ; and the freeing of the European women and children also on the Monday suggests that Chilembwe and his men had come to the conclusion that resistance was useless. It appears that the engagement with the European forces on the Monday morning had created some demoralization amongst Chilembwe's followers, and this had grown throughout the night : so that, when any who remained within the bounds of Mbombwe village heard the approach of the troops and Volunteers from Chiradzulu, they scattered rapidly in all directions. Their retreat was so rapid that they made no attempt to stay together ; and to which group John Chilembwe attached himself no answer, it seems, can be given. From the fact that unfinished cups of warm tea were found on the table in Chilembwe's house [108] when a search was being made of the area, it is likely that he himself was in Mbombwe until the last moment. There is no apparent evidence to indicate whether Chilembwe experienced the kind of panic which some of his men so obviously showed on the Tuesday morning, or whether he was possessed of the same degree of resignation which he seems to have shown on the Monday. But one thing is clear : that he and his men, now scattered in fugitive groups, were fleeing in the direction of Mlanje with the hope of escaping into Portuguese East Africa. Parties were detailed to follow up the rebels from amongst the African police and soldiers. It was a wet day ; yet, had they but known it, there was good reason for the spirits of the Europeans to be high, for the news could be taken to read that the Rising was as good as over.

The sack of the rebel headquarters produced box-loads of documents and correspondence which acted as valuable intelligence for the Government when it came to try Africans who were suspected of complicity in the rebellion. But the capture of all these papers revealed even more : it showed, for anyone who required such a demonstration, that the rebel headquarters had been captured, and that any further resistance which could be expected would not be that of determined men who were fighting for a cause but of fugitives who had once had a cause but who, at that moment, possessed no other aim, it seems, than escape and self-preservation. One item which was discovered was a book on military tactics ; it was much thumbed.[109] Yet if this provided evidence of the measure of planning which had gone into the Rising, nothing, apparently, was discovered to suggest that Chilembwe had made any preparations for an underground movement against the Europeans if he should fail in his immediate objectives.

As a symbol of their conquest and as a measure of safety, in case a counter-attack should come, the huts and houses of the village were burnt, after the intelligence material was taken away, and attempts were made to set Chilembwe's church on fire. But it was too stout a building to succumb to simple flames, and had to await demolition by dynamite a week later.[110] It stood amid the ruins of his village as a sign of the aspirations which the Providence Industrial Mission had possessed. And on the outskirts of Mbombwe another sign was found by the searching troops, a symbol both of the origins of the Rising and its imminent end : the head of William Jervis Livingstone.[111]

Yet, at that time, although it was clear that the initiative had passed to the Europeans, with the exception of the four insurgents captured at the time of the attack on Mandala, and the few who had been taken after the first unsuccessful brush by the Government troops with Chilembwe's forces, the rebels were still at large and still, apparently, had the capacity to do damage to any person or place that might come their way. Thus, with the escape of the insurgent leaders and forces after the capture of Mbombwe, rumour ran more rife than ever. On the Wednesday, Zomba residents were not allowed to leave their laager during the day for their homes 'in view of the very doubtful loyalty of one or two Chiefs near at hand'.[112] And L. S. Norman, the Mikalongwe planter, has provided further evidence of such rumours :

> . . . reliable information reached us that the rebels were that night [Wednesday, 27 January, the day after the sack of Mbombwe] to burn the buildings and wreck the properties throughout our planting district. . . . Over this great extent of country . . . extending over one hundred miles . . . the estates, the tobacco plantations, cotton ginneries, fibre and tea factories and the numerous European dwellings, cattle and other property, had been abandoned. Everything lay completely at the mercy of any small band of raiders, who might burn, destroy or rob almost to their hearts' content.[113]

There was little to prevent the carrying out of such a programme of incendiarism. That it was not even attempted suggests that the rebels were being painted blacker than they were. The 'abandoned' property was, in fact, in the hands of house-boys and watchmen, often enough because an unwilling and sceptical European had been ordered by Government into laager. Few had any reason to complain of the stewardship of their servants and tenants. Indeed, if Chilembwe's chances of support from a 'canny' local African population were slender while he was still in possession of his headquarters at Mbombwe, when he was in flight they were infinitesimal. Authority, from the tribal and slave-raiding days, the days of the Portuguese and Arabs, down to the epoch of the British, had changed hands often enough for the locals to be very well aware of the dangers of backing a cause before it had given clear evidences of its chances of success.

Those chances were now hopeless—with the rebels in flight, and the Government troops and the Nyasaland Volunteers in pursuit of them. All indications were that the fugitives would seek to escape into Portuguese territory ; but the two colonial governments saw eye to eye on the subject of insubordinate natives, and the border was heavily patrolled on the Portuguese side, while Portuguese East African troops (56 native soldiers and 3 white officers [114]) were sent from Sena to Blantyre to reinforce the British levies if they should be needed. Furthermore, railway officials in both colonies were in touch with each other in order that the railway could be kept open, should it prove necessary for further troops to be rushed into the Protectorate, or for supplies to be introduced into Nyasaland from as far afield as the Chinde mouth of the Zambezi.[115]   A net of pursuers was thus stretched tightly over all the important areas and the rebels' chances of escape were slight.   Their only hope of getting across the border was to make for the difficult country at the north end of Mlanje mountain, across the plain of the Tuchila and Phalombe rivers.   But the force which had set out after the adherents of the rebellious Zomba headman, Kimu, was still in existence, and was already moving across the northern margin of the plain ; and motor-transported riflemen could easily cover the length of Mlanje mountain on the east, and in this way were able to follow up every report of suspicious movements or appearances.   The story, then, of the remaining days of the Rising, from Wednesday, 27 January, the day after the capture of Chilembwe's headquarters, to 3 February when the rebel leader was shot, is the story of the rapid and relentless tightening of the net on the fleeing insurgents.

The movements of the various police and Volunteer detachments, to whom the military left the tracking down of the insurgents once it was clear that there would be no more concerted resistance, are confused and are of no great importance except to the villagers who found themselves involved in their incursions.   Not all the Volunteers were competent investigators of the rights and wrongs in a village reported to be harbouring rebels ; and not all native policemen and very few armed irregulars were disinterested judges of the activities of villagers not of their own kin.   On the other hand, an insurgent was not to be distinguished from any ordinary villager apart from his arms—which by this time, in many cases, he had either thrown away or hidden—and his hostile attitude, which was equally capable of concealment.   And among these villagers were men who had done murder.   It was the eternal problem of identifying enemies among an alien population whose day-to-day equipment and culture provided possible means of hostile action ; and, in the circumstances, reliance had to be placed on native agents.   The imposition of rewards on the heads of the rebels ensured that there was no lack of these.

The general pattern into which the many individual patrols and tiny actions of the police and Volunteer detachments with their African allies and assistants may be fitted was succinctly described by the *Nyasaland Times* in its issue for Saturday, 30 January, by which time most of the effective work of bringing in the main rebels was completed. The paper noted that

> Blantyre has sent a strong detachment of the N.V.R. [Nyasaland Volunteer Reserve] to Mlanje to operate from that end. The Resident of Mlanje is using his native police to help in the round-up and the Mikalongwe section of the N.V.R. have been doing excellent work and are hot on the trail and further strong detachments are operating from Chiradzulu Boma, Magomero, and a force of Angoni under Mr. Thorneycroft and Mr. A. J. Williams is trying to head them off in the Shirwa direction.

With this ring of forces closing in on Chilembwe and his men, the *Nyasaland Times* was justified in noting that 'The Government has now got the situation well in hand'; and, as if to give increased assurance to its readers, could clinch the point with the statement that 'the arrival of Captain Collins with reinforcements makes the position secure'.

The arrival in the Shire Highlands of Collins from Karonga, with his double company of the 1st Battalion of the King's African Rifles and a seven-pounder gun, provided a notable episode in the story of the Rising. On the Rising itself his force seems to have had little more than an effect on morale—though this should not be under-estimated, either on the Europeans of the Protectorate or on the rebels themselves. When he arrived with his men on Friday, 29 January,[116] only small isolated parties were left to round up, for the main work of defeating and scattering the rebels had been done by the forty-odd British Volunteers and the hundred King's African Rifles recruits under Captain L. E. L. Triscott. Apart from the fact that the absence of Collins and his men from Karonga depleted for a time the already scanty numbers of troops available for the defence and patrolling of the northern border of Nyasaland against the Germans, what gives him and his force its secure place in the history of British Central Africa for this time is the march which they made of eighty-six miles in forty-seven hours. The adjective 'remarkable' [117] is often used in the description of this march and it is not unjustified. After a journey down Lake Nyasa, the force had reached Fort Johnston at its southern end on the evening of Wednesday, 27 January. Though this was the day after the capture of Chilembwe's headquarters, it has been seen that there were still fears for the security of life and property in the Shire Highlands. Therefore Collins and his men subjected themselves to severe tests of endurance to get to the affected centres as soon as possible. One detachment went off immediately to Ncheu, where, for all they knew, trouble from the remnants of Filipo Chinyama's men might still be expected. The remainder, dragging their seven-pounder gun over a distance of eighty-six miles which rose from one thousand six hundred to three thousand feet in altitude, reached Zomba in forty-seven hours.[118] They were then ready for action to assist the local forces in rounding up the last scattered parties of rebels. Above all, they stood by the seat of government in the Protectorate as a symbol of the military power behind the British State in Nyasaland, and as a very obvious warning to any disaffected African who, then or later in the course of the War, might think of emulating John Chilembwe.

On the Wednesday when Collins and his men were approaching Fort Johnston, the Mikalongwe force of Volunteers—there were about twenty-five of them [119]—was ready for further adventures. As the *Nyasaland Times*, which has just been quoted, put it: the Mikalongwe force was 'hot on the trail'. Dawn on the Wednesday morning saw the Volunteers up, after a night of resting at Nguludi near the Marist Fathers Mission. Having searched rebel property in their own area and done what they could to help the Nguludi mission, they had now received instructions to proceed to the main area of the Rising, Chiradzulu. With their tatterdemalion collection of native allies, they began an early morning march up to the Chiradzulu Boma, a climb of over two thousand feet which for some of the untrained and middle-aged men was as epic in its quality as Collins's own march! The magistrate, who had returned by this time, was glad to see them, for his own protective force that morning had been sent off on another job. 'A number of rebels, hidden in the high table-top hill at the back of his station, seeing the other troops depart, had spent the morning hurling insults and threats as to his coming fate that night.' [120] But it seems that the arrival of the Mikalongwe Volunteers was noticed by the jeering rebels, and they remained silent for the rest of the day. Yet the Volunteers themselves were in no unduly happy frame of mind, for not only was there the thought of the rebels on the hill, but also the rumour was abroad that an insurgent attack on their property was imminent during the night. It appears that some of the Volunteers went down to Mikalongwe to look into the situation but were reassured by the news that measures would be taken to safeguard their property and that Portuguese troops had arrived in the Protectorate. Nothing occurred

Plate 23(*a*). The last photograph of Chilembwe—probably taken between 1913 and 1914. He is standing on the steps of the P.I.M. church with the Rev. John Chorley of the Chipande station of the Zambesi Industrial Mission

Plate 23(*b*). Chilembwe's church and headquarters as they would appear to attacking Europeans

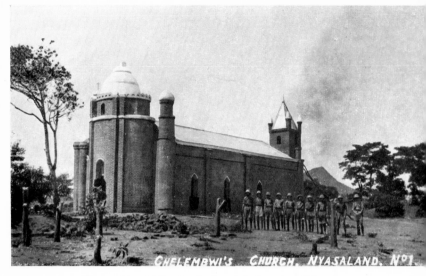

Plate 24(*a*). Chilembwe's church before demolition, 1915

Plate 24(*b*). Chilembwe's church after demolition, 1915

during the night, the rebels' bark having proved worse than their bite, and the Mikalongwe Volunteers, after a night spent guarding the Chiradzulu magistrate and his Boma, felt free to leave. A new patrol was expected to take their place, and they had themselves received orders that, on Thursday, 28 January, they were to join in the chase for the fleeing rebels.[121]

This Thursday was to be another exciting day for the Shire Highlands. News of a relieving character came that Chilembwe's men were making for the Fort Lister Gap at the north end of Mount Mlanje, opening into Portuguese territory. In Zomba a leading native of Chilembwe's following had reported to the authorities, and others were expected to follow in his footsteps.[122] Yet in spite of this reassuring news the Government, which had been caught napping once, demonstrated that it was not to be lulled again. The Government Gazettes announced that martial law, which had been proclaimed some weeks ago over the North Nyasa district where contact with the Germans was relatively close, had, from 26 January, been extended to the southern parts of Nyasaland. Thus, one by-product of the Chilembwe Rising was that it succeeded in bringing the whole Protectorate under martial law. These were all exciting tidings, yet probably none of the Europeans of the Shire Highlands had greater cause for excitement or congratulation than the Mika-longwe Volunteers. For, on the Thursday, they were to begin the process that was to end in the capture of the second-in-command of the rebels, John Gray Kufa.

In the morning they had set out to scour the countryside around Chilembwe's church. It seems that the Government troops who had attacked and sacked the Mbombwe area on the Tuesday morning had not got away with all the loot, for the Mikalongwe Volunteers and their African allies found that there were still some valuable pickings.[123] Some of Chilembwe's cattle were left, and two of the beasts provided the Volunteers and their Africans with a meal. Lunch was taken inside Chilembwe's church. It was a not altogether unworried meal, for news was brought in by a friendly native that Chilembwe was about eight miles away. The group immediately went into action again, and moved off to the village nearest to the place where Chilembwe was reported to have been seen. The Volunteers were told that he had spent the night about two miles away in a rough shelter that he had built. It seems that he had some of his men with him, and that those who had escaped capture were trying to link up with him. A scouting party was therefore sent out by the Volunteers to check on Chilembwe's camp of the night before. After they had left, two natives brought the news that some of the spearmen who were fleeing with Chilembwe had visited their village, only three miles away, and had killed four of its inhabitants. The news worried the Mikalongwe Volunteers who had been left behind after the scouting party had left to reconnoitre. As one of them said, 'It was now getting grey, the moon was up, and our ten men had not returned'.[124] And so they cleared away the maize which surrounded the huts in the village at which they were resting, in order that a clear field of view might be secured, should any surprise attack be made upon them. In an hour's time the reconnaissance patrol returned. It had learned that Chilembwe was collecting his scattered followers together and making for another part of the country—obviously the Portuguese border. 'All the side paths were "shut" by having a mark put upon them so that John Chilembwe's followers would understand which way he had gone and would be able to follow him.' [125]

If the reconnaissance patrol could bring such valuable information into the temporary camp of the remaining Mikalongwe Volunteers, those who had been left behind had meanwhile acquired news which was just as exciting and which promised to be more immediately fruitful—the tidings that John Gray Kufa was in hiding, close to their camp.

This intelligence was provided by 'a wily old native character, a carpenter' [126] who was employed by one of the Volunteers and who had joined them in the hope of obtaining loot of some kind. The fact that a Government reward of £20 [127] was on John Gray Kufa's head no doubt stimulated the old man to provide a personal reconnaissance patrol among the local villagers. He thus brought in the news that the rebel second-in-command was not far away; that he was, indeed, out in the bush, hiding behind a small hill. A force of six Africans,[128] armed with rifles, was sent out to capture John Gray. The old carpenter went with them and played a leading part in taking him. The incident had begun before the Mikalongwe Volunteers' patrol had returned with the news that Chilembwe's men were rallying to him along marked paths; it was not to be finished until the following day. It appears that for the latter part of the night of Thursday, 28 January, and for the early morning of Friday, 29 January, the old carpenter and the six armed Africans were out in the bush after John Gray, while the main body of the Mika-longwe Volunteers, all together again, were in the village about eight miles from Chilembwe's church.[129]   What adventures befell John Gray's captors cannot be clearly determined : but if the story which one of them told later is to be believed, that John Gray had drawn a knife on them,[130] then they were not without excitement.   For the Volunteers who had spent the night in spells of sentry duty and disturbed sleep, the sight of the six Africans, the old carpenter, and John Gray was a welcome one.   All the news they had gathered on the previous day about Chilembwe and his men had led them to fear that their own men, and not John Gray Kufa, had been captured. But the stimulus of the prize money had had its effect, and John Gray Kufa, tied up by his African captors, was brought to the Mikalongwe Volunteers in the early hours of Friday morning.[131]

The next step was to get him to the nearest railway station, fifteen miles away.   It was a determined procession which set off : a number of natives first ; two Europeans with loaded rifles immedi-ately behind them ; then the prisoner himself with ropes bound around his waist and wrists, and two natives holding each end of the ropes ; a pair of native riflemen on either side of the Africans who were holding the ropes ; two more Europeans with loaded rifles ; and a number of natives to bring up the rear.[132]   Next to Chilembwe, John Gray Kufa was the greatest capture of the Rising, and neither Volunteers nor native helpers, for prestige or prize money, were willing to risk the chance of losing him.

The question may be asked at this stage why John Gray Kufa had not caught up with Chilembwe in his escape.   Perhaps that was his intention when he was captured.   Yet is there not something significant in the story of his hiding alone behind a hill in the bush,[133] and the comparative ease with which he was taken ?   Had he become separated from the others not by chance but by intention, because he had not played the part in the Rising that was expected of him ? This is, of course, pure speculation.   But there is the story that John Gray had been put in charge of the attack on Mandala and that his heart had failed him at the last moment.[134] Could this have been the reason for his isolation at this time when the remainder of Chilembwe's men were making attempts to rally to their leader ?   Certainly, when John Gray was taken prisoner he seems to have spoken freely to his captors.   European accounts which are given of his utterances after capture do not suggest the figure of a rebel second-in-command.[135]

When judging his sentiments at this time, it has, of course, to be remembered that they come from European evidence and that John Gray himself may have been completely dispirited and demoralized. Yet John Gray's words do not seem to have the ring of some of the rebels' utterances at the trials which they faced after the Rising: 'Go to, ye rich men, weep and howl for your miseries that shall come upon you'.[136] There was none of this defiance about the interview which John Gray had in his death cell later with his old employer, A. L. Bruce of the Magomero Estates, who, on hearing of the news of the disasters on his property, had hurried down from the north of the Protectorate, where he was serving with the Army, to see the situation for himself. John Gray told him that there was no feeling against the Estates and W. J. Livingstone by the rebels: a sentiment which—unless one is prepared to suppose that the owner of Magomero was exaggerating—John Gray must have known to be incorrect. There is a similar air of demoralized deception about remarks to his captors before they handed him over to the armed guard on the train that was to take him to Blantyre. One of those captors, William Sanderson, an employee of the African Lakes Corporation at their Gotha Estate, has left an account of their last interview with him. After noting that he could speak English 'as well as you or I', Sanderson went on:

> This prisoner of ours denied having anything to do with the rebellion. He admitted that John Chilembwe had sent for him twice, and because he was afraid that John C. would come or send men to kill him, he had cleared out from his own brick house and village. We asked him why he had not gone to the Boma officials at once or at least told some European about it all. 'Well', he said, 'that was the only mistake I made', and he inferred that this was all they would be able to bring against him at the trial.[137]

Here, of course, John Gray was wrong; and a few weeks later, after trial, he was executed.[138] When he was put on the train for Blantyre in the early afternoon by the detachment from the Mikalongwe Volunteers, he must have known that such could be his only fate.

By the time of the arrival of John Gray Kufa in Blantyre on the forenoon of Friday, 29 January, it was becoming clear, to any who still had doubts, that the Rising as a threat to European life and property in the Protectorate was as good as over. But rumour was still rife, and it was yet possible for an idle tale to put fear into people's hearts again. In the afternoon, for example, it was reported that Chilembwe had been seen with his spearmen 'in the vicinity of the lower Mombezi Stream, near the Blantyre/Mlanje road some ten miles from the former place'.[139]   This was only a rumour ; but it was enough for the deconcentration orders that had been given in the morning to the Europeans in laager at Mandala, Blantyre, to be withdrawn.   An additional protective patrol was organized for the safeguard of Mandala.   By the morning it was able to report 'all clear' and the people at Mandala could get ready to return to their homes.   In fact, all that the Friday had seen, apart from the arrival of Collins and his King's African Rifles contingent at Zomba, was a series of further captures of Africans who had conspired with Chilembwe, amongst whom was the 'leading warder' on the Mago-mero Estates who was 'shot owing to being deeply implicated'.[140] His execution provides further evidence which helps to localize the Rising and to throw some light on its motivation.

On the Friday before they had handed John Gray Kufa over to the custody of armed guards on the train that was to take him to Blantyre, the Mikalongwe Volunteers had obtained from him some information which was to secure the arrest the following day of another of Chilembwe's leading followers.   John Gray Kufa had told them quite freely that Hugh Mataka, on whose head a price had also been set, was in his own village, about half a mile from his 'office' which the Volunteers had already burnt.[141]   The Volunteers did not hurry out to capture him.   They felt confident that the task could be accomplished on the morrow, and spent the evening at a local planter's having their first bath and shave for a week.   Their confidence proved justified, for the operation to capture Hugh Mataka on Saturday, 30 January, was a simple one : six armed Africans and a spearman surrounded his house ; a reconnaissance was made, and a small group was then sent out to bring him in.   'In about ten minutes', wrote one of the Volunteers, 'our men returned with a native dressed in trousers and jacket of khaki.   He was a wily-looking customer with a small beard.'[142]   Mataka, unlike Chilembwe and John Gray Kufa, did not live in a brick house : but his wattle-and-daub hut was a large one, and the search of it revealed other evidence of the conspiracy in the form of letters and papers.   Though the insurgents appear to have learnt as much as they could about European techniques of conspiracy, their knowledge evidently did not extend so far as the burning of documents before they might fall into the hands of the enemy.   Mataka was put on a train and sent to

Blantyre, together with another African who had been 'found trying to conceal himself in the long grass near Hugh Mataka's place, having what was taken to be a bloodstained matchet in his possession'.[143] They arrived in Blantyre about noon.

The Blantyre residents in the Mandala laager no longer had any fears for their safety, and on the Saturday morning, with the exception of a few Blantyre ladies and some dwellers in the outer districts who returned to Mandala for the night, the laager broke up. By this time most of the other concentrations of Europeans in the Shire Highlands had dispersed, or were about to break up. The sights in the concentration camps—as such gatherings of Europeans could be described then quite unashamedly: of the summary justice which was handed out to captured rebels; the news that came in of the pursuit of the fugitive Chilembwe and his men; the knowledge that troops had arrived from Karonga, and that the local populations, if not always as co-operative as they might be, showed no open signs of disaffection: all brought about a state of mind amongst the Europeans of the Shire Highlands which no longer made necessary their stay in the laagers. On the Saturday some cattle, the property of Chilembwe and John Gray Kufa, about fifty-six in all, were brought into Blantyre.[144] It was another symbol that the Rising which had broken out seven days before with the attacks on Magomero and Mandala was almost over.

All intelligence from the forces who were chasing Chilembwe suggested that the rebels who had not been captured while escaping had managed to come together and were making a concerted attempt to escape by way of the Machemba Pass (Fort Lister Gap) into Portuguese territory. One by one, rebel leaders had been captured or shot. But Chilembwe was to be a more successful fugitive. Four days later, however, on Wednesday, 3 February, 1915,[145] a small Mlanje police force, which had been sent out to patrol the Portuguese border, had fired on a group of fleeing rebels in the bush. It was a light engagement but it was enough to cause the death of the rebel leader. Later, it was stated that a Church of Scotland African teacher from Mlanje had had much to do with tracking him down,[146] though the Administration claimed this honour for its own police.[147] A planter member of the Volunteer Reserve, Hayter, identified one of the dead men who was brought in by the patrol and who was found to be wearing gold-rimmed glasses, as John Chilembwe.[148] His body was taken to the Boma at Mlanje the following day,[149] where three more witnesses identified it.[150] Chilembwe's body was then handed by the District Officer, Colin Grant, to John R. Downs, a commercial man and another Volunteer. He was instructed to bury it. With two African policemen to carry the body, Downs buried it amongst thick bush about two miles from the Boma, far away from any associations of Chilembwe in life.[151] But the operation was carried out so quietly—whether intentionally or not, is not clear—that many Africans refused to believe that Chilembwe was dead. He had escaped from his pursuers, they claimed, and one day would return to liberate them from European rule in the Protectorate. It was the beginning of a John Chilembwe legend.

Thus, by 4 February 1915, not a fortnight after the Magomero and Mandala attacks, the Rising was over.[152] There was no protracted partisan warfare. The European Volunteers could get ready to go home, with the blessing of the Government, to await the end of the War and the special bar in commemoration of their services in the Rising of 1915 which would be added to their Victory medals.[153] Quick trials of most of the captured rebels had taken place by this time,[154] and all that remained was the ending of the 'clearing-up' process. Had the Government not carried on with this, it is more than likely that most of the rebels would have assimilated themselves easily into the local societies again. But the Government had not only the task of stamping out all elements of the conspiracy : it also had to save face before the attacks that were directed against it by angry Europeans in the Protectorate for allowing the rebellion to begin at all. Thus, for over two years after the Rising, a police patrol was sent every month from the Mlanje Boma along the Portuguese border. Its task was to try to get information about escaped rebels. But it was a hopeless task. The ruthless and summary way in which the rebellion had been put down scared away Africans, and the patrol could go for miles without seeing a single native.[155]

Some of the rebels managed to remain in hiding for a long time after the effective ending of the Rising. Such a one was Andrack Jamali, Chilembwe's secretary, who was not caught until December 1915.[156] He had been working quite openly as a wood-boy in Zomba and might have continued for long in that role if he had not been given away by some of the rebels who were held as prisoners at Zomba. Jamali passed them quite cheerfully each day as they were at their hard-labour tasks in Zomba. One of them, no doubt frustrated by the cheerful 'moni' ('morning') which Jamali gave them as he passed by, betrayed him to the police. Indeed, it was the Africans rather than the Europeans of the Protectorate who brought the remaining rebels to light. It was a process which was greatly stimulated by the official rewards that were given. At least one semi-professional informer was thus created. He was the 'wily old carpenter' who had been responsible for John Gray Kufa's capture. The old man had obtained a kind of roving commission to spy out rebels from the Blantyre judge, with a food allowance of ten shillings a week instead of the usual sixpenny allowance. 'Abandoning carpentry for a time he roamed about the country and succeeded in piling up a substantial sum in rewards.'[157] Yet for one such man, how many Africans in the villages around Magomero kept their knowledge of the conspiracy a close secret, and did all they could to shield any rebels who were known to them, in spite of all the frequent forays of Government troops and informers? This question has never been, and is unlikely to be, documented. Yet, from the Chilembwe legend which was springing up at this time, there is some circumstantial evidence to suggest that such Africans were not a few.

One story which, in various versions, had its roots in this period and which was to be told later by mothers to their children, has had the effect of making something of a mythical folk-hero out of Chilembwe. The story, which spread into the villages around the Providence Industrial Mission, told of how Chilembwe was chased into his church by the troops who came to attack his village. They saw him enter the church, and, when they emerged at the other exit, saw his footprints in the wet ground outside. They followed these footprints with a hope of catching him. Soon, however, they found that one human footprint of each two was replaced by a hyenas' footprint, and then that both became those of a hyena.[158] They drew the conclusion that Chilembwe had turned himself into this animal in order to escape. Later, some of the villagers would claim that in this and similar fashions he had flown like a bird invisibly to America, from which he would eventually return to emancipate them. The 'American' story exists in many forms—some connected more with Joseph Booth than with 1915 and John Chilembwe. All of these tales bear witness to the enduring memory of John Chilembwe amongst those Africans and their children, and wider native circles with whom they came into contact, whom he and his mission had influenced. Together with the growth of the story that his mother was Nyangu, a famous Maravi chieftainess, they illustrate that the death of John Chilembwe was but the beginning of the legend.

Another legend which sprang up at this time had a shorter but, for its period, a no-less-effective life. It concerned the callousness of the prison official who had been charged with the execution of most of the rebels. He was John Archer. When the Rising scare was over, Archer, an ex-Regular soldier and veteran of the Omdurman campaign in the Sudan, who was a member of the Nyasaland Volunteer Reserve, had gone with this force to serve in the campaign against the Germans in Rhodesia. Many of its African members had not joined up out of pure free-will, and this made the problem of getting work out of them under difficult conditions no easy one. The *Nyasaland Times* for 27 September 1917 reprinted an article on the Nyasaland Volunteers' reinforcement column at Fort Hill which demonstrated that to Archer, at least, there was no problem. Together with two French Fathers, he was then in charge of the force's transport, which consisted in the main of *tenga-tenga*, native carriers. The French Fathers, said the paper,

> could not get anything like the amount of labour out of the natives that the executioner did. He had hanged a considerable number of rebels [159] who were concerned with the John Chilembwe rising in the early part of 1915. He had sent these mutinous ones west at a fee of £3 per head and it was averred that he had expressed his willingness to hang the whole population at this rate of remuneration. If ever a Tenga-tenga complained about the size or weight of his load the appearance of the soldier hangman was sufficient to make the protesting porter jump to deeds that would have shamed Atlas.

Would it, then, be too much to say that another by-product of the Chilembwe Rising was that it enabled at least one group of the British forces who were fighting against the Germans to get more labour out of their native porters ? If so, it forms but another ironical side to a story which has more than its share of irony.

VII

THE SMALLER MISSIONS AND EUROPEAN
INVOLVEMENT IN THE RISING

Your Commissioners express it as their opinion . . .
that the causes which have led to the late Rebellion
among the slaves in this Island are . . . from a mischiev-
ous abuse existing in the system adopted by different
religious sects in this Island, turned Baptists, Wesleyan
Methodists and Moravians, by their recognizing grada-
tion of rank among such of our slaves as have become
converts to their doctrines, whereby the less ambitious
and more peaceable among them were made the dupes of
the artful and intelligent who had been selected by the
preachers of those particular sects to fill higher offices in
the chapels under the denomination of rulers, elders,
leaders and helpers.

*Report from the House of Assembly, Jamaica,
as to the Injury sustained during the Recent
Rebellion, 1832*

THE SMALLER MISSIONS AND EUROPEAN INVOLVEMENT IN THE RISING

1. Watch Tower; Zambesi and Nyassa Industrial Missions; Seventh-day Adventists

No sooner was the Rising effectively over and the trial and punishment of the rebels and their African sympathizers well in hand than suspicion and rumour began to attach themselves to possible European supporters of Chilembwe and his men. Of course Booth's name was on everyone's lips, though he had been out of Nyasaland for over a decade. He was still remembered as the volatile and negrophile missionary who had disturbed the apparently peaceful pattern of Church and State relationships by his introduction into the Protectorate of a number of highly independent missions and movements, to which radical and ambitious Africans, like Chilembwe, Booth's first convert, could attach themselves : the Zambesi Industrial Mission ; the Nyassa Industrial Mission ; the Baptist Industrial Mission of Scotland ; the African Christian Union and the first African separatist church in the Protectorate which he had planned with Chilembwe and Malinki ; his pro-African petition of 1899 ; the Seventh Day Baptist Mission ; the Seventh-day Adventist Mission ; the Watch Tower movement ; the Church of Christ Mission ; the petition which he had sponsored with Nyambo in 1914 just before the War broke out ; and a whole host of enthusiastic and ephemeral activities amongst Nyasaland Africans, inside and outside the Protectorate. It was natural, therefore, that any person or institution which had been in any way connected with him should fall under suspicion as in some way linked to the Rising. His name and its associations ('Ethiopian', 'Africa for the Africans', 'Seventh Day', 'Watch Tower', 'Adventist') became a convenient series of symbols for a movement which, under war-time conditions of alarm, resentment, and suspicion, acquired something of the character of a 'witch-hunt' against both Africans and Europeans who did not fit into the patterns of conduct that were acceptable to the ruling circles of the Protectorate.

Though he was unconnected with the Rising, Charles Domingo, who had been Booth's chief African intermediary with the independent African Seventh Day Baptist churches, went down in the 'general cataclysm'.[1] After its experience with the P.I.M. as a focus for discontent, it was obvious that the Government was going to keep the strictest possible control over the African independent schools and churches; and, whether by Government order or by his own reading of the signs of the times, Domingo closed up his school and church. Nevertheless his influence, if only indirectly, seems to have made itself felt at the time of the trial of African rebels. Domingo's use of texts from the 'radical' Chapter V of James's Epistle has already been noticed.[2] Identical texts with a similarly radical interpretation appear to have been used by some of Chilembwe's followers when they were put on trial for their part in the Rising:[3] 'Go to, ye rich men, howl and weep for your miseries that shall come upon you. . . .' Whether such texts were used for defence or defiance, or both, is of small importance compared with the suggestion they carried of strong elements of Watch Tower teaching.

Though, as has been noted,[4] Chilembwe himself had no apparent connection with the American Watch Tower movement and attempts to link his insurrectionary projects with this organization in the United States seem misguided, there was, nevertheless, a significant amount of its literature in Nyasaland on the eve of the Rising. Some of it had come into the Protectorate at the time when Booth was toying with the teachings of Pastor Russell of Pennsylvania, and when Kamwana was threatening to set off a poll-tax rebellion amongst the Lake shore people to the west; much of this literature had passed into the stream of Domingo-supervised separatist schools and churches and seems to have been used less as a doctrinal medium than as exercise and teaching material for a small, independent African reading-public. Further Watch Tower literature had come in after Booth's break with Russell and after Kamwana's deportation: this was posted or brought to those members of Kamwana-ite Watch Tower congregations who were still attached to the new creed in spite of Government intervention against its African leader. Much of this material would have fallen easily into the hands of Africans [5] who, while not particularly interested in the dogmas of the American sect, found its implicit and explicit criticism of all Governmental institutions attractive. And in at least two of Russell's *Studies in the Scriptures*, the radical verses from Chapter V of James's Epistle might be found with appropriate comment. In the first and most widely circulated volume, *The Plan of the Ages*, in a chapter called 'The Day of Jehovah', there is a compelling essay on their theme. In spite of Russell's assertion that 'the worst government, and the most expensive, is vastly better than no government at all',[6] he had no hesitation in pointing out that one of the signs of the impending End was a 'growing opposition between the wealthy and labouring classes';[7] and he declared that 'the Apostle James points out this day of trouble and tells of its being the result of differences between capital and labour'.[8] The point is put even more strikingly in the fourth volume of Russell's *Studies*, *The Battle of Armageddon*, in a manner which could not fail to have had meaning for those workers on the Magomero Estates who followed or were influenced by Chilembwe, and who may have read the volumes themselves, or have heard of their tenor from preachers who found a platform in the P.I.M. and the circles of African independent churches. Some of these workers, it must be remembered, nursed the grievance that they were being defrauded of their lands and traditional privileges, and most of them had often accused the manager of paying them short or of delaying their wages. Russell's comments almost seem to have been specially written for this group, and the modern translation which he gives of these scriptural passages underlines their radical implications. After a reference to 'the very striking prophecy respecting the closing days of this Gospel age, as recorded by the Apostle James',[9] he adds : 'He seems to point out the condition of things precisely as can now be seen by all careful observers, adding in *explanation* of the matter—that it is the result of a *fraud*'. He says : 'Behold, that reward which you ['rich men'] have fraudulently withheld from those labourers who harvested your fields cries out : and the cries of the labourers have entered into the ears of the Lord of armies'.[10] As if to make the point clearer, the chapter in which this analysis occurs is entitled 'The Cries of the Reapers'; and the general section in which the chapter is set seems almost to be looking directly towards the tragedy of Magomero—it is called 'The Day of Vengeance'.

In such reasoning, of course, there must be much of the circumstantial element. Yet it seems something more than a coincidence, something more than an unaided reading of the Holy Writ, that at the trials of the rebels many of them quoted from Chapter V of James's Epistle. Because of this, and in spite of the fact that the

American Watch Tower Bible and Tract Society had no representative in Nyasaland or the Rhodesias before 1925,[11] loose accusations of 'Watch-Towerism' were flung against the Chilembwe movement. Yet, as has been seen, in a seemingly representative list of the fugitives after the defeat of the first insurrectionary attempts, only one is mentioned as having a clear affiliation with the Watch Tower movement : 'Wilson Daniel Kusita. A Ngoni. Resided formerly at Chilembwe's, lately Watch Tower preacher in Upper Shire District.' [12] However, from this time many wild rumours against Watch Tower were to spread in Nyasaland : all of them the result, t appears, of panic or the desire to find a scapegoat, and the product of a misconception that was based on a failure to distinguish between an American society and African individuals and groups who had no closer connection with the parent organization than the reception of its literature. Had the Watch Tower Bible and Tract Society possessed European representatives in Nyasaland in 1915, there is no doubt that they would have been forced to leave summarily by the Government. As it was, such scapegoats had to be found from other sectarian missions in the Protectorate.

At first, perhaps, some of the Europeans of Booth's original ventures, the Zambesi and Nyassa Industrial Missions, may have felt that the axe would descend on them. Some of them had been friendly with Chilembwe at the P.I.M. and had attended the opening of his brick church. Such a one was John Chorley,[13] Z.I.M. missionary at Chipande, on the other side of Chiradzulu mountain from Mbombwe ; and the Z.I.M. missionaries noted that the Chilembwe 'trouble [had] started on an Estate adjoining our Chipande station'.[14] It was, then, perhaps in a mood of some trepidation that H. J. Rayment of the Nyassa Industrial Mission at Cholo wrote to the local press [15] on 10 February 1915. His letter defended the missions against attacks which were being made on them as raisers and educators of African agitators, and laid the blame for the Rising squarely on Booth, Ethiopianism, and Government negligence altogether. But no accusations, he claimed, could be substantiated against the Z.I.M. and N.I.M. Europeans who, since their break in the 1890's with Booth, had engaged in the most peaceful and non-political industry. Yet there is a curious note in a subsequent Z.I.M. publication which suggests that, while no possible accusation could be brought against any European of this mission, however indirectly, of connection with Chilembwe's conspiracy, there were, nevertheless, some bonds, direct or indirect, whether of sympathy or of more active support, between some of their African converts and the Rising. It is a note which indicates a certain degree of demoralization after the Rising in those areas of the Z.I.M. that were close to Chilembwe's mission and the Bruce Estates :

> The work at Numulu and Maela churches has gone down consider-ably since the Chilembwe native rising. This district used to be the background of the Chipande work. Some of our most reliable native boys married second wives.[16]

Yet this may indicate nothing more than a certain marginal Z.I.M. African radicalism that may have felt the force of the Chilembwe movement. Something more substantial was required to confirm the many accusations which were then rife about the complicity of the smaller missions in the Rising. To some over-suspicious Euro-peans in Nyasaland, attacks on the Seventh-day Adventist Mission seemed likely to be more profitable. Indeed, at that time, the appellation 'Adventist' was capable of provoking a reaction amongst European 'witch-hunters' as powerful, if not more powerful than the tag 'Watch Tower'. For example, in an editorial published on 4 February 1915, the day after Chilembwe was shot, the *Nyasaland Times* claimed that the Seventh-day Adventists were associated with Ethiopianism, and hinted at the moral of this a week later with the quite unjustifiable statement that 'John Chilembwe was an Adventist and a very immediate one'. The implication was taken to a much higher level when a question was raised in Parliament on 29 April 1915 about the Rising. It was brought up by Sir John Rees, a director of the British Central Africa Company and a persistent raiser of Nyasaland questions in the Commons. It was a query about Booth's part in the Rising, and Rees dubbed him, with all the contemporary confident vagueness, 'a Seventh Day Adventist mis-sionary', and asked what could be done to prevent 'this person and his American negro supporters from propagating their doctrines in this British Protectorate'.[17] Booth's position as the founder of the first Seventh-day Adventist Mission at Malamulo in Nyasaland naturally brought the denomination under suspicion ; and this was strengthened by the fact that Peter Nyambo, whose Rhodesia-Nyasaland appeal of May 1914 had been circulating in the Pro-tectorate before the Rising, had been for long one of its leading converts. Furthermore, one of the Seventh-day Adventist European missionaries during the period 1908–14 was an American with the German-sounding name of S. M. Konigmacher—and, when assessing European suspicions in Nyasaland at this moment, it must be remembered that the United States did not enter the Great War until 1917, and, until then, pro-German groupings amongst American descendants of German immigrants were known to be common. Konigmacher, moreover, in the past had had his difficulties with the Government over the opening of mission schools ; [18] and, whilst engaged in an evangelistic campaign in Portuguese Angoniland, close by the Nyasa border, had been accused of upsetting the minds of native Christians.[19] The gravest causes for suspicion of him, however, were that he was known to have been friendly at one time with Filipo Chinyama, to have had some correspondence with him, and to have taken an interest in Chinyama's career as a preacher.[20] Yet both Konigmacher's name and his activities were innocent enough : but they could be calculated to add to the atmosphere of suspicion that was then winding itself around the Seventh-day Adventist missions in Nyasaland.[21]

In response to these suspicions, C. J. Robinson, an English Seventh-day Adventist and superintendent since 1911 of the Malamulo mission, availed himself of the main means of public defence then open in Nyasaland : the press. He wrote a letter to the *Nyasaland Times* in which he objected to its statement that the Seventh-day Adventists were implicated in the Ethiopianist movement. So scornful, however, of their position was the *Nyasaland Times* that it did not bother to publish Robinson's letter but made it instead the subject of a sneering leader in its issue of 11 February 1915 entitled 'Nondescript Missions'. Whilst it admitted that no direct connection could be found between the Seventh-day Adventist missions in Nyasaland and the Rising, the paper nevertheless made abundantly clear its view-point that they had been indirectly concerned with the Rising. Its first charge against the Seventh-day Adventists was part of a general criticism of all missionary activity in the Protectorate : 'a tendency to over-educate the natives not only beyond what they can really assimilate but also beyond the economic needs of the community'. Its second charge was more direct and menacing : 'To speak very plainly, we think that hair-splitting over the observance of Sunday is calculated to do immense harm to the natives and we go further and say that the Government would be well advised to stop all such propaganda'.

It was obvious from this kind of suspicion that, if the work of his mission was not to be impeded, the Malamulo superintendent would have to produce some clear evidence that his mission stations and schools had not been centres of sedition. For several months after the Rising, therefore, he indulged in a spate of correspondence [22] to Commissioners of Districts where the Seventh-day Adventists had schools or churches, to the Nyasaland Government, and to his co-workers in South Africa, where Booth had his base. The upshot of it all was that it appeared that few, if any, Africans who had been directly attached to Seventh-day Adventist missions on the eve of the Rising had taken any part in it.[23] This, however, did not mean that Africans who had at one time been connected with Malamulo or its kindred churches and schools could be completely absolved. Indeed, it became clear that in 1907 Filipo Chinyama had been attached to the Malamulo mission, and that one of the members of his following, Joshua Chona,[24] had been there in 1911. Yet both of them, like any other of the direct or indirect participants in the Rising who may have been associated at one time with the Seventh-day Adventists, had left them before the insurrection took place; they seem to have gone into more independent African missions, either Chilembwe's, Chinyama's, or any of the other little African 'nondescript missions'. Perhaps the greatest single defence that the Seventh-day Adventists could provide was the conduct of Kalindi Morrison Malinki who, in spite of his original associations with Booth and Chilembwe, had resisted all overtures to join the Rising. Malinki had gone over to Malamulo in 1904, had become its first African pastor and, by 1915, one of its most valued workers. This did not prevent the general atmosphere of suspicion from overtaking him, however; and he was taken to Zomba in 1915, put into leg-irons, and questioned on his knowledge of the Rising.[25] The subsequent liberation of Malinki was a sign that the Seventh-day Adventists in Nyasaland were free from direct complicity in the Rising. The worst, perhaps, that could be said against them was the extremely indirect statement that there was evidence 'that certain rebels implicated in the rising in the Ncheu Division were attempting to make for Matandani', a mission station of the Seventh-day Adventists which had been set up in 1908.[26] By June 1915 Robinson had produced his master stroke: an extract for 18 January from the 1907 minute-book of the South-African Seventh-day Adventists in which, in the critical year after the Natal Rebellion of 1906 when there was in South Africa a similar atmosphere of suspicion to that in Nyasaland after the Chilembwe Rising, the South African Union Conference of the denomination had passed a resolution that expressed its 'unqualified disapproval of the "Ethiopian Movement"'. Copies were sent to the Governor of Nyasaland and to the Commission which had been appointed to inquire into the Rising. The result was that, when the Commission produced its Report in 1916, though it was critical of 'small missions which run contrary to ordinary ideas and tend to unsettle the native mind . . . [by preaching] that Saturday is the divinely appointed day of rest and that the end of the world is at hand',[27] it did not mention the Seventh-day Adventists by name. With the exception of Malinki's mistaken arrest and the very short period when some of their African-supervised schools were closed by Government decree, they were left to conduct their work without impediment. 'Adventist' still continued to be a vague term of suspicion; but the Malamulo *milieu* of 1915 had produced no scapegoats to satisfy the agitations of the Government or local European settlers.

These were to be provided by the two 'small Missions, insufficiently financed, conducted by unsuitable persons and under no proper control',[28] in the words of the Commission of Inquiry into the Rising, which it thought fit to mention by name in its Report : the Seventh Day Baptists and the Churches of Christ Mission.

2. The Seventh Day Baptist Scapegoat

It should be obvious, from what has been said in the account which has already been given of the immediate prelude to the Rising, who the scapegoat in Nyasaland for the Seventh Day Baptists would be : the independent American missionary, Walter Cockerill of Berlin, Wisconsin, whose zealous activities amongst the remnants of the Boothian S.D.B. churches to the west of Lake Nyasa before the battle of Karonga had caused the Government to restrict his movements to the neighbourhood of Blantyre before the Rising had broken out at all. To the authorities he was clearly marked out as a 'dangerous element' and one that should be removed as soon as possible.[29]

From the middle of October 1914, when he had come back to the Shire Highlands after crossing swords with the authorities over his evangelizing among the Ngoni and Tonga, to the time when the Rising broke out, Cockerill's activities had been peaceful enough. He had taken himself off to Booth's old Shiloh station at Chikunda, some five miles to the north of Blantyre, and from there had carried on normal missionary work with the purpose of confirming in their faith the small group of Africans who still adhered to it, and of extending, through mission and school, the Seventh Day Baptist beliefs to other natives of the Protectorate. That it was not all plain sailing was indicated by a laconic statement in his diary for Saturday, 14 November : 'Hosea, 7 ; 15'. The verse in question reads : 'Though I have taught and strengthened their arms, yet do they imagine mischief against me'. It is a cryptic reference and may well refer to the increasing Government suspicion of his activities. More probably, however, it seems to illustrate the demands which were made on his resources by local Africans who thought that they saw in him another missionary of the Booth stamp : an American who would dispense his money and attention freely to all. Cockerill had already made it clear that he was not prepared to support the rump of the African Russellites in Nyasaland, when they had originally welcomed him with open arms. The demands of the supporters of his own denomination were more than enough for him. Yet it was quite obvious that he had a soft heart. 'I have come to love the people here in spite of their faults', he had written home from Mzimba on 20 September 1914 'I cannot see how anyone can help loving the negro. . . . I am convinced that the only way to under-stand the African is to love him.' When, therefore, the flow of his financial charity to some of the Africans in his following did not come up to their expectations, some grumbling could be expected. It was slow work, too, in face of the suspicious attitudes of surround-ing missions. Nevertheless, by the end of 1914 he had constructed some rudimentary buildings and carried on preaching and teaching to ensure for himself a regular congregation. Less than a fortnight before the Rising broke out, on 11 January 1915, he started a little school with twelve pupils ; and, the Saturday before the attacks on Magomero and Mandala, he could report an attendance of sixty at a Communion service. After his repulses in the northern territories of Nyasaland, it was not an unfavourable beginning.

Then, on the Sunday morning, 24 January, he received a note from a friendly neighbouring planter, Ritchie, which told him of Chilembwe's work of the night before. From that time Cockerill was given little peace by the authorities, or scope to carry on his work. Like most of the other local Europeans, he was called to the Boma and spent four nights in laager there before he was allowed to go back to his station at Chikunda on 30 January. The next day his main African helper, Alexander Makwinja, left the little mission station, and two days afterwards Cockerill received news of his arrest on a charge of complicity in the Rising. Later he heard that three others of his flock had been arrested on similar charges. The Government round-up of suspects and the summary justice meted out to those who were found guilty struck fear into the hearts of his African adherents. As the word spread around that the Government was suspicious of all the small, independent missions, especially those which had had any contact with Bwana Booth—and which of them had not, at some time?—and that it was prepared to make quick arrests, often on what must have seemed to many Africans to be 'guilt-by-association' charges, then, obviously, Cockerill might expect some diminution of his flock. By March the children at his school had left him. A week later he heard that his subsidiary school at Lunzu, close to Chikunda, had been closed, and that the African women there, out of fear of possible Government reprisals because of their association with Seventh Day Baptists, had torn down his church. It was clear that, directly and indirectly, every obstacle was being put before what Cockerill considered to be the path of his duty. He was not the sort of man to take it without protest.

By this time, on Wednesday, 24 February, his dwelling had been searched, his correspondence taken, and as he wrote home to America 'the officer in charge even threatened my life . . . saying that he would have me shot if I tried to run away'.[30] And, to crown it all, the Government had asked him to leave the Protectorate. Cockerill could see no good reason for this, and so availed himself of his main line of defence : protest to the nearest American Consulate. In his case this was the U.S. Consul at Cape Town some seventeen hundred miles away ! The letters which he wrote to the American Consul brought sympathetic but belated and ineffective replies. 'I would advise you to remember', wrote the Consul to him on 6 April, 'that, while martial law is in force, certain procedure is warranted which at other times might seem harsh and unjust, and that consequently it would be apt to weaken your case if you now claimed rights which you would not be fully entitled to in times of peace.' By the time this letter reached him, however, Cockerill was in no position to weigh the finer points of procedure. On Friday, 16 April, he had received through the District Resident at Blantyre a letter from the Chief Secretary's Office at the centre of government, Zomba, which made quite clear the Governor's attitude towards him. Under the powers of the Nyasaland Defence Ordinance, 1914, the Governor, stated this letter, 'had decided that the continued presence in this country of certain persons, of whom you are one, is politically un-desirable in existing circumstances by reason of their teaching which, in His Excellency's judgement, tends to unsettle and disturb the minds of the native population'. Therefore, it went on, 'since it is understood that you have refused to obey the order directing you to leave this Protectorate, a warrant has been issued under the Governor's hand authorizing your arrest and removal by force should you be so ill advised as to persist in this attitude'. Then—no doubt with a memory of Cockerill's interview with the Governor in October in mind—the letter concluded that 'it must be understood that the Governor cannot enter into any further discussion on the subject and that unless his order is obeyed at once it will be enforced in the manner indicated'. The point was driven home by a visit from a Government Officer on the following day, who brought the warrant with him in case Cockerill needed any further evidence that the Government meant business! But the unfortunate missionary required no further assurance of this, wound up what few affairs he had, said a hasty good-bye to the few Europeans he knew, made his last farewells to his dwindling African congregation, and on Monday 26 April 1915, was on the train from Blantyre to Port Herald and thence, down the Zambezi, to Quilimane and home. Just over a year before he had been going up the Zambezi, full of high hopes for the success of his mission!

What lay behind the action of the Government in deporting Walter Cockerill from Nyasaland? Some of the reasons have already been suggested in the previous account of his expulsion from the districts of Mombera's and Gomani's Ngoni. Nevertheless, because the entire affair is so typical of the whole process of Government reaction to the course of African discontents from Booth's arrival in the Protectorate in 1892 down to Chilembwe's revolt of 1915, it is worth while to bring together in a summary all the possible reasons for the Administration's action in the case of Walter Cockerill in 1915.

First of all, one must adduce the fact that Cockerill had already fallen foul of the authorities in his evangelizing trips into the Ngoni and Tonga districts on the western shores of Lake Nyasa. Had he not been deported from those regions, the Government might have looked more leniently upon the character of his Seventh Day Baptist Mission at Chikunda in 1915. But Cockerill was unfortunate enough to have been caught between the two fires of Kamwana-ism and Chilembwe-ism. He got the worst of both worlds. Memories of Kamwana's agitations in 1908, and fear of African reaction to his Watch Tower prophecy that the world would end in October 1914, had forced the Government's hand against Cockerill in the first months of the Great War after the battle at Karonga. Furthermore, it is significant that Cockerill had been told by an indiscreet District Officer, during the period of his deportation to the Shire Highlands, that the Government was afraid that his presence might act as an agency to start off disturbances amongst the rival African independent sects which were scattered along the Lakeside : amongst, mainly, the Watch Tower faction which had deserted Booth and had given its allegiance to Elliot Kamwana, and the series of African Seventh Day Baptist Churches which owed some allegiance to Booth at the Cape, through Charles Domingo, but that were already beginning to show signs of turning into pro- and anti-Booth factions. It would have been a complicated *mêlée* if it had been touched off : a process which would have had some analogy with the bitterness of the old tribal rivalries—and might, indeed, have brought to the surface again some of the old Tonga-Ngoni tension and turbulence. It would have created a whole intersecting sequence of religious feuds, vehicles of a number of ambitious and competing personalities who had been brought out by the White Man's new order and for whom the old order could find no place.[31] At a time when the German armies still threatened the Protectorate, such a situation would have been an open invitation for von Lettow to invade Nyasaland. After Chilembwe's movement, too, the Administration would have no desire to see the leaders of the various independent African sects—many of whom had been deprived of the, at least nominal, leadership of John Chilembwe who had possessed, it must be remembered, the ambition of bringing them together into a single Nyasaland African church—plunged into a whirlpool of rivalry over the now disputed leadership of the African independent churches. Again, Cockerill's presence, as an heir of Booth, could have added stimulus to this movement.

At the time of both of his deportations, Cockerill's connections, though only superficial, with Booth and his movements must have been a powerful factor in adding weight to the Government's final decision. It may or may not have been known that Cockerill had had some correspondence with Booth over the Chikunda land on which the Seventh Day Baptist Mission stood. If the Government had known of this, it would certainly have construed this correspond-ence, innocent in intention though it may have been, as a very definite black mark against Cockerill; a form of 'guilt by associa-tion'—this time against a European.

Other forms of 'guilt by association', however, may have helped to create that climate of opinion inside which the Government of Nyasaland shaped its decisions against Cockerill. These com-prised, in the main, his friendship with neighbouring planters of German descent. Though the Government had not scrupled to use the services of local Germans and prisoners-of-war in the actual period of emergency during the Rising, and though it afforded very liberal conditions to the Germans in Nyasaland during the War, it was still aware of the fact that it was fighting against Germany. Too much association with Germans, therefore, would cause suspicion of anyone. To Cockerill it was a perfectly innocent matter. He came from a part of the United States which had been strongly influenced by German settlement; his home town, in fact, was called Berlin. (Is it just possible that Cockerill's letters to Berlin—if only Berlin, Wisconsin—reinforced suspicions of him? In the atmosphere of official panic in many parts of Nyasaland at this time it is at least not improbable.) Furthermore the United States was not yet at war with Germany, and Walter Cockerill, as a free, Mid-Western, highly independent and democratic American, saw no reason for not speaking freely about the War to Germans or to anyone else. From them, indeed, he had learned of many African grievances, and had openly discussed these with them. And some of the letters which he had written home, in spite of the censorship in Nyasaland, had been critical of the Government. Later Cockerill saw the moral of all this when he wrote to a friend in Berlin, Wisconsin, that 'few Americans realise . . . the animosity that there was between the English and the Germans before the war . . .',[32] though how far he was correct when he ascribed this to 'the great German trade on the east side of Africa' was more debatable. Nevertheless, in some way, Walter Cockerill's innocent-enough meetings with local Germans, his references in correspondence and conversations to German affairs, and his refusal, as an independent American, to adopt what he called 'the same degree of patriotism as the English bishop who goes about recruiting',[33] seem to have had something to do with his eventual deportation. He was quite clear on this himself. 'I am suspected', he wrote home, 'of being an American (or German) spy, and of teaching sedition to the natives. An Englishman sees in every American a rebel and a filibuster. One of the grim jokes of war is the spy madness of the people of the nations engaged in this war. An alien is an enemy in these countries.'[34]

However much substance there may have been in his feeling that he was being taken for a spy, he was on sure ground when he claimed that the Government felt that he was 'teaching sedition to natives'. This was clear from the letter in which he was informed that he would be arrested if he did not leave the Protectorate. The matters for speculation here lie not in the fact that the Government considered Cockerill's teaching as unsettling to the native mind but, first, how far all of this was simply the general effect of Cockerill as a representative of a 'nondescript mission' which taught doctrines that ran contrary to the general tenor of Christian teaching in the Protectorate—that is to say, Cockerill's teaching as the recipient of criticism that was stronger, but similar to that which the Seventh-day Adventists were enduring ; and, secondly, how far the unsettling effect of his work was due to a more direct connection between his mission and the Rising. On the first count, there is no doubt that as a representative of the Seventh Day Baptists, with all that this denomination had meant in the Protectorate through its associations with Joseph Booth, as far as the Government and its Commission of Inquiry into the Rising were concerned, Cockerill was at fault. He was not mentioned by name in the Commission's Report—in fact, there are no references to his case, presumably because of the Protectorate censorship, in the local press—but his denomination was mentioned by name as a type of small mission which was insufficiently controlled and, therefore, liable to give the Africans too much scope for discussion of points which they barely understood but on which they placed the fullest possible radical interpretation. Had the Commission possessed the knowledge that some of the Seventh Day Baptists in the Old World were the Fifth Monarchy Men of the days of Cromwell and the English Revolution,[35] some of them might have been tempted to put this point more strongly !

On the second count, the matter is more complex.[36]   There seems
no reason whatsoever to suppose that Cockerill was in any way connected with John Chilembwe's plans.   He had himself never seen
Chilembwe or even been into the immediate area of his Providence
Industrial Mission.   It is true that Cockerill had received from some
African or other a hint that the Rising was intended.   But he had
dismissed this as improbable, and had not thought it worth mention-
ing to any Government agency.   The apparent fact that the Government itself had originally treated similar news with a good deal of
scepticism indicates that Cockerill's reaction to this rumour was not
unusual.   What made it, in his case, the more serious must have been
the fact that a number of Africans from the Seventh Day Baptist
Mission were known to have been implicated in the Rising.   Foremost amongst these was Alexander Makwinja.   Cockerill knew that
Makwinja had been connected with Booth at the time of both his
Watch Tower and Seventh Day Baptist ventures.   Furthermore he
knew, from conversations with him, that Makwinja was a great
admirer of John Chilembwe and his Providence Industrial Mission.
There is, indeed, an interesting, if small, item of evidence in existence which suggests close contacts between Makwinja and Chilembwe
as far back as 1911.   It consists of some words written by Booth in
the margin of a leaflet which advertised the African Industrial Society
that was proposed by leading Africans at the P.I.M. in 1911.   Next
to Chilembwe's name on the leaflet, as one of the sponsors of the
Society, Booth wrote to his Seventh Day Baptist colleagues in
America : 'My first convert.   He will help Alexander [Makwinja.—
AUTHORS] in translating from English [for the circulation of S.D.B.
leaflets].')   Cockerill knew, too, that Makwinja was a man of an
independent spirit.   Makwinja had told him that one of the local
planters had knocked from his head the jaunty green hat he liked to
wear, because Makwinja had not raised it to him.   (The enforced
raising of hats by Africans before Europeans was a common grievance
of native witnesses before the Commission of Inquiry into the Rising.)
Makwinja was highly insulted by the action ; for the green hat, a
European article, was to him a symbol of his status as a leader amongst
many of the local Africans and a mark of his aspirations to emulate
the Europeans.   When Makwinja told the story to Cockerill he had
concluded with the words, 'We can fight, too !'   At the time they
were lost upon Cockerill, though he saw their implications after the
Rising when Alexander Makwinja was arrested.   Cockerill had been

aware, too, that Makwinja had made a trip into Ngoniland just before himself. While there is little clear evidence to connect this trip of Makwinja's with Chilembwe's plans, it is not unlikely that this was a journey to sound out Ngoni support for Chilembwe. Makwinja, as Cockerill knew, was always raising funds for postage and other objects. Indeed, on one occasion he and a group of other Africans were instrumental in getting Cockerill to help them in cutting down a mahogany tree, which they then cut up and sold for funds. Again, Cockerill was not to know the purpose of these funds before the attack on Magomero. Afterwards, it was only too clear to him what end the money had served. Yet for several days after the Rising, Cockerill was apparently assured by the Resident at Blantyre that there was nothing against Makwinja.[37] It was not until 5 February 1915 that Makwinja was arrested by the Resident at Chiradzulu and the charges brought against him that were to give him a sentence of nine years' imprisonment. By this time Cockerill could put together all the strange scraps of conversation and encounters which he had had with one of the chief African Seventh Day Baptists of the Protectorate, and their full intent was then evident. Yet, until then, they had raised no suspicions in Cockerill, and he had seen no reason for reporting Makwinja to the authorities.

One piece of evidence that fell into his hands at the time of the Rising, however, Cockerill did hand over to the authorities. This was a letter which he had received from Filipo Chinyama to say that 'three natives of the Watch Tower faction had been captured by the Resident Magistrate . . . [at Ncheu], and that he was in danger of being taken himself'.[38] Cockerill had taken this letter straightway to the Resident at Blantyre. Yet he was not then aware, it seems, that Chinyama was the leader of the branch of the Rising amongst Gomani's Ngoni which was planned to link up with the movement around Blantyre and Chiradzulu. Nevertheless this letter that passed from Chinyama to him during the Rising, together with the fact that he had visited Chinyama at his church on his way through the country of Gomani's to the area of Mombera's Ngoni, in the prevailing atmosphere of suspicion, and with all the other circumstantial evidence against him, must have made Cockerill appear to the Administration a figure of the utmost suspicion.

Cockerill, indeed, even if he had not met Chilembwe, had had some contact, albeit of the most innocent kind, with leading figures in the movements of African discontent out of which came the

Rising of 1915 : Booth, Kamwana, Chinyama, Domingo, and a host of lesser lights of which Makwinja was a fair sample. And at one time he may even have had a copy of Nyambo's and Booth's 1914 Rhodesia-Nyasaland Appeal, though he seems to have made no attempt to propagate it. Inevitability is a dangerous concept to use in a historical narrative, yet if ever it had any validity then, surely, it was in this case of Walter Cockerill, Seventh Day Baptist missionary from the backwoods of Wisconsin ? What other outcome of his genuine idealism could there have been than the deportation which awaited him from the chosen field of his missionary activity ? In the first six months of the War in Nyasaland, a frightening event for White and Black alike, the dice were too heavily loaded against Cockerill for it to be possible for him to succeed in his chosen endeavour. He was, indeed, an innocent abroad : and from his own standpoint—that of an independently minded early twentieth-century American—he was undoubtedly harshly treated. Yet from the view-point of the Government, in an atmosphere of suspicion, panic, and fear, with all the novelty of an international war and a new type of African rebellion, and the pressure of local settler groups to contend with, what other course was open than deportation ? Cockerill, as has been pointed out, was caught between the fires of the Kamwana and the Chilembwe movements, and he was brought low by them.

So, although he was not mentioned by name in the report of the Commission of Inquiry into the Rising, the innocently intentioned Cockerill, by the general stigma that was placed on the Seventh Day Baptists by the Commission, suffered accordingly. What he and the smaller, independent missions were taken to stand for in Nyasaland was indicated by A. G. B. Glossop, High Anglican Archdeacon of Likoma in the Universities Mission to Central Africa (U.M.C.A.), and the one clerical representative on the Commission of Inquiry. To keep the African under control, to allow him to develop along 'proper' lines, a very different kind of teaching was needed than that which was provided by these small missions, said Glossop : [39]

> What the African wanted was that kind of teaching which the U.M.C.A. stood for, that was to say the full Catholic Faith with its organization of fellowship and discipline. . . .

The old African way of life was based on a 'communistic not the individualistic' system. When this collapses, as it was collapsing

under the impetus of the new European system of values and politica
and economic relationships, moral restraints on the individua
African disappear. Glossop continued :

> This shows that the Church which professes to aid him must be
> strong Church with discipline, one which will claim for herself some
> thing of the obedience which of old an African gave to his chief an
> tribe. The stronger we make the claims of the Catholic Church, wit
> its discipline and its sense of corporate responsibility, the better for th
> African individual who wills to be saved. For all the bad characters w
> find among Africans, heathen or Christian, collapse for this reason
> they have lost the old props of tribal discipline based chiefly, it may be
> on self-interest and fear, and the newer and higher principles an
> motives which have not had time really to hold them.

Then Glossop came to his point against the smaller, independen
missions, against the American idealists like Cockerill :

> Are these the sort of people to whom we should preach an ultra
> Protestant individualism ? The overwhelming majority of the boys le
> away by John Chilembwe . . . were members of this type of Chris
> tianity. This is the type which prints and proclaims as chief doctrine
> 'the Bible the sole guide of truth and doctrine'. This means that ever
> half-educated native who can just read the Bible in the vernacula
> proceeds to prove everything and anything he likes from Ezekiel an
> Daniel. As a logical result, in practice, each teacher secedes from th
> other on any little pretext and forms a new so-called Church upon an
> private quarrel, and proves that he is right from Isaiah and the Apoca
> lypse. The rebel easily proves to his own satisfaction—which is al
> that is required—that the powers that be are to be destroyed, that a nev
> reign, when Christ will reign upon the earth, is immediately at hand
> and that there will be no Government and no taxes and no white ma
> control.

Then, finally, Glossop stressed the moral again : not a full Pro
testantism but the Catholic Church, either in its Roman form or i
the guise of the High Anglicans :

> As someone said in Blantyre after the rising, 'A Christianity withou
> sacraments is of no use for Africans'.

In this impassioned statement one is carried back almost to the
eve of the Reformation in Europe : and the cries that were hurled
at Luther, and the charges that were thrown by the first Reformers
against the Anabaptists and the less orthodox 'separatist churches

of the new era of a divided Christendom, seem to fill the air once more. And in his reply to such attacks, with his spirited defence of the lower orders' right to interpret the scriptures in their own way, Cockerill added his own characteristic note of democracy against authority, of the Reformation fighting back for its essential principle of individual liberty against the backsliders to Rome within its midst. In Central Africa, indeed, at this time, the Old World and the New seem to meet in a religious controversy which is as old as the Reformation, if not older, and which reveals clearly in statements like Glossop's and in Cockerill's counter-attack, the social and political implications of such struggles. For, in his reply to authoritarian attacks of this sort, Cockerill claimed with equal fervour :

> It is only a relic of Roman Catholicism that is still cherished by Protestant societies when they express by deeds, if not by words, that the lower classes of humanity, and especially heathen races, are not capable of reason, and therefore must have their religious convictions moulded by a hierarchy or council. In most cases such councils cater for political power and, failing to achieve this end, they form a federation of councils. As if by their numbers they may humble God to change his laws to suit their fads and fancies ! [40]

3. THE CHURCHES OF CHRIST SCAPEGOAT

It was with something of this spirit that the original Churches of Christ Mission had been set up amongst the Africans of Nyasaland in 1908.[41] This was the mission, together with the Seventh Day Baptists, that was singled out by the Commissioners, who inquired into the Rising, for providing teaching and examples which helped to touch off the Chilembwe movement. And it was from the Nyasaland Churches of Christ Mission in 1915 that there had come the second European deportee of the Rising. He was George Hubert Hollis.[42]

From the little evidence that is readily available about him, Hollis seems to have been a man of profound convictions, like Booth. In Chapter IV [43] it has been noticed that he came into contact with Booth at some time between 1906 and 1908, and under his inspiration had gone up to Nyasaland from the Cape and had founded there a Churches of Christ Mission on some of Booth's old land at Chikunda. Though the British and South African European Churches of Christ had not sponsored Booth's original scheme for a mission under their auspices, they had given their blessing and backing to Hollis. Yet this should not be taken to mean that Hollis lost all his connections with Booth, for many of the Africans who came to learn or to teach at the schools and churches which Hollis set up were often from the little missions that had been under Booth's influence, and some of them had known Booth at the Cape, when they had made the hard journey down to the extremity of Africa from their homes in Nyasaland. But, on the eve of the Rising, it would probably be an exaggeration to suppose that there was any firm organizational connection between Booth and Hollis, or even that there was any close connection by correspondence at all. What mattered, it seems, was the affinity in spirit, in many ways, between the two men.

Hollis, for all his dozen years or so in Africa, was an Australian (born Lillydale, 1876), and had much of the independence of spirit and disregard (often disrespect) for authority which is often associated with the Southern Continent, although for a period he was a member of the South Africa police in Cape Town. Service in the Imperial Forces during the Boer War had brought him to Africa. At this time, like many another Australian—if Booth's experiences with atheists among the Melbourne miners before he had left for Nyasaland are any indication—he was a 'disbeliever'.[44] Then, like Booth, who was also a disbeliever, even an atheist at one time, he was converted to Christianity, and probably made his way to Nyasaland under the impetus of a relatively recent conversion. If so, this would again be another point of similarity in spirit with the experience of Joseph Booth. The similarity continued when Hollis was in the mission field. He believed with Booth that the Christian missionary must be prepared to 'live rough', and had arrived at one of Booth's old stations at Chikunda with his wife, with nothing more than an African-style mud hut to live in at first. As a European 'living native' he was, from the outset of his Nyasaland experience, therefore, an object of scorn for many of the Europeans of the Shire Highlands. His pronounced outspokenness on African affairs, furthermore, was not likely to overcome their attitude. Unfortunately, few recorded pronouncements of Hollis's exist for this period ; but the words of the colleague, George Hills, another Boer War veteran who had been through the siege of Ladysmith, and who accompanied him on the preliminary survey of the Shire Highlands mission field, may be taken not unfairly as representative of Hollis's own feelings throughout his missionary work in the Protectorate

They are sentiments not unlike the sweeping charges which Booth had levelled originally at the Europeans in Central Africa :

> I am more and more convinced that many of the [African] atrocities of the past have been aggravated by the intolerant attitude of the visiting European, who, seeking only his own selfish ends, has taken every advantage of the natives' lack of knowledge.[45]

It was a spirit which, if it did not make him indulgent towards the African point of view, certainly predisposed Hollis to allow the African to take greater responsibility in the running of mission work than many Europeans were prepared to sanction. And, to add to it all, Hollis had opened up some small stores and was prepared to trade at close quarters with the African. That this was Hollis's way of providing money for his missionary work—indeed, because of this, he was able, from time to time, to dispense with his salary from the metropolitan Churches of Christ [46]—would not be taken as an excuse, and his petty trading activities would not endear him to many Europeans of the Protectorate who would see in them a backstairs invasion of the commercial field, like the planting enterprises of the industrial missions. And then, to cap it all, Hollis had become a pacifist. This was nothing strange for a member of the Churches of Christ, for there was a strong pacifist strain amongst them before the First World War. Yet it was another tenet which brought Hollis closer in spirit to Booth. In the early days of the War, he was writing home :

> I now look upon war more as a relic of barbarism than anything else. I do not see how I could take up a gun with the intention of shooting my fellow man now I am a disciple of Him who is the Prince of Peace.[47]

In the patriotic atmosphere [48] of Nyasaland at that time, pacifism was the last thing to make a man popular !

Thus, from the beginning, the personality of Hollis and the background of association with Booth were calculated to bring the Churches of Christ Mission in Nyasaland into disfavour. Hollis, furthermore, as he went up to Nyasaland for the first time, had a premonition that there might eventually be trouble with the authorities : he discussed with a friend in Bulawayo, *en route*, the uneasiness that he felt in following in the footsteps of a man (Booth) who had already had so much trouble with them. From the first, the Church of Scotland Mission saw in the Churches of Christ another intrusion into their 'territory', and the establishment of a new series of centres,

Boothian in character, to which ambitious and discontented Africans from their own missions might repair in order to set up their own incipient, independent schools and churches under the wing of a friendly European whose principles and preoccupation with other tasks would not allow him to inquire too deeply into what was taught in them. And as early as 1910, reports had been spreading in the Protectorate that the Churches of Christ Mission was advising Africans not to pay the hut tax. These reports were discovered to be groundless. But the affair provided the Churches of Christ with an occasion for stating their position on relations with the civil power. 'We recognize', they stated, 'that it is our duty to obey the laws of the land in which we carry on our Mission unless'—and the addition is surely significant—'these laws be in flagrant violation of the laws of God. Then we must obey God rather than man. . . .' [49]

To the Administration, with its memories of the disturbing effects of Kamwana's movement, the licence which the Churches of Christ Mission seemed to allow their African teachers and evangelists was not to be encouraged. Furthermore, many Europeans, official and unofficial, were unable to distinguish between the Churches of Christ and the independent African Seventh Day Baptist churches, many of which, following the model of the American S.D.B. churches, were inclined to dub themselves 'Churches of Christ'. It was not difficult, therefore, to see why, even before the Rising, the Churches of Christ Mission in Nyasaland had more than its share of annoyances [50]—difficulties over the acquisition and situation of land, the running of schools—from the Government and the local Europeans.

Yet were these pre-Rising troubles, which the European missionaries of the Churches of Christ in Nyasaland endured, sufficient to account for the harsh handling that they received during the emergency period? Doubtless, if there had been no suspicion of them—particularly of Hollis—before January 1915, they would have received milder treatment.

There is no better guide to their predicament than the diary for 1915 of one of the Churches of Christ missionaries. This was Mary Bannister, who had arrived at Namiwawa, the headquarters of their mission, on 5 June 1912,[51] to help Hollis and his wife in their work. She was a simple but sincere woman who had, in her own way, many of the qualities which make Mary Slessor of Calabar famous in the history of African Christian missions. Like her, she had had a hard life before going out to the mission field.[52] She had lost both parents at the age of twelve, and had been sent to work in a Lancashire mill at an early age. As into so many of the lives of the industrial workers of the nineteenth and early twentieth centuries, membership in a small, back-street, nonconformist church—in Mary Bannister's case, the Church of Christ of Burnley, Lancashire—brought for her a new aim and purpose. By 1902, when she was twenty-four, Mary Bannister had formed the resolution to dedicate her life to missionary work. One might speculate how much of this was the result of compensation for personal, emotional troubles—for there was a time when she lapsed in her membership of the church for the 'pleasures of life', and yet she was never married. Whatever its cause, she threw herself zealously into preparation for missionary work, and between 1908 and 1912 took a maternity course in a Glasgow hospital, and then worked amongst some of the worst of the Glasgow slums at the Shamrock Street Mission. It was a thorough, practical apprenticeship for the African mission field. It enabled her to take charge very quickly of the medical side of Hollis's work ; and through this, and her own lovable personality, and her determination to command the African vernacular—in spite of only an elementary education—she helped to swell the congregations, particularly amongst African women, of the Nyasaland Churches of Christ. Yet she, too, was to be a victim of the Government drive against the Churches of Christ after the 1915 Rising. The careful diaries which she kept throughout her African stay help to estimate the suffering which this caused, for one sensitive soul at least. Therefore, as an illustration of the predicament of the Churches of Christ missionaries during the period of the emergency, her journals will be drawn upon frequently.

On the eve of the Rising there were five adult European Churches of Christ missionaries in Nyasaland : Hollis and his wife, Mary Bannister, and Henry and Etta Philpott, two new missionaries from England, who had arrived at Namiwawa in November 1913.[53] Furthermore, the Hollises had four young children to look after, three boys and a girl, with ages ranging from one to five years. On the Monday, 25 January 1915, all of them, together with other local Europeans, were ordered into laager in Zomba. (It was typical of Hollis's independent turn of mind that although he allowed his wife and family to enter the camp with the other Churches of Christ missionaries, he originally refused to go in himself, until specifically ordered by the authorities, on the grounds that he could look after himself and that the natives were not likely to harm him.) They were the last to arrive in the camp and had to be housed in tents which, in the wet season, with their low flies, made it difficult to keep their bedding dry. Then began the sad process of watching the prisoners who were brought into the camp, and the even sadder fact of realizing that some of them were from their own mission, or had had connections with it at one time. It was a miserable situation, especially when the Hollis's children became sick. After a week of this, by Sunday, 31 January, the remainder of the Europeans who wished to leave the camp permanently were allowed to do so. But the Churches of Christ missionaries and their children, though they were moved to better quarters, were kept inside. It was a sign of the suspicions that attached to them. 'We are prisoners', wrote Mary Bannister, 'in the plain sense of the word . . . to be held up before all people in suspicion is to me a fearfully unjust thing.'[54] For another week, neither they nor their African 'boys' were allowed to leave the camp. No explanation of this discrimination was given, and although they were later to be allowed out into the town, the Churches of Christ missionaries were kept in the Zomba camp for seven weeks.[55]

On Monday night, 1 February, Mary Bannister went down with fever : 'last night was a wild cold night. I wrote to the Governor asking for permission to go out but have not yet received any reply . . . it is wretched in here.' Letters and cables to the Governor by the imprisoned missionaries received no answer until Friday, 5 February, by which time Chilembwe had been shot—but, even so, the reply was non-committal. All that they could learn was that it was 'desirable' that they should stop teaching for a while.[56] 'Bro. P.', wrote Mary Bannister, 'is in bed to-day, where we shall all be if we have to stay here. A fearful wet day. It is miserable, indeed, when it rains here : it is so cold. . . .'[57] They were allowed to walk out in the neighbourhood by Monday, 8 February : but that was a small compensation for their other tribulations. 'They seem to be bringing in fresh prisoners every day . . .' Mary Bannister noted on the morrow. Then, on the following Thursday, the Philpotts were taken out to watch a search of the Churches of Christ's missionaries' houses. And on the Friday, 12 February, Mary Bannister 'went out to find the scaffold . . . the first I have ever seen'. 'They have been busy all day', she wrote on the Saturday, 'building a new scaffold. It is awful. This has been the most miserable day I have had since I came here. . . .' But worse was to come when the hangings started. '. . . Six more were hung to-day', she noted on the Monday. 'I could not get it out of my mind. . . .' The effect of it all was to bring on acute nervous pains in Mary Bannister : 'Had a bad head all day', she wrote at the end of the week, 'and was obliged to stay in. They are bringing in fresh prisoners every day : quite a number have been shot and hung. It fills one with pity for the poor things. I don't know when I had such a headache lasting so long. . . .' By Tuesday, 23 February, when the rest of the Europeans in the area were taking their ease at home, she noted that the depression had had similar effect on her fellow missionaries : 'Mr. Philpott is in bed. He seems to be all upset.' And then, the next day, when she herself was feeling a little better and had been out for an hour, more prisoners came in to remind her of the wretchedness of her state and the suspicion in which they were all held : '. . . they brought in another prisoner in a machila ; they have got the man whom it is supposed cut off Mr. Livingstone's head. . . .' (Unfortunately for the historian, she gave no further account of him or his name, and one is still left in ignorance of the African to whom the chance fell, either by plan or passion, of making an end of the manager of the Magomero Estates.)

Her diary leaves no doubt, however, that by this time the greater part of Chilembwe's following were being rounded up by the local forces. She noted on Thursday, 25 February : 'A lot of prisoners came in to-night from Mlanje, Frederick among them and poor old women who could hardly walk'. (The 'Frederick' she mentions was Frederick Singani Khonda, a leading teacher of the Churches of Christ Mission, whose implication in the Rising will be considered when a final examination is made of Hollis's role in it.) The large numbers of African prisoners in the Boma at Zomba, all of them living close to the Churches of Christ missionaries, brought further trials : '. . . it gets more and more wearying and the native habits are too disgusting for words. . . .' [58] And so this wretched routine continued for them all. By the end of the fifth week of their captivity, Mary Bannister put together some hasty words in her journal which illustrate not merely the spiritual and physical states of the Churches of Christ missionaries but also the continued drive that the Administration was making to bring in and punish as many rebels as possible in order that no lesson might be left unlearnt by the local African population :

Six more of our teachers have been taken prisoner. I am so sorry for them all. A note this morning tells us that the Christians [of the

Churches of Christ missions] have been told they were not to meet together. Things seem to get blacker but our hope is in God from whence our help is sure to come. Mrs. P. has been in bed all day. But flogging of prisoners goes on just the same. I do think they might have some consideration for us and punish them outside the place. A European ought not to be allowed to stay in a place like this. Sunday of all days is the worst : our hearts and minds travel homewards often. . . .

The sixth week of their captivity brought a similar series of plaints in her journal and further evidence of the success of the Administration in searching the country for Africans who had supported or were suspected of supporting the Rising. On Monday, 8 March, she noted that 'more prisoners from Angoniland are expected', and, on the Tuesday, reports their arrival, 'and amongst them the faithful Simon'—a reference, it seems, to Simon Kadewere who was sentenced to death on the following Friday. Meanwhile, in addition to Mrs. Hollis and her children becoming 'queer',[59] Mary Bannister noted on Thursday, 11 March, that 'Mrs. P. is still far from well, and no wonder. They lashed more prisoners to-day. It is too awful for anything. . . .'

The seventh week of their imprisonment provided Mary Bannister with further melancholy material for entry into her diary. Monday, 15 March, she noted that 'George [60] [Masangano] was sentenced to 7 years ; Ronald and Jackson, 2 years. . . .' On the Thursday, 'two more were flogged . . . and given ten year's imprisonment. It teemed with rain during the night. Oh, to be home. . . .' And then, on the Friday, 19 March, by which time it was obvious to the authorities that the Rising was well under control, and when, presumably, some official recognition was at last being taken of the repeated letters and cables which the Churches of Christ missionaries had sent to the Administration, Mary Bannister could report the final blow of many that had fallen upon them in seven weeks : 'After dinner we did get a shock. We three [she and the Philpotts] may go home to-morrow on conditions but Mr. Hollis must leave the country. . . .' The conditions were drastic : they were to give an undertaking in writing that they would do no teaching nor hold any meetings, and that they would remain in the district until permission to the contrary was given. If they did not abide by these conditions, the three of them would be liable for deportation.[61]

It was a heavy blow to lose Hollis, on whom the burden of building up the mission had fallen. But it was an even heavier blow to learn, when they returned to Namiwawa from captivity at Zomba, that something very much like an all-out drive to destroy their mission work had taken place during the period of their imprisonment.[62] The majority of their African teachers had suffered because of their association with the Churches of Christ missionaries. Those who had been living at some distance from their homes had been sent back to their villages. By the middle of February all of their village schools had been closed by Government decree, and at least one—at Palombe—had been burned down. 'The respective chiefs were given a free hand', reported Henry Philpott at the end of the year to his British base.[63] One can imagine with what relish some of the chiefs would have undertaken this task of closing down these independent African schools. With their ambitious and independently minded African teachers, they seemed in many instances to be a threat to the traditional power of the chiefs, who, by this time, were clinging to those powers which remained to them after the British Administration had clipped their wings; some of the chiefs, indeed, were the creation of the alien Administration, and would have no desire to feel the effective substance of their power undermined by the emergence of an insubordinate class of African teachers and scholars in their villages. And so the Government drive went on against the remnants of Churches of Christ influence in the Protectorate. In Mlanje their school was destroyed, and the African teacher's house razed to the ground because he had held a meeting after being told that assembly was forbidden. The whole number of the African Churches of Christ members in Mlanje (fifteen), after this, were arrested and sent to Zomba. Examination revealed that there was apparently nothing against them, and they were released—with the instruction that they must hold no more meetings but, if they wished to worship, must attend the local Church of Scotland Mission.[64] Similar stories could be reported from other areas in which the Churches of Christ had churches or schools, and it became obvious by the end of the year that the work of the mission in the Protectorate had been brought, abruptly and by order, to a standstill.

While the distressing news of all these impediments to their work was coming in, Hollis was preparing to leave the Protectorate. He had been told that he had to quit Nyasaland by 2 April,[65] and yet his movements were restricted, because he was ordered to sleep at the

Zomba Boma until Tuesday, 30 March.[66] For all this, as Mary Bannister noted, there was 'no reason given. How they expect him [Hollis] to get away by next Friday I cannot tell. Their treatment is most unreasonable. . . .' [67] Hollis had the task of winding up his store, of handing over to the remaining Europeans of the Churches of Christ Mission at Namiwawa what was left of the mission's assets, and of making ready for himself and his family to leave the Protectorate. And, all this while, his youngest child, the baby boy of the family, was, according to Mary Bannister's report, 'very ill'.[68] Nevertheless, the authorities were determined to keep Hollis under the closest observation. Because he reported in late to the Boma on the night of Tuesday, 30 March, he was not allowed to go down to see his fellow missionaries at Namiwawa until 2 April, when he was to leave the Protectorate. 'Really it is too bad', wrote Miss Bannister in her journal.[69] The fact that the boat to the coast did not leave until 12 April, however, gave him and his family a week's grace, during which they managed to put themselves and their effects in some sort of an order, and to leave Zomba by 10 April. For Mary Bannister, spinster, their departure had a note of personal sadness because she was deeply attached to the children. On Thursday, 8 April, she wrote in her diary : 'Mr. Hollis came to-day to say that they were all to be in Zomba before dusk. What a struggle saying good-bye to the bairns—I dare not think they are not coming back '. But Hollis was not coming back—the Government was making very sure of that.

Why had he been pursued with such relentlessness since the outbreak of the Rising ? Was he in any way directly implicated in the conspiracy of John Chilembwe and his men ? Until the official papers which still remain in existence [70] are available for the public inspection—if they ever are—the question remains an open one. Yet on the basis of the evidence which the authors of this book have been able to gather, it appears that Hollis was a victim of 'guilt by association' like Walter Cockerill. Hollis's case seems to have caught the public eye much more than Cockerill's at the time. Four days after the outbreak of the Rising, Cockerill himself could reflect this in a letter [71] home in which he stated casually that 'the Government has some evidence against a Mr. Hollis'—a fact which must have been drawn from local hearsay, for there was no mention in the Nyasaland press at this time or later, owing to the censorship, of Hollis's affairs. Yet such reports have little more than the vague substance of rumour, and, in Hollis's instance, could have drawn much of their animus from European feeling which had been growing against him and his influence amongst Africans since he first arrived in the Protectorate with the mantle of Booth hanging over him.

The main basis of the Government's case against Hollis appears to have been, first of all, that he had had previous knowledge of the Chilembwe conspiracy [72] but that he had failed to report it to the authorities ; and secondly, that a number of Africans who had been found guilty of complicity in the Rising were members of his mission, or had at one time been members, and that Hollis had apparently been on very good terms with them.[73] They are the same main charges which had led to Cockerill's deportation. But Cockerill's treatment, however brusque and irksome it may have been, did not have the harshness of that which Hollis received—for Cockerill was an American citizen and America was still neutral. Hollis, as a British subject, however, could and did take the full force of official disapproval.

Had he been guilty of concrete complicity in Chilembwe's conspiracy, it is likely—indeed, it would have been incumbent upon the Government—that he would have been charged with high treason and have met the supreme penalty. That this did not happen is evidence that his 'guilt' was circumstantial only. Two facts, moreover, support this point : Hollis's pacifism, which would, surely, have prevented him from becoming involved in an armed insurrection ; and the fact that in 1914 he had announced to the British Foreign Missions' Committee of the Churches of Christ that, 'as the long residence in Africa [had] been telling on his health',[74] he wanted to go on a furlough to his friends in Australia in March 1915. Unless this is to be construed as the careful deceit of a cunning conspirator —which seems highly unlikely—it does not suggest that Hollis would have got himself entangled in a plot that was likely to spoil his plans for a much-needed and overdue vacation.

To the first charge that he had failed to report the rumour which he had heard of an impending Rising, it might be answered, as it was when dealing with the similar charge against Cockerill, that it had seemed so absurd to Hollis that he had not bothered to report it ; and that, anyway, the Government itself had treated such rumours with a good deal of apparent nonchalance when they were first made known to it. To the second charge—that he had had friendly relations with some of the conspirators—more detailed examination must be

given : not merely because it throws light on the degree of relationship between them and Hollis but also because it provides evidence
of the kind of Africans from the Nyasaland Churches of Christ
missions who supported Chilembwe, and indeed, because it gives
further details of the social composition of Chilembwe's movement.

There is no evidence to suggest that Hollis knew or bothered
about Chilembwe. The Churches of Christ had schools [75] in the
Chiradzulu district ; but their literature had no mention of him or
his work. Hollis, however, was clearly, but, it seems, innocently
interested in the extension of their mission work into the Tonga-
Ngoni regions around Bandawe on the Lake, the area from which
the Kamwana movement had come. In 1911 he had reported home
that 'Brethren George and Ronald' had recently returned from there,
where there were 'several thousands of Atonga Christians entirely
without a shepherd'.[76] And the following year he had noted more
carefully the character of this mass of independent African congregations which the Kamwana and the Watch Tower [77] movements
had deposited in this area : 'churches more or less resembling those
of primitive times'.[78] Hollis was, therefore, keen to begin work in
the very region that had brought Cockerill to grief in 1914 at the
time of his first deportation to the Shire Highlands. The Government would not be likely to encourage Hollis's ambitions in this
area which they hoped would not degenerate into a mass of African
sectarian strife but would settle down as quickly as it could. (It is
interesting to note that both 'Brethren George and Ronald' whom
Hollis had sent into this part in 1911 were found guilty of complicity
in the Rising.[79] Can this in any way be taken to suggest that
Chilembwe had, if not agents amongst the tribes on the western
side of the Lake which had felt the influence of Booth, at least
active organs of intelligence ?)

Hollis, furthermore, had some interests in the Ncheu area where
Filipo Chinyama had organized the subsidiary rising. The Churches
of Christ had a school in 'Central Angoniland',[80] and Hollis had
hopes for establishing a mission there, just before the War broke
out.[81] Above all, there is evidence that he knew Chinyama, though
his interest in him appears to have been nothing more than an
interest in a promising teacher ; Chinyama had helped the Churches of
Christ Mission at Chikunda at one time, it seems.[82] It is not unlikely
that Hollis kept up his contacts with him, and that the Authorities
would have noted this fact, and would not have received it favourably.

Chinyama was one of a number of Africans whom Hollis had come to know, presumably, because of his original connections with Booth. But, in their previous relations with Booth, either in Nyasaland or in South Africa, such Africans, having been stimulated by him to reach out for equality with the European, would often then proceed to demonstrate their egalitarianism by breaking away from Booth on slight pretexts in order to set up their own tiny churches and to assert their own authority by independent baptizing. In Hollis's case a similar process was at work. Though he and his fellow European missionaries tried to keep control over indiscriminate baptizing by ensuring that no-one was accepted by the mission who had not been properly taught, many of the independently minded Africans who, after a varied career of religious attachments along the lines of Joseph Booth, had come to the Churches of Christ, began to resent even this light measure of control. On the eve of the Rising, therefore, many of them had actually broken away from the Churches of Christ Mission and had swollen the ranks of the keepers of small African independent churches [83] which were entirely free of European control. In this way, many of the Africans who had supported Chilembwe and who, it was claimed by the authorities, were members of the Churches of Christ Mission at Namiwawa or one of its outlying stations, were, in fact, by January 1915, not attached to any European-led mission at all. Furthermore, some of the Churches of Christ Africans who could be fairly accused of complicity in the Rising and who still retained a nominal connection with the Churches of Christ Mission, had been on the point of breaking away from the control of the European missionaries at Namiwawa. It is apparent that Hollis was not on good terms with a number of them [84]—another fact which clears him of direct participation in the planning of the Rising. His role, and the role of the Churches of Christ, with their 'primitive Christianity' concepts, had been, in many ways in spite of themselves, to provide a transitional mechanism whereby certain Africans who were breaking away from one mission, or who were working in their minds towards the logical outcome of Booth's teaching of African independence, could become leaders in their own churches.[85] It was even more natural that, when they reached this stage, they should gravitate to Chilembwe's general leadership, for he provided an avenue not merely for the airing of grievances against the European occupation, but also a focal point for the whole African independent church movement in the Shire Highlands.

Even Frederick Singani Khonda,[86] the cherished pupil of Mary Bannister, was restive under the light discipline of the Churches of Christ Mission. It was Frederick S. Khonda who had told Hollis five weeks before the Rising that an insurrection was planned.[87] Though Khonda himself appears to have taken some trouble to dissuade the conspirators, nevertheless he was caught up in the general punishment and received a seven-year sentence.[88] Like so many others of the Churches of Christ Africans, he had been down at Johannesburg, and had had enough English to serve as a police interpreter. Here, again, like numerous other Africans in this mission, he had, it seems, come into contact with Russell's 'Millennial Dawn' volumes, and on the eve of the Rising had been observed studying them.[89] He was aware, too, of the Seventh Day Baptist teaching, and was, in all, typical of an African proto-intellectual of the period.

But Frederick S. Khonda, though unsettled, had not been, it appears, within the inner circle of the conspirators. One of the Churches of Christ Africans who does seem to have been within this circle was a certain 'Barton'. Mary Bannister had noted dispiritedly in her diary for 1 February that 'Barton was shot to-day'; and shooting was the punishment which the authorities apparently reserved for those whom they could prove quite clearly as close Chilembwe-men. Barton had been one of the heady characters who had either broken away from the Namiwawa missionaries or was in process of being disciplined by them on the eve of 1915. His full names appear to have been Barton Makwangwala, and he may have been a brother of the Zomba headman, Kimu,[90] who has already been noted as being fully aware of Chilembwe's conspiracy. Barton was originally a member of the Church of Scotland Blantyre Mission, like so many rebellious Africans of this time, whose independent spirits had found in the Boothian African separatist churches *milieu* an appropriate field for action.

The other Churches of Christ Africans who were charged with knowledge of the Rising do not seem to have suffered the supreme penalty. From any survey of punished Africans, however, it is difficult to say which of them were really practising members of the Namiwawa mission or its subsidiary churches; not merely because many had, in an independent frame of mind, drifted away from Hollis's leadership but because the very term 'Church of Christ', in the scatter of African independent churches that was left by the ramifications of Booth's activities, was capable of several constructions, and the Administration was not skilled in distinguishing between the many fine shades of African Christian sectarianism.

And so the Churches of Christ Mission—though it was allowed to resume its work in Nyasaland after the war, in 1928—went down in the general collapse of the African independent church structure after the Chilembwe Rising. Its Foreign Missions Committee at home complained in a long correspondence with the Colonial Office : but the Colonial Office, with the reports of the Governor of Nyasaland before it, was unmoved.[91] By 1917 the European missionaries who had been left after Hollis's deportation quitted the Protectorate. There now remained only those little communities of Africans who still retained the principles of the Churches of Christ, and who, through their subsequent correspondence with Miss Bannister,[92] made a reopening of the mission possible after the War. (Nevertheless, the fissiparous processes inside this body which have already been noted, continued and, after the War, an 'African Church of Christ' [93] was set up as well as a mission under European leadership.)

With the Europeans of the Churches of Christ and the Seventh Day Baptists out of the Protectorate, and with the activities of the Seventh-day Adventists under a watchful and suspicious official eye, much of the pattern of African church separatism which Booth had moulded in Nyasaland was broken. Watch Tower had already been made illegal before the Rising, when Kamwana had been deported. Booth's original three missions (the Zambesi Industrial Mission, the Nyassa Industrial Mission, and the Baptist Industrial Mission of Scotland) had by now become thoroughly respectable. There remained, then, but one thing for the Government to do in its attempt to put an end for ever to Boothism and revolt in the Protectorate at this time : to reach out and strike down Booth himself. When he was out of Africa, the Government would undoubtedly feel that it had finished—at least for a while—with the last of its radical critics.

4. JOSEPH BOOTH AND THE RISING

There is some doubt as to the exact way in which the Nyasaland Government of 1915 went about settling its final score with Booth.[94] But that he was very much in its mind at this time is indisputable. This is clear from what has been said at the beginning of this chapter of the way in which Booth's name was on everyone's lips when the reasons for Chilembwe's plans were being bandied backwards and forwards across the Protectorate. It becomes even clearer from the Report of the Nyasaland Native Rising Commission :

> If a more remote source [of the Rising] is sought [said the Commissioners to the Governor] it will be found in the machinations of Joseph Booth. . . . Your Commissioners have not seen evidence to suggest that Joseph Booth was actually cognisant of the intended rising, but we have come to the conclusion that Booth's teaching sowed the seeds of racial animosity in the Protectorate, and that his correspondence with Chilembwe influenced the latter and others in rebelling against the Government.[95]

Yet by the time that the Commission's charges against Booth appeared in print in 1916, official action had already been taken against him.

At some time between June and July 1915 he had received fourteen days' notice to leave Basutoland,[96] to which, as was noticed in Chapter V, he had gone to conduct independent educational and missionary work after Peter Nyambo had set sail for England with the petition, the 'Rhodesia-Nyasaland Appeal', that Booth had helped him to organize. Booth and his wife were brought down hastily from Basutoland by the South African police ; were given a curt opportunity to say good-bye to their daughter in Cape Town ; and were then bundled on to the ship for the United Kingdom. By the third week in October 1915, the two of them arrived, penniless and dispirited, in England.[97] Booth himself believed that this deportation had been 'on account of his anti-war doctrine' : [98] that is to say, he related it to South African circumstances. Yet it is more than likely that the Nyasaland Government played a part in it. When the chairman of the British Central Africa Company, Sir John Rees, had raised his question about Booth in the House of Commons on 29 April, the Colonial Secretary had replied that Booth's case was 'under notice'. It is, indeed, more than probable that both Governments, the South African and the Nyasaland, had a hand at this time in the deportation of Booth. It is likely that the Nyasaland Government's conception of Booth as a source of the 1915 Rising spurred on the Colonial Office to have him removed from the British territory of Basutoland, and that the South African Government, which had its own special troubles with native problems in that year,[99] and which was well aware of Booth as a 'dangerous' egalitarian, was only too willing to co-operate. His pacifism was a last straw, perhaps.

Yet it is this very pacifism, which ran throughout Booth's life from the time when he was questioning his parents' conceptions of Christianity to the last days of his criticisms of European governments in Africa for the use of force against Africans, which surely clears him of anything but the remotest connection with the Rising of 1915. His correspondence with his daughter in America during his Basutoland period of 1914–15 shows that he was still as clearly opposed to war as he was when he first went to Africa. He recognized the 'sanguinary tyranny the German slaughter system would impose',[100] but his principles were still absolutely anti-war. And at this time he was sixty-four. 'We are old and poor and have not the vim and go of past years', he had written to his daughter in the United States.[101] Though to his last days he continued working to the best of his ability in the ways which seemed to him appropriate for the advancement of causes of justice and liberty for Africans, age brought declining fire, and he was hardly the man to encourage revolt, even if his confirmed pacifism could have found an exception for the case of Chilembwe and Nyasaland.

It is doubtful, indeed, if Booth was aware of Chilembwe's Rising in 1915 and at the time of his expulsion from South Africa. The Commissioners of Inquiry had been forced to admit this. It is, too, a matter for some doubt whether Booth heard of the Rising for some years after the tragedy of Magomero. Evidence on this point is provided by a number of autobiographical documents which Booth seems to have written shortly after the War.[102] In these, which were written undoubtedly under the stimulus of the harshness of his last deportation and in war-time circumstances of an enforced lessening of activity, he reviews his whole career as an African missionary. One of them deals exclusively with Chilembwe [103] and seems to be Booth's last recorded assessment of his first African convert. Its final paragraphs deserve quotation as they put more clearly than anything else could do, the force and the pathos of Booth's relationship with Chilembwe, at the same time as they establish his apparent late knowledge of the Rising.

About 1919, then, he wrote : '. . . in 1914 or 1915 Sir Harry Johnston informs me that Chilembwe was the leader of a "crackbrained" rebellion, during which he was shot in action'. (Booth's very vagueness of the date which Johnston mentioned is further evidence of his lack of interest in the Rising *qua* rising. His interest in Chilembwe after 1900 was, on the whole, personal rather than practical; for, after his break with him in America, Booth had realized that any attempt of his to influence British Central Africa would have to be through other Africans.) He goes on :

> The writer gathers from the said letter of Sir H. H. Johnston that the writer is supposed by the ingenious officials of Nyasaland after some sort of one-sided enquiry, and without any opportunity for the writer to rebut false statements, to be more or less responsible for this rebellion during 1914 or 1915, although it occurred 12 years after we [Chilembwe and Booth] parted in Philadelphia [Booth's memory is some five years out here] and about 10 years after Nyasaland was closed to me. Such [comments Booth] are the pitifully unjust ways of hidden enemies of fair play, against which I protest and ask for a further open enquiry.

And then, the old man's indignant reactions to yet another 'insolence of office' stop, and his mind goes right back to the first days when he went out to Africa and the isolation and dangers of that period. Booth here is no longer the injured innocent but an old man remembering the bygone days and a faithful friend of his prime :

> Poor kindhearted Chilembwe, who wept with and for the writer's fever-stricken and apparently dying child; nursed and fed the father with a woman's kindness during 10 months of utter prostration; wept, laboured with and soothed the dying hours of my sweet son John Edward [18 years old] at the close of a 2 month's toilsome journey to the ocean post, for food and goods, in flood time of rainy season, 1894, the Writer being away. . . .

And finally, a last compassionate comment which seems to sum up, better than any other source, the relationship of the essential Booth to the Rising :

> Yes, dear Chilembwe, gladly would I have died by my countrymen shot, to have kept thee from the false path of slaying : far better die a slave than die stained with others' life blood.

The Commissioners of Inquiry may have seen in Booth a 'remote source' of the Rising : yet, after comments like this, it seems so remote as to be well beyond the immediate bounds of effective analysis. His guilt—if, indeed, it were guilt—was, even more than Cockerill's or Hollis's, 'guilt by association', and a very remote association, to be sure, by 1915. Certainly, Joseph Booth's influence on British Central Africa goes deeply into the first two decades of the Protectorate : but it is not the influence of militant action. Booth may have supplied the spark that set the pile on fire. But other hands than his had to bring it to the pile. And who, anyway, in the first place heaped up the discontents which comprise the pile : the isolated Englishman who criticized the results of the Scramble for Africa, or the intricate processes of that mad rush itself ? Surely only a confirmed believer in the individualist interpretation of history will answer in the first category ?

And so, with these final sad comments on Chilembwe and his story, Joseph Booth passes from the effective scene of British Central African history. He was to live for about another twelve years and was eventually to be allowed back into the Union of South Africa. He was to write and speak and struggle forcibly still for the African causes which he believed to be just : but, all the time, with a decreasing vigour. His second wife, the valiant little nurse from St. Thomas's Hospital in London who had shared almost from the first his strange career in Africa, America, and Europe, died, and late in life he married an impecunious South African school teacher. In failing health, the two of them went back to England, and on Wednesday, 4 November 1932, Joseph Booth, an octogenarian, died at Weston-super-Mare. But memories of his work, often misguided but always passionately sincere, and motivated consistently by a deep and genuine desire to improve the lot of the African, have lived on in the minds of countless Africans from Lake Nyasa to Cape Town. A Booth legend [104] has come into being in much the same way as a Chilembwe legend has been created. Each, indeed, is a vital element in the other's story. So that if, with the removal of Joseph Booth from Africa by the middle of 1915, the British authorities had got rid of one who seemed to them a major source of European involvement in the intricate chain of circumstances which had caused John Chilembwe and his men to attack Magomero and Mandala, the spirit of Booth had not been suppressed in Nyasaland—or, indeed, in those other parts of Africa which he visited, and out of which the clash of European and African cultures produces continually even stranger patterns of African reaction than anything that Booth had ever conceived.

VIII

THE AFTERMATH OF THE RISING

> 'Africa for the Africans' has been our policy from the first, and we believe that God has given this country into our hands that we may train its people to develop its marvellous resources for themselves.
>
> Scottish Blantyre missionaries in
> *Life and Work in British Central
> Africa*, January 1895

THE AFTERMATH OF THE RISING

1. THE SCOTTISH MISSIONS' REFUTATION

THE attack on the smaller, less orthodox missions for their role in the Chilembwe Rising was only the prelude to a more general onslaught by Nyasaland settler groups on all missionaries in the Protectorate. The *Nyasaland Times* in its issue for 4 February 1915 expressed their sentiments well when it wrote that 'In a sense all Missions are responsible as it [the Rising] is due to the effect of ill-digested teaching on the native mind . . . it is very plain that to educate natives very highly and then not find suitable employment for them is a mistake'. Its contemporary, the *Beira Post*, which spoke for a wide range of Europeans in South-East Africa, was even more outspoken in its denunciation of the Christian missions. 'It will be interesting', it wrote shortly after the Rising, 'to see . . . the number of discovered scoundrels for which each mission is responsible.' [1] 'Missionary enterprise', the paper noted later, 'in this continent has in most cases meant well [but] general results have not proved that it has done well. Endless trouble has been incurred by the doctrine of equality of race and missionaries as a rule have had to be followed by armed battalions.' [2] The accusation was raised to a more serious level when the Governor himself, in his opening speech to the Nyasaland Legislative Council on 9 March 1915, showed his own suspicions of mission teaching. He said of the Rising that 'its effect has been to shatter some of our beliefs in the efficacy of past attempts at christianizing and civilizing the native population'. [3] And the point was even carried as far as Parliament by the chairman of the British Central Africa Company, Sir John Rees, who informed the Commons on 21 July 1915 that there was 'much reason for believing that the real trouble arose from the missionary schools'. [4]

The Scottish missionaries could not be silent in the face of such charges. They were well aware that they themselves, as much as the smaller, less orthodox missions, were under fire, for it was well known that almost all of the ringleaders in the Rising had begun their early education in the Scottish missions, although later they may have deserted to one of the more sectarian bodies. And that John Gray Kufa had been until the very last a trusted elder in the Blantyre Church was for many of the critics of the missions something of a trump card. It was apparent, then, to the Scottish missionary leaders that they were in a period of crisis similar to, but in many ways more serious than those early days of the establishment of the Protectorate when rifts had appeared between missions and settlers and Administration. If they were not to lose much of the freedom and prestige which they had gained even before the beginning of British rule in Central Africa, the Scottish missions would have to fight back against their accusers, and fight back hard. Luckily for them, their leaders, Robert Laws of Livingstonia and Alexander Hetherwick of Blantyre, were not the sort of men to flinch before a fight. Furthermore, in addition to their own strength of character they had behind them the sure knowledge of support from home. To many people in Scotland the pioneering role of the Scottish missions in Central Africa was a matter of national pride, and they would not stand ineffectively aside before an attack on Blantyre and Livingstonia, both of which had strong associations with the national hero, David Livingstone. And to back them in their protests— should these become necessary—were the powerful Foreign Missions Committees of the Church of Scotland and of the United Free Church. These bodies, through the ramified network of Scots in business and politics, when the occasion demanded it, could act as strong 'pressure groups' at Westminster. From the start of the attack on their missions, Laws and Hetherwick kept their home Committees carefully informed of the trouble that was brewing in the Protectorate : thereby, their rear was guarded while they repelled the attacks of their critics in the African field.

It was Laws who had to bear the weight of the first battle. In 1915 he was one of the three nominated unofficial members of the Nyasaland Legislative Council. After the first day of the Council— at which the Governor had shown suspicion of the missionaries—it fell to Laws on 10 March to ask whether the Government intended to appoint a Commission of Inquiry into the Rising, such as the Nyasaland Chamber of Commerce at their meeting of 23 February 1915 had outlined when they drew up a petition to the Governor. Hetherwick himself had moved for this Commission in the Chamber of Commerce.[5] It is noteworthy that the demand for a Commission of Inquiry was first put forward formally by the leading representatives of the Scottish missionaries, for it seemed to indicate that they had nothing to fear from an inquiry, and was probably arranged between the two of them as a preliminary tactical manœuvre to spike the guns of the anti-missionary faction. But this faction was not easily silenced. On the following day, 11 March, Alexander Livingstone Bruce, owner of the Magomero Estates, who was also a member of the Legislative Council, brought forward a motion that struck directly at the missions.

On hearing of the outbreak at Magomero, Livingstone Bruce had hurried down from service with the forces at the northern end of Lake Nyasa in order to safeguard the interests of his Estates. The motion which he introduced into the Legislative Council had something of a defensive character, for, by this time, word had spread abroad that conditions on the A. L. Bruce Estates had had much to do with the Rising. His motion was 'That pending the finding of the Commission about to be appointed by the Government all schools in charge of native teachers in the Protectorate be closed at once'.[6] To his mind, 'the fact that the rebellion had been entirely engineered by . . . educated natives was . . . the most pernicious feature of the whole affair . . . it was a rebellion of mission trained natives'. His seconder was another planter, the Hon. James Fiddes, and when he had finished his supporting remarks, the Governor interjected that 'From the remarks of the introducer and seconder of the motion he took it that they made no distinction between missions in any way'. To this A. L. Bruce replied with a simple and affirmative 'No'. It was thus clear that his motion and his speech were a general attack on mission education. Though in subsequent discussion he seemed to realize that he had gone too far, and stated that it was not his intention to suggest that Laws or 'any [other] responsible missionary should close down the entire work of their missions',[7] nevertheless that had been the tenor of his remarks, and Laws replied accordingly.

His answer, on the whole, was given with care and dignity, although it was impossible that a little acrimony should not creep into it, for Laws had been in Nyasaland for almost forty years and his leadership in the field of higher and technical education for Africans had been a primary factor in creating the reputation of the Nyasaland skilled worker throughout South and Eastern Africa. There was thus an understandable touch of sarcasm in his statement that, while he admitted that 'there was room for improvement' in education in Nyasaland, 'he would be glad to visit any school on the Hon. A. L. Bruce's estate to learn from it any better method or form of education than he [Laws] had followed during these years'.[8] Laws knew very well when he said this that the Bruce Estates were notorious for their opposition to native schools or churches on their land. He rammed the point home when, after he had pointed out that he was always being asked by Nyasaland employers for Africans with higher education, he noted that 'from the Hon. A. L. Bruce's own estate came such an application a number of years ago'. However, added Laws, 'One lad was sent, but after serving his term and returning home, he refused to go back for work on the Hon. A. L. Bruce's estate'. Yet, with these exceptions, Laws's argument in defence of missionary education was conducted on a dignified, impersonal plane. He indicated that the missions bore the greater part of the burden of education in the Protectorate : indeed, the Government grant for education was under twopence for each scholar, as compared with fifteen shillings in the Cape Colony. Laws took the South African analogy further when he pointed out that the South African Government had recognized that 'the opposition from many quarters to the giving of higher education to the native had proved a powerful factor in producing' Ethiopianism, and that 'the Governments of the different States had been compelled in self-defence to found an inter-state college for the higher education of natives as the best preventative of their going to America in search of it, and too often coming back with notions which were not suited for South Africa'.[9] Perhaps Laws's most telling point, however, was that the missions attempted to inculcate a spirit of loyalty to the Government, and that this had been proved by the manner in which Africans had assisted in the suppression of the Rising. (Had the debate taken place later in the year, Laws would have been on even stronger ground here, for he could have pointed out that in September 1915,[10] when Chimtunga of Mombera's Ngoni to the north tried to resist Government levies on his people for food and carriers for the Karonga forces, the Livingstonia missionaries had persuaded him to change his mind, and had probably prevented disturbances in the area.) Finally, Laws brought his case to a close with the remark that 'the arguments brought forward by him proved the necessity for a greater and better education than for any attempt to set back the hands of the clock as this motion indicated a desire to do'.

Although A. L. Bruce ultimately withdrew his motion, the debate had obviously brought into the open, even more than before, suspicion and distrust of missionaries in the Protectorate ; and the question of the education of Africans had been so nicely poised that, as the missionaries could see, a slightly more concerted push by their critics might well set back the condition of teaching and preaching in Nyasaland by many years. When Hetherwick, therefore, reported the debate in his letters to the Church of Scotland Foreign Mission Committee at home, some clear reaction might be expected from it. One of the Committee's first responses was a sentiment of complete surprise at Livingstone Bruce's action. 'It was an extraordinary thing', its secretary commented, 'that a grandson of David Livingstone should actually propose the closing of Mission Schools. I believe it would create a sensation in this country if it were known. . . .'[11] When this surprise had been expressed, however, the Committee's feeling was one of confidence, for it seemed clear to it that if the critics of missions were opposed to African education 'they would have to face up to maintaining that the education of mankind generally was a mistake'.[12] The point was well taken, for if the Scottish churches had been forced to take the issue to the country, they realized that they could count on not merely the supporters of Scotland's national pride but also upon that wide segment of the British people which was hoping for an extension of popular education after the War, and which might see in the arguments of some of the ruling, richer groups in Nyasaland against schools for Africans the thin end of the wedge against the spread of popular education anywhere.[13] But, above all, the Scottish Churches knew that they could rely on powerful influences at Westminster to support their case : in particular, on Arthur Steel Maitland, Under-Secretary of State for the Colonies, a Scot who had presided at a big missionary meeting during the 1915 General Assembly of the Church of Scotland, and who could be relied on as 'a good friend at court'.[14] In the long run, this feeling of confidence was to be justified.

In the short run, however, there seemed less reason for confidence. Though Laws's spirited discussion had forced Livingstone Bruce to withdraw his anti-missionary motion at the Legislative Council in March, the criticism of missions and their influence on the Chilembwe *milieu* continued. That these had sunk into the official consciousness was apparent from the terms of reference of the Commission of Inquiry, whose composition was announced on

28 April 1915.[15]   These terms included some of the points which Laws and Hetherwick had asked for when they began their agitation for a Commission of Inquiry into the Rising.   But there was a new element in them, and one which was to disturb the missionaries and to make them realize that the battle was not yet over.   This was the fourth term of reference :   'The effects of mission teaching— religious, education or industrial—on the native mind and character'.   And, from the point of view of the non-Catholic missionary groups in the Protectorate, the final blow was that there was but one missionary representative on the Commission :   the Venerable Arthur George Bernard Glossop, Archdeacon of Likoma and a member of the Universities Mission to Central Africa, a priest of High Anglican views who would not be likely to be over-sympathetic to the more Protestant view-point.   His attitude on mission and African education in general has already been illustrated in the previous chapter, when the expulsion of Walter Cockerill was dealt with,[16] and it will be realized from this that the fears of the Scottish missionaries were not altogether unjustified.

Not only were many of the witnesses from the smaller missions who gave evidence before the Commission when it began its inquiry in May 1915 handled rather brusquely,[17] but the Scottish missions themselves, in their opinion, were not treated much better.[18]   So far as Hetherwick was concerned, the only member of the Commission to show any impartiality and fairness at all was Robert Lyall Grant, Judge of the High Court of Nyasaland.[19]   The others seemed to be hostile to all missions, except the Anglican and Romanist ;   and the leader of the Church of Scotland in Nyasaland was forced to feel that he had not had a full opportunity to put his case.   With, no doubt, the instance of John Gray Kufa in mind, and with a full awareness of the capital which had already been made of the role of this Blantyre elder in the Rising by anti-missionary critics, Hetherwick had asked for permission to appear on behalf of the Church of Scotland and to examine the witnesses.   Naturally, permission was refused ;[20] but it seemed to the Scottish missionary just another instance of the anti-Protestant mission bias of the Commission.   The irony of the situation was that the interpreter on whom the Commission had to rely was an African elder of the Blantyre Church, one of the same educated Africans which the anti-missionary party criticized so vehemently.[21]

When Hetherwick's time came to give evidence, he was ready

for the Commissioners. They, no doubt with the realization of all the harsh things he had said against some of them in his public and private defence of the Scottish missions, were, it seems, also ready for him ! He was examined and cross-examined for four and a half hours ; and, according to his biographer, 'during this time not one friendly question was put to him. The whole trend of the queries was to discover whether there were any weaknesses in the work and policy, and even in the Government of the Church.'[22] Hetherwick was now in the position in which Laws had been when he had replied to Livingstone Bruce's criticisms in the Legislative Council. At that time, elements in the Church of Scotland had wished that Hetherwick had been there, for they felt that he could have fought a case better than Laws.[23] Now he had his chance. He rose, it appears, fully to the occasion.[24] He had marshalled facts and figures on the extent and responsibility of mission education in Nyasaland, and he used his statistics tellingly before the members of the Commission. Of the £11,000 which was spent annually on education less than a tenth came from the Government : all the rest was provided by the missions, he pointed out.[25] His impressive array of statistics seems to have calmed the censoriousness of the Commissioners. But Hetherwick's *coup de grâce* was reserved for the end of his four-and-a-half-hour spell of questioning. A Government member then aired the European grievance—which, it must be remembered, was also, from their own point of view, a grievance of many of Chilembwe's men who were being tried at this same time for their part in the Rising—that Africans were no longer so respectful to Europeans as they used to be, because they did not take off their hats when they passed a white man. Hetherwick, in high dudgeon, pointed out that the European himself was to blame. 'I have seen many Europeans absolutely ignore a boy's salutation', he claimed. 'The smallest drummer boy in the British Army if he salutes Lord Kitchener receives a salute in return. There will be no difficulty if the European makes acknowledgement : it indicates that two gentlemen have met and not only one.'[26] This was Hetherwick's climax and there his cross-examination closed. It had obviously been something of a personal triumph. But, in the long run, what did it amount to ?

Perhaps Hetherwick's statements, together with those of Laws and the criticisms behind the scenes of the missionary boards in Scotland, had something to do with blunting the worst edge of the anti-missionary party, which otherwise might have cut more deeply into the final report of the Commission. Certainly, the Government did not close down all mission schools. But the report of the Commission, when it was published on 31 January 1916, contained material which seemed to the Scottish missions to threaten their whole future in Nyasaland. The contest, therefore, had now to go on to a third round; the first had been against the effects of Livingstone Bruce's statements in the Legislative Council; the second had been Hetherwick's fight with the Commissioners of Inquiry; the third would now have to be fought out by the missionary 'pressure groups' in the Home Country itself.

The first censures on missions which appeared in the published Report of the Commission were, as has been noted in the previous chapter, trenchant condemnations of the role of the smaller and less orthodox missions before the Chilembwe Rising. But, just as similar charges shortly before the end of the Rising had been the prelude to a wider attack on missions, so now, in the Commission's Report, they acted as something of an introduction to more general charges against all missionary teaching. It was to these that Livingstonia and Blantyre, with their proud and pioneering traditions in Central Africa, took exception and against which they marshalled influential support in the mother country.

With many of the Report's points on secular matters (improvements in relations with the Africans on questions of land, labour, and taxation) the Scottish missions had no fault to find. But they felt at the start that the Commissioners, under their term of reference to inquire into the effects of mission teaching, might 'have made at least some reference to what the old and established missions have done for and among the natives of the country'. But of the good things that these missions had done—'Of these not a word ! . . . all the Commission say[s] is "This is a wide subject" '.[27] To the Blantyre and Livingstonia missionaries this rather feeble statement was further weakened by the fact that the Commissioners had made only very limited inquiries. 'They took no steps to make local enquiries as to the effect or results of Missions in various parts of the country. Instead of holding such enquiry at local centres throughout the Protectorate, the Commission sat only at Blantyre.'[28] There was no doubt that, from the beginnings of this controversy, the pride of the Scottish missions had been deeply wounded, and they were not, therefore, in the mood to appreciate any good intentions which the Government might have—even if such intentions could be read between the lines of subsequent sections of the Report, which to the Scottish missionaries seemed extremely doubtful. Their experience under the Commissioners' questioning had created in them no feeling of confidence in the Government's good intentions whatsoever.

This was the frame of mind in which the Scottish missionaries approached Paragraph 195 (b) of the Commissioners' Report which recommended 'The examination by Government of the credentials of religious sects which seek to be established in the Protectorate and the exclusion of those which are likely from any cause to lead to disaffection or unrest among the native population'. With the second part of this recommendation the Scottish missions had no quarrel. Nor would they object if by 'credentials' were meant 'bona fides', though this might be construed to contain 'the germs of inquisitorial power'.[29] What they were afraid of was that 'credentials' was intended to mean 'creed'. This to them was 'Erastianism with a vengeance', and they rose with all their force against this interpretation. They based their belief in this kind of interpretation on their experiences during the sittings of the Commission when, for several hours on end, members of the Blantyre Mission were examined on the Creed and practice of the Church of Scotland, and a copy of the Westminster Confession of Faith and other Standards was handed into the Commission for examination.[30] Their feelings may well be appreciated when it is recalled that the only churchman on the Commission was the High Anglican Archdeacon Glossop. It would have been bad enough for the Scottish missionaries to have been examined in this way by a Commission which was composed entirely of secular elements; but it was adding insult to injury when one of its members was a High Anglican. Something, then, of the old religious radicalism of the days of the Covenanters, of the national religious struggle with the English, seems to make itself felt in their reaction to the term 'credentials' in the Commission's Report. But reason triumphed over emotion, and—may it be said 'in typically Scottish fashion'—the missionary agencies of the Scottish churches had recourse to the law.

In their struggle against the Commission's recommendation they called to their aid Article VI of the Berlin Act of 1885, that formative document of the Scramble for Africa. This Article had bound the Powers who signed the Treaty—and Great Britain was one—to grant full freedom and protection to religious institutions within the Conventional Basin of the Congo: and Nyasaland fell clearly within this area. Both of the missionary journals of the Scottish missions published the article in full,[31] and their supporters at home used it as ammunition in their fight. Yet its use at times proved somewhat embarrassing, for the Scottish missions found themselves compelled to defend not only their own Christian freedom but also the liberty of Islam,[32] if they wished to claim the cover of the Berlin Treaty for themselves ; and at this time in particular—as will be seen later—they were very much afraid of the spread of Islam in Central Africa.

But Paragraph 195 (b) had not exhausted the threat—so it seemed to them—to missionary freedom in the Report. There were other, more dangerous and more insulting, statements to which they had to give their full, militant attention.

These were contained in fourteen sections at the end of the Report (35-48) which examined in detail 'the effects of mission teaching on the native mind and character'. At the beginning was a doubtful statement on 'properly accredited missions' and the Scottish missionaries felt that this harked back to the 'examination . . . of credentials' and all that that implied. Then followed a series of comments on the industrial and educational work of the missions which appeared, by omission, to overlook all that Livingstonia and Blantyre had done for the Protectorate over four decades ; and which seemed to question the capability of their African teachers. The attempts of the Commissioners to force a close European supervision on all education, 'if it is not to be attended by the growth of un-settling ideas', was not only against the whole tradition of the Scottish missions to encourage the African to become his own teacher and preacher, but was, according to them, contrary to the policy 'followed in all other British colonies—to work through properly trained and qualified native teachers'.[33]

What really roused the ire of the Scottish missionaries and their supporters at home was the Commission's implication that their educational system was not to be trusted, whereas those of the Roman Catholics and Anglicans were wholly reliable. 'There is a certain danger', commented Paragraph 44 of the Report, 'that in the absence of adequate supervision religious instruction may possibly be made a vehicle for undesirable political propaganda by native teachers.' But, went on the Commissioners, 'In the Roman Catholic and Anglican Missions this danger does not exist to the same extent owing to the nature of the religious teaching entrusted to native teachers'. It was obvious that, in the face of such innuendoes, the Scottish missionaries would not be silent. 'That Protestant methods open a door to disloyalty which is closed by Romanism and Anglicanism is a doctrine new to us', thundered the Blantyre missionary journal, 'and, we think, to those of our readers who know anything of Church history. It is to be regretted that this invidious comparison found a place in the report.' [34] The point was echoed in countless discussions and motions both in the Protectorate and at home ; and it was not only the Scottish missionaries who considered that it was a slur on their integrity. The missionaries of the Dutch Reformed Church, too, felt that their Protestant bona fides had been unjustifiably attacked. 'What is "the nature of the religious teaching entrusted to native teachers" by . . . the Roman Catholic Church ? asked one of them. 'It is obedience to the Pope of Rome, a spiritual and *temporal* head of the Church. . . . Place over against this the teaching of the Protestants who, in obedience to the command of the New Testament, indicate submission to the powers that be. . . .' [35]

And so, for a time, an acrimonious little controversy was touched off. Indeed, it does seem strange that the Commissioners should have gone out of their way to include such a statement in their report, especially as in a later paragraph (48) they deplored the rivalry which existed in some parts of the Protectorate between Roman Catholic and Protestant missions because it often led to 'serious friction' and 'a spirit of fanatical sectarianism'.[36] How much of this apparently pro-Anglican and Catholic view-point in the Report was due to a High Anglican being the sole representative of missionary interests on the Commission, and how much of it may be attributed to lay members' preference for a centralized church with a stake in the country, is not clear. Some of it, perhaps, may have been due to the fact that it is not unusual for British officials—for they constituted the majority of the Commission—to assume that Anglicanism ('C. of E.') is the norm in religious matters.

From all this, it was clear to the Scottish missionaries that the battle for the preservation of religious freedom in the Protectorate was not yet over. The best opportunity for making their position clear on the Report was the next meeting of the Legislative Council, with Laws as their spokesman. At the opening session, 14 March 1916, however, their hopes were dampened when the Governor stated that he was not able to submit any proposals for the consideration of the members of the Legislative Council until he had received instruction from the Home Government, to whom he had sent the opinions of the Nyasaland Government on the Report but from whom he had not yet received a reply. This was tantamount to putting a ban on discussion of the Report in the Legislative Council, and Laws spoke to the Governor about it immediately after the opening session. The Governor asked him to send him a letter with the points he wished to raise. Laws did so on the same day. It was a letter which summed up the feelings of the Scottish missionaries, and asked for an opportunity to discuss the Report in the meetings of the Legislative Council. He received from the Governor on the following day a friendly but temporizing and non-committal reply; and so, on the last day of the Legislative Council, Thursday, 16 March, Laws stood up and asked that his protest that no opportunity had been given to discuss the Report should be recorded in the official minutes. His intention was to safeguard the position of the Scottish missions in the future, and to put on record that an opportunity for discussion had been denied them in the Legislative Council.[37] When he had done this, he went to Blantyre and he and Hetherwick put their heads together and drew up a formal memorandum for their churches at home. This was completed by 22 March, and it included in a succinct form the main points of the Scottish churches' objections to the Report.

Letters, memoranda, and telegrams now began to pass between the missionaries on the spot, their home Committees,[38] and the International Missionary Council in London [39] at an increased pace. That faithful son of the Church of Scotland, Arthur Steel Maitland at the Colonial Office, gave an attentive ear to all the appeals and protests which the Scottish missionaries sent to him, either formally by post, informally by proxy at Westminster, or when he was attending the 1916 General Assembly of the Church of Scotland. The slowness of mails during the War did much to delay negotiations, and they dragged on until August 1916. By this time the hand of the Church of Scotland had been strengthened by a resolution in the General Assembly on 25 May 1916, which instructed the Foreign Mission Committee, together with its counterpart in the United Free Church of Scotland, to 'take all needful steps to secure the well-being of the Nyasaland Mission',[40] and, if necessary, to send a deputation to the Colonial Office. This would throw the whole weight of the Church of Scotland, if the need arose, behind the Nyasaland missionary cause.[41] It did not, however, become necessary, because, at the beginning of August, Steel Maitland was able to give an

Plate 25.   John Gray Kufa (from Chilembwe's own photograph album)

assurance that the Governor of Nyasaland's dispatches on the Report of Inquiry into the Rising had been read, and that they showed that he was 'absolutely satisfied with the work and teaching of the Scottish missions'.[42] With that, it appeared, the missionary situation in the Protectorate had stabilized itself for a while.[43]

While the Scottish religious 'pressure groups' at home were using all the influence on Westminster which they could command, there was still disquiet amongst their missionaries in Nyasaland. Nor was this entirely subdued until the end of the War. For one thing, Laws's terms of office as an unofficial member of the Legislative Council came to an end in 1916. The new member in his place as representative of African interests was to be Bishop Fisher of the Anglican Universities Mission to Central Africa, a fellow-worker with Glossop. Consequently the Scottish missionaries were rather suspicious of him, and, as Laws cautiously wrote home at the time, 'How the Bishop may act regarding the other missions, should matters arise affecting all, remains to be seen'.[44] The Bishop, let it be noted, did little to justify these suspicions of him, though in the 1918 Legislative Council he did express the opinion that it would be 'a good thing' if the Government had the power to ban literature which was critical of Roman Catholics.[45] Yet the suspicions of the Blantyre missionaries continued. They wanted to set up schools and churches in Chilembwe's old district during 1916, and found themselves prevented at every turn by the Government, which seemed to be giving preferential treatment to the Roman Catholics. As the Secretary of the Church of Scotland Foreign Mission Committee wrote to Hetherwick:

> The worst of it is that this is just the sort of incident to which we cannot very effectively make an *ad hoc* approach to the Colonial Office. It rather seems to us that the Government sets up a fairly plausible case for their own action, except perhaps as regards their initial step in sanctioning a Romanist mission in what appears to have been really a Protestant area. . . . It raises one's choler unboundedly.[46]

The circumstances of this incident are not clear but it indicates that, although a superficial peace had been made by August 1916, between the Scottish missions in Nyasaland, the Government, and the Anglican and Roman Catholic bodies, much of the bad feeling which had been released by the rather tactless questioning and references of the Commission of Inquiry was still very active beneath the immediate surface.

A further indication that these mutual suspicions had not disappeared was an extraordinary exercise of censorship by the Government in the last quarter of 1916. In October the journal of the United Free Church of Scotland Mission in Nyasaland, the *Livingstonia News*,[47] published an article called 'Notes on Report of Commission', which was a series of comments on the published findings of the Commission of Inquiry into the Rising. It appeared with six gaps in the text, each heralded by the self-explanatory term '[Censored]'. Fortunately copies of the passages which were struck out by the authority have survived,[48] and they demonstrate that the official censorship [49] was apparently exercised in an atmosphere of unreasonable panic, which affords a good example of Hetherwick's point from another context that the 'Government lost their heads, and made more of the trouble than there was any necessity for'.[50] It indicated, furthermore, the Government's determination to control, as far as it possibly could, criticism of the Report. A brief review of these six censored passages is, therefore, not only a useful illustration of the continuing mutual suspicions of Authority and Scottish mission in 1916, but affords also further evidence of the somewhat hasty reactions of elements in the Nyasaland Government to the new circumstances of world war and internal rebellion.

The first censored passage merely noted of the Commission's findings and recommendations that

> The views expressed in these are of a very serious nature and we do not see how some of them can be accepted by the public or acted on by the Government.

The second was a comment on the Commission's recommendation that the Government should have the power to regulate schools and churches on Crown and private land in accordance with the amount of European control available. The words struck out at this place were simply that

> [here] we are on very dangerous ground indeed.

But the third censored passage was even briefer. The text of the article ran at this point: 'Now we come to what the Commission . . .' The censored portion which should have followed read

> have left unsaid.

It is scarcely possible to follow the workings of the official mentality here !

The next passage which was removed was longer and more strongly worded, but its tenor seems to be hardly that which would promote further disaffection amongst His Majesty's subjects in Nyasaland. It took up the point about Protestant criticisms of Roman Catholic missions, and said :

> With regard to the 'publication in the native language of intolerant criticisms of rival missions'. No Church or Mission can give up the right to advocate and explain its beliefs in a reasonable way even though it rejects and seeks to refute doctrinal positions held by other Churches or Missions. Such freedom is part of the liberty of conscience and religious toleration provided for in the Berlin Act. Nor do we see how any Government can take powers to suppress literature discussing these subjects. Truth cannot be hid, and no attempt to extinguish it has succeeded permanently in its suppression.

It is difficult to see how different in essence this criticism was from that of the Blantyre missionaries in their journal,[51] and yet their criticism was left completely untouched by the censor. Similar considerations apply to the fifth censored passage which followed a section that was critical of the Report's distinction between Protestant and Catholic and Anglican methods of African education. The censored passage runs :

> Expressing such opinions, it was surely inadvisable for the Commission itself to stir up the 'spirit of fanatical sectarianism' by insertion of Section 44, without the production of any evidence for the assertion. Do the Commission expect that the non-Roman, and non-Anglican missions are, without protest, quietly to submit to be told without proof that in their methods of evangelization there is a certain danger that the religious instruction given may possibly be a vehicle for undesirable political propaganda by native teachers, whilst such danger does not exist to the same extent in the Roman Catholic and Anglican missions ?

It is very difficult to see in what way this passage was liable to impede the successful prosecution of the War in the Nyasaland Protectorate.

The last section to be struck out was a simple comment on those portions of the Report which referred to conditions on the A. L. Bruce Estates :

> The sad outstanding fact set forth in the Report of the Commission is, that in a given area of the Protectorate it was the policy 'not to allow any Christian Church' and 'schools were refused'.

If the censor was prepared to strike out passages like this, one wonders why he allowed the published Report of the Commission in the first place to contain material that was critical of conditions on the Bruce Estates. The surprising fact of the whole affair is that, if any part of this *Livingstonia News* article could be supposed in the slightest way to encourage future African trouble, it was the concluding words which might, in some very remote manner, be looked upon as an expression of sympathy with Chilembwe's rebels. But these words the censor left alone. They are :

> This policy [on the Bruce Estates] set at nought the last command of the Lord Jesus Christ and denied to the people their legitimate aspirations for the education of themselves and their children. In due time Nemesis appeared in the shape of the John Chilembwe Rising, with its attendant horrors. We hope one such lesson will be enough.

Perhaps the censor thought that this passage was safe because the Africans had not attained the benefit of a classical education, and that, therefore, any of them who might chance to read the article would be unaware of the significance of 'Nemesis' ? Perhaps it was the censor who did not know the meaning of Nemesis ?

Why did the censor cut so savagely into this article from the *Livingstonia News*, which was produced so far away from the main scenes of the Rising and had its main circulation outside the Shire Highlands, and yet leave completely alone the equivalent article in the Blantyre missionary journal, which certainly did not lack its passages of strong comment, and which was produced and circulated in the Chilembwe country ? Whim or accident may perhaps be the reason. And yet it is not unlikely that the causes go deeper. At the time of Cockerill's first deportation from the Ngoni and Tonga areas to the north of Lake Nyasa (the areas, indeed, of the Livingstonia Mission and its main spheres of influence), it has been noticed that the Government was afraid of trouble in these districts : trouble from the Ngoni ; trouble from the rumps of the rival factions of African separatist churches left after the wave of Kamwanaism. By 1916 the Government was still not happy about conditions in these parts, and at least one Ngoni chief, Chimtunga of Mombera's Ngoni, had shown himself hostile to the exactions of the War. Because of these facts, the Government, with memories of the Shire Highlands Rising still fresh in its mind, may, in its prevailing mood of suspicion and semi-panic, have been very wary of any publication from these districts—even though it were backed by a veteran like Laws of Livingstonia—which might, by criticism of the Government, seem likely in some way to stimulate unco-operative, quasi-rebellious activities amongst its Ngoni or Tonga subjects. Even so, the action of the censor towards the October issue of the *Livingstonia News* has an unreasonable and hysterical ring about it.

Thus, by the end of 1916, with suspicion still in the air, the Christian missions of Nyasaland entered into a new period of their history. As the fortunes of the War turned towards the Allies, the Government became more lenient towards them ; and after the War even the smaller, less orthodox missions (amongst which was Chilembwe's old mission, the P.I.M.) were allowed to begin their work again.[52] But the suspicions which the Rising engendered died hard, if they died at all, and the anti-missionary factions in East, Central, and South Africa did not scruple when the occasion arose to use the example of the Chilembwe Rising against Christian missionary work—in particular against the activities of the Protestant missions.

Perhaps, however, in Nyasaland this may have had a more positive effect, and may have done something to heal the divisions amongst the Protestant missions themselves. It may, in this respect, be significant that the censored article of the *Livingstonia News*, in its attempt to fight back against the implied slurs on the principle of missionary freedom in the Report of the Commission of Inquiry, had come out in defence of all missions, however small or strange they might seem to be. In this, though the authors of the article may not have intended it, there was not only commentary on, but also some exculpation for, the Booth heritage amongst the missions of Nyasaland ; for the Cockerills and the Hollises ; for the individualist missionary and the tiny congregation ; and, indeed, for the African independent congregations themselves. Thus this defence from Livingstonia merits quotation, for it shows that, if from the attack on the smaller missions had come the onslaught on the greater, at least one of those greater missions had followed the wheel full circle and was now ready to speak in defence of the little missions themselves :

> Most of the advances of Religion and Society have come by means of a 'Freak' Mission or a 'Freak' Missionary, and though the sneer pleased contemporaries, the truth such stood for became the heritage of the world. Such a solitary Missionary appeared and gathered a few followers. The Church of the day denounced the teaching given, the

Government of the day crucified the Teacher, and scattered his followers, but the truth proclaimed by that 'Freak' Mission has outlasted the Roman Empire and dominates the moral judgement of the world at the present hour. Christ's definition of a Church was 'two or three gathered together in my name'. Which things are a parable, not to be lightly disregarded.[53]

Finally, what was the significance of this whole war of paper and words for and against the missionaries and the education of Africans which the Rising had touched off in Nyasaland, and to which the Report of the Commission of Inquiry had given a new lease of life, so that a bitter controversy was kept up in the Protectorate and in interested circles abroad for almost two years? Perhaps some clue to this may be found in the words of the first Commissioner and Consul-General to British Central Africa, Harry (then Sir Harry) Hamilton Johnston. In 1916 Johnston, who was living in Great Britain in retirement a life of liberalism and literature, published an article with the provocative title, 'The Bitter Cry of the Educated African', from which the following words may be quoted as a last commentary on this whole episode :

> The white man [said Sir Harry Johnston] who controls in every direction the negro's destinies would in his collective opinion like to thrust the negro back into helotry and into exclusively manual work of a more or less unskilled kind, in connection with land, with mining, and the general development of the money-making resources of Africa, the money-making to remain chiefly with the white controller. In short, all Governments, most Government officials, and nearly all the masters of Europe's trade and industry connected with Africa, would prefer if they spoke their utmost thoughts to re-establish slavery all over Africa. . . . But the time for such a phase in African history has gone by . . . the missionaries have sown the dragon's teeth of education. . . .[54]

2. OTHER ASPECTS OF THE COMMISSION

But the missionaries, with their 'dragon's teeth of education' were not the only people in the Protectorate to express criticism of the Commission of Inquiry into the Rising. As soon as the Government announced, in its *Gazette* for 8 April 1915, the composition and terms of reference of the Commission, a current of muttering against them arose from settler groups in the Shire Highlands. Of the five members of the Commission, only one could be said properly to represent their interests : Claud Metcalfe of Blantyre, General Manager of the British Central Africa Company. Glossop, Archdeacon of Likoma, could hardly be looked on as a representative of Shire Highlands planting and business interests. And for the other three members of the Commission, who could be relied upon to act together and to cast a majority vote where necessary, the Government had appointed nominees from its own ranks : Robert William Lyall Grant of the High Court ; Aubrey Marriott Dalway Turnbull, Assistant Chief Secretary ; and Joseph Charles Casson, Superintendent of Native Affairs. By thus making sure of having the final word in the Report which the Commission would produce, it seemed to many that the Government, which had obviously been taken unawares by the outbreaks at Magomero and Mandala, was seeking to save its own face.

It was in this way that criticism against the Government gathered force in the Shire Highlands. The outcome was a public meeting under the auspices of the Nyasaland Chamber of Agriculture and Commerce in the Queen Victoria Hall, Blantyre, on the afternoon of Saturday, 5 June 1915. From reports of this meeting it is clear that it was well attended—there were sixty present, many from long distances, which was a large number for that particular time—and the scene of vigorous discussion.[55] The Government was accused of betraying its promise to Laws in the March Legislative Council for a complete and impartial inquiry. The personnel of the Commission was criticized, and a motion was carried, 'enthusiastically and unanimously', which revealed that those present—and they were not all business men, for Hetherwick had a hand in drafting and carrying the motion—were anxious that the Government, as well as themselves, should take its full share of responsibility for the Rising. Or, perhaps, it might even be truer to say that many of those present, by this motion, showed a desire, by putting the Government in a difficult position, to absolve themselves of any part in the long and involved train of circumstances which had led to the Rising. The motion requested that, as the Chamber of Commerce had originally proposed, there should be five, not four terms of reference. To the terms set out in the Government *Gazette* (origin, causes, and objects of the Rising ; native grievances which may have led to it ; the adequacy of the means in the Protectorate for obtaining information on native feeling ; and the effects of mission teaching on the native mind) the meeting proposed a fifth : 'Whether any warning had been given to the authorities. If so, what was the nature of such warnings and what measures were adopted to safeguard the interests of the community by taking advantage of them ?' Those who voted for this motion knew very well that the Government had received warnings about possible trouble from Chilembwe and his mission, and that it had done very little about them until its hand had been forced by the Magomero and Mandala attacks. Because of this, some, indeed, amongst Central African settlers had even gone so far as to suggest that the Commission should be appointed by the Colonial Office in Great Britain, and not by the Nyasaland Government.[56] The motion was thus an implicit criticism of a Government which, by its narrowly interpreted war-time censorship, was clamping down on discussion of the Rising. Metcalfe's seems to have been the only voice at the meeting which was raised in defence of the Government, and he had been appointed a member of the Commission whose sittings had already begun. But the meeting was not without its humour—if this is the correct word to apply to a manifestation of some Scottish nationalism in what was, after all, a predominantly Caledonian colony, with many economic and political grievances not unlike those of metropolitan Scotland. This manifestation appeared in the words of one member who criticized the Commission on the grounds that 'English criminal law is [not] suitable or adaptable to such a rising as they have been called upon to judge'.

Within a week's time the Chamber of Commerce had received assurances from the Government that the terms of reference of the Commission had been couched broadly, that they were not exclusive of the meeting's points, and that the Government was as anxious as the Chamber was to secure the fullest possible evidence.[57] For a while this seems to have quietened the criticisms of the settler groups in the Shire Highlands, though not for long. This was evident from a letter in the *Nyasaland Times* for 1 July, which revealed the sensitiveness of Nyasaland settlers at this period. The writer claimed that the Commissioners in their sittings seemed unable to discriminate between a civil trial and a commission of inquiry, for they followed the High Court practice when taking evidence. Instead of the witnesses sitting around the table with the Commissioners, the Commissioners sat up on the Judge's platform at Blantyre, while the witnesses, one and all, had to occupy the ordinary witness-box.

The correspondent may have been impelled by offended dignity, but he certainly had a point : for the effect of this procedure on many of the witnesses must have been to make them feel that they were almost on trial themselves.

News of the manœuvres of the Nyasaland Chamber of Commerce, which focused so much criticism of the Government by settler groups in the Protectorate, drifted, through the press, overseas. It was in this way that that hardy fighter for the African standpoint, the Anti-Slavery Society in Great Britain, sent yet another epistle to the Colonial Secretary. It had noticed that the Chamber of Commerce was petitioning the Nyasaland Government for a full inquiry into the Rising, and it added its mite to this process when its Committee resolved to send a letter to the Colonial Secretary, 'associating itself with this request . . . for a representative commission'. [58] The Society then wrote to the Nyasaland Chamber of Commerce, and the Chamber, perhaps with memories of Booth and his anti-slavery efforts in mind, replied with nothing more than an official letter to inform the Society that a Commission was sitting.[59] But if nothing else, this minor action of the Anti-Slavery Society must have given the Chamber of Commerce and its adherents amongst the Shire Highland settlers some feeling that they were not entirely alone, and some encouragement to take action in the future should the Commission's findings make this seem necessary.

The Chamber of Commerce,[60] however, does not appear to have taken any further action : no doubt because, as the editor of the *Nyasaland Times* pointed out in his notice of the Commission's Report on 24 February 1916, the censorship of the time prevented free discussion. But, more fundamentally, it seems the Chamber was inactive because the Report did not implicate in any very direct fashion the general European settler community in the Protectorate. There was, perhaps, a very mildly implied censure under the heading of 'Native Grievances' where Paragraph 25 of the Report had stated that there was 'the understanding that a native wearing a hat should salute a European by raising it'. But that was all. The Report had reserved its more direct censure for two bodies : the Protestant missionaries and the A. L. Bruce Estates. With the former's response, the previous section of this chapter has already dealt. But a word must now be said about the reaction of the Bruce Estates to this censure on their land-holdings and management.

That the owner of the Estates, Alexander Livingstone Bruce, was not altogether unprepared for the charges which were made against them seems likely, if his conduct in the Legislative Council the year before is recalled. At that time it had appeared that he had tried to shift the blame away from his own Estates and on to the shoulders of the missionaries. But the Report of the Commission left the Estates no alternative but to face the fact that the Commissioners had included the 'unsatisfactory conditions' on them as one of the causes of the Rising. A. L. Bruce had, no doubt, presented the best case he could to the Commissioners when he was called upon for evidence. He had been questioned for three or more hours, and had then been congratulated by the Chairman, Judge Lyall Grant, for his evidence.[61] But this had not prevented the Commissioners from coming to the conclusion that 'the treatment of labour and the system of tenancy on the Bruce Estates . . . were in several respects illegal and oppressive and . . . directly conduced to the rising'. And when extracts from the Report appeared in the press outside the Protectorate, at least one influential journal expatiated on the restrained language of the Commissioners. This was Horatio Bottomley's *John Bull*, and its wide circulation would have ensured for the Estates additional unfavourable publicity. Under the heading of 'Living Livingstones in Darkest Africa' the sharp-tongued paper commented that 'to judge from the Report the present Directors [of the Bruce Estates] appear to have departed widely from the precepts of their distinguished forerunner. . . .'[62]

The character of the Estates' reactions to all such charges is shown clearly in a letter which the Secretary of the Company wrote to the *Scotsman*, 24 March 1916. (The choice of the national Scottish paper was, presumably, because the Bruce Estates was a Scottish company, registered at the Scottish Companies Office; and perhaps because it was felt that the Estates owed some sort of an explanation to a people that looked upon Nyasaland as its own special colony.) He began by pointing out that he had been instructed to say that the Company had not received fair treatment from the Commission. The rest of his letter was then an attempt to demonstrate that labour conditions on the Estates had not been oppressive, and that the 'principal contributory cause [of the Rising] was the negligence of the Nyasaland Government'. This attempt to implicate the Government revealed an apparent shift of tactic by the Bruce Estates in their defence. Their letter to the *Scotsman* had no mention of A. L. Bruce's charge of the year before that the Chilembwe movement had been the outcome of missionary education of the African. From the manner in which this had been handled by Laws and Hetherwick in Nyasaland, it must have been clear to the Company's representatives in Scotland that the implication of even the faintest of connections between the missions and the Rising would have drawn down upon the Company a storm of letters and well-documented counter-accusations from the scholarly Scots of the Foreign Mission Boards who were at this time already in action with their petitions and protests to the Colonial Office against the slurs upon them in the Report of Inquiry. Instead, the Secretary of the A. L. Bruce Estates contented himself with the charge on which all the Europeans in Nyasaland, settlers and missionaries alike, were in agreement : Government negligence. William Jervis Livingstone, he claimed, had more than once pointed out to the Government that Chilembwe was preaching sedition at the Providence Industrial Mission ; but the Government had done nothing about it. This attempt to shift responsibility on to the Government was carried further when, in a defence of the labour-rent system on the Estates, the Secretary claimed, very correctly, that the *tangata* system, in one form or another, was widespread in the Protectorate, and implied that it was the result of the Government's policy of imposing a hut tax on the Africans, and represented a method whereby the African was saved the trouble of grappling with the new-fangled economic ways of the white man. 'The taxes', he pointed out, 'are "purchased" from the Government by the planter', and the natives then work off the required amounts instead of paying them directly to the planter who has 'purchased' them. Furthermore, went on the Secretary, of the two months of the year which were worked for the Estates by their African tenants, neither of them was rent in the strict sense. One month went for the hut tax, and, for the other, current wage rates were paid. From this, another charge was implied against the Government : for this month's labour, it was claimed, many planters, 'including, it is believed, the Government', gave no money wage and exacted more than a month's work. The rest of the letter was a defence of the Estates' manager and his staff : that, for all the accusations made against them, they had a larger labour reserve than other planters ; that their policy of disciplining native churches on their land was directed against the seditious Chilembwe's mission only ; that their concern for their employees' welfare was shown by the hospital for natives on the Estates 'at the expense of the Bruce family'; and finally, that, so far from having started the Rising, the Europeans of the Bruce Estates had stopped it spreading—but for the 'heroic resistance' of John Robertson and his wife at Mwanje the Rising might not have been so easily suppressed.

The only comment on this particular letter which seems to have survived is that from the secretary of the Foreign Mission Council of the Church of Scotland to Hetherwick in Nyasaland : 'It seems to me a poverty-stricken, and most injudicious production'.[63] For all that, a defence through the press of the mother country was a wiser approach for the Estates than an attempt to address the Nyasaland public through the papers of the Protectorate. As the editor of the *Nyasaland Times* pointed out in his edition of 24 February 1916, in which he noticed the issue of the Commission's Report, it was impossible to speak freely of it because of the censorship then in operation in the Protectorate. Indeed, when the Report was laid before the members of the Legislative Council at its sixteenth session, 14 March 1916, the Governor himself put a virtual ban on discussion of it by stating that he could submit no proposals about it for the consideration of the members until the Nyasaland Government received instructions from the Government at home to whom it had sent its 'considered views'.[64] This ban on discussion did not go without a protest, which, as has been seen, was voiced the following day by the veteran Laws. But the Governor was adamant, though he held out vague hopes for 'fullest consideration' at some future date.

Nevertheless the Government was not allowed to have it all its own way, for, on the first day of the Council, the planter James Fiddes, who had supported A. L. Bruce's criticism of the missionaries at the Legislative Council the year before, slipped in two questions which must have caused the Government some embarrassment to answer, for they both concerned the common charge of Government negligence before the Rising. The first question asked whether Chilembwe's premises had been searched while he was under suspicion ; to which the Government's answer was that they had not been searched until after the Rising, though Chilembwe's correspondence had been intercepted for three months before. The second question had something of the character of a very indirect defence of the Bruce Estates, while, like the Estates' letter in the *Scotsman*, it was pointed directly at the Government. 'If', asked Fiddes, 'the conditions under which the natives lived on the Magomero Estates were so oppressive as to directly conduce to the recent rising, why did the Government not take steps to remedy this state of affairs ?' The Government's reply was a model usage of non-committal officialese : 'The allegation of oppressive methods had only now been brought to the notice of the Government by the recent Report of the Special Commission which rested upon evidence touching the internal affairs of the Magomero Estate to which the Government had no access'.[65]

With these questions, which seemed to bring into the Legislative Council not merely a touch of the last public defence of the Bruce Estates but also an echo of the meeting, ten months earlier, when the Nyasaland Chamber of Commerce had shown its own suspicions of the Government's willingness to take any share of responsibility for preventing the Rising, and with Laws's protest on behalf of the missionary interests at the lack of opportunity for discussing the Report, its immediate repercussions on the plane of specially interested personalities and groups may be said to have ended. If nothing else, during the eight months in which the Commissioners had been taking evidence and drafting their Report, it had brought into Blantyre and Zomba numbers of Europeans, some of whom had not been into the principal centres of the Protectorate for years, so that some opportunity for social reunions was a measure of compensation for any of the indignities or inconvenience which particular Europeans may have felt they had suffered under the cross-fire of the Commissioners. And, in spite of all the criticisms made of it by missionary or secular interests, the Commissioners, it must be said, had produced a very succinct and well-drafted document which, if the existing conditions are taken into consideration, is no bad general guide to the factors behind the Rising.

Fundamentally, however, the calling and the course of the Commission of Inquiry had provided an opportunity for the three groups into which the Europeans of the Protectorate fell (Government, settlers and business men, and missionaries) to pit themselves against, and with each other, in a variety of combinations so that any suggestion of responsibility for the Rising, however slight, might be shifted from their own particular group to some other. They were, perhaps, too near to the scene of the Chilembwe movement to realize that, as parts of a total European culture, they were all, in some sense, responsible.

3. Some Results of the Rising and Commission

When, late in life, Hetherwick of Blantyre came to write his biography, he gave as his opinion that 'nothing came of the Commission and the whole matter was speedily forgotten'.[66] How far was this true?

In one respect, certainly, it is incorrect. After the Rising, the Government had to enforce a number of administrative measures whose effects, if slight amongst the Europeans of the Protectorate, were by no means small for the Africans. For instance, there was the whole range of punitive measures which the Government felt obliged to introduce. These covered not merely the public shootings in the first few days of the Rising when the Chilembwe-men were still in flight, or the hangings of rebels who were convicted and tried later—all of which made a deep impression on the Africans of Chilembwe's area and in many other parts of the Shire Highlands, so that for years afterwards they were very guarded in their discussion of the whole affair with Europeans or Africans for the fear, real or imaginary, of possible victimization on the official or the private level. But they included also four exercises by the Government of its powers under the Collective Punishment Ordinance of Nyasaland, 1909, by which fines were levied, in June 1915, of four shillings on every male African hut-owner in parts of the Mlanje, Zomba, Ncheu, and Chiradzulu areas for 'colluding with, or harbouring, or failing to take all reasonable means to prevent the escape of rebels'.[67] Though the fines were paid quietly and with no show of resistance, it must not be supposed that they were not resented. With the earlier and more militant manifestations of the Government's wrath, they continued to provide material for anti-European discussions for many years to come. But, for the historian of the Chilembwe movement at least, the use of collective punishment ordinances in 1915 has some value : it enables him, in the absence of other records, to indicate with some degree of exactitude the areas over which Chilembwe and his followers had direct influence.[68]

And there were other Government actions which were remembered and discussed discreetly by Africans for years after the Rising. There was the blowing-up of Chilembwe's headquarters and the symbol of his power : the brick church which he had built at Mbombwe, Chiradzulu. Much African money and work had gone into it, and there would be many Africans who felt that its destruction was a wanton waste. Chilembwe's sponsors in America, the National Baptist Convention, apparently thought so : they submitted a claim to the Nyasaland Government for compensation for the dynamiting of the church, which Chilembwe's American Negro sponsor, L. G. Jordan, valued at forty thousand dollars.[69] Needless to say, the claim was not met. Furthermore, there were the fines that were claimed from the Africans who had destroyed the Marist Fathers Mission : though it is clear from the amount of damages for which the mission asked, £1400,[70] that the Government must have paid them. Indeed, by April 1915, the announcement that the expenses incurred in the suppression of the Rising amounted to £2200 and that these would be met from local revenue [71] must have caused a little discussion, too, amongst local European taxpayers.

Furthermore, European critics of the Government—and, as has been seen, there were many at this period—found additional ammunition for their attacks in the attempts which the Administration made after the Rising to group the villages of the Chiradzulu, Zomba, Blantyre, and Mlanje areas [72] into aggregates of not less than fifteen huts in order that they might be more effectively controlled.[73] Critics of the system claimed that the Ncheu district, the centre of Chinyama's subsidiary rising, had experienced some measure of concentration under the District Administration (Native) Ordinance of 1912, but that this had not prevented trouble there.[74] The Government's actions at this time seem to be in direct line with their expressed intentions—which the coming of the War had overshadowed—to tighten up the system of African local government. It has been noticed in Chapter V on the prelude to the Rising that, by disturbing the traditional pattern of African life, this may have added to the complication of circumstances which created the Chilembwe movement. A similar point was made by European critics of the Government's attempts to concentrate native huts in the main areas of the Rising : 'the whole movement', it was claimed, '[was] premature and [was] condemning a system of native life which was much better than the new system proposed'.[75] What the Africans had to say about the concentration-of-huts policy is not noticed by available European sources. But it does not seem unjust to suppose that they would have looked upon it not as part of a plan which had lapsed as a result of the coming of the War, but as a direct adjunct to the Government's general policy of punishment and control after the Rising. It would be added to the growing fund of grievances against the Government and the white man which the Rising had emphasized, and which supplied endless material for mutterings against them in future years. In sum, it would not be true to say that the Government's policy of punishment and control after the Rising was 'speedily forgotten'. It was certainly not forgotten quickly by the Government when, following the recommendation of the Commission of Inquiry, it put out a Seditious Publications (Prohibition) Ordinance in 1918,[76] and did not hesitate to use it in later years.[77]

Nor could the Government forget that some settlement had to be made for the Chilembwe family in order that it could be controlled in case, in future years, with the growth of the Chilembwe legend, it might become the centre or the symbol of a new anti-European movement. The Government appears to have made some provision for Chilembwe's sons, Donald and Charlie;[78] and the death of Mrs. Ida Chilembwe not long after the Rising[79] helped to break up the family as a nucleus for possible future discontent. Yet, if the story recorded by Hector Livingstone Duff, Chief Secretary to the Nyasaland Government during the Rising period, is correct, it would appear that Chilembwe's family, with the knowledge of the punishment of rebels in mind, was in no way anxious to fulfil such a role. Duff noted that, some time after Chilembwe's death, he had received a 'letter from his [Chilembwe's] son in the United States', in which,

> after referring to his deceased parent as 'that late perfidious man, my father', the writer went on to say that, being fully conscious of the justice of British rule and the benefits which it had conferred on his countrymen, he wished to make such atonement as he could in his own person, for Chilembwe's ingratitude and folly. To that end, he said, he had decided to volunteer for active service with the American Army in France, and expressed the hope that if he fell there, the sacrifice of his life might be accepted in expiation of his father's guilt.[80]

Whatever was the author's exact degree of relationship with John Chilembwe,[81] the letter would serve to remind the Government that there were a few Nyasaland Africans in the United States; and it would keep this fact and the Rising alive in the Government's mind as consequences of the 'Ethiopian' relationship between Central Africa and American Negroes and their organizations whenever they attempted to begin work again in Nyasaland. That it was not until 1926 that the Providence Industrial Mission was allowed to reopen,[82] under the auspices of the National Baptist Convention, Inc., and its representative, Dr. Daniel Malekebu (Miss DeLany's former pupil, who had followed her back to the States in 1907 and had taken a medical degree in a Southern Negro college), was another indication that the Rising was not 'speedily forgotten'.

In the same year as the Providence Industrial Mission was re-admitted to work in Nyasaland, the Protectorate's first Director of Education was appointed. With his arrival in April 1926, Nyasaland's first Education Department was set up ; and between then and 1930, after discussions with missionary bodies, new Ordinances were promulgated to standardize and encourage education amongst Africans.[83] Though the attempt to standardize African education in the Protectorate goes back to a joint-missionary conference at Livingstonia in 1900, the Government had paid little attention to educational problems until the time of the Rising when the Scottish missionaries, inside and outside of the Legislative Council, in defence of their own schools, drew the Government's attention forcibly to its lack of concern for education in Nyasaland. The point was repeated less personally but none the less clearly by the Commission of Inquiry into the Rising when it recommended the appointment of a Director of Education.[84] Thus, while some might not welcome a greater incursion by the Government into what had been a traditional missionary sphere in Nyasaland, and politically conscious Africans might complain that the new policy represented an attempt to condition the natives of the Protectorate in the manner which seemed safest to the authorities, the increase of Government grants-in-aid and interest in education generally might be linked to the shock which it was given in 1915 when the results of some of the poor and uncontrolled African independent schools manifested themselves in the Chilembwe outbreaks. The Rising, though it appears to have been rarely mentioned in open discussion of educational problems in the Protectorate between 1916 and 1930, has nevertheless a very definite place in the history of educational extension amongst Africans in Nyasaland.[85]

Some Africans, too, have claimed that, after the Rising, there was an improvement of European behaviour towards them : that the raising of hats or compulsory salutations by Africans towards Europeans was no longer insisted on so rigorously by the white settlers, and that social relations between the two groups generally improved. The point should not be pressed too far; but there do seem some grounds for supposing that Chilembwe's militant demonstration had some effect on the dominant groups of Nyasaland: the new society which had created the 'educated' and 'aspiring' African must find a place for him not only by a more sympathetic understanding of the personal difficulties of his position but also by making some attempt—however difficult this might be because of the character of Nyasaland's economy—to fit him into a job.

But, above all, the Rising appears to have affected Nyasaland most in the sphere of land questions. Again, as with education, its effect seems to have been to speed up consideration of, and action on, a number of difficult problems which were recognized before the War and the Rising but which, for various reasons, had been neglected.

It has been seen that, in 1914, the Government had had under consideration measures to regularize the position of Africans on private European estates in Nyasaland. War and the general difficulties which had attended a settlement of the land question in the Protectorate since Sir Harry Johnston's 'Certificates of Claim' in (1890's had prevented their realization. The Rising, however, and its exposure of conditions on the Bruce Estates forced these problems afresh upon the Government. The Commission of Inquiry had appealed for greater security of tenure for African tenants, and had revealed something of the abuse of the *tangata* system by European land-owners. It had recommended 'an ordinance to regulate the position of native tenants on Europeans' estates', and had suggested its terms in further recommendations. These were

> the abolition of work in lieu of rent, except at the option of the tenant; the securing that the tenant pays a reasonable rent; that he receives reasonable notice to quit [so as to enable him to ingather his crop]; and ... eviction [should] only be carried out by order of the Court.[86]

It was impossible for the Government to avoid the implications of these recommendations, and in 1916 it had issued the draft of 'A Bill to amend the law as to Native Tenancies on Private Estates'. These proposals had been shown to the Nyasaland Chamber of Commerce —no doubt the Government had in mind the sensitivity which the Chamber had displayed in 1915 when the character of the Commission of Inquiry was in dispute. Then, when the Chamber had made suggestions about the Bill, it was laid before the seventeenth session of the Legislative Council, 13-15 March 1917, for discussion. It emerged finally as the Native Rent (Private Estates) Ordinance of 1917 which decreed that no labour service, unless voluntary, was to be exacted from African tenants on Europeans' estates, 'nor . . . any restriction or obligation as an equivalent for permission to reside'. Furthermore, some measure of protection for African tenants on the rates and conditions of their money rental was indicated, and six months' notice was stipulated before the tenants could be evicted from European land.

The connection between these measures and the recommendations of the Commission had been noted by the Blantyre missionaries in their journal for December 1916, and they went on to make an appraisal of them which indicated the difficulties that the Government would face in the future over the land question in Nyasaland

> The Bill so far as it goes is good [they said] but it is only a fragment of a very wide and important subject—the whole position of the native on the land. Something will have to be done soon to secure an ample reserve of land to meet the future needs of the native population This is specially clamant in the Shire Highlands where there is little land left now in the hands of the Crown, and consequently very little left to form native reserves in the event of an increase in the development of European agricultural enterprise. . . . The existing Native Locations Ordinance provides for the setting apart of one tenth of each European estate as a provision for the natives resident thereon. But this is far from sufficient for the natives on European estates in the Shire Highlands. Some other provision will have to be made if this question is ever to be definitely and satisfactorily settled. We see no other way out of the present *impasse* than that the Government should buy over some of the undeveloped land in European hands. . . .[87]

These words were more prophetic than the missionaries probably realized at the time. In 1919 one of their members, the Reverend James Reid, suggested at the Legislative Council that the land situation was little better, and that a special commission should be set up to deal with this. This was done in July 1920 ; and when the Land Commission reported in 1921, it was clear that the provisions of the 1917 Ordinance had failed to ameliorate the basic position of African tenants *vis-à-vis* European landowners. The Land Commission connected the 1917 Ordinance with the Chilembwe Rising and its own Commission of Inquiry but added that the Ordinance had not achieved its objects : 'In practice on the majority of private estates the native is still only the tenant of his landlord as long as he is also an employee'[88]—which was another way of saying that labour-rent was still being exacted. Furthermore, the Land Commission went on to indicate that, if the 1917 Ordinance had laid down that six months' notice should be given, it had not prevented evictions of African tenants from European estates.[89] It made a plea for some instrument to secure the African security of tenure :

> This is what the native most desires and what he now has not, whether on private estates or Crown land. We believe that the possibility of removal from their homes is a source of real anxiety to many.[90]

Debates, discussions, Commissions, Ordinances followed down the years, through the depression of the 1920's, into and beyond the period of the Second World War.[91] In 1946 another Land Commission in Nyasaland reported that the problem 'is intensified by very much greater pressure on the land, and is exposed in its seriousness by the failure of the Legislature to settle the differences between estate owners and resident natives' ;[92] and put at the head of its recommendations the suggestion which the Blantyre missionaries had made in 1916 as the only way out of the impasse—Government acquisition of privately owned land.[93] But, as the missionaries had also noticed, it was 'a plan which we are certain the Government will be very unwilling to do'.[94] The practical difficulties which faced such purchase and resettlement in 1916 had advanced at a galloping geometrical ratio by the 1950's. The Government was not inactive, and between 1946 and 1954 had taken over some 300,000 acres of estates' lands.[95] Nevertheless its policy fell between the two stools of advancing African nationalism and political organization on the one hand, and European opposition on the other. In 1953 serious African disturbances[96] broke out in the Cholo, Chiradzulu, Mlanje, Zomba, and Blantyre areas over land and allied questions, and, in a memorandum to the Colonial Secretary, the European Convention of Associations and Landowners Association, after reviewing the land situation in Nyasaland and the attempts to settle it, headed its summary of salient points with the significant words, 'The territory is faced with a crisis'.[97]

Thus, looking back to the Rising, its Commission of Inquiry, and the Ordinance of 1917 which emerged from it, it is clear that if, perhaps, in the sphere of education and social relations, the repercussions of the Rising had done something to change the lot of the Africans in the Protectorate, its effects on the land situation were limited to bringing into existence an Ordinance which became a dead letter almost as soon as it was passed.[98] Here, essentially, Hetherwick was right when he wrote of the Commission that 'nothing came of it'. The land situation in the Shire Highlands had been one element behind the Chilembwe Rising; the Rising had stimulated a new review of the situation and some hasty legislation to meet it. But there its effects had stopped.

The fact of the Rising remained as a warning of what could happen again if some satisfactory solution of the land problem were not reached. Yet in the printed reports of Commissions, debates, discussions, memoranda, after the 1921 Land Commission, very few references to the Rising appear. It seems almost as if a conspiracy of silence had overtaken it.[99] Those who might be said to be most closely connected with it as a portent of land difficulties—settlers, employers, shareholders, missionaries, tenants, administrators—seem to have closed their lips at the mention of it, almost as if the words 'Chilembwe', 'Native Rising', 'tangata' might touch off more troubles with the Africans. Thus it has been left mainly to academics to give it a passing mention in its context of land problems.[100] Even these are few. Miss Lucy Mair, for example, in her *Native Policies in Africa* (London, 1936) has noticed that:

> Discontent with the existing [land] system, in which the period of work demanded by the landlord constantly increased, and the practice common further south of refusing to allow squatters to seek work elsewhere began to be followed, was found to be one of the causes of the Chilembwe Rising of 1915 (p. 109).

And Professor W. M. Macmillan in his *Africa Emergent* (London, 1938) has said of the Rising that:

> The occasion undoubtedly was the disposition shown by some landowners to make the shortage of native land, and the preference shown by natives for the better land, an occasion to exact more onerous labour services. Here, for once, the people were sufficiently independent to resist (p. 144).

But there are few other serious references which put the Rising into its perspective of the problems of land tenure in Nyasaland.[101]

It might seem, then, that on this fundamental question Hetherwick was right when he said of the Rising that 'the whole matter was speedily forgotten'. However, in view of the explosive nature of the land situation in Nyasaland, it is perhaps more appropriate to say that it had been relegated to that uneasy category of 'things best forgotten'.

And finally, it must never be overlooked, when judging Hetherwick's sweeping statement, that it has been pointed out that he was one of the most surprised men in Nyasaland when the Rising took place.[102] Sir George Smith, the Governor, was also surprised at the news but his estimate of the Chilembwe movement is of more solid substance : it opened 'a new phase in the existence of Nyasaland'.[103]

IX

THE RISING IN PERSPECTIVE

But our golden age is not in the past. It is in the future,—in the good time coming yet for Africa and the world.

DAVID LIVINGSTONE to his son, Thomas,
24 September 1869

IX

THE RISING IN PERSPECTIVE

I. IN CENTRAL AFRICA

How far is Sir George Smith's statement that the Rising 'opened a new phase in the existence of Nyasaland' correct? It was made soon after the end of Chilembwe's movement, when Europeans in the Protectorate were still concerned about the prospect of similar outbreaks, a concern that was not lightened by the continuing peril of the German war on their borders. It would have been natural, then, as some were inclined to suggest, for the Governor to exaggerate the crisis. A South African emissary of the Dutch Reformed Church, who visited Nyasaland in early 1916 and discussed the Rising with Hetherwick and other Europeans, summed up this outlook when he commented that 'to one like [himself] who was born near the eastern frontier of the Cape Colony at a time when the alarm of the Kaffir wars was a matter of everyday occurrence, it [seemed] as though the white population of the Protectorate were thrown into a very great fright over a very little thing'.[1] Similarly, Hetherwick, in accordance with his line of discouraging any general European distrust of Africans by emphasizing the limited extent of Chilembwe's movement, was to stress repeatedly that 'it was in no sense a "Native Rising" '.[2]

Certainly, if viewed statistically from the aspect of casualties on both sides, the Chilembwe Rising makes only a tiny score. Three Europeans killed and a handful wounded, and the small number of Africans—never exactly ascertained [3]—killed and wounded on both sides, comprise a modest total in comparison with the casualty lists of the Arab, Yao, and Ngoni wars in the Protectorate's early days. Compared with the numbers killed and wounded in armed outbreaks elsewhere in southern Africa before 1915, its figures are almost negligible. In the Mashona and Matebele rebellion of 1896 in Rhodesia over 3000 Africans and 200 Europeans were killed.[4] By the time the Maji-Maji rebellion against German rule in what is now southern Tanganyika had been suppressed in 1906, it is estimated that 120,000 Africans had died.[5] In the Bambata rebellion of 1906

399

in Natal, over 4000 lost their lives ;[6] and in what has been called 'the greatest rebellion in Africa in the twentieth century', the 1947 revolt in Madagascar, probably 40,000 Malagasies died.[7] Nevertheless in spite of its comparatively small casualty list, Government agencies habitually referred to Chilembwe's movement as the 'Native Rising'; and the Government *Gazette* for 27 February 1915 described it as a 'serious emergency'.[8]

The Government's reasons for this attitude are clear. The Rising occurred at an embarrassing time, during a general war against the Germans. It could have been more than a local danger, and support to repress it might not have been readily available. At the same time it seemed to open up prospects of future active African discontent. Though taken unawares by the outbreak, the officials could not have been ignorant of the fact that the harmony of European and African relations in Nyasaland, though better maintained than in some other colonial territories, had not been left entirely undisturbed. Kamwana's movement was evidence enough of this. The 1915 Rising, then, was not simply a temporary lapse in a placid record of mutual acceptance.

If the oblique approach is taken of recognizing why the Rising failed to achieve its aims, and was brought under control so quickly, its significance in wider Central African history may emerge. First of all, Chilembwe and his immediate adherents were 'marginal men' between the simple African village way of life and the complex European culture, which offered great opportunities at the cost of accepting frightening because unassessable risks. They were, as has been noted, confused in their aims : they wanted both to destroy and to preserve ; to stage both a demonstration and a revolution ; to assert a traditional dignity by martyrdom, and by the same activity to mould a new community. The ambivalence of their aim reflected itself in their organization,[9] with its mixture of short-term and long-term elements. Their very position on the bridge of transition between ways of life which had neither traditions nor prospects in common was responsible for their failure to understand the type of movement which, in a frustrated and incoherent way, they were creating. The Government, though slow to realize what was being built up around the Providence Industrial Mission, was well qualified to identify what had happened when the movement passed from the stage of conspiracy to that of insurrection. The Government had at its disposal the vast legacy of Imperial experience in India and elsewhere; while the disproportion in physical resources between the Chilembwe-ites and the Europeans made its success in repressing rebellious activity well-nigh inevitable.

It was clearly aware that it had at last met not simply primitive tribal revolt against alien rule,[10] but an organization which aimed to create what had always been foreseen with apprehension : a unity in opposition to European rule [11] that transcended the tribal and other divisions of the subject people. Yet it was this all-embracing inter-tribal aspiration of Chilembwe's movement which, as much as anything, caused it to fail; for in 1915 the majority of Nyasaland Africans were tribesmen first and foremost, disinclined to abandon customary associations and subordinations. Among those de-tribalized to some extent by education, most found security in attachment to a European person or a community that was un-questionably endowed by nature with European power and prestige, rather than by participating in the fortunes of a 'new man'. Many who agreed substantially with Chilembwe's grievances and others who admired his achievement in appropriating so much of the European endowment, were not prepared to be carried into armed rebellion against all that Chilembwe had come to regard with enmity. Their discontent with things as they were stopped short of attacking the system of government. To revolt was not only to profess ability to handle the new complexities of cash economy and wide territorial and international relations, but also to challenge immediate conflict with the power that had within living memory imposed its authority on the tribal chiefs, the fathers who were axiomatically better men than their children. That Chilembwe was able to inspire a measure of unity among adherents of different tribes was one of the most significant features of his achievement. But that measure of unity had neither the strength nor the range to arm him adequately against the British Administration. He lacked even the measure of force that the solid backing of one tribe would have conferred on him. He counted himself a Yao, and had made his initial appeal as missionary to that tribe on his return from the United States; but the Yao had never in living memory acted together as a tribe,[12] and none of their sectional chiefs had any desire to see himself sup-planted by a 'new man'.[13] The tribal notables preferred the rule of the British to whatever might emerge from Chilembwe's success. They knew the worst of British rule, and had accommodated them-selves to it. They had no means, other than a jealous suspicion,

THE RISING IN PERSPECTIVE

of assessing the other. The African population was, in fact, still politically heterogeneous, for little more than two decades of centralized rule by aliens could scarcely create much strong sense of membership of a quite artificially demarcated state. Thus the small African 'petty-bourgeoisie' in Nyasaland which owed its existence to the social example and requirements of the dominant Europeans, found it impracticable to enlist allies among the traditional reservoir of power in Africa, the self-conscious tribes. It had to rely mainly on what has been called 'the worst of all possible allies',[14] the violent, vacillating 'lumpenproletarians'[15]—in Nyasaland, the uprooted Nguru immigrant labourers. Furthermore, has any petty-bourgeoisie, whatever its racial composition, ever maintained its unity? The apparent defection of Chilembwe's lieutenant, John Gray Kufa, in the later stages of the Rising suggests that this question is applicable to Chilembwe's movement, and it should not be left out of account in speculations on what its achievement might have been.

Some of the disgruntled individuals who might have sided with Chilembwe in his outburst were probably dissuaded by recollection of the fate of earlier protest movements against European rule in Nyasaland : not merely the original tribal revolts against the first pressure of administrative discipline, but, more particularly, those movements which had derived their ideas and, in part, borrowed their tactics from the Europeans themselves. There can be little doubt that the summary treatment which the Nyasaland Government had meted out to Booth, which compelled him to reside outside the Protectorate after 1903, was noted by many Africans who had sympathized with his schemes and his standpoint. If an aggrieved Government could deal so brusquely and effectively with one of its own people, what might Africans expect who tried to walk in his footsteps? Notably, the determined deportation of Elliott Kamwana, with his anti-hut-tax policy and his anti-European ambitions, may probably have deterred potential supporters from openly siding with Chilembwe. It is quite possible that, if Kamwana and the Nyasaland African Watch Tower movement had not provoked various small-scale cautionary repressions between 1906 and 1909, John Chilembwe would have found a wider following in 1915, which in all probability would have included some of the Tonga, whose abstention, in spite of their presence as fellow labourers with the Nguru, has been noted in Chapter V ; for Kamwana had found a fruitful field in the Tonga country on the Lake Nyasa shore.

Yet a more probable reason for the abstention of the Tonga labourers from Chilembwe's movement springs from the fact that the Shire Highlands was not in their estimation part of their country. It was, like Rhodesia and South Africa, one of the places they resorted to for paid employment. It was for many of them simply a stage on the way to those more profitable fields. If there had been no such economic safety-valve allowing tribesmen, whose ambition and sense of earning-power chafed under the limited opportunities available in the Protectorate, to drain away out of the country, it is probable that they would have built up a considerable force of exasperation at the disposal of such a movement as Chilembwe's. But while Chilembwe's mission station was at the centre where the mobile labourers crossed, and often enough paused for a time, their mobility was such that the Tonga and the Ngoni (the majority of whom were Chewa and Chipeta serfs of Ngoni chieftains) and other incomers from the areas remote from European development never had time or opportunity to realize any unity that might have been organized to support a general movement. Against this background of a population poorly integrated, whose most efficient members had their eyes on distant fields of promise, the wonder is not that Chilembwe's movement failed, but that it ever found it possible to start.

Even so, once it had started, two other factors interfered with its success. First, the properly indigenous part of the population, the villagers who were descendants of the Mang'anja refugees in the hills from Yao slave-catchers, remembered enough of the old days of indecisive and recurrent wars to refuse to come out in support of such a dubious enterprise as that of challenging the power which controlled the army and the police. There is no evidence of any whole-hearted partisanship for the Government's interest, but the wait-and-see attitude of the tribal villagers deprived the Rising of that local support and encouragement which it needed as soon as it had come into the open. Secondly, the household staffs, and senior employees and adherents of the Europeans in the area, in the main stood by them. In part, they felt the attachment of long association ; in part, they saw that their interests were best served by that association ; and, in part, they were conscious of enjoying a relatively privileged position in the existing scheme of things that they were unlikely to be accorded in any revolutionary reorganization. They conveyed warnings, stood by abandoned households, and generally prevented the collapse of the visible pattern of European existence which would have been one of the most powerful assurances that Chilembwe had properly assessed the situation and had struck an effective opening blow.

But, above all, the Rising failed because it was too closely identified with Chilembwe as an individual. It was his weakness that the only positive emotional bond that he could provide for his supporters was that of personal friendship ; and that was prepotent only for those who lacked other social ties. This weakness might have been deduced from the relative isolation of the Providence Industrial Mission before 1915 ; but it only became apparent when tested by the demands of the Rising ; and when it was recognized by the Europeans, it could be employed deliberately in their activities of suppression. Chilembwe perhaps failed to assess realistically the general condition of Nyasaland, and took the concurrent views of other sufferers from European discourtesy, and other seekers in vain for a hearing for native protests and native points of view, as implying acceptance of his attack on the situation. The unstable alliance of such interests, which he was able to assemble out of the heterogeneous population which resorted or drifted to his independent settlement, broke up when he was compelled to go into concealment as a fugitive, and was finally killed. When the personal centre of the association was removed, it could no longer exist.

It will be seen, then, in these reasons for the failure of the Rising, that it marked the emergence of the spokesman for the angry discontent of those who had no longer a tribe to give them an effective voice ; but neither those detribalized by entry into civilized activities and ambitions, nor the immigrant or mobile manual labourers, were as yet able to see any ground for perseverance or indeed for acceptance of direction and discipline, beyond the luck of the leader. The leader himself was sensitive enough to realize what an accumulation of discontent existed, as it were, in parallel with his own increasing sense of outrage ; but he did not allow sufficiently for the underlying sense of the compensating benefits of European rule, in spite of all its drawbacks, that was present in the minds of many whose support he needed. Probably, like any sensitive person, Chilembwe was incapable of estimating the deadening force of sheer inertia on most people ; and he certainly assumed too readily that African suspicion was concentrated on non-Africans : so far, at least, Hetherwick was justified in denying that Chilembwe's movement was a 'Native

Rising', in the sense that the Europeans feared and Chilembwe initially hoped. But it did mark the beginning of a stage at which the native population would realize that the future offered more possibilities than the alternatives of helplessly accepting whatever, good or bad, the Europeans might offer, or of returning to tribal allegiances. It provided the 'new men' with an example of action, a pattern of practicability, and a martyr ; and it shocked a thoughtless group of the Europeans into considering their ways, and into recognizing that the Africans could not simply be taken for granted.

Some aspects of this reassessment of African feeling deserve more detailed examination. While the independent African churches were regarded with distrust, it was not because they were thought of as centres where tribal antagonisms would be sunk and common supra-tribal aspirations developed. It was felt, rather, that such a dangerous role would be played by Islam. Throughout the nineteenth century Great Britain had been learning in its social laboratory of imperialism, India, that Islam was a revolutionary faith. The attempt to restore the Mogul Empire through the great Mutiny of 1857–8 was simply the most notable of a series of outbreaks, of which the Moplah risings from 1836 to 1896 in Malabar are typical.[16] At the end of the century the Islamic messiah, the Mahdi, Mohammed Ahmed, had given the Sudanese tribesmen 'the enthusiasm they lacked' [17] to make common cause against Egyptian domination, and had cost Britain, as Egypt's guardian, over thirteen million pounds in money, the lives of two thousand officers and men, and seven thousand invalids, to overthrow the movement.[18] General Gordon's death at Khartoum, publicized as that of a Christian hero, had reawakened in Protestants the traditional Catholic sense of the eternal enmity of Cross and Crescent. Gordon himself had drawn attention to the social revolutionary aspect of Islam when he wrote of Mahdism that it was 'a question of property, and is more like Communism under the flag of religion'.[19] Africa offered the most promising field for this threatening infection of militant religion.[20] Sudanese Mahdism was the most virulent case, but there were others. In Nyasaland the Muslim Arab [21] and Yao slavers had fought stubborn wars to repel the imposition of British rule ; though it was not to be forgotten that the Arab Jumbe of Kota-Kota,[22] obedient, as his co-religionists were not, to the Sultan of Zanzibar, by his alliance with the British had helped considerably to bring about their victory. In the early twentieth century a new Mahdi in Somaliland, the so-called

'Mad Mullah',[23] was able to maintain forces of fierce nomads in long and successful campaigns which painfully embarrassed the British Empire—and supplied the 2nd (Nyasaland) Battalion of the King's African Rifles with its historic tragedy, when one of its companies was ambushed and completely wiped out.[24] The British apprehensiveness that Islam might inspire and unite the separate tribes in her colonial territories was so apparent that Germany had no hesitation in encouraging the pan-Islamic movement, and in using agents to stir up trouble wherever a basis of Islam could be discovered.

In Nyasaland this Islamic basis went back to the pre-European days of the slave trade, and it was reasonable for the Europeans to expect that their power would be challenged from that quarter, anti-European and insubordinate by religious prescription, and smarting from the overthrow of a way of life satisfactory and profitable in its time. The Nyasaland Government might naturally consider that the ferment of reformism and sectarianism which was stirring so much else of the Islamic world would spread to Nyasaland.[25] Indeed, as has already been noted,[26] it may have been that which for so long prevented officials, and influential and informed missionary-statesmen like Hetherwick, from noticing the real threat to European government that was growing in the work of John Chilembwe and the African independent churches.

Warnings about Islamic aggression were common in the territory's missionary literature. In 1900 the Livingstonia missionaries, working in the area of the last stubborn stand of the Arabs, concluded that a general native rising in the Protectorate under the Muslim banner was possible.[27] The Anglicans working at the permanent Muslim centres of Kota-Kota and Mponda's spoke constantly of this possibility, and were particularly explicit in 1905, perhaps in view of the Muslim elements in the unexpected and staggering Maji-Maji revolt in the German territory between them and their mother diocese of Zanzibar.[28] Two years later the Blantyre missionaries noted the social factors which might inspire such a rising, in discussing *Chinasala*, a term which might denote either the Swahili language, or 'a spurious kind of Mohammedanism' which would pander to the aspiring African's ego by giving him a quickly obtained status higher than that possessed by 'the common run of the natives'.[29] But what they did not take into account was that, although the Turkish Revolution and Egyptian independence movements were in the air and promised modern types of Islamic culture, yet, for aspiring Africans of the Chilembwe type, Islam was identified with a non-technical civilization which offered none of the power and comforts to be had from acquiring the civilization of the Christian West. Nevertheless, in Central African history, Islam had first offered a way of advance beyond rigid tribalism, and still provided a possible alternative for the African who sought some status or dignity *vis-à-vis* the European. It is impossible to say how many of Chilembwe's fellow Yao had found in Islamic profession a mode of asserting that discontent with the European order which others found in membership of separatist churches. Yet the traditional Yao association with the Coast and the Islamic outposts there [30] clearly supplies another reason, in addition to sectionalism and jealousy, for the lack of support for Chilembwe from his father's tribe.

On the eve of the War, all the colonial Powers were apprehensive of Muslim risings, and lay and clerical observers of Nyasaland's affairs agreed in pointing to the danger.[31] But Chilembwe's movement, the agency which did, in fact, realize to some extent the Islamic threat of uniting tribesmen in revolt, was one which, though troublesome, had been in the eyes of most Europeans a much less potent danger to their dominion. From their own angle the Germans seem to have shared the common expectation, for the letter to Chilembwe from the 'judge' at Tunduru addresses him as 'sultan',[32] as if assuming him to be a Muslim. And from another angle one of the strange consequences of the Rising was, on the witness of the Blantyre Mission's paper, that 'it made many natives take up Islam, lest the faintest suspicion of having been influenced by [Christian] missions might lead to the same difficulties as the rioters'.[33] How far this apparent increase in the number of even nominal Muslims suited the German policy is hard to say; but there is evidence that in pursuance of the design of directing Islam against the Allies,[34] the Germans had infiltrated African agents into Nyasaland. Non-officials, as well as Government, were concerned about this,[35] and the *Beira Post* of 16 February 1915 put the point as part of its criticism of the local character of the Commission of Inquiry into the Chilembwe Rising, when it linked that incident with the question of a Muslim 'fifth column' working against European rule in Central and East Africa :

... the general seriousness of the affair in its inception at this juncture ... and the underlying question of the Jehad [the Muslim Holy

War against unbelievers] renders a more general inquiry than one of local origin essential.

Towards the end of 1915 there were scares, the more readily entertained in view of the recent Chilembwe affair, of Islamic risings in both southern and northern Nyasaland;[36] and in July of that year a missionary of the U.M.C.A. reported 'much talk of the coming of Mzilima [a sort of Mohammedan messiah-mahdi]'.[37] In 1916, when the outcome of the Inquiry into the Rising was being debated, the discovery of a letter from Count Falkenstein, commander of the German forces on the Nyasaland borders, 'to a certain Mwalimu Isa who exercised great influence on the large Mohammedan population living on both sides of the British Portuguese border near Lake Nyasa',[38] raised uneasiness to a new height. The letter asked for the names of Ngoni who, like Chimtunga of Mombera's district, or the few who followed Chilembwe, refused to support the British war effort. The scare was apparently over by August of 1916;[39] but until the end of the war and later the missionaries, at least, continued to point to Islamic dangers.[40] Yet their apprehensions were ideological rather than political, for by the end of 1916 the local tide of war had clearly turned against the Germans, and the subversive adherents of Islam had lost all hope of effective support.[41] The divisions of Nyasaland's African society which derived from diverse origins and traditions, and from complicated and internally conflicting patterns of alliances with and against the European order, had overcome another potential unifying factor in opposition to that order.

But though it is now apparent that Chilembwe's movement is not unique as an attempt to work on a supra-tribal level, this must not obscure its importance as a stage in that development. There had been earlier alliances in British Central Africa between tribal units and the heterogeneous bands of henchmen who followed the Coast slavers, in the latter years of the nineteenth century: for example the 'concerted plan' of the three Yao chiefs Zarafi, Kawinga, and Matipwiri, who controlled the slave road which rounded the south end of Lake Nyasa and passed the bottlenecks at either end of the precipices of Mount Mlanje. They allied themselves with Nguru from beyond Mlanje to drive out the British and open the road again.[42] The last stand of Mlozi's Arabs in 1895 had been in alliance with the Bemba of what is now Northern Rhodesia.[43] But such alliances were purely temporary matters of convenience, with no intention or prospect of enduring beyond their immediate purpose. It is not misleading, then, to say that Chilembwe's was the first Central African resistance to European control which looked to the future, not to the past, and which did not assume that tribal potentates, whether by inheritance or by usurpation, would head the new state. He did not propose to reject or destroy the traditional order, since he sought the support of the headmen who were his neighbours at Zomba and Mlanje, and of certain sections of the nearly monarchical Ngoni—though, if he had succeeded, he would probably have had the usual experience of combining new wine and old wine-skins. Nevertheless, the prospect for which Chilembwe began to fight was one of founding a nation rather than of restoring the fortunes of the tribes. It is true that Kamwana's movement, though relying mainly on the Lake-shore Tonga, included other tribesmen, and this deserves more attention than it has been given as a link between the old resistance and the new, and as an important incident in the growth of Ethiopianism in Africa.[44] But, on the whole, Kamwana's effort was akin to the tribal reactions of the past. It lacked the secrecy and sense of wide purpose which marked the movement that grew out of the first Providence Industrial Mission; and it was of John Chilembwe, not Elliott Kamwana, that an African informant said: 'He was not of one tribe, but for all tribes'.

There is little possibility of doubt that Chilembwe himself felt this. The symbolical character of the decapitation of William Jervis Livingstone has already been noticed. He and his two assistants at Magomero were not the first white men to suffer violence at the hands of Africans in Nyasaland. In the days before the Protectorate a brother of Cecil Rhodes, who had entered the country with the Elton expedition of 1878, was burned to death in a hut at Liwonde's village on the upper Shire in 1880. In spite of assertions that it was simple accident,[45] the incident remains mysterious, and stories are handed down that it was a deliberate act of native revenge. In 1884 George Fenwick, who had come to the country with the Blantyre Mission and subsequently became a trader, having killed the Makololo chief, Chipatula, when both were in liquor and were arguing over a commercial dispute, was run down and speared to death by the chief's people, who thereafter cut off his head.[46] Even when it had become obvious that European control had strong backing, John Buchanan, while acting as Consul and head of the British community, had been held and whipped at the orders of Makanjira, a

Yao slaving chief; [47] and at the end of the century two unscrupulous European traders had been attacked by Ngoni sufferers from their double-dealing and rape.[48]   Other examples might be quoted, but, in all of them, a local tribal group was avenging a tribally felt injury. The point has been made [49] that the Magomero tragedy was due to a vendetta between Chilembwe and Livingstone.   Yet if one compares it with Fenwick's affair, while Chipatula's successor went on to demand the surrender of Fenwick's wife, Chilembwe with his enemy's whole household at his mercy was careful to provide for their safety.   Chilembwe struck only where the necessities of his war compelled him.   It is a further significant point in determining the Rising's place in Nyasaland's history.

Now, what of the feature that is most commonly connected with the Chilembwe Rising : its expression of African resentment over the complex land situation in the Shire Highlands with its vexed question of the rights of African tenants and European managers on private estates ?   It has been apparent in previous chapters that the Rising was in part a reaction to economic changes as the territory developed ;   nevertheless, the matter of European land-holding, involving a complicated superstructure of labour inducements, discipline, and grievances, has been given undue predominance in analyses of the movement.   Every African reaction anywhere to the introduction of European regulation and settlement has had some reference to land questions ;   but, in this particular instance, that factor has been allowed to overlay the many other elements which were of particular significance : the attempts to 'organize the unorganizable' under the leadership of Africans who had dipped quite deeply into the new, European education ; its connection with the African church separatist movements, with their strange ramifications in South Africa and as far afield as America ;   and the above-noted inter-tribal outlook and emergence of 'new men' as authorities.

A further disregarded factor which deserves attention was Chilembwe's consistent opposition to Africans becoming embroiled in the white man's wars.   From his objection, shortly after his return from the United States, to the use of Nyasaland troops in the Ashanti and Somaliland campaigns, this broadened into a clear manifesto against their employment in the African campaigns of the Great War in the interest of what the Europeans had demarcated for them as their country.   As this point has an obvious importance for the general history of relations between Africans and European administrations, it will be considered more fully when an attempt is made to estimate the significance of the Chilembwe movement for Negro history in general. But, at this stage, it may be pointed out that in the Central African territories overt resistance to participation in the 1914 war was offered by about forty so-called African Watch Tower preachers in Rhodesia, who asserted that war was anti-Christian and were imprisoned for their principles;[50] and a Ngoni chief, Chimtunga, objected to soldiers and military transport carriers being recruited from his people. But Chilembwe's attitude was probably more deeply considered than these.

It was this basis of conviction, derived from deep and long consideration, that marked Chilembwe's movement as something new in Central African resistance. All former movements of African resistance to European rule had aimed at recovering old conditions rather than at creating new ways of life. The Arabs had sought to preserve free hunting-grounds for slavers and their Yao satellites to continue in enjoyment of the irresponsible profits and prestige of middlemen in the business. The Ngoni, whose commoners were a motley crew of diverse origins, looked to the Zulu ancestors of their chiefs, the robber-kings Shaka and Zongendaba, as patterns for their ideal future. The handful of Makololo chiefs thought nostalgically of the days when, as 'friends of the British' who appeared only on occasional expeditions, and as sophisticated gun-men, they had lorded it over the tribes of the lower Shire Valley. Kamwana's glimpse into the future, as he sought to inspire his first Watch Tower adherents, did not look beyond destruction : 'The Government will go . . . we shall build our own ships [ships on the Lake were gun-boats or potential gun-boats.—AUTHORS], make our own powder ; import our own guns'.[51] Chilembwe's ideas may have been utopian ; they may have sprung up in a soil of insecurity, and have grown in the atmosphere of the African independent church movement which is fitly expressed in the slogan *Kairos*, 'the due season [is here]' ;[52] and they may have borne their fruit in action dictated by despairing frustration. But, at their heart, there was a solid matter-of-fact element that was constructively forward-looking, and kept for the most part within the bounds of practical, even if remote, possibility. This detached Chilembwe from vain dreams of the past, and set him in a central position in the new, non-tribal way of life which was developing.

African strivings towards this new way of life were already taking three forms in Nyasaland. First, there was the purely individual reaction, open to capable and adventurous spirits : escaping from the home situation, temporarily or permanently. Mostly, this took the line of trekking overland to the Rhodesias or South Africa, though it had been extended by some to making their way as far afield as America. Among the numerous Nyasaland expatriates there were individuals who rose to considerable prominence : Daniel Malekebu, who grew up in Chilembwe's fold, left it in 1907, secured medical qualifications at Selma University in Alabama and Meharry Medical College,[53] and was able to return to Nyasaland in 1926 to re-establish the Providence Industrial Mission ; [54] Clements Kadalie, the Tonga teacher of the Livingstonia Mission who went away from the Protectorate in 1915, and by 1919 had founded in the Cape the Industrial and Commercial Workers' Union, the first modern labour union amongst South African native workers, which convulsed the whole labour scene between 1919 and 1926 and caused a Cabinet crisis ; [55] Hastings K. Banda, a Livingstonia pupil who left home in 1915, worked his way through South Africa to America, took one medical qualification, came on to Britain and took another (which made him the first Nyasaland African to hold full British medical qualifications), and played a leading part in the agitation against Central African Federation in the early 1950's ; [56] Peter Nyambo, Booth's follower, who had taken the 1914 anti-war petition to Britain, and remained out of Nyasaland for twenty-seven years ; [57] and J. G. Phillips, who founded the 'Holy Catholic Apostolic Church in Zion',[58] one of the main African secessionist churches in South Africa. The many expatriates who made no such mark in history are simply, to those with whom they work, 'the Nyasas' or 'Blantyres', of good reputation among employers. But in the country which they have left they are *machona*, 'the lost legion', many of whom never return. Chilembwe, with his independent stay in America, pioneered the way and its possibilities for all of them.

Secondly, African organization in Nyasaland has assumed the form of religious separatism, often with a distinctly political air : the new Providence Industrial Mission, the African Church of Christ, the African Methodist Episcopal Church, the African Presbyterian Church,[59] the Watch Tower congregations both regular and independent,[60] and many others. Several of these bodies have been objects of official and unofficial suspicion. Some have broken the bounds of permitted self-expression and have caused 'disturbances', like Wilfred Good and the 'Sons of God' in Cholo, and the African Seventh Day Baptists at Mlanje in 1938.[61] Others have had a transcendental kind of air about them ; for example, the universalist type of church which Peter Nyambo founded when, as an old man, he returned to Nyasaland in 1943, preaching, in the spirit of the teachings of Sri Ramakrishna, a conception of the best that is to be found in all religions. Some endeavours which have not taken the title of 'church' seem to have affinities with independent African religious movements in general ; for example, the *mcapi* movement of the mid-1930's, which professed to control the witchcraft which, it was asserted, found fresh room to flourish in European-regulated Africa.[62] In general, as the Nyasaland disturbances of 1953 indicated,[63] all forms of African political organization in the Protectorate tend to express themselves in Christian forms : Bible quotation, prayer at meetings, and a general pulpiteering structure of activities to secure effective action. Here too Chilembwe, from the time in 1895–6 when he was helping Booth to organize the first independent church in the country,[64] to the day when Government forces blew up his brick church at Mbombwe as a measure of suppression, was laying foundations which have endured.

In the third type of organization adopted by disquieted Nyasaland Africans the religious element is not prominent. These organizations are bodies which have modelled themselves on the more secular sort of European association. Clements Kadalie's South African Industrial and Commercial Workers' Union, founded far from Nyasaland but nevertheless in the country with the greatest number of separatist African churches, was professedly secular :

> The I.C.U. . . . . regards religion as a purely private matter concerning members individually. Personally I do not subscribe to any religious doctrine in the generally accepted sense of the term. In the words of Ingersoll, 'The world is my country, and to do good is my religion', and it seems to me that my life can be more usefully employed in endeavouring to improve the lot of my fellow-creatures here than bothering about a chimerical life above.[65]

Kadalie, however, paid tribute to 'the good missionaries in Nyasaland who taught me that all men were equal and their lives valuable' [66] as an important source of his radicalism, while he toyed with the extreme Left in European politics. This isolation and approval of Christian social doctrines permitted such secular bodies, whose literate members had perforce been associated with Christian missions in a period when no other instructors in literate skills were available, to retain an occasional tinge of religious expression and procedure, and some claim to 'respectability'. Yet some of these organizations were (and are) strongly suspect to the authorities; in 1927, for example, one of Kadalie's people in Nyasaland was imprisoned for distributing the radical literature of the Union; [67] but others, such as the 'self-help' organizations which grew up after the Great War, were safely respectable. One such was the Mombera Native Association, formed in 1920, with the constitution :

1. *Aim* : The aim of the Association is neither directly nor indirectly to subvert the authority of the Government, or any lawful establishments ; nor to induce the community to do so. It is rather one of the helpful means of developing the country, in the hands of the two necessary connecting links—the Government and the Governed. Being Natives of the country, and acquainted with all the habits and customs of the people, it could adequately express their desires and needs to the Government ; and being educated, it could fully explain the mind of the Government to the people.

2. *Order and Industry* : It aims at making the people understand the necessity and value of order, and at the importance of becoming law-abiding citizens ; and also the necessity and value of industrious labour, and in short the value of civilization as against ignorance, laziness, disloyalty and anarchy.[68]

Between this cautious type of association, acceptable to the authorities it engaged to support, and the disreputable Kadalie type of defiant trade-unionism, there were bodies like the Nyasaland African Congress (whose origins, it is suggested, may be traced as far back as 1912,[69] and which was obviously influenced, as its name indicates, by the South African Native National Congress that was constituted in that year) and expatriate organizations such as the Nyasaland Native National Association which was created in South Africa in 1920 [70] to embrace the migrant workers in mines and industries. Livingstonia Mission, and particularly the Overtoun Institute for advanced education, founded in 1894 at Kondowe, its head station, was the seed-bed from which grew Kadalie's enterprise, the Nyasaland African Congress,[71] and the Mombera Native Association. Most of those more secular organizations were founded by, and seem mainly to have appealed to, 'second-generation' mission adherents. Kadalie was born, for example, in 1896, about a quarter-century after Chilembwe, and twenty years after the establishment of the pioneer mission stations in Nyasaland. But the first generation had shown the way : as, for example, in the African Industrial Society formed at the P.I.M. centre in 1911—surely the prototype of native self-help associations in the Protectorate. Chilembwe's own concern with such non-evangelistic matters as dress and deportment, labour conditions of the people in general, the welfare and dignity of women, and his anti-militarism, link him with the secular interests of the later bodies, respectable and disreputable alike.

As a result his memory has lived on among them, a symbol of achievement and frustration, hope and disappointment, courage and sacrifice. To many Africans he is the chief of the detribalized, who clarified the conflict which they cannot escape : his death marked the end of an episode which showed not that the European Powers were right, but that they were too strong to be forced. But many Africans deny that he is dead. To the simple, he is a liberator who will come again ; to those who, like him, have emerged from courses of education which have given them wider knowledge and a sense of criticism, his career is taken as an example of achievement. They are aware of Chilembwe's final insurrection as an understandable conclusion to his career, in his particular circumstances, at the same time as they recognize that those circumstances were of his own time, and that his fate is not laid on all who share his starting-point.

Chilembwe has his place in the record of the emergence of a concept and sentiment of African Nyasaland nationality.[72] Only at first did he include the tribal name *Ajawa* (Yao) in the title of his mission.[73] In his later writings he uses wider territorial expressions such as 'Nyasaland' in speaking of the African people of the Protectorate. Chilembwe's anti-War statement which preceded the actual outbreak in the restricted and special area of the Bruce Estates, had clearly national implications, and he signed it 'on behalf of his countrymen'. His conception of Nyasaland nationality was not multi-racial, though he apparently considered that the state which would emerge from a successful rising would accommodate some Europeans as mentors and specialists. When discussing in 1911 the African Industrial Society, he had criticized the Indian traders for sending the money they made out of the country, thus depriving the community of capital. It is unlikely that he regarded them as potentially full members of his state.

Whatever communication Chilembwe had with the Germans

seems to have led them to regard him as a national rather than tribal representative; and, as the Commission of Inquiry found: 'it was part of his scheme to form a union between their various sects [the African independent churches] and his own mission'.[74] Chilembwe may have had some inkling of the role that a national church can have in creating national feeling. Furthermore, the place of expatriates in the European revolutions of 1848 offers an interesting parallel with the activity of the returned expatriate Chilembwe, and the prominence of other expatriates and socially rootless immigrants in his movement. It is a commonplace that residence abroad breeds a feeling for home which over-rides the sectional antagonisms of those who have known no life but that of the land of their origin. In both of these respects, in Chilembwe's groping towards a national church and in his typification of expatriate nationalism, there is the suggestion that events in Nyasaland followed a pattern familiar in European history. Thus, while the Rising failed to elicit much national response there was an element of nationalism in its ideology and composition.

The native people of Nyasaland have no myth, like that of the old civilization of the Ghana kingdom which inspires much communal self-confidence, on which to rest a claim to national dignity and in which to find emotional satisfaction. The nearest parallel, the 'empire' south of the Zambezi of that Monomotapa, 'Lord of the Goldfields', with whom the Portuguese made a treaty in the seventeenth century, seems too remote to appeal to Africans who live north of the river and in lands where no mines exist. The memory of Chilembwe, then, may be utilized in the creation of such a myth, for his story is still alive, and growing. It survived—perhaps was fostered by—the way in which discussion of him was discouraged in Nyasaland after the Rising. The facts grew dim in a mist of embroidery, on the whole laudatory and awe-inspiring among the Africans, trivializing and derogatory among the Europeans.[75] Much of the European view was no doubt due to disappointment of the hope that as the tribal cultures yielded to civilized training and example the native population would behave with progressive docility. The Rising of some of the least savage men in the country opened up a vista of dilemma, whether to leave savagery untouched, with all its economic fecklessness and narrow social range, or to educate more Chilembwes. Christian education was no guarantee of peace, for it was apparent that the African Christian would be no more inhibited on political issues than the European Christian had been in the course of his tumultuous history, and no more ready to be content with only a spiritual endowment. The Rising served notice that the quite real virtues of paternalism would not excite gratitude enough to swamp the demands of emergent Africans for adult rights and privileges. Chilembwe appeared, in the eyes of many Europeans, a classic example of the relapse into savagery and superstition which inevitably awaits the African who is given the authority and responsibility of a clergyman.[76] It is not to be wondered at that some Europeans after the Rising read John Buchan's South African novel *Prester John* more as prophecy than fiction.

One of the more colourful additions to the European legend of Chilembwe is the persistent assertion that he was an adherent of the Watch Tower movement. In previous chapters it has been shown that such a belief ignores what this actually teaches, and that the real exponent of that teaching in Nyasaland was not Chilembwe, but Kamwana.[77] Yet Chilembwe is spoken of as the centre of a vast Watch Tower conspiracy which has been behind practically every disturbance in Central Africa : in the Rhodesias from the Mwana Lesa movement of the 1920's [78] to the Copper Belt riots of the middle 1930's ; [79] in Tanganyika in the early 1920's ; [80] and, above all, in the Belgian Congo from the Simon Kimbangu 'Prophet' troubles after the First World War, through the emergence of the Kitawala (the Ngwana rendering of 'tower') or African Watch Tower movement, to the outbreaks during the Second World War and after.[81] In 1936 a Belgian senator in a debate on the Congo budget expressly linked Chilembwe, Kimbangu, and Watch Tower together as proof of the political danger of permitting scope to Protestant missions, very much in the manner of Archdeacon Glossop on the 1916 Commission of Inquiry.[82] The Nyasa dispersion to wherever industrial wages could be earned—even into the Belgian Congo [83]—gives the wide canvas on which such fanciful pictures can be painted ; but the demonstrable fact is that Chilembwe had no more connection with the Watch Tower than was imposed on him by the adherence of a few Africans who may have been influenced at some point by millenarian teaching.[84]

If Nyasaland's neighbours want to learn from the Rising, it is not to be regarded as a centre of infection from which otherwise contented subjects continue to contract sedition, but as a case record by which to assess clinically the nature and probable course of discontents which arise at least primarily within their own boundaries, from sources within their control. At this stage, then, we may attempt to sketch, not only for Central Africa but for Negro history as a whole, the application of the Rising as a clue to developments which are apt to be either over-simplified or given up as incomprehensible. As Norman Leys realized when in 1924 he used it to illumine his analysis of nascent African political organization in Kenya, Chilembwe's story has wide applications.

2. THE CHILEMBWE MOVEMENT AND NEGRO HISTORY

With a few exceptions, notice of the Rising, its leader, and the Providence Industrial Mission which provided its base and headquarters, has been confined to contemporary records of institutions directly affected, and to later publications of reminiscences. More detached studies draw heavily on two sources : the findings of the 1916 Commission, which, since they were published at Zomba, are not readily available ; and Leys's pioneer analysis, which is in many ways still the best. But as he used his account 'as a footnote to the analysis of the situation in Kenya',[85] employment of this source has often had the effect of bracketing the two situations.[86] Attention is concentrated on the common factors, and the larger territory's interest tends to overshadow any that may be aroused by one of the smallest and poorest British dependencies. In the hectic context of violent settler agitations in Kenya, the menace of Indian immigration, and the issue of closer union with the other East African territories, it was remarkable that the Chilembwe affair was noticed even as a footnote.

Even in literature, which might be expected to be particularly interested, that of anti-Imperialism and labour agitation, it has very often been overlooked. For example, *The Life and Struggles of Negro Toilers*, by the West Indian writer Mr. George Padmore, published in 1931 for the Red International of Labour Unions (Profintern), traces in detail forms of Negro resistance to European rule in Africa and across the Atlantic, but does not mention anything about the Rising.[87] One of its first appearances in such literature was in *A History of Negro Revolt* (London, 1938) by another West Indian journalist, C. L. R. James,[88] and this time it was linked with the Belgian Congo Kimbangu agitations. As the 1915 Rising has

418

often been treated simply as an appendage to discussion of Kenya affairs, so Nyasaland Ethiopianism has frequently been treated in subordination to the African 'Prophet' movements which worry the Belgian authorities and the Roman Catholic church in the Congo. German writers, on the other hand, lacking immediate colonial concern, have dealt with it in a more detached spirit. From Julius Richter's *Geschichte der evangelischen Mission in Afrika* of 1922 [89] to Dr. Katesa Schlosser's comprehensive *Propheten in Afrika* of 1949,[90] they give due independent weight to the socio-religious aspects of Ethiopianism in Nyasaland. Oskar Karstedt and Peter von Werder, publishing *Die afrikanische Arbeiterfrage* in 1941 under the Nazi régime, link it with criticism of British land regulation ('. . . der Landfrage in religiösen Motiven . . .'),[91] a useful counter to assertions that it was Germany alone that had oppressed African peasants.

Thus it would appear that when writers after 1915–16 have noticed the Chilembwe movement, the tendency, on the whole, has been to be interested in it less for its own sake—for its colourful story, its particular place in British Central African history—and more for its use as a standard of comparison with other African movements of socio-religious discontent and with phases of general European colonial policy. Although such attention has tended to smother research into the Rising's specific detail by drawing on a few convenient sources such as Leys or the 1916 Commission's Report, nevertheless it has, if only in a small way, kept alive some interest in the place which the Chilembwe movement occupies in general Negro history.

Writers who have compared the Nyasaland Native Rising of 1915 with other outbreaks have pointed out that it was not supported by a tribe or headed by a tribal leader, as were most of the earlier African resistance movements. Leys spoke of it as '. . . a new kind of unrest . . . with other leaders than tribal authorities and other motives than tribal independence'.[92] The echo of this in James's brief *History of Negro Revolt* is unmistakable : 'In 1915 we have a new type [of rising]—a rising led not by a tribal chief but by a Negro who has had some education'.[93] In so saying, such writers had in mind movements like the Zulu wars in South Africa which culminated in the Bambata Rebellion of 1906 ; in Southern Rhodesia, the Matebele War of 1893 and the later Mashona-Matebele Rebellion of 1896 ; in German East Africa, the fierce Chagga and

Hehe wars in the early 1890's, and the fighting in German South-West Africa which came to a head in the major military operation of the Herero Rebellion of 1903–7 ; the 'little wars' with the Sultan of Witu, and with Kamba, Kikuyu, and Nandi tribesmen in East Africa, with Kabarega of Bunyoro in Uganda, and, as has been noticed, with Yao and Ngoni chiefs in Nyasaland ; and, perhaps, lesser known movements in Portuguese territories such as the Bailundu war of 1902 and the 1913–15 Buta revolt in Angola.[94] One of the last of such tribal risings was an interesting but little-known outbreak of the lower Zambezia Tonga (a people quite distinct from the 'plateau Tonga' of the Rhodesian Zambezi and from the Lake-shore Tonga so frequently mentioned in this book), who were brought out against the Portuguese by Chief Makombe in 1917.[95]

By the time of the Great War it had become apparent that tribal organization had not the political or military strength to react effectively against European domination. A new type of revolt, for those Africans who might look to such a method of attacking their difficulties, was needed : one led, not by traditional chiefs followed by their own henchmen, but by men with a reputation for their success in following European ways, who were able to lay equal claim to support from people of all tribes. Here Chilembwe's movement marks a new stage in action. Yet it has to be remembered that the break was less sharp than may appear. Two earlier movements, at least, had overridden tribal divisions to considerable effect. The Mahdist revolt in the Sudan had the effective support of desert nomads and riverain pastoralists, of Arabic-speaking Muslims and pagan Nilotes ; and in German East Africa the majority of the people of the Southern Province between Lake Nyasa and the sea took part in the Maji-Maji Rebellion.[96] This took its name from the battle-cry *Maji, Maji* ('Water' or perhaps 'The Water'), reminding the insurgents both that they were serving a pagan water-snake spirit whose prophets had incited the first acts of defiance, and that they were protected by a water-medicine which turned enemies' bullets to water as they flew. The semi-official *Handbook of Tanganyika* asserts that the rebellion 'was chiefly remarkable for the combined effort of a number of tribes, for while it was never doubted that any one tribe might at any time give trouble, concerted action by many tribes was generally considered to be out of the question'.[97] Closer study in the field, however, indicates that the profusion of sectional names in the area gives a rather misleading picture of tribal diversity,[98] and that the Maji-Maji Rebellion in fact appealed mainly to members of the widespread Ngindo linguistic and cultural unit. The Tanganyika Ngoni split on the issue, the eastern section whose commoner stratum was of Ngindo-Ndendeuli origin rebelling, while the westerners rejected appeals from the Maji-Maji leaders. The old recalcitrants, the Hehe and the Yao, remained quiet. Nevertheless Maji-Maji marks an advance beyond the enforced unification by a despotic war-leader, or the stultifying mutual jealousies of tribal neighbours, which had set the patterns of African revolt up to that time.

Yet, in another respect, Chilembwe differed from the Mahdi and the Maji-Maji leaders. They revolted against the whole new and alien system of European rule. He, on the other hand, was protesting forcibly as a last resort, against those features only which seemed to him a betrayal of the promise of the first European emissaries, that the Africans who accepted their training and direction would enjoy the fruits of civilization which were displayed in everyday European life.

In this record of violent African reaction the mutinies of African troops in European service are not to be overlooked. A good example is the mutiny of Sudanese elements in the British Uganda forces in 1897.[99] Such movements often took place amongst men of different tribes. But, where they were anything more than the embittered protest of men unaccustomed to sustained discipline, and exasperated by poor conditions, they aimed at making predatory use of their acquired fighting power and equipment once they had destroyed or escaped from their European commanders to return to the old tribal way of life ; or, as in the example of the ambitious group of Muslim Sudanese officers who conceived the idea of supplanting the British as rulers of Uganda in 1897,[100] envisaged no type of government very much different from what they had always known. Yet the fact that they broke out against officers who often enough were popular with their men, and that former mutineers returned to discipline equably enough after due punishment of the 'ring-leaders', suggests that in many pre-Chilembwe African revolts there has been a conservative function, if not always purpose ; and that we have to take account of what Professor Max Gluckman has identified as 'the rebellious structure of [a] type of stationary society',[101] which he has suggested is characteristic of many traditional African societies. Most, if not all, East, Central, and South African native risings before 1915—and probably many West African ones too [102]—which had inter-tribal elements in them were, it seems, of this type.

The more strictly regulated tribal societies permitted expressions of hostility to chiefs which in practice ensured that ordinary men and women could feel that they had asserted themselves, but yet did not affect the chiefly authority in anything that mattered. Neither civil nor military regulation under European rule allowed for such a safety-valve, partly because those concerned had forgotten the classical lesson of the Roman Saturnalia ; partly because of a not unjustified feeling that a subject people, given an inch, may take an ell. This repressed self-assertion no doubt helped to excite support for Chilembwe's deviation into violence, but it is not likely to have inspired his own attitude of revolt. He wanted, not the continuance of any established society which he had known, but a new African society. Many of his ideas had been formed in the United States, where the white man's world was most dynamic. Like another passing sojourner in a new world, the American writer Lincoln Steffens who visited Russia in the utopian days just after the decisive successes of the 1917 Revolution, Chilembwe had seen the future, and it worked !

For all this, he was no career politician, though again he may be regarded as a prototype of that class which since 1945 has changed so conspicuously the political complexion of the African dependencies. His politics, his simple journalism, his activities in organizing Africans, were all part of his role as leader of an independent African church. Despite some useful studies [103] and the spate of books and articles deriving from the Mau-Mau outbreak, the close connection which often exists between membership of independent African churches and anti-European political activity has not been fully explored ; but two points are unlikely to be set aside : first, that an independent outlook in one sphere is likely to be carried over into the other ; and second, that John Chilembwe's movement, with its ramifications which reach back to Joseph Booth's arrival in British Central Africa in 1892, has an important place in the history of the relationship between African politics and churches.

In tracing the growth of Chilembwe's mission and the background of the Rising in previous chapters, something has been said of its connection with other Negro independent church movements. But a recapitulation of these points, and the addition of a few new ones, may make clearer Chilembwe's place in the socio-political history of

African independent churches. His heritage goes back to the beginnings of Negro congregations among the plantation slave labour in predominantly Protestant America, and ultimately to the 'social sources of denominationalism' [104] in Western Christendom. The effective starting-point, however, may be found in George Lisle, a former Virginia slave who went to Jamaica in 1783 as a Baptist missionary and set up the first Negro dissenting chapel there. From that time Baptists, and especially Negro Baptists, were linked with all emancipatory movements amongst the slaves in Jamaica and elsewhere.[105] More than once they were imprisoned for the levelling content of their teaching. One of them, for example, was tried on a charge of 'teaching sedition and stirring up the slaves to rebellion' when at a service he gave out Dr. Watts's hymn, one verse of which runs :

> We will be slaves no more
> Since Christ has made us free,
> Has nailed our tyrants to the cross
> And brought us liberty.[106]

The slave disturbances of 1831 in Jamaica were spoken of as 'the Baptist war',[107] and after the abolition of slavery two years later, the Baptist name was linked to the whole train of troubles which resulted in the Jamaica Rebellion of 1865 under Governor Eyre.[108] It was a tradition of Negro protestantism—elaborated along a Baptist stem with roots that went back to the revolutionary Anabaptists of the European Reformation—which stretched from the West Indies to America. In America, in the cotton States, Negro Baptists were often at the fountain-head of revolt, notably the prophetic Nat Turner ; and after the emancipation which followed the Civil War, two great alliances of independent Negro churches emerged, the African Methodist Episcopal Church and the National Baptist Convention, through which Ethiopianism was encouraged in South and Central Africa.

The pattern of that tradition as it was followed in the Virginia to which American Negro Baptists sent Chilembwe for his education, has been described by a white observer of the Negro scene in 1889, only a few years before Chilembwe's arrival. His description indicates not only the functions of the independent Negro churches in the United States at that time and later, but also the part played in Africa by the corresponding institutions in the growth of native political consciousness. Indeed, it might almost be taken for a prophetic view of the whole trend of Nyasaland African independent church activities which had, amongst its other results, the 1915 Rising:

The preachers of the negroes are their most active politicians, as a rule, but even when they are not they have much political influence, for they constitute, individually, the natural leaders of their race, being elevated to their clerical position not because they are men of greater holiness of life or eloquence of tongue than the rest of their fellows, but because they have more energy and decision of character. Each one brings these qualifications to bear on all occasions of public agitation from that conspicuous coigne of vantage, his pulpit, which thus becomes a rostrum, the religious doctrines enunciated from thence, taking the color of his political principles, just as, on the other hand, his political harangues have a religious echo. The two parts of minister and orator are played so skilfully at one and the same time that it is impossible to distinguish them ; and the affairs of the Hereafter and a contemporary political canvass are mixed in inextricable confusion. His church is thus converted into a political organization that is consolidated by the religious fervour that pervades it, and propelled towards a single political end by a religious enthusiasm that expects to be rewarded spiritually for the performance of partisan duties. The preacher playing alternately upon the political passions and religious fears of his congregation, or upon both at once, excites an emotional responsiveness that is prepared to obey his slightest injunctions ; and he does not hesitate to turn this exalted state of feeling to the most useful account.

The political mass-meeting of the negroes is held after nightfall, for it is only at that late hour the labourers can attend. The spot selected is illuminated by the glare of torches; and what with the waving lights, the darkness of the background of the forest, the gleaming of the foliage overhead, the dimly outlined forms of men huddled together, the strident voices of the speakers, and the low murmurs of assent rising from their auditors, the scene is strangely picturesque in its physical aspects and impressive in its political suggestions. It is a strong proof of the timidity of the negroes that they have not often been impelled by these occasions, the influences of which are always violent and incendiary, to inflict the grossest injury upon the white people, but excepting a certain moroseness and sullenness of demeanour, their employers observe no evidence even on the following day of the emotions of anger and hatred that had inflamed their minds recently.[109]

It was this tradition which was to become the much-feared Ethiopianism of South Africa ; and it has been too readily assumed that that was a purely South African development. It has been overlooked that the Central African Ethiopianism of the period 1892 to 1915 [110] was much more than a branch or reflection of native church separatism south of the Limpopo. The movements had their link in Joseph Booth, and through him were, in great part, one : [111] a network of Ethiopianist centres, mainly African independent churches, that spread from the Cape to the north end of Lake Nyasa. This widespread movement was no conspiracy, but a unity shaped by the general conditions in British-ruled territory, both restrictive and permissive. But in the 'classical' pre-war period of Ethiopianism—for the term has been employed much more loosely since 1918 [112]—it had less of the mere safety-valve character than the dissipation of African unity in increasing numbers of churches and professingly Christian cults has since imposed on it. In that period it often provided a medium for direct political activity, inspired and fostered by groups of American Negroes both in the United States and in Africa. Since 1918, however, more secular forms of political organization, some of which have not entirely cast off all the forms of their predecessors, have taken over active agitation ; and the American Negroes, too, have shifted their interests.

Chilembwe has an important place in the Ethiopianist pattern. He made a mark at once as introducer of the Negro National Baptist Convention of America as a rival to the African Methodist Episcopal Church in offering focal points for African secession in South and East Central Africa.[113] He and his associates created an impressive experiment in economic and intellectual betterment of Africans by Africans through the industrial mission ; and in the end they were responsible for the first revolt in southern Africa which had strictly Ethiopianist character ; for while Ethiopian elements were present in the Bambata Rebellion,[114] they were subsidiary to the Zulu material grievances which built up the movement. In Nyasaland in 1915 it was the native preacher, the Ethiopian—taken popularly to be a synonym for pro-African and anti-European native working through a church organization—who was at the heart of the affair.[115] John Buchan, writing *Prester John* in 1910, had indeed been prophetic, though he had seen his Ethiopian preacher raise the people of the Transvaal border—country which, like Chilembwe's Chiradzulu, looks out to Portuguese territory.

The nearest approach to the Nyasaland Ethiopian situation of Chilembwe's time seems to have been in the German Cameroons, where a Native Baptist Church that seceded from the Basler Mission in 1888–9 had a total of forty thousand members by 1913.[116]   These *hosennegers*, as the Germans contemptuously dubbed them, became the centre of protest against German rule, and African political agitation developed early over land questions, reaching its height in 1911 when the Germans expropriated a large area of Duala tribal territory.   There had also been some trouble over taxation.   The Cameroons Baptist movement, however, did not produce anything like a planned rising; though, during 1922–3, the expression of African Baptist independent feeling, under the rebellious pastor Lotin Same, threatened to assume the proportions of a serious anti-European movement.   Elsewhere in West Africa, although there has been rapid growth of African religious sects and 'Ethiopianism' has been used as a general term for African nationalism by some native writers,[117] the independent native churches and other religious groups do not seem to have made themselves centres of quite the same kind of political activity as in the southern horn of Africa.[118] Perhaps the absence of white settlement with its delimitation of 'reserves' and its demonstration of the establishment of permanent European interests may have had much to do with this, for outside the small, formerly German territories of Cameroons and Togoland it is hard to see in West Africa any movement approaching Chilembwe's,[119] although the American Negro Baptists before the Great War were taking as much interest in west coast missions as in any other part of Negro Africa.[120]

In many ways, the closest parallel to the work of John Chilembwe was provided by the sequence of events in Kenya between June 1921 and April 1922, which is commonly associated with the name of Harry Thuku.   Leys himself noted the similarity, and it was not accidental that he opened his account of Chilembwe's movement with a reference to Thuku.[121]   Thuku, a Kikuyu who was employed at the Treasury in Nairobi, took the leading part in canalizing into a political form the discontent which his people felt against European rule in Kenya at the time of the financial and economic depression of the early 1920's.   As a retrenchment measure, European employers of native labour decided to reduce African wages by about a third;   Government manipulation of the currency, and the introduction of a new shilling in the place of the old rupee, had confused the native mind;   there was an increase of taxation, and, with a storm of African grievances against the *kipande* (labour registration system) and the Government's policy of labour 'encouragement'—particularly of

women and children—for coffee estates, and with the rumour abroad
that the European was about to take away more native land, it was
obvious that an explosive situation existed. Heading a wave of
African discontent, Thuku held protest meetings ; formed a political
body, the Young Kikuyu Association [122] (sometimes called an East
Africa Native Association [123] and sometimes the Kikuyu Central
Association [124]) ; criticized Government, settler, and missionary
alike, and called on the Africans, at one meeting of about five
thousand, to dump their labour certificates on the drive of Government House, Nairobi, so that all would know that they meant
business ! His influence stretched out beyond the Kikuyu, and he
had immense meetings of Kavirondo natives. 'A polyglot *nation*
was beginning to emerge from among certain of the highland and
lake tribes—and it was a hostile nation.'[125] On 15 March Thuku
was arrested. Africans swarmed to his place of imprisonment and
there was an ugly scene when, in a panic, the native troops who
faced the irate Thuku supporters fired at the crowd and killed
eighteen of them. The incident was followed by patrols of the
King's African Rifles in near-by villages. At length, after police
action and inquiry, what seemed then, to many, a danger to European
rule was held in check. Thuku was deported for some years to
Jubaland, and discontent went underground.

Thuku was not a preacher ; but he was, like Chilembwe, a
'marginal man'. Though, again like Chilembwe, in relation to the
Zambesi Industrial Mission, he was ready to enlist the services of
missionaries when it was possible and expedient, he was in general
critical of their approach to the social situation. The missionaries, on
their side, were critical of a movement which embraced many lapsed
communicants of their own churches, people who, from their point
of view, 'had only snatched the coveted boon of education, which
the missionaries offered free, and had then decamped with it'.[126]
Thus there was considerable similarity in the kind of support which
the Chilembwe and Thuku protests commanded ; and leaders of
Thuku's movement made a religious as well as political appeal.
African Christians were asked to pray for Thuku and his elders
'who have been set apart by God to be our guides in our present
condition of slavery which we knew not . . . before the Europeans
came. . . .' Sympathizers were told to remember

how that our God brought the Children of Israel out of the house of
bondage of King Pharaoh . . . and to Him let us pray again, for He is

our God. And also let us have faith since in the eyes of God there is no distinction of white or Black. All are sons of Adam, and alike before Him, Jehovah our Living God. . . . Thou Lord Jehovah, our God, it is Thou who hast set apart to be our Master and Guide Harry Thuku ; may he be chief of us all.[127]

This recalls what Leys learned from followers of Chilembwe : that he 'got his inspiration from the Old Testament . . . and preached to many hundreds every week sermons in which the example of the Jews in their national struggle with Egyptians, Philistines and others was held up for their admiration and imitation'.[128]

Like Chilembwe, Thuku was driven to exasperation by the obstruction he encountered in trying to get a hearing for the Africans' sense of outrage. It is true that, at the dramatic meeting at Dagoretti on 24 June 1921,[129] he reached the ear of the Government, and was thus more successful than the Nyasaland spokesman ; but he was given no more than a cold hearing. For the rest, his movement created disturbances but did not issue in a planned rising, and eventually he was released from detention, with liberty to return home. He did so, and settled down as owner of a landholding, becoming a stabilizing, even a conservative, influence among the Kikuyu. He has consistently opposed the Mau-Mau kind of reaction against European culture and control.[130] Indeed, Thuku's history raises the speculation whether, if Chilembwe had been treated less brusquely before he committed himself to a policy of armed violence, he might have been brought through his crisis in the same way to a patient 'elder statesman' attitude.

But similarities between the Nyasaland and Kenya situation must not be pressed too far. The manner in which, since 1922, the Kikuyu separatist churches and their attached independent African schools have acted as channels for political discontent [131] cannot be considered as quite analogous to the work of the first Providence Industrial Mission. They may be better compared with some of the less orthodox bodies in Nyasaland, Kamwana's for example ; for Chilembwe's mission appears to have had no 'deviationist' Christianity about it. In spite of assertions that he conducted 'certain hideous rites' [132] over the head of W. J. Livingstone when it was brought to Mbombwe, which remain bare assertions by, in this respect, unreliable authorities, it is evident that his tenets and his pattern of worship were little influenced by residual old pagan cults, or defiantly devised new ones. There was none of the approval of polygamy which has characterized some of the Kikuyu sects. One could hardly conceive of the neat Chilembwe, with his congregation exemplifying Sunday-go-to-meeting meticulousness of dress, echoing such invective as that of the cult of Mumbo, among the Central and Southern Kavirondo in 1913 :

> The Christian religion is rotten [*mbovu*—it stinks] and so is its practice of making its believers wear clothes. My followers must let their hair grow, never cutting it. Their clothes shall be goatskins, and they must never wash. All Europeans are your enemies and the time is shortly coming when they will all disappear from our country.[133]

Chilembwe might have echoed the last line in his heart, but the rest, like the frantic Mau-Mau resort to the polar opposites of European standards, would have been remote from one who saw only that Europeanism had much to add to what he and others, by emulation, had already acquired. He wanted to break the European monopoly of the power, wealth, and dignity which their culture conferred, not to reject that way of life.

Chilembwe was equally remote from the standpoint of the so-called Malaki religion [134] which came to notice in Uganda just before the Great War. It sprang from Biblical exposition dictated by ancestral African views of the world. It sanctioned polygamy, and claimed that man should submit to disease since it is ordained of God. One chief deduced from this that he should refuse to pay land tax, which contributed to the support of Government doctors, and refused to have his cattle inoculated against rinderpest. The movement attracted about ninety-one thousand adherents who found in it a rallying-point against the incomprehensible activities of Government and resented obtrusiveness of well-meant medical and veterinary services.

In Uganda, too, the Bataka party came into being principally as a protest against the mistaken ideas about indigenous land tenure which Sir Harry Johnston wrote into the Uganda Agreement of 1900 [135]—just as some of the inadequately based decisions in his 1892 settlement of European land claims in Nyasaland laid the foundation of grievances which brought disgruntled tenants on European estates into Chilembwe's following. But the two movements have little in common. Though some of the more recent Bataka who figured in the disturbances of April 1949 [136] 'seemed to believe that they were waging a semi-holy war . . . and soon became a collecting bag for all who had complaints against the Church or the Government',[137] yet, among the sophisticates of the modern period in Uganda, they seem to have a rather anachronistic quality, and the lack of dignity in their speeches, as reported,[138] lends them an air of somewhat comic pathos. Chilembwe in the context of his time was a forward-looking modern, and while the precariousness of his position confers some pathos, there is no record that he was undignified in his protestations.

It is this very pathetic dignity of John Chilembwe which serves to introduce a further point about his place in Negro history. There has been a tendency to group many Negro movements, particularly those in Africa, which do not fit into easily understandable European categories, under the general heading of 'prophet movements', and to call their leaders 'prophets' or 'Messiahs'.[139] Yet, to re-echo a point which has already been made, Chilembwe does not fit conveniently into such a category. His preaching, to be sure, had enthusiasm and fire; he could invoke the imagery of the Bible in a way which his African hearers were able to appreciate in the light of their political and economic status; he may have felt that he had to make some gesture towards the 'deliverance' of his people; he employed the open-air baptism in which the 'prophets' of the so-called African 'Zionist' churches of South Africa take so much delight; [140] but Chilembwe elaborated no cult, or made no claims to special insight into the future. Though he was a striking personality with an appeal to many Africans, he was no 'prophet', no 'Messiah'. He saw no visions like Nat Turner, leader of the 1831 Negro revolt in Virginia. He had none of the assurance of the Central Africa Watch Tower adherents that the millennium had started in October 1914. He lacked the fanatical conviction of Enoch Mgijima and his 'Israelite' African followers who refused to remove themselves from their settlement at Bulhoek commonage, near Queenstown in the Ciskei, South Africa; resisted eviction by units of the Defence Force; charged their guns in May 1921, and suffered a hundred and sixty-three killed and a hundred and twenty-nine wounded.[141] Nor could Chilembwe, for all the support which he had received from American Negroes and from the United States, be said to be possessed by that messianic faith in their power to deliver their peoples from all their sorrows which has characterized the leaders of many under-privileged groups in colonial territories.[142] He made none of the claims of the more modern type of African 'prophet' such as

Wellington Butelezi of the Transkei, South Africa, who told his adherents in 1921 that all Americans were Negroes ; that they would soon be coming to free their brother Africans from European rule ; that they would arrive in aeroplanes, the white man would be driven into the sea, and the Bantu would have to pay no more taxes.[143] Chilembwe had little of the 'prophetic' in common with figures of this sort. Indeed, if he had possessed more of their spirit, he might have swayed his followers to greater carnage during the first two days of his rising, when they had plenty of opportunity for killing many more than the three Europeans whom they put to death on the Bruce Estates. Chilembwe's place in the history of Negro revolt, from this point of view at least, seems to be distinguished, then, by the absence of those 'prophetic' elements which are so often associated with Negro protest movements.

It is only necessary to compare the letter of protest against African implication in the Great War which he sent to the *Nyasaland Times* in the few months before the Rising with another letter that was written on the eve of the war by a Watch Tower supporter in Nyasaland—both of which have been quoted above, pages 234-5 and 230—to see the distinction between Chilembwe's attitude and that of the African who had been strongly influenced by the 'prophetic' type of religious teaching. Chilembwe's letter has courage, criticism, fervour ; but it has none of the eschatological flavour of the Watch Tower epistle.[144]

His criticism of the international war into which the African had been plunged without so much as a 'by your leave' from his European masters draws attention to what is, perhaps, one of the most significant aspects of Chilembwe's movement : his consistent opposition to the African's being drawn into the white man's wars. As has been noted, emphasis on the undoubted African grievances about land and labour as a cause of his conspiracy has had the effect of overshadowing other aspects of the movement, of which its reaction to the whole complicated change of scene that the Great War brought to Central Africa is an important part. Similarly, what comparative judgement there has been about Chilembwe and the Nyasaland Rising in the general history of African revolts has tended to stress its non-tribal leadership and character as distinguishing features, and has passed over completely its importance as a reaction to the first great international war of modern times. Chilembwe, in his criticism of the War to the *Nyasaland Times*, linked questions of

African political and economic advancement with the more general issues of the conflict, and thus showed in his own way something of the spirit which the American Negro scholar, Benjamin Brawley, revealed in his book, *Africa and the War*, which was published in New York in 1918. Brawley's comments round off, as it were, the implications of Chilembwe's statement : 'The great war of our own day is to determine the future of the Negro in the World. Alsace, Lorraine, Belgium, the Balkans, and even Russia all become second in importance.' [145]

Yet Chilembwe's opposition to the Europeans and their war could not be entirely consistent : he had to consider the possibility of allying himself with one party, the Germans, in order to fight against the other, the British. However much he may have deplored it, the extension of their 'balance of power' system which the Europeans had introduced into Africa had Chilembwe, almost as much as them, in its grip. But, within these limitations, he did display a conscious attitude of opposition to the War which he carried to its logical extreme. In this he differed from most of the American Negroes who, in spite of the indignities they suffered before and during the War, did not oppose the entry of the United States into it.[146] And in this, too, he was different from most of the Africans not only in his own country but in other parts of European Africa. The attitude of the African Negro towards the Great War is a subject which calls for a serious and intensive study. But, until this is made and more evidence is available, it does not seem an exaggeration to say that, although many Africans in the European colonies may have mumbled against it, very few of them expressed open opposition to the War, or used the occasion it provided to rise against their foreign rulers. There were riots in Dahomey and Liberia,[147] it is true, and the Mullah in Somaliland kept the British embarrassed. But these episodes and the few other minor outbreaks appear to have been largely traditional in character.[148] Their leaders, unlike Chilembwe, do not seem to have had a conscious opposition to the War, or to have calculated as closely as he did that it provided a chance, however slender, to break the power of the European. In this respect, then, however ineffective his protests against Negro participation in the white man's wars may have been, Chilembwe's stand in the first months of the Great War has no small place in the history of African reaction to the European way of life.[149]

There was something of Chilembwe's spirit in the air at the great conference that was held in New York, in August 1920, by Marcus Garvey's Universal Negro Improvement Association. It was this conference with its thousands of Negro delegates from many lands which drafted the 'Declaration of Rights of the Negro Peoples of the World'. And amongst its provisions were statements against the participation of Negroes in Europeans' wars.[150] 'The first dying that is to be done by the black man in the future', Garvey told the delegates, 'will be done to make himself free.' When this had been achieved, he went on, 'if we have any charity to bestow, we may die for the white man.' And then, in words which his biographer points out 'had an ominous portent for every colonial government',[151] he added, 'But as for me, I think I have stopped dying for him.' Garvey's Association, with its fervent expressions of Negro nationalism, its 'Back to Africa' movement, and the hopes which it inspired in the hearts of thousands of Negroes all over the world, has been called the 'first and only real mass movement amongst Negroes in the history of the United States',[152] 'the largest Negro movement of its kind in history'.[153] At least, in their criticism of European wars, there was an identity of spirit between Garvey and Chilembwe. But one American Negro scholar has claimed a connection between the two men which is stronger than that.

In an article, 'Some New Light on the Garvey Movement', Mr. Robert Hughes Brisbane writes that Garvey

> became interested in the condition of the African Negro as a result of the followers of Chilembwe of Nyasaland and Kimbangu of the Congo. As a result of these experiences, Garvey's vision broadened perceptively.[154]

When and where Garvey came into contact with these followers it is difficult to say. Some might even be inclined to show scepticism that he had such contacts at all. Yet it would not do to dismiss the assertion out of hand, and Mr. Brisbane's claim that the names of Chilembwe and Kimbangu were common currency among street-corner agitators for the Garvey movement in New York [155] is not so bizarre as it may at first sight appear. Not only had Chilembwe been in the United States for two years but, as has been noted, he had connections with the 'Back to Africa' movement a long time before Garvey.[156] He had been introduced to this by Booth, whose book, *Africa for the African*,[157] had been printed by an American Negro press, and used as its title, a quarter of a century before the Universal Negro Improvement Association was founded, the slogan [158] which the Garvey-ites later made famous in many parts of the world. As an apparently leading member of a 'Back to Africa' movement with its centre at his place of education, Lynchburgh, Virginia, Chilembwe has a place in the uneven course of this tortuous American Negro dream which stretches from the days of slavery down to the fiasco of Marcus Garvey's 'Black Star Line' in the 1920's. Furthermore, from what has been said in earlier chapters, it is certain that Chilembwe had friends and relations—'followers', indeed—in the United States : his whole web of connections with American Negroes of the National Baptist Convention, whose journal noted his rising in 1915 ; [159] the Rev. L. N. Cheek who had married into Chilembwe's family ; the young Nyasas who had gone back to America with Cheek and Miss DeLany from the Providence Industrial Mission ; and Chilembwe's mysterious 'son' in the United States.[160] And, of course, there was that complicated train of wandering and enterprising Nyasaland Africans in many parts of the world who could have carried the Chilembwe story with them— and, perhaps, some of Kimbangu's tale too, for Nyasas were not strangers to the Belgian Congo. But the whole subject of connections between the Chilembwe and Garvey movements, direct and indirect, bristles with difficulties, for both of them, like most movements of protest and revolt, left few easily accessible records.[161] Yet, whatever may be said of the postulated connections between the spheres of influence of Chilembwe and Garvey, there are obvious places where they interpenetrate : the history of the 'Back to Africa' movement ; their attempts to increase Negro status ; their criticisms of the Negro in the European's armies ; and the parts they both played in the growth of Negro nationalism.

At the end of the Great War, an expression of this nationalism was the Pan-African Congress [162] which the American Negro scholar, Dr. W. E. B. DuBois, who had known Joseph Booth in America,[163] secured Clemenceau's permission to hold in the Grand Hotel in Paris in February 1919. It was infinitely smaller than Garvey's conference of the following year, but it called together Negro peoples from America, Africa, and the West Indies, and served to show the world that Negroes as well as Whites were interested in the deliberations that were then being held by the Allied Powers in Paris.[164] DuBois and Garvey, though they were bitter political opponents with fundamental disagreements on tactics, were, in reality, both working for the same end : to raise the status of the Negro, materially and spiritually, in his own eyes, and in the eyes of the world at large. Were not the aims of John Chilembwe the same, though his effective field was a smaller one, and his final tactics different from either of them? And may it not be said, then, that in his own, smaller way, the work of John Chilembwe has its place in the Pan-African movement?

The character of this place was indicated by the writer of an article which was published at much the same time as Garvey and DuBois were crossing swords. Analysing the Pan-African movement, Captain J. E. T. Phillips wrote in the *Journal of the African Society* for 1921–2, that

> At one end of the scale the National Congress of British West Africa is developed sufficiently to be discreet in its public utterances. At the other end the young Ethiopians of Nyasa [in 1915] over-estimated their own importance. . . .[165]

Though, perhaps, it might be truer to say that Chilembwe had not so much over-estimated his own importance as that he had felt in 1915 that only one course, the way of insurrection, was open to him, this passage, nevertheless, draws attention to the position his movement occupies in the history of African nationalism in the European colonies. It is a very immature position, as Chilembwe's staking his all on the desperate gamble of 1915 reveals. But, if he lacked the means to realize his ideal, he had no doubt about the end: a primarily African state, with selective European assistance, in which the African inhabitants, as his master Booth had taught him, would run their own industries and enterprises. Chilembwe seemed to realize, too, that such a state would need spiritual, ideological sources of strength as much as its own political and economic foundations: for him this was to be achieved by a union of all the independent African churches. It was a concept of a national African church which has more than a little in common with similar processes at the heart of the European Reformation. The white man had brought to Africa new political, economic, and ideological practices and conceptions. Out of these African nationalism matured, and if it wished to develop further it had to master them and turn them to its own account. The unhappy John Chilembwe knew this, though he lacked the means to realize it. But his consciousness of this and the feeble attempts of himself and his followers to achieve it, give to the Chilembwe movement its own special place in the history of African nationalism.

What can be said by way of conclusion ? A lament for the lost at Magomero, Mandala, Mbombwe ? The loss not merely of lives, European and African, but the wreckage of hopes of the living as well as of the dead, white and black, in those few days of January and February 1915 ? This would, indeed, be appropriate ; for it is impossible to study at close quarters the long trail which leads to those few fatal days without feeling an intense sympathy for all who were forced along it. It is a sympathy which must include such completely contrasting figures as Joseph Booth and William Jervis Livingstone : the one of whom lost two of his children and many of his hopes in Africa ; the other of whom lost his hopes and his all when his life was taken away from him by some of the very men whom Booth had trained. Neither would have had it so : yet, looking back, the issue seems never to have been in doubt. But, faced with such a problem, the historian is tempted to hand over his responsibilities to the philosopher, perhaps to the theologian. Yet even they may be ill-equipped for explaining the wider issues of the role of the individual and the mass, of the idea and the material force, of free will and predestination, which, for all his sympathy, the historian who tries to survey closely that small group of figures, whose lives in their interactions brought about the disasters at Magomero and Mbombwe, cannot avoid having forced on his attention. Perhaps the only appropriate word in such a situation is the poet's

... word over all, beautiful as the sky,
Beautiful that war and all its deeds of carnage must in time be utterly lost. ...

But Time, not the Transcendent, is the historian's orbit. And so, if we must strike our concluding notes from material which is more congenial to our task, perhaps we may find it in quotations from the works of two men who knew their Africa well.

The first provides a note of sympathy, which is, in its way, also something of an explanation for the character who, perhaps more than any other in this story, is deserving of sympathy : John Chilembwe himself. It is provided by comparing him, as we did at the start of this book, with the Reverend John Laputa, the leader of the African revolt in John Buchan's romance, *Prester John*. In one of the exchanges between Laputa and Buchan's hero, David Crawfurd, the young Scot asks the rebel leader, 'What in God's name are you doing in this business ? You that are educated and have seen the world ? '

Then he goes on to condemn him for his part in instigating the revolt and to criticize his following : 'Supposing you were Oliver Cromwell you could make nothing out of such a crew.' Laputa's response, as Chilembwe's might have done in similar circumstances, comes immediately :

'They are my people', he said simply.[166]

And the second quotation is from Lord Lugard's great work, *The Dual Mandate in British Tropical Africa*. He is dealing with: native peoples and their movements of protest against colonial rule

Their very discontent is a measure of their progress.[167]

NOTES AND REFERENCES

THE following abbreviations are used throughout these notes and references: *Z.I.M.O.P.*, Zambesi Industrial Mission Occasional Paper; *L.W.B.C.A.*, Life and Work in British Central Africa, Blantyre Mission Supplement; *L.W.N.*, Life and Work in Nyasaland, continuation of *L.W.B.C.A.*; *R.C.N.R.*, Report of the Commission to Inquire into . . . the Native Rising within the Nyasaland Protectorate (Zomba, 1916).

CHAPTER I

INTRODUCTION

1. G. C. Rawlinson, 'Some Lessons from the Chilembwe Rebellion', *Central Africa: a Monthly Record of the Universities Mission to Central Africa* (London, 1917), p. 61. The same comparison is made in Isaac F. Marcosson, *An African Adventure* (New York, 1921), p. 94; Donald Fraser, *The New Africa* (London, 1927), p. 89; Eric Rosenthal, *Stars and Stripes in Africa* (London, 1938), pp. 260, 264.

2. Norman Leys, *Kenya* (London, 1924), p. 334.

CHAPTER II

ORIGINS: JOSEPH BOOTH AND JOHN CHILEMBWE
1892–1897

1. Cyrus T. Brady, *Commerce and Conquest in East Africa* (Salem, Mass., 1950), pp. 74-5.

2. *The Last Journals of David Livingstone* (London, 1874, ed. Horace Waller), ii, p. 39.

3. Sir Richard Burton, *First Footsteps in East Africa* (London, 1856), p. 49; G. L. Sullivan, *Dhow Chasing in Zanzibar Waters* (London, 1873), p. 163; Livingstone, op. cit. i, pp. 109, 345; Joseph Thomson, *Ulu* (London, 1888), i, pp. 42-3, 46; F.O.2.55, p. 314 (Public Record Office, London); F. D. Lugard, *The Rise of Our East African Empire* (London, 1893), i, p. 191; ed. Margery Perham, *Ten Africans* (London, 1936), p. 98; *Slave Boy to Priest. The Autobiography of Padre Petro Kilekwa* (London, 1937), pp. 15, 17; Alice Werner, *Chapenga's White Man* (London, n.d.), p. 21.

4. Ed. William Monk, *Dr. Livingstone's Cambridge Lectures* (Cambridge, 1858), p. 45; Henry Rowley, *The Story of the Universities' Mission to Central Africa* (London, 1866), pp. 171-2; Livingstone, *Last Journals*, op. cit. i, p. 60, ii, p. 39; W. A. Elmslie, *Among the Wild Ngoni* (Edinburgh, 1899), p. 171; D. R. Mackenzie, *The Spirit-Ridden Konde* (London, 1925), p. 102. Cf. also W. Holman Bentley, *Pioneering on the Congo* (London, 1900), i, p. 431. But cf. Duff MacDonald, *Africana* (London, 1882), i, pp. 213-14, 222-3; *L.W.B.C.A.*, April 1888, p. 1. Alice Werner, *The Natives Tribes of British Central Africa* (London, 1906), pp. 84-5, 98; C. Snouck Hurgronje, *Mekka in the Latter Part of the Nineteenth Century* (London, 1931), p. 20.

5. Jessie Monteath Currie, *The Hill of Goodbye* (London, 1920), p. 78.

6. In one form or another, this 'white men are cannibals' rumour has continued to exist in Nyasaland. Dr. Daniel Malekebu, who took over in 1926 the mission that John Chilembwe founded and who was one of Chilembwe's early pupils, has told us that his parents tried to stop him when he wanted to go to America in 1905 because of fears for his safety that were based on this rumour. For examples of its force in modern times, see *East Africa and Rhodesia* (London), vol. 29, 1507, 1953, p. 1653 ; Mr. Colin Legum's report in *The Observer*, 6 September 1953 ; *Nyasaland Protectorate. Report of a Commission of Inquiry appointed by the Governor on the 20th August 1953* (Zomba, 1953), p. 5 ; Don Taylor, *Rainbow on the Zambesi* (London, 1953), pp. 82-3 ; Arthur Loveridge, *I Drank the Zambesi* (New York, 1953), p. 280.

7. For the Rhodes-Johnston dispute, see especially Public Record Office, Africa, F.O.2.55, pp. 107-42, Johnston to Roseberry, Zomba, 8 October 1893 (Central Africa, No. 52), with enclosures, Johnston to Rhodes, Zomba, 8 October 1893, etc., etc. There are interesting criticisms of Rhodes's actions in British Central Africa by the Scottish Blantyre missionaries in their journal, *L.W.B.C.A.*: e.g. April 1893, pp. 4-5, etc. For a fully considered examination of the dispute, see A. J. Hanna, *The Beginnings of Nyasaland and North-Eastern Rhodesia* (Oxford, 1956), pp. 245 et seq.

8. See Sir Harry H. Johnston, *British Central Africa* (London, 1898), pp. 112-113 ; Raymond Leslie Buell, *The Native Problem in Africa* (New York, 1928), i, pp. 245-6 ; Hanna, op. cit. pp. 177-8, 190-4, 229-38. Cf. also Johnston, F.O.2.54 (Public Record Office, London), in Central Africa, No. 6 : '. . . there are other Land-Holders who are proceeding to treat the natives living on native reserves within their estates, as their serfs.' This point should be compared with the Nunan reference 49, Chapter IV.

9. *Nyasaland Protectorate. Land Commission, 1946. Report by the Rt. Hon. Sir Sidney Abrahams, P.C.* (Zomba, 1947), p. 8.

10. William Robertson, *The Martyrs of Blantyre* (London, 1892), p. 50.

11. The Blantyre church had another symbolism : of European community with Africans (cf. Robertson, op. cit. pp. 50-1).

12. *Cyclopaedic Dictionary* . . . (Edinburgh, 1892), p. xxii.

13. *Illustrated Missionary News* (London), xxvi, p. 147.

14. Cf. 'The Greatest Work in the World—A Plea for Missionary Enterprise', *Missionary Review of the World* (New York), v, 1892, pp. 573-80.

15. Obituary notice by Emily Booth Langworthy in *The Sabbath Recorder* (U.S.A.), 28 November 1932, gives Booth's date of birth as 1849. However, in his own *Africa for the African* (Baltimore, Md., 1897), p. 42, he states that his thirty-fifth birthday was on 26 February 1886, which would make his date of birth 1851. The main sources for Booth biographical details in this section and later are : (1) A group of autobiographical manuscripts written by Booth which, in some mysterious fashion, found their way into the papers of the Anti-Slavery Society, London, where they were discovered by George Shepperson. They are now in Rhodes House Library, Oxford : Anti-Slavery Papers MSS. Brit. Emp. S18. C154 1-9. They will be referred to as 'Booth MSS.', and, where possible, the title of each separate MS. will be given to facilitate reference. (2) Booth's own short book, *Africa for the African* (Baltimore, Md., 1897), particularly its autobiographical sketch, 'The Author's Apology', pp. 42-8. (3) Letters and other materials by and about Joseph Booth from his acquaintances and relations : in

particular, from his daughter, Mrs. Emily Booth Langworthy. Some of this material is too scattered for adequate reference; but other parts of it (such as Mrs. Langworthy's own writings) are easily available for reference

16. Booth MSS., 'Other Calls', p. 1.

17. *Seventh Day Baptists and Mission Work in Nyasaland, Africa. A Report by N. Olney Moore* (a duplicated report, dated 4 January 1949 and published 27 February 1950, Chicago, Ill.), p. 1.

18. Booth MSS., op. cit. pp. 1-3.

19. Ibid. p. 4.

20. Ibid. pp. 5-6.

21. Ibid. p. 6.

22. Ibid. p. 7.

23. Ibid. pp. 8-9.

24. See A. H. Oussoren, *William Carey—especially his Missionary Principles* (Leiden, 1945), pp. 92-8, 180, etc.

25. *Missionary Review of the World*, op. cit., from which the following quotations in this section are taken. See also *The Christian* (London), p. 595, 7 July 1892: letter from Booth, 'Industrial Mission for Africa'.

26. As the majority of the early papers of the Zambesi Industrial Mission (the present-day Zambesi Mission) were lost in the London 'blitz', the best general guide to its history is in the Occasional Papers it published from 1892 (*Z.I.M.O.P.*). There does not seem to be a complete collection of these in existence; but a fairly comprehensive collection is in the British Museum Library and at the headquarters of the mission. The Library of the Royal Empire Society also has a number of copies. See also four articles by Emily Booth Langworthy, '"Early Days" of the Zambesi Mission', *The Polished Shaft. Organ of the Zambesi Mission* (London), January-March, April-June, July-September, October-December 1949.

27. Booth MSS. op. cit. pp. 10-11.

28. Ibid. pp. 11-13.

29. *Z.I.M.O.P.*, September 1893, p. 6.

30. *Z.I.M.O.P.*, January 1894, p. 2.

31. Booth MSS. op. cit. p. 13.

32. Emily Booth Langworthy, *This Africa Was Mine* (Stirling, 1952), p. 24. The 'John' of this book is John Chilembwe; and the value of Mrs. Langworthy's evidence about him here and elsewhere is that the manuscript on which the book is based was written several years before she knew of Chilembwe's role in the 1915 Nyasaland Rising.

33. W. P. Livingstone, *Laws of Livingstonia* (London, n.d.), pp. 258-9.

34. *Z.I.M.O.P.*, 1892, p. 2.

35. Booth's quotation is a reference to p. 55 of Drummond's book.

36. Communication from Mrs. E. B. Langworthy.

37. *Africa for the African*, op. cit. p. 43. Cf. *Proceedings of the Sixth General Council of the Reformed Churches Holding the Presbyterian System* (Glasgow, 1896), Appendix, p. 116, for complaint lodged by the Church of Scotland against Booth's mission; and *L.W.B.C.A.*, October 1894, pp. 2-3.

38. *Z.I.M.O.P.*, 1892, p. 2.

39. *Church of Scotland Home and Foreign Mission Record* (Edinburgh), xix, pp. 270-1.

40. Ibid. p. 292.

41. *The Nyasa News* (Likoma), May 1894, No. 4, p. 110.

42. Ibid., 6 November 1894, p. 211.

43. Cf. the 'Blantyre Controversy' of 1880–1 : *Laws of Livingstonia*, op. cit. pp. 169-74 ; A. Chirnside, *The Blantyre Missionaries, Discreditable Disclosures* (London, 1880).

44. Booth MSS. op. cit.

45. Langworthy, op. cit. pp. 39-41.

46. Ibid. p. 53.

47. There is a mass of conflicting evidence about Chilembwe's early schooling. In the long quotation used above (reference 45) from Mrs. Langworthy's book, it will be noted that she states that '. . . at a mission school somewhere he had learned to speak and write a few English words'. If this is so, it must have been the main Blantyre Mission school, as the outlying Church of Scotland Mission schools did not teach English but carried out vernacular instruction. Furthermore, Mrs. Langworthy, op. cit., states elsewhere (p. 53) that Chilembwe had chosen his Christian name '. . . himself before we knew him. At a mission school he had learned that "the disciple whom Jesus loved" was named John. So he asked for that same name.' We have not checked any baptismal rolls or school records which may still remain at the Blantyre Mission ; but the Rev. F. S. Chintali of the Church of Scotland Mission informs us that Chilembwe was educated at Blantyre. Cf. also Rev. Harry K. Matecheta (one of the first ordained African ministers of the Church of Scotland), *Blantyre Mission. Nkhani za Ciyambi Cace* (Blantyre, 1951), p. 27 : Chilembwe started his education at a village school at Cilomoni where Blantyre township now stands. Chilembwe's niece, Harris (in an interview with Mr. P. L. Bridle), infers that family background may have had something to do with Chilembwe's education : his parents 'were well educated and ate white man's food and not native food. . . . John was sent to the Church of Scotland Mission in Blantyre for education.' Another African informant of Mr. P. L. Bridle has claimed that he was at school with Chilembwe at Blantyre. Cf. also a statement by a witness, who obviously knew the Nyasaland scene well, in *Daily Chronicle* 14 April 1915 : Chilembwe was educated at 'the Mission Church'—i.e. Blantyre. Against such statements, however, must be set the claim of Pastor K. M. Malinki (in an interview with Mr. S. G. Maxwell), who was also one of Booth's early helpers, and, as will be seen, was associated closely with Booth and Chilembwe in an independent missionary venture, that Chilembwe 'had not been to school and was still a heathen'. The story which is credited to Chilembwe by an American Negro source (see reference 72 below), that he kept away from the Blantyre Mission because of the baptismal practices it employed, and the fact that Chilembwe himself claimed that his conversion did not take place until 1893, a year after he met Booth (see reference 70 below), do not suggest a degree of close association between him and the Blantyre Mission. Nevertheless, as Rev. F. S. Chintali points out, Chilembwe may have left the mission for Booth before he was baptized. That the Chilembwe family had come under some European educational influences is suggested by the fact that at least two of them taught at the independent African mission which Chilembwe set up after 1900 : Morris Chilembwe, his nephew, and Mary Chimpele, daughter of John Chilembwe's elder brother (information kindly supplied by Mr. Gibson Mbela who was taught at the Providence Industrial Mission of John Chilembwe from 1904–11). Cf. also the statement in *Z.I.M.O.P.*, October 1911, that Booth 'secured the help of several natives who had been educated

at the Blantyre Mission. . . . These natives acted as interpreters' (p. 4). While Chilembwe is not mentioned by name here, it is certain that he was one of Booth's earliest African interpreters.

48. William Garden Blaikie, *The Personal Life of David Livingstone* (London, 1880), pp. 285-6 ; Jack Simmons, *Livingstone and Africa* (London, 1955), p. 98. For the troubled state of the Magomero-Chiradzulu region, see Henry Rowley, *Story of the Universities' Mission*, op. cit.

49. *Martyrs of Blantyre*, op. cit. pp. 122-3.

50. *L.W.B.C.A.*, following p. 8. Cf. also Albert Grey of the British South African Company to Cecil Rhodes, 25 December 1891 (Rhodes House, 3A, Charters 1889–91, Folio for 1891, 199a) : 'I am afraid dear little H. H. Johnston is rushing ahead a bit too fast'. His interfering too much with natives—burning native villages with Sikhs—may make natives unable to compare British policy favourably with that of Germany or the Congo Free State. Johnston's policy may be misunderstood : 'I fear there is some truth in the statement that he is adopting too largely objectionable German methods'.

51. L. G. Jordan, *In Our Stead* (Philadelphia, Pa., 1914), p. 12.

52. Booth MSS., 'Re John Chilembwe the Yao Native Messenger to the Negroes of the U.S.A.', p. C.

53. This information is based largely on oral evidence, which has been conveniently summarized for us by one of Chilembwe's former followers in a memorandum entitled 'Maziko a Prov. Ind. Mission. Chiradzulo. Nyasaland, 1900 A.D. By Andrew G. Mkulichi' (The Founding of the Providence Industrial Mission . . .). This will be referred to subsequently as 'Mkulichi'. Chilembwe's nieces (daughters of his brother, James) have also stated that the parents were Kaundama (Yao) and Nyangu (Maravi.).

54. A useful basic account of Nyasaland tribal history is Mary Tew, *Peoples of the Lake Nyasa Region* (London, 1950). Its bibliography may be supplemented by the bibliographical section of J. A. Barnes, *Politics in a Changing Society. A Political History of the Fort Jameson Ngoni* (London, 1954), which, although it is orientated towards the Ngoni, is also a valuable guide to other materials on Nyasaland tribal history, particularly those in the Public Record Office, London. In particular, for useful commentary on the Yao under the impact of Arab and European cultures, see J. Clyde Mitchell, 'The Political Organization of the Yao of Southern Nyasaland', *African Studies* (Johannesburg), September 1949 ; and his *The Yao Village* (Manchester, 1956).

55. Rowley, op. cit. p. 188, for an example of Mang'anja women who married Yao men.

56. T. Price, 'More about the Maravi', *African Studies* (Johannesburg), vol. 11, 2 June 1952, pp. 75-9. See also J. Bruwer, 'Note on Maravi Origin and Migration', *African Studies*, vol. 9, March 1950, pp. 32-4.

57. For 'Nyangu', see Alice Werner, *The Natives of British Central Africa* (London, 1906), p. 256 ; Samuel Yosia Nthara, *Mbiri Ya Acewa* (Zomba, 1945), pp. 3, 4, 9, etc. ; J. M. Winterbottom, 'Outline Histories of Two Northern Rhodesian Tribes', *The Rhodes-Livingstone Journal* (London), viii, 1949, pp. 21-3 ; Price, op. cit. p. 77 ; Bruwer, op. cit. p. 32. Cf. also *L.W.B.C.A.*, January 1896, p. 4 : 'Bessie Nyangu'.

58. See also H. C. Stannus, 'Notes on Some Tribes of British Central Africa', *Journal of the Royal Anthropological Institute* (London), xl, 1910, p. 308 ; A. G. O.

NOTES AND REFERENCES

Hodgson, 'Notes on the Achewa and Angoni of the Dowa District of Nyasaland', ibid. lxiii, 1933, p. 127.

In this book 'Chilembwe' is used throughout as the spelling of this name—it was used in this way by John Chilembwe himself—but many other variants exist, amongst which are : Chelembwe (common amongst members of the 1915–16 Nyasaland Administration) ; Chirembwe (frequently used by members of the Blantyre Mission) ; Cilembwe (usage of linguistic purists) ; Tschirembwe (German variant) ; and a host of corruptions and misconstructions of which 'Caglombwe' in *Glasgow Herald*, 4 February 1915, is the most outstanding.

59. Cf. his references to his father as a 'prince', when he was in America : Chapter III, references 102-3.

60. Mkulichi, op. cit. See also Alice Werner, *Myths and Legends of the Bantu* (London, 1933), pp. 126-7.

61. *Central African Times*, iv, 10, 8 December 1900, p. 10.

62. Mkulichi, op. cit., puts it as 1847 ; but, as his time-scale appears often to be ten years too early, he probably means 1857. The youthful appearance of Chilembwe in the photographs of him when he was in America (see frontispiece, and Lewis G. Jordan, *Negro Baptist History*, *U.S.A.*, *1750–1930*, Nashville, Tenn., 1930, p. 64) does not suggest that he was a man in his forties, which this estimate would make him. The estimate of 1871 is more likely, if these American photographs are taken as a fair indication of his age : for Chilembwe would then be in his middle twenties when he went to America. This would put him in the forties, or early fifties at the most, when he was shot in 1915. This calculation agrees with the statement of Chilembwe's niece, Harris, another daughter of his brother James, that John Chilembwe was about forty when he died (from information kindly collected by Mr. P. L. Bridle).

63. Cf. Rev. L. N. Cheek (American Negro minister who lived for a time with Chilembwe in Nyasaland) in 'Reminiscences of a Missionary', *The Mission Herald* (U.S.A.), vol. 44, September-October 1940, pp. 17-18.

64. Chilembwe's niece, Harris (see reference 62 above).

65. Chilembwe's niece, Miriam, says that his mother and father came from outside Nyasaland, and settled in Michiru near Blantyre (information kindly supplied by Mr. P. L. Bridle).

66. John Rebman, *Dictionary of the Kiniassa Language* (Basle, 1877), cf. pp. iii-vi.

67. The conclusion of field investigations by T. Price.

68. Cf. Frank Debenham, *The Way to Ilala* (London, 1955), pp. 221, 228-9.

69. Cf. *Z.I.M.O.P.*, October 1911, p. 4, for Booth's use of Blantyre mission boys.

70. *Central African Times*, iv, No. 10, 8 December 1900, p. 10.

71. Note in Booth's handwriting on the back of a leaflet headed 'African Industrial Society', in possession of the Seventh Day Baptist Historical Society ; also, p. 4, *The African Sabbath Recorder* (Cape Town), 6 January 1913, p. 4. Cf. also *Missionary Review of the World*, 1896, p. 293.

72. *The Missionary Herald*, February 1907, p. 3 : cf. reference 47 above.

73. Langworthy, op. cit. p. 53.

74. There is a revealing photograph, opposite p. 50 in Robertson's *Martyrs of Blantyre*, op. cit. It is titled 'Manganja and Yao', and portrays young Africans of the two tribes in European clothes. The Yao boy who carries a book—which

the Manganja boy does not—seems almost to have been designed to fit especially Mrs. Langworthy's description—as, indeed, does the Mang'anja.

75. Langworthy, op. cit. p. 53.

76. Booth MSS., 'Makololo Call', pp. B-C.

77. Langworthy, op. cit. p. 68.

78. Booth, op. cit. pp. C-D.

79. Ibid p. D.

80. Langworthy, op. cit. p. 82.

81. This and the following quotation are from Booth MSS., 'The Native African's Call for Pacifists', page reference unclear.

82. It should be noted to supplement Booth's account of this Ngoni country that the Blantyre Mission had a station there staffed by two women, one of them being Alice Werner; and that the great Ngoni raid of '84 had been turned by 'men without guns', the Scottish missionaries, Scott and Hetherwick

83. Langworthy, op. cit. pp. 91-5.

84. Ibid. pp. 98-100, 103-4.

85. Ibid. pp. 89-90.

86. Ibid. pp. 99-102.

87. *Z.I.M.O.P.*, September 1894, p. 4. Cf. also Langworthy, ' "Early Days" ', *Polished Shaft*, op. cit., October-December 1949, p. 4.

88. Langworthy, op. cit. pp. 107-11.

89. Cf. Rowley, op. cit. p. 155 ; Lewis Gann, 'The End of the Slave Trade in British Central Africa : 1899-1912', *Rhodes-Livingstone Journal*, No. 16, 1954, pp. 31, 38, 40 ; H. S. Stannus, 'The Wa Yao of Nyasaland', *Harvard African Studies* (Cambridge, Mass., 1922), iii, p. 354 ; *L.W.B.C.A.*, July 1902, No. 160, pp. 4-5.

90. Langworthy, op. cit. pp. 58-9.

91. *Z.I.M.O.P.*, September 1893, p. 6.

92. Langworthy, op. cit. p. 134.

93. Ibid. p. 135. Cf. Booth's moving testimony to this on last page of Booth MSS., 'Re John Chilembwe . . .'

94. *Central African Planter*, No. 5, January 1896, p. 63. See also *The Sabbath Recorder* (Plainfield, N.J.), vol. 73, No. 22, 25 November 1912, p. 701 ; and *Illustrated Missionary News* (London), 1 February 1895, pp. 25-6. The steamer was also often called the *Good News*, another translation of the Nyanja, *Mtenga Wabwino*. Cf. also *Accounts and Papers* (London), 1896, lviii, c. 8254, pp. 16, 27 ; *L.W.B.C.A.*, August 1894, p. 5, and February 1895, pp. 2-3.

95. Mkulichi, op. cit.

96. In Booth's *Africa for the African*, op. cit., opposite p. 49, there is a photograph of a group of Zambesi Industrial Mission workers. The African in the back row bears some resemblance to early pictures of John Chilembwe, and he is wearing a kind of sailor's costume. *Z.I.M.O.P.*, December 1895, indicates that Alexander Dickie, another Z.I.M. missionary with whom Chilembwe was in close contact (see *Africa for the African*, p. 51), was working with the Z.I.M. barges at the Chinde mouth of the Zambezi. Johnston, *British Central Africa*, op. cit., has a picture of a Mang'anja river pilot (p. 457), and pays tribute to the Nyasa Africans' nautical ability. Circumstantial evidence of this sort suggests that Chilembwe may well have worked on a river steamer, possibly the *Glad Tidings*.

97. *L.W.B.C.A.*, August 1890, p. 1. This indicates that before baptism he

was known simply as 'Kufa'. Rev. F. S. Chintali reports that this name was given to him by his own father whose name was Mapantha : 'To begin with, his father called him Gopani Kufa, which means Opani Kufa [Fear Death—AUTHORS]. As John Gray Kufa grew up, the name Gopani slowly faded away, leaving Kufa instead.' It is not clear from which European or Europeans John Gray Kufa took his Christian names.

98. *L.W.B.C.A.* No. 46, December 1892, p. 2 ; No. 67, September 1893, p. 1.

99. *Z.I.M.O.P.*, 23 November 1894.

100. The book appears to be E. D. Young, *The Search After Livingstone* (London, 1868).

101. Booth MSS., 'The Call of the Mang'anja People for Pacifists', p. 1.

102. Ibid.

103. Ibid. pp. 1-2.

104. Ibid. pp. 2-3.

105. Ibid. p. 3.

106. Ibid. pp. 3-4. For Mbona see Rowley, op. cit. p. 151 ; Werner, *Native Tribes*, op. cit. pp. 60-1 ; W. H. J. Rangeley, 'Mbona the Rainmaker', and T. Price, 'Mbona's Waterhole', *The Nyasaland Journal* (Blantyre), vi, No. 1.

107. Booth MSS., 'The Call of the Mang'anja People . . .', p. 4.

108. Ibid. pp. 4-6.

109. Ibid. p. 6.

110. Ibid. p. 7.

111. *Africa for the African*, op. cit. p. 23 and especially p. 45, '. . . my policy to the natives was severely challenged as too liberal by my co-workers'. Some idea of the troubled state of Booth's mind when making his decision to go to America is provided by an 1895 (undated) letter of his to Miller of the Z.I.M. that was found among the mission's remaining papers. In it Booth says : 'If found necessary to go to America, as I am often advised to, I suppose I must : but I am weary in spirit—His & yours, J. B.—pray for me, *do please*'.

112. Cf. *The Scottish Baptist Magazine* (Edinburgh), ix, 1895, p. 242 ; *The African Sabbath Recorder* (Cape Town), 6 January 1913, p. 5 : certified copy of a letter from Caldwell to Booth, '. . . your severance from the Mission came as a result of doctrinal differences in relation to Baptism, and to some extent a difference as to the Sabbath Day'.

113. *Scottish Baptist Magazine*, ix, 1895, pp. 241-3.

114. *Missionary Review of the World*, loc. cit., and vii, 1894, pp. 562-3.

115. *L.W.B.C.A.* No. 83, January 1895, p. 4.

116. *Z.I.M.O.P.*, July-August 1896, p. 9.

117. Rev. F. S. Chintali reports that he was a village headman.

118. *Africa for the African*, op. cit. p. 48. This brother appears to have suffered a change of heart later. A letter from Booth's wife, 17 October 1899, reports that he was teaching in a Zambesi Industrial Mission school on the borders of Portuguese territory (p. 27, pamphlet, *The Sabbath Evangelizing and Industrial Association*, No. 1 [Seventh Day Baptist Historical Society]).

119. *L.W.B.C.A.* No. 99, p. 3 ; cf. also No. 79, 1894, p. 4. See Public Record Office, London : BT.31.6671.46912, The African Missions Transport Company Limited ; BT.31.8627.62906, British Central Africa Transit Company Limited. These two files appear to indicate that a company of some kind existed from 1896 to 1903, though there is little indication of the volume of its business.

II: JOSEPH BOOTH AND JOHN CHILEMBWE

After the initial incorporation, Booth's share seems to have been slight in this particular project. But cf. reference 58, Chapter IV.

120. Booth MSS., 'The Zulu Call (or Challenge)', p. 1.

121. Ibid.

122. Ibid. p. 2.

123. As long ago as 1864, however, Horace Waller had taken a group of twenty Nyasa Africans to the Cape (Rowley, op. cit. p. 492).

124. Booth MSS., 'Zulu Call', p. 3.

125. For a general essay and bibliography on Ethiopianism, see George Shepperson, 'Ethiopianism and African Nationalism', *Phylon* (Atlanta, Ga.), xiv, 1, 1953, pp. 9-18. To this should be added two important sources on Ethiopianism : *Cape of Good Hope. Blue Books on Native Affairs*, especially *1898*, pp. 118-20; *1899*, pp. 16, 118; *1900*, pp. 4, 25, 49; *1902*, pp. 24, 54, 84; *1903*, pp. 34, 44-5; *1904*, pp. 30, 123; *1905*, pp. 22, 76; *1906*, pp. 7, 22, 32, 53-4; *1907*, pp. 17, 37; *1908*, pp. 30, 40 ; *South African Native Affairs Commission, 1903–5* (Cape Town, 1904–5), five volumes, 'Ethiopianism' fully indexed under 'Politics' and 'Religion'. Index to Subjects, Volume V.

126. 'Mr. Booth in Durban', *L.W.B.C.A.* No. 106, December 1906, pp. 10-11.

127. For this and the three above quotations, see Edward Roux, *Time Longer Than Rope. A History of the Black Man's Struggle for Freedom in South Africa* (London, 1949), pp. 92-4. Cf. also *The Central African Planter* (Zomba), 15 January 1897, pp. 3-4.

128. *L.W.B.C.A.* No. 106, December 1896, p. 11. Cf. also *Africa for the African*, op. cit. p. 45, where Booth speaks of 'the difficulty of bridging the *gulf between* the European and the native'.

129. Booth MSS., 'Zulu Call', p. 4.

130. J. Stuart, *A History of the Zulu Rebellion* (London, 1913), p. 556.

131. *Africa for the African*, op. cit. p. 35.

132. Booth MSS., 'The Native African's Call for Pacifists', p. 8.

133. Ibid.

134. Cf. *Z.I.M.O.P.*, July-August 1896, p. 8 ; October 1896, p. 9 ; January 1897, p. 3 ; April 1897, p. 5. Cf. also *The History of Pastor K. M. Malinki* (Malamulo, n.d.), an autobiographical pamphlet.

135. The other African trustees were Peter Michita, Stephen Luyo, and Ebury Ngalama.

136. Kindly loaned by Mrs. E. B. Langworthy.

137. 'The supreme authority and sufficiency of the Holy Scriptures of the Old and New Testaments as the Revelation of the Will of God to Man. The Unity of the Father, the Son and the Holy Ghost in the Godhead. The love of God to the world. Man's fall and spiritual death. Redemption from sin and from the wrath to come only through the propitiatory sacrifice of the Lord Jesus Christ. Justification by Faith. The necessity of the direct work of the Holy Spirit to impart and sustain spiritual life. Baptism of believers by immersion.'

138. *Africa for the African*, op. cit. pp. 49-51. See Appendix 1.

139. *The Central African Planter*, ii, 13, 1 March 1897.

140. The *Oban Times*, No. 3141, 6 February 1915, p. 5. The *Glasgow Herald* 2 February 1915, states that W. J. Livingstone went out to Nyasaland in 1891.

141. *Central African Planter*, No. 8, April 1896, p. 102.

142. Ibid. No. 12, February 1897.

143. Ian Carmichael, *Lismore in Alba* (Perth, 1951), pp. 65, 86, 103, 129, 138, 171-81. See also the *Oban Times*, No. 3141, 6 February 1915, p. 5; No. 3142, p. 2; No. 3146, obituary column; No. 3153, p. 2; No. 3159, p. 5. There are photographs of William Jervis Livingstone in this newspaper: No. 3141, p. 5, and No. 3159, p. 5.

144. For an opposing point of view see an anonymous manuscript, 'The Bachul, or Pastoral Staff of St. Moluag', Class XD, in the Reference Department of the Edinburgh Public Libraries. This document, which appears to be based on some local tradition, includes a highly coloured version of the 1915 Rising.

145. *The Times*, 29 November 1893, p. 7.

146. Ibid.; also the *Scotsman*, 28 November 1893, p. 5; and A. Z. Fraser, *Livingstone and Newstead* (London, 1913), chapters xxvii-xxviii.

147. A. L. Bruce, *The Cape to Cairo : Britain's Sphere of Influence* (Edinburgh, 1892).

148. *Scottish Baptist Magazine*, April 1915, p. 51.

CHAPTER III

CHILEMBWE AND BOOTH IN AMERICA
1897–1900

1. *L.W.B.C.A.* No. 126, 15 August 1898, pp. 5-6.

2. Ibid. Nos. 114-18, August-December 1897, pp. 10-11.

3. Ibid. No. 107, January 1897, p. 3.

4. Mkulichi, op. cit.

5. Booth MSS., 'Re John Chilembwe . . .', p. B.

6. Langworthy, op. cit. p. 103.

7. Roland Oliver, 'Some Factors in the British Occupation of East Africa, 1884–1894', *The Uganda Journal*, March 1951, pp. 52-5, for the Arab 'conspiracy'.

8. Booth MSS. op. cit. pp. B-C.

9. Booth quotation in reference 128, Chapter II.

10. Booth MSS. op. cit. p. C.

11. Ibid.

12. *Africa for the African*, op. cit. pp. 23, 45.

13. *Central African Times*, iv, 10, 8 December 1900, p. 10.

14. *Mission Herald*, vol. 19, No. 5, May 1915, p. 2.

15. Booth MSS., 'The Native African's Call for Pacifists', p. 8.

16. *L.W.B.C.A.* No. 126, August-December 1897, p. 11.

17. Ibid.

18. Was John Chilembwe ever in South Africa, either before or after his return from America? Some slight oral evidence exists for supposing that he was; but, again, the matter is puzzling.

19. Letter from Booth to his daughter Emily, of 9 April 1897, from c/o Professor Brown, Principal, Lincoln School, 924, 24 St. N., Washington (kindly loaned by Mrs. E. B. Langworthy).

20. It is not clear whether this Professor Brown is the same Brown who later befriended Chilembwe (see references 94-6 below).

21. *Africa for the African*, op. cit. passim, and especially pp. 23-5, 45.

22. See Roux, op. cit. passim.

23. *The African Sabbath Recorder*, 6 January 1913, p. 4.

24. *Missionary Review of the World*, xiv, 1901, p. 421.

25. Ibid. xx, 1907, p. 205.

26. Booth MSS., 'Re John Chilembwe . . .', pp. C-D.

27. Ibid. pp. D-E, for quotations in this paragraph.

28. Ibid. p. E.

29. *R.C.N.R.* pp. 4, 6.

30. Rayford W. Logan, *The Negro in American Life and Thought : the Nadir, 1877–1901* (New York, 1954).

31. *Africa for the African*, op. cit. p. 23.

32. *Virginia. A Guide to the Old Dominion.* Compiled by workers of the Works Projects Administration in the state of Virginia (New York, 1952), p. 82.

33. Ibid.

34. Ibid.

35. Herbert Aptheker, *A Documentary History of the Negro People in the United States* (New York, 1951), pp. 806, 813-14.

36. John Hope Franklin, *From Slavery to Freedom. A History of American Negroes* (New York, 1947), pp. 431-2, 435.

37. See Carter G. Woodson, *The History of the Negro Church* (Washington, D.C., 1921) ; Aptheker, op. cit. pp. 48, 67-9, 205, etc.

38. See Edward A. Freeman, *The Epoch of Negro Baptists and the Foreign Mission Board, National Baptist Convention, U.S.A., Inc.* (Kansas City, 1953), pp. 69-90.

39. Cf. ed. W. E. B. DuBois, *Efforts for Social Betterment among Negro Americans* (Atlanta, Ga., 1909), p. 17 : 1906 figures for National Baptist Convention—18,534 organizations ; 2,261,607 members ; $24,437,272 worth of church property. Cf. also *Virginia*, op. cit. p. 83.

40. Ed. W. E. B. DuBois, *Economic Co-operation among Negro Americans* (Atlanta, Ga., 1907), pp. 82-3.

41. See L. L. Berry, *A Century of Missions of the African Methodist Episcopal Church* (New York, 1942).

42. Cf. Rev. Chas S. Morris, 'African Coloured Baptists, 1899–1901' in *Christianity and the Natives of South Africa* (Lovedale, n.d.), ed. Rev. J. Dexter Taylor.

43. *Ecumenical Missionary Conference, New York, 1900*, pp. 469-71.

44. Blaikie, *Livingstone*, op. cit. p. 395.

45. See, in general, Wilber C. Harr, *The Negro as an American Protestant Missionary in Africa* (Ph.D. thesis, University of Chicago, 1945).

46. Booker T. Washington, *Up from Slavery. An Autobiography* (first published, 1901 ; 'World's Classics' edition, London, 1945), p. 88.

47. Ibid. p. 166.

48. George P. Marks, iii, 'Opposition of Negro Newspapers to American Philippine Policy, 1899–1900', *The Midwest Journal* (Jefferson City, Missouri), iv, 1, Winter 1951–2, p. 23.

49. See Franklin, op. cit. pp. 437-41 ; William Z. Foster, *The Negro People in American History* (New York, 1954), pp. 416-25.

50. August Meir, 'The Emergence of Negro Nationalism', *Midwest Journal*, iv, 2, Summer 1952, pp. 93-103 ; Wilson Record, 'The Negro Intellectual and Negro Nationalism', *Social Forces* (Chapel Hill, N.Ca.), xxxiii, 1 October 1954, pp. 13-15.

449

51. Rufus L. Perry, *The Cushite, or the Descendants of Ham* (Springfield, Mass., 1893), p. x (quoted in Meir, op. cit. p. 99).

52. Cf. Franklin, op. cit. pp. 402-5.

53. One may guess that Chilembwe had read the books of the great Negro hero, Frederick Douglass, for Booth in *Africa for the African* (e.g. pp. 23-4) shows an acquaintance with them, and Douglass's name was revered by all American Negroes. Also, it is most likely that he read Booker T. Washington's *Up from Slavery*—cf. Lewis G. Jordan (Chilembwe's mentor), *Negro Baptist History, U.S.A., 1750–1930* (Nashville, Tenn., 1930), end-paper in which Booker T. Washington takes the central place.

54. 'The Conservation of Race', *American Negro Academy Occasional Papers*, No. 2 (Washington, D.C., 1897), p. 10 (quoted in Robert Ernst, 'Negro Concepts of Americanism', *The Journal of Negro History* (Washington, D.C.), xxxix, 3, 1954, pp. 206-19).

55. George Padmore, *The Gold Coast Revolution* (London, 1953), p. 255.

56. Cf. here the Pan-African implications of 'Yours for Africa' with which Chilembwe concluded some of his letters to American Negro friends when he was back home : e.g. *Journal of the Twenty-Fourth Annual Session of the National Baptist Convention*, Austin, Texas, 14-19 September 1904 (Nashville, Tenn.), p. 37 ; *The Mission Herald* (Philadelphia), vol. 19, No. 1, May 1913, p. 2.

57. Ed. W. E. B. DuBois, *Economic Co-operation*, op. cit. pp. 49-54 ; Foster, op. cit. p. 364.

58. See, in general, Aptheker, op. cit. pp. 70, 287, 326-8, 329-30, 367-8, 670-1, 751 ; Record, op. cit. pp. 11-12 ; Franklin, op. cit. pp. 234-8.

59. George Brown Tindall, *South Carolina Negroes, 1877–1900* (Columbia, 1952), pp. 309-10.

60. *Illustrated Missionary News* (London), 1897, pp. 70-2, 105, 113 ; Gustav Warneck, *Outline of a History of Protestant Missions* (Edinburgh, 1901), p. 232. Cf. also Heli Chatelain and his 'Phil-African' League of 1896 (*Dictionary of American Biography*).

61. P. 195, *Africa and the American Negro. Addresses and Proceedings of the Congress on Africa held under the Auspices of the Stewart Missionary Foundation* (Atlanta, Ga., 1896). Cf. also Aptheker, op. cit. p. 751 ; E. Merton Coulter, *The South during Reconstruction* (Baton Rouge, La., 1947), pp. 98-9 ; *Dictionary of American Biography*.

62. See reference 42 above.

63. Cf. 'Back to Africa' imagery in slave songs, Miles Mark Fisher, *Negro Slave Songs in the United States* (Ithaca, N.Y., 1953), passim.

64. Herbert Aptheker, *Essays in the History of the American Negro* (New York, 1945), pp. 209-10.

65. Aptheker, ibid., and *American Negro Slave Revolts* (New York, 1943), passim.

66. See Aptheker, *Slave Revolts*, op. cit. ; Leonard L. Hayes, Jnr., *The Negro Community in American Protestantism* (Boston, 1953), pp. 144-57 ; *Virginia*, op. cit. p. 76.

67. Chilembwe's main town in the U.S., Lynchburg, Virginia, was not without its associations of Negro revolt : e.g. cf. Aptheker, *Documentary History*, op. cit. pp. 56-7, on connections between the 1812 slave conspiracy in Virginia and the Negroes of Lynchburg.

68. Aptheker, *Slave Revolts*, op. cit. p. 98 ; see also pp. 41-4.

69. C. L. R. James, *The Black Jacobins* (New York, 1938) ; Ralph Korngold, *Citizen Toussaint* (London, 1945) ; John W. Vandercook, *Black Majesty* (New York, 1928).

70. Aptheker, *Slave Revolts*, op. cit. p. 82, quotes Robert Alexander Young's pamphlet, *The Ethiopian Manifesto. Issued in Defence of the Black Man's Rights in the Scale of Universal Freedom* (New York, 1829), which foretells the coming of a mulatto saviour, huge, bearded, and invincible, from Grenada's Island, who was to destroy slavery.

71. See *Accounts and Papers*, 1831-2, xlvii, 482, Communications relative to Slave Insurrections and Trials of Missionaries, and 561, Report from the House of Assembly, Jamaica, on the Injury sustained during the Recent Rebellion ; James M. Phillipo, *Jamaica, its Past and Present State* (1843), pp. 270-1, 279, 293, 295, 356, 358, 426, 457, 460 ; John W. Clark, etc., *The Voice of Jubilee, a Narrative of the Baptist Mission, Jamaica, from its Commencement* (London, 1865), pp. 3, 25, 30, 32-9, 57, 59, 61-3, 113, 284, etc. ; W. J. Gardner, *History of Jamaica* (London, 1909), pp. 277-9, 285, 344, 351, 359, 473-4 ; Lord Olivier, *Jamaica* (London, 1936), pp. 63, 98, 125, 174 ; Philip D. Curtin, *Two Jamaicas. The Role of Ideas in a Tropical Colony, 1830-1865* (Cambridge, Mass., 1955), pp. 31-8, 85-9, 164-8, 195-6, etc.

72. Berry, op. cit. p. 34 ; Haynes, op. cit. pp. 150-1 ; Aptheker, *Slave Revolts*, op. cit. p. 275.

73. Cf. Haynes, op. cit. pp. 147-50, 154-7 ; 'Nat Turner's Confessions' reprinted in Harriet Beecher Stowe, *Dred* (London, 1856), pp. 498-505 ; Leys, op. cit. p. 328. The comparison between Nat Turner and Chilembwe suggested itself to Chilembwe's American Negro backers during their first reactions to the 1915 Rising: *Mission Herald*, vol. 19, No. 5, May 1915, p. 2.

74. Haynes, op. cit. p. 152.

75. Aptheker, *Slave Revolts*, op. cit. p. 327.

76. Cf. Gardner, op. cit. p. 285 ; Haynes, op. cit. p. 153.

77. Franklin, op. cit. p. 399.

78. Miles Mark Fisher, *The Negro Baptists and Foreign Missions* (B.D. thesis, Northern Baptist Theological Seminary, Chicago, 1922), p. 187.

79. The full title-page reads : 'AFRICA FOR THE AFRICAN. DEDICATED First, to VICTORIA, QUEEN OF GREAT BRITAIN. Second, to the BRITISH and AMERICAN CHRISTIAN PEOPLE. Third and Specially to the AFRO-AMERICAN people of the United States of America.—By JOSEPH BOOTH, MISSIONARY, NYASALAND, EAST CENTRAL AFRICA.' The 1897 edition used here—and for quotations in previous chapter—is marked on the front cover, 'Second Edition. Revised and illustrated.' So far, we have not been able to trace a copy of the first edition, for there seem to be few copies at all of this book left in the United States. It has fifty-eight pages of very close print, and, therefore, deserves to be called a book rather than a pamphlet.

80. See Chapter IX, reference 158.

81. *Africa for the African*, op. cit. p. 45.

82. Ibid. pp. 35, 45.

83. Ibid. p. 46.

84. From a Booth letter of 1899 in private American hands.

85. The imprint at the back of *Africa for the African* reads : 'Press of the Educator of Morgan College, Edmondson and Fulton Avenues, Baltimore, Md.'

John F. Wagner was the Principal of the College from 1888 to 1901. Unfortunately the College (to-day Morgan State College) has no records about the publication of Booth's book. Furthermore, the records of its branch school at Lynchburg (Chilembwe's main American place of education), the Virginia Collegiate and Industrial Institute, were destroyed by fire in 1917.

86. See reference 118, Chapter II.

87. See reference 138, Chapter II, and Appendix.

88. See Chapter IX, references 152-3.

89. *Africa for the African*, op. cit. p. 38.

90. Fisher, thesis, op. cit. p. 187.

91. See *Report of the Baptist Industrial Missionary Society of New York, 1897*, pp. 547, 554—information kindly supplied by the American Baptist Foreign Mission Society—which indicates that the main period of Booth's attempts to interest the white American Baptists in his mission proposals was September-November 1897.

92. Fisher, thesis, op. cit. p. 187 ; *Mission Herald*, 1907, p. 3.

93. *Who's Who in Colored America* (New York, 1927–40), v, pp. 2, 4, and 5 ; Freeman, *Epoch of Negro Baptists*, op. cit. pp. 86-7, etc. For a personal biographical statement, etc., see Jordan's own book, *Negro Baptist History*, op. cit. pp. 128, 239-40, etc. There is a good photograph of Jordan on p. 237, *The Baptist World Congress . . . Proceedings* (London, 1905).

94. Carter G. Woodson, op. cit. p. 278.

95. Porter W. Phillips, *W. W. Brown, Host* (New York, 1941), p. 58 (quoted from Jordan, *Negro Baptist History*, op. cit. p. 241).

96. Information kindly supplied by Miss Nannie H. Burroughs of the National Baptist Convention, U.S.A., Inc.

97. *Virginia*, op. cit. pp. 264-72. For a useful general review by a Southern white on conditions amongst Lynchburg Negroes in Chilembwe's day, see B. W. Arnold, Jnr., 'Concerning the Negroes of the City of Lynchburg, Virginia', *Southern History Association Publications*, x, 19-30, 1906.

98. Jordan, op. cit. p. 290, and end-paper, 'Some Negro Baptist Pathfinders', for biographical sketch and photograph (No. 56).

99. *Virginia*, op. cit. p. 270.

100. *Negro Education : a Study of the Private and Higher Schools for Colored People in the United States* (Washington, D.C., Government Printing Office, 1917. Bureau of Education Bulletin, 1916, No. 39), pp. 618-19.

101. *The Negro Caravan*, ed. Sterling Brown, etc. (New York, 1941), pp. 351-5. Cf. also James Weldon Johnson, *Along This Way* ('Penguin' edition, London, 1941), p. 181.

102. Communication from Mrs. Anne Spencer.

103. Ibid. President Madison C. Allen of the Virginia Theological Seminary and College to-day confirms the 'Che-Prince' story. Cf. H. S. Stannus, 'Notes on the Tribes of British Central Africa', *Journal of the Royal Anthropological Institute* (London), xl, 1910, p. 308 : 'Every Clan a . . . [Prince] *Chilembwe*'.

104. Cf. the Nyasa trade-union leader, Clements Kadalie, who also claimed to be of the 'royal blood' (from an unpublished Kadalie autobiographical MSS kindly supplied by Mr. George Padmore).

105. See R. H. Boyd, *A Story of the National Baptist Publishing Board* (Nashville, Tenn., 1924) ; Freeman, op. cit. pp. 91-104 ; DuBois, *Economic Co-operation*, op. cit. pp. 63-9.

III: CHILEMBWE AND BOOTH IN AMERICA

106. *Central African Times*, iv, No. 10, 8 December 1900, p. 10.

107. Information kindly supplied by President Madison C. Allen.

108. Cf. *Central African Times* letter (reference 106 above).

109. See reference 27 above.

110. This statement is based on a circumstantial assumption. The National Baptist Convention missionary journal, *The Mission Herald* (Philadelphia, Pa.), vol. 19, No. 5, May 1915, p. 2, states that 'Rev. John Chilembwe was a member of the Zion Baptist Church of this city'. But the whole matter is very puzzling, and one would like very many more details of Chilembwe's American Negro church membership.

111. Fisher, thesis, op. cit. p. 187; *The Sabbath Recorder* (Plainfield, N.J.), 1 and 22 August and 31 October 1898.

112. See Fisher, thesis, op. cit. p. 187; ed. Rev. J. Dexter Taylor, *Christianity and the Natives of South Africa* (Lovedale, n.d.), p. 79; Rev. Charles S. Morris, 'African Coloured Baptists, 1899–1901', *The Baptist World Congress, 1905 . . . Proceedings* (London, 1905), pp. 81, 325; Freeman, op. cit. p. 124.

113. See Appendix 2.

114. Woodson, op. cit. p. 278.

115. Cf. E. L. Fox, *The American Colonization Society, 1817–1840* (Baltimore, 1919), p. 92; L. Minor Blackford, *Mine Eyes Have Seen the Glory* (Cambridge, Mass., 1954), p. 284 n.; Ellis P. Oberholtzer, *A History of the United States* (New York, 1917), i, p. 79.

116. Cf. reference to 'the Adventists' Industrial Mission in Matabeleland', *Africa for the African*, op. cit. p. 18; *The Sabbath Recorder*, 22 August 1898. In general, for American religious sects mentioned in this book, see Elmer T. Clark, *The Small Sects in America* (Nashville, Tenn., 1937).

117. Pamphlet (Seventh Day Baptist Historical Society), *To the Pastors and Evangelists* (21 Sept. 1911), Booth: 'About fifteen years ago when, as an Evangelist, I first visited and preached to the Manganja people at Masanji, Port Herald, I was very much surprised by the questions of the Chief Chatyika, as to why we White Preachers put the law of God and the words and acts of Jesus, as to the Seventh Day Sacred Sabbath, away from us and "under our feet". Pastor John Chilembwe, of Chiradzulu, was present and saw that I could not answer from scripture.'

118. For Booth's shift to the Seventh Day Baptists and their financing of his new mission, see Joseph Booth, 'Why I abandoned Sunday-keeping', *The Sabbath Recorder* (Plainfield, N.J.), 1898, pp. 794 et seq.; William C. Hubbard, 'The Sabbath Evangelizing and Industrial Association', pp. 577-83, *Seventh Day Baptists in Europe and America. A Series of Historical Papers written in Commemoration of the One Hundredth Anniversary of the Seventh Day Baptist General Conference : celebrated at Ashaway, Rhode Island, August 20-25, 1902* (Plainfield, N.J., 1910), vol. i; a series of four pamphlets, *The Sabbath Evangelizing and Industrial Association*, 1899 (and other materials of the Seventh Day Baptist Historical Society); *The Sabbath Recorder*, 1898–1900, especially 1 and 22 August 3, 27, and 31 October, 26 December 1898, and passim.

119. See letter from Booth, *Central African Times*, No. 18, 27 January 1900.

120. Letter from F. B. Pearce, Government Secretary's Office, Zomba, 28 August 1912, to Rev. Edwin Shaw, Secretary of the American Sabbath Tract Society, Plainfield, N.J. (Seventh Day Baptist Historical Society).

121. *Sabbath Recorder*, 1900, p. 344.

122. Pamphlet, *The Sabbath Evangelizing and Industrial Association*, 1899, No. 4, pp. 5-6.

123. For the whole episode see Public Record Office, London : 1899, F.O.2.207, F.O. No. 210; F.O.2.209, Central Africa Nos. 184, 200; F.O.2.210, Central Africa Nos. 207, 219; F.O.2.211, p. 45; F.O.2.248, correspondence with Seventh Day Baptists, etc. See also *Sabbath Recorder*, vol. 56, 1900, pp. 27, 123, 548-9, etc.; Hubbard, op. cit. pp. 577-80; *Central African Times*, 22 July 1899, etc.

124. *Mission Herald*, February 1907, p. 3. This story was confirmed independently by Mr. Andrew Mkulichi, a former follower of John Chilembwe.

125. *Journal of the Twenty-Fourth Annual Session of the National Baptist Convention*, 14-19 September 1904 (Nashville, Tenn.), p. 363.

CHAPTER IV

THE FIRST WAVE OF ETHIOPIANISM IN BRITISH CENTRAL AFRICA
1900–1912

1. The exact date of Chilembwe's return to Nyasaland is difficult to determine. Reference 108 in Chapter III indicates that there is some confusion about this. Booth MSS., 'Re John Chilembwe . . .' speaks of Chilembwe's being two years at the Virginia Theological Seminary, Lynchburg. But a letter from L. G. Jordan to the Foreign Mission Board of the Seventh Day Baptists says that Chilembwe was brought to America in 1897 and that he was three years at the Lynchburg Seminary (*Sabbath Recorder*, 6 February 1911, p. 171). These three pieces of evidence would put the date of his return to Nyasaland either just before, or well into 1900. *Journal of the Twentieth Annual Session of the National Baptist Convention*, 12-17 September 1900 (Nashville, Tenn.), pp. 48-9, seems to infer that Chilembwe was back in Africa shortly before this Session was held. Two references in *Central African Times* point to his return at some time towards the end of the third or the beginning of the fourth quarter of 1900 : 1 September 1900, 'pitiable travesty of Christianity'; and Chilembwe's own letter in the issue of 8 December 1900. This seems very likely, as the Rev. Charles S. Morris, who went back to Africa with him, was speaking at the Ecumenical Missionary Conference, New York, 25 and 27 April 1900 : see *Ecumenical Missionary Conference, New York, 1900* (New York, 1900), i, p. 469; ii, p. 156. But Fisher, thesis, op. cit. p. 187, says that Chilembwe sailed for Africa on 23 January 1901. However, that Chilembwe was back in Nyasaland at some time in 1900 seems confirmed by African oral evidence and by D. S. Malekebu, 'The History of the Providence Industrial Mission' in Appendix I, *Nyasaland Education Department. Report for 1931*.

2. *Central African Times*, 8 December 1900, p. 10.

3. This is the meaning of the initials 'A.P.I. Mission' at the end of Chilembwe's letter to the *Central African Times* of 8 December 1900. See also *Journal of the Twentieth Annual Session of the National Baptist Convention*, 12-17 September 1900 (Nashville, Tenn.), p. 45. This also gives the names of the original American Negro trustees of Chilembwe's mission.

4. The Providence Missionary Baptist District Association is noted at the beginning of Chapter IV, p. 63, 'Early Baptist Organizations' in Jordan, *Negro Baptist History*, op. cit.

5. Freeman, op. cit. pp. 28, 35, 43. *N.B.* also that Dr. D. Malekebu, head of the Providence Industrial Mission since 1926, says that it may have been named after a church in Brooklyn, New York. That Chilembwe had associations with Brooklyn is known; but it seems impossible to trace any church there with which he was connected that has 'Providence' in its title. Cf. the Negro Providence Baptist Church in Chicago of which Thomas L. Johnson was pastor, 1873–6: Johnson, *Africa for Christ. Twenty-eight Years a Slave* (London, 1882), pp. 5, 25; also the 'Mr. Providence' in P. T. Stanford, *From Bondage to Liberty: being the life story of the Rev. P. T. Stanford who was once a slave and is now a recognized pastor of an English Baptist Church* (Smethwick, 1889), p. 22; and the Providence Baptist Cathedral, etc., in F. D. Price, *Liberian Odyssey* (New York, 1954), pp. 15, 28.

6. Cf. reference 75, Chapter II. Cf. also statement by Chilembwe's niece, Harris, that not all of the Chilembwe family understood Chinyanja in the early days (from Mr. P. L. Bridle).

7. Cf. figures of National Baptist Convention holdings given in reference 39, Chapter III. The Convention's foreign mission expenditure rose from nearly nine thousand dollars in 1900 to over forty-three thousand dollars in 1909.

8. *L.W.B.C.A.* No. 144, March 1900, p. 7, in an article called significantly 'The Parting of the Ways'.

9. Cf. Sir Harry H. Johnston, *British Central Africa* (London, 1898), pp. 203-4; John Buchan, *A Lodge in the Wilderness* (London, 1906), p. 140.

10. Later, such criticisms would appear: see reference 143 below.

11. See James Wells, *The Life of James Stewart* (London, 1909); *General Assembly Reports of the United Free Church of Scotland* (Edinburgh, 1901), pp. 64, 71.

12. *Journal of the Twentieth Annual Session of the National Baptist Convention*, 12-17 September 1900 (Nashville, Tenn.), pp. 45-6; *Journal of the Twenty-Fourth Annual Session . . .* , 1904, p. 37; Rev. L. N. Cheek, 'Reminiscences of a Missionary', *Mission Herald*, vol. 44, September-October 1940, p. 17; also private information kindly supplied by the Rev. L. N. Cheek.

13. From a letter by Sir Alfred Sharpe in private hands.

14. Mkulichi, op. cit.

15. See *British Central Africa Gazette*, v, No. 7, 1898, p. 3.

16. Public Record Office, London, F.O.2.308, British Central Africa, July-October 1900: Central Africa No. 216.

17. *British Central Africa Gazette* (Zomba), iii, 1901: No. 129, 3 August 1901, Rex *v.* W. L. Livingstone. See also *Central African Times*, iv, No. 47, 24 August 1901. The 'W. L.' instead of 'W. J.' in the initials seems to be a misprint.

18. Cf. *Central African Times*, viii, No. 51, 16 September 1905, for a murder case amongst Chiradzulu Nguru.

19. Chilembwe's niece, Miriam, and others have claimed American origins for Mrs. Ida Chilembwe. However, Chilembwe's first American Negro helper, Rev. L. N. Cheek, states that she was a local woman, and that he saw the marriage take place. One of Chilembwe's early pupils, Mr. Maynard Gibson Mbela declares that she was Chilembwe's second wife and was a half-caste: her mother was probably a Sena and her father probably of Portuguese East African origin. Dr. D. Malekebu of the post-1926 Providence Industrial Mission supports this

view, and states that Chilembwe never married an American Negro woman. Existing photographs of Mrs. Chilembwe do not suggest that she came from the United States.

20. *Journal of the Twentieth Annual Session of the National Baptist Convention,* 12-17 September 1900 (Nashville, Tenn.), pp. 45-6.

21. From information kindly supplied by Mr. Maynard Gibson Mbela.

22. Hubbard article, *Seventh Day Baptists* . . . op cit. p. 580. M. Ellsworth Olsen, *A History of the Origin and Progress of Seventh-day Adventists* (Washington, D.C., 1925), p. 493, gives $12,500 as the purchase price.

23. *Sabbath Recorder*, 20 January 1902, p. 45; 3 February 1902—Booth's project for an 'African Repatriation Society', which was supported by a number of American Seventh Day Baptist pastors.

24. Hubbard, op. cit. pp. 582-3; also *Sabbath Recorder*, 1900-2, passim.

25. Olsen, op. cit. pp. 493-4; unpublished MSS., 'Historical Sketch of the Work of the Seventh-day Adventists in Nyasaland, 1902-1915', kindly provided by Mr. V. E. Robinson; Public Record Office, London, F.O.2.607, July-October 1902—Central Africa No. 226; information kindly supplied by Mrs. Josephine Cunnington Edwards; *The History of Pastor K. M. Malinki* (Malamulo, n.d.), pp. 1-6.

26. *Central African Times*, iv, No. 31, 4 May 1901.

27. Ibid. No. 34, 25 May 1901.

28. *Ruo District Book*, under 'Missions'; *Nyasaland Times*, 11 February 1915, letter from H. J. Rayment; see also letter from F. B. Pearce (reference 120, Chapter III).

29. *Central African Times*, No. 34, 25 May 1901.

30. Cf. H. T. (Chiana) Harrington, 'The Taming of North-Eastern Rhodesia', *The Northern Rhodesian Journal*, vol. ii, No. 3, 1954, p. 16.

31. This section is based on information kindly supplied by the Rev. L. N. Cheek himself, and his 'Reminiscences', op. cit.; *Journal of the Twentieth Annual Session* . . . , op. cit. pp. 48-9; *Journal of the Twenty-Eighth Annual Session of the National Baptist Convention*, 16-21 September 1908, p. 85; L. G. Jordan, *In Our Stead* (Philadelphia, 1914), p. 24.

32. Cheek, 'Reminiscences, op. cit. p. 17.

33. Ibid.

34. *Central African Times*, viii, No. 49, 2 September 1905, quoting from *The Richmond Planet*.

35. This section is based on: a cyclostyled pamphlet on Miss DeLany of 1910 by Miss Rose M. Miller for the Epworth League of the Seventh North Street Methodist Episcopal Church, Lorain, Ohio; material under reference 31 above; 'Hear Miss DeLany', *Journal of the Twenty-Fourth Annual Session of the National Baptist Convention*, 1-19 September 1904 (Nashville, Tenn.), pp. 358-63; *The Spelman Messenger* (Atlanta, Ga.), vol. 18, No. 1, October 1901, p. 2, and vol. 18, No. 5, February 1902, p. 5. Emma B. DeLany, 'Why I go as a Foreign Missionary', material kindly supplied by Miss Florence Read of Spelman College.

36. National Baptist Convention figures for Chiradzulu given in ed. W. E. B. DuBois, *The Negro Church* (Atlanta University Publications, 1903), p. 120: 5 pastors and workers; 3 churches; 35 members.

37. Mkulichi, op. cit. It is just possible that this story is confused with a similar tale by L. G. Jordan, p. 171, *Sabbath Recorder*, 6 February 1911, p. 171.

IV: FIRST WAVE OF ETHIOPIANISM

38. Cf. Cheek, 'Reminiscences', op. cit. p. 17 : 'We continued our extension into Portuguese Territory East . . .'

39. Mkulichi, op. cit. Cf. *Journal of the Twenty-Fourth Annual Session,* op. cit. p. 37.

40. See *Journal of the Twenty-Third Annual Session of the National Baptist Convention,* 16-21 September 1903, p. 37 : '. . . one of our native helpers . . . in Rhodesia . . . is Noah Chinzinga . . . one of the first baptized by Bro. Chilembwe. . . .' (Cf. reference 30 above.)

41. *N.B.* the first reference to the P.I.M. by the Blantyre missionaries in their journal was in October 1903, *L.W.B.C.A.* No. 175, p. 6. Information that Chilembwe preached in Nyanja comes from his niece, Miriam.

42. 'Hear Miss DeLany', op. cit.

43. *Central African Times,* viii, No. 49, 2 September 1905.

44. L. G. Jordan, 'What the Brethren in Black are doing in Missions', *Missionary Review of the World,* xviii, No. 8, 1905, p. 600. Cf. also Cheek article, *Central African Times,* viii, No. 49, 2 September 1905 : 'seventy-one in school and eleven awaiting baptism'.

45. National Baptist Convention data in DuBois, *Economic Co-operation,* op. cit. pp. 70 and 83, mentions Cheek and Miss DeLany but not Chilembwe, thereby suggesting that they were looked upon as over him in authority, at this time. But (see reference 3 above) Chilembwe had originally been designated by his sponsors 'pastor and superintendent' of the P.I.M. A draft from the Convention of $1800 through the African Lakes Company to the P.I.M. was sent, in the first place, to Cheek, not to Chilembwe : p. 70.

46. *L.W.B.C.A.* No. 186, September 1904, p. 1. Cf. a similar story in more detail in Major-General Sir Francis de Guingand, *African Assignment* (London, 1953), pp. 87-8.

47. R. R. Kuczynski, *Demographic Survey of the British Colonial Empire* (London, 1949), pp. 629-32, etc.

48. See reference 9, Chapter II above.

49. Supervisor of Native Affairs *v.* Blantyre and East Africa, Limited, High Court of British Central Africa, Blantyre, 28 April 1903, p. 5, *British Central Africa Gazette,* x, No. 4, 30 April 1903. *N.B.* also the reference in this important judgement to the 'philanthropic efforts of Mr. Joseph Booth of the Plainfield Mission' to inform the Africans of their land rights.

50. *Scottish Baptist Year Book, 1915-16* (Glasgow), p. 24. Cf. *Year Book, 1899,* p. E.27. In the first of these, the name is spelt 'Makwangala'; in the second, there is a second 'w'. Cf. *L.W.N.* (reference 172, Chapter V below) where the 'w' is also omitted. 'Makwangwala' is used here and later because this was the spelling employed by the District Resident, C. A. Cardew (see reference 174, Chapter V below).

51. *L.W.N.* No. 246-7, November-December 1909, p. 2.

52. These revolts will be discussed in the last chapter.

53. No. 31, 5 May 1906.

54. No. 39, 30 June 1906.

55. Information kindly supplied by Mr. Maynard Gibson Mbela. Cf. the experience at this time of another African preacher, K. M. Malinki, friend of Chilembwe and former co-worker with him and Booth at the Zambesi Industrial Mission. Following Booth, Malinki had switched his allegiance to the Seventh-day

Adventists, and in 1902 was helping the Negro, Thomas Branch, to extend their mission. 'I taught the Sabbath of the Lord to everybody and found that the schools were progressing. But other denominations tried to threaten and stop me. Some of the Europeans came to my schools with a whip and said : "Why are you deceiving our people and letting them rest on the wrong day ?" But I boldly answered, "Please, you don't have your people here, these people belong to my tribe and are the people of God" ' (*History of Pastor K. M. Malinki*, op. cit. p. 6).

56. *Nyasaland Government Gazette*, xv, 1908, p. 75 ; xvi, 1909, p. 83 ; xvii, 1910, p. 81. See also reference 141 below. Cf. also Chilembwe to Foreign Mission Board of the National Baptist Convention : 'Elephant hunting in this part of Africa is profitable, but we must pay the Government $125 a year for a licence. Will the Board give me this amount ?', *Journal of the Twenty-Fourth Annual Session*, op. cit. p. 37. Also on Chilembwe as a hunter, see Rev. Harry K. Matecheta, op. cit. (reference 47, Chapter II above), p. 27.

57. Cf. *Sabbath Recorder*, vol. 73, No. 22, 1912, p. 726.

58. Booth MSS., 'The Native African's Call for Pacifists', p. 8B. Mr. A. A. Carscallen, a former Seventh-day Adventist missionary in East Africa, informs us that when he went up-country in British East Africa in 1906, one Government official in particular whom he met was very bitter against the Seventh-day Adventists because of Booth's influence. In similar fashion, Booth's name had been raised by the authorities in South Africa in 1903 at the time of an official inquiry into native affairs : *South African Native Affairs Commission* (Cape Town, 1904), ii, pp. 219-20. This also reveals that Booth was still interested in a kind of Central African transport company : cf. reference 119, Chapter III.

59. There is a good photograph of Peter Nyambo in *Missionary Worker* (Watford), vol. 15, No. 25, 1911, p. 199. See also reference 48, Chapter V below.

60. Letter by C. Robinson to Government Secretary, Zomba, 17 June 1915 (kindly copied by Mr. S. G. Maxwell).

61. There is the suggestion of a link between Booth's activities in South Africa from 1896 onwards and the circumstances which led to the Natal Zulu Rebellion of 1906 in Frederick B. Bridgeman, 'The Ethiopian Movement in South Africa', *Missionary Review of the World*, xvii, 1904, pp. 434-43.

62. A. C. Watters, *History of the British Churches of Christ* (Indianapolis, 1948), p. 109 and *passim*.

63. *The Bible Advocate* (Birmingham), vol. 17, No. 13, 30 March 1906, p. 203.

64. Ibid. vol. 18, No. 3, 20 September 1907, p. 620 ; No. 47, 1907, p. 764 ; vol. 19, No. 24, 12 June 1908, p. 382, etc.

65. *L.W.N.* No. 244-5, September-October 1909, p. 13.

66. Private letter of Booth in American hands ; *The Watchtower* (New York), xxviii, No. 4, 15 February 1907, p. 3943, and for subsequent quotation.

67. Russell wrote six main volumes, which were published eventually together under the general title of *Studies in the Scriptures* : I, The Divine Plan of the Ages (Alleghany, Pa., 1886) ; II, The Time is at Hand (Alleghany, Pa., 1891) ; III, Thy Kingdom Come (Brooklyn, New York, 1891) ; IV, The Battle of Armageddon (Brooklyn, N.Y., 1897) ; V, The At-one-ment between God and Man (Brooklyn, N.Y., 1886) ; VI, The New Creation (Brooklyn, N.Y., 1904).

68. Minna Edgar, *Memoirs of Dr. John Edgar* (n.d.), p. 14, states that he was always giving away copies of *The Divine Plan of the Ages*. It is probable that

Booth was introduced to Russell's writings in this way. A private Booth letter in American hands also suggests this.

69. See *Dictionary of American Biography*; K. S. Latourette, *A History of the Expansion of Christianity*, *IV* (London, 1941), pp. 443-4; and works in subsequent references.

70. Cf. Ira V. Brown, 'Watchers for the Second Coming: The Millenarian Tradition in America', *Mississippi Valley Historical Review*, xxxix, 3 December 1952; Shirley Jackson Case, *The Millennial Hope* (Chicago, 1918).

71. *Studies in the Scriptures*, IV, op. cit. pp. 604, 622, quoted in Milton Stacey Czatt, *The International Bible Students. Jehovah's Witnesses* (Scottdale, Pa., 1933), p. 8. See also Royston Pike, *Jehovah's Witnesses* (London, 1954), pp. 57-66.

72. *Millennial Dawn. III, Thy Kingdom Come* (Alleghany, Pa., 1891), p. 20.

73. Herbert Hewitt Stroup, *The Jehovah's Witnesses* (New York, 1945), pp. 54, 131, 158, etc.; *Studies in the Scriptures*, IV, op. cit. pp. 485-7. Cf. also the place given to millennial elements in the American socialist tradition in Donald Drew Egbert and Stow Persons, *Socialism and American Life* (Princeton, N.J., 1952), i, index.

74. *Millennial Dawn*, op. cit. p. 23.

75. Ibid.

76. Russell quoted in *Livingstonia News*, vol. ii, 1909, p. 73.

77. *The Watchtower*, xxviii, No. 4, February 1907, pp. 3942-3. A private Booth letter in American hands indicates that Booth visited Russell in November 1906, and that he spent three weeks with him.

78. Ibid. p. 3943.

79. This oral evidence seems to be based on a rumour which was reflected in an editorial on Ethiopianism in *Central African Times*, x, No. 20, 16 February 1907, that Booth was returning to Nyasaland.

80. *The Watchtower*, xxx, No. 13, 1 July 1909.

81. Ibid.

82. There is a good succinct account of the Kamwana movement based on Nyasaland evidence (European and African), Booth's letters, and some Watch Tower material in *Sabbath Recorder* (Plainfield, N.J.), vol. 73, No. 22, 25 November 1912, pp. 719-23. See also *Livingstonia News*, vol. ii, 1909, pp. 22, 52-3, 56-9, 68, 72-5, 81, 83, 90; iii, 1910, pp. 14, 46-7. *The Watchtower*, xxx, 1909, pp. 4316, 4359, has further references; and see especially its article 'The Good Tidings Spreading in Africa', No. 13, 1 July 1909. It is interesting to notice that the official Nyasaland annual reports for this time have no mention of the movement. Some of the Kamwana material to follow is based on private Booth letters in American hands.

83. *Tenth Foreign Mission Report. United Free Church of Scotland* (Edinburgh, 1910), p. 9; *Missionary Record of the United Free Church of Scotland*, vol. ix, p. 321.

84. *Twelfth Foreign Mission Report. United Free Church of Scotland* (Edinburgh, 1913), p. 81; *1912 Annual Report, Livingstonia* (Glasgow, 1913), pp. 19, 21.

85. *Seventh Day Baptist and Mission Work in Nyasaland, Africa. A Report by N. Olney Moore*, op. cit. pp. 14-15; *World Missionary Conference, 1910. Reports of Commissions* (Edinburgh, 1910), III, A. MacAlpine, pp. 193-4.

86. *Nyasaland Annual Reports, 1907-8* (Cd. 3729-38, No. 574), p. 22; *Z.I.M.O.P.*, July-September 1909, p. 12. Cf. *Nyasaland Times*, 2 November 1911: disaffection in Fort Johnston district over increased hut tax; ring-leaders deported.

NOTES AND REFERENCES

87. In R. D. McMinn, 'The First Wave of Ethiopianism in Central Africa', *Livingstonia News*, vol. ii, 4 August 1909.

88. A private Booth letter in American hands says that Kamwana was deported in June 1909.

89. *Twelfth Foreign Mission Report. United Free Church*, op. cit. p. 81; *1912 Annual Report, Livingstonia*, op. cit. pp. 19, 21.

90. *Livingstonia News*, vol. iii, 6 December 1910, pp. 92-4.

91. See Johnston's report, 'The Harvest Work in Africa', *The Watchtower*, xxxii, No. 2, 15 January 1911.

92. *1909 Annual Report, Livingstonia* (Glasgow, 1910), p. 4. It may be suggested that one element that may have had something to do with creating at least part of the formal conditions inside which the Kamwana movement emerged was the encouragement of the revivalistic spirit in the area by Livingstonia missionaries. Cf. *Missionary Record of the United Free Church of Scotland*, 1902, p. 357; 1904, p. 214 (four thousand people at Communion at Ekwendeni); 1906, p. 448, photograph; 1909, p 450, photograph; 1910, pp. 168, 409; 1911, p. 30. See also Rev. Chas. Inwood, *An African Pentecost* (London, 1911). On the 'spiritual upheaval that took place during Dr. Inwood's visit' of evangelization to Livingstonia, see Donald Fraser, 'Work in Nyasaland', *Missionary Record*, op. cit., 1911, pp. 410-411.

93. *Tenth Foreign Mission Report. United Free Church*, op. cit. p. 91.

94. *1911 Annual Report, Livingstonia* (Glasgow, 1912), pp. 23-4.

95. *Livingstonia News*, 1909, p. 74.

96. *1911 Annual Report, Livingstonia*, op. cit. p. 24.

97. *Sabbath Recorder*, No. 22, 1912, op. cit. p. 727.

98. See W. P. Livingstone, *Laws of Livingstonia* (London, n.d.), pp. 194, 257, 277, 309, 327.

99. Mary Hall, *A Woman's Trek from the Cape to Cairo* (London, 1907), p. 78.

100. *L.W.N.* No. 157, October-December 1901, pp. 14-15.

101. Leaflet in the possession of the Seventh Day Baptist Historical Society, 'A Native Pastor's Pleas' (24 September 1911). See also W. P. Livingstone, op. cit. pp. 339-40; and *Sabbath Recorder*, vol. 73, No. 22, 25 November 1912, pp. 714-15 and especially p. 723.

102. Livingstone, op. cit. pp. 339-40.

103. Vol. iii, 6 December 1910, p. 92.

104. Olney Moore, op. cit. pp. 4-5; *Sabbath Recorder*, 8 August 1910, pp. 163, 186-7; Booth/Domingo leaflets and materials in Seventh Day Baptist Historical Society.

105. 'The Report of the Visit to South and Central Africa by N. O. Moore and Wayland D. Wilcox', pp. 695-735, *Sabbath Recorder*, vol. 73, No. 22, 25 November 1912, which has already been quoted several times, must be considered a basic source for the history of independent churches in Central Africa.

106. Leaflet, 'The African Industrial Society', in the possession of the Seventh Day Baptist Historical Society, note in Booth's own hand that Chilembwe would help with English translations.

107. From a study of report forms from these little churches which came to Booth at the Cape (from Mrs. E. B. Lnagworthy).

108. J. H. Morrison, *Streams in the Desert. A Picture of Life in Livingstonia* (London, n.d.), p. 57. Cf. *Livingstonia News*, vol. iii, 1910, pp. 2-3.

109. Cf. Chief Makwangwala (reference 50 above) who shifted his whole village to be near a European-style school.

110. E.g. pamphlet, 21 November 1911, 'To all S.D.B. Pastors . . .' (in Seventh Day Baptist Historical Society) : 'We have resolved to follow or stand and fall by the name of Christ, not Elliott, or Booth, nor Russell, or any other man's or woman's chosen name' ; Moore-Wilcox Report, 1912, op. cit. pp. 704, 714, 732, etc.

111. *The African Sabbath Recorder*, No. 2, June 1912, Booth : 'It needs to be borne in mind that the leading pastors are in frequent correspondence with free and able South African leaders, such as President J. L. Dube and Editor Tengo Jabavu, who both know their language and have read their letters here'.

112. At least six of these were issued—probably more—and five are in the Seventh Day Baptist Historical Society files.

113. Pamphlet (in Seventh Day Baptist Historical Society), 'To the Pastors and Evangelists', 21 September 1911.

114. Ibid.

115. Cf. Chapter VII, reference 2.

116. Moore-Wilcox Report, 1912, op. cit. p. 722.

117. Cf. ibid. p. 723.

118. See *Sabbath Recorder*, 1912, 25 November, pp. 675-723 ; 19 August pp. 229-30, etc.

119. Cf. W. P. Livingstone, op. cit. pp. 339-40.

120. *World Missionary Conference. 1910. Reports of Commissions* (Edinburgh), ii, p. 379. The detailed inquiry form which Chilembwe must have filled in for this purpose (see ibid. p. 277) appears to be lost : information from Dr. J. Oldham and the International Missionary Council. This is a major loss, undoubtedly, of Chilembwe records.

121. Cf. ed. Alexander Hetherwick, *Robert Hellier Napier in Nyasaland* (Edinburgh, 1925), p. 68 ; *Z.I.M.O.P.*, July 1910, p. 4, 'John Chilembwe . . . carrying on good work' ; *Sabbath Recorder*, 6 February 1911, p. 171.

122. *Census of Nyasaland Protectorate, 1911* (Zomba), p. 13.

123. *Journal of the Thirtieth Annual Session of the National Baptist Convention*, 14-19 September 1910 (Nashville, Tenn.), p. 59. Cf. figure of 105 members in 1905, reference 44 above.

124. *Journal of the Thirty-Second Annual Session of the National Baptist Convention*, 11-16 September 1912 (Nashville, Tenn.).

125. A letter from Chilembwe to Booth (see Appendix 4), dated 6 November 1911, indicates that it was at this time that work began on the brick church.

126. Leaflet headed 'African Industrial Society', with annotations by Booth in his own hand (copy with Seventh Day Baptist Historical Society). The leaflet was, apparently, printed on the Blantyre Mission press for distribution ; but the number of copies and the extent of distribution is not known. Subsequent quotations about the Society are from this source.

127. 'A sign of the times is the opening up of small retail stores by enterprising natives . . . in competition with the Banyan', *Annual Report. British Central Africa*, 1904 (Cd. 2684-18, No. 472).

128. *Sabbath Recorder*, 6 February 1911, p. 171.

129. See Appendix 4 for 1911 Chilembwe-Booth letter.

130. Ibid.

131. Cf. *R.C.N.R.* p. 5 : 'It was part of his [Chilembwe's] scheme to form a union between their [African] various sects and his own Mission'.

132. Cheek took back with him to the United States two of the Njilimas : Matthew and Fred.

133. *Journal of the Thirty-Second Annual Session of the National Baptist Convention,* 11-16 September 1912, pp. 119-22. In this account Chilembwe appears to have over-estimated the distances.

134. Mr. Maynard Gibson Mbela, to whom we are indebted for this and above information.

135. *Journal of the Thirty-Second Annual Session,* op. cit. pp. 119-22.

136. This list of schools by G. A. Shakespeare supplements Chilembwe's own above : 'Sangano at USIIRAINA ; Ndunde at JUMANYUMBE ; Namkundi at LILIMITSA ; Jumalowe at CHITAMBULI ; Chingoli at CHINGOLI ; Matili at CHITAMBULI'. Cf. here the statement by Rev. Harry K. Matecheta, *Blantyre Mission. Nkhani za Ciyambi Cace* (Blantyre, 1951), p. 27 : 'His [Chilembwe's] teaching at this school was, "God gave the Europeans their land, and black men theirs ; let us save our country" '. Unfortunately, this statement is undated.

137. Mkulichi, op. cit.

138. *Journal of the Thirty-Second Annual Session,* op. cit. pp. 119-22.

139. Ibid.

140. Mkulichi, op. cit. For the Blantyre Mission's knowledge of Chilembwe's hunting trips at this time, see *Sabbath Recorder,* No. 73, 1912, p. 727.

141. See reference 56 above. For dates of gun and game licences issued to Chilembwe and his hunting cronies, Rev. L. N. Cheek and John Gray Kufa, see *Nyasaland Government Gazette,* 1902, p. 1 ; 1903, p. 78 ; 1904, pp. 231, 293 ; 1905, pp. 398, 451 ; 1906, pp. 564, 574, 579 ; 1907, pp. 716-17, 726 ; 1908, pp. 75-76 ; 1909, pp. 83, 119 ; 1910, p. 81 ; 1911, p. 117 ; 1912, p. 264 ; 1913, p. 148 ; 1914, p. 95 ; etc. It should be noticed that the references for 1912-14 are to '*Wm.* Chilembwe' (our italics).

142. *Sabbath Recorder,* 6 February 1911, p. 171 : L. G. Jordan, apparently reporting from a Chilembwe letter—Chilembwe 'has been making a tour of the East Portuguese Province. . . . The treatment the subjects receive is very bad ; they live in extreme poverty. . . . The authorities did not want [Chilembwe and his men] to remain because they spoke against the bad habits and wicked living, with the cruel treatment of the natives . . . they finally had them arrested.'

143. *Sabbath Recorder,* No. 73, 1912, p. 727. Cf. also the statement (kindly supplied by the Rev. L. N. Cheek) that he and Chilembwe baptized on admission of faith only.

144. Ibid.

145. Cf. references 56 and 141 above. Hetherwick's protest against Chilembwe's elephant-hunting was certainly not the first time he had spoken out against an African who indulged in this sport. For many years the Blantyre missionaries had had trouble with members of their own African congregations and staff who had neglected mission work for elephant-hunting, or who had used the mission as a protective screen behind which to extend the profitability of their shooting. See *L.W.B.C.A.,* January 1889, p. 2 ; May 1889, p. 2 ; November 1889, p. 3 ; etc.

146. See Jordan, *Negro Baptist History,* op. cit. p. 241 ; also *Journal of the Thirtieth Annual Session,* op. cit. p. 59 : Chilembwe had written a letter to the National Baptist Convention appealing for payment for four of his teachers in out-

IV: FIRST WAVE OF ETHIOPIANISM

stations, and for school supplies. His letter was placed before American Negro Baptist business men and others 'with the result that Dr. C. First Johnson, of Mobile, Ala., pledged $50 a year and Rev. J. B. Raynor, of Calvert, Tex., pledged $25 a year on the salary of Brother Chilembwe'. Six others also promised $25 each a year for the four teachers.

147. Mbela, op. cit.

148. The late Rev. James Reid, former Church of Scotland missionary in Nyasaland, told us of the annoyance to many Europeans that was caused by Chilembwe's buying European-style clothing for his wife in the local stores.

149. *Journal of the Thirty-First Annual Session of the National Baptist Convention*, 13-18 September 1911 (Nashville, Tenn.), pp. 199-200.

150. This account of Chilembwe's growing tensions with the Bruce Estates is based on African evidence which has already been mentioned, as well as on a large amount of European and African oral evidence and testimony. Cf., here, Parliamentary question, 19 February 1908 (*Parliamentary Debates*, 1908, pp. 294-5), on and concessions to Europeans in Chiradzulu and other districts, and petition by natives against alienation.

151. See reference 9, Chapter II.

152. *L.W.N.* No. 2, April-May 1911, p. 18. This important article by Dr. A. M. Caverhill on 'Ethiopianism' is given in a fuller form in *Life and Work (Scotland)*, xxxiii, 1911, p. 383 et seq., and xxxiv, 1912, p. 30 et seq. In this version it should be noted that some of the Nyasaland material (which might possibly have given offence if it had been published in full in the Blantyre version of the paper) is expanded : e.g. in the Scotland version, the last line of this quotation reads, 'The native here does not greatly take to his black brother over the water, if we may judge from the success of John Cheek's [*sic*] mission'.

153. *The Aurora*, vol. iv, 1 October 1900, No. 23, pp. 48-9, 'Wanted—a New Religion'.

154. *L.W.N.* Nos. 214-15, January-February 1907, pp. 13-14, and No. 5, October-December 1911, for figures in Nyasaland : estimated 15,000 Muslims in excess of Christians in the Protectorate. For 'Chinasala' see T. Price, 'The "Arabs" of the Zambezi', *The Muslim World* (Hartford, Conn.), xliv, 1, 1954, p. 36; also *L.W.N.* No. 1, 1911, p. 22, '*Kuchotsa nasala . . .* to liberate from Mohammedanism'.

155. E.g. Norman McLean, *Africa in Transformation* (London, 1914), pp. ix-x ; also Robert Laws, *World Missionary Conference, 1910*, op. cit. iii, p. 196.

156. E.g. *Central African Times*, No. 5, 4 November 1905 : 'Where Mohammedanism flourishes, there is a unity which, when extended, becomes a source of unrest. . . .' Cf. also H. Brode, *British and German East Africa* (London, 1911), p. 83 : '. . . signs of a pan-Islamic agitation were noticed only two years ago, and it is certain that a religious rising in one part of East Africa would soon spread all over the country'.

157. Winston Spencer Churchill, *The River War* (London, 1899), chapter ii, especially p. 34.

158. From conversations with Dr. Hastings K. Banda.

159. Information kindly supplied by Dr. W. E. B. DuBois.

160. E.g. *Central African Times*, No. 41, 14 July 1906, editorial on Upton Sinclair's *The Jungle*, and No. 46, 25 August 1906, letter from Keir Hardie to Bankole Bright, an African living in Edinburgh, in support of the rebels in the

NOTES AND REFERENCES

Natal Native Rising of 1906; *Livingstone Mail*, No. 115, 6 June 1908, quotes Jack London's *Revolution*, and discusses socialism with reference to North-Western Rhodesia and the British South Africa Company—ends with the remark, 'What wonder if the revolution is coming'—and 11 December 1909, 'Social Reform', etc. etc.

161. *L.W.N.* No. 2, 1911, p. 17 (see reference 152 above).

CHAPTER V

PRELUDE TO REVOLT
1912–1915

1. *L.W.N.*, July-September 1913, No. 4, p. 1.

2. *L.W.N.*, July-September 1913, No. 4, p. 4. Cf. H. Moyse-Bartlett, *The King's African Rifles* (Aldershot, 1956), p. 195.

3. Nyasaland *Annual Reports*, No. 732, 1911–12 (Cd. 6007-32), pp. 5, 7, 17-19; No. 772, 1912–13 (Cd. 7050-13), pp. 8-9, 14, 21-2 ; No. 832, 1913–14 (Cd. 7622-23), p. 31.

4. Sir Philip Mitchell, *African Afterthoughts* (London, 1954), p. 24.

5. *L.W.N.*, November-December 1912, No. 5, p. 13. Cf. *Nyasaland Government Gazette*, xix, 1912, pp. 116-17, The Native Foodstuffs Ordinance of 1912 which forbade the sale or resale of native foodstuffs in many parts of southern Nyasaland.

6. *L.W.N.*, April-June 1913, No. 3, p. 3 ; Nyasaland *Annual Report* No. 772, 1912–13 (Cd. 7050-13), pp. 8-9. On the incidence and effects of Nyasaland labour migration in general, see *South Africa. Correspondence relating to the recruitment of Labour in the Nyasaland Protectorate for the Transvaal and Southern Rhodesia Mines, 1908*. (Cd. 3993) ; Margaret Read, 'Migrant Labour in Africa and its Effects on Tribal Life', *International Labour Review*, xlv, No. 6, June 1942, pp. 606-31.

7. Cf. Nyasaland *Annual Report*, No. 772, 1912–13 (Cd. 7050-13), pp. 8-9.

8. Mitchell, op. cit. p. 24.

9. Alexander Hetherwick, *The Romance of Blantyre* (London, n.d.), p. 206.

10. *The Mission Herald*, vol. 19, No. 1, May 1913, p. 2.

11. *L.W.N.*, April-June 1913, No. 3, p. 3.

12. *The Mission Herald*, vol. 19, No. 6, June 1913, p. 4.

13. See photograph, p. 158. Cf. also letter from a Blantyre woman of 21 February 1915, in *Daily Chronicle*, 14 April 1915 : Chilembwe 'baptized in the river, had steps made to descend to it, and was always attended by four deacons'.

14. Cf. R. R. Kuczynski, *Demographic Survey of the British Colonial Empire* (London, 1949), ii, p. 633, etc.

15. Mitchell, op. cit. p. 27.

16. Ibid. p. 26.

17. Kuczynski, op. cit. p. 619.

18. See Chapter IV, reference 134.

19. *A Handbook of Nyasaland*, compiled by S. S. Murray (Zomba, 1932), p. 129.

20. Ibid.

21. Ibid. p. 133.

22. *Livingstonia News*, No. 2, vol. viii, April 1915, p. 24. Cf. also A. W. Lee, *Charles Johnson of Zululand* (London, 1930), pp. 108-9, on Bantu church separatism.

V: PRELUDE TO REVOLT

23. For an excellent commentary on this and kindred points, see J. Clyde Mitchell, 'The Political Organization of the Yao of Southern Nyasaland', *African Studies* (Johannesburg), September 1949, pp. 141-59. Cf. also Max Gluckman's concept of rebellion/revolution in his *Rituals of Rebellion in South-East Africa* (Manchester, 1954), pp. 23-6.

24. *Handbook of Nyasaland*, op. cit. p. 129.

25. Nyasaland *Annual Report*, No. 772 (Cd. 7050-13), p. 22.

26. *Handbook of Nyasaland*, op. cit. pp. 133-40.

27. Ibid. p. 289. See also, in general, *A Report by Mr. Eric Smith . . . on the Direct Taxation of Natives in the Nyasaland Protectorate* (London, 1937), pp. 6-8, etc.

28. E.g. Nyasaland *Annual Report*, 1912–13, p. 21.

29. Cf. *R.C.N.R.* p. 5, paragraph 13 (e) ; p. 7, paragraph 22.

30. *R.C.N.R.*, paragraph 29.

31. *R.C.N.R.*, paragraph 22 states that 'headmen and well-to-do natives would prefer a flat 5/- tax to the present 8/- with a 4/- rebate on production of a signed labour certificate'.

32. *R.C.N.R.*, paragraph 23.

33. In general, on the Nyasaland land situation, see *Report of a Commission . . . 19 July 1920 to enquire into Certain Matters connected with the Occupation of Land in the Nyasaland Protectorate* (Zomba, 1921, 10582) ; *Nyasaland Protectorate. Land Commission 1946* (Zomba, 1947), I, Abrahams Report.

34. 1920 Land Commission *Report*, op. cit. p. 13.

35. *Nyasaland Times*, 23 April 1914.

36. *L.W.N.*, July-September 1913, No. 4, pp. 1-2. Cf. also May-August 1914, No. 8, pp. 2-3.

37. E.g. *Nyasaland Times*, 1914—23 April, report on Legislative Council discussion ; 7, 21 May, correspondence ; 28 May, editorial ; 9 June, 'Native Tenants' article ; 2 July, letter from 'No Bible Thumper' ; etc.

38. Nyasaland *Annual Report*, 1912–13, op. cit. p. 21.

39. Ibid. 1913–14, p. 34.

40. *L.W.N.*, July-September 1913, No. 4, p. 2.

41. 17 September 1914.

42. *L.W.N.*, March 1913, No. 2, p. 14.

43. *L.W.N.*, March 1913, No. 2, p. 5.

44. Information kindly supplied by Professor D. D. T. Jabavu. Cf. also *Seventh Day Baptists and Mission Work in Nyasaland, Africa. A Report by N. Olney Moore* (Chicago, 1950), pp. 9-10 : 'He seemed to feel the brotherhood of all races so deeply that he would be willing, he told us, for his daughter to marry a native African'.

45. This and subsequent quotations and details are taken from a four-page British Christian Union leaflet of February 1913, kindly supplied by Mrs. E. B. Langworthy.

46. Other names included : 'Dr. Lyman Abbott, Editor, *Outlook*, New York ; Dr. Burghart Du Bois, Editor, *Crisis*, New York'.

47. Sol. T. Plaatje, *Mhudi* (Lovedale, 1930). See Edward Roux *Time Longer than Rope* (London, 1949), pp. 118-19.

48. Material on Peter Nyambo is based on his own answers to questionnaires; on an interview with him by Pastor S. G. Maxwell, formerly of the Seventh-day

NOTES AND REFERENCES

Adventist Mission, Blantyre; information kindly supplied by Pastor A. A. Carscallen, who was with Nyambo at the Seventh-day Adventist Mission in British East Africa (see references 58-9, Chapter IV); *The Missionary Worker* (Watford), No. 5, vol. 12, 25 December 1908; and No. 25, vol. 15, 4 December 1911, 'Peter Nyambo and the Nyasa Mission Work', p. 199, etc.; 'Peter's Plaint', a single-page leaflet which reprints a letter from Nyambo to the *S.A. Spectator* of April 1913, in which he gives biographical details and a number of criticisms of white rule (kindly supplied by Mrs. E. B. Langworthy).

49. Maxwell interview, op. cit.

50. 'Peter's Plaint', op. cit.

51. Cf. Roux, op. cit. pp. 118-19, for a similar petition of the South African Native National Congress.

52. Cf. *Nyasaland Times*' comments, 2 July 1914.

53. *R.C.N.R.* p. 6, paragraph 18.

54. These and subsequent quotations from the 1914 Petition are taken from a copy kindly supplied by Mrs. E. B. Langworthy.

55. From a private Booth letter kindly supplied by Mrs. E. B. Langworthy.

56. We are most grateful to Mr. Walter Cockerill for putting at our disposal personal papers and memoranda which have enabled not only much of this section to be written but have also made it possible to trace many other details for this book. Unless otherwise stated, quotations, etc., in this section are taken from this material.

57. David Duncan Wallace, *South Carolina* (Chapel Hill, N.Ca., 1951), p. 298.

58. Mary Tew, *Peoples of the Lake Nyasa Region* (London, 1950), p. 98.

59. Ibid. pp. 95-6.

60. Sir George Smith, 'Nyasaland and General Northey's Campaign', in *The Empire at War*, edited by Sir Charles Lucas (London, 1924), iv, p. 260. Cf. also *British Central Africa Gazette*, 1898–1901, troubles in Central Angoniland; Judge Nunan sent to investigate. These were the result of Ngoni reaction to two unscrupulous European traders, Sehlmann and Ziehl. There were five executed, one of whom, Malota, was 'an educated and nominally Christian native who had visited Europe, who was himself a planter, and who was drawing a large salary from a local planting firm' (*Central African Times*, 23 February 1901). Nunan drew a moral: 'Certain native teachers . . . had shown a tendency to abuse their power. . . . Personally he was opposed to allowing unorganized mission stations to be established in a district like Angoniland.' For further troubles involving Ngoni, land and taxation, see *Central African Times*, 9 March 1901, etc. Cf. also Donald Fraser, 'The Chief Who Would Not Help', *The Record of the Home and Foreign Mission Work of the United Free Church of Scotland*, xvi, 1916, pp. 147-8.

61. *The Berlin Courant* (Berlin, Green Lake County, Wisconsin), lxi, 19, Thursday, 19 November 1914, quotes in full a letter from Cockerill to his mother, Mzimba, August 1914: 'I stopped first at Uchinda where Filipo Chinyama has a school near Chiole and Ncheu. . . .'

62. Ibid.

63. 'Filipo Chinyama . . . seems to have been connected at one time with the 7th Day-adventist Mission, judging from correspondence between him and Mr. Konigmacher' (a Seventh-day Adventist missionary in Nyasaland): from 301/15 No., 10 August 1915, Zomba, A. M. D. Turnbull, Assistant Chief Secretary,

Nyasaland, to Superintendent, Malamulo Mission, Blantyre. (Copy kindly supplied by Mr. S. G. Maxwell.)

64. *Bible Advocate*, vol. 22, 1911, No. 43, 27 October, p. 683.

65. *Scottish Baptist Year Book*, 1915–1916 (Glasgow), Baptist Industrial Mission of Scotland, Twentieth Annual Report, pp. 9, 10. Cf. also statement by C. A. Cardew, Ncheu 1915 Resident (kindly collected by Mr. F. M. Withers), that 'When the Baptist Industrial Mission abandoned their mission at Dzunje Filipo established what he called "the Church of Christ" there'.

66. *Handbook of Nyasaland*, op. cit. p. 422.

67. See Sir George Smith and Donald Fraser, reference 60 above. Some authors have inadvertently suggested that Chimtunga's opposition to Government recruitment linked him with Chilembwe. E. H. Lane Poole in *The Native Tribes of the Eastern Province of Northern Rhodesia (Notes on their Migrations and History)* (Lusaka, 1938), p. 9, states that Chimtunga 'spent a period of years in the seclusion of exile at Zomba, for his share in the "rising" of 1915 . . .' Mary Tew, op. cit. p. 97, follows Lane Poole, and notes 'he was deposed after a rising in 1915'. Mr. Lane Poole, in correspondence, kindly confirms that the Chimtunga affair had nothing to do with Chilembwe. In fact, it took place around October 1915 (see *Nyasaland Times*, 7 October, 4 November 1915)—though, obviously, the origins of the trouble went back to the beginning of the War.

68. Cockerill's fellow Seventh Day Baptists, Moore and Wilcox, had noticed similar happenings during their tour of inspection of Booth's Nyasaland centres.

69. Cf. Mrs. Tamar Davis, *A General History of the Sabbatarian Churches* (Philadelphia, 1851), pp. 54-5. Cf. also a letter from S. H. Davis, Treasurer, Seventh Day Baptist Missionary Society, Ashaway, R.I, 7 June 1915, to Cockerill. This letter indicates the close interest of his denomination in Sabbatarianism in Ethiopia : 'Before our first missionaries went to China Seventh Day Baptists had learned that Abyssinia was practically a Sabbath keeping nation. . . . Mr. Joseph Booth of Cape Town gave us quite a little information, the accuracy of which we would like to have ascertained.'

70. It should also be remembered that the inveterate African Bible readers of the area would know that 'Ethiopian' was the only Scriptural term which referred to them with any degree of status ; and others were not unaware of the Abyssinian defeat of the Italians at Adowa in 1896.

71. No. 6, 11 February 1915.

72. Sir George Smith in *The Empire at War*, op. cit. p. 259.

73. *Kenya* (London, 1924), p. 329.

74. It is unlikely that this was a misprint. The same error occurs in R. C. F. Maugham's *Nyasaland in the Nineties* (London, 1935), p. 54. The value of Mr. Maugham's account of the Rising, etc., is that it was derived directly from the Governor's private dossier. (Information kindly supplied by Mr. R. C. F. Maugham.)

75. *Peace Handbooks. Issued by the Historical Section of the Foreign Office. Vol. XV . . . Nyasaland* (London, 1918–19).

76. Cf. L. G. Jordan, *In Our Stead*, op. cit. p. 12.

77. Ibid. 'During 1913 he has completed one of the largest houses of worship in British Central Africa.' Many other Europeans noted the church's costly and elaborate character : cf. letter of 21 February 1915 from a Blantyre woman, in *Daily Chronicle*, 14 April 1915, where it is claimed that it cost £1500 to build.

Mkulichi, op. cit., says that it was opened by a 'Bwana Cole' of the Zambesi Industrial Mission. Is this a confusion with the Z.I.M. missionary, John Chorley, whose association with Chilembwe's church is clear? See photograph (p. 310) and Chapter VII, reference 13.

78. *The Times*, 22 April 1915 (copy of this particular edition in *The Times* Library), quoting from *Natal Mercury*. See also *Nyasaland Times*, 5 February 1915 : '. . . seemed to be built almost as a fort. . . .'

79. Herbert Aptheker, *American Negro Slave Revolts* (New York, 1943), p. 299, 'Turner and his followers set out for the country seat, Jerusalem, where there was a considerable store of arms'.

80. John W. Vandercook, *Black Majesty* (New York, 1928).

81. See, for example, *L.W.N.*, January-February 1914, No. 6, p. 2 ; *Robert Hellier Napier in Nyasaland*, edited by A. Hetherwick (Edinburgh, 1925), p. 91. Cf. also photograph of African-built Churches of Christ church (p. 231).

82. Mkulichi, op. cit.

83. Cf. W. P. Livingstone, *Laws of Livingstonia* (London, n.d.), p. 339.

84. Cf. a statement by Pastor K. M. Malinki (in an interview kindly obtained by Mr. S. G. Maxwell), Chilembwe's friend of the early Z.I.M. days : 'Things went well for a few years when, later, Chilembwe hated the European. His hatred grew more bitter that he definitely made up his mind to destroy all the Europeans in Nyasaland. But, as he could not do all this by himself, he at once got busy interesting all his believers and his friends to join him in his plan. "The European is here to make you his slave for ever, let us get rid of him", he told them. One day John Chilembwe came to my house. "Why do Europeans trouble us ?" he asked. "Let us plan to kill them all !" "How can we do that ?" I asked. "They came here in peace and have patiently taught us many things, including the Word of God." "You are a coward," cried Chilembwe, and he went away and told all his followers to keep away from me because I was their great enemy and would one day betray them. That was the last I saw of Chilembwe and the end of our friendship.' Cf. also statement by Rev. Harry K. Matecheta (one of the first ordained ministers of the Church of Scotland in Nyasaland) in his *Blantyre Mission. Nkhani za Ciyambi Cace* (Blantyre, 1951), p. 27 : 'One day on my way back from Ndunde I slept in his [Chilembwe's] house ; he and his people and I did not sleep, speaking about his hate of Europeans. I told them that the white people came here to help us and our country ; they refused [to see it that way—AUTHORS' gloss].' (Translation from Nyanja original.)

85. Cf. a statement (kindly obtained by Mr. P. L. Bridle) from Chilembwe's niece, Harris : 'During the final year before the Rising Chilembwe taught non-payment of taxes but that had not been a part of his early teachings. Before becoming antagonistic to the Government his teachings were much the same as other religions except that he was more zealous than most in taking the message from house to house over a wide area of the Southern Province.'

86. See reference 127 below.

87. Scottish Companies' Office, Edinburgh · Bruce Estates, file No. 8650.

88. *Nyasaland Times*, 23 April 1914.

89. This point was made by Sir Robert Grant (amongst others), who was in charge of the trials of most of the Chilembwe rebels.

90. For an additional biographical detail on W. J. Livingstone, see *Nyasaland Times*, 24 April 1913.

V: PRELUDE TO REVOLT

91. Cf. *R.C.N.R.* p. 7, paragraphs 25, 27-8. Mr. M. G. Henschel, a Director of the Watch Tower Bible and Tract Society, summarizing field investigations into Chilembwe by the Society's workers, states that there was 'some trouble' over forestry reserves, as a result of which Chilembwe again wrote to the Government. (Information kindly supplied by Mr. Henschel.)

92. *South Africa. Correspondence . . . 1908* (Cd. 3993), op. cit. p. 54.

93. *Nyasaland Times*, 12 March 1914.

94. Ex Harris (see reference 85 above).

95. *R.C.N.R.* p. 5, paragraph (e).

96. From the late Rev. James Reid.

97. As reference 95 above. Cf. *Peace Handbooks . . . XV*, op. cit. p. 70 : Bruce Estates over 20,000 acres of holdings. The figure of 1000 for the labour force was provided in an interview by Mr. John Robertson, one-time section manager of the Bruce Estates (see reference 18, Chapter VI). For map of the original Bruce Estates, see Johnston *Report . . . of British Central Africa* (London, 1896, C. 8254), facing p. 25. See also Denis D. Lyell. *Memoirs of an African Hunter* (London, 1923), p. 53, from 1908 *Handbook of Nyasaland*, Bruce Magomero estate had 939½ acres under cotton; Bruce Lukulezi estate had 300 acres under cotton. See also in this work pictures of the Bruce Estates at Mlanje and Lukulezi.

98. *R.C.N.R.*, p. 5, paragraph (e).

99. Cf. Lieutenant-Colonel Charles Hordern, *History of the Great War . . . Military Operations. East Africa. I* (London, H.M.S.O., 1941), pp. 525-9; Heinrich Schnee, *German Colonization* (London, 1926), p. 81.

100. Sir Hector Duff, *African Small Chop* (London, 1931), p. 195.

101. Sir George Smith in *The Empire at War*, op. cit. pp. 272-5.

102. Ibid. pp. 270-2. See also Duff, op. cit. pp. 187-8, 200.

103. E.g. W. A. Elmslie, *Among the Wild Angoni* (Edinburgh, 1899), pp. 170-1 ; Alice Werner, *Myths and Legends of the Bantu* (London, 1933), p. 239.

104. *Livingstonia News*, Nos. 5-6, 1914, pp. 61-2.

105. *Scottish Baptist Year Book* (Glasgow), end, 19th Annual Report of the Baptist Industrial Mission of Scotland, letter from A. Smith, 11 September 1914.

106. Hordern, *Military Operations*, op. cit. p. 180.

107. References to Chilembwe and Watch Tower range from Lord Hailey's relatively mild note on p. 73 of his *Native Administration in the British African Territories, Part II* (London, 1950), to such assertions as Chilembwe's organization of 'the Watchtower Movement, a strange mixture of distorted Christianity and darkest heathenism, with rites that led to numerous murders' in Eric Rosenthal, *Stars and Stripes in Africa* (London, 1938), p. 264—though Mr. Rosenthal does distinguish Chilembwe's supposed 'Watchtower Movement' from the American body—to the mixture of misconstructions in such a work as W. Lloyd Jones, *K.A.R.* (London, 1926). Here (pp. 207-8) Chilembwe becomes, after a Watch Tower education in America—the Nyasaland 'leader of the sect . . .' which is so called because its adherents 'build towers from which to watch for the end of the world' !

108. *R.C.N.R.* p. 6, paragraphs 18, 19.

109. Cf. *Nyasaland Times*, No. 9, 4 March 1915, 'Notice. Published for Public Information. List of Natives Still Wanted' : No. 13, 'Wilson Daniel Kusita. A Ngoni. Resided formerly at Chilembwe's, lately Watch Tower preacher in Upper Shire District.'

110. See reference 137, Chapter II. Chilembwe's theology in 1915 seems to

have been that of his sponsors, the National Baptist Convention : see Freeman, *Epoch of Negro Baptists*, op. cit. pp. 84-6.

111. See reference 114-15, Chapter IV.

112. *Studies in the Scriptures. IV, The Battle of Armageddon* (Brooklyn, 1897), pp. 11, 392.

113. E.g. Frederick S. Khonda of the Churches of Christ Mission : 'Our brother is familiar with the English Bible and we found him studying Isaiah. He is a possessor of several of "Pastor" Russell's books, and receives their periodical' (*Bible Advocate*, vol. 25, No. 29, 4 December 1914, p. 729).

114. Russell's culling of the contemporary press for his arguments (e.g. *The Battle of Armageddon*, op. cit.) was extensive.

115. *Studies in the Scriptures. I* (Alleghany, Pa., 1886), pp. 338-42, etc. etc.

116. Leys, op. cit. p. 328 : 'church . . . said to have cost £380, most of it raised in Nyasaland, an immense sum in a country where the standard wage was five shillings a month'. Cf. reference 77 above : another Blantyre witness's estimate was £1500.

117. See reference 10 above.

118. See references 56 and 141, Chapter IV.

119. Freeman, *Epoch of Negro Baptists*, op. cit. p. 129 : 'In 1910 Mr. M. C. Treat for three consecutive years gave donations averaging $1,200.00 per year to be applied to the salaries of the Reverend E. Murff, South Africa, and a native worker, Reverend John Chilembwe. . . .' From Jordan, *Negro Baptist History*, op. cit. p. 241, it appears that Treat was a white man.

120. *The Mission Herald*, No. 10, October 1914, p. 3.

121. Sir George Smith in *The Empire at War*, op. cit. p. 257.

122. Cf. Sir Hector Duff, op. cit. pp. 181-2.

123. Chilembwe seems to have shown some awareness of the Berlin Act ; cf. reference 99 above.

124. For source, see reference 126 below. After reading this letter, one wonders at the widespread belief of which this statement from the *Annual Register, 1915* (London, 1916), p. 319, is typical : 'The rising was quite unconnected with the Anglo-German War'.

125. Kindly supplied by Mr. Walter Cockerill.

126. This date was reached as a result of checking a file of the *Nyasaland Times* in the British Museum Newspaper Library for the period 30 July 1914 (No. 31) to 31 December 1914 (No. 53). The issue for 26 November 1914 (No. 48), p. 7, column 6, bears an article, 'Censorship or Absolutism', which refers to the restrictions by the Government on the activity of Reuter's Nyasaland agent. At the bottom of this column, a section of about 1¾ inches has been cut out of the paper. The issue of 3 December in its weekly comment, and also in the rhymed critical verses that follow, seems to refer not only to the Chilembwe episode but also to the Reuter's trouble. Chilembwe's letter was apparently to be published as a separate sheet to be inserted inside the paper—this type of 'stop press' practice was quite common with the *Nyasaland Times*. After the Resident's action, it would be quite a simple matter to remove these 'insets', and any small notice that referred to the letter could then be cut with scissors from the main body of the paper.

We are most grateful to Mr. Maynard Gibson Mbela, a former P.I.M. pupil, for a statement (kindly collected by Mr. O. E. Chirwa) which first drew our attention to this important episode. Mr. Gibson writes 'As a rule this letter was sent

470

to the Resident Commissioner, Blantyre, who stopped its publication. The Editor accordingly published the fact that John Chilembwe's letter had been withheld by the censor. A copy of the paper was sent to John Chilembwe, but afterwards the Resident Commissioner went as far as banning the paper as a whole. The issue had the notice about Chilembwe's letter cut out, and was not sent off.' We are indebted to Mrs. K. Livingstone who allowed us to examine what is, apparently, one of the few copies left of the 'insets' of this letter that were prepared for the *Nyasaland Times*. It is from this that the Chilembwe letter printed in the text is taken.

Cf. also Mkulichi, op. cit., on the episode (translation and paraphrase from the original Nyanja) : 'The *Nyasaland Times* announced that large numbers of Africans had been killed at Karonga. This moved every African's heart, to see the black man come to such an end, when they had no idea of the causes at issue, and in a job the wages of which were a meagre price for a man's life. Because of this Chilembwe questioned the Governor through a letter to the *Nyasaland Times*. . . . The Editor was charged by the D.C. at Blantyre for making trouble.'

A date at some time in November for the episode is also suggested by the official assertion that Chilembwe's 'postal correspondence, both to and from him, was intercepted and examined for three months before the rising' (Hector Duff, Chief Secretary, *Nyasaland Government Gazette*, No. 4, xxiii, 1916, p. 5). But, against this must be set Duff's statement that this examination of Chilembwe's correspondence 'revealed nothing incriminating or even suspicious'.

127. From a letter by Bishop Auneau of the Nguludi Mission (kindly supplied by Mr. F. M. Withers). See also Sir Philip Mitchell, *African Afterthoughts*, op. cit. pp. 248-9 ; and *R.C.N.R.* p. 4, paragraph 10. Cf. also reference 131 below.

128. Mr. Maynard Gibson Mbela, op. cit., states that the Nguludi mission was attacked 'because Roman Catholics indulged in the practice of rivalry against the P.I.M.—building their own churches where the P.I.M. had its own'. Cf. *L.W.N.*, January-February 1914, No. 6, p. 2, 'The Marist Brothers of the Roman Church, whose head station is at Nguludi, 14 miles from here [Blantyre] have lately shown an unwanted zeal in planting schools in our neighbourhood'. Also, *The Scottish Baptist Magazine* (Glasgow), xiii, 1908, p. 161, for criticisms by B.I.M. missionary of 'the Roman Catholic invasion' ; J. H. Morrison, *Streams in the Desert. A Picture of Life in Livingstonia* (London, n.d.), pp. 120-1, for African criticism of Catholic educational facilities ; *Bible Advocate* (Birmingham), No. 17, 26 April 1912, for Churches of Christ criticism of Marist Fathers.

129. *Military Operations. East Africa. I*, op. cit. p. 179. Cf. also Duff, *African Small Chop*, op. cit. p. 200.

130. *R.C.N.R.* p. 4, paragraph 13 (c).

131. Cf. the statement kindly supplied by Col. A. Livingstone Bruce of the Magomero Estates : 'If memory serves me right, it was in the year 1913 that my attention was first drawn to the activities of John Chilembwe. At that time we employed John Gray Kufa . . . as hospital dispenser at Magomero. He came to me one day to ask if he might go to Chilembwe's church . . . the following Sunday. That was the first time I had heard of Chilembwe so I asked John Gray many questions about him. He gave me the impression that he was uncomfortable about answering. In consequence I made it my business to obtain through native sources what information I could about Chilembwe's activities. What little evidence I did obtain, I imparted privately to the Governor. . . . At that period there

was nothing to show that Chilembwe was interested in the natives resident on Magomero.'

132. Cf. the three months' period when Chilembwe's correspondence was opened officially (reference 126 above).

133. Mkulichi, op. cit. Cf. also a statement from Mr. M. G. Henschel's independent inquiry (reference 91 above) : '. . . he [Chilembwe] did his best to stop men from volunteering for the 1914 war. Some cases came to his attention of ill-treatment of soldiers' wives living on European estates because they could not afford the rents in their husbands' absence. He wrote letters to the Government about this [and other matters] . . . but all his protests were ignored. At last a letter came to him from the Government stating that representatives were being sent out to see him. Guessing that this meant that they were coming to arrest him because of his continual complaints against authority, Chilembwe called all his supporters to rise in rebellion with him. . . .'

134. R. C. F. Maugham, *Nyasaland in the Nineties*, op. cit. p. 55 : '. . . arrangements had actually been made [to deport Chilembwe] and in a few days he would have been on his way to the Seychelles Islands when the blow fell'. (See reference 74 above.)

135. Mkulichi, op. cit.

136. Ibid. In an earlier part of his Chilembwe testament Mr. Mkulichi departs from his Nyanja and gives in English three statements which he implies Chilembwe used frequently : '1. I hear the crying of my Africans. 2. My people are destroyed through lack of knowledge. 3. It is better for me to die than to live.'

137. *R.C.N.R.* p. 4, paragraph 13 (b) ; p. 6, paragraphs 15, 16.

138. Leys, op. cit. p. 326.

139. *Laws of Livingstonia*, op. cit. p. 355.

140. See reference 84 above.

141. See Everett V. Stonequist, *The Marginal Man* (New York, 1937).

142. See references 97-9, Chapter II ; reference 1, Chapter III ; reference 140, Chapter IV ; reference 131 above.

143. Mbela, op. cit., says John Gray Kufa was a Sena ; A. Livingstone Bruce, op. cit., calls him a Yao. It is, however, most improbable that a Yao would originate from the Chinde area at the time of Kufa's childhood.

144. A member of the Mikalongwe Volunteers, Mr. W. Sanderson, and a member of the party which took John Gray to Blantyre after his capture, has left an account of his 1915 experiences. This was a long letter home which he wrote into an exercise-book under the title 'A Planter's Experiences in the Nyasaland Rising [letter from Willie Sanderson] Gotha Estate, Nyasaland, 7th Feb. 1915'. This will be known henceforth as 'Sanderson'. In this (kindly supplied by Mr. Sanderson himself) he suggests that John Gray 'was afraid that Chilembwe would come or send men to kill him' if he did not co-operate. A. Livingstone Bruce, op. cit., however, in an interview with John Gray in the condemned cell, has no mention of this. Gray's statement to Sanderson may well have been an attempt to exculpate himself before he was actually brought to trial.

145. See reference 29, Chapter VI.

146. For this and following two quotations, see reference 131 above.

147. *Nyasaland Times*, as reference 109 above, No. 3 on 'Notice'.

148. Sanderson, op. cit.

149. *British Central Africa. Report on First Three Years' Administration, 1894*

V: PRELUDE TO REVOLT

(Cd. 7504), p. 40 : 'growth of a desire among the more intelligent natives to possess personal property rather than hold an inalienable share in the tribal lands. . . .'

150. Cf. Joseph Bismarck's purchase of fifty acres of land at five shillings an acre, p. 115, *Central African Planter*, No. 9, May 1896 ; 'A sign of the times is the opening of small retail stores by enterprising natives . . . in competition with the Banyan'. Nyasaland *Annual Report*, 1904 (Cd. 2684-18, No. 472), and the *Report*'s comments on the increased circulation of cash since the return of labourers from the Transvaal mines, etc.

151. Mbela, op. cit.

152. Sanderson, op. cit.

153. Very probably a relation of Gordon Mathaka, whom Booth had taken to South Africa in 1896 (see references 121-3, Chapter II).

154. *Nyasaland Times*, as reference 109 above, No. 14, on 'Notice'. For evidence on occupational stratification amongst Nyasaland Africans from the early days of the Administration, see Appendix 3.

155. Cf. *Nyasaland Times*, 12 April 1915, reporting a visit of a representative of the British Cotton Growers' Association : he speaks of cotton as a 'permanent native industry', and of the native growers as 'quite swells some of them . . . though their huts are wattle and daub they actually have European furniture in them. *They are as enthusiastic and patriotic as Lancashire people.*' (Our italics.)

156. Cf. also another member of the Mikalongwe Volunteers who rounded up the 1915 rebels : 'We arrived . . . at the small farms owned by several of the rebel leaders. These farms were compact premises with well-built brick houses, tobacco-curing barns and other improvements such as orchards and cattle enclosures', L. S. Norman, 'Rebellion', *Blackwood's Magazine*, December 1931, pp. 865-6.

157. From a memorandum kindly supplied by Sir Hector Livingstone Duff.

158. Cf. Lord Hailey, *Native Administration in the British African Territories*, Part II (London, 1950), p. 22. See also *Handbook of Nyasaland* (Zomba, 1932), p. 386.

159. *L.W.N.*, June-July 1911, No. 3, pp. 8-13, 'Education—a Retrospect'.

160. *Nyasaland Times*, 16 December 1915.

161. L. S. Norman, *Nyasaland Without Prejudice* (London, n.d.), p. 114.

162. Cf. Duff, *African Small Chop*, op. cit. p. 50, 'a thousand or so' ; *The Times*, 1 February 1915, 'some 500 followers' ; Sir George Smith in *The Empire at War*, op. cit. p. 258, gives an estimate of 200 Chilembwe-ites who attacked the Magomero estate ; Maugham (see reference 74 above), p. 57, says about 800 were arrested ; Mr. Walter Cockerill in a private communication gives a figure of about 2000. Cf. also Nyasaland *Annual Reports* for 1915 and 1916 : increase in cases tried in Blantyre High Court in 1915 (146 in 1915 as opposed to 7 in previous years and 17 in 1916) ; in addition, 116 persons came before subordinate courts as opposed to 67 in 1913–14 ; in all, 3740 offences in 1915 as opposed to 3264 in 1914— Cd. 8172-9, xix, 1915, pp. 14-15 ; Cd. 8434-6, xxii, 1916, p. 9.

163. Cf. also Mbela, op. cit. : 'It is not true to say that [Chilembwe's] following was only Nguru—that was the story which people coined after the reign of terror which had been ushered in after the Rising'.

164. The evidence for this is difficult to trace, and there are a number of cryptic statements about the Ngoni and the 1915 Rising. For example, *Report of*

the Universities Mission to Central Africa (London, 1915), p. 11 ; this account of the Rising says that 'The other raid was on the Angoni Hills behind Kota Kota. . . .' Cf. also Chapter VI, reference 36. One thing seems clear—that this statement by Mr. Maynard Gibson Mbela, op. cit., is no exaggeration : 'The Ngonis knew all about the Rising. . . . Chilembwe's staff and pupils at the Mission in Chiradzulu included a number of influential Ngonis. There were connections with the Ngonis in the highlands, and meetings had been held where the Rising had been planned.' The *Nyasaland Times*'s notice of 'Natives Still Wanted' of 4 March 1915 includes four Ngoni : Nos. 13, 31, 32, 36.

However, in assessing the support which Chilembwe received from the Ngoni, it should be remembered that 'Ngoni' in Gomani's country did not simply mean an inheritor of conquest and suzerainty but, in many instances, Chipeta serf of a Shona-Ndonde survivor of the flight from the Gwangwara country after the clash of the Ngoni east of Lake Nyasa. Such 'Ngoni' were remarkably like the marginal Mangoche Yao : fugitives who were anxious to live down their flight, and so lapsed into brittle aggressiveness.

Nevertheless it should be noted that the Blantyre missionaries in 1891 spoke of large numbers of Ngoni at work in the Shire Highlands (*L.W.B.C.A.*, April 1891, p. 2 ; June 1891, p. 3) ; and in 1897, Alfred Sharpe estimated about 5000 Ngoni wage labourers in the Highlands (Hanna, *Beginnings of Nyasaland*, op. cit. p. 239).

165. Leaflet, 1899 (in Seventh Day Baptist Historical Society collection), 'The Sabbath Evangelizing and Industrial Association—No. 4', p. 27, statement by Annie S. Booth.

166. See references 117-18, Chapter II.

167. Mbela, op. cit.

168. Ibid.

169. Rev. F. S. Chintali states that Chinyama was not related to Gomani but was 'one of the descendents of [a] war commandant of Gomani's'.

70. References 61-5 above.

171. *Bible Advocate*, vol. 22, 1911, No. 43, p. 683.

172. See reference 50, Chapter IV.

173. *L.W.N.*, August-September 1911, No. 4, p. 8.

174. From statement by C. A. Cardew, 1915 Ncheu resident, in Withers, op. cit.

175. Suggested by Cardew statement, op. cit. : 'The day before the rising broke out I had word that the Dzunje natives were holding meetings'.

176. See J. Clyde Mitchell, op. cit., reference 23 above.

177. Field investigation by T. Price. Malemia's support for the Government is illustrated by the fact that he was appointed one of the assessors of the Blantyre High Court at the time of the Rising Trials (*Nyasaland Times*, 11 February 1915).

178. *Nyasaland Times*, 4 February 1915. See also *Report on the Schemes of the Church of Scotland with Legislative Acts passed by the General Assembly* (Edinburgh, 1916), p. 137. Were the main three of these, Kaduya, Fundi, and Mkanda, three Mlanje District chiefs who were each fined four shillings after the Rising, under the punitive ordinances ? (*Nyasaland Government Gazette*, 1915 : No. 129 of 1915, p. 99). Certainly one of Chilembwe's main followers was a David Kaduya (see photograph, Plate 9) who was later shot (*Nyasaland Times*, 30 January, 11 February

1915). David Kaduya was, apparently, a relation of the Mlanje chief, Kaduya. For the Kaduyas see *L.W.N.*, September-December 1910, No. 254-5, p. 19.

179. He is called 'Makangwala' and 'Makwangwala' in the references to him in *Nyasaland Times*, 4 February 1915. Mr. Geoffrey Thorneycroft, who raided his village in 1915, writes (in Withers, op. cit.): 'A Headman named Kim whose village was some 15 miles from Zomba near Pirimiti Hill to the East of Zomba threatened to attack the town. . . .' Clearly he is not to be confused with Makwangwala of Ncheu. Rev. F. S. Chintali of the Church of Scotland Mission, Blantyre, writes that there was 'another Makwangwala at Pirimiti who was captured and executed in 1915. The village is the same which you now know as Kimu. Makwangwala was at first a member of our church and he was called Barton Makwangwala. He was a leading Christian in Pirimiti at that time. Later he joined Mr. Horace [a phonetic-style African reference, apparently, to Mr. G. H. Hollis of the Churches of Christ Mission—see reference 42, Chapter VII]. He was a brother of Kimu.' Despite some confusion, 'Kimu' and 'Makwangwala' seem references to the same person. If Rev. F. S. Chintali is correct about the name Barton, he would appear to be one of the members of the Churches of Christ Mission whose execution is mentioned in the diary of one of their European missionaries, Mary Bannister, for 1 February 1915 : 'Barton was shot to-day'.

180. See *Nyasaland Times*, 25 February 1915 : amongst list of principal natives condemned one Wilson Azimba Chimbaira is noted as a Tonga.

181. *R.C.N.R.* p. 6, paragraph 17.

182. E.g. *Nyasaland Times*, as reference 109 above, 'Notice' : Nos. 1, 3, 7, 9, 42, etc.

183. See Sources, pp. 505-6.

184. The late Mr. L. S. Armitage told us that they included Alexander Hetherwick of the Church of Scotland Mission, and 'Bambo' Smith of the Baptist Industrial Mission of Scotland. The Blantyre carpenter, John McIlwain (cf. W. P. Livingstone, *A Prince of Missionaries*, London, n.d., pp. 23, 194), has also been suggested.

185. *R.C.N.R.* p. 6, paragraph 14.

186. *R.C.N.R.* p. 5, paragraph 13 (d).

187. Cf. Appendix 1.

188. *Nyasaland Times*, 29 April 1915.

189. Duff memorandum, op. cit.

190. *The Empire at War*, op. cit. pp. 259-60. There is a mystery about the 'Chief Judge at Tunduru'. Field investigations by T. Price at Tunduru, Tanganyika, indicate that the first European to stay there came in 1912 : a junior under the Bezirksamtmann at Lindi. He was home on leave when the War was declared, and brought the news to the district. The 'Judge', then, could have been a Swahili *akida* or *liwali*, and not necessarily a high-ranking European. That Sir Hector Duff has some suspicion of this is clear from his memorandum, where he states that the letter to Chilembwe was 'signed by a person describing himself as "the Chief Judge of Tunduru"'. But another memorandum (kindly supplied by the late Mr. Keith Coutanche) on this subject, who went out to Nyasaland two months after the Rising and, after the War, acted as Assistant Attorney-General in charge of the prosecution against the African who bore Chilembwe's letter, refers to its being 'typed in Swahili and signed by a high-ranking German official (I think it was the Chief Judge at Tunduru)'. It is said, it should be

NOTES AND REFERENCES

noted, that native renderings of the German administrative hierarchy in Tanganyika were, in Swahili: 'Bwana Major' (Provincial Commissioner), 'Bwana Judge' (District Commissioner, Bezirksamtmann), and 'Bwana Mdogo' (Cadet).

191. Duff memorandum, op. cit., 'I know of no evidence connecting any German military officer with the affair'.

192. Duff memorandum, op. cit. Mr. Coutanche's memorandum, op. cit., says that the bearer of Chilembwe's letter 'had exciting adventures on his journeys, being detained and afterwards released at various places and eventually escaped to South Africa, where he was traced and sent back to Nyasaland after about four years' delay'. Mr. Coutanche, as prosecuting attorney at his trial, says that he could not be tried for treason 'as a Portuguese native sergeant, who had caught the accused with the reply letter and who would have been a damning witness had died'. (This statement seems to be at variance with Sir Hector Duff's account of the dropping of the letter on the road.) He was, therefore, charged with Unlawful Assembly in the Chiradzulu District at the time of the Rising, and given two years' imprisonment, the maximum sentence.

193. In connection with Chilembwe's communication with the Germans, three other points are worthy of note. (1) There is some evidence that the Germans around Tunduru spoke to the Africans about Chilembwe. T. Price, in a field investigation, interviewed Canon Kolumba Msigala of the Universities Mission to Central Africa about eight miles from Tunduru. He was imprisoned at Lukuledi when the War broke out, and says that the Germans told the prisoners that there was a big man of the Nyasaland Yao who was on their side, and gave them Chilembwe's name. (2) Mr. Coutanche, in his memorandum, op. cit., states that, apart from Chilembwe, the only other Nyasaland African, to the best of his knowledge, who tried to help the Germans during the War was a native who was caught putting dynamite into the firewood that was stacked for the Lake Nyasa steamers. 'He was tried by a military court in Zomba, found guilty and sent back to Fort Johnston where he was shot. That was *in 1915* when I was stationed at Fort Johnston.' (Our italics.) (3) Did Chilembwe send his messenger to Tunduru, or thereabouts, because of the predominance of Yao in the area? A few of these had been in the 1905 native rising in German East Africa—cf. Chief Kadewele at Tunduru who was executed for complicity.

194. F. W. Pick, *Searchlight on German Africa. The Diaries and Papers of Dr. W. Ch. Regendanz* (London, 1939), section ii, 6. See also Robert Williams, *German Penetration in Central Africa* (London, 1918).

195. Cf. references 34, 38, Chapter IX.

196. *Military Operations. East Africa. I*, op. cit. p. 180. Cf. also H. Brode, *British and German East Africa* (London, 1911), p. 83.

197. *Nyasaland Times*, 4 February 1915.

198. See reference 29, Chapter VI.

199. *Nyasaland Times*, 11 February 1915. Cf. reference 94, Chapter VI.

200. 'We heard that the natives had cut the wires between Mikalongwe and Blantyre, between Blantyre and Zomba, and between Blantyre and Tete. The Mikalongwe wire was cut only a couple of miles above the railway station so that this was quickly repaired . . .' (Sanderson, op. cit.).

201. See reference 128 above. It is also possible that the attack on the Nguludi mission was not premeditated but was the result of the mission's lying in the line of retreat from the P.I.M. of one section of Chilembwe's men who had decided to

withdraw from their base. Would they have burned the mission—it might be asked from this point of view—if one European, Father Swelsen, had not been present? But, against this point of view must be set the fact that the retreating rebel section did not burn the mission until after they had searched it, and left Father Swelsen apparently for dead, and had found no other Europeans there. (Statement by Bishop Auneau in Withers, op. cit.)

202. See reference 134 above.

203. Mkulichi, op. cit., etc.

204. E.g. Norman article, *Blackwood's*, op. cit. p. 869; Daniel Thwaite, *The Seething African Pot. A Study of Black Nationalism, 1882–1935* (London, 1936), p. 64; etc.

205. It is just barely possible that Chilembwe held his fire until he saw what was the outcome of the Rhodesia-Nyasaland Appeal of May 1914 (Booth-Nyambo Petition) which had asked that its terms should come into operation at the end of 1914. See p. 206 above.

206. A mysterious figure in the Chilembwe-ite organization—of whom one would like to know much more—was a certain John Nkologo. Mrs. Josephine C. Edwards, a former Seventh-day Adventist missionary in Nyasaland, kindly informs us (from her independent investigations, and especially from her questioning of Chilembwe's former friend, K. M. Malinki) that Nkologo had been closely connected with Booth, and then worked intimately with Chilembwe, and was something of an emissary for him. Malinki told her that it was Nkologo who was sent to secure his co-operation for the Rising. He is mentioned in Rev. Harry K. Matecheta, op. cit. (see reference 84 above), p. 27. Matecheta seems to posit a connection between Nkologo and Booth—cf. Malinki who told Mrs. Edwards that he was originally one of Booth's house-boys. Matecheta writes: 'Kaamba ka kulalikira kotere Boma linamcotsa [Booth] m'Nyasaland, koma anatumiza Ce John Nkologo, atate wace Ce Cilembwe'. A literal translation of this cryptic Nyanja passage would be: 'Because of this kind of teaching [Booth's radical message—AUTHORS] the Government made him [Booth—AUTHORS] go away from Nyasaland, but he sent Mr. John Nkologo, the "father" of Mr. Chilembwe'. It is not likely that the Nyanja sentence is meant to imply that Nkologo was Chilembwe's father. In this context, 'atate' seems to be used as a term of respect, and suggests that Chilembwe regarded himself as a junior to Nkologo.

207. *R.C.N.R.* p. 5, paragraph 13 (d).

208. Official diary of the African Lakes Corporation, 1915, from copy in Withers, op. cit., by courtesy of Mr. J. A. Marshall, O.B.E.: Tuesday, 26 January. And Norman, *Blackwood's*, op. cit. p. 867.

209. Norman, op. cit. p. 867.

210. Cf. Sanderson, op. cit., 'They had been sending letters to their friends written on Boma paper, or rather typed, encouraging this disloyalty to Britain. The letters have been got since.' Could the Zomba Administration supporter have been one Moses, who is mentioned in the *Nyasaland Times*, 30 January 1915, among the list of 'Wanted' Africans, and who is set down as a clerk in the Zomba Treasury?

211. Amongst the many observers who have noticed the relatively good treatment that the rebels meted out to the captured women and children, the comment of Hetherwick's biographer, W. P. Livingstone, in his *A Prince of Missionaries* (London, n.d.), may be cited as typical: 'Curious and characteristic features

marked the event. The ladies who were seized were treated kindly and set free and sent back. Native women nursed the children . .' (p. 155).

It should be noted that African orders for the safe-conduct of women and children were also a feature of the Natal Zulu Rebellion of 1906 (J. Stuart, *Zulu Rebellion*, op. cit. pp. 506-7).

212. Norman, *Blackwood's*, op. cit. p. 868, seems to attribute this to the 'number of trained ex-soldiers assisting' Chilembwe.

213. Cf. *Nyasaland Times*, 25 February, 1 April 1915, on the solitary sergeant of the K.A.R. who was tried for complicity in the Rising.

214. Cf. *Reminiscences for his Sons*, by the Reverend Alexander Burnett (1949, Northumberland and Berwickshire newspapers, privately printed), pp. 26-7.

215. Cf. *Livingstonia News*, vol. viii, 1915, p. 24 : no articles stolen from Magomero by the rebels.

216. Testimony by African participant in the Rising.

217. Cf., for example, Hetherwick, *Romance of Blantyre* (London, n.d.), p. 213, Chilembwe's motive : 'revenge for some private grudge [against] a neighbouring planter'. But cf. also Livingstone Bruce memorandum, op. cit., which reports a personal interview with John Gray Kufa after he was sentenced to death : 'Gray swore to me that there was no personal vendetta against W. J. Livingstone or Magomero'.

218. Mkulichi, op. cit.

219. Cf. William Monk, editor, *Dr. Livingstone's Cambridge Lectures* (Cambridge, 1858), Lecture II, p. 43.

220. F. L. M. Moir, *After Livingstone* (London, 1924), p. 129 ; Sir Harry H. Johnston, *British Central Africa* (London, 1898), pp. 69, 470.

221. Cf. reference 128, Chapter IX.

222. It is interesting to notice that this Epistle, with its emphasis on works rather than faith, was relegated to a place at the end of Luther's German Bible.

223. *Thirty-Eighth Annual Report, 1913* (Glasgow, 1914), p 28.

CHAPTER VI

THE RISING
23 January–3 February 1915

1. Cf. Captain J. Brander Dunbar, 'African Notes', *Chambers's Journal* (Edinburgh), vol. viii, 1904-5, p. 552.

2. Cf., for example, *Reminiscences for his Sons*, by the Reverend Alexander Burnett, missionary at Blantyre, Nyasaland, 1900-25 (1949, Northumberland and Berwickshire newspapers, privately printed), p. 26, '. . . so suddenly and unexpectedly' ; L. S. Norman, *Nyasaland Without Prejudice* (London, n.d.), p. 114 ; testimony by Mr. John Robertson (reference 21 below) ; etc. etc.

3. L. S. Norman, *Blackwood's*, op. cit. p. 863. Cf. story (kindly supplied verbally by Father Martin) of Father Guimard of the Marist Fathers Mission at Nguludi who was out on the day after the first attacks, and was stopped by a gang of Africans who asked, 'Don't you know that this is the day of war ?' He escaped by the exercise of phlegm.

4. Nyasaland *Annual Report*, No. 883, 1914-15 (Cd. 8172-9), p. 14. One European rumour, however, has it that this magistrate knew of the impending

Rising, was afraid of the consequences it might have for him, and got away before the trouble began.

5. Some of these points are from the African Lakes Corporation Diary, 24-30 January 1915, in Withers, op. cit. Roach wrote an account of the attack on Magomero (information kindly supplied by Mrs. K. Livingstone): see *Oban Times*, 1 May 1955, p. 2, 'Appin Lady's Terrible Ordeal'; *The Times* (Royal edition), 22 April 1915. This seems one of the best immediate accounts of the affair, and makes it clear—a point which is confused in some accounts—that the white women at Magomero were not all under the Livingstones' roof on the night of the attack; Mrs. Roach and her sister were in a house about a hundred yards away from the Livingstones.

6. African Lakes Corporation Diary, op. cit.; *Nyasaland Times*, 30 January 1915. Roach in his account, op. cit., puts it 'at about 9.30 P.M.'

7. *Nyasaland Times*, 30 January 1915.

8. Testimony of Mrs. K. Livingstone.

9. Some hearsay evidence has it that Chilembwe went with the column that attacked Livingstone's house. But Mrs. K. Livingstone has told us that she does not believe that he was present, and (see Chapter V, p. 261) it seems most likely that he was co-ordinating the attacks from his Mbombwe church. See also reference 23 below.

Yet Mr. John Robertson of Mwanje, when fleeing with his wife from rebels who had attacked his part of the Estates, came across an African herd-boy whom he knew, and who told him that 'Mrs. Livingstone and Mrs. Roach passed only a short time ago, led by Chilembwe himself' (statement in Withers, op. cit.). But this does not prove that Chilembwe was actually present at the Magomero attack. The statement by Mkulichi (Chilembwe follower), op. cit., suggests very strongly that Chilembwe was waiting at his church to receive Livingstone's head: 'Those who went to the Magomero area, the Nguru, cut off the head of Bwana Listonia and brought it back with them to the hands of Rev. J. Chilembwe' (from Nyanja original). Mkulichi, op. cit., also speaks of reports being brought in to Chilembwe in a manner which suggests that he spent most of his time during the Rising at the Mbombwe church.

10. Information kindly supplied by Miss Lena Mackeachan, sister of Mrs. Ranald MacDonald. Some accounts (e.g. African Lakes Corporation Diary and Roach, op. cit) seem to imply that Mrs. MacDonald was actually in the room when Livingstone's head was cut off. But it is by no means certain that she was.

11. *Oban Times*, 13 February 1915, has a photograph of Duncan MacCormick and a brief biography; see also 19 June 1915. See also *Glasgow Herald*, 2 February 1915.

12. This point is corroborated by Roach, op. cit., and in an account by Mr. John Robertson of the Estates Mwanje section (in Withers, op. cit.). But they differ on one important detail: Roach has it that MacCormick was awakened by the 'watchman' and was begged to take his rifle; Robertson says that Livingstone sent an African servant to tell MacCormick that there was trouble and that he should bring his gun.

13. The exact manner in which the three ladies were rounded up is not clear: time, and the darkness of the night, have added to the confusion of accounts. Roach's account, op. cit., states that, while Africans were attacking his house, Mrs. Livingstone met his wife and sister outside and told them of her husband's fate.

Roach, however, does not indicate clearly whether she was under armed African guard at that time or whether she was apprehended with the two other ladies at this particular moment. It is most likely that she was under guard when she spoke to Mrs. Roach.

14. Cf. reference 211, Chapter V.

15. *Nyasaland Times*, 30 January 1915.

16. Roach, op. cit.

17. The statement in the African Lakes Corporation Diary, op. cit., 24 January 1915, that Robertson was from Lismore like Livingstone and MacCormick is incorrect.

18. Account by Mr. John Robertson in Withers, op. cit., on which most of the following section on the Mwanje attack is based. An interview with Mr. Robertson helped to clear up a number of doubtful points.

19. African Lakes Corporation Diary, op. cit., 24 January 1915, says, 'The outstation of Mwanje was attacked simultaneously with Magomero. . . .' However, *Nyasaland Times*, 30 January 1915, implies that the Mwanje raid followed after the Magomero attack : 'Possibly the same lot [i.e. the Magomero attackers] *then* [our italics] razed an outstation of Magomero nearer Chiradzulo. . . .' This implication, that there were not two parties who attacked the Bruce Estates but only one, does not seem justified, and seems to be a reflection of contemporary European confusion.

20. *Glasgow Herald*, 2 and 4 February 1915.

21. African Lakes Corporation Diary, op. cit., 24 January 1915. Robertson (in Withers, op. cit.) says, 'We at Mwanje never heard any rumours of trouble brewing, we were completely taken by surprise. When I returned from Karonga the Natives at Mwanje and Chiradzulu were quite friendly and we never dreamed that there was anything in the wind.' Mr. Robertson in a subsequent interview said that he was unaware that any warning had been received by Ferguson.

22. Information kindly supplied by Mr. John Robertson.

23. Would this suggest that Chilembwe was with the column that attacked Magomero (cf. reference 9 above), and that by his presence he managed to maintain a superior discipline to that of the attackers of Mwanje ?

24. L. S. Norman in *Blackwood's*, op. cit. p. 867, after his description of the Magomero attack, and before his account of the assault on Mwanje, declares that 'The main rebel body went to another plantation, where, however, they found that the European had fled, he having obtained news of their approach'. It is not clear whether this obvious piece of hearsay evidence refers to Kemper's plantation or not. It is not improbable that the rebels in their withdrawal from their immediate objectives did look into other European centres : but, apart from this statement, there seems to be no direct evidence for it. The majority of the attacking parties appear to have gone straight back to their Mbombwe headquarters.

25. Burnett, op. cit. pp. 26-7, states that on the night of the attack 'we heard the muffled noise of crowds of natives passing through the Mission' but did not connect this with a native rising.

26. In the main, the details of this raid are from the African Lakes Corporation Diary, op. cit., in Withers. Information on the Blantyre raid is even more confused than that of the Magomero attack, and it is difficult in the extreme to be sure that any account of the Chilembwe-ite movements at Mandala is more than generally true. See reference 32 below.

VI: THE RISING

27. Sanderson, op. cit. (see reference 200, Chapter V).

28. Ibid. This story may be compared with the tale that was told to Mr. Walter Cockerill shortly after the Rising: natives informed him that the rebels placed small potted plants near the houses of Europeans who were marked out for slaughter.

29. A. L. Bruce memorandum, op. cit.: 'He himself had been put in charge of a party of rebels who were to attack Blantyre, but he told me that his heart failed him so nothing came of it'.

30. '. . . at a point midway between the European Store and the Ammunition Store [they are some 400 yards distant from each other], and about 50 yards in front of the house tenanted by Mr. McCash . . .', African Lakes Corporation Diary, op. cit., 24 January 1915.

31. Diary, ibid., states that this raised the alarm at 2.30 P.M. It is thus quite possible that the rebels had been on the objective for some little time before this.

32. It is not even certain that the Ammunition Store was raided after the European Store. Diary, op. cit., for 24 January 1915, states that the raids took place 'about the same time' but then adds that the native watchman who was shot 'followed the depredators *after* [our italics] they had broken into the European Store'. Sanderson, op. cit., gives an account which he derived from Morrison, an African Lakes Corporation employee who was present at the time of the attack, which implies but does not state clearly that the attacks on both the European Store and the Ammunition Store took place after the shooting of the watchman. The contemporary *Nyasaland Times* account (30 January 1915) gives little help in solving this puzzle.

33. E.g. Norman, *Blackwood's*, op. cit. p. 869 ; Thwaite, op. cit. p. 64.

34. Sanderson, op. cit.

35. G. H. Wilson, *The History of the Universities Mission to Central Africa* (London, 1936), pp. 165-6.

36. Canon G. H. Wilson kindly supplied us with this account of how he heard the story: 'In 1915 or for some years after, Kampelusa's people were in the Fort Johnston district [South Nyasa] and they used to come to Fort Johnston on King's Birthdays and such like. In 1914 (I think) the Governor made an official visit to Fort Johnston and a party of Kampelusa's Angoni came to dance a war-dance before him. I went to see that dance. . . . The party was in charge of Kampelusa's son. But he had a fever and could not dance, and sat wrapped up in a blanket. I went over and had a chat with him and he looked an awfully nice young fellow and I was told that he was greatly beloved by the clan. Later, when the Chilembwe rising came on and I heard of the murder at the African Lakes Store, my boys told me that it was Kampelusa's son, with whom I had talked at the war-dance.' Two unsolicited comments seem to support the story that the watchman was an Ngoni: Mr. Maynard Gibson Mbela, op cit., who speaks of 'the Ngoni watchman'; and Mr. Walter Cockerill, who comments on his reference to the 'native watchman' in a letter home of 27 January 1915 that he was a 'Zulu msikari' (soldier)—'Zulu' was then a common enough synonym for 'Ngoni'. Miss K. Smith of Nyasaland kindly informs us that Kampelusa was an Ncheu headman. It should be noted that the map, *Nyasaland Protectorate* (G.S., C.S., No. 2136, 1906), shows a 'Kampalusa' village some four miles south-south east of Livilezi mission, and about thirteen miles north of Ncheu Boma.

37. Verbal communication to T. Price by Father Martin of the Marist Fathers.

NOTES AND REFERENCES

38. Sir George Smith in *The Empire at War*, op. cit. p. 258. About 1 P.M., *Nyasaland Times*, 30 January 1915.

39. Memorandum in Withers, op. cit.

40. *History of the Great War. Military Operations. East Africa*, op. cit. p. 180.

41. Memorandum by James Aitchison, Mlanje planter and member of the Volunteer Section, in Withers, op. cit.

42. Norman, *Blackwood's*, op. cit. pp. 862-4.

43. Memorandum by Bishop Auneau, 1915 Resident of the Nguludi Mission, in Withers, op. cit.

44. Mr. L. S. Norman's statement in *Blackwood's*, op. cit. p. 868, that a European and native force attacked Chilembwe's headquarters on Sunday morning is incorrect.

45. Maugham, *Nyasaland*, op. cit. p. 56.

46. Mkulichi, op. cit.

47. Ibid., Nyanja original : 'Ife kuno tagwira ncito yathu bwino lomwe. Ndipo tiri kudikira kufa kwa zoona zace tatumidza dona wace uyo wa moyo alongosole kwa inu zimene anaziona usiku wa lero uno za imfa yamwamuna wace.'

48. *Nyasaland Times*, 30 January 1915.

49. *Third Supplement to the London Gazette*, Tuesday, 1 August 1916, No. 29,692, p. 7651.

50. *Military Operations. East Africa*, op. cit. pp. 179-80.

51. Rev. J. F. Alexander, Church of Scotland Mission, Zomba : verbal communication.

52. Information kindly supplied by Miss Ethel Parsons.

53. *Nyasaland Diocesan Chronicle*, No. 48, 1915, p. 19 : 'The chief Kung'eng'eni was very keen to hear about the war . . . he seemed very much puzzled to hear that America was neutral and at last said "But did not the Americans start the war down in Blantyre ?" It took me some time to realise that he was speaking of the John Chilembwe rising and of his original connection with some American mission.'

54. See reference 44 above.

55. Reference 3 above.

56. Memorandum by C. E. Ingall in Withers, op. cit.

57. Nyasaland *Annual Report*, 1914–15 (Cd. 8172-9), p. 14.

58. L. S. Norman, *Blackwood's*, op. cit. p. 870.

59. *Nyasaland Times*, 4 February 1915.

60. See reference 179, Chapter V.

61. Thorneycroft in Withers, op. cit.

62. Unless otherwise stated, the details here are based on 'A Short Account of the Ncheu Native Rising', by C. A. Cardew, Resident at the time, in Withers, op. cit. See also *London Gazette*, 1916, op. cit. p. 7651.

63. Mbela, op. cit.

64. It is not clear from the accounts we have seen whether the Ncheu rising broke out on 23 January or not. From the Governor's statement in *The Empire at War*, op. cit. p. 258, that 'news reached Zomba on the 26th [of January] of a similar rising in the Ncheu district', it would appear that, although the affected areas were some seventy miles from Zomba and there was then no telephone, perhaps, and news would, therefore, take a little longer to reach the Government centre than news from Blantyre or Magomero, the Ncheu rising broke out later than the Magomero-Mandala attacks, possibly 24 or 25 January.

VI: THE RISING

65. E.g. Sanderson, op. cit.

66. *Sabbath Recorder*, 24 May 1915, pp. 653-4, letter of 10 February 1915.

67. Letter from A. M. D. Turnbull, member of the Commission of Inquiry, Secretariat, Zomba, to the Superintendent, Malamulo Mission, 2 August 1915 (copy kindly supplied by Mr. S. G. Maxwell). See also Chapter VII, reference 20.

68. Cf. note on Kampelusa, reference 36 above : did this have anything to do with bringing numbers of the Ngoni to the Administration's assistance ? Or was it due chiefly to envy or dislike of Chinyama—cf. reference 177 and appropriate text, Chapter V.

69. *Nyasaland Times*, 4 February 1915.

70. *Scottish Baptist Year Book* (Glasgow), 1901, Fifth Annual Report, Baptist Industrial Mission.

71. Ibid., 1915–16, Twentieth Annual Report . . . p. 10.

72. Ibid. p. 11.

73. See references 172 and 179, Chapter V.

74. *Scottish Baptist Year Book*, op. cit. pp. 21-4. Cf. Rev. F. S. Chintali, who writes that he shot himself 'because he was greatly disappointed in the way his people were killed'.

75. Johnston, *British Central Africa*, op. cit. p. 144—*N.B.* 'He was of the Achewa race, but was allied to the Angoni, and had under him Angoni headmen'.

76. *Scottish Baptist Year Book*, op. cit. pp. 21-4.

77. In the attempt to discover—rather unsuccessfully—what actually did happen in the freeing of the Magomero ladies, in addition to other accounts, the following evidence has been used : correspondence and interview by kind permission of Mrs. K. Livingstone ; African Lakes Corporation Diary in Withers, op. cit. ; memorandum by Mr. John R. Downs, member of the Volunteer force which met the ladies, in Withers, op. cit. ; Sanderson, op. cit. ; extract from a letter of 31 January by Rev. Napier, also with the Volunteers, in Hetherwick, *Robert Hellier Napier*, op. cit. p. 92 ; Roach, op. cit. ; Mkulichi, op. cit. Roach's account—presumably noted down from his wife shortly after her release—is probably the best European statement. All the others are either blurred by memory or, if set down at the time, are based on hearsay evidence or hasty and partial observation. Roach states : 'The women and children were taken away and forced to walk about six miles through the bush to a village, where they were given a little food and then forced to walk. They were hurried on all day long [i.e. Sunday, 24 January—AUTHORS] through the hills. They dared not stop to rest for fear of the consequences. In the evening they were told to go to the Boma, but begged to be allowed to rest, so they gave them a hut and left them. First thing next morning a party came and put them on the road to the Boma, when, finding that the soldiers were coming, they left them and ran away.'

78. Mkulichi, op. cit.

79. Information kindly given orally by Mrs. K. Livingstone.

80. African Lakes Corporation Diary, in Withers, op. cit.

81. *Nyasaland Times*, 25 February, 1 April 1915.

82. African Lakes Corporation Diary, in Withers, op. cit. The members of the party were : Messrs. Roe, Morrison, Fairbrother, Apps, Miskin, Haarseth, Jones, and J. A. Brown (compiler of the Diary).

83. Sanderson, op. cit. : his source of information was Morrison of the firing party.

84. Fred L. M. Moir, *After Livinsgtone* (London, 1924), p. 49.

85. African Lakes Corporation Diary, op. cit.

86. Sanderson, op. cit.

87. See reference 152, Chapter V.

88. Memorandum by Bishop Auneau, in Withers, op. cit.

89. Ibid.

90. Sanderson, op. cit. Another version of the same story is given in a memorandum kindly supplied by Mr. E. Borthwick, on leave from Karonga in 1915, who served with the Mikalongwe Volunteers. In his version, the disturber of the Volunteers' tranquillity was 'a lean old cow'.

91. Auneau, op. cit.

92. See references 128 and 201, Chapter V.

93. L. S. Norman, *Blackwood's*, op. cit. p. 866.

94. Verbal information kindly given by Father Martin. According to an African informant of Mrs. J. C. Edwards—to whom we are indebted for this information—David Kaduya is the man with the cap in photograph, Plate 9. Cf. also the fact that all male hut-owners under the jurisdication of the Mlanje chief, Kaduya, were each fined four shillings after the Rising (*Nyasaland Government Gazette*, 1915, p. 99). It is clear also that Duncan Njilima had something to do with the attack on Nguludi : damages were claimed later by the Marist Fathers against Njilima's representatives (see reference 70, Chapter VIII).

95. Auneau, op. cit.

96. Ibid. Norman's account, *Blackwood's*, op. cit. p. 866, says that 'he managed to battle his way into a banana grove, where he fell unconscious and was left for dead'.

97. Information kindly given by Father Martin.

98. Auneau, op. cit.

99. Sanderson, op. cit.

100. Sanderson, op. cit.—confirmed verbally by Father Martin.

101. Verbal information kindly given by Father Martin.

102. Sanderson, op. cit.

103. Cf. F. R. Spindler, 'A Week in a Concentration Camp', *Central Africa* (London), 1915, p. 115.

104. *Z.I.M.O.P.*, July 1915, p. 3. (In Royal Empire Society Library.)

105. African Lakes Corporation Diary, op. cit., Tuesday.

106. Memorandum by C. E. Ingall, member of the attacking forces, in Withers, op. cit.

107. John R. Downs, in Withers, op. cit.

108. Ingall, op. cit.

109. African Lakes Corporation Diary, op. cit., Tuesday.

110. *Nyasaland Times*, 4 February 1915.

111. Downs, op. cit. Cf. Norman, *Blackwood's*, op. cit. p. 868: 'The head of the murdered man was found still stuck on a pole placed as a prominent ornament in the church'. As Downs was present at the attack, his account of the discovery of the head seems the more accurate.

112. African Lakes Corporation Diary, op. cit., Wednesday.

113. Norman, *Blackwood's*, op. cit. p. 871. This rumour is repeated in African Lakes Corporation Diary, op. cit., Wednesday, which attributes it to 'native sources'.

114. African Lakes Corporation Diary, op. cit., Wednesday.

115. *The Rhodesia Herald*, 5 February 1915, quoting *Beira Post*.

116. *Military Operations. East Africa*, op. cit. p. 180.

117. Ibid. ; Smith in *Empire at War*, op. cit. p. 259, etc.

118. There is a difference of an hour in the length of the march given in the two official accounts mentioned in reference 117 above.

119. Norman, *Blackwood's*, op. cit. p. 865.

120. Ibid. p. 871.

121. Sanderson, op. cit.

122. African Lakes Corporation Diary, op. cit., Thursday.

123. Sanderson, op. cit.

124. Ibid.

125. Ibid.

126. Norman, *Blackwood's*, op. cit. p. 872.

127. Sanderson, op. cit.

128. Ibid.

129. Our main sources here, Sanderson, Norman, and the African Lakes Corporation Diary, op. cit., differ slightly in a number of chronological details. Our estimate of the time involved is an attempt at compromise.

130. Information kindly communicated verbally by Mr. Sanderson.

131. The statement in the African Lakes Corporation Diary, op. cit., that John Gray Kufa's village was burned was denied in an interview with Mr. W. Sanderson.

132. Sanderson, op. cit.

133. Ibid.

134. A. L. Bruce memorandum, op. cit. : see reference 29 above.

135. Bruce, Sanderson, op. cit., etc.

136. Information kindly supplied by Canon A. M. Jenkin.

137. Sanderson, op. cit.

138. *Nyasaland Times*, 25 February 1915.

139. African Lakes Corporation Diary, op. cit., Friday. It is possible that the writer of the Diary meant 'Chisombezi', not 'Mombezi'.

140. Ibid.

141. Sanderson, op. cit.

142. Ibid.

143. African Lakes Corporation Diary, op. cit., Saturday.

144. Ibid.

145. Smith in *Empire at War*, op. cit. p. 259. Cf. also *Nyasaland Times*, 4 February 1915 : reports a telegram from Mlanje Resident to Blantyre that Chilembwe was killed 'yesterday'. There is no further evidence to support R. C. F. Maugham's statement in his Nyasaland, op. cit. p. 57, that Chilembwe was shot dead 'in the act of savagely resisting capture'. John R. Downs, in his statement in Withers, op. cit., speaks of a 'light engagement', and other accounts appear to support this view.

146. *Reports of the Schemes of the Church of Scotland with Legislative Acts passed by the General Assembly* (Edinburgh, 1916), p. 137.

147. Nyasaland *Annual Report*, 1914–15 (Cd. 8172-9), p. 14.

148. Information kindly supplied verbally by Father Martin.

149. Memorandum by James Aitchison, planter and member of the Mlanje

Volunteers, in Withers, op. cit. Agreement with 4 February as the date for the bringing in of the body seems implied in the Resident's telegram mentioned in reference 145 above.

150. Telegram mentioned in reference 145 above. It is possible that Hayter was one of these three witnesses rather than a separate witness, as verbal report has it.

151. Downs, in Withers, op. cit. Mr. Downs notes : 'So far as I am aware no reference has ever been made to the burial or where it took place, and assume that I am the only one who knows of its whereabouts'. Cf. Aitchison, op. cit., who speaks of Chilembwe's being 'duly interred in the Boma compound'. The official telegram mentioned in reference 145 above gives no indication of place and merely says 'Buried to-day'.

152. Something, perhaps, of an official statement of the ending of the emergency followed a little later : the publication on 12 February of a Government announcement which publicized a congratulatory message from the Colonial Secretary in London on the 'successful manner in which the recent rising [had] been dealt with' (*Nyasaland Government Gazette*, p. 27, No. 31 of 1915). Another indication of the official conception of the emergency period is provided by the length of service which qualified for the 'Nyasaland, 1915' clasp to the Africa General Service medal. This was the period 24 January-17 February 1915 (*The Times*, 6 March 1916).

153. The Volunteers' C.O., Captain Thorburn, was mentioned in dispatches (*London Gazette*, 1916, op. cit. p. 7649).

154. Cf. a note on the sixtieth birthday of the first meeting of the Blantyre town council in the *Scotsman*, 13 August 1955, p. 10 : '. . . the Blantyre council solemnly discussed whether, when future hangings in connection with the revolt took place, they should call on the principal headmen to witness them. These hangings were done from a large tree which still stands outside the Town Hall.' (This note seems to have been based on the Blantyre town council's minute books.)

155. From a memorandum kindly supplied by the late Mr. Keith Coutanche, Assistant Attorney-General in Nyasaland for the period.

156. *Nyasaland Times*, 16 December 1915.

157. Norman, *Blackwood's*, op. cit. p. 877.

158. Cf. Alice Werner, *Myths and Legends of the Bantu* (London, 1933), p. 202 : 'I recall a curious statement made by a Giryama, Aaron Mwabaya, at Kaloleni in 1912 : "When the print of a human foot is seen side by side with those of a hyena's spoor the traces are those of a sorcerer who is on one side human, on the other a hyena". This I have never heard elsewhere—people in Nyasaland had a different way of accounting for human footprints beside a hyena's track, but that is "another story".' It is unfortunate that Miss Werner did not give this other story—it might have thrown light on the emergence of the form, at least, of a powerful part of the Chilembwe legend. However, in her *The Native Tribes of British Central Africa* (London, 1906), pp. 64, 84-5, writing of Chilembwe's people, the Yao, she states : 'The dead may manifest themselves in the shape of animals. . . . The Yao theory seems to be that none of the departed will do this, unless they mean to turn nasty. . . . [But] witches often turn into hyenas without dying first.' Similarly, Duff MacDonald in his *Africana* (London, 1882), i, p. 62, states that in Nyasaland witches return as hyenas. May such references be taken to suggest that Nyasaland African legend which associates Chilembwe's name with

the hyena thus attributes to him not merely magical powers but also something of the malevolent? Cf. in general here W. F. Willoughby, *The Soul of the Bantu* (London, 1928), pp. 164-5.

159. If the account given in Leys, *Kenya*, op. cit., that 'less than twenty were executed, and the rest sentenced to long terms of imprisonment' (p. 329), is correct—and the list of natives executed and condemned to death (of whom at least two are known to have been pardoned later) in *Nyasaland Times*, 25 February 1915, suggests that he was not far from the truth—the total amount of fees involved cannot have been so great as the *Nyasaland Times*'s account implies. But *N.B.* Maugham, *Nyasaland*, op. cit. p. 57, states that forty-six were condemned to death.

CHAPTER VII

THE SMALLER MISSIONS AND EUROPEAN INVOLVEMENT
IN THE RISING

1. Livingstone, *Laws*, op. cit. p. 355.

2. See reference 115, Chapter IV.

3. Information kindly supplied by Canon A. M. Jenkin.

4. See Chapter V, references 106-15.

5. Cf. *Nyasaland Times*, 11 February 1915, 'Nondescript Missions'.

6. *Plan of the Ages*, op. cit. p. 312.

7. Ibid.

8. Ibid. pp. 313-14.

9. *Battle of Armageddon*, op. cit. p. 392.

10. Ibid.

11. *The Watchtower Story* (pamphlet, New York, 1948), p. 6.

12. See Chapter V, reference 109.

13. See Chilembwe photograph from *Journal of the Thirty-Fifth Annual Session of the National Baptist Convention*, 8-13 September 1915, between pp. 112-13. The 'John Charley' of this picture, who is called Chilembwe's 'English Friend', is clearly the Z.I.M. missionary, John Chorley.

14. *Z.I.M.O.P.*, July 1915, p. 3.

15. *Nyasaland Times*.

16. *Z.I.M.O.P.*, May 1920, p. 3.

17. *Parliamentary Debates* (London), Commons, lxxi, 808.

18. *The Missionary Worker* (Watford), 1911, vol. 15, No. 8, report from S. M. Konigmacher.

19. From an unpublished 'Historical Sketch of the Seventh-day Adventists in Nyasaland, 1902–1915', kindly shown to us by Pastor V. E. Robinson.

20. A. M. D. Turnbull, Assistant Chief Secretary's Office, Zomba, Superintendent, Malamulo Mission, 2 and 10 August (Ref. 301/15 No.) 1915 (copies kindly supplied by Pastor S. G. Maxwell). Cf. also reference 63, Chapter VI. This refers to the Turnbull letter of 2 August, where it is stated that 'there is evidence to show that certain rebels implicated in the rising in the Ncheu division were attempting to make for Matandani'. Shortly after his arrival in Nyasaland in 1908, Konigmacher and his wife had pioneered the Seventh-day Adventist Mission at Matandani, and from this centre they had carried out much of their work (V. E. Robinson, 'Historical Sketch', op. cit.).

21. As typical of the vague rumours about the Seventh-day Adventists and the Rising, cf. *Report of the Universities Mission to Central Africa* (London, 1915), p. 11 ; *Beira Post*, 16 February 1915, 'the prime movers and offenders are the Ethiopian and Seventh Day Adventists and a clean sweep should be made of this danger to South Africa and their stations razed to the ground'.

22. We are grateful to Pastor S. G. Maxwell for sending us copies of a selection of Robinson's correspondence, with replies, of this time.

23. E.g. L. T. Moggridge, Resident, Blantyre, 25 March 1915, to Robinson : '. . . no member of your mission has been convicted before me of complicity in the late rising . . .', etc.

24. Turnbull to Robinson, 301/15 No., 1915, op. cit. ; Robinson's reply, 17 August 1915.

25. Memorandum by Pastor K. M. Malinki, kindly supplied by Pastor S. G. Maxwell.

26. See reference 20 above.

27. *R.C.N.R.* paragraph 13 (d).

28. *R.C.N.R.*

29. Again, we are indebted to Mr. Cockerill for putting his personal papers at our disposal and thus making the writing of this section possible.

30. *Berlin Courant* (Berlin, Green Lake County, Wisconsin), Thursday, 24 June 1915, p. 1.

31. Cf. the troubles with the Roman Catholic, 'Wa-Fransa', and Anglican, 'Wa-Ingleza', factions in the early British occupation of Uganda.

32. *Berlin Courant*, op. cit.

33. Ibid.

34. Ibid.

35. *Sabbath Observer* (London), No. 3, p. 7.

36. In this respect it is unfortunate that one of the files which bears on the Rising in the Zomba branch of the Central African Archives is not open to public inspection : 'Implications of members of the Seventh Day Baptist Mission' (Ref. No. 484/19).

37. *Sabbath Recorder*, 24 May 1915, pp. 653-4, letter of 10 February 1915, from Blantyre.

38. Ibid.

39. Subsequent Glossop quotations from *Central Africa* (London), xxxiv, 1916, pp. 178-9.

40. *Sabbath Recorder*, 7 December 1914, p. 717.

41. See Chapter IV, references 62-4.

42. For material for this section we are indebted for memoranda and documents to Mrs. Winifred Hollis (second wife of Mr. G. H. Hollis) ; Miss Florence Hollis (his third child) ; Mr. F. L. Hadfield, M.B.E., 1908 supporter of the Nyasaland Churches of Christ Mission and a lifelong friend of Mr. Hollis ; Mr. H. Philpott, Churches of Christ missionary in Nyasaland, 1913-15 ; Rev. and Mrs. George E. Barr, Mr. C. S. Slater, and Mr. W. McL. Wishart for bringing to our attention and supplying the diaries of Miss Mary Bannister, Churches of Christ missionary in Nyasaland, 1912-15.

43. Chapter IV, reference 64.

44. *Bible Advocate*, xxv, 6 November 1914, No. 45 : letter from Hollis of 10 August.

VII: THE SMALLER MISSIONS

45. *Bible Advocate*, xix, 13 November 1908, p. 748. Because at this time the Churches of Christ found it impossible to support two European missionaries in Nyasaland, by August 1909, Hills had withdrawn from the field.

46. *Churches of Christ Year Book, 1913* (Birmingham), p. 86.

47. *Bible Advocate*, xxv, 6 November 1914, No. 45 : letter from Hollis of 10 August.

48. E.g. the patriotic poems in *Robert Hellier Napier of Nyasaland*, op. cit.

49. *Bible Advocate*, xxi, 1910, p. 252.

50. E.g. *Churches of Christ Year Book, 1911* (Birmingham), p. 92, 'After experiencing very much difficulty the Government agreed to rent us an acre of land at Namiwawa . . .' ; *Year Book, 1913*, p. 100, 'At the present time we are a little embarrassed by the action of the authorities in banishing all the inhabitants from a thousand acre plot of land, in the middle of which our dwelling houses and meeting house stand' (*N.B.* this may have been a premature application by the authorities of the District Administration (Native) Ordinance of 1912—see Chapter V, references 19-21, etc.) ; *Year Book, 1914*, p. 94, 'at present the obstacles in the way of acquiring land are insurmountable . . .', etc. etc.

51. *Churches of Christ Year Book, 1912*, p. 81.

52. Some of the details which follow are based on a brief, private biographical study of Mary Bannister kindly supplied by Mrs. G. E. Barr.

53. *Churches of Christ Year Book, 1914*, p. 78.

54. Bannister diaries, 31 January 1915. Unless otherwise stated, subsequent Mary Bannister quotations are from her diaries.

55. *Churches of Christ Year Book, 1915*, p. 110.

56. Ibid.

57. Diaries, 5 February 1915.

58. Ibid., 27 February 1915.

59. Cf. report by H. Philpott in *Bible Advocate*, xxvi, 23 April 1915, No. 17, p. 200.

60. *Bible Advocate*, xx, 1909, p. 649, says that George Masangano had been an interpreter in the Resident Magistrate's office, Zomba, but gave up this job for three shillings a month mission work with the Churches of Christ. It is possible that George Masangano was related in some way to the rebellious Yao chief of the Mangoche area (Chilembwe's boyhood territory) who, with two other Yao chiefs, Kawinga and Matipwiri, in 1895 had been part of a 'concerted plan to drive the white man from the country' (*Handbook of Nyasaland*, Zomba, 1922, p. 21). As *L.W.B.C.A.*, November 1895, p. 3, points out, Zarafi's native name was Masangano. See also *Bible Advocate*, xxvi, 1915, p. 261 ; *Nyasaland Government Gazette*, 9 June 1915, p. 92, No. 120 of 1915 (Appendix 6 below) ; and reference 83 below.

61. *Churches of Christ Year Book, 1915*, p. 110

62. Ibid. pp. 111-14.

63. Ibid. p. 111.

64. Ibid.

65. This date is calculated from the entry for 26 March 1915, in Bannister diary.

66. Ibid.

67. Ibid.

68. Diary, 24 March 1915.

69. 31 March 1915.

70. E.g. the file in the Zomba branch of the Central African Archives : 'Implications of teachers and members of the Churches of Christ Mission' (Ref. No. 486/19).

71. Extract kindly supplied by Mr. Walter Cockerill.

72. *Bible Advocate*, xxvi, 21 May 1915, pp. 260-1, reports an interview by H. E. Tickle of the British Churches of Christ with the Colonial Office. Then—apparently quoting from a Colonial Office letter which had drawn on dispatches from the Nyasaland Governor—the paper states : '. . . and that although there is not sufficient evidence forthcoming to charge Mr. Hollis with implications in the matter, his conduct throughout has been suspicious ; that he admitted at his sworn examination that five weeks before the rising the intentions of the rebels had been communicated to him by one of his leading teachers, who has since been convicted ; and that he failed to bring the matter to official notice. . . .' Cf. also article by H. E. Tickle, 'Difficulties in Nyasaland', pp. 107-9, *The Open Door on the Regions Beyond. Magazine of the Churches of Christ* . . ., No. 12, July 1915.

73. Mr. F. L. Hadfield, in a memorandum which he has kindly drawn up for us, states that Hollis was 'quite definite' that he had been deported because he 'refused to give an undertaking not to undertake any more work among the Natives till the trouble was over and the Government gave them permission to carry on. He explained that all he wanted to do was to preach the Gospel, nothing else. They would not allow this, and his attitude was that he could not possibly give such a pledge. "Imagine the Apostles giving such a pledge," he said.' This may well have been Hollis's personal feeling : but the attitude of the Nyasaland Government, as the material quoted in reference 72 above shows, was much more closely linked to the immediate circumstances of the Rising.

74. *Churches of Christ Year Book, 1914*, p. 80.

75. There is a list of Churches of Christ outlying mission schools in Nyasaland in *The Open Door*, January 1915, p. 83.

76. *Churches of Christ Year Book, 1911*, p. 92.

77. Cf. *Bible Advocate*, 1911, p. 731, and 1912, p. 108, for information on Hanson Tandu, a former Tonga link in the Booth-Kamwana chain, who had approached Hollis to found schools in the Bandawe area. Tandu had been imprisoned at one time for deserting from the Army. For other members of the Churches of Christ who were interested in the Watch Tower teaching, see Chapter V, reference 113.

78. *Churches of Christ Year Book, 1912*, p. 97.

79. Bannister diary, 15 March 1915.

80. *Churches of Christ Year Book, 1912*, p. 96.

81. Ibid., 1914, p. 94.

82. *Bible Advocate*, 1911, p. 683.

83. E.g. George Masangano who 'went off and started a new sect a few miles away, which remains to this day, styled African Church of Christ' (from a memorandum kindly supplied by Mr. H. Philpott).

84. E.g. Simon Kadewere whose death sentence is mentioned in Mary Bannister's diary for 12 March 1915 : Mr. Philpott reports a 'certain truculence' about him and says that Hollis always had to visit him and not *vice versa*.

85. Cf. here Hollis's statement in *Churches of Christ Year Book, 1911*, p. 92, that 'Half-an-hour's conversational English before we commence the students' class serves as a bait (the natives like learning English). . . .'

VIII: THE AFTERMATH

86. See *Bible Advocate*, xxv, 4 December 1914, p. 729, etc. *The Open Door*, No. 7, April 1914, 'Frederick, one of Mr. Hollis' most trusted teachers'; January 1915, p. 83, 'the faithful Frederick'; p. 85 for photograph, etc.

87. *Bible Advocate*, 1915, p. 261.

88. Cf. *Bible Advocate*, xxvii, 1916, p. 397: '. . . we feel there was a miscarriage of justice in his case; he was not tried in the open court like the other prisoners . . .'

89. See Chapter V, reference 113.

90. From information kindly supplied by Rev. F. S. Chintali.

91. *Churches of Christ Year Book, 1915*, p. 90; *1916*, pp. 59-61, 75-7. *Bible Advocate*, 1915, pp. 260-1; 1916, pp. 396-7. *The Open Door*, 1915, p. 124; No. 14, January 1916, *passim*; April 1916, p. 146; 11 January 1917, p. 180, Government gave £50 for the Namiwawa buildings which they took over. Etc.

92. See *Churches of Christ Year Books, 1916–1928, passim*.

93. *Handbook of Nyasaland* (Zomba, 1932), pp. 400-1. See also *Nyasaland Protectorate. Blue Book, 1927* (Zomba, 1927): Government subsidy of £96 : 10s. to the African Church of Christ.

94. Again, this point will not be clear until recent South and Central African papers are open for public inspection.

95. Paragraph 13.

96. Booth MSS. op. cit.

97. *Sevenoaks Chronicle and Kentish Advertiser*, 17 December 1915, p. 6.

98. Ibid.

99. Cf. Eric Walker, *A History of South Africa* (London, 1947), p. 546, for land troubles on the Basutoland border.

100. Booth letter from Sekebu, N. Basutoland, 24 April 1915, to Mrs. E. B. Langworthy (kindly loaned by Mrs. Langworthy).

101. Ibid.

102. In Booth MSS. op. cit.

103. 'Re John Chilembwe, the Yao Native Messenger to the Negroes of U.S.A.', op. cit., from which the following quotations are taken.

104. E.g. Edward Roux, *Time Longer Than Rope*, op. cit. p. 92, where Booth is made into a Negro.

CHAPTER VIII

THE AFTERMATH OF THE RISING

1. No. 14, 16 February 1915.

2. No. 38, 11 May 1915.

3. *Nyasaland Protectorate. Summary of the Proceedings of the Legislative Council, Fourteenth Session* (Zomba, 1915), p. 3.

4. *Parliamentary Debates*, Commons, lxxiii, 1915, pp. 1554-5; see also lxxii, 17 June 1915, p. 801.

5. W. P. Livingstone, *A Prince of Missionaries* (London, n.d.), p. 155.

6. *Summary Legislative Council Proceedings* (Zomba), op. cit. p. 11.

7. Ibid. p. 14.

8. Ibid. p. 13.

9. Ibid. p. 13. This seems to be a reference to the South African Native College at Fort Hare.

NOTES AND REFERENCES

10. *United Free Church of Scotland. Report on Foreign Missions*, 1915 (Edinburgh, 1916), p. 44; *Nyasaland Times*, 7 October 1915. See also Chapter V, reference 60.

11. *Church of Scotland Letter Book No. 29*, p. 485, 6 May 1915. (These *Letter Books* and many other foreign mission materials of the Church of Scotland and the former United Free Church are now in the National Library of Scotland.) The Secretary went on to say : '. . . but of course at present the least said about these things in public the better'. See also p. 676, 3 June 1915.

12. Ibid.

13. Cf. linkage of Nyasaland and British educational questions in *Church of Scotland Letter Book No. 31*, p. 849; linkage by Sir J. D. Rees in Parliamentary debate of 21 July 1915 (*Parliamentary Debates*, Commons, lxxiii, 1555. See also lxxii, 801).

14. *Letter Book No. 29*, op. cit. p. 677.

15. *Nyasaland Government Gazette*, 1915, p. 50.

16. See Chapter VII, reference 39.

17. Cf. *Bible Advocate*, 1915, p. 501, etc.

18. *United Free Church of Scotland. Report on Foreign Missions, 1915*, op. cit. p. 45; etc.

19. Livingstone, *Prince of Missionaries*, op. cit. p. 156; *Letter Book No. 29*, op. cit. p. 228; etc.

20. *Prince of Missionaries*, op. cit. pp. 155-6.

21. Ibid.; Mrs. Chalmers, 'Memories of Nyasaland' *Nyasaland Times*, 18 June 1953, p. 4.

22. *Prince of Missionaries*, op. cit. p. 156.

23. *Letter Book No. 29*, op. cit. p. 676.

24. Livingstone, *Laws*, op. cit. p. 354.

25. *Prince of Missionaries*, op. cit. p. 157.

26. *Laws*, op. cit. p. 354.

27. *L.W.N.*, 1916, No. 1, p. 3.

28. From *Memorandum relative to the Report of the Commission of Enquiry into the Native Rising. Prepared for the Foreign Mission Committees of the Church of Scotland and the United Free Church by the Reverend Dr. Laws, Livingstonia, and the Reverend Dr. Hetherwick, Blantyre* (22 March 1916, Blantyre), typescript copy in Church of Scotland records.

29. Pencil note by Committee member on copy of *R.C.N.R.* circulated among Church of Scotland Foreign Mission Committee members.

30. *Livingstonia News*, vol. ix, February-October 1916, Nos. 1-5, p. 6; *L.W.N.*, 1916, No. 1, p. 3. Laws-Hetherwick *Memorandum*, 22 March 1916, op. cit.

31. *Livingstonia News*, 1916, Nos. 1-5, p. 29; *L.W.N.*, 1916, No. 1, p. 4.

32. Cf. pencil note by Committee on *R.C.N.R.* circulated among Church of Scotland Foreign Mission Committee members : comment on paragraph 46 that Government should 'regulate the establishment of Mohammedan mosques and schools'; writer noted that they should be on the 'same footing as X^n schools as regards qualifications'. See also Laws-Hetherwick *Memorandum*, op. cit.

33. Committee pencil note on Church of Scotland copy of *R.C.N.R.*

34. *L.W.N.*, 1916, No. 1, p. 7.

35. J. Du Plessis, *Thrice Through the Dark Continent* (London, 1917), p. 347.

36. For subsequent discussion on missionary 'spheres of influence' in Nyasa-

land, see Du Plessis, op. cit. p. 347; *Livingstonia News*, 1916, Nos. 1-5, p. 9; *L.W.N.*, 1916, No. 1, p. 7; etc.

37. From Laws's letter, Zomba, 14 March 1916; a copy of the Governor's reply; and Laws's Legislative Council statement in Church of Scotland foreign mission records.

38. The Secretary of the Church of Scotland Foreign Missionary Committee at this time was J. N. Ogilvie. He appears to have put some of his experience of this episode into his book, *Our Empire's Debt to Missions—The Duff Missionary Lecture, 1923* (London, 1924), especially into chapter vi, 'Concerning Criticisms' —in particular pp. 202-7.

39. We must express our indebtedness to the International Missionary Council for allowing us to consult their files on the Rising and on Central African missions. We are also indebted to Dr. J. Oldham who played an important part in the negotiations with the Colonial Office at this time. He tells us that the proposed regulations for the control of foreign missions in Nyasaland included a clause which would have made missionaries liable to imprisonment for infringement of certain regulations. He took up the matter with Arthur Steel Maitland, and the regulations were changed, so that it came to appear that missionary activity in the Protectorate under responsible direction was welcome.

40. Cf. *Reports on the Schemes of the Church of Scotland, 1916* (Edinburgh), p. 129.

41. *Church of Scotland Letter Book No. 32, 1916,* has a valuable selection of correspondence on these points.

42. Letter from A. Steel Maitland to Dr. John Ogilvie, 4 August 1916 (Church of Scotland records).

43. See also *Reports on the Schemes of the Church of Scotland, 1917* (Edinburgh), p. 190, where it is indicated that the Church was still worried about the Nyasaland missionary situation. But the 1918 *Reports* are free from any mention of the affair.

44. To Rev. F. Ashcroft, from Blantyre, 22 March 1916 (Church of Scotland records).

45. *Summary of the Proceedings of the Legislative Council . . .* (Zomba, 1918). p. 7.

46. *Letter Book No. 32*, op. cit. p. 844.

47. Vol. ix, Nos. 1-5, February-October 1916, pp. 1-4.

48. In Church of Scotland papers.

49. Presumably under the Censorship Ordinance of 3 December 1914 (*Ordinances of the Nyasaland Protectorate, 1913–1915*, Zomba, 1915, p. 47).

50. Letter from Hetherwick to Miss Gibson of the International Missionary Council, 27 April 1926 (in the Council's files).

51. *L.W.N.* No. 1, 1916, pp. 3-6.

52. It is interesting here to note that Dr. J. Oldham in his letter to us states that the one thing he remembers clearly about the Rising was that it was the starting-point of long-continued negotiations and of a growing understanding between missions and Government.

53. *Livingstonia News*, op. cit. p. 6.

54. *New Statesman* (London), 8 July 1916, p. 321.

55. *Nyasaland Times*, 10 July 1915.

56. *Beira Post*, No. 14, 16 February 1915; *Nyasaland Times*, No. 11, 18 March 1915, p. 3.

NOTES AND REFERENCES

57. *Nyasaland Times,* 10 June 1915.

58. 7 May 1915 : Anti-Slavery Society Minute Book, C2/13 (Bodleian Library, Oxford).

59. Buxton files, Anti-Slavery Society Papers (Bodleian) : 11 June 1915, 21 July 1915.

60. We have not consulted any minute books which the Chamber may possess ; such books would, presumably, give the story in greater detail.

61. From private A. L. Bruce memorandum, op. cit.

62. *John Bull,* xix, 1916, No. 519, p. 8.

63. *Letter Book No. 32,* op. cit. p. 15, 24 March 1916.

64. *Summary . . . Legislative Council, Sixteenth Session* (Zomba, 1916), p. 2.

65. Ibid. p. 5

66. *Romance of Blantyre,* op. cit. p. 215. Cf. here evidences of European memories of the Rising in *Nyasaland Times,* 27 April 1926, p. 3, and 30 April 1926, p. 2.

67. *Nyasaland Government Gazette,* 1915 : pp. 92-3, 99, Nos. 120-2 and 129 of 1915.

68. See Appendix 6.

69. Miles Mark Fisher, B.D. thesis, *Negro Baptists,* op. cit. p. 198.

70. *Nyasaland Times,* 19 August 1915 : Case in the High Court of Blantyre, 10 August, of The Company of Mary and the Roman Catholic Lord Bishop of Shire, Plaintiffs *v.* The Representatives of John Chilembwe, Defendants. Damages against the representatives of Duncan Njilima'.

71. *Nyasaland Times,* 15 April 1915.

72. Ibid., and for 20 May 1915.

73. Nyasaland *Annual Report,* 1914–15 (Cd. 8172-9), pp. 20-1.

74. *Nyasaland Times,* 15 April 1915.

75. *Nyasaland Times,* 22 April 1915, 'The Week'; also letter from 'Old Planter', 27 April 1915.

76. *Summary . . . Legislative Council. Nineteenth Session* (Zomba, 1918), pp. 6-7.

77. See *Parliamentary Debates* for the deportation of Ira Macdonald Lawrence for importing into Nyasaland six copies of *Negro World* (Philadelphia) and two copies of *Workers' Herald,* edited by Clements Kadalie : vol. 200, 1926, column 1365 ; vol. 202, 1927, columns 541-2, 1381, 855. *Nyasaland Times,* 24 September 1926, p. 3, reports this case ; the P.I.M. was linked with the principals.

78. There is a document (not open for public inspection) in the Zomba branch of the Central African Archives about this : 'Government Assistance towards the maintenance of Charlie and Donald Chilembwe' (Ref. No. 3049/22).

79. In a memorandum from Mr. Maynard Gibson Mbela it is stated that Mrs. Chilembwe died of influenza in 1918.

80. Duff, *African Small Chop,* op. cit. p. 51. This letter was also mentioned by Sir Hector Duff in a private memorandum for the authors. Cf. also *Nyasaland Times,* 29 April 1915 : letter from Abraham Z. Twalu, a Zulu. This obsequious letter suggests that other Africans were anxious to dissociate themselves from Ethiopian-style movements after the Chilembwe Rising, and to keep free from official wrath. Cf. *Nyasaland Times,* 24 July 1915, List No. 18 of subscribers to Nyasaland Relief Fund : a 'George Chilembwe' of Limbe gave 3s. 6d. This and subsequent lists, with their numbers of native subscribers, suggest that this

VIII: THE AFTERMATH

was one way in which Africans could demonstrate their loyalty to the Government after the Rising.

81. It is not clear which of Chilembwe's sons wrote this letter. Information from Chilembwe's relatives indicates that his son Donald went to America eventually. But the fact that the Government made a maintenance grant to Chilembwe's two sons in Nyasaland in 1915 suggests that Donald Chilembwe at this time was not old enough to consider migration to America—indeed, the date his relations suggest (ex Mr. P. L. Bridle) is the mid-1930's. The confusion of testimony about Chilembwe's marriage or marriages (see reference 19, Chapter IV) makes it possible that it was quite another son who wrote this letter. It is also possible that Sir Hector Duff misunderstood the exact degree of relationship with Chilembwe that the letter implied—in which case it is not unlikely that the writer was an offspring of the union between the Rev. L. N. Cheek and Chilembwe's niece, Rachael.

82. There is an interesting file of correspondence on the reopening of the P.I.M. in the International Missionary Council offices, London. This reveals official suspicions of the mission and its American Negro contacts.

83. *Handbook of Nyasaland* (Zomba, 1932), pp. 383-9.

84. *R.C.N.R.* paragraph 41.

85. It is interesting to notice that a group of papers on the Rising which was found in the Church of Scotland offices, Edinburgh, was filed with a collection of papers on education in Nyasaland in the 1920's. Cf. also a criticism of the proposed Education Ordinance in 1927 by the Livingstonia missionary, Donald Fraser, in a letter to Dr. J. Oldham, 27 December 1927, which indicates that the Government still had memories of 1915 in its mind : Fraser claimed that the Government wished to control all education through the Ordinance but 'we maintain that if we guarantee no seditious teaching, we are at liberty to provide what education we can . . .' (File with International Missionary Council : Nyasaland, Educational Ordinance, Correspondence with Scottish Churches).

86. *R.C.N.R.* paragraph 30 (a).

87. *L.W.N.* No. 3, 1916, pp. 1-3.

88. *Land Commission. Nyasaland, 1921* (Zomba, 10582), p. 14.

89. Cf. Harry Johnston's optimism in the 1890's that his land settlement would 'completely free the natives from any dependency on the white settler . . .' *British Central Africa*, op. cit. p. 113.

90. *Land Commission, 1921*, op. cit. p. 19.

91. There is a useful summary of these in *Land Commission, 1946, I, Report by Sir Sidney Abrahams* (Zomba, 1947).

92. Ibid. p. 7.

93. Ibid. p. 34.

94. *L.W.N.* No. 3, 1916, p. 3.

95. *East Africa and Rhodesia*, 3 June 1954, p. 1256, and 6 December 1956, p. 477 ; A. J. Hanna, *The Beginnings of Nyasaland and North-Eastern Rhodesia* (Oxford, 1956), p. 233.

96. For useful summaries of the events during these disturbances, see *East Africa and Rhodesia*, vol. 29, 1953, pp. 1148-9, 1312-13, 1371-2, 1378-9, 1385, 1689 ; vol. 30, 1953, pp. 45, 68-9, 74, 95-100, 107, 160, 172, 189-90, 287-9, etc. See also *Report of a Commission of Inquiry . . 20th August 1953* (Zomba, 1953).

97. Ibid., 27 May 1954, p. 1232.

NOTES AND REFERENCES

98. For evidence of a continuation of land troubles in the Chiradzulu area, see, for example : *Nyasaland. Annual Reports on Native Affairs* (Zomba), *1933*, p. 9, greatest percentage of native evictions from European estates in Chiradzulu district, and *1937*, p. 13, bad feeling on Bruce Estates ; *Nyasaland. Annual Reports of the Provincial Commissioners* (Zomba), *1937*, p. 16, evictions from Bruce Estates, and *1939*, pp. 12-13, trouble on Magomero Estates ; etc.

99. And this in spite of the publicity which the Rising and its connections with land questions had received in Norman Leys's *Kenya* of 1924, which soon became a basic source for subsequent accounts of the Rising.

100. E.g. Raymond Leslie Buell, *The Native Problem in Africa* (New York, 1928), i, pp. 245-50.

101. C. K. Meek's *Land Law and Custom in the Colonies* (London, 1946) gives an excellent, succint examination of Nyasaland land problems but does not link them to the emergence of African discontents.

102. L. S. Norman, *Nyasaland Without Prejudice* (London, n.d.), p. 114.

103. *Summary . . . Legislative Council. Fourteenth Session* (Zomba, 1915), p. 3.

CHAPTER IX

THE RISING IN PERSPECTIVE

1. Du Plessis, *Thrice Through the Dark Continent*, op. cit. p. 347.

2. *Romance of Blantyre*, op. cit. p. 214 ; *L.W.N.*, 1916, No. 1, p. 1.

3. There appear to be no official figures for the numbers of dead and wounded. It is very doubtful—at a rough estimate—if the Chilembwe-ite casualties went much beyond fifty—if, indeed, they reached that figure at all.

4. J. Stuart, *A History of the Zulu Rebellion*, 1906 (London, 1913), pp. 555-6.

5. *The Handbook of Tanganyika* (London, 1930), p. 75.

6. Roux, op. cit. p. 104.

7. Edwin S. Munger in *Africa To-day*, edited by C. Grove Haines (Baltimore, 1955), p. 178.

8. P. 27.

9. Cf. Maugham, *Nyasaland*, op. cit. p. 55 : 'It was a conspiracy which only failed through imperfect organization'. Also Du Plessis, op. cit. p. 347 : 'badly organized'. And see also general analysis of the conspiracy in Chapter IV.

10. H. L. Duff, *Summary . . . Legislative Council. Fourteenth Session* (Zomba, 1915), p. 14 ; *R.C.N.R.* paragraph 16.

11. Cf. Lewis Gann, 'The End of the Slave Trade in British Central Africa', *Human Problems in British Central Africa. Rhodes-Livingstone Journal* (Manchester, 1954), No. 16, p. 46, for view of Harry Johnston in 1898 on dangers of African combination. Cf. also Captain J. Brander Dunbar, 'African Notes', *Chambers's Journal*, viii, 1904-5, pp. 551-2.

12. Gann, op. cit. p. 46.

13. Cf. Chapter V, references 23, 176-7.

14. Friedrich Engels, *The Peasant War in Germany* (London, 1927), p. 18.

15. This characterization of the Nguru, however, should not be over-generalized, as it is, by some writers. Cf. J. Clyde Mitchell on the 'progressive' characteristics of the Nguru in his 'Political Organization of the Yao of Southern Nyasaland', *African Studies*, September 1949, p. 151.

16. L. Natarajan, *Peasant Uprisings in India* (Bombay, 1953), p. 66, etc.

IX: THE RISING IN PERSPECTIVE

17. Winston S. Churchill, *The River War* (London, 1899), p. 55.

18. Sir Harold Macmichael, *The Anglo-Egyptian Sudan* (London, 1934), p. 63.

19. Churchill, op. cit. p. 34.

20. In general, for Islamic 'prophets' of protest against European rule in Africa, see Schlosser, *Propheten in Afrika*, op. cit. pp. 59-228.

21. See Chapter III, reference 7.

22. Cf. Public Record Office, F.O.84. 2051, Africa No. 7, 1 February 1890, Sir Harry H. Johnston ; see also F.O.2. 54, January-August 1893, p. 66, Johnston, private letter to Sir P. Anderson : 'It may certainly be said that Jumbe has several times held our fate in his hands . . .' ; etc.

23. Carl Brockelmann, *History of the Islamic Peoples* (London, 1949), pp. 414-15.

24. Cf. *Glasgow Herald*, 27 April 1903 : 'Col. Cobbe sent out one company of the 1st K.A.R. . . . [and] one company of the 2nd K.A.R. . . . They were surrounded and overwhelmed' ; see also Lloyd-James, *K.A.R.* op. cit. pp. 91-3.

25. Cf. *L.W.N.* No. 2, 1916, pp. 7-10, 'Islam'.

26. See Chapter IV, section 8, where some of these points on Islam are first introduced.

27. *The Aurora*, iv, 1 October 1900, No. 23, pp. 48-9, 'Wanted—a New Religion'.

28. File in U.M.C.A. offices, London : I.D.I/4.

29. *L.W.N.* Nos. 214-15, 1907, pp. 13-14.

30. Cf. Clyde Mitchell, op. cit. p. 151.

31. E.g. Sir Harry H. Johnston, *A History of the Colonization of Africa by Alien Races* (Cambridge, 1930), p. 449 ; Norman Maclean, *Africa in Transformation* (London, 1914), pp. ix-xi.

32. See Chapter V, reference 190.

33. *L.W.N.*, 1916, No. 2, p. 8. Cf. also Lothrop Stoddard's racialist, *The Rising Tide of Color against White World Supremacy* (New York, 1920), pp. 95-6.

34. Smith in *The Empire at War*, op. cit. p. 260.

35. From memorandum kindly supplied by Canon A. M. Jenkin of Nyasaland U.M.C.A. in 1915. See also *Reports . . . of the Church of Scotland* (Edinburgh, 1916), p. 128.

36. Ibid., and *Bible Advocate*, No. 39, 24 September 1915, letter from H. Philpott, 6 August 1915, Namiwawa.

37. *Nyasaland Diocesan Chronicle*, July 1915, p. 9.

38. *The Times*, 14 January 1916, p. 7. See also *Nyasaland Times*, 9 March 1916.

39. *Nyasaland Times*, No. 32, 10 August 1916.

40. Cf. *Report of the Universities' Mission to Central Africa* (London, 1916), p. xvii ; *Reports . . . of the Church of Scotland* (Edinburgh, 1917), p. 125 ; *Church Missionary Review* (London), lxix, 1918, p. 269 ; Livingstone, *Prince of Missionaries*, op. cit. p. 177.

41. It is interesting here to notice that a party of Mohammedan political deportees was sent from East Africa to Mauritius towards the end of 1917 (*The Empire at War*, op. cit. iv, p. 559).

42. *Handbook of Nyasaland* (Zomba, 1922), p. 21.

43. Ibid. p. 22.

44. Ibid. p. 23 reads : 'With the exception of the semi-religious rising in January 1915, the Protectorate has been free from internal trouble since 1897'.

45. Johnston, *British Central Africa*, op. cit. p. 67 footnote.

46. Ibid. pp. 68-9 ; F. L. M. Moir, *After Livingstone* (London, n.d.), p. 129.

47. Ibid. p. 77.

48. For the case of William Robert Ziehl and Albert Bolle, see *The Aurora* (Livingstonia), 1 June 1899, No. 15, pp. 17-18, 21-3 ; *British Central Africa Gazette*, vii, 24 June 1899, Ziehl tried, 25-7 May 1899 ; 31 August 1899, p. 4 ; etc. Cf. also reference 60, Chapter V.

49. E.g. Hetherwick, *Romance of Blantyre*, op. cit. p. 213.

50. R. L. Buell, *Native Problem*, op. cit. i, p. 243. See also *The Watchtower*, vol. xxxix, 1918, p. 6195 : '. . . several of the leading brethren [Nyasas, presumably—AUTHORS] have been deported and are now interned in Flat Island, Mauritius'.

51. In R. D. McMinn, 'The First Wave of Ethiopianism in Central Africa', *Livingstonia News*, 4 August 1909.

52. Cf. Paul Tillich, *The Protestant Era* (London, 1951), chapter iii, 'Kairos'.

53. *Spelman Messenger* (Atlanta, Ga.), vol. 61, February 1945, No. 2, pp. 2, 7-9.

54. See National Baptist Convention, U.S.A., Inc., pamphlet, *My Vision—East, Central and South Africa of To-day*, by Daniel S. Malekebu, M.D., D.D.

55. See Roux, *Time Longer Than Rope*, op. cit. passim ; Eric Walker, *A History of South Africa* (London, 1928), pp. 615-16.

56. See *Our African Way of Life*, edited by Cullen Young and Hastings Banda (London, 1946), pp. 26-7 ; pamphlet, *Federation in Central Africa* (London, 1951), by Hastings K. Banda and Harry Nkumbula.

57. See Chapter V, section 2.

58. Bengt G. M. Sundkler, *Bantu Prophets in South Africa* (London, 1948), p. 49.

59. In general see *Nyasaland Protectorate. Blue Books* (Zomba), *passim*, for very brief details of some of these churches.

60. By kind permission of the South African Branch of the Watchtower Bible and Tract Society, we publish a translation of a letter in Nyanja of 7 March 1947, from the leader of an African independent Watch Tower grouping in order to demonstrate the emergence of such independent bodies with no connection with the parent American body :

'The Watchman Mission has no time to waste on rumour, because the Blacks and the Europeans know that the Watchman Mission is separate from the Watchtower Bible and Tract Society of Europeans. The Watchman Mission represents the Healing Prince Jehovah, the Healing Prince Michael, the Kingdom and Righteousness. *The power of man to fear Jehovah comes from heaven not from Brooklyn of America or elsewhere.* [Our italics.] Hating and arguing with one another is of no assistance, for such destroys the work of righteousness. Elliott Kamwana Cirwa.

'Holiness Watchman Welfare Mission' (Maela Mlonda Mishoni Yocirisa).

It is not clear from this letter whether it was written by the original Elliott Kamwana as an old man, or by a disciple who had taken his name.

61. *Annual Reports of the Provincial Commissioners*, year ended 31 March 1938 (Zomba, 9060-175), p. 15.

62. Audrey I. Richards, 'A Modern Movement of Witch Finders', *Africa*, viii, 1935, pp. 448-60 ; M. G. Marwick, 'The Social Context of Cewa Witch Beliefs', *Africa*, xxii, 1952, pp. 120 and 215 et seq.

63. Cf. statement on African meetings to draw up a petition to Parliament and

IX: THE RISING IN PERSPECTIVE

U.N.O. by Rev. Michael Scott : 'The meetings, which were generally on Sundays, invariably began and ended with prayers and hymns, and were much more religious in tone throughout than any meetings on the same subject held in Britain', *East Africa and Rhodesia*, 25 June 1953, p. 1378.

64. See Chapter II, references 135-7.

65. Clements Kadalie, 'The Aims and Motives of the I.C.U.', *Seventh General Missionary Conference of South Africa* (Lovedale, 1928), pp. 125-31.

66. For this and a number of other points on Kadalie we are indebted to Mr. George Padmore for allowing us to examine an unpublished typescript of Kadalie's autobiography.

67. See Chapter VIII, reference 77.

68. Quoted from a letter by its secretary, Yesaya M. Chibambo, Ekwendeni, to Rev. T. Ashcroft, 27 June 1924, in Church of Scotland papers. In the same papers, a 1924 Livingstonia missionary comments : 'These native associations, if rightly guided, are going to be very useful. They are excellent safety valves. . . . The Governor has wisely taken notice of them. . . .' Cf. also Donald Fraser, *The New Africa* (London, 1927), p. 162 : 'Their minutes are submitted to the Governor and allow him to see what people are thinking'.

69. Verbal comments kindly supplied by Dr. Hastings K. Banda.

70. *Africa and Orient Review*, vol. i, 5, May 1920, p. 39.

71. From Dr. Hastings K. Banda.

72. Cf. statements by Laws of Livingstonia in *World Missionary Conference*, 1910 (Edinburgh, 1910), iii, p. 196. Cf. also Sir Hector Duff in a letter to *Sunday Times*, 13 September 1953 ; Leys's use of the term 'national struggle' in his account of Chilembwe's Rising, *Kenya*, op. cit. p. 328.

73. Cf. Chapter IV, references 3 and 6.

74. *R.C.N.R.* paragraph 13 (d).

75. E.g. Lothrop Stoddard, *The Rising Tide of Color* (New York, 1920), p. 9 ; W. Lloyd Jones, *K.A.R.* (London, 1928), pp. 206-9 ; Carl Von Hoffmann, *Jungle Gods* (London, 1929), pp. 49-50 ; R. C. F. Maugham, *Nyasaland in the Nineties* (London, 1935), pp. 54-5 ; Daniel Thwaite, *The Seething African Pot* (London, 1936), pp. 63-5 ; Eric Rosenthal, *Stars and Stripes in Africa* (London, 1938), p. 264 ; *Official History of the Great War. Military Operations. East Africa* (London, 1941), i, p. 180 ; H. Maclear Bate, *Report from the Rhodesias* (London, 1953), pp. 226-8 ; etc.

76. Cf. Johnston, *British Central Africa*, op. cit. pp. 203-4.

77. This is implied clearly enough in *Report of His Britannic Majesty's Government on the Mandated Territory of Tanganyika, 1923* (Colonial No. 2, London, 1924), p. 22. See also Buell, op. cit. i, p. 242—though Buell himself shows confusion about the effect of Watch Tower on Chilembwe.

78. Hoffmann, op. cit. ; Buell, op. cit. p. 242 ; George Padmore, *How Britain Rules Africa* (London, 1936), p. 53 ; etc.

79. *Report of the Commission . . . into the Disturbances on the Copper-belt, Northern Rhodesia* (Cmd. 5009, 1935), pp. 42-51, 114, etc. ; *Central Africa. News and Views* (Blantyre), i, 3, 1936, pp. 1-8.

80. See reference 77 above. Also W. J. Roome, *Can Africa Be Won?* (London, 1927), p. 63.

81. In general on Kimbangu, see Buell, op. cit. ii, pp. 601-9 ; Georges Balandier, *Sociologie Actuelle de l'Afrique Noire* (Paris, 1955), pp. 427 et seq.

NOTES AND REFERENCES

R. H. Carson Graham, *Under Seven Congo Kings* (London, n.d.), pp. 182-94, for the movement in the Portuguese Congo. More particularly for the supposed Chilembwe-Kimbangu link, see 'Le prophétisme dans les églises protestantes indigènes d'Afrique (digest of an article by R. P. Brou), *Congo* (Brussels), i, 1931, pp. 711-12 ; *Bulletin des Jurisdictions Indigènes et du Droit Coutumier Congolais* (Elizabethville), July-August 1944, 'Kitawala', pp. 231-6 (e.g. p. 232—'Dès 1915 le mouvement s'était déjà étendu au Nyassaland').

82. *Le Courrier d'Afrique*, 26 March 1936.

83. Cf. *Nyasaland Times*, 29 April 1915.

84. Correspondence with M. Jean Comhaire (whose article, 'Sociétées Secrètes et Mouvements Prophétiques au Congo Belge', *Africa*, xxv, January 1955, may be consulted for more recent information on Congo Kimbanguism) has helped to clear up this point.

85. *Kenya*, op. cit. p. 326.

86. E.g. C. L. R. James, *A History of Negro Revolt* (London, 1938), pp. 47-52.

87. The Rising, however, is noted in later works by Mr. Padmore.

88. Pp. 47-8 : monograph in September 1938, 'Fact' Series (London).

89. (Gütersloh), iii, pp. 566-8, 572-3, 646, etc.

90. (Braunschweig), pp. 368-80.

91. Karstedt and von Werder, op. cit., pp. 149-50, 153-4. See also Karstedt's *Der Weisse Kampf im Afrika* (Berlin, 1937), pp. 231-2

92. Leys, op. cit., p. 326.

93. James, op. cit., p. 47.

94. For these Angola movements, see H. W. Nevinson, *A Modern Slavery* (London, 1906), pp. 82, 140-1, 157, and *More Changes, More Chances* (London, 1925), p. 65 ; R. H. Carson Graham, *Under Seven Congo Kings* (London, n.d.), pp. 132-72, 236-7. Cf. also on the 1916 revolt in Mbunda and Luchazi country, C. M. N. White, 'The Balovale Peoples and their Historical Background', *Rhodes-Livingstone Journal*, viii, 1949, p. 39. In movements such as the Buta outbreak, which arose out of cocoa plantation conditions, the interesting question arises as to how far such Portuguese native outbreaks represent inter-tribal movements.

95. *Arquivo Histórico Colonial, Moçambique index, No. 379, Revolta do Barue, 1917.*

96. *The Handbook of Tanganyika* (London, 1930), pp. 72-5 ; Karl Weule, *Native Life in East Africa* (London, 1909), pp. 27 et seq., 31, 50-1, etc. ; J. H. Driberg, 'Yakan', *Journal of the Royal Anthropological Institute* (London), lxi, 1931, pp. 413-20 ; R. M. Bell, 'The Maji-Maji Rebellion in the Liwale District', *Tanganyika Notes and Records* (Dar-es-Salaam), No. 28, January 1950. The principal German source is Graf von Götzen, *Deutsch-Ostafrika im Aufstand, 1905-6* (Berlin, 1909).

97. *Handbook*, op. cit., p. 72.

98. When von Götzen, op. cit., listed twelve tribes as participating in the Rebellion, he gave an impression that some factor had arisen which overrode ethnic divisions and united diverse peoples. Free play of speculation on what such a factor might be has produced, at either extreme, the notions that it was atavistic barbarism and bloodlust, or patriotic rejection of alien domination.

On examination of the groups indicated by these tribal names, they are found to fall into two categories—those which were wholly involved, and those which split, part either remaining quiet or contributing to the German auxiliary forces. The

IX: THE RISING IN PERSPECTIVE

former were the Pogoro, Kichi, Ikemba, Bunga, Donde (better rendered as Ndonde) and Ngindo. But these all belonged to one linguistic unit, with which the Mwera and Matumbi, other proscribed tribes, are also connected. Culturally, they are not much differentiated, and are not reckoned a single tribe mainly because they had not developed or been subjected to any paramount chiefship or other central authority.

The others are tribes on the borders of this Ngindo-Mwera heartland, which is roughly the basin of the Rufiji river-system. The Zaramo and Sagara on the north were chronically excitable, lying as they did in the line of any operations against or initiated from Dar-es-Salaam. The Bena on the west had not yet quietened down after much unsettlement by local wars with their Hehe and Ngoni neighbours.

The Ngoni, the only one of the notorious warlike and domineering tribes to join, in fact split sharply on the issue. The western group refused to respond to emissaries from the Maji-Maji leaders. The easterners under Tschabruma (Chaburuma) eventually joined in the Rebellion, but were too late to do much except prolong the repressive and punitive period. Not only was there contention between the section chiefs, but the eastern Ngoni were mostly servile adherents of local origin but Ngindo speech. Nowadays, they prefer, for the most part, to be known by their old name of Ndendeuli.

Neither the Hehe nor the Yao, who might have held that they had old scores to settle with the Germans, joined in any very great numbers. The unity of the Maji-Maji rebels was much more one of communications, linguistic and geographical, than of policy or emotion.

99. J. V. Wild, *The Uganda Mutiny* (London, 1955). Cf. also the early mutinies in the Belgian Congo native armies.

100. Wild, op. cit. p. 97.

101. Gluckman, *Rituals of Rebellion in South-East Africa* (Manchester, 1954), p. 24.

102. Cf. Buell, op. cit. ii, p. 737 : 'About 1875 the seaboard tribes between Grand Cess and San Pedro formed the G'debo Reunited Kingdom and attempted to drive out the civilized Liberian settlements'.

103. E.g. Roux, Sundkler, Schlosser, Balandier, op. cit., and two pioneering studies : Maurice Leenhardt, *Le Mouvement Ethiopien au sud d'Afrique* (Cahors, 1902); Allen Lea, *The Native Separatist Church Movement in South Africa* (Cape Town, 1926). For further bibliography see footnotes to the above and to George Shepperson, 'Ethiopianism and African Nationalism', *Phylon* (Atlanta, Ga.), xiv, 1, 1953 ; and to references below.

104. H. Richard Niebuhr, *The Social Sources of Denominationalism* (New York, 1929). Cf. also Max Weber, 'The Protestant Sects and the Spirit of Capitalism', in H. H. Gerth and C. Wright Mills, editors, *From Max Weber : Essays in Sociology* (London, 1947); A. Victor Murray, *The School in the Bush* (London, 1929), appendix.

105. See Chapter III, reference 71.

106. John W. Clark, etc., *The Voice of Jubilee* (London, 1865), pp. 34-5.

107. W. J. Gardner, *History of Jamaica* (London, 1909), pp. 277-8.

108. Ibid. pp. 473-4.

109. Philip A. Bruce, *The Plantation Negro as a Freeman. Observations on his Character, Conditions and Prospects in Virginia* (New York, 1889), pp. 73-4.

110. E.g. Sundkler, op. cit. p. 72, notices the Chilembwe movement only in passing.

111. The link between South and Central African Ethiopianism is implied by Lord Lugard in a footnote to his *The Dual Mandate in British Tropical Africa* (Edinburgh, 1922), p. 117

112. E.g. Jomo Kenyatta, *Facing Mount Kenya* (London, 1938), p. 269.

113. But cf. Rev. Chas. S. Morris, 'African Coloured Baptists, 1899–1901', in Rev. J. Dexter Taylor (editor), *Christianity and the Natives of South Africa* (London, n.d.).

114. *Correspondence relating to the Native Disturbances in Natal* (Cd. 2905, 1906), pp. 3-5, 11, 15, etc.; *Further Correspondence . . . Native Disturbances* (Cd. 3027, 1906), pp. 82-7, etc.; *Further Correspondence . . .* (Cd. 3247, 1906), pp. 7, 21, 28-33, 34, 87, etc.; J. Stuart, *A History of the Zulu Rebellion* (London, 1913), pp. 97, 128, 420, 521; Anon., *A Question of Colour* (Edinburgh and London, 1906), pp. 249-65; etc.

115. It is interesting to notice that Lothrop Stoddard in his racialist *The Rising Tide of Color* (London, 1920) brings the Natal and Nyasaland Ethiopian Risings together (pp. 98-9) but gives greater mention to the latter.

116. Thomas Hodgkin, 'The French Cameroons', *West Africa*, 27 November 1954, p. 1109. See also H. R. Rudin, *Germans in the Cameroons* (London, 1938), pp. 340, 356, etc.; Buell, op. cit. ii, pp. 272-3, 302-5.

117. E.g. Bandele Omoniyi, *A Defence of the Ethiopian Movement* (Edinburgh. 1908), p. 4; Casely Hayford, *Ethiopia Unbound* (London, 1911), p. 173.

118. On West African church separatism, see in general John H. Harris, *Dawn in Darkest Africa* (London, 1912), p. 288; Georgina A. Gollock, *Sons of Africa* (London, 1928), pp. 207-11; Arthur T. Porter, 'Religious Affiliation in Freetown, Sierra Leone', *Africa* (London), xxiii, 1953, especially pp. 7 and 10; Geoffrey Parrinder, *Religion in an African City* (London, 1953), chapter 6 and appendices iv-v; Thomas Hodgkin, *Nationalism in Colonial Africa*, chapter 3 and pp. 198-200; etc.

119. Nevertheless some of the sentiments expressed by West African separatist churches have a strong spirit of political independence. Cf. A. F. Beyioku in Parrinder, op. cit. p. 126: 'I have little faith in political emancipation without spiritual independence'. The spirit of the so-called National Church of Nigeria and the Cameroons is overtly political. Its *Hymns and Prayers* contains politically orientated parodies of Christian hymns. Its pamphlet by J. A. Iwuna, *Bishop Heerey of the National Church of Rome versus the National Church of Nigeria and the Cameroons*, calls upon the examples of the Waldenses, Albigenses, Lollards, Hussites, and Huguenots in its objections to foreign religious control. For similar examples in the Gold Coast cf. the African nationalist adaptation of the Lord's Prayer, the Apostles' Creed, and the Beatitudes, pp. 80-1, 101-2, Bankole Timothy, *Kwame Nkrumah* (London, 1955).

120. See E. A. Freeman, *The Epoch of Negro Baptists and the Foreign Mission Board* (Kansas City, 1953), passim.

121. *Kenya*, op. cit. p. 325.

122. W. MacGregor Ross, *Kenya From Within* (London, 1927), p. 225.

123. Buell, op. cit. i, p. 374.

124. L. S. B. Leakey, *Mau Mau and the Kikuyu* (London, 1953), p. 86.

125. Ross, op. cit. p. 228.

126. Ibid. p. 225.

127. This and the above quotation are from *Native Disturbances in Kenya* (Cmd. 1691, 1922), pp. 5-6.

128. *Kenya*, op. cit. p. 328. But it must also be remembered that Chilembwe was not uninfluenced by the 'radical' passages in the New Testament.

129. Ross, op. cit. p. 225.

130. Leakey, op. cit. p. 93. Cf. also *East Africa and Rhodesia*, 8 September 1955, for Thuku's support of the Moral Re-armament World Mission.

131. See Kenyatta, op. cit. chapter xi, 'New Religion'; Negley Farson, *Last Chance in Africa* (London, 1953), pp. 120-31, 218-39; Leakey, op. cit., and *Defeating Mau Mau* (London, 1954), pp. 41-76, etc.; D. H. Rawscliffe, *The Struggle for Kenya* (London, 1954), chapter iii, 'The Dinis', etc.

132. R. C. F. Maugham, *Nyasaland in the Nineties* (London, 1935), p. 55.

133. 'Nyangweso', 'The Cult of Mumbo in Central and South Kavirondo', *The Journal of the East Africa and Uganda Natural History Society*, No. 38-9, p. 13.

134. Buell, op. cit. i, pp. 565, 612-17; H. B. Thomas and Robert Scott, *Uganda* (Oxford, 1935), pp. 337-8; Sir Albert Cook, *Uganda Memories* (1897-1940) (Kampala, 1945), pp. 323-4.

135. Buell, op. cit. i, pp. 594-5.

136. *Report of the Commission of Inquiry into the Disturbances in Uganda during April*, 1949 (Entebbe, 1950), pp. 85-99.

137. E. M. K. Mulira, *Troubled Uganda* (pamphlet, London, 1950), p. 37.

138. Cf. pp. 88-9, *Report . . .* (Entebbe), op. cit.

139. E.g. W. C. Willoughby, *The Soul of the Bantu* (London, 1928), pp. 112-35; Gollock, op. cit. pp. 203-27; Lloyd Allen Cook, 'Revolt in Africa', *Journal of Negro History*, iv, 1933, p. 396; Sundkler, op. cit.; Schlosser, op. cit.

140. Sundkler, op. cit. passim.

141. Buell, op. cit. i, pp. 120-3; Roux, op. cit. pp. 143-7.

142. Cf. the 'Cargo' cults of the Pacific, for which see *Oceania* articles in bibliography below; Peter Worsley, 'The Trumpet Shall Sound', *The Listener* (London), 13 October 1955, pp. 597-8; Jean Guiart, 'Culture Contact and the "John Frum" Movement in Tanna, New Hebrides', *Southwestern Journal of Anthropology* (Albuquerque), xii, 1956. See also Aarne A. Koskinen, *Missionary Influence as a Political Factor in the Pacific Islands* (Helsinki, 1953), pp. 101-4, 107, 110, 223, etc.

143. Roux, op. cit. pp 147-9; Monica Hunter, *Reaction to Conquest* (London, 1936), pp. 570-1.

144. Chilembwe's remark, 'Pray that God in his Chariot may bring messengers of peace . . .' in his 1914 letter to his American Negro supporters (Chapter V, reference 120) might be construed as an example of his usage of apocalyptic imagery. In its context, however, it seems that he was doing nothing more than employing the conventional imagery of contemporary missionary journals.

145. Brawley, op. cit., first page of preface.

146. Cf. John Hope Franklin, *From Slavery to Freedom* (New York, 1947), chapter xxiv; William Z. Foster, *The Negro People in American History* (New York, 1954), chapter 40.

147. Buell, op. cit. i, p. 920; ii, p. 738.

148. Cf. *Proceedings of the Church Missionary Society for Africa and the East* (1914-15), p. 55, which reports a native rising in the Giriama country north of

Mombasa (see also Buell, op. cit. i, pp. 361, 373-4) in August 1914 : 'It was in no wise connected with the European war'.

149. It is worthy of note that some Nyasaland Africans appear to have served in Flanders during the Great War—presumably as a result of going down to South Africa and of joining its armed forces : cf. Donald Fraser, *The New Africa* (London, 1927), pp. 9-10, who speaks of a meeting between himself and two Nyasas, a trade-union leader and a Nyasaland African who had served in France. In his unpublished autobiography Clements Kadalie confirms this information and identifies himself with the trade-union leader.

150. Buell, op. cit. ii, pp. 965-76, Articles 16, 47-8.

151. Edmund David Cronon, *Black Moses. The Story of Marcus Garvey and the Universal Negro Improvement Association* (Madison, Wisconsin, 1955), p. 66.

152. John Hope Franklin, op. cit. p. 483.

153. Franklin, foreword to Cronon, op. cit. p. ix.

154. *Journal of Negro History*, xxxvi, 1, 1952, pp. 56-7.

155. Information kindly supplied by Mr. Brisbane. See *Nyasaland Times*, 24 September 1926, p. 3, for further circumstantial evidence of links between Chilembwe-ites and Garvey-ites.

156. See Chapter III, section 4, and Appendix 2.

157. See Chapter III, section 3.

158. It has been claimed that Booth was the originator of this slogan. See *Mission Herald* (National Baptist Convention, Philadelphia), May 1915, vol. 19, 5, p. 27 ; Schlosser, op. cit. p. 233, footnote 90. Booth was certainly using the slogan extensively in 1897 : e.g. *Central African Planter* (Zomba), 15 January 1897, 'Mr. Booth in Durban', 1 March 1897, 'African Opinion of Mr. Booth', etc. But this should not be taken as implying that Booth originated 'Africa for the Africans'. This is clear from p. 16 of Booth's *Africa for the African*, op. cit., where he quotes from Mackay of Uganda who seems to suggest that the slogan goes back to the Negro, W. Edward Blyden (author of *Christianity, Islam and the Negro Race*, London, 1887, etc. ; West Indian Negro who settled in Sierra Leone ; later Liberian minister in London). It is probable that the slogan has earlier origins. However, it is certain that Booth, after his first visit to America, did much to popularize it many years before Marcus Garvey took up active political life.

159. *Mission Herald*, May 1915.

160. See Chapter VIII, reference 80.

161. Cf. Cronon, op. cit. p. 227. We are grateful to Mrs. Amy Jacques Garvey, second wife of Marcus Garvey, for supplying us with material. In none of it is there any mention of Chilembwe. The only reference, indeed, that we have been able to find to Nyasaland in Garvey's major printed works is in *The Tragedy of White Injustice* (New York, 1927), p. 20.

162. See Chapter III, references 54-6. For the Pan-African movement in general, see W. E. Burghardt DuBois, *The World and Africa* (New York, 1947), pp. 7-12, 235 et seq., 240-5 ; Hodgkin, op. cit. pp. 21, 23-4, 161, 175, 181-2, 184, 188.

163. See Chapter IV, reference 159.

164. Franklin, op. cit. p. 462.

165. xxi, 'The Tide of Colour. I', p. 130.

166. Buchan, *Prester John* (London, 1910), pp. 275-7.

167. London, 1922 edition, p. 618.

SOURCES

THE collection of adequate materials for this work has been made difficult by the non-existence and non-availability of records of persons and institutions which would seem to have importance for the study of the Chilembwe movement and its *milieu*. A special difficulty here was the fact that the British official records are not open to public inspection beyond 1902 ; nor was it possible to obtain permission to consult the group of documents which deals with the Rising in the Zomba branch of the Central African Archives. These documents are :

1. Summary of Sir George Smith's confidential dispatch of 13 March 1916 to the Colonial Office on the activities of smaller Nyasaland Missions. (Ref. No. 488/19.)
2. Release of political prisoners, with copies of early correspondence on their connection with the Rising. (Ref. No. 927/19.)
3. Native Tenants (Agreement) Ordinance 1915, and subsequent ordinances. (Ref. No. 172/19.)
4. Report on political prisoner Lot Collection Chimwembwe detained for complicity in the Chilembwe Rising. (Ref. No. 89/92.)
5. Implications of the teachers and members of the Churches of Christ Mission. (Ref. No. 486/19.)
6. Implications of members of the Seventh Day Baptist Mission. (Ref. No. 484/19.)
7. Government assistance towards the maintenance of Charlie and Donald Chilembwe, sons of John Chilembwe. (Ref. No. 3049/22.)
8. Effects of mission teaching and the Chilembwe Rising in 1494/19.
9. An account of the Rising compiled by Sir George Smith in 946/19.
10. Adoption by the Government of the Recommendations of the Commission of Inquiry. (Ref. No. 1304/19.)
11. Seditious teachings of Biseyi Kachewanda and Peter Kalemba of the P.I.M., 1922–4. (Ref. No. C8 55/22.)

Furthermore, even if such records are opened eventually for public inspection, future investigators of this period will face an insuperable difficulty : a fire in the Nyasaland Secretariat in 1919 destroyed all Secretariat records up to that date (see *Central African Archives in Retrospect and Prospect, 1935–47*, Salisbury, 1947, p. 47). When it is considered that these would no doubt have contained many of Chilembwe's seized papers, their loss must be counted as one of the greatest impediments to the detailed investigation of the Rising. Some indication of the character of the loss is provided by a paragraph from the *Nyasaland Times* of 11 February 1915 :

> The papers, consisting of letters, registers of names, etc., which were seized in the house of John Chilembwe have thrown considerable light on the plot which was hatched at Chiradzulu and have given valuable clues to the authorities in discovering who were the prime movers. Apart from the information thus obtained, it would have been very difficult to piece together and assign to their true place the various items of information that have come to hand during the trials.

And some suggestion, at least, of the literary style of the seized Chilembwe-ite papers is afforded by the remark of the Nyasaland Chief Secretary, Hector Duff, in a Legislative Council debate of 11 March 1915 :

> The confiscated papers of these plotters of murder and of their correspondents teemed with professions of piety couched in the language of educated or partially educated men.

But these two tantalizing glimpses remain, perhaps, the only evidence or the nature of these conspiratorial papers which now seem to be irretrievably lost. There may, indeed, be a certain consolation for the non-existence or non-availability of official papers in Henry Adams's remark in his *Education* that 'material furnished by a government seldom satisfies critics or historians, for it always lies under suspicion'. Nevertheless the seizure of Chilembwe's own papers by the Government after the Rising and their apparent destruction in the 1919 Secretariat fire make up a loss of the first magnitude.

Similarly, time, fire, human error, and suspicion have been at work on other important records of this subject. For example, a fire in the office of the National Baptist Convention, U.S.A., Inc., destroyed papers on Chilembwe and the P.I.M.—another major loss of material. In a smaller way, the destruction by fire in 1917 of the records of the Lynchburg branch of Morgan State College, Baltimore, Maryland—it should be remembered that Chilembwe was educated at Lynchburg, and that Booth's *Africa for the African* was printed at Morgan College—has removed what might have been a useful source of information on Booth's and Chilembwe's relations with American Negro centres. These examples could easily be multiplied. Yet one more must be mentioned : the ravages of the London 'Blitz' amongst the records of the Zambesi Mission (formerly Zambesi Industrial Mission) which destroyed possible sources for Booth's early relations with Chilembwe.

Nevertheless, in spite of all these obstacles, it has surprised us continually to discover what records do survive, however scattered and difficult of access they may be. In particular, it has been gratifying to discover the number of photographs still in existence. Chilembwe's own photograph album—a souvenir of war that was taken by a member of the Mikalongwe Volunteers—is an important example of this type of material.

Wherever possible, we have tried to trace all major living witnesses (or their relations or friends) of the events which we have attempted to describe and analyse. It has been a process which has afforded us pleasure and embarrassment in equal proportions. Again, we have been surprised to find out how many such witnesses can be traced. It has been equally remarkable to discover how many of them—by far the greater part of those who were approached—were willing to co-operate with us by supplying material which ranged from the brief memorandum to masses of personal papers and comments. Many of these witnesses of both races have been interviewed personally, and a vast body of oral evidence has been collected. All such material, of course, suffers from the defects of memory and partisanship. Yet when it has been checked against more reliable primary sources, out of it all has come a picture of the Nyasaland Native Rising, its antecedents and its consequences which we believe does not distort their essential form—for it is clear that many of the details are, by now, utterly lost. We hope, however, that this book will act as a stimulus to bring to light other details which, at the present moment, are buried out of sight.

Our assault on our objective has combined something of the frontal attack and the flanking movement ; and, all the time, we have been carrying out a kind of guerrilla warfare to bring to light the more recondite materials. In fact, very often it has been by indirections that we have found directions out. In this way, much of our investigation has had the joint character of a complicated chain-letter system and a series of long-range patrols. Thus, our list of acknowledgements to the many persons and institutions who have answered our letters and our questions, and have directed us to further materials, follows logically the list of the more obvious sources : for without these persons and institutions, in face of the formidable barrier of non-existent and non-available records, this book would have been impossible.

Finally, we would point out that, because of the recondite character of many of our materials, we have been confronted with no small problem of classification when presenting them under the heading of 'Sources'. The method of classification which we have decided to adopt is by no means entirely satisfactory ; but we hope that it will give some indication

SOURCES

of the very wide range of materials we have used and, perhaps, some sugges-tions as to the way in which we have employed them. Under the heading of 'Primary Sources' we have included a number of items which might conventionally be described as 'Secondary Sources'. Thus, some printed books and articles will be found under 'Primary Sources' because, in the absence of other materials, that is, in fact, what they have become. For example, Norman Leys's account of the Rising in his *Kenya*, which has been used as a basic source by so many other writers who have noted the Chilembwe movement, is the only surviving record of this acute observer's interviews with some of Chilembwe's followers, and of his witness of the aftermath of the Rising. His brother, Dr. Duncan Leys, has told us that Norman Leys destroyed all his Nyasaland notes and records almost im-mediately after writing his book. To us, then, the Leys *Kenya* account of the Rising, although printed nine years after it, is, in effect, a primary rather than a secondary source.

I. PRIMARY SOURCES

A. *Statements (oral or written) in response to questionnaires and/or personal interviews with persons who had connections with John Chilembwe, Joseph Booth, or the milieu of Nyasaland African discontents, 1892–1916.*

(*N.B.*—1. Statements marked with an asterisk were collected originally by Mr. F. M. Withers, who generously placed them at our disposal. 2. Int. = Interview. 3. Titles, decorations, etc., have only been included in this list when, to the best of our knowledge, they were held during the actual 1892–1916 period. We must apologize for any omissions.)

*AITCHISON, James (planter and Volunteer, Mlanje, 1915).
ARMITAGE, L. S. (Church of Scotland missionary, Nyasaland, 1901–23). Int.
*AUNEAU, Bishop (Montfort Marist Fathers Mission, Nguludi, 1915).
BANDA, Hastings K. (African pupil teacher, Livingstonia Mission, 1915). Int.
BORTHWICK, G. H. (on leave from Karonga, 1915 : served with Mikalongwe Volunteers against Chilembwe).
BRUCE, A. Livingstone (of A. L. Bruce Estates. Member of Nyasaland Field Force and Legislative Council, 1915).
*CARDEW, C. A. (Resident, Ncheu, 1915).
CARSCALLEN, A. A. (American Seventh-day Adventist missionary; with Peter Nyambo in British East Africa, 1905–7).
CHARD, W. H. (Australian member of Zambesi Industrial Mission, 1895).
CHEEK, Rev. L. N. (American Negro Baptist missionary at P.I.M., 1901–6).
CHILEMBWE, Harris (niece of John Chilembwe). Int.
CHILEMBWE, Miriam (niece of John Chilembwe). Int.
CHINTALI, Rev. F. S. (Church of Scotland Mission ; later minister, Church of Central Africa, Presbyterian ; collateral relative of various adherents of John Chilembwe). Int.

SOURCES

COCKERILL, Walter B. (American Seventh Day Baptist missionary in Nyasaland, 1914–15).

COUTANCHE, Keith (Nyasaland Government Service, 1915; Assistant Attorney-General, 1918–19).

*DOWNS, John (commercial man; Volunteer, Nyasaland, 1915).

DUBOIS, Dr. W. E. B. (American Negro scholar; acquaintance of Booth about 1912).

DUFF, Hector L. (Acting Chief-Secretary, Nyasaland, 1915).

FERGUSON, Rev. J. S. (with Zambesi Industrial Mission, Dombole, 1915).

GRANT, R. W. Lyall (Chairman of the Commission of Inquiry into the Rising, and Judge of the High Court, Blantyre, 1915–16).

HADFIELD, F. L. (Rhodesian member of the Churches of Christ, 1915, and close personal friend of G. H. Hollis, missionary for the Churches of Christ, Nyasaland, 1908–1915).

HOLLIS, Mrs. G. H. (second wife of Mr. G. H. Hollis).

*INGALL, Cecil E. (planter and Volunteer, Nyasaland, 1915).

JENKIN, Rev. A. M. (U.M.C.A. missionary and Anglican chaplain to Blantyre and Zomba Europeans; Volunteer, 1915).

LANGWORTHY, Emily Booth (first daughter of Joseph Booth; with him in Nyasaland, 1892; Chilembwe was her first African friend).

LIVINGSTONE, Mrs. K. (Magomero, 1915).

MALEKEBU, Daniel (early scholar of P.I.M.; followed its American Negro missionaries to United States in 1907; in charge of new P.I.M. since 1926). Int.

MALINKI, K. M. (co-worker of Booth and Chilembwe, 1892–7; subsequently first Nyasaland African Seventh-day Adventist pastor).

MANN, Nora L. (U.M.C.A. Mission, Nyasaland, 1915).

MARTIN, Father (Nguludi Mission, 1915). Int.

MAY, J. C. (commercial employee, Blantyre; Volunteer, 1915).

MBELA, Maynard Gibson (pupil at P.I.M., 1904–11).

MITCHELL, Philip (Government Service, Nyasaland, 1913–15; temporarily in charge, Chiradzulu, end of 1914).

MKULICHI, Andrew (Member of P.I.M.; follower of Chilembwe during the Rising). Int.

NYAMBO, Peter (African friend and co-worker of Booth, 1901–14).

PARSONS, Ethel (U.M.C.A. Mission, Nyasaland, 1915).

PHILPOTT, Henry (Churches of Christ missionary, Nyasaland, 1913–15).

REID, Rev. James (Church of Scotland missionary, Mlanje, 1915). Int.

*ROBERTSON, John (manager, Mwanje section, Bruce Estates, 1915). Int.

ROBINSON, C. (Superintendent of Seventh-day Adventist Mission, Malamulo, 1911–19).

ROGERS, J. C. (Seventh-day Adventist missionary, Malamulo, 1907–31, intermittently).

SANDERSON, W. (planter on Gotha Estate; Volunteer, 1915). Int.

SPENCER, Anne (American Negro student at Virginia Theological Seminary and College while Chilembwe was there).

*THORNEYCROFT, Geoffrey V. (planter, Chimpeni Estate, Zomba district; Volunteer, 1915).

WILCOX, Wayland D. (American Seventh Day Baptist who went to Nyasaland in 1912 to report on the strength and character of Booth's African congregations).

SOURCES

B. *Manuscript, non-printed or unpublished materials*

AFRICAN LAKES CORPORATION : Headquarters Diary, Nyasaland, 24-30 January 1915 (copy kindly provided by Mr. J. Marshall for Mr. F. M. Withers, who placed it at our disposal).

ANTI-SLAVERY SOCIETY : Minute Book, 1915–16 (Anti-Slavery Society Papers, C2/13, Bodleian Library, Oxford).

BANNISTER, Mary (Churches cf Christ missionary in Nyasaland, 1912–15) : Diaries, 1912–40.

BOOTH, Joseph : Papers. The most important group of these found its way by some mysterious process into the London office of the Anti-Slavery Society. This group comprises papers which were all written towards the end, or shortly after the Great War, and represents Booth's stock-taking of his African work up to that time. It is possible to arrange them in nine sections : (i) 're John Chilembwe, the Yao Native Messenger to the Negroes of U.S.A.'; (ii) 'Foreword to the African Friendly Settlements Proposal'; (iii) 'To Conscientious Objectors and Others, being a Leaflet chiefly relating to an Appeal for Friendly Settlements in Africa, by Joseph Booth, Fourfold Deportee, of 34 Mill Mead, Staines, Bucks'; (iv) 'The Call of the Man'ganja People for Pacifists'; (v) 'The Native African's Call for Pacifists'; (vi) 'Other Calls'; (vii) Untitled—Makololo 'Call'; (viii) 'The Call of the Chipeta'; (ix) 'The Zulu Call'. The papers are now conveniently placed in the Bodleian Library, Oxford : Anti-Slavery Papers, MSS. Brit. Emp. S18. C. 154/1-9.

A second group of Booth papers which has been used includes a selection of his personal correspondence, notes, mission reports, memoranda, etc., in the possession of his first daughter, Mrs. Emily Booth Langworthy of Gloversville, New York.

CHILEMBWE, John : two letters in possession of Mr. W. Sanderson and Mrs. N. O. Moore.

CHURCH OF SCOTLAND : Missionary Records. Now held by the National Library of Scotland. (This collection includes records of the old United Free Church of Scotland.) Papers examined include : Livingstonia files, 1896–1910; Church of Scotland, Letter Books, Africa, 1888–1926 (Nos. 28-35 of 1914–18 period are the most useful of this group).

Another group of Scottish church papers which was examined in the Church of Scotland offices, Edinburgh, before the transfer of the Missionary records to the National Library of Scotland comprised an informal file on the 1915 Rising. This included : copies of correspondence between J. N. Ogilvie and A. Steel Maitland for the Colonial Office, 1916; letters and papers from the Blantyre and Livingstonia missionaries on the Rising and the Commission of Inquiry; an annotated version of the Commission's Report; and a copy of the censored passages from *Livingstonia News*, 1916.

COCKERILL, Walter B. : Nyasaland diaries, 1914–15; letters to America from Nyasaland, 1914–15.

INTERNATIONAL MISSIONARY COUNCIL (London) : file on Nyasaland Native Rising in 1915 (correspondence with Colonial Office, Church of Scotland, etc.; contains what seems to be the only unprinted account of the Rising, by Dr. Alexander Hetherwick in existence).

SOURCES

KADALIE, Clements : South African trade-union leader (Tonga tribesman by origin), typescript autobiography.

LIVINGSTONE, Mrs. K. : letters, testimonials, etc., on the subject of Mr. W. J. Livingstone.

MILLER, Rose M. : hand-duplicated pamphlet for circulation amongst members of the Epworth League of 7nth Street M.E. Church, Lorain, Ohio, with extracts from letters and conversations of Miss E. B. DeLany on early P.I.M. history.

MKULICHI, Andrew G. : 'Maziko a Prov. Ind. Mission. Chiradzulo. Nyasaland. 1900 A.D.' (Account, written in 1951 by former Chilembwe follower, of Chilembwe's life and influence.)

MOORE, N. O. (companion of Wayland D. Wilcox on Seventh Day Baptist journey of investigation into Booth's African activities in 1912) : miscellaneous African materials.

NYASALAND DISTRICT BOOKS : Blantyre ; Chiradzulu ; Chikwawa ; Cholo ; Ruo District.

PUBLIC RECORD OFFICE, London : F.O.2. 207-12 (1889) ; F.O.2. 247-8 (1899) ; F.O.2. 306-8 (1900) ; F.O.2, 605-9 (1902) ; BT.31.6671.46912, The African Missions Transport Company Limited ; BT.31.8627.62906, British Central Africa Transit Company Limited. This group of official papers contains the main references to Booth's Nyasaland activity in the Public Records up to 1902, when the Records are closed to public inspection.

ROBINSON, V. E. : unpublished typescript, 'Historical Sketch of the Work of Seventh-day Adventists in Nyasaland, 1902–1915'.

SANDERSON, William : unpublished MSS., 'A Planter's Experiences in the Nyasaland Rising (letter by Willie Sanderson). Gotha Estate. Nyasaland. Sunday, 7th Feb. 1915.'

SCOTTISH COMPANIES OFFICE, Edinburgh : A. L. Bruce Estates, file No. 8650.

SEVENTH-DAY ADVENTIST NYASALAND MISSION : copies of correspondence with Government bodies on the Rising.

SEVENTH DAY BAPTIST HISTORICAL SOCIETY : miscellaneous material on Booth and Chilembwe.

WILCOX, Wayland D. (companion of N. O. Moore above) : 1912 African diary.

C. *Photographs*

The illustrations which accompany the text of this book give some indication of the surprising range of photographic material which still survives. The camera habit seems to have been well established among the British Central Africa Europeans by the 1890's ; and it is fortunate for the recording of Nyasaland history that the Americans who visited the country as a result of Booth's influence were all, apparently, keen photographers.

The photographs which we have examined fall into four groups :

1. *Chilembwe/P.I.M. material.* (a) Photographs in Booth's *Africa for the African.* (b) Photographs of Chilembwe taken by National Baptist Convention agencies in the United States. (c) Chilembwe/P.I.M. photographs taken during the period 1900–15. These include photographs from Chilembwe's personal album. (Each of these is rubber-stamped on the back 'M. M. Chisuse, The African Photographer, Blantyre, Nyasaland' ; Chisuse, apparently, followed Chilembwe during the Rising.) Thomas Branch, the American Negro Seventh-day

Adventist missionary, took a number of photographs of Chilembwe and his *milieu*. Photographs of the blowing up of the P.I.M. church, and also some from Chilembwe's own album, appear to have been made up into postcards by Europeans in Nyasaland after the Rising and sold in aid of War charities.

2. *Booth material.* This group includes material in the possession of Booth's relations and friends ; a range of items from various missionary publications ; the illustrations to his *Africa for the African* ; the photographs taken by Messrs. Moore and Wilcox on their mission of investigation in 1912 into Booth's South African and Nyasaland activities.

3. *Other Nyasaland African independent church material.* The Wilcox-Moore photographs, op. cit., are an important source here. G. H. Hollis of Namiwawa left some valuable photographs of Churches of Christ activity. The periodicals and publications of the Seventh-day Adventists, the Seventh Day Baptists and the Churches of Christ are also a useful source for illustrations.

4. *Photographs of other European and African personalities.* Photographs have been traced, either from the press or private sources, for almost all the leading characters of the movements, etc., which culminated in the 1915 Rising. We were unable to trace contemporary photographs of Elliott Kamwana, Filipo Chinyama and Robert Ferguson.

Individual details of these photographs will be found in the text and 'Notes and References'.

D. *Works printed and produced mainly during the 1892–1916 period. (Some works which, although printed and published after 1916, have special relevance for the Rising and thus appear to qualify for the description of primary sources are also included.)*

1. Press

(a) *Newspapers*

(A useful quick general guide is provided by a press-cutting book of the Anti-Slavery Society, 1914–16 volume, p. 47, in Rhodes House Library, Oxford.)

Beira Post, The : 1915–16.

Berlin Courant, The (Berlin, Wisconsin) : 19 November 1914 ; 24 June 1915.

Central African Planter, The (Songani, Zomba) : 1895–7.

Central African Times, The (Blantyre) : 1900–8. (The first two volumes of this valuable source are not in the British Museum Newspaper Library.)

Glasgow Herald, The : 1915–16.

Livingstone Mail, The (Rhodesia) : 1908–15.

Nyasaland Times, The : 1911–18.

Oban Times, The : 1915.

Rhodesia Herald, The : 1915–16.

Scotsman, The : 1893, 1915–16.

Times, The : 1915–16. (The Royal edition in *The Times* Library has been checked for the Rising reference of 22 April 1915, which is not in normally filed 1915 editions.)

(b) *Periodicals*

African Sabbath Recorder, The : 1911–13. (Sometimes no more than a leaflet, this was Booth's own magazine which he edited from Sea Point, Cape Town, and distributed through African agencies in Nyasaland and South Africa. Nos. 1-4 and 6 (16 December 1911–January 1913) are with the Seventh Day Baptist Historical Society, Plainfield, N.J.; a copy of No. 5 is in the possession of Mrs. E. B. Langworthy. It is not known whether any numbers were issued after January 1913.)

Aurora, The (Livingstonia): 1897–1902.

Bible Advocate, The (Birmingham): 1905–16. (Churches of Christ journal.)

Blackwood's Magazine, ccxxx, No. mccxciv, December 1931: L. S. Norman, 'Rebellion'.

Central Africa (London): 1883–1917. (Universities' Mission to Central Africa journal: especially F. R. Spindler, 'A Week in a Concentration Camp', 1915, p. 115; Glossop statement, 1916, p. 177; and G. C. Rawlinson, 'Some Lessons from the Chilembwe Rebellion', 1917, p. 61.)

Church Missionary Intelligencer, later *Review*: 1892–1916. (Church Missionary Society journal.)

Church of Scotland Home and Foreign Mission Record, later *Life and Work*: 1891–1918.

Journal des Missions Évangéliques (Paris): 1892–1919.

Life and Work in British Central Africa, later *Life and Work in Nyasaland*: 1888–1916. (Blantyre Mission journal.)

Livingstonia News, The: 1908–18.

London Gazette, The, Third Supplement to, Tuesday, 1 August 1916, No. 29692, pp. 7649–53.

Mission Herald, The (Philadelphia). (This American Negro missionary organ of the National Baptist Convention began publication in 1896. But there seems to be no readily accessible complete file of it in the United States. There is no complete file in the Library of Congress; and even the National Baptist Convention, U.S.A., Inc., appears to lack a full collection—neither L. G. Jordan nor E. A. Freeman, historians of National Baptist Convention missionary activity, used full sets in their work, according to their bibliographies. The files of *The Mission Herald* for 1907–9 in the New York Public Library, and from 1911 to date in the Yale University Library, seem to be the most immediately useful sources. See L. N. Cheek, 'Reminiscences of a Missionary', vol. 44, 1940.)

Missionary Record of the United Presbyterian Church, later *Missionary Record of the United Free Church of Scotland*, finally *Record of the Home and Foreign Mission Work of the United Free Church of Scotland*: 1892–1917.

Missionary Review of the World, The (New York): 1888–1916.

Missionary Worker, The (Watford): 1908–19. (Seventh-day Adventist journal.)

Nyasaland Diocesan Chronicle (Likoma): 1914–18.

Nyasaland Government Gazette, formerly *British Central Africa Gazette*: 1894–1918. (Contains Summaries of the Proceedings of the Legislative Council.)

Nyasa News, The (Likoma): 1893–4. (U.M.C.A. journal.)

Open Door on the Regions Beyond, The (Birmingham): 1914–25. (Churches of Christ journal.)

Parliamentary Debates (London): 1892–1939.

Sabbath Recorder, The (Plainfield, N. J.): 1898–1915. (Seventh Day Baptist journal.)

South Africa Pioneer, The: 1915–18. (South Africa General Mission journal.)

SOURCES

Spelman Messenger, The (Atlanta, Ga.), 1901–2, 1921, 1945. (Material on Emma B. DeLany, etc. See especially Emma B. DeLany, 'Why I go as a Foreign Missionary', xviii, 1902 ; 'Spelman Women in Africa', lxi, 1945.)
Watch Tower, The (New York) : 1892–1918.
Zambesi Industrial Mission, Occasional Papers : 1892–1918.

(c) *Pamphlets and reports*
Churches of Christ Year Books (Birmingham) : 1911–29.
Ecumenical Missionary Conference, New York, 1900.
JORDAN, L. G., *In Our Stead* (Philadelphia, 1914–17).
LEENHARDT, Maurice, *Le Mouvement éthiopien au sud de l'Afrique de 1896 à 1899* (Cahors, 1902).
Livingstonia, Annual Reports (Glasgow) : 1909–16.
MALEKEBU, Daniel S., *My Vision. East, Central and South Africa of To-day* (Philadelphia, n.d.).
'The History of the Providence Industrial Mission.' (In Appendix I, *Nyasaland Education Department. Report for 1931.*)
MALINKI, K. M., *The History of Pastor K. M. Malinki* (Malamulo, n.d.).
MATECHETA, Harry K., *Blantyre Mission. Nkhani za Ciyambi Cace* (Blantyre, 1951).
MOORE, N. Olney, *Seventh Day Baptists and Missionary Work in Nyasaland, Africa* (duplicated report, dated 4 January 1949 ; published Chicago, 27 February 1950).
Natal. Correspondence relating to the Native Disturbances in Natal, 1906 (Cd. 905, Cd. 3027, Cd. 3247, London, 1906).
National Baptist Convention, U.S.A. : *Journals of the Annual Sessions of the National Baptist Convention* (Nashville, Tenn.), 1900, 1903–4, 1907–13, 1915, 1918–19 ; *A Year of Prayer. Suggested Monthly Prayer Calendar for Missions of the Foreign Mission Board* (National Baptist Foreign Mission Board, 1911).
NYAMBO, Peter, *Peter's Plaint* (26 March 1913, from Ndabeni Location, Cape Town. Reprinted from *South African Spectator*, April 1913).
Nyasaland Protectorate. Report of the Commission appointed by His Excellency the Governor to inquire into Various Matters and Questions concerned with the Native Rising within the Nyasaland Protectorate (Zomba, 1916).
Nyasaland Protectorate. Annual Reports (London) : 1894–1927.
Proceedings of the Church Missionary Society for Africa and the East (London) : 1914–15.
Proceedings of the General Council of the Reformed Churches Holding the Presbyterian System. Fifth, Toronto, 1892 (London, 1892) ; Sixth, Glasgow, 1896 (London, 1896).
Reports on the Schemes of the Church of Scotland with Legislative Acts passed by the General Assembly (Edinburgh) : 1892–1918.
Scottish Baptist Year Books (Glasgow) : 1899–1918 (with annual reports of the Baptist Industrial Mission of Scotland).
South African Native Affairs Commission, 1903–5 (Cape Town, 1904–5), five volumes.
United Free Church of Scotland. General Assembly Reports (Edinburgh) : 1901–16.
Universities' Mission to Central Africa. Annual Reports (London) : 1914–16.
World Missionary Conference. Reports of Commissions (Edinburgh, 1910).
Zambesi Industrial Mission (London) : miscellaneous pamphlets.

SOURCES

2. BOOKS

BOOTH, Joseph, *Africa for the African* (published by Joseph Booth, Press of the Educator of Morgan College, Edmondson and Fulton Avenues, Baltimore, Md., 1897).

BURNETT, Alexander, *Reminiscences for his Sons, by the Rev. Alexander Burnett. Missionary at Blantyre, Nyasaland, 1900–1925* (privately printed : Northumberland and Berwickshire newspapers, 1949).

DUFF, Sir Hector, *African Small Chop* (London, 1932).

DU PLESSIS, J., *Through the Dark Continent. A Record of a Journey across Africa during the Year 1913–1916* (London, 1917).

HETHERWICK, Alexander, *The Romance of Blantyre* (London, n.d.).

HETHERWICK, Alexander (editor), *Robert Hellier Napier in Nyasaland. Being his Letters to his Home Circle* (Edinburgh, 1925).

INWOOD, Charles, *An African Pentecost. The Record of a Missionary Tour in Central Africa, 1910–11* (London, n.d.).

JOHNSTON, Sir Harry H., *British Central Africa* (London, 1898).

JOHNSTON, James, *Reality versus Romance in South Central Africa* (London, 1893).

JORDAN, Rev. Lewis G., *Negro Baptist History, U.S.A.* (Nashville, Tenn., 1930).

LANGWORTHY, Emily Booth, *This Africa Was Mine* (Stirling, 1952).

LEYS, Norman, *Kenya* (London, 1924).

LIVINGSTONE, W. P., *Laws of Livingstonia* (London, n.d.).

LUCAS, Sir Charles (editor), *The Empire at War* (London, 1924), IV (for article by Sir George Smith, 'Nyasaland and General Northey's Campaign').

MAUGHAM, R. C. F., *Nyasaland in the Nineties and other Recollections* (London, 1935).

MITCHELL, Sir Philip, *African Afterthoughts* (London, 1954).

PHILLIPS, Porter W., *W. W. Brown, Host* (New York, 1941).

Seventh Day Baptists in Europe and America. A series of papers written in Commemoration of the One Hundredth Seventh Day Baptist Conference : celebrated at Ashaway, Rhode Island, August 20–25, 1902 (Plainfield, N.J., 1910), I (for article by William C. Hubbard, 'Sabbath Evangelizing and Industrial Association, 1898')

II. SECONDARY SOURCES

A. *Periodicals*

(*N.B.*—1. Unless otherwise shown, a check has been made of the whole range of the periodical in question. 2. Some articles of interest are mentioned in parenthesis.)

Africa. Journal of the International African Institute (London).
(Audrey Richards, 'A Modern Movement of Witchfinders', viii, 1935 ; E. de Jonghe, 'Formation récente de sociétés secrètes au Congo Belge', ix, 1936 ; Max Gluckman, J. C. Mitchell, J. A. Barnes, 'The Village Headman in British Central Africa', xix, 1949 ; J. C. Mitchell, 'An Estimate of Fertility in some Yao Hamlets', xix, 1949 ; M. G. Marwick, 'Another Modern Anti-witchcraft Movement in East Central Africa', xx, 1950 ; M. G. Marwick, 'The Social Context of Cewa Witch Beliefs', xxii, 1952 ; Arthur T. Porter, 'Religious Affiliation in Freetown, Sierra Leone', xxiii, 1953 ; George Shepperson, 'The Politics of African Church Separatist Movements in British

Central Africa, 1892–1916', xxiv, 1954; Jean Comhaire, 'Sociétés secrètes et mouvements prophétiques au Congo Belge', xxv, 1955.)

African Monthly (Grahamstown). 1910.

(W. Y. Stead, 'The Order of Ethiopia and its relation to the Church', 1910.)

Africa and Orient Review (London), i, 1920.

African Studies (Johannesburg).

(J. C. Mitchell, 'The Political Organization of the Yao of Southern Nyasaland', 8, 1949; J. Bruwer, 'Notes on Maravi Origin and Migration', 9, 1950; T. Price, 'More about the Maravi', 11, 1952.)

All Nations. An Illustrated Monthly Missionary Magazine (London). 1900–17.

Anthropological Quarterly (Washington, D.C.). 1953.

(Jean L. Comhaire, 'Religious Trends in African and Afro-American Urban Societies', xxvi, 1953.)

Anti-Slavery Reporter and Aborigines Friend (London). 1914–18.

Bulletin de juridictions indigènes et du droit coutumier congolais (Elizabethville). 1944.

('Kitawala', pp. 231-6, No. 10, 1944.)

Cahiers internationales de sociologie (Paris). 1953–4.

(Georges Balandier, 'Messianismes et nationalismes en Afrique Noire', xiv, 1953; 'Sociologie de la colonisation', xvii, 1954.)

Chambers's Journal (Edinburgh). 1904–5.

(Captain J. Brander Dunbar, 'African Notes', viii, 1904–5.)

Congo (Brussels). 1931.

(R. P. Brou, 'Le Prophétisme dans les Églises protestantes indigènes d'Afrique', i, 1931, pp. 208-20.)

East Africa and Rhodesia (London).

Human Problems in British Central Africa (Journal of the Rhodes-Livingstone Institute).

(J. M. Winterbottom, 'Outline Histories of Two Northern Rhodesian Tribes', 1949; Lewis Gann, 'The End of the Slave Trade in British Central Africa, 1889–1912', 1954.)

Illustrated Missionary News (London). 1892–6.

International Labour Review (Montreal). 1942.

(Margaret Read, 'Migrant Labour in Africa and its Effects on Tribal Life', xlv, 1942.)

International Review of Missions (London).

John Bull (London). 1915–16.

Journal of the African Society, The, later *African Affairs* (London).

(Captain J. E. T. Phillips, 'The Tide of Colour. I, Pan-Africa and Anti-White', xxi, 1921–2.)

Journal of the East Africa and Uganda Natural History Society (Nairobi).

('Nyangweso', 'The Cult of Mumbo in Central and South Kavirondo', Nos. 38-9, pp. 13-17.)

Journal of Negro Education, The (Washington, D.C.).

(Wilson Record, 'Negro Intellectuals and Negro Movements: Some Methodological Notes', xxiv, 1955.)

Journal of Negro History, The (Washington, D.C.).

(Lloyd Allen Cook, 'Revolt in Africa', xvii, 1933; Robert Hughes Brisbane, Jnr., 'Some New Light on the Garvey Movement', xxxvi, 1951; Robert Ernst, 'Negro Concepts of Americanism', xxxix, 1954.)

SOURCES

Journal of the Royal Anthropological Institute, The (London).
> (L. T. Moggridge, 'The Nyasaland Tribes', xxxii, 1902 ; A. Hetherwick, 'Some Animistic Beliefs Among the Yao of British Central Africa', xxxii, 1902 ; H. C. Stannus, 'Notes on the Tribes of British Central Africa', xl, 1910 ; H. W. Garbutt, 'Witchcraft in Nyasaland', xli, 1911 ; J. H. Driberg, 'Yakañ', lxi, 1930 ; A. G. O. Hodges, 'Notes on the Achewa and Angoni in the Dowa District of the Nyasaland Protectorate', lxiii, 1933.)

Journal of Southern History, The (Lexington, Ky.).
> (Elsie M. Lewis, 'The Political Mind of the Negro, 1865–1900', xxi, 1955.)

Listener, The (London). 1955.
> (Peter Worsley, 'The Trumpet Shall Sound', October 1955.)

Midwest Journal, The (Jefferson City, Missouri). 1951–2.
> (George P. Marks, III, 'Opposition of Negro Newspapers to American Philippine Policy, 1899–1900', iv, 1951–2 ; August Meier, 'The Emergence of Negro Nationalism', iv, 1951–2, 1952.)

Mississippi Valley Historical Review, The (Cedar Rapids, Iowa).
> (Ira V. Brown, 'Watchers for the Second Coming : the Millenarian Tradition in America', xxxix, 1952.)

Muslim World, The (Hartford, Conn.). 1954.
> (T. Price, 'The "Arabs" of the Zambezi', xliv, 1954.)

Negro History Bulletin, The (Washington, D.C.). 1952.
> (George Shepperson, 'The Story of John Chilembwe', January 1952.)

New Statesman, The (London). 1915–16.

Northern Rhodesia Journal, The (Livingstone). 1954.
> (H. T. (Chiana) Harrington, 'The Taming of North-Eastern Rhodesia, ii, 1954.)

Nyasaland Journal, The (Blantyre).
> (W. H. J. Rangeley, 'Mbona the Rainmaker', vi, 1953 ; T. Price, 'Mbona's Waterhole', vi, 1953 ; and *passim*.)

Oceania (Sydney).
> (Jean Guiart, 'Forerunners of Melanesian Nationalism' and 'John Frum Movement in Tanna', xxii, 1951–2 ; R. M. Berndt, 'A Cargo Movement in the Eastern Central Highlands of New Guinea', xxiii, 1952–3 ; K. O. L. Burridge, 'Cargo Cult Activity in Tangu', xxiv, 1953-4.)

Phylon. The Atlanta University Review of Race and Culture (Atlanta, Ga.).
> (George Shepperson, 'The United States and East Africa', xiii, 1952 ; 'Ethiopianism and African Nationalism', xiv, 1953.)

Scottish Baptist Magazine (Edinburgh and Glasgow). 1895–1918.

Social Forces (Baltimore, Md.). 1954.
> (Wilson Record, 'The Negro Intellectual and Negro Nationalism', 33, 1954.)

Southern History Association Publications (Washington, D.C.). 1906.
> (Benjamin W. Arnold, Jnr., 'Concerning the Negroes of Lynchburg, Virginia', x, pp. 19-30, 1906.)

Southwestern Journal of Anthropology (Albuquerque). 1956.
> (Jean Guiart, 'Culture Contact and the "John Frum" Movement in Tanna, New Hebrides', xii, 1956.)

Tanganyika Notes and Records (Dar-es-Salaam).
> (R. M. Bell, 'The Maji-Maji Rebellion in the Liwale District', January 1950.)

SOURCES

Uganda Journal, The (Kampala).
(Roland Oliver, 'Some Factors in the British Occupation of East Africa, 1884–1894', xv, 1951.)
West Africa (London).
(Thomas Hodgkin, 'The French Cameroons', November 1954.)

B. *Pamphlets and reports*

AXENFELD, Karl, *Der Aethiopianismus in Südafrika* (Berlin, 1906).
BANDA, Hastings K., and NKUMBULA, Harry, *Federation in Central Africa* (London, 1951).
Baptist World Congress. July 10-20, 1905. Proceedings (London, 1905).
BOONE, Theodore Sylvester, *A Social History of Negro Baptists* (Detroit, 1952).
BOWEN, J. W. E. (editor), *Africa and the American Negro. Addresses and Proceeding of the Congress on Africa, December 13-15, 1895* (Atlanta, Ga., 1896).
BOYD, R. H., *A Story of the National Baptist Publishing Board* (Detroit, 1952).
BRUCE, A. L., *The Cape to Cairo. Britain's Sphere of Influence* (Edinburgh, 1892).
CHIRNSIDE, Andrew, *The Blantyre Missionaries. Discreditable Disclosures* (London, 1880).
Christian Action in Africa. Report of the Church Conference on African Affairs held at Oberlin College, Westerville, June 19-25, 1942 (New York, 1942)—chapter on 'The Contribution of the American Negro to Africa'.
GLUCKMAN, Max, *Rituals of Rebellion in South-East Africa* (Manchester, 1954).
JAMES, C. L. R., *A History of Negro Revolt* (London, 1938).
JOHNSON, Thomas L., *Africa for Christ. Twenty-Eight Years a Slave* (London, 1882).
LEA, Allen, *The Native Church Separatist Movement in South A'rica* (Cape Town, 1926).
MULIRA, E. M. K., *Troubled Uganda* (London, 1950).
NATARAJAN, L., *Peasant Uprisings in India, 1850–1900* (Bombay, 1953).
Negro Education : a Study of the Private and Higher Schools for Colored People in the United States (Washington, D.C., Government Printing Office, 1917. Bureau of Education Bulletin, 1916, No. 39).
NTHARA, Samuel Yosia, *Mbiri Ya Acewa* (Zomba, 1945).
Nyasaland Protectorate :
   Ordinances, Regulations, Proclamations and Notices (Zomba), 1894–1918.
   Report of a Commission . . . 19 July 1920 to enquire into Certain Matters connected with the Occupation of Land in the Nyasaland Protectorate (Zomba, 1921, 10582).
   Blue Books (Zomba), 1927–38.
   Annual Reports. Provincial Commissioners (Zomba), 1934–8.
   Report on the Nyasaland Natives in the Union of South Africa and Southern Rhodesia by J. C. Abraham (Zomba, 1937).
   A Report by Mr. Eric Smith . . . on the Direct Taxation of Natives in the Nyasaland Protectorate (London, 1937).
   Report of the Royal Commission on the Rhodesias and Nyasaland, 1938–9 (Cmd. 5945).
   Land Commission 1946 (Zomba, 1947), I, Report by Sir Sidney Abrahams.
   Report of a Commission of Inquiry appointed by the Governor on the 20th August 1953 (Zomba, 1953).

SOURCES

OMONIYI, Prince Bandele, *A Defence of the Ethiopian Movement* (Edinburgh, 1908).

Parliamentary Papers (miscellaneous) :

> *Communications relative to Slave Insurrections and the Trials of Missionaries* (xlvii, 482, 1831–2).

> *Report from the House of Assembly, Jamaica, on the Injury sustained during the Recent Rebellion* (xlvii, 561, 1831–2).

> *Papers relating to Native Disturbances in Kenya* . . . *1922* (Cmd. 1691).

> *Report on the Mandated Territory of Tanganyika* . . . *1923* (Colonial No. 2 1924).

> *Report of the Commission* . . . *into the Disturbances on the Copperbelt, Northern Rhodesia* (Cmd. 5009, 1935).

Report of the Commission of inquiry into the Disturbances in Uganda, during August 1949 (Entebbe, 1950).

South Africa :

> *Cape of Good Hope. Blue Books on Native Affairs* : 1898–1908.

> *Report of the South African Native Affairs Commission, 1905* (Cd. 2399, 1905).

> *South Africa. Correspondence relating to the Recruitment of Labour in the Nyasaland Protectorate for the Transvaal and Southern Rhodesia, 1908* (Cmd. 3993).

> *Report of the Native Church Commission* (Cape Town, 1925).

> *South Africa. General Missionary Conference Reports* : 1925, 1928, 1932.

STANFORD, P. T., *From Bondage to Liberty* (Smethwick, 1899).

The Reason why the Colored American is not at the World's Columbian Exposition (Philadelphia, 1893).

The Watchtower Story (Watch Tower Bible and Tract Society, Brooklyn, N.Y., 1948).

WILD, J. V., *The Uganda Mutiny* (London, 1955).

C. Books

ABDALLAH, Yohanna B., *The Yaos*, translated and edited by Meredith Sanderson (Zomba, 1919).

ALLIER, Raoul, *La Psychologie de la conversion chez les peuples non-civilisés* (Paris, 1925).

ANON, *A Question of Colour* (Edinburgh and London, 1906).

Annual Register, The (London), 1915–16.

APTHEKER, Herbert, *American Negro Slave Revolts* (New York, 1943).

APTHEKER, Herbert, *Essays in the History of the American Negro* (New York, 1945).

APTHEKER, Herbert, *A Documentary History of the Negro People in the United States* (New York, 1951).

Arquivo histórico colonial, Moçambique index, No. 379 : *Revolta do Bárue, 1917*.

ATTWATER, D., *The White Fathers in Africa* (London, 1937).

BALANDIER, Georges, *Sociologie actuelle de l'Afrique Noire. Dynamique des changements sociaux en Afrique Centrale* (Paris, 1955).

BARNES, Bertram H., *Johnson of Nyasaland* (London, 1933).

BARNES, J. A., *Politics in a Changing Society. A Political History of the Fort Jameson Ngoni* (London, 1954).

BATE, H. Maclear, *Report from the Rhodesias* (London, 1953).

BENTLEY, W. Holman, *Pioneering on the Congo* (London, 1900).

SOURCES

BERRY, Lewellyn L., *A Century of Missions of the African Methodist Episcopal Church* (New York, 1942).

BLACKFORD, L. Minor, *Mine Eyes Have Seen the Glory. The Story of a Virginia Lady* (Cambridge, Mass., 1954).

BLAIKIE, William Garden, *The Personal Life of David Livingstone* (London, 1880).

BOUNIOL, J., *The White Fathers and their Missions* (London, 1928).

BRADY, Cyrus T., *Commerce and Conquest in East Africa* (Salem, Mass., 1950).

BRAWLEY, Benjamin, *Africa and the War* (New York, 1918).

BROCKELMANN, Carl, *History of the Islamic Peoples* (London, 1949).

BRODE, H., *British and German East Africa* (London, 1911).

BROWN, Sterling (editor, etc.), *The Negro Caravan* (New York, 1941).

BRUCE, Philip A., *The Plantation Negro as a Freeman. Observations on His Character, Condition, and Prospects in Virginia* (New York, 1889).

BUCHAN, John, *The African Colony* (Edinburgh, 1903).

BUCHAN, John, *A Lodge in the Wilderness* (London, 1906).

BUCHAN, John, *Prester John* (London, 1910).

BUELL, Raymond Leslie, *The Native Problem in Africa* (New York, 1928).

BURTON, Sir Richard, *First Footsteps in East Africa* (London, 1856).

CABRAL, A. A. Pereira, *Raças, usos e costumes dos indígenas da provincia de Moçambique* (Lourenço Marques, 1925).

CAREY, William, *An Enquiry into the Obligations of Christians to use Means for the Conversion of Heathens. Reprinted in facsimile from the Edition of MDCCXCII* (London, 1891).

CADDOCK, Helen, *A White Woman in Central Africa* (London, 1900).

CARMICHAEL, Ian, *Lismore in Alba* (Perth, 1951).

CASE, Shirley Jackson, *The Millennial Hope* (Chicago, 1918).

CHURCHILL, Winston S., *The River War* (London, 1899).

CLARK, Elmer T., *The Small Sects in America* (Nashville, 1937).

CLARK, John W., *The Voice of Jubilee, a Narrative of the Baptist Mission, Jamaica . . .* (London, 1865).

COLSON, Elizabeth, and GLUCKMAN, Max (editors), *Seven Tribes of British Central Africa* (London, 1951).

COOK, Sir Albert, *Uganda Memories (1897–1940)* (Kampala, 1945).

COULTER, E. Merton, *The South During Reconstruction* (Bâton Rouge, La., 1947).

COX, F. A., *History of the Baptist Mission from 1792 to 1842* (London, 1842).

CRONON, Edmund David, *Black Moses. The Story of Marcus Garvey and the Universal Negro Improvement Association* (Madison, Wisconsin, 1955).

CURRIE, Jessie Monteath, *With Pole and Paddle down the Shire and Zambesi* (London, 1918).

CURRIE, Jessie Monteath, *The Hill of Goodbye. The Story of a Solitary White Woman's Life in Central Africa* (London, 1920).

CURTIN, Philip D., *Two Jamaicas. The Role of Ideas in a Tropical Colony* (Cambridge, Mass., 1955).

CZATT, Milton Stacey, *The International Bible Students. Jehovah's Witnesses* (Scottdale, Pa., 1933).

DAVIDSON, Basil, *The African Awakening* (London, 1955).

DAVIES, Morton, and SHEPHERD, R. H. W., *South African Missions, 1800–1950* (London, 1954).

SOURCES

DAVIS, Mrs. Tamar, *A General History of the Sabbatarian Churches* (Philadelphia, 1851).

DEBENHAM, Frank, *The Way to Ilala. David Livingstone's Pilgrimage* (London, 1955).

DEBENHAM, Frank, *Nyasaland—Land of the Lake* (London, 1955).

DREWRY, William S., *Slave Insurrections in Virginia* (Washington, D.C., 1900).

DRUMMOND, Henry, *Tropical Africa* (London, 1899).

DUFF, H. L., *Nyasaland under the Foreign Office* (London, 1903).

DuBois, W. E. B. (editor), *The Negro Church. A Social Study* (Atlanta University Publications, No. 8, Atlanta, Ga., 1903).

DuBois, W. E. B. (editor), *Economic Co-operation Among Negro Americans* (Atlanta University Publications, No. 12, Atlanta, Ga., 1907).

DuBois, W. E. B. (editor), *Efforts for Social Betterment Among Negro Americans* (Atlanta University Publications, No. 14, Atlanta, Ga., 1909).

DuBois, W. E. B., *The World and Africa* (New York, 1947).

DU PLESSIS, J., *A History of Christian Missions in South Africa* (London, 1911).

DU PLESSIS, J., *The Evangelization of Pagan Africa* (Cape Town, 1929).

DWIGHT, Henry Otis, *The Blue Book of Missions for 1905* (New York, 1905).

EDGAR, Minna, *Memoirs of Dr. John Edgar* (n.d.).

ELLENBERGER, Edmund D., *A Century of Mission Work in Basutoland, 1833–1933* (Morija, 1938).

ELLIOTT, Scott F. G., *A Naturalist in Mid-Africa* (London, 1898).

ELMSLIE, W. A., *Among the Wild Ngoni* (Edinburgh, 1899).

ENGELS, Friedrich, *The Peasant War in Germany* (London, 1927).

FARSON, Negley, *Last Chance in Africa* (London, 1953).

FERGUSON, Charles W., *The Confusion of Tongues* (London, 1929).

FISHER, Miles Mark, *Negro Slave Songs in the United States* (Ithaca, N.Y., 1953).

FOSTER, William Z., *The Negro People in American History* (New York, 1954).

FOX, E. L., *The American Colonization Society, 1817–1840* (Baltimore, 1919).

FRANKLIN, John Hope, *From Slavery to Freedom. A History of American Negroes* (New York, 1947).

FRASER, Agnes, *Donald Fraser of Livingstonia* (London, 1934).

FRASER, Alice Z., *Livingstone and Newstead* (London, 1913).

FRASER, Donald, *The Future of Africa* (London, 1911).

FRASER, Donald, *Winning a Primitive People* (London, 1914).

FRASER, Donald, *The Story of Our Mission* (London, 1915).

FRASER, Donald, *African Idylls* (London, 1923).

FRASER, Donald, *The Autobiography of an African* (London, 1925).

FRASER, Donald, *The New Africa* (London, 1927).

FRAZIER, E. Franklin, *The Negro People in the United States* (New York, 1949).

FREEMAN, Edward A., *The Epoch of Negro Baptists and the Foreign Mission Board. National Baptist Convention, U.S.A., Inc.* (Kansas City, 1953).

GARDNER, W. J., *A History of Jamaica* (London, 1909).

GARVEY, Marcus (edited by Amy Jacques GARVEY), *Philosophy and Opinions of Marcus Garvey* (New York, 1923).

GARVEY, Marcus, *The Tragedy of White Injustice* (New York, 1927).

GOLLOCK, Georgina, *Sons of Africa* (London, 1928).

GÖTZEN, Graf von, *Deutsch-Ostafrika im Aufstand, 1905-6* (Berlin, 1909).

GRAHAM, R. H. Carson, *Under Seven Congo Kings* (London, n.d.).

SOURCES

GROVES, C. P., *The Planting of Christianity in Africa, iii, 1878–1914* (London, 1955).

GUINGAND, Major-General Sir Francis de, *African Assignment* (London, 1953).

HAILEY, Lord, *An African Survey* (London, 1945).

HAILEY, Lord, *Native Administration in the British African Territories. Part II, Central Africa* (London, 1950).

HAINES, C. Grove (editor), *Africa To-day* (Baltimore, 1955).

HALL, Mary, *A Woman's Trek from the Cape to Cairo* (London, 1907).

A Handbook of German East Africa (London, 1923. Naval Intelligence. I.D. 1055).

A Handbook of Portuguese Nyasaland (London, n.d., Naval Intelligence. I.D. 1161).

The Handbook of Tanganyika (London, 1930).

HANNA, A. J., *The Beginnings of Nyasaland and North-Eastern Rhodesia, 1859–1895* (Oxford, 1956).

Harvard African Studies (Cambridge, Mass., 1922), for H. S. Stannus, 'The Wa Yao of Nyasaland'.

HAYFORD, Casely, *Ethiopia Unbound* (London, 1911).

HAYNES, Leonard L., Jnr., *The Negro Community in American Protestantism* (Boston, 1953).

HELLMAN, Ellen (editor), *A Handbook of Race Relations in South Africa* (London, 1949).

HODGKIN, Thomas, *Nationalism in Colonial Africa* (London, 1956).

HOFFMAN, Carl von (edited by LOHRKE, Eugene), *Jungle Gods* (London 1929).

HOOKER, Richard T. (editor), *The Carolina Backcountry on the Eve of the Revolution. The Journal of Charles Woodmason, Anglican Itinerant* (Chapel Hill. N.Ca., 1953).

HORDERN, Lieutenant-Colonel Charles, *History of the Great War. Military Operations. East Africa. Volume I, August 1914–September 1916* (London, 1941).

HUNTER, Monica, *Reaction to Conquest* (London, 1936).

HUXLEY, Elspeth, *White Man's Country* (London, 1935).

JABAVU, D. D. T., *The Life of Don Tengo Jabavu* (Lovedale, 1922).

JACK, James W., *Daybreak in Livingstonia* (Edinburgh, 1901).

JALLA, Louis, *Du Cap de Bonne Espérance au Victoria Nyanza* (Florence, 1905).

JAMES, C. L. R., *The Black Jacobins* (London, 1938).

JOHNSON, James Weldon, *Along This Way. The Autobiography of James Weldon Johnson* ('Penguin' edition, London, 1941).

JOHNSTON, Sir Harry H., *The Black Man's Part in the War* (London, 1917).

JOHNSTON, Sir Harry H., *A History of the Colonization of Africa by Alien Races* (Cambridge, 1930).

JOHNSTON, Ruby F., *The Development of Negro Religion* (New York, 1954).

KARSTEDT, Oskar, *Der weisse Kampf im Afrika* (Berlin, 1937).

KARSTEDT, Oskar, with WERDER, Peter von, *Die afrikanische Arbeiterfrage* (Berlin, 1941).

KENYATTA, Jomo, *Facing Mount Kenya* (London, 1938).

KILEKWA, Petro (translated by SMITH, K. A. Nixon), *Slave Boy to Priest. The Autobiography of Padre Petro Kilekwa* (London, 1937).

KORNGOLD, Ralph, *Citizen Toussaint* (London, 1945).

KOSKINEN, Aarne A., *Missionary Influence as a Political Factor in the Pacific Islands* (Helsinki, 1953).

SOURCES

KUCZYNSKI, R. R., *Demographic Survey of the British Colonial Empire. Volume II* (London, 1949).

LANE POOLE, E. H., *The Native Tribes of the Eastern Province of Northern Rhodesia* (Lusaka, 1938).

LATOURETTE, Kenneth S., *A History of the Expansion of Christianity, IV* (London, 1941).

LAWS, Robert, *Reminiscences of Livingstonia* (Edinburgh, 1934).

LEAKEY, L. S. B., *Mau Mau and the Kikuyu* (London, 1953).

LEAKEY, L. S. B., *Defeating Mau Mau* (London, 1954).

LEE, A. W., *Charles Johnson of Zululand* (London, 1930).

LETTOW-VORBECK, General Paul von, *My Reminiscences of East Africa* (London, 1920).

LETTOW-VORBECK, General Paul von, *Heia Safari. Deutschlands Kampf in Ostafrika* (Leipzig, 1920).

LETTOW-VORBECK, General Paul von, *Meine Erinnerungen am Ostafrika* (Leipzig, 1921).

LITTLE, David Shaw, *Letters from David Shaw Little* (privately printed, 1952).

LIVINGSTONE, David, *Dr. Livingstone's Cambridge Lectures*, edited by MONK, William (Cambridge, 1858).

LIVINGSTONE, David, *The Last Journals of David Livingstone in Central Africa*, edited by WALLER, Horace (London, 1874).

LIVINGSTONE, W. P., *A Prince of Missionaries. The Rev. Alexander Hetherwick* (London, n.d.).

LLOYD-JONES, W., *K.A.R., being an Unofficial Account of the Origin and Activities of the King's African Rifles* (London, 1928).

LOGAN, Rayford W., *The Negro in American Life and Thought : the Nadir, 1877–1901* (New York, 1954).

LOVERIDGE, Arthur, *I Drank the Zambezi* (New York, 1953).

LUGARD, Captain F. D., *The Rise of Our East African Empire* (London, 1893).

LUGARD, Lord, *The Dual Mandate in British Tropical Africa* (London, 1922).

MACDONALD, Duff, *Africana : or, The Heart of Heathen Africa* (London, 1882).

MACKENZIE, D. R., *The Spirit-Ridden Konde* (London, 1925).

MACKINTOSH, C. W., *Coillard of the Zambesi* (London, 1907).

MACLEAN, Norman, *Africa in Transformation* (London, 1914).

MACMICHAEL, Sir Harold, *The Anglo-Egyptian Sudan* (London, 1934).

MACMILLAN, W. M., *Africa Emergent* (London, 1936).

MAIR, L. P., *Native Policies in Africa* (London, 1936).

A Manual of Portuguese East Africa (London, 1920. Naval Int. I.D. 1189).

MARCOSSON, Isaac F., *An African Adventure* (New York, 1921).

MAUGHAM, R. C. F., *Africa as I have known it* (London, 1929).

MEEK, C. K., *Land Law and Custom in the Colonies* (London, 1946).

MILLIN, Sarah Gertrude, *The Coming of the Lord* (London, 1928).

MITCHELL, J. Clyde, *The Yao Village* (Manchester, 1956).

MOIR, Fred. L. M., *After Livingstone* (London, 1929).

MORISON, J. H., *Streams in the Desert. A Picture of Life in Livingstonia* (London n.d.).

MOYSE-BARTLETT, H., *The King's African Rifles* (Aldershot, 1957).

MURRAY, A. Victor, *The School in the Bush. A Critical Study of the Theory and Practice of Native Education in Africa* (London, 1929).

SOURCES

MURRAY, S. S., *A Handbook of Nyasaland* (Zomba, 1922).
MURRAY, S. S., *A Handbook of Nyasaland* (Zomba, 1932).
MYRDAL, Gunnar, *An American Dilemma* (New York, 1944).
NEVINSON, H. W., *A Modern Slavery* (London, 1906).
NEVINSON, H. W., *More Changes, More Chances* (London, 1925).
NIEBUHR, H. Richard, *The Social Sources of Denominationalism* (New York, 1929).
NOBLE, Frederick Perry, *The Redemption of Africa* (Chicago, 1899).
NORMAN, L. S., *Nyasaland Without Prejudice* (London, n.d.).
NTARA, S. Y. (translated and edited by YOUNG, Cullen), *Headman's Enterprise. An Unexpected Page in Central African History* (London, 1949).
OBERHOLTZER, Ellis, *A History of the United States since the Civil War* (New York, 1917).
OGILVIE, J. N., *Our Empire's Debt to Missions* (London, 1924).
OLIVER, Roland, *The Missionary Factor in East Africa* (London, 1952).
OLIVIER, Lord, *Jamaica, the Blessed Isle* (London, 1936).
OLSEN, M. Ellsworth, *A History of the Origin and Progress of Seventh-day Adventists* (Washington D.C. 1925).
OUSSOREN, A. H., *William Carey—especially his Missionary Principles* (Leiden, 1945).
PADMORE, George, *The Life and Struggles of Negro Toilers* (London, 1931).
PADMORE, George, *How Britain Rules Africa* (London, 1936).
PADMORE, George, *Africa—Britain's Third Empire* (London, 1939).
PARRINDER, Geoffrey, *Religion in an African City* (London, 1953).
Peace Handbooks. Issued by the Historical Section of the Foreign Office. Volume XV, Nyasaland (London, 1918–19).
PERHAM, Margery (editor), *Ten Africans* (London, 1936).
PHILLIPO, James M., *Jamaica : its Past and Present State* (London, 1843).
PICK, F. W., *Searchlight on German Africa. The Diaries and Papers of Dr. W. Ch. Regendanz* (London, 1939).
PIKE, Royston, *Jehovah's Witnesses* (London, 1954).
PLAATJE, Sol. T., *Mhudi* (Lovedale, 1930).
PLATT, W. J., *An African Prophet. The Ivory Coast Movement . . .* (London, 1934).
PRICE, F. D., *Liberian Odyssey* (New York, 1954).
RAWSCLIFFE, D. H., *The Struggle for Kenya* (London, 1954).
REBMAN, John (edited by KRAPF, L.), *Dictionary of the Kiniassa Language* (Basle, 1877).
RICHTER, Julius, *Geschichte der evangelischen Mission in Afrika* (Gütersloh, 1922).
ROBERTSON, William, *The Martyrs of Blantyre* (London, 1892).
ROOME, W. J. W., *Can Africa Be Won ?* (London, 1927).
ROOME, W. J. W., *A Great Emancipation. A Missionary Survey of Nyasaland* (London, 1920).
ROSENTHAL, Eric, *Stars and Stripes in Africa* (London, 1938).
ROSS, W. McGregor, *Kenya from Within. A Short Political History* (London, 1927).
ROUX, Edward, *Time Longer than Rope. A History of the Black Man's Struggle for Freedom in South Africa* (London, 1949).
ROWLEY, Henry, *The Story of the Universities Mission to Central Africa* (London, 1866).

SOURCES

RUDIN, H. R., *Germany in the Cameroons* (London, 1938).

RUSSELL, Charles Taze, *Studies in the Scriptures* :

    I, *The Divine Plan of the Ages* (Alleghany, Pa., 1886).

    II, *The Time is at Hand* (Alleghany, Pa., 1891).

    III, *Thy Kingdom Come* (Brooklyn, N.Y., 1891).

    IV, *The Battle of Armageddon* (Brooklyn, N.Y., 1897).

    V, *The At-one-ment between God and Man* (Brooklyn, N.Y., 1886).

    VI, *The New Creation* (Brooklyn, N.Y., 1904).

SCHLOSSER, Katesa, *Propheten in Afrika* (Braunschweig, 1949).

SCOTT, David Clement, *A Cyclopaedic Dictionary of the Mang'anja Language* (Edinburgh, 1892).

SHEPHERD, Robert H. W., *Lovedale, the Story of a Century* (Lovedale, 1941).

SIMMONS, Jack, *Livingstone and Africa* (London, 1955).

SPEER, Robert E., *Missions and Modern History* (New York, 1904).

STEWART, James, *Dawn in the Dark Continent* (Edinburgh, 1903).

STODDARD, Lothrop, *The Rising Tide of Color against White World Supremacy* (New York, 1920).

STONEQUIST, Everett V., *The Marginal Man. A Study in Personality and Culture Conflict* (New York, 1937).

STOWE, Harriet Beecher, *Dred. A Tale of the Great Dismal Swamp* (London, 1856).

STROUP, Herbert Hewitt, *The Jehovah's Witnesses* (New York, 1945).

STUART, James, *A History of the Zulu Rebellion, 1906* (London, 1913).

SULLIVAN, G. S., *Dhow Chasing in Zanzibar Waters* (London, 1873).

SUNDKLER, Bengt G. M., *Bantu Prophets in South Africa* (London, 1945).

TAYLOR, Don, *Rainbow on the Zambezi* (London, 1953).

TAYLOR, J. Dexter (editor), *Christianity and the Natives of South Africa. A Handbook of South African Missions* (London, n.d.).

TEW, Mary, *The Peoples of the Lake Nyasa Region* (London, 1950).

THOMSON, Joseph, and HARRIS-SMITH, Miss, *Ulu. An African Romance* (London, 1888).

THWAITE, Daniel, *The Seething African Pot. A Study of Black Nationalism, 1882–1935* (London, 1936).

TIMOTHY, Bankole, *Kwame Nkrumah* (London, 1955).

TINDALL, George Brown, *South Carolina Negroes, 1877–1900* (New York, 1952).

VANDERCOOK, John W., *Black Majesty* (New York, 1928).

Virginia. Guide to the Old Dominion. Compiled by workers of the Works Projects Administration in the state of Virginia (New York, 1952).

WALKER, Eric, *A History of South Africa* (London, 1947).

WALLACE, David Duncan, *South Carolina. A Short History* (Chapel Hill, N.Ca., 1951).

WALLIS, Wilson D., *Messiahs, Christian and Pagan* (Boston, Mass., 1915).

WARNECK, Gustave B., *Outline of a History of Protestant Missions* (Edinburgh, 1901).

WASHINGTON, Booker T., *Up from Slavery* ('World's Classics' edition, London 1945).

WATTERS, *History of the British Churches of Christ* (Indianapolis, 1948).

WELLS, James, *The Life of James Stewart* (London, 1909).

WERNER, Alice, *The Native Tribes of British Central Africa* (London, 1906).

WERNER, Alice, *Myths and Legends of the Bantu* (London, 1933).

WERNER, Alice, *Chapenga's White Man : A Story of Central Africa* (London, n.d.).

SOURCES

WEULE, Karl, *Native Life in East Africa* (London, 1909).

Who's Who in Colored America (New York, 1927–40).

WILLIAMS, Robert, *German Penetration in Central Africa* (London, 1918).

WILLOUGHBY, W. C., *Race Problems in the New Africa* (Oxford, 1923).

WILLOUGHBY, W. C., *The Soul of the Bantu* (London, 1928).

WILSON, G. H., *The History of the Universities Mission to Central Africa* (London, 1936).

WOODSON, Carter G., *The History of the Negro Church* (Washington, D.C., 1921).

YOUNG, Cullen, and BANDA, Hastings, *Our African Way of Life* (London, 1946).

YOUNG, T. Cullen, *Notes on the History of the Tumbuka-Kamanga Peoples in the Northern Province of Nyasaland* (London, 1932).

YOUNG, E. D., *The Search after Livingstone* (London, 1868).

YUILLE, George (editor), *History of the Baptists in Scotland from Pre-Reformation Times* (Glasgow, 1926).

D. *Theses*

FISHER, Miles Mark, *The Negro Baptists and Foreign Missions* (B.D., Northern Baptist Theological Seminary, 1923).

HANNA, Alexander John, *The History of Nyasaland and North-Eastern Rhodesia, 1875–1895* (Ph.D., London University, 1948).

HARR, Wilber C., *The Negro as an American Protestant Missionary in Africa* (Ph.D., University of Chicago, 1945.)

ACKNOWLEDGEMENTS

1. *To persons for direct assistance in securing materials*

We wish to express our gratitude to the following persons who, by answering our questions and by checking and discovering materials for us, have made possible the work of assembling the scattered sources for this study :

Dr. Madison C. Allen, Principal, Virginia Theological Seminary and College ; Rev. and Mrs. George E. Barr (for materials on the Churches of Christ) ; Miss Jean Blackwell (curator, the Schomburg Collection, New York Public Library, for checking sources of American Negro history and, in particular, for examining copies of the *Mission Herald*) ; the late Mrs. Joseph Booth (*née* Lillian Webb) ; Mr. P. L. Bridle (of the Watch Tower Bible and Tract Society, for interviews with Nyasaland Africans) ; Miss Dorothy W. Bridgewater (of Yale University Library, for checking sources of American Negro history and, in particular, for examining copies of the *Mission Herald*) ; Mr. Robert Hughes Brisbane (for information on the Garvey movement) ; Miss Nannie H. Burroughs (of the Women's Convention, National Baptist Convention, U.S.A., Inc.) ; Mr. O. E. Chirwa (for Nyasaland African materials) ; Mrs. Josephine Cunnington Edwards (for materials on the Seventh-day Adventists in Nyasaland, the Chilembwe *milieu*, etc.) ; Dr. Miles Mark Fisher (for materials from his own study of Negro American Baptist history) ; Mrs. Amy Jacques Garvey (for comments on possible connections between Chilembwe and Booth and the Garvey movement) ; Sir Charles and Lady Griffin (for a Chilembwe photograph) ; Mr. Leopold Harris (of the Zambesi Mission, England, for materials on the early history of the Zambesi Industrial Mission) ; Mr. M. G. Henschel (Director, the Watch Tower Bible and Tract Society, Brooklyn, N.Y., for materials on the Society and Central Africa) ; Miss May Hetherwick (for information on Dr. Alexander Hetherwick) ; Dr. Charles S. Johnson (President, Fisk University, Nashville, Tenn., for references to individuals and institutions in the United States which made possible the assembly of much material on Chilembwe's American Negro *milieu*) ; Mr. R. E. Kachelenga (of the School of Oriental and African Studies, London, for a commentary on some Nyanja materials) ; Dr. and Mrs. H. W. Langworthy of Schenectady, N.Y. (for additional Joseph Booth materials) ; Miss Lena Mackeachan (sister of Mrs. Ranald MacDonald, for Nyasaland, 1915, materials) ; Mr. W. McL. Wishart (Chairman of the Churches of Christ Missionary Committee) and Mr. C. S. Slater (of the Church of Christ, Burnley) for providing us with Miss Mary Bannister's diaries ; Rev. Walter J. Main (for information on the early history of the Zambesi Industrial Mission) ; Dr. R. M. MacFarlane ; Rev. H. B. Make (for information on John L. Dube) ; Mr. R. C. F. Maugham ; Pastor S. G. Maxwell (for materials on the Seventh-day Adventists in Nyasaland, the Chilembwe *milieu*, etc.) ; Miss Rose M. Miller (for early National Baptist Convention materials) ; Mrs. Mary W. Moore (for supplying a Booth-Chilembwe letter and other important African materials gathered by her late husband, Mr. N. O. Moore) ; Mr Raymond P. Morris (Librarian, Yale

ACKNOWLEDGEMENTS

University Divinity School for arranging to copy a photograph of Chilembwe in the *Mission Herald*); Mr. George Padmore (for allowing us to examine an unpublished typescript autobiography of Clements Kadalie); Mrs. Dorothy B. Porter (Supervisor, Moorland Foundation, University Library, Howard University, Washington, D.C., for checking sources of America Negro history and, in particular, for examining copies of the *Mission Herald* and printed *Journals* of the National Baptist Convention); Mrs. B. E. Read (of the Home Department, American Baptist Foreign Missionary Society, for information on Joseph Booth's early connections with American Negro Baptists); the late Mr. Corliss Fitz Randolph (President and Librarian, Seventh Day Baptist Historical Society); Mr. V. E. Robinson (for permission to examine an unpublished typescript history of Seventh-day Adventist missionary activity in Nyasaland); Miss Elizabeth de W. Root (of the Case Memorial Library, Hartford Seminary Foundation, for help in discovering and examining Joseph Booth's *Africa for the African*); Mr. F. M. Withers (for putting at our disposal his own collection of materials on the Rising of 1915).

We would express, in particular, our gratitude to those persons whose surnames are mentioned in capital letters under the heading of *I. Primary Sources. (A.) Statements,* and who are also mentioned frequently in the text and references. Often at the cost of very unpleasant memories for themselves, they have given us generous assistance from their recollections and records. We wish to point out with particular reference to this group of persons—and, in general, with reference to all the persons and institutions whose names appear under our Acknowledgements —that we alone are responsible for the use which we have made of the materials with which they have supplied us.

2. *To persons for indirect assistance in securing materials*

We wish to express our gratitude to the following persons whose assistance to us, through correspondence and personal interview, although it has made a more indirect contribution to the progress of our work than the help that was given to us by those whose names are mentioned under the first group of acknowledgements, has, nevertheless, in the long run, been invaluable :

Dr. C. C. Adams of the National Baptist Convention, U.S.A., Inc.; Mr. John C. Anderson; Dr. Guy Atkins; Dr. Michael Banton; Canon G. W. Bloomfield, D.D.; Mrs. A. J. C. Bond; Mr. Arna Bontemps; Rev. E. D. Bowman; Rev. Henry A. Boyd; Mr. E. D. Branch; Dr. Jean Comhaire; Mr. and Mrs. John L. Dawson; Rev. James Dougall, D.D.; Miss Mabel E. Epp; Dr. Lorenzo Greene; Rev. C. P. Groves; Mr. R. Hamilton; the Very Reverend Thomas Hannay, Lord Bishop of Argyll and the Isles; Dr. Wilber C. Harr; Mrs. L. R. Hildebrand; Miss Elizabeth Holland; Dr. G. Isaacs; Professor D. D. T. Jabavu; Pastor Leon R. Lawton; Mr. F. Macauly; Rev. J. McGeachy; Miss M. H. Moore; Mr. Samson Morris; Colonel H. Moyse-Bartlett; Mr. S. S. Murray; Rev. Melvin G. Nida; Rev. E. W. Nielsen; Dr. J. H. Oldham; Dr. Benjamin Quarles; Dr. L. Reddick; Mr. L. B. Reynolds; Mr. E. B. Rudge; Mrs. M. Sales; the Editor of *The Scotsman*; Lady Smith; Miss Alison Smith; Miss K. Smith; Mrs. A. R. Stark; Dr. J. Stewart; Dr. Bengt G. M. Sundkler; Mr. E. W. Tarr   Mr. F. M. Trefusis; Canon G. H. Wilson; the late Rev. T. Cullen Young.

ACKNOWLEDGEMENTS

3. *To institutions*

We wish to express our gratitude to the following institutions and their staffs for help in carrying out our researches :

American Baptists Foreign Missionary Society; the Anti-Slavery Society; the Baptist Union of Scotland; the British Museum Library (especially the Newspaper Library at Colindale); the Bodleian Library; the University Library, Cambridge; the Central African Archives; the Church of Scotland (especially its Foreign Mission Library and the General Assembly Library); the Case Memorial Library, Hartford, Connecticut; the Colonial Office Library; the Commonwealth Relations Office Library; the Library of Congress; the University Library, Edinburgh; Fisk University Library; Howard University Library; the International African Institute Library; the International Missionary Council; the Mitchell Library, Glasgow; the National Baptist Publishing Board; the National Baptist Convention, U.S.A.; the National Library of Scotland; New College Library, Edinburgh; the New York Public Library; the Nyasa Mission; the Office of the Commissioner for Nyasaland; the Public Record Office, London; the Public Relations Department, Zomba; Rhodes House Library; the Royal Botanic Gardens Library, Kew; the Royal Empire Society Library; the Scottish Companies Office, Edinburgh; the Selly Oak Colleges Library, Birmingham; the Seventh-day Adventists in both Great Britain and the United States; the Seventh Day Baptist Historical Society; Spelman College, Atlanta, Georgia; *The Times* Library; Universities' Mission to Central Africa; Virginia Baptist Historical Society; Virginia Union University; War Office Library, London; the Watch Tower Bible and Tract Society (in Brooklyn, N.Y., London, and Cape Town); Yale University Library, and the Day Missions Library of Yale University; the Zambesi Mission.

APPENDICES

I

AFRICAN CHRISTIAN UNION SCHEDULE, 14 JANUARY 1897
(From Joseph Booth, *Africa for the African* (Baltimore, Md., 1897),
pp. 49-51)

Objects of the Society :

1. To unite together in the name of Jesus Christ such persons as desire to see full justice done to the African race and are resolved to work towards and pray for the day when the African people shall become an African Christian Nation.

2. To provide capital to equip and develop Industrial Mission Stations worked by competent Native Christians or others of the African race ; such stations to be placed on a self-supporting and self-propagating basis.

3. To steadfastly demand by Christian and lawful methods the equal recognition of the African and those having blood relationship, to the rights and privileges accorded to Europeans.

4. To call upon every man, woman and child of the African race, as far as may be practicable, to take part in the redemption of Africa during this generation, by gift, loan, or personal service.

5. To specially call upon the Afro-American Christians, and those of the West Indies to join hearts and hands in the work either by coming in person to take an active part or by generous, systematic contributions.

6. To solicit funds in Great Britain, America and Australia for the purpose of restoring at their own wish carefully selected Christian Negro families, or adults of either sex, back to their fatherland in pursuance of the objects of the Union ; and to organize an adequate propaganda to compass the work.

7. To apply such funds in equal parts to the founding of Industrial Mission centres and to the establishing of Christian Negro settlements.

9.* To firmly, judiciously and repeatedly place on record by voice and pen for the information of the uninformed, the great wrongs inflicted upon the African race in the past and in the present, and to urge upon those who wish to be clear of African blood in the day of God's judge-

---

* In the original text, the eighth paragraph is numbered '9'.

ments, to make restitution for the wrongs of the past and to withstand the appropriation of the African's land in the present.

10. To initiate or develop the culture of Tea, Coffee, Cocoa, Sugar, etc. etc., and to establish profitable mining or other industries or manufactures.

11. To establish such transport agencies by land, river, lakes or ocean as shall give the African free access to the different parts of his great country and people, and to the general commerce of the world.

12. To engage qualified persons to train and teach African learners any department of Commercial, Engineering, nautical, professional or other necessary knowledge.

13. To mould and guide the labor of Africa's millions into channels that shall develop the vast God-given wealth of Africa for the uplifting and commonwealth of the people, rather than for the aggrandisement of a few already rich persons.

14. To promote the formation of Companies on a Christian basis devoted to special aspects of the work ; whose liability shall be limited, whose shares shall not be transferable without the society's consent ; whose shareholders shall receive a moderate rate of interest only ; whose profits shall permanently become the property of the Trustees of the African Christian Union, for the prosecution of the defined objects of the Union.

15. To petition the government of the United States of America to make a substantial monetary grant to each adult Afro-American desiring to be restored to African soil, as some recognition of the 250 years of unpaid slave labor and the violent abduction of millions of Africans from their native land.

16. To petition the British and other European governments holding or claiming African territory to generously restore the same to the African people or at least to make adequate inalienable native reserve lands, such reserves to be convenient to the locality of the different tribes.

17. To petition the British and other European governments occupying portions of Africa to make substantial and free grants of land to expatriated Africans or their descendents desiring restoration to their fatherland, such grants to be made inalienable from the African race.

18. To provide for all representatives, officials or agents of the Union and its auxiliaries, inclusive of the Companies it may promote modest,

economical yet efficient and as far as may be, equable, maintenance, together with due provision for periods of sickness, incapacity, widowhood or orphanage.

19. To print and publish literature in the interests of the African race and to furnish periodical accounts of the transactions of the Society and its auxiliary agencies, the same to be certified by recognized auditors and to be open to the fullest scrutiny of the Union's supporters.

20. To vest all funds, properties, products or other sources of income in the hands of Trustees, not less than seven in number, to be held in perpetuity in the distinct interest of the African race and for the accomplishment of the objects herein set forth in 21 clauses.

21. Finally, to pursue steadily and unswervingly the policy :

'AFRICA FOR THE AFRICAN'
and look for and hasten by prayer and united effort the forming of a united
AFRICAN CHRISTIAN NATION
By God's power and blessing and in His own time and way.

[Signed]   JOSEPH BOOTH,
English missionary.
JOHN CHILEMBWE,
Ajawa Christian Native.
Dated January 14th, 1897,   ALEXANDER DICKIE,
at   English missionary.
Blantyre, Nyassaland,   MORRISON MALINKA,
East Central Africa.   Native Christian Chipeta Tribe.

2

LYNCHBURG 'AFRICAN DEVELOPMENT SOCIETY', c. 1899
(From a private source in the United States of America. These details are found on a leaflet measuring six by twelve inches.)

Prof. G. W. Hayes, Pres., Lynchburg, Va.
Rev. J. A. Taylor, Vice Pres., Washington, D.C.
Rev. B. F. For, Sec., Salem, Va.
Rev. W. C. Hall, Asst. Sec., Danville, Va.
Mrs. Mary Hayes, Treas., Lynchburg, Va.
Rev. W. F. Graham, Asst. Tres., Richmond, Va.
CHE. JOHN CHILEMBWE, of EAST CENTRAL AFRICA,
Gen. Solicitor.

533

APPENDICES

AFRICAN DEVELOPMENT SOCIETY (To be incorporated) Capital $50,000 in $1.00 Shares.

Whereas certain Christian natives of East Central Africa have sent messengers to the Afro-American people, bearing a petition, asking their co-operation and direction in the development of the rich resources of their country, and

Whereas some of the tribes represented by the petitioners own vast areas of country in their own right of disposal, notably the Ajawa, Chipeta and Angoni peoples of Nyassaland, East Africa, and

Whereas certain very advantageous offers of extensive blocks of valuable plantation land have been made by certain of these Chiefs, at a cost of less than one cent per acre ; and

Whereas it is beyond doubt that large fortunes have been made and are being made in that country from the production of coffee, sugar, tobacco, oil, nuts, cotton, rubber, etc., by a few enterprising Europeans ; and

Whereas the climate has been proven to be temperate and healthy ; the natives friendly and earnestly desiring Christian civilization ; the market easy of access and the present opportunities of vast importance to the Afro-American people,

It is Proposed to form the aforementioned society and conduct its operations in a thoroughly Christian spirit, sending in the field only men of an approved Christian standing who are believed to have the best interests of the African race at heart. It is intended that the transactions of the society in Africa shall be missionary in spirit, though not in name.

The society proposes to take the following powers :

1. Power to acquire land in Africa by purchase or grants from native Chiefs or others holding possession, and to retain, sell, or develop the same, as the Directors may see fit.

2. Power to establish manufactures, mining, or other industries, or the cultivation of coffee, tea, sugar, tobacco, cotton, fruit, or other profitable products, and to export or import, as they may desire.

3. Power to purchase, charter, or construct the means for transport by land, river, lakes or ocean.

4. Power to provide, construct, or organize such means of defense as the Directors may consider necessary in order to retain and develop the territories they may acquire in Africa by purchase or grant.

5. Power to increase the capital of the society at the discretion of a two-thirds majority of the Board of Directors.

The society proposes to pay an interest not exceeding 7 per cent yearly upon the paid-up shares, but does not guarantee to pay that figure unless it be fully earned : any surplus profit earned to be applied, first, to the creation and maintenance of a reserve fund equal to one-fourth of the whole paid-up capital (such reserve fund to be invested in government securities in the U.S. of America) and second, to the founding of settlements of Afro-Americans desiring to settle in Africa on the basis of Schedule D.*

The society proposes to establish at each of its stations or townships African schools where such elementary knowledge and Christian instruction shall be imparted as may be approved by the Station Superintendent.

The Directors propose to solicit contributions from the general Christian public for the special purpose of forwarding the Christian settlement scheme referred to as Schedule D.

A special feature relating to the issue of the first 30,000 shares is that the Directors purpose giving each shareholder of not less than five paid-up shares a preferential right to a grant of 50 acres of land in East Africa under such title as the society may be able to furnish, with right to hold, occupy or sell to any Afro-American or African purchaser. Such preferential shareholders shall not be permitted to purchase more than 1,000 shares or be entitled to a grant of more than 10,000 acres of the society's estate : such preferential shares to be open only to Afro-American shareholders.

The registration and preliminary floating expenses to be paid by the Directors out of the sale of shares.

The following persons have agreed to act as provisional Directors and to take up the number of shares affixed to their respective signatures :

> G. W. Hayes, 25 shares ; T. J. Minton, 10 shares ; H. T. Kealing, 10 shares ; Matthew Anderson, 10 shares ; Bernard Tyrrell, 10 shares ; George W. Scott, 2 shares ;
>
> VIRGINIA SEMINARY PRINT

---

* This may well have been based on the Schedule D of Booth's *Africa for the African*, op. cit. pp. 55-6. This 'Negro Christian settlement programme' envisaged : ten families to a settlement ; each settlement to consist of 2000 acres; each family to have 200 acres of this ; £3000 capital to be available for each settlement ; 'during the first seven years modest maintenance to be provided and such allowance further as the executive considers to be merited'; after seven years, each 200-acre estate and all its appliances becomes the absolute property of the settler.

APPENDICES

3

Occupational Stratification, baptized African Adults, Blantyre and Domasi, 1899

(From *Life and Work in British Central Africa*, No. 154, January–March, 1901, p. 13.)

Occupations	In Mission Employment	In Outside European Employment	Working on Their Own Account	At Present Out of Work	Total	Lapsed
In charge of Mission Stations	6				6	
Teachers	49			2	51	
Hospital Attendants	6	1			7	
Assisting Collector		1			1	
Overseers of Estates		3	2	1	6	2
Overseers	8	24		1	33	3
Printers	15	9		1	25	
Carpenters	15	14	2	2	33	
Builders	6	13			19	1
Agents for Trading Companies		2			2	
Clerks	1	6			7	1
Clerks in Post Office		6			6	1
Telegraphists		5			5	
Interpreters		7			7	
Salesmen in Stores		6			6	2
Sergeant-Interpreters in C.A. Rifles		4			4	1
Private in C.A. Rifles		1			1	
Gardeners	7	1			8	
Cattlemen	1			1	2	
Coffee-pruners	4	8			12	
Coffee-workers	3				3	
Orra-man ★	1				1	
Coachman		1			1	
Sewing Machinists	2				2	
Cobblers	3		1		4	
Tailor		1			1	
Beadle	1				1	
Blacksmith	1				1	
Cooks	2	7			9	1
Personal and House Servants	4	10			14	1
Taking odd work			2		2	2
Headmen of Villages			4		4	1
Old men and Invalids			3		3	
Living native fashion in their villages			21		21	7
Schoolboy	1				1	
Unaccounted for			5		5	3
TOTAL	136	130	40	8	314	26

★ Odd-job man.

536

APPENDICES

4

Letter from Chilembwe to Booth, 1911
(from the original in the possession of Mrs. Mary W. Moore, widow of
Mr. N. O. Moore.)

Providence Industrial Mission,
Chiradzulo,
Blantyre.

6. ii. 1911.

Prof, J. Booth.

Dear Father—*

I beg to acknowledge the receipt of
your kind & thoughtful letter dated 1st Oct 1911, and
to state that I am appreciated most
highly for your loving remberance.
I am assure you, that you will not
know how happy I was when I recei
ved your letter and to note that you
are the one who sent us an English
syllable roll.   Indeed it is very help
ful to us.   Regarding your kind
invitation I thank you most
heartly, but regret to say that I am
unable to fulfil for reason that
I am almost overwhelmed by
most important duty to perform ; I am
busy making bricks as our old
Chapel is too small to hold our
Christian congregation, therefore
they Church devoted herself to
build a large church.   As to be
understood you are aiming
that we should work together by changi
ng Sunday into Sabbath day.   Father
what profit can a man got on Sunday
or on Sabbath, are both days essential
to the Salvation of the Souls of truth
you have said.   Certainly the truth

* 'Father' in this context implies no blood relationship between Booth and
Chilembwe. Used in the vernacular, it was a form of address by Nyasaland Africans
to Europeans in whom they placed particular trust and towards whom they felt a
special affection.

of God will not part us for all the
work I am doing and my life is partial
to your Crown. For Joseph Booth's fe
[tear at edge of letter *]
as the people call it is still living
in B.C. Africa. But as the changing
of the day is the question of the feture [future ?—AUTHORS].
I wish if I could see you tomorrow &
try to accomodate you in your
important request. Dear Papa Booth
think not that I am unkind to you, you
have my sympathy in all your suffering.
I know you are God's fearing man,
and as long as God living we are
together. Desiring that God's blessing
may rest upon you and succeful [*sic*—AUTHORS]
dignify your effort. I am Father

Yours very dear Son in
Christ,

John Chilembwe

5

SPECIMEN LIST OF CHILEMBWE'S FOLLOWING
(From a Government notice published in the Nyasaland Times, No. 9
vol. xviii, 4 March 1915.)

NOTICE

Published for Public Information

List of Natives Still Wanted

1. Johnston Zilongolola alias Jei alias of Johnston's village, Mombezi
   river and of Nawani's village, Magomero, Nephew of Nawani—A
   Nyanja. Formerly road capitao at Magomero, elder of Chilembwe's
   Church.

* The 'fe' appears to be followed by an 'r' or a 'v', and the whole word is
probably 'fever' or 'fervour'.
N B —The circumstances of this letter appear to be an appeal by Booth to
Chilembwe either to visit him at the Cape in order to be recruited into Booth's
network of African Sabbatarian churches, or to assume in Nyasaland a position
of special responsibility in the leadership of these churches.

2. Jonathan Maniwa alias Henry, Brother of No. 1. A Nyanja, employed as a groom at Magomero. Elder of Chilembwe's Church and bell ringer, probably in possession of a .303 rifle. Nephew of Headman Nawani.

3. Lemeck of Mwandama's village, Nephew of Mwandama's (brother of Forti-Matewera). Formerly capitao at Magomero, further employed at Cotton Ginnery Magomero and left and was employed as capitao at John Grey Kufa Mapatha. A Mkokhola.

4. Kavea alias Solomon (son of Chimpeni) headman of small village under Headman Mwandama, close to Magomero. Has one ear only. A Nyanja.

5. Forti alias Matewera (son of Kachera) of Mwandama's village, Magomero. A Mkokhola. (Mwandama's Nephew.)

6. Makina alias Archie of Mwalula's village Chief Mwandama. A. L. Bruce Estates. Employed as ox waggon driver at Magomero. A Nguru.

7. John Cameron of Tamangisa village, Chief Mwandama. Employed in Cotton Ginnery Magomero.

8. Mainda or Maida alias Bardeni of Kambwiri village (married Mlanga's village, Namisewe) near Mailmen's rest house. Employed as ox waggon driver at Magomero. A Nyanja.

9. Fred Maganga of Mulowa village (son of Mulowa) Muruma stream Magomero. Employed in Magomero Ginnery to sew and mark cotton bales. A Nguru.

10. Yotam S. Bango alias Saiti of Chilembwe's village, Chikunda tribe. Cooked for Stephen Mkulichi.

11. Master Nyimbili of Nyimbili's village, A Nyanja, Magomero. Deacon of Chilembwe's Church at Nangundi, Chiradzulo sub-district.

12. Wilfrid Natambo of Chingoli's village, Chiradzulo. A Yao, worked as native Clerk in Mandala store, Blantyre. Chilembwe's teacher at Chingoli. Short and thick-set. Clean shaven.

13. Wilson Daniel Kusita. A Ngoni. Resided formerly at Chilembwe's, lately Watch Tower preacher in Upper Shire District. Slight moustache. About 5 feet 4 inches in height and thick-set square and rather large head.

14. Thomas Lulanga. Owner of small estate on Bombwe stream. Close to Chilembwe's.

15. Samuel alias Nyarisa of Chikuni's village, Magomero. Son of Chimpeni.

16. Chikwete (son-in-law of Tipa) of Chimbia's village, Magomero.

17. Makunganya of Dikia's village, Chief Mbombwe, Chiradzulo.

18. Matimati alias Yolama of Mavila's village, Headman Mwandama, Magomero Nguru.

19. Foster of Abraham Chimbia's village, Magomero.
20. Wallace alias Manyamba Chimbia's village (son of Chirombo—dead).
21. Nacheya of Kambwiri's village, Magomero.
22. Jerman of Kambwiri's village, Magomero.
23. Malango of Mwandama's village, Magomero.
24. Jackson of Dikiya's village, Son of Dikiya, Magomero.
25. Makawa of Makawa's village, Chief Mbombwe, Magomero.
26. Sanama alias Juma of own village, Chief Mbombwe, Magomero.
27. Mtipa of Makawa's village, Chief Mbombwe, Magomero.
28. Isaac of Kasongo's village, Chief Mbombwe, Magomero (has a wife at Chikuni's village).
29. Dikiya of own village, Magomero.
30. Andack Jamali of Chilembwe's village. A Yao. Chilembwe's Secretary and Church Clerk. Was clean shaven.
31. Anderson Puka of Chinpesa's village, Chief Chingoli Chiradzulo Angoni.
32. Laiti Puka of Chinpesa's village, Chief Chingoli Chiradzulo Angoni.
33. Simon Chiwayula Yao—son of Chiwayula near Chiradzulo Boma and of Chilembwe's School.
34. Fred Chifunya son of Chifunya of Kachomba, Chinkunda and of Chilembwe's School.
35. Yekoniya Matengo, Yao—son Matengo, Matengo's village Chipande and of Chilembwe's School.
36. Whiskers Matengo. A Ngoni with a store at Chinkwenzule's village, Chiradzulo.
37. Nelson Storo of Mwalula's village (married at Mavila's village). Ox waggon driver at Magomero.
38. Morris of Chikuni's village. Has wife at Mlipwe's village, Chief Chikoja, Chiradzulo.
39. Malidadi son-in-law of No. 18.
40. Burnett Kadangwe. A Nyanja, one of Chilembwe's teachers.
41. James Gordon Matoga of Chilembwe's village.
42. Moses, A Nyanja—son of Nyambili village Chief Ndala, Magomero. Employed as a capitao at Chikomwe Station Magomero.
43. Costa, of Mchocholo's village, Msoni.

Zomba,

27th February, 1915.

APPENDICES

6

PUNITIVE AREAS OF THE RISING

(These areas are included in the following copies of Collective Punishment Orders from the *Nyasaland Government Gazette*, 1915.)

No. 120 of 1915. Collective Punishment Ordinance, 1909. Order. By virtue of the powers vested in him by section 2 of the above-mentioned Ordinance, His Excellency the Governor has been pleased to order that a fine of four shillings (4/-) be levied on every male native hut owner in the under-mentioned areas in the Zomba district in respect of the following offences :—Colluding with, or harbouring, or failing to take all reasonable means to prevent the escape of the rebels in the late native rising.

AREAS

(a) That portion of Magomero estate lying within the Zomba district ;

(b) All that area lying within a radius of one mile from the late Makwangwala's church and house and that lying within a radius of one mile from George Masangano's house.

By Command of His Excellency the Governor,

ZOMBA, NYASALAND,   H. L. DUFF,
    8th June, 1915.   Chief Secretary.

No. 121 of 1915. Collective Punishment Ordinance, 1909. Order. By virtue . . . etc. (as for No. 120 of 1915) . . . in the undermentioned areas in the Ncheu division of the Upper Shire District . . . etc. (as for No. 120 of 1915). . .

AREAS

(a) An area bounded on the West by the Dzunje Mountain, on the North by a line drawn in a North North-Easterly direction from Dzunje to Mwalayoera [should this be Mwalaoyera ?—AUTHORS] Hill, on the East by a line drawn due South from Mwalayoera to meet the Tambala stream, thence up-stream along the Tambala stream in a South South-Westerly direction to the source of the Tambala on Dzunje mountain and known as the villages of Siriya and Nemo ;

(b) An area bounded on the West by a wooded ridge running due North and South called Kwakwera, on the North by the Chiole stream from where it passes the Kwakwera ridge down stream, on the East by a line drawn due South at a distance of one mile from Kamwala's present hut, which line will also be 1½ miles from the Chikombola stream, which line will meet northward the Chiole stream, and southward the Napwati stream ; on the South by the Napwati stream, from where it meets the

Eastern boundary, up-stream to where it passes the Kwakwera ridge and known as Kamwala Village.

By Command . . . etc. (as for No. 120 of 1915).

No. 122 of 1915. Collective Punishment Ordinance, 1909. Order. By virtue . . . etc. [as for No. 120 of 1915] . . . in the undermentioned areas in the Chiradzulu sub-district . . . etc. [as for No. 120 of 1915]. . . .

AREAS

(1) That portion of the Magomero estate lying within the Chiradzulu sub-district.

(2) All that area in the aforesaid sub-district lying South of the Magomero estate and bounded on the East by the Mlanje district, on the South by the Blantyre-Mlanje road and on the West by the Magomero-Chiradzulu-Mombesi-Nguludi road with the following exception of the inhabitants living under the undermentioned Chiefs :—

> (a) Onga ;
> (b) Chinkwenzuli ;
> (c) Tsumani ;
> (d) Masikini ;
> (e) Njusi ;
> (f) Chiniko ;

or under the following headmen :—

> (a) Kaparamula
> (b) Nkwanda.

By Command . . . etc. (as for No. 120 of 1915).

(The above three orders may be found on pp. 92-3 of the *Nyasaland Government Gazette*, 9 June 1915.)

No. 129 of 1915. Collective Punishment Ordinance, 1909. Order. By virtue . . . etc. (as for No. 120 of 1915] . . . on every male hut owner living under the jurisdiction of the following Chiefs in the Mlanje district . . . etc. (as for No. 120 of 1915) . . .

CHIEFS
Kaduya.
Fundi.
Mkanda.

By Command of His Excellency the Governor,

ZOMBA, NYASALAND,   H. L. DUFF,
  16th June, 1915.   Chief Secretary.

(The above order may be found on p. 99 of the *Nyasaland Government Gazette*, 30 June 1915.)

INDEX

Abyssinian church, 217, 467

Adowa, 72, 467

Africa Emergent, W. M. Macmillan, 395

Africa for the African, Booth, J., 109-12, 117, 118, 134, 254, 433, 450, 506, 531, 534-5

'Africa for the Africans', 75, 79, 91, 109, 245, 254, 323, 361, 434, 533
   Joseph Booth as originator of slogan, 504

African Baptist Church, Chiradzulu, 220
   first, 169
   first in Richmond, 98

African Baptist Industrial Mission, 116, 119

African Baptist Society, 116

African Christian Union, 70 ff., 74, 76, 77, 78, 79, 90, 109, 110, 111, 145, 168, 202, 323, 531-3

African Churches of Christ, 161, 213, 355, 412, 490

African Colonial Enterprise, 104

African Industrial Society, 166, 167, 168, 169, 171, 222, 246, 337, 415

African Lakes Company, 12, 32, 48, 81, 159, 457

African Lakes Corporation, Blantyre, 58, 59
   raid on ammunition and general stores, 259, 261, 262, 279-82
   native watchman, 280, 282
   laager, 298 ff.

African Methodist Episcopal Church, 73, 92, 97, 99, 101, 107, 412, 423, 425

African Missions Transport Company, 69, 70

African Presbyterian Church, 412

African Russellites, 232, 331, 352, 412

African Sabbath Recorder, 163

African separatist church, first in Nyasaland, 78-9

African Seventh Day Baptists in Nyasaland, 160, 166, 168, 211, 214, 241, 323, 334, 338, 413

African 'Zionist' churches, 430

Afro-American Council, 101

Ahmed, Mohammed, *see* 'Mahdi'

Aitchison, James, 508

Ajawa, 127, 128, 140, 194, 415, 533.
   See also Yao

Ajawa Providence Industrial Mission, 127, 140, 194, 415, 454

Alabama :
   and Tuskegee Institute, 100
   and L. G. Jordan, 113
   and Selma University, 412
   Mobile, 463

Albigenses, 502

Alexander, Rev. J. F., 251

Alicia (Nguludi mission orphan), 301, 302

Alleghany, Penn., and C. T. Russell, 152

Alliance of Reformed Churches holding the Presbyterian System, Foreign Missionary Council of the, 36

American Baptist Home Missionary Society, 112

American Baptist Missionary Union, 112

American Civil War, 94, 98, 99, 103, 122

American Colonization Society, 104

American Constitution, 94
   Reconstruction constitutions, 94
   Fourteenth and Fifteenth Amendments, 94, 95, 101

American Negro :
   and Joseph Booth, 42, 65, 79, 93 ff., 425
   arrival in Nyasaland, 133 ff.
   after Civil War, 93-109
   exclusion from franchise, 95
   and segregation, 95-9
   and lynching, 96
   religion and independence, 97-100
   and ideal of Booker T. Washington, 100-2
   and W. E. B. DuBois, 101-2
   and revolt, 105-9
   See also African Baptist Church, first in Richmond ; African Baptist Industrial Mission ; African Baptist Society ; African Methodist Episcopal Church ; Afro-American Council ; American Negro Academy ; American Negro coloniza-

INDEX

Chiole, 294, 466, 541
Chipande, 326-7, 540
Chipasala, 41
Chipatula, 298, 409, 410
Chipeta, 403, 474, 533
Chiradzulu, 39, 40, 41, 42, 43, 46, 116, 127, 128, 136, 166, 173, 226, 236, 244, 256, 259, 261, 268, 269, 282 ff. 305, 309, 310, 326, 338, 352, 388, 389, 394, 425, 539-40
Chiromo, 38, 58, 59, 269
Chisombezi, 289
Chisusi, A. M., 170
Chitambuli, 462
Chiwayula, Simon, 540
Choctaw Indian tribe, 113
Cholo, 134, 148, 203, 304, 326, 394, 413
Chona, Joshua, 329
Chorley, John, 326, 468
Church of Christ, Burnley, Lancashire, 345
Church of Scotland, 371
  General Assembly of 1915, 367
  General Assembly of 1916, 374
Church of Scotland Foreign Mission Committee, 364, 367, 369, 374-5, 386
Church of Scotland Mission, Nyasaland, 13, 16, 39, 40, 90, 250, 251, 316, 343, 349, 363-80. *See also* Blantyre Mission
Churches, independent African and Negro, 78, 98, 107, 161, 178, 211, 237, 240, 242, 263, 323, 325, 334, 340, 343, 353, 354, 404, 406, 410-13, 416, 422-6, 435. *See also* Ethiopianism, Providence Industrial Mission
Churches of Christ, British, 149
Churches of Christ Mission, Nyasaland, *see under* Missions, Nyasaland : Other Missions
Churches of Christ, South Africa, 149
Churchill, Winston S., 184
Cikomwe, 226, 540
Ciskei, 430
Civil Rights Act of 1875, U.S.A., 95
Cleland, Robert, 40
Clemenceau, Georges, 434
Cobbe, Lt.-Col. A. S., 497
Cockerill, Walter B., 209-18, 235, 250, 292, 330-41, 350, 352, 358, 368, 378, 379, 481, 509
Coffee planting in Nyasaland, 35, 134, 141
Coker, Rev. Daniel, 99

Colenso, Bishop ('Sobantu'), 71, 76
Collective Punishment Ordinance of Nyasaland, 1909, 388, 541, 542
Collins, Captain H. G., 286, 309-10, 315
Colonial Office, London, 355, 374-5, 382-3, 385
Commission of Inquiry into the 1915 Rising, *see* Nyasaland Native Rising Commission
Companhia de Moçambique, 257
Confessions of Nat Turner, 187
Congo, 255, 433-4
  Conventional Basin of, 371
Congo, Belgian, 417-19
Convention of Associations and Landowners Association, Nyasaland, 394
Copper Belt riots, Northern Rhodesia, 417
Costa, of Mchocholo's village, 540
Cotton, 473
  P.I.M., 141, 222
Councils of Headmen, Nyasaland, 193-4
Coutanche, Keith, 475-6, 509
Covenanters, 263, 371
Crawford, David, 436-7
Cromwell, Oliver, 262, 265, 336, 437
Crown Lands Ordinance of 1911, 197
Cruise, Assistant Magistrate, Chiradzulu, 226
Cuba, 104
Cuffee, Paul, 104
Cyclopaedic Dictionary of the Mang'anja Language, 17

da Gama, Vasco, 44
Dagoretti, 428
Dahomey, 432
Daniel, Book of, 340
Dar-es-Salaam, 256, 501
'David Livingstone', African assistant of Joseph Booth, 49, 50, 51, 55, 87
Declaration of Rights of the Negro Peoples of the World, 1920, 433
Dedza, 212
DeLany, Emma B., 138, 139, 140, 141, 142, 166, 172, 391, 434
Dickie, Alexander, 79, 533
Die Afrikanische Arbeiterfrage, 419
'Diggers', 24
Dikiya, 540
Dinizulu, 76, 77
District Administration (Native) Ordinance, 1912, Nyasaland, 193, 195, 199, 207, 389
Disturbances of 1953, Nyasaland, 394, 413

549

INDEX

Jenkin, Rev. A. M., 509
Jerman, 540
'Jerusalem', 223
Johannesburg, 154
John the Baptist, 39, 44, 48
John Bull, 384
John the disciple, 39
Johnson, Dr. C. First, 463
Johnston, Sir Harry, 7, 11, 12, 13, 14, 15,
   49, 50, 51, 52, 70, 85, 246, 380, 429,
   443, 497
   land settlement in Nyasaland, 14-16,
     33, 143, 179, 197, 227, 392, 429, 495
   relations with Joseph Booth, 34, 52,
     357-8
   See also Nyasaland, Governors of
Johnston, Dr. James, 64
Johnston, William W., 157
Jordan, Lewis Garnett, 112, 113, 117,
   122, 174, 389, 454
Jordan, river, 40
Journal of the African Society, 435
Jubaland, 427
Jumalowe, 462
Jumanyumbe, 462
Jumbe, headman, 271
Jumbe of Kota-Kota, 405, 497

Kachewanda, Biseyi, 505
Kadalie, Clements, 155, 185, 252, 412,
   413, 414, 452, 504
Kadangwe, Burnett, 540
Kadewele, Chief at Tunduru, 476
Kadewere, Simon, 348, 490
Kaduya, David, 259, 301, 302, 484
Kaduya, Mlanje chief, 475, 542
Kaffir wars, 399
Kalemba, Peter, 505
Kaloleni, 486
Kamba, 420
Kambwiri's village, 540
Kampalusa village, 481
Kampelusa, 282, 481, 483
Kamwala, 541, 542
Kamwana, Elliott (sometimes called
   Kenan), 153-9, 163, 166, 170, 182,
   196, 210, 211, 212, 214, 215, 232,
   252, 324, 339, 355, 402, 411, 417
Kamwana movement, 160, 184, 344,
   352, 378, 400, 409, 428
Kankhomba, Mang'anja chief, 43
Kansas, 103
Kaparamula, 542
Kapeni, 43, 86
Karonga, 213, 216, 244, 257, 286, 304,
   309, 316, 366

Karonga—*contd.*
   Battle of, 1914, 223, 233, 235, 238, 267,
     276, 284, 297, 330, 334, 471
Karstedt, Oskar, 419
Kasungu, 263, 295
Katanga, 12
Katunga, 49, 50
Kaundama, 42, 43, 443
Kavea, 539
Kavirondo, 427, 429
Kawinga, 86, 408, 489
Kazembe, 133
Kealing, H. T., 535
Kemper, Mr., 277, 278
Kenya :
   Kikuyu Central Association in, 4, 427
   subject in Leys' *Kenya*, 4, 418-19,
     508
   African political organization in, 418
   comparison with Nyasaland, 419, 426,
     428
   Thuku, Harry and, 426-8
   Young Kikuyu Association in, 427
   Kikuyu separatist churches in, 428-
     429
Khonda, Frederick Singani, 347, 354,
   470
Kichi, 501
Kikuyu, 148, 420, 426-9
Kikuyu Central Association, 4, 427
Kikuyu separatist churches, 428-9
Kimbangu, Simon, 417-18, 433-4
Kimberley, 77
Kimu, 251, 258, 290, 308, 354
King Christophe, 106, 221
King's African Rifles, 229, 233, 262,
   286, 297, 303, 309, 315, 406, 427
Kipande, 426
Kitawala, 417, *see* Watch Tower
Kitchener, Lord, 369
Kondowe, 153, 253, 414
Kongoni, 243
Konigmacher, S. M., 328
Kota-Kota, 405, 406, 474, 497
Koyi, William, 159
Ku chita gain, 190
Ku Klux Klan, 94, 105
Kucha-wa-dzua, 60
Kufa, John Gray, second in command
   to John Chilembwe :
   names of, 445-6
   native deacon, 59
   takes medical training, 85
   medical assistant, Blantyre, 192
   career and meeting with J. C., 243-
     245

INDEX

INDEX

INDEX

Shona-Ndonde, 474
Sierra Leone, 99, 104, 504
Sinclair, Upton, *The Jungle*, 463
Singleton, Benjamin 'Pap', 103
Siriya, 541
Sixty Years of an Agitator's Life, 20
Skye, 81
Slave risings, American, 106
Slave trade, 46. *See also* Arab slavery
Slessor, Mary, 344
Smith, Alexander ('Bambo'), 293-5, 475
Smith, Sir George, 189, 198, 217, 239, 396, 399, 505. *See also* Nyasaland, Governors of
Soanga, 216
'Sobantu', *see* Colenso, Bishop
Soche Hill, 43
Socialism, 151, 184, 464
Somaliland campaigns against the 'Mad Mullah', 133, 143, 234, 405, 410, 432
'Some New Light on the Garvey Movement', 433
'Son of Man', Kasungu prophet, 263
Songani, 167
'Sons of God' at Cholo, 413
South Africa :
    and Ethiopianism, 92, 102, 105, 148, 155, 330, 366, 412, 424, 425
    emigration/immigration : Tonga, 154-155, 158, 252
    education, African, technical, 365 ; higher, 366
    comparison with Nyasaland, 366
    Zionist churches in, 412-30
    Negro prophets in, 430-1
    Booth and, 72, 73, 77, 92, 150, 184, 353
    Mathaka and, 72
    Turner and, 73, 105
    Kamwana and, 154-5
    Kadalie and, 155, 252, 412
    Njilima and, 246
South African Native National Congress, 184, 202, 203, 253, 414
Southampton Country, Virginia, 106
Souza, 132
Spanish-American War, 1898, 101
Spelman Seminary, 138
Spencer, Anne, 114, 115, 509
Spurgeon, Rev. Charles, 21
Spurgeon, Rev. Thomas, New Zealand Tabernacle, 21
s.s. *Induna*, 136
s.s. *Oroya*, 27

Stanton, Mrs. Emily, 269, 272
Steffens, Lincoln, 422
Stewart, James, 130, 160
Stoddard, Lothrop, 502
Store, Nelson, 540
Studies in the Scriptures, 152, 185, 230, 231, 324-5
Sudanese, 421
Supervisor of Native Affairs *v.* Blantyre and East Africa, Limited, 1903, 143, 197, 457
Suppression of the African Slave Trade to the United States, 1638-1870, The, 101
Swahili, 406
Swelsen, Father, 301, 302, 303
Symes, Joseph, 23, 24

'Tabernacles', working men's, 24-5
Tambala stream, 541
Tandu, Hanson, 490
Tanganyika, 399, 417, 421
Tangata, see *Thangata*
Taxation, native, 40, 133, 137, 154, 216, 223, 370, 385, 426, 429. *See also* Hut tax
Taylor, Rev. J. A., 533
Tembu, 73
Tenga-tenga, 229, 299, 319
Tennessee, 95
Texas, 462
Thangata or labour-rent, 179, 181, 198 224, 228, 385, 392, 395
Thorburn, Captain, 486
Thorne, Dr. Albert, 104
Thorneycroft, G. V., 284, 290, 309, 509
Thuku, Harry, 5, 426-8
Tickle, H. E., 490
Tile, Nehemiah, 73
Times, 3
Togoland, 426
Tonga, Lake Nyasa, 35, 153, 154, 155, 210, 211, 212, 214, 216, 217, 251, 252, 290, 331, 334, 352, 378, 402, 403, 409, 412, 420, 490
Tonga, Lower Zambezia, 420
Transkei, 431
Transvaal, 425
Treaty with Mangoche Yao, 40
Treaty of Vereeniging, 205
Tribal involvement in the Rising :
    Inter-tribalism, 240-53, 401-2, 409, 415, 419-21, 538-40, 541-2
    Chikunda, 539
    Mkokhola, 539
    Ngoni, 249-50, 403, 408, 539

INDEX

INDEX

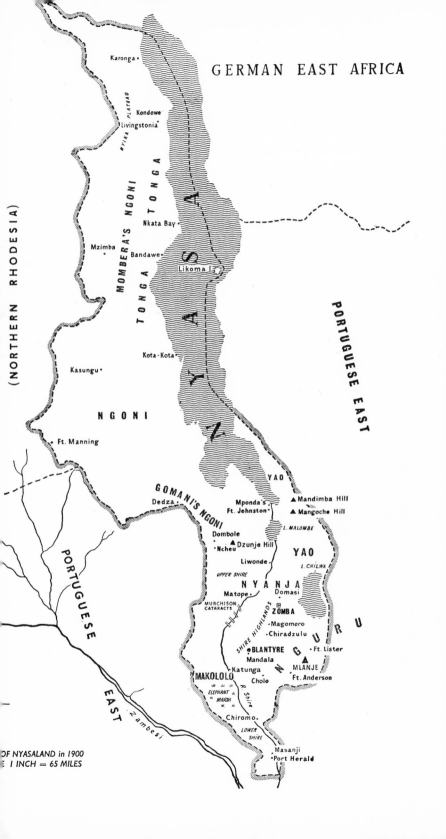

GERMAN EAST AFRICA

(NORTHERN RHODESIA)

PORTUGUESE EAST

Karonga

NYIKA PLATEAU
Kondowe
Livingstonia

MOMBERA'S NGONI

TONGA TONGA

Nkata Bay

Mzimba
Bandawe

Likoma Is.

Kota-Kota

Kasungu

NGONI

Ft. Manning

GOMANI'S NGONI
Dedza

YAO

Mponda's ▲ Mandimba Hill
Ft. Johnston ▲ Mangoche Hill

L. MALOMBE
Dombole
Ncheu ▲ Dzunje Hill

Liwonde YAO *L. CHILWA*

UPPER SHIRE
Matope NYANJA
Domasi

PORTUGUESE

MURCHISON
CATARACTS ☐ ZOMBA

SHIRE HIGHLANDS
•Magomero
•Chiradzulu
•BLANTYRE •Ft. Lister
Mandala

MAKOLOLO Katunga MLANJE
Cholo •Ft. Anderson
ELEPHANT
MARSH

EAST

Zambesi

Chiromo

LOWER
SHIRE

Masanji
•Port Herald

NGURU

OF NYASALAND in 1900
E I INCH = 65 MILES

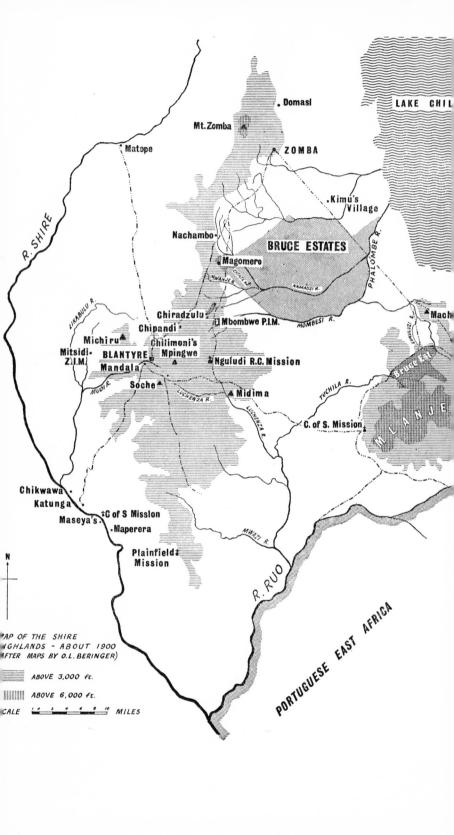

Domasi

Mt. Zomba

ZOMBA

LAKE CHIL

Matope

Kimu's
Village

Nachambo

BRUCE ESTATES

Magomero

R. SHIRE

PHALOMBE R.

LIKABULU R.

Chiradzulu

Chipandi

Mbombwe P.I.M.

Mach

Michiru

Chilimoni's
Mpingwe

MOMBESI R.

Mitsidi-
Z.I.M.

BLANTYRE
Mandala

Nguludi R.C. Mission

MUDIR.

Soche

Midima

LUCHENZA R.

TUCHILA R.

C. of S. Mission

LANDE

Chikwawa

Katunga

Maseya's

‡C of S Mission

Maperera

MWAZI R.

Plainfield
Mission

N

R. RUO

MAP OF THE SHIRE
HIGHLANDS – ABOUT 1900
(AFTER MAPS BY O.L. BERINGER)

ABOVE 3,000 ft.

ABOVE 6,000 ft.

SCALE   10 2 4 6 8 10   MILES

PORTUGUESE EAST AFRICA